ROOTS OF THE BIBLE

FRIEDRICH WEINREB (c. 1985)

FRIEDRICH WEINREB

ROOTS *of the* BIBLE

AN ANCIENT VIEW FOR A NEW VISION

The Key to Creation in Jewish Tradition

Angelico Press

Originally published in Dutch (1963) as "De Bijbel als Schepping"
by N.V. Servire, Den Haag.
The English translation is by Mrs. N. Keus, MA,
and grateful thanks are extended to Mrs. J. M. Francis
for her help in completing the index.

This edition © Angelico Press 2021

All rights reserved:
No part of this book may be reproduced or transmitted,
in any form or by any means, without permission

For information, address:
Angelico Press, Ltd.
169 Monitor St.
Brooklyn, NY 11222
www.angelicopress.com

pb 978-1-62138-803-6
cloth 978-1-62138-804-3

Cover design
by Michael Schrauzer

Contents

Publisher's Note 5

Preface and Apologia 7

Part One: The Universe of the Word
1. *Counting to Four* 19
2. *The Secret of the Word* 42
3. *In the Beginning* 55
4. *The Miracle of the Name* 73
5. *Male and Female* 87
6. *The Bounds of this World* 102
7. *The Coming World is Beyond Our Boundaries* 114
8. *The Chronology of the Bible* 149

Part Two: Expanding
9. *The Story of the Two Trees* 183
10. *Cain's Death* 221
11. *Sons of the Gods* 236
12. *The Word Carries Life Through Time* 245
13. *How Time is Measured* 262
14. *The Eye and the Ear of the Servant* 269
15. *Destruction in Multiplicity* 278

Part Three: The Curve
16. *Facing the Others* 285
17. *The Incredible* 292
18. *The Offering and Paradise* 297
19. *The Twins* 303
20. *Blindness and Vision* 308
21. *Life Expresses Itself as Subtlety Facing Subtlety* 315
22. *The Reversal* 323
23. *The Colours of Time* 327
24. *The Disappearance of Life* 335
25. *This World as Centre of the Universe* 339
26. *The Game* 341

Part Four: The Return
- 27 *The Threshold to the Eighth* 369
- 28 *The Pangs of Development* 376
- 29 *The Laws Governing the Return* 387
- 30 *How the World is Left* 398
- 31 *The Principle of the Half* 402
- 32 *Crossing the Border* 413
- 33 *The Conditioning: Creating Order* 418
- 34 *The Structure of Man* 421
- 35 *The Circle and the Fragments* 434
- 36 *The Method of Counting* 448
- 37 *The Secret of the Reversal of the Laws of Nature* 454
- 38 *The Fourth Dimension* 463
- 39 *Economic Problems* 468
- 40 *Looking Into the Future* 477
- 41 *At the End of the Journey, the Giants* 484
- 42 *A Realistic and Serious Conclusion* 491

Epilogue 497

Appendix
- *Notes and Records* 504
- *Statement of the Sources of Sagas Employed* 511
- *Bibliography of the Main Sources of Tradition* 516
- *Index* 519

Publisher's Note

Friedrich Weinreb (born Lemberg, 1910, died Zürich, 1988) was an exceptional figure in twentieth-century Judaism. With his path-breaking book *Roots of the Bible: An Ancient View For a New Vision*, he opened the depths of the "word-hoard" of Jewish wisdom. Weinreb taps, as a source of inspiration for our present world, "the sacred oral teaching" preserved for millennia in scholarly redoubts remote from the ways of the world. As writer and lecturer, he left behind an extensive body of work, in which often astonishing connections can be found between the Biblical worldview and that of today.

When it first appeared in Dutch in 1963, this book heralded the veritable rediscovery of a foundational stratum of the Old Testament. For the first time, those keen to penetrate what the Bible has to say, but confused by what on the surface often seems an impenetrable narrative, were offered a key to unlocking the mystery of its *way* of telling stories (from narrative, to word, to letter, to "number") in a cosmologically-expanded "gematria" suited also to those unfamiliar with the original Hebrew. Weinreb communicates so vivid and profound a knowledge of Hebrew that through his work the reader quickly comes to experience the spirit and richness of the original text.

The stories of the book of Genesis — from the Creation of the World and of Humanity, Cain and Abel, the Flood, the Tower of Babel, Abraham and Isaac, Jacob and Esau, to the story of Joseph — are explored in detail, as are also the Exodus of Israel from Egypt, the Crossing of the Red Sea, and the many events on the Journey through the Wilderness to the very brink of the Promised Land.

For Weinreb, the aim is always insight into the complex phenomena of the world — indeed, of all that lives — through the core-text of the Bible. Readers may find here answers to hitherto intractable obstacles to their understanding of the Bible — answers not only satisfying, but often astonishing! How are we to understand stories that sometimes provoke moral doubts, such as the matriarch Sarah sending Hagar into the wilderness, or Jacob receiving blessing despite having betrayed his brother Esau and even his own father, or Joseph being sold into slavery by his own brothers? Why are there so many sacrifices in the Bible, especially of animals? Why all the genealogical tables with their hundreds of names that no longer seem to say anything to us? The reader will find these, and many other perplexing questions answered in a breathtaking new light, a light which, once lit, they can carry further on their own path of thrilling discovery.

The book is enriched with an extensive appendix containing the author's notes and references, a bibliography of the most important sources of the tradition, biographical and bibliographical details, and indexes of persons and subjects, of Hebrew words, of figures, and of Biblical passages.

Preface and Apologia

Why was this book written? This book definitely requires a few words of introduction for it is rather an unusual book. It deals with problems of life, of the world, of the Bible, in a way unknown in publications up to the present. One will look in vain for writings, in any language, containing this matter communicated in this way. This book will, therefore, be a sensation to the interested and understanding reader. The author is well aware of the fact, but on careful consideration has thought fit to communicate to a limited extent this knowledge which has so far not been published and even for the most part forgotten.

The knowledge set forth in this book dates back to prehistoric times; it is definitely no discovery of the author's. It practically got lost, however, in these latter centuries, partly even in the latter millenium, in those circles, too, where acquaintance with it might have been of illimitable significance. With the loss of this knowledge many certainties in regard to the purpose of life got adrift or altogether lost.

Yet the material, fundamental to this knowledge, has remained intact throughout the ages. Not in the form of scrolls hidden in caves or ancient potsherds and parchments retrieved in archeological expeditions. The manner in which it remained intact is much more surprising and imposing: it has been with us all the time, and during the latter centuries even printed many times in numerous books. The only thing is that it has for a long, long time not been recognized as such; the quintessence was overlooked; people simply did not see it; primarily because they had lost the key. It has rarely been more manifest that the gods thinking they could lead the world 'had eyes but could not see'.

Once the key is retrieved, as will appear after perusal of this book, one will realize that regaining this knowledge from the profuse material at hand is a simple and, at the same time, uncommonly fascinating matter easily accomplished in one's lifetime. One will see that regaining it does not depend on endless complicated research, in which subtlety, abnormal penetration or a photographic memory play a decisive part, and that neither screwing up to a special spiritual condition nor application of mystical practices are required. It is nothing except a simple human affair which merely requires normal common sense, besides goodwill and an attitude to life directed towards the real.

By now one will wonder what this mysterious, yet often printed, material is and how it is that the key for understanding such important things got lost.

The material is found in the enormous complex known as ancient Jewish lore. An exact, serious, intellectually justified approach of this tradition proves to lead to astonishing results, to unknown possibilities. Without any exaggeration a new universe may be said to loom up.

This ancient tradition, as any tradition at any time, is based on knowledge of the meaning of life. When the study of this ancient wisdom approaches the domain where the one thing that matters is to penetrate to the ultimate cause regarding the reality of this world, of life and death, it changes its character of typical, general formulations, resulting from mechanical, material and exterior relationships, to that where the single personality, the manner of life, thought and desires of the man facing this tradition, become decisive for the powers of understanding and his mental scope.

The approach of the essential in the world is closely related to the essential in man and because of it has a very personal character. Every man gives expression to the world in a different manner.

Therefore it was an ancient custom merely to transmit this profounder and wider approach from teacher to pupil, taking into account the natural disposition and character of the pupil correctly to understand the greatness and depth of the meaning of life. It required wisdom and restraint on the part of the teacher to impart this to the pupil — with regard to the latter's personality — which under the circumstances formed the maximum. For the reverse of the knowledge of ultimate causes and forces implies a potential, unchecked, immense power over matter. The chances of abuse of this power for the sake of narrow-minded selfish purposes often caused the teacher to limit the extent of the pupil's initiation. Modern man who has barely tasted the consequences of penetrating into a few secrets of matter as expressed in conceptions such as nuclear energy, modern psychology and biology, will not look upon this disposition in regard to initiating pupils as strange or narrow-minded or wrong any more.

In consequence of the serious loss in depth in the views and the ways of life of humanity through the externalization which has been in progress for centuries, the knowledge of the essence of things could no longer be transmitted or at least only partially. People lost sight of the correct, systematic all-embracing approach to reality. They forgot that it is man's personality which determines the depth of his knowledge; and that which through deficiency of the personality could not be comprehended any more, was called 'the secret'. In this way there ensued an erroneous estimation, a misconception of the meaning of the secret. It brought in its wake trifling with mysteriousness, with unwarranted secrecy, indulgence in strange, misunderstood expressions. The ever-expanding domain of ignorance about the real became a hotbed for queer and alarming reactions, indicating that man realized intuitively that he might come to knowledge, *it is true,* but that he no longer knew *how.* It was the domain where ignorance of things one was certainly able to grasp, made a mockery of the secret; where profound human sentiments were debauched.

Because of all this the rendering of what would have been regarded in ancient times as knowledge of the meaning of the world has become vague, confused, desultory, not to mention the numerous entirely wrong approaches, based on misjudgement of the significance of this wisdom. All in all there arose an unsatisfactory picture, rightly to be rejected by those who seriously wanted to find out the purpose of existence and live in accordance therewith.

Neither did the teachers in general know how to approach the reality of things by means of the material they had read and studied. Large numbers of them do not even realize any more that there is a knowledge of the reality of things; they believe that the Bible and biblical lore are merely information dating back to olden times concerning the history and customs of an ethnic group, mixed up with myths and legends and sagas, illuminated with conceptions on justice, morals, hygiene or ethics, whether acceptable or otherwise.

Considering the ever growing loss of knowledge about the why and wherefore of this life, and mankind losing control of itself and feeling dissatisfied and miserable, I judged that such times justified my pointing to this reservoir of knowledge esteemed impossible and of wisdom of an altogether different order. This knowledge offers firm standards, it does not deal with vaguenesses or speculations. It gives certainties throughout life, it gives insight into the purpose of existence and it is logical, systematic, all-embracing. Consequently it satisfies the warranted desire for intellectual acceptability. It will undoubtedly appeal to straightforward modern people in quest of truth.

At the same time it brings solid human standards instead of the chilly world-picture of a mechanical infinity in space-time, and the relativity of human morals, so dispiriting to man as a live personality. Besides it will prove to be a continuation of the lost ancient path of religious man, the way about which modern man, in spite of all the progressist-complexes dominating his mind, intuitively knows it existed at some time and of which he cherishes an inexpressed hope that he shall find it back one day.

It is the way which man lost through the obtruding superficiality, vagueness and hypocrisy; the way which he tries in vain to find back through various theories in the domain of philosophy, metaphysics, theology, ethics and history; all the while getting more and more discouraged and sceptical because of his hopeless and vain search. It is also the way he vainly hopes to regain through experimenting with and forcing of all kinds of schemes social or political, efforts which therefore can only eventuate in deadly pessimism, cynicism and opportunism. The only thing actually gained was that the goal, the retrieving of the essence of things, had to make way for a ruthless, harsh, scientific world-picture with statistic standards based on the law of big figures, instead of the expected all-embracing, all-pervading human standards.

The need of anaesthetics and diversion, and recreation – which indeed whatever form it presents itself in, amounts to excluding reality, creation of a fictitious world – all these things are the exterior signs of this despair of ever finding back the path of religious man. So many people, too, clinging to every kind of strange 'spiritual' school of thought, veiling what is truly human as long as it makes the impression or even merely pretends to be complete or having descended from other spheres, from regions, seemingly inspiring one with belief and faith, from worlds beyond the sensory perceptible, all these things are indications of human need and human search, but above all, indications of human loneliness and deep human sorrow.

These times of tragic pessimism demand restoration of certainties round which there is sense in building up a new life and a new world. For that reason I thought it was not only justified, but even urgent to lift a tip of the veil and point at the existence of this unknown world which has contained the certainties of life ever since the beginning of human life.

More than this I cannot accomplish in a book which is the first and only one ever published in this field, and which, considering the entirely new and foreign subject-matter, cannot but have the character of a cautious, general introduction. It does not nearly contain a hundredth part of what I could write with the help of the elaborate material in my possession. But even this brief and cursory glance into the new world, opening up to us, is so fascinating, opens up such new vistas, that one will never stop wondering how all this can really be and how it could be so close to us without our ever having the slightest suspicion of it. One will also wonder how it was that one 'had eyes yet could not see'.

The Public Secret

Is handing on information about material touching the essence of things not at variance with the above mentioned custom, maintained throughout the ages, of handing these problems merely from teacher to pupil and such only if and in so far as the pupil in his disposition and practice of life inspires the confidence that this knowledge will not develop in him in the wrong direction? That I myself should ask this question, shows that I have given this problem my careful consideration. On the one hand a world which spiritually, as seen from the human standpoint, lives on the edge of the abyss, which, since it does not know any longer the why and wherefore of things, loses itself in its search for all kinds of subtle anaesthetics and intoxicants for the purpose of driving away despair, a world which lives in hard-heartedness, opportunism, cynicism, egoism, and because of it threatens to end in catastrophe. On the other hand the knowledge and the experience that the deepest essence of things must remain hidden, as the soul in the body, the seed in the fruit, the nucleus in the atom; that this deepest truth can only be transmitted in silence to the one who shows he can take it in, whose attitude of life is in harmony with it. None but such a man will understand that the essential is approached in a way different from exteriorizing the soul, extricating the seed, or releasing the atom's nucleus. He will know that pushing the essential into the sphere of the universal mechanistic, the statically measurable, is suicidal and that it may destroy others as well. It is only through the essential remaining hidden from sensory perception, through its being protected by the perceptible material sheath with which, in its contrast, it forms a unity, that existence in this world is at all possible.

Here we see facing each other, on the one hand this world, precipitating itself intoxicatedly into the abyss; pathologically set on making sensorily perceptible the essence of things, the nucleus, existence, that which has life-informing sense as long as it is maintained in its state of sensory non-perceptibility, and on the other hand the presence of a knowledge of the same qualities as this essence, which similarly requires a protective sheath, so as not to be destroyed and not to act destructively. The tension between these two extremes is heightened by the knowledge that only restoration of the knowledge of the essential can cause the certainties to be found back, which will again make of life a humane joy and give the world a humane foundation. It is only the gift of this profoundest and holiest essence to the world which might avert calamity.

The solution to this dilemma of opposing contrasts lies in the principle that one of the most important missions of mankind is making known the wonders of the world, the unsuspected depths of the structure of life. This principle for instance expressed in the Bible as: 'Declare His Glory among the heathen, His Wonders among all people' (Ps. 96:3) or in the: 'Give thanks to the Lord; make known His deeds among the people ...; talk ye of all His wondrous works' (Ps. 105:1–2).

Talking about these 'wonders' is a serious matter; therefore, like all teaching – and teaching in fact is nothing but telling about 'wonders' – it should be straightforward aspiration after truth. Most emphatically it is not something to be handed to the credulous with half-heartedness and vagueness. The wonder should not evoke emotions in hazy minds, but to the contrary in the alert man. Such a man in his joyous surprise will surely find his way to the reality of things and the purpose of existence. It will then also prove to be his personal way and it will depend on himself what he will meet on that way and what will abide with him. He will then be able to say that he has seen the wonder and yet lives.

This book speaks about this 'wonder'. It grants a view, unknown as yet, of the wonder of the world, as it unfolds itself in that creation known as the 'Bible'. With creation in this connection I mean something which like the universe or life cannot definitely have been made by man but which as a surprising, inescapable datum ever faces man, whose existence is found therein. In this book the Bible is not presented as a historic tale, nor as a source of morals, justice, theology, ethics, hygiene or any other thing people have ever taken the

Bible for, but as a pure wonder, a wonder just as demonstrable as the universe of life.

The essential being of things, the knowledge of the essential, which is to be materialized, is not touched upon, as these things are subject to the personality of the man who approaches them; they cannot even be touched upon in a book like this without creating a dangerous confusion.

For this reason there remains a wide gap, sedulously defined no man's land, between the farthest reaching communication in this book and the domain of the deepest reality of things. But with the same sedulousness it has been seen so that the reader, through his disposition, can repeatedly cast a glance at this domain, can set foot on elevations which reveal to him its existence and its nature. From this viewpoint he will be enabled to gaze into another world. For I wanted emphatically to fulfil the primary intention of this book to create the possibility of finding the way back to lost certainties. In times of serious danger during devastating epidemics the Thora, which is otherwise to remain in the house of instruction, according to ancient Jewish usage, is carried through the streets of the town threatened with destruction so that the pestilence may come to an end.

Apart from these motives, decisive in themselves, there is the fact that especially in the latter centuries so much has been written about the Bible and tradition in utter ignorance of their meaning and purpose, that an entirely false and misleading general opinion has arisen concerning them. Ancient sources of condensed wisdom, only to be understood by adepts, are printed in bulk, often in translation, analysed by inexpert people and of course wrongly commented upon, hence foolishly interpreted. And all this ever remains uncontradicted, thus creating the impression as if these interpretations were acceptable, just as if silence gives consent. Watching silently how mankind from misconception pulls down the most important thing, that which can give sense to life, is an attitude showing an alarming indifference towards the essential, which allows such considerations to prevail as social status, national pride, scientific and technical progress, etc. It very often means that people do not know any better, that they content themselves with a partial world, with a sham world. It is also for this very reason in order not to leave this situation uncontradicted, that this book was written.

Knowledge of the real is not a secret one person can take possession of begrudging another's participating of it, excluding the other from it. The secret of this knowledge exists so that anybody may seek it, it is there to grant man the joy of finding it. It absolutely wants to be found, because in finding arises that unity of essence and phenomenon, the unity of the opposites. Whoever has experienced the wonder of the world as it stands revealed in the Bible, finds himself on the threshold of the domain of this secret.

Knowledge of the essence of things forms a closed system which contains the proof of its reality within itself, as it is also the case with the universe. Just as one can only agree full of admiration that the universe is an imposing creation, in perusing this book one will be able to state that the Bible is an even more imposing creation. More imposing because it does not only show the wonder of an unsuspected mechanical relationship, as it also exists in the universe and in life, but because together with this mechanical coherence it also reveals its purpose. The mechanical relationship proves to contain the structure of the events, it likewise contains the standards by which to form judgements, and actions get colour and sense as determining forces in the course of the world. With it man regains the certainties concerning the purpose of existence without which his life is cheerless and unacceptable, without which, in fact, he cannot live.

This system, as will be seen at the perusal of the book, cannot be tampered with any more than the existence of the planets' orbits or the phenomenon of gravity. It is built with just as wonderful relationships, embracing the smallest details and penetrating into the heart of things. This book indeed proves that the Bible is a creation, that even more than the universe and life it has all the characteristics thereof.

That is why this book has nothing in common with the endless variety of discussions between theories or theologies which regard the Bible as a book produced in ancient times. A creation cannot be discussed; it can be seen or ignored. One cannot, however, enter into considerations whether the solar year on earth embraces 365¼ days or not. One cannot be for or against it either. The number of days of the solar year forms a certainty. Therefore ancient Judaism boasted neither theory nor theology of the Bible. It merely contained the life-practice which in people's lives gave form to the structure which the Bible revealed about this life.

The presentation of the system will undoubtedly spring one surprise after the other on the reader, it will touch him more deeply than the discovery of the structure of the universe, of the laws of nature. It is more sensational, since it was not suspected, yet secretly rather expected all the same.

A few Remarks on the Sources and the Form

Although this book is based on the knowledge of ancient Judaism, it has been arranged and written so as to enable anybody to read it without any difficulty, whatever conviction or denomination he may adhere to. It may be read as people generally do without any further considerations of their conviction, or denomination in much the same way as one reads a book, revealing the structure of the universe or of life. One may be stirred by the information, one will perceive a new wonder. Subject to one's personality one will then see the way leading to the real. It is the way which will lead towards God.

From all directions, from a wide circle, there are paths leading to the centre. Everybody will go towards the essential from his place, also from the milieu in which he has grown up or with which he feels affinity. There in that goal all ways converge. The author of this book, as a Jew, only felt justified to speak from his point of view, his path, conscious however that the wonder, which urged him to follow it like so many others in ancient times, can cause anybody to strike the path *he* is destined to follow in this world. So that from all directions people can come, flocking towards the one goal, the place where God can be found. On all ways life is realized. This book merely points to the significance of *going* the way towards the essential. Everybody has only to fill in what is relevant to his way, that he may strike it with joy and conviction.

Ancient Judaism was the knowledge of the Bible as creation. As the conception 'Bible' only the Old Testament was known of course. Where the Bible is mentioned in this book, it is exclusively the Old Testament which is meant. Besides, this knowledge was especially based on that which was considered fundamental, i.e. the root story of the Bible. It was this very root story which was known as a creation. It is formed by the first five books, the so-called Pentateuch. As I follow the path of this ancient knowledge, all the information in this book is similarly based on the Pentateuch, although for convenience sake I shall go on using the word 'Bible' which refers to the whole.

In this book special passages in the Bible are repeatedly referred to without quoting them. The book would have become too bulky, if all texts referred to were printed verbatim. It is therefore a piece of practical advice to readers not well versed in the Bible to read passages as well and particularly to have the text ready at hand. Any translation anyhow has its fundamental defects. From this book it will be apparent that in fact translations exclude understanding of the essential and that therefore our approach takes place in an entirely different way. So in this case the translation is practically of no importance. It is merely an intelligible medium, which enables us to come into contact with the original text. And in that case it does not matter whether the translation is correct or no. The reader can use any translation.

This book in fact is based on the original text of the Bible as it exists in Hebrew. The remarkable thing about the Hebrew text is that it has remained unaltered throughout the ages. It does not only refer to the purport and the words used, but above all it applies to every letter. Here we see the phenomenon unknown in any other book, that even the so-called defective spellings continue 'wrongly spelled', that redundant letters are not crossed out, that letters unmistakably missing are not inserted, that some letters are unwarrantably written in big capitals or very small size, in the middle of a text often even in the middle of a word, that unexpectedly letters are turned upside down, etc. This fact in itself shows that we are here faced with something very peculiar; that these letters evidently have an entirely different function, besides that of forming a word. Otherwise in the course of so many centuries things would certainly have been altered, 'corrected'. In translations such facets cannot possibly become evident. We shall therefore follow a way completely different from that of the translation to make the reader familiar with the purpose of this original text.

The same thing applies to the way in which the pronunciation of the Hebrew words is rendered. I have on the whole chosen the rendering generally met with in translations. For here too it is irrelevant since our manner of approach has nothing to do with this pronunciation or that, this spelling or that, in English.

The conception 'tradition' has not been set out in greater detail in the text. It will be a matter of indifference to most readers whether the names of the sources used are mentioned or no. Those names are meaningless and are rather wearisome. As sources I have selected those which incontestably date back to antiquity. Moreover I have preferred such sources and such data as are fairly well known to those readers posted up or specialized in this direction, so that even without statement of the sources of information they will know the derivation. I have avoided the use of less well-known sources. Most of the sources used are even known in translations. The interested reader can trace back the principal sources in an index at the back of the book and also a limited bibliography containing the most important published general sources in this field.

For the sake of continuity and readability of the text, the explanatory notes and the expatiatory notes have also been printed at the back under the heading 'notes and annotations'.

To wind up with, an extensive register of references will help the reader to compare the various passages dealing with a certain subject. Very often this comparison will deepen his insight in the various subjects.

It was exceedingly difficult to find a suitable form in which to render the material. For indeed we are concerned with an entirely new field; there were hardly any points of contact with subjects already well known to the reader, no reference could be made to existent literature. Neither was there a terminology of this field intelligible to modern man. So I felt like one belonging to these modern times who had to explain our present-day scientific and social world to an Egyptian of Pharaonic ages. How was I to begin, how was I to describe the terms even our secondary schoolchildren are familiar with nowadays, lest the ancient Egyptian should misunderstand me? How was I to discuss the principles of atom-structure, of chemistry, modern mathematics, economic structure when I could not refer to anything in the Egyptian world picture?

The comparison is not far-fetched; the distance is at least just as big. Especially the danger of being misunderstood loomed up as I was writing. For nothing is more disastrous than the premature conclusion of the reader who with it connects things with well-known conceptions of his own world. Once such a wrong connection is made, the reader will continue in the wrong direction. For that reason I have approached the matter under discussion most cautiously, at first sight perhaps too elaborately. For the same reason I could not help repeating myself on various points. Also I have tried to prevent the reader's forming mistaken conceptions by inserting parenthetic clauses or explanatory interpolations, which may create the impression of superfluous, irritating reiterations. Considering this new explosive matter, the danger of misunderstanding seemed more serious to me than the risk of irritating people with my redundance and the repetitions, perhaps unnecessary to some and therefore rather trying. It goes without saying I could not take these measures everywhere. I do hope, however, that the reader, because of the very form of the elucidations, will avoid coming to rash conclusions and drawing rapid comparisons. For that reason I advise the reader urgently to stick to the sequence of the book. Passages or chapters skipped may make the rest unintelligible or, which is worse, cause misunderstanding.

I was also faced with the alternative whether this first book as a general introduction should be of a purely scientific nature destined for a very limited circle of persons interested or that it should reach as many readers as possible through its popular scientific character. There were many objections attaching to either extreme. That is why I tried to strike the happy mean. The scientific reader trying to penetrate deeper will find an immense quantity of surprising material, and the person generally interested will find the book fairly easy to read and yet intuitively feel the deep significance of this regained image of the world. It will assuredly not leave him unperturbed.

I have purposely avoided in this book to try and bring the reader in a desired frame of mind through pathetic language. In my use of language I have on the analogy of ancient commentators in this field purposely limited myself to the most sober, simple, generally intelligible, unequivocal choice of words. The facts must speak for themselves, words must only pave the way. This implies that I have also conscientiously avoided plausible, speculative vaguenesses, which can be explained in various ways. The facts communicated, the wonders shining forth from the creation, called the 'Bible', have to rouse the pathos and give one the feeling of having come across something most extraordinary.

It seemed necessary also to give an account in this preface of the manner of expression used in this book lest there should be any misunderstanding. The subject is too important and I think that the contents of this book can best be expressed in the simplest possible form. The reader will then be able to allow those feelings to develop which pertain to his personality and his place in the world. Thus he will find his own way too. That is what I sincerely wish for him.

Geneva, August 1963   *Friedrich Weinreb*

PART ONE

The Universe of the Word

1
Counting to Four

The tale of creation in the Bible faces many people with a number of problems. To illustrate our approach to the subject I selected the first two chapters. And I shall for the present leave the standards of science and history out of consideration. Let us begin with merely noticing what it says in the Book and try to discover in it some sort of systematic order. Such order may well indicate the presence of a leading thought and give it structural support.

When reading the tale we are struck at once by opposites forming a duality. Thus at the very beginning there are the two extremes of heaven and earth. In each of the next six days in which creation is completed according to the biblical story we again meet with sets of opposites. The first day there is that between light and darkness. The second day the waters under the firmament are divided from the waters above the firmament. The third day we first see the waters as opposed to dry land and afterwards on the same day a division is made in primeval life, plant-life, between the herb yielding seed and the tree yielding fruit.

This principle is carried on in the fourth, fifth and sixth days. In the fourth day there is the great light for the day and the lesser light for the night. The fifth day offers the contrast of the life of winged fowl flying above the earth in the open firmament of heaven and the moving creatures brought forth from the waters under the firmament. Finally on the sixth day there is first the contrast between the cattle and the wild beasts, after which another act of creation takes place, i.e. that of man, when duality is expressed in woman opposite to man.

Confining ourselves to the first chapter of Genesis even a casual perusal of the tale of creation establishes the impression that creation also means the formation of a polarity in each of its components. Through the creation of this polarity another duality presents itself, at first rather indefinitely, but afterwards more distinctly, viz. that of the male and female sexes. With the plants it must have been present already, with the beasts on the fifth day it becomes more apparent in the words: 'be fruitful and multiply', and in the case of man duality is brought forward as a definite principle. This principle of duality clearly extends still further and penetrates more deeply in the tale of creation. To discover this fact one has to arrange the material in a system which proceeds from the story itself.

The first day there is the light and the division of the light from the darkness. We observe the tale refers to light and darkness again on the fourth day as the lights of sun, moon and stars whose function it is to divide light from darkness. The second day mentions the division of waters above and waters under the firmament. This division is not referred to again until the fifth day when life is noticeable in the waters above the firmament and under the firmament. The third day in contrast with the previous days shows two creations mentioned emphatically and separately on the same day. The sixth day in its turn is likewise characterized by two different kinds of creation on that same day. To keep things as simple as possible we can take the events of the initial part of the third day as the creation of conditions of life on earth in general, whereas in the second half of that day the first manifestations of life begin to take shape. The sixth day shows a parallelism in that the biological conditions for the existence of man on earth are created during the first part of the day, after which man makes his appearance as a live creature during the second part.

So there is an undeniable correspondence between the first and the fourth days, the second and the fifth, the third and the sixth. And the fourth, fifth and sixth days represent a certain development, a concretion and elaboration of the phenomena of the first, second and third days respectively.

Indeed there are two groups of three days corresponding as depicted above, the first triad and the second.

For the sake of clarity let us arrange these correspondences systematically:

1st day:

light
darkness

4th day:

sun
moon and stars

2nd day:

waters above
waters under

5th day:

life directed to waters above
life directed to waters under

3rd day:

A
water
land
biological conditions for life in general

A
6th day:

cattle
wild beasts
biological conditions for the life of man in particular

B
seed-bearing plants
fruit-yielding plants
appearance of life in general

B
man
woman
appearance of life of man in particular

In this scheme and the preceding comment all the facts have been kept as concise as possible in order to stick to the main outlines at our first approach and not get entangled in details unintelligible as yet.

The diagram can also be arranged in a different way, owing to which the systematism becomes more distinct. It may be done by placing the first and fourth days, which both show forth the elements of light, on the right side, and the second and fifth days, which show forth the element of water, on the left side; the third and sixth days, both showing forth a duality, being placed in the middle. As the third and sixth days each complete a group of three days, they are placed lower down in the diagram, according to the principle of

All this merely to suit our convenience and give us a clearer insight. The scheme might be arranged differently again. For the purpose of our further investigation, however, we shall stick to the above scheme, since things were done this way in antiquity and there are no logical or practical reasons for abandoning it. So now the diagram is:

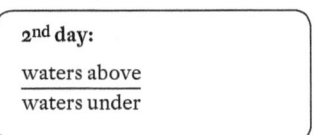

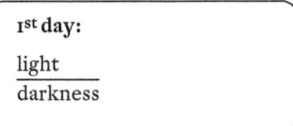

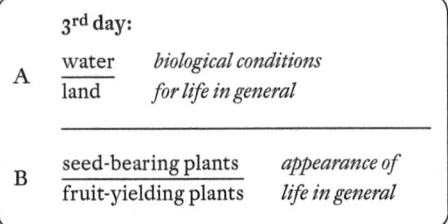

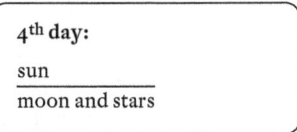

In this diagram it is clearly shown that the fourth day represents a kind of projection of the first day into another realm, as does the fifth day as compared with the second and the sixth with the third. Besides we see the group of the fourth, fifth and sixth days as a complete whole repeating the first, second and third days after their projection into another realm.

Indeed we may conclude from this diagram that there is but one development from the first day via the second to the third, and that a further unfoldment of things, as laid down in the first triad, manifests itself in the group formed by the fourth, fifth and sixth days.

So the principle of duality is now manifest in various ways. We found it in the duality ensuing on each day of creation, we recognized it in the male-female character manifesting through the initial duality, we came across the typical duality on the third and sixth days, and finally we pointed out this duality in the polarity of light and water, placed respectively on the right and the left of our diagram and also in the occurrence of the two triads, each with their specific characteristics, owing to which they too form a duality. The first triad forms a unit and thus a cycle is completed; the second triad similarly forming a cycle presents itself as a kind of projection, elaboration, specialization of the first. With due discretion one might look upon the second triad as a further concretion of the more abstract first.

At any rate our first approach of the tale of creation, although superficial, has supplied us with a certain systematism. The tale evidently contains more than a mere catalogue of events during those six days. The facts related show a barely disguised systematism, indicating deeper levels even in this cursory perusal.

We have already referred to the number 'three' as having a function in the scheme of creation in that it completes a unit; something is rounded off by it. Besides we see four acts of creation in either triad, each of them introduced by the formula 'and God said', and so, owing to the dual character of the third and sixth days, this formula occurs four times in either triad. The cycle of three days includes four acts of creation.

The Bible mentions three Patriarchs: Abraham, Isaac and Jacob. The third, Jacob, rounds off the tale of the patriarchs. It also strikes us that Jacob is a 'dual', exactly like the third day in the cycle of the tale of creation. For Jacob is Esau's twin brother. Jacob even has two names, viz. Jacob and Israel. Besides he has two wives of the same social status, Leah and Rachel, who each in their turn form a duality with their 'handmaids', Bilhah and Zilpah. Whereas Abraham and Isaac play their role as singles, Jacob is born in conflict with, in opposition to another. A conflict which has a decisive influence on the course of events.

So there is a manifest parallelism between the duality of the third day in either cycle and that of the third of the patriarchs. And in either case the cycle is completed by the third. Other instances of the systematism as found in the tale of creation can be discovered in the subsequent chapters of the Bible. I shall restrict myself to a few examples.

The first day in the cycles of the tale of creation is characterized by the creation of light, resp. lights. Now one of the outstanding features in the story of the first patriarch is the mention of light, fire, heat. In the so-called 'covenant of the pieces' (Gen. 15) great emphasis is laid on the 'smoking furnace' and the 'burning lamp'. Abraham is visited by the three angels when he sits 'in the tent-door in the heat of the day' (Gen. 18). Abraham witnesses the destruction of Sodom in fire (Gen. 18–19). Abraham is to sacrifice his son Isaac in a fire (Gen. 22). Oral tradition has it that Nimrod had Abraham thrown into a lime kiln. So we see light, heat and fire emphasized in the story of Abraham, analogous to the emphasis on light on the first day of the cycle of three days.

The Bible deals more briefly with Isaac, the second patriarch. But we get a detailed description about the strife with Abimelech on account of the wells, i.e. water (Gen. 26:16–33). Now the second day in both cycles of three days in the tale of creation is the day characterized by 'water'. It strikes us that immediately after Isaac's birth Abraham has a dispute with Abimelech concerning a well, just as if the appearance of Isaac is bound to evoke the idea of water (Gen. 21:25–33). Also when Isaac meets Rebekah for the first time, he comes from the direction of a well. It appears utterly irrelevant to the story, it even causes surprise to read about Isaac's coming from the direction of a well. Nevertheless this apparently irrelevant detail is significant, since it mentions 'coming from the direction of water'. Isaac's sole activity – for the rest Isaac is markedly passive, a point which will be amply discussed later on – is with the four wells contested by Abimelech.

The third patriarch, Jacob, besides showing the aforementioned characteristic duality, displays great activity, not with fire, nor with water, but with the things of the third day in the cycle of creation. Jacob is concerned with plants, beasts, and in a very specific way with the 'generating' of man. Just think of the pottage of lentils with which he bought Esau's birthright (Gen. 25:29–34), of the peeled rods of green poplar and of the hazel and chestnut tree, with which he hoped to get the spotted and ring-straked cattle and flocks from Laban (Gen. 30:25–43). We refer to the venison with which he obtains the blessing destined for Esau (Gen. 27), to the flock he herds and increases for Laban (Gen. 30:25–43), to the beasts he offers Esau so emphatically as a present (Gen. 32:13–21; and Gen. 33:8–11). And last but not least, the creation of man and the conflict of man play a conspicuous part in Jacob's life. He generates the twelve tribes, who carry on the story of the children of Israel in the Bible, he is mixed up in the husband-and-wife-conflict with Rachel and Leah, and in consequence he undergoes the experiences with Joseph, the son kidnapped and regained.

Obviously the point at issue is the biblical principle that in a cycle we are primarily concerned with light and everything pertaining to it, secondly with water, and thirdly with something of dual character, having to do with plants, beasts and the generating of man, which at the same time completes the cycle. Both, emphasis and parallelity, are too evident to be dismissed as mere coincidence. Besides, I have so far only adduced the story of the three patriarchs by way of illustration.

I have already referred to the concurrence of the three days of creation with the four acts of creation, and how every cycle of three days embraces four acts of creation, owing to the dual character of the third day. The acts of creation make things perceptible, manifest, they give form to the principle. Correspondingly we see the three patriarchs together having four spouses, the four matriarchs: Sarah, Rebekah, Rachel and Leah, who bring forth the further generations, manifesting them, shaping them. here again, a triad involving a quaternary.

This systematism which we extracted from the biblical story appears to have been well known also in the realms outside the Bible. Let me illustrate this point too.

As we know even in antiquity the stars were classified into twelve zodiacal signs. Ancient tradition founded on the Bible and dealing with the Bible also uses this classification. The scope of this book does not allow of expatiating on the significance and the names of these signs. I merely want to point out in connection with the aforementioned dual character of the thirds in the system, that the third sign of the Zodiac bears the name of Gemini, meaning Twins. The name of that sign therefore corresponds with the dual character of the third day of creation and with the duality of the third patriarch, who himself is a twin. Apparently there was a knowledge based on a fixed system which implied that the 'three' always has the character of duality.

Another example: the first day of creation has to do with light, so has the first patriarch. Now the first day of the week obtained the name Sunday in antiquity. The second day of creation, like the story of the second patriarch, is connected with water. The second day of the week was given the name of Moonday (Monday). Now the moon, according to antique tradition has to do with water. Proof of this correspondence will repeatedly he given in due course. It goes deeper than the obvious connection between the moon and the sea-level, or the frigidity of the moon as contrasted with the heat of the sun.

Thus the names of the first two days of the week have resulted from knowledge of the systematism as described above. The names of the other days of the week need not be discussed here; all this merely seves as an illustration from realms outside the Bible.

Antiquity likewise knew a fixed classification of metals. The prime metal was gold, which was also connected with the sun and with light. The second metal was silver and it was juxtaposed with the moon and water.

Besides there was in antiquity a systematism for the generations. In it man was placed first, hence ranking with light, sun, gold; and woman came second, hence she ranked with water, moon, silver. The relation between man and the sun, woman and the moon, is emotionally accepted even nowadays, although the intrinsic knowledge of this systematism has got lost. Last not least, there is the fact of the monthly period of woman, normally corresponding with the lunar-month period; and the sun giving light and the moon receiving light.

Therefore in our scheme, coinciding with antique usage, the right side or the side of the first day can be called the male side, the left side or the side of the second day, the female side. Consequently the third place, a little lower down the centre of the diagram, is called the place of the child. It is the place where on the third day appears the first sign of life and where in the corresponding place of the second triad arises the life of beasts and of man. The child too has a dual character, pertaining to that of the father and of the mother, since the joint existence of the father and the mother forms the *sine qua non* for the appearance of the child.

In this first approach I intend merely to mention a few points of correspondence without entering into things more deeply. It only serves to point out to the reader that the systematics, prominent in the first chapter of the Bible were apparently well known and generally used and that they still obtain in the biblical story, though the reader may not be aware of the fact. Hence we had better not enter as yet into the details of the information given, which might invite all kinds of questions. These questions will be duly answered in the course of the argument. One might, for instance, rightly ask, what about the male-female systematism in the case of the patriarchs. The first patriarch is Abraham and we see that fire plays a prominent part in the information given about him. The second patriarch is Isaac, with the emphasis on water. Isaac too is a man, so in this case the male-female systematics would not be applicable. Although the story of Isaac will be dealt with circumstantially lower down, I will here deal with this question just to show that any questions offering themselves can be answered and that systematism in regard to Isaac actually points to the female side just as it points to the male side in the case of the first patriarch, Abraham. In the life of Abraham it is invariably he himself who takes decisions. Even when his wife, Sarah, comes into prominence, it is Abraham who takes the lead, takes the decisions. Abraham is active, he is the man of initiative.

In the life of Isaac, on the other hand, we see passivity preponderant. As ordained by God Isaac is led to the sacrificial spot by Abraham to be sacrificed. Clearly demonstrating passivity. When Isaac is to find a wife, Abraham takes the initiative and sends a servant to find her for Isaac (Gen. 24). The servant's search is circumstantially described. Isaac merely accepts her. As we shall see by and by when Isaac was going to be sacrificed and passively accompanied his father, merely asking a few questions, he was thirty-seven and when his wife was found for him, he was forty. Not an age, generally speaking, to undergo things passively. Again, when Isaac actually should have taken the initiative in his most important act, decisive for the subsequent course of biblical events, viz. giving his blessing to his sons, he is markedly passive, his wife Rebekah taking things in hand. In fact, it is Rebekah, who determines that the blessing shall be given to Jacob and not to Esau (Gen. 27). And it is Rebekah, who sends Jacob to Laban (Gen. 27:42–46). So it is woman taking the second place in the scheme after all. The only instance in which we see Isaac acting for himself is the story of the water-wells. Here the water-character is implicitly indicated by the locality. Isaac's so-called blindness, his decisions ever taken by other people, all this stamps him with the female principle, the receptive principle, that which undergoes things, that which exerts no perceptible influence on the development. So the second patriarch is characterized by passivity, as it is not only manifested by woman towards man, but also by water as regards fire, and by the moon as regards the sun.

Finally, let us point out the difference between male and female, between active and passive, as it manifests in the right side and the left of man himself. Generally speaking in man's physical life it is the right side, the right hand which is active, the left hand which is passive.

The reader is requested not to ascribe undue importance to all this illustrative material. It merely serves to make things easier for us to point out that the systematism found in the tale of creation is not an arbitrary theory of our own concoction, but that it is related to the systematics in use elsewhere. Hence all this is bound to have a far wider scope than one is apt to think.

The various examples introduced into the scheme as drawn up for the tale of creation present the following diagram:

Second day		*First day*
left		right
female		male
moon		sun
water		fire
Isaac		Abraham
Monday		Sunday
silver		gold
passive		active
receptive		giving
left hand		right hand
	Third day	
	middle	
	child	
	dual character	
	Gemini	
	Jacob-Esau	
	Rachel-Leah	

I will now revert to the fact of the four acts of creation in the three days of creation, hence the relation between the numbers three and four. Either of them shows the completion of an identical cycle. What follows is a repetition of this three-four relationship. The leader is begged to remember the repetition occurring in the second triad of creation.

Just as the four acts of creation are correlated with the three days in which they take place, thus the four matriarchs are correlated with the three patriarchs. In either case the three and the four are interrelated as an indissoluble unity. The three may be called the number which represents the male character as the three patriarchs do and the four the number which represents the female character as expressed in the four matriarchs. In antiquity the numbers three and four were actually looked upon as the male and female numbers respectively. The number five applied to the child. This relationship between three, four and five is not arbitrary. We have already pointed out the man-woman relationship in the case of the three days of creation which offers the opportunity of materializing, concretizing, to the four acts of creation, just as man gives it to woman, as the three patriarchs give it to the four matriarchs.

However, this relationship may also be approached from another point of view, the arithmetical. In doing so a word must be said about one of the ways numbers are looked upon in the world of the Bible.

The number 'one' is not – at least not exclusively – looked upon as part of a complexity built up of many component parts, but first and foremost as an expression of the conception of unity which embraces everything. The number 'one' represents a world outside which nothing exists, since it includes everything, literally everything. Hence the conception 'two', as we know it, meaning two different or at any rate separate things, is non-existent in the realm of the 'one'. As soon as there are 'two', it means that 'one' has divided itself into two parts. All at once another world has come into existence. Multiplicity has become prominent over against the inclusive unity previously existent. The transition from 'one' to 'two' consequently means an altogether new situation. For now the 'three' has become conceivable as well, since three is the condition of 'one', undivided as yet, plus the condition of the two parts now come forth. Thus there are three different situations to be discerned. It may be represented this way:

1 (undivided)	
either of the two	the other one of the two

The forthcoming of the 'two' proves to have still further consequences. For the 'two' can be brought into relation to itself. This is expressed in the form of four possibilities, the 'twice two', and may be represented as forming a square, like this:

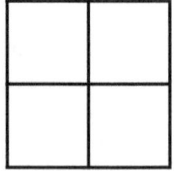

Since the 'one' is as yet only divided into two parts, the 'two' is the ultimate possibility for the 'two' to be related to itself. For multiplication by 'two' means multiplication by the greatest possible number in the realm where 'two' is the ultimate possibility. Therefore squaring always means multiplication by the greatest possible number, if the number which is to be squared, itself contains the ultimate possibility of division. As regards the condition where division into two represents the extreme limit, the number four is the ultimate possibility offered by the division into two. In the 'four' the 'two' has fulfilled itself, has related itself to itself.

It may be useful to point out here the consequences of the above line of thought in regard to the tale of the Bible as we have considered it so far. We have seen that the tale of creation begins with a duality and how this duality is worked like a weaving-pattern into the developments of the six days of creation. We also see on the one hand the 'two' eventuating in the 'three' of the three days of creation and on the other hand in the 'four' of the four acts of creation. Thus the systematism of the tale of creation makes it clear that if there is a duality, this duality has the three and the four as its consequence. And that the cycle is completed with the coming of the four. For what comes afterwards is in a sense a repetition in a different quality. In a world of duality, in a world of opposites, the conception 'four' is the ultimate real possibility. And that is why the cycle is completed with the fourth act of creation.

It is what is sometimes called mystery, this knowledge about the 'four'. It is said that in the school of Pythagoras a neophyte at his initiation was made to count: one, two, three, four. When he had uttered the number 'four', he was told to stop, 'since you have uttered our oath'. There was no need to continue counting. Whoever knows what is contained in this one, two, three, four, is able to open the door to the secret.

Here 'four' is indeed represented in a way altogether different from our method of counting nowadays. Four is the highest number in the systematics we have discovered, both in the cycle of the tale of creation and in that of the patriarchs and matriarchs. Keeping this in view, we may come to command a little more understanding of the four elements known to antiquity, as we shall realize that they belong to an altogether different conception of the world and so have nothing to do with the ninety-two or more elements of modern chemistry. There is no sense in manipulating the word 'primitive' reciprocally when judging the points of view concerning the elements.

We shall repeatedly come across the number 'four' as the expression of the extreme stage of development, as the completion of the cycle resulting, if there is duality. With the 'four' the cycle of the three phases, the three days, is likewise completed. In the diagram of the tale of creation the four are to be arranged like this.

```
left                                                              right
 2                                                                  1
                          middle
                            3
                            4
```

With this 'three' of the three phases and the 'four' as the corresponding extreme stage of development all the rest is settled. It was quite apparent from the systematism of the tale of creation. Now if we proceed with our argument about the numbers just as we commenced, we shall in yet another way get a confirmation of the fact that 'four' must be considered the extreme development.

We saw that the existence of the 'two' creates the presence of three conditions. Thus the resulting 'three' as a phase of the process of completion of the 'two', when brought in relation to itself, contains the potential presence of six situations. For then there is the genuine 'three', the quantity which appears in reality, but this 'three' contains within itself the preceding 'two' together with the original 'one'.

Presented in a diagram it would look like this:

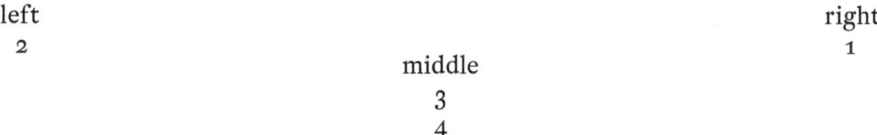

		1 (the undivided 'one')	
'one' plus 'two' in the background	one of the two		the other of the two
the genuine 'three'	one of the three	the second of the three	the third of the three

Thus the three days of creation, as soon as manifest, potentially contain within themselves the six, i.e. the next three days of creation. At the manifestation of the first triad, the subsequent manifestation of the second triad, completing the six, has become a definite fact.

The same argument applies to the 'four' as ultimate development of the 'two'. The 'four' is the exterior value, that which actually becomes manifest. Previous to this there is the intermediate stage, the aforementioned 'three', which in its turn is preceded by the 'two' with which division set in and finally by the state of the 'one', undivided as yet. So the 'four' presupposes the existence of 4+3+2+1=10 different conditions. With it the 'four' actually proves to be the basis of a system underlying the whole structure of the world and of thought. With it the 'four' actually proves to be that which is contained in the conception of the four elements.

We have now found the 'six' of the six days of creation resulting as a consequence from the three which served as their basis. But where in the tale of creation can we find the 'ten', proceeding from the 'four', existing as the extreme development of a condition of duality? Just as 'four' represents the extreme in a cycle, so the 'ten' must bring its completion. In our numerative system the 'ten' has that function. Indeed, in the tale of creation the 'ten' actually achieves completion. Just as the six days of creation proceed logically from the three as the root of the tale, so also must we find ten acts of creation, resulting from the four acts in the nucleus of the tale. As a matter of fact there are 10 acts of creation in the story.

We find that every act of creation is introduced by the words 'and God said'. The story states that the word of God crystallized into an event, that the word caused things to come forth. And in the tale of creation in the first chapter of Genesis we actually find that God spoke ten times, calling things forth with the word. We have already come across the two groups of four words of creation in twice three days. On the sounding of the eighth word man comes forth. Then follows the ninth word of God, saying that man 'be fruitful and multiply', and at the tenth word man is given 'every herb bearing seed and every tree yielding fruit, for meat'. In the tale of creation being fruitful and multiplying, as also taking food, are aligned to the creation of light and the creation of man. They form part of the complete cycle of the ten acts of creation. Ten times an act of creation is called forth by God's word. With the tenth word the tale of creation is completed and this is emphatically stated in the story at the advent of the seventh day. Hence there are ten acts of creation in the six days, proceeding from the four acts in the nucleus in the first triad of days. So here again the 'four' as the end of a cycle is completed with the 'ten' as conclusion of the whole.

Armed with this knowledge about the conception of numbers let us return to our discussion of the numbers 'three', 'four' and 'five'. The number by which is expressed the conception man, the 'three', finds its completion in the number 'nine'. The three has then been related to the highest attainable in the world of the three, i.e. It has been squared. Viewed in the same manner, the number of woman, the 'four' has for its extreme development four to the square, i.e. sixteen. 'Man' and 'woman' together, when they have become united in the condition in which they have reached the highest attainable, the extreme in their be-ness, are $9 + 16 = 25$. And 25 is the square, the completion of the 'five'. Now *that* is what is meant with the 'child'. It is the fruit of the unity of the 'man' and the 'woman', each completed in themselves. It is then that something new is born. So it is not true that man + woman = child. For indeed $3 + 4$ do not make 5. But it is a fact that man (in fulfilment of his existence) + woman (in fulfilment of her existence) = child (in fulfilment of its existence). Man and woman face each other as opposite conceptions in order to make the child, as the fulfilment of themselves. And the child cannot be, unless it has the fulfilment of both the man and the woman for its basic condition. If one has to a certain extent mastered the knowledge of the antiques, then what is now known as the Pythagorean proposition, may be taken for an expression of a universal law of life, embodied in a geometrical form, a rectangle, showing how the male and the female principles, related to each other as thesis and antithesis effect the child-principle as a synthesis, which unites the 'parents' as a hypotenuse.

The three, four and five, apart from their multiples, of course, are the only whole numbers to express this proposition. Therefore, in their direct sequence, they are of very special significance in the systematism to be discussed further down. The Pythagorean proposition can be visualized as follows:

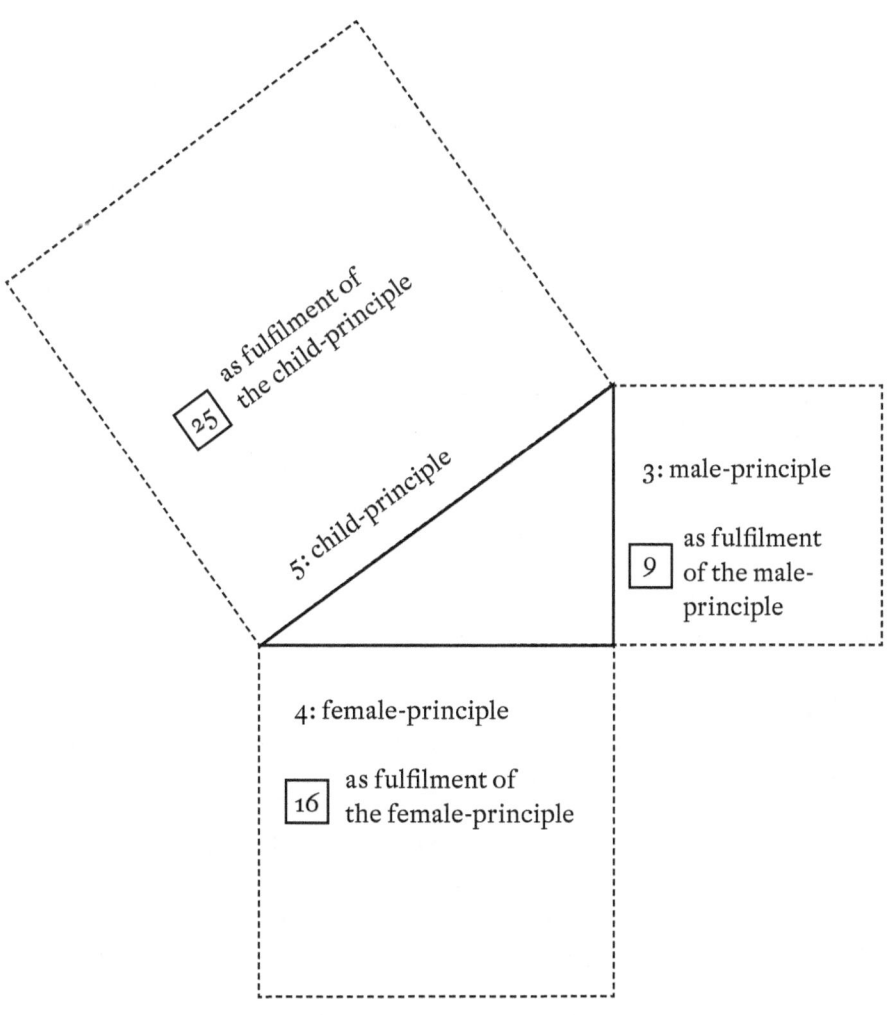

The reader may, for himself, have made the combination of 3+4=7, and 3×4=12. We shall discuss it later on. The numbers 7 and 12 require ample discussion. It may be pointed out, however, that neither the 7 nor the 12 have the character of completion, as have the 5 and the 25.

We have ventured upon an initial approach, a very simple approach of the tale of creation. In doing so we have struck upon a few general principles, evidently operative in other realms as well. At any rate we have discovered that there is more in the tale of creation than we would suspect when merely reading it as a story, trying to put the images vividly before us, and finally deciding, if we believe or do not believe, whether things could have been like that. So far I have purposely avoided entering into the significance of the words and images. And just as deliberately I have put forward an almost mechanical systematism. To impart life to this mechanical systematism we shall have to go more deeply into the matter. For the sake of simplicity let us restrict ourselves to the further analysis of the tale of creation, since we have started in that way and it has at our first approach revealed an interesting systematism.

At the same time we shall discuss another facet of the tale of creation. Every reader will have noticed that we are actually concerned with two tales of creation. One in the first chapter and the other in the second chapter of Genesis. And these two tales of creation contradict each other in various ways. Here we have one of those passages which makes the well-meaning reader sigh why things were not told a little more intelligibly, why the two chapters do not show more correspondence. The less well-meaning reader will find occasion to suppose there were a number of authors with diverse conceptions. But everybody is faced with this contradiction and even though many well-meaning commentators have tried to adjust the second tale to the first by means of various interpretations, we cannot say any interpretation has succeeded in removing our confusion. It is difficult to see the sense of these further specifications with so much different and often contradictory information.

In the second story man is present at the very beginning, the beasts are brought to him afterwards and even the trees come after man. It will also strike the reader that the first tale of creation speaks of God, whereas the second tale, without exception, speaks of the Lord God.

However, let us not enter, just yet, into the meaning of the words, but confine ourselves to finding the systematism, if possible. We shall have plenty of opportunity to give due consideration to the meaning of the words and images, when we know a little more about this systematism.

Now starting with Gen. 2:4 we notice a different line of development and when we try to arrange the events in due order we find:

There was not anything, because it had not rained yet, but there went up a mist from the earth. Then we hear that man was formed. The third act is the planting of a garden in Eden and there He put the man whom He had formed.

The fourth thing we are told is that the Lord God made to grow all kinds of trees and that the tree-of-life was made to grow in the midst of the garden together with the tree of the knowledge of good and evil. The fifth act is that a river went out of Eden and formed out into four streams. As the sixth there is man again put into the garden to dress it and to keep it. The seventh is the commandment that he might freely eat of every tree in the garden, but of the tree of knowledge of good and evil he should not eat. The eighth is the statement that man was alone and that it was not good that he should be alone. And therefore the Lord God formed every beast of the field and every fowl of the air and brought them unto him. As this did not lead to the purpose in view, the ninth act is a deep sleep falling upon man and a rib taken from him. After which the tenth act reveals that the Lord God made a woman out of the rib and brought her unto the man.

These ten events are not set apart from each other by the words: 'and God said', as in the first tale of creation, but they are mentioned in the strict sequence of their occurrence. Now, if we make a diagram of these ten events, as we did with the ten words of creation of the first chapter, we get the following picture:

2. Man   1. Mist

    3. Garden in Eden
    4. The trees, and especially
      the two trees in the midst

6. Man in the garden to   5. River forking out
  dress it and keep it   into four streams

    7. Commandment as to
      eating and non-eating
    8. Not good that the man
      should be alone and the
      beasts are brought to him
    9. The deep sleep and the
      taking of the rib.
    10. Making the woman and
      bringing her to man.

This graphic also clearly shows ten parts, but it has nothing in common with the scheme resulting from the ten words of creation. Yet here too is seen a distinct regularity. On the right side of the diagram we read 'a mist watering the earth' and 'the river to water the garden', which river forks out into four streams. So we notice a typical coherence: both mentioning water which is moistening things.

Again on the left side we see man mentioned twice. First man is made and then man is put in the garden to till it and keep it. So just as in the first tale of creation, what comes lower down in the scale is a kind of elaboration of that which was stated higher up.

In the middle part of the scheme we also notice a certain coherence. First we see the Garden made in Eden and details described concerning the trees; then there is a kind of relationship between man and the garden, as expressed in the rules about his eating of the trees of the garden; afterwards there is man's being alone and finally the making of woman.

So the scheme does show a certain purpose, when one considers it in itself. It does not show any coherence, however, with that of the first tale of creation. For in the first scheme the right side is that of light and fire, in the second it is the side of water. There, on the left, we found the separation of the waters above the firmament from the waters under the firmament and the life in those waters. Here, on the left, it is man's coming; but it *does* show some connection with the first scheme after all, for man has also to do with water here. The mist was first needed to moisten the earth, and the garden into which man is put is likewise watered, in this case by rivers. Both sides, left and right, have to do with water. Everything connected with light and fire is emphatically left out of the picture. It is a typical tale of water.

The events in the middle column show a little more connection with the first scheme. Both in the second and the first schemes there are the plants, the trees and afterwards the beasts. And as the last item the man as man and woman. For the man who is made at the beginning in this second tale of creation, at this stage appears to be merely a human being, not yet subdivided into man and woman.

However, there is an altogether different connection to be perceived with the first tale of creation. The first tale of creation has light as the first appearance, as the beginning of the scheme of things, and water as the second. We were able to trace back this principle of first light then water, in a number of examples chosen at random. According to this scheme the second tale of creation must have the character of the conception 'second', and this character is actually the water-character. Hence the second tale of creation is a story in which water plays the prominent part. Indeed, when we continue to read, we shall find in the third chapter that it is the story of woman. For it is emphasized that nothing can happen until the man has the woman. And as soon as he has got her she takes the initiative. It is the woman who speaks with the serpent, it is the woman who eats and offers man to eat. Man is passive, in the same way as the second patriarch, Isaac, is passive.

As the first tale of creation begins with light, so the second must begin with water. In systematics the second tale as a whole is placed on the 'left', opposite the first tale which is placed on the 'right'. So the water-character of this second tale of creation fits in completely, both as to sequence and significance.

Although there is otherwise no appreciable connection between the systematism of the first tale of creation and that of the second, the tales in themselves actually show a definite system. It seems as if this sytematism compels us to pay attention to a connection which lies much deeper. For when a story is presented like this — and nobody can maintain it has required any but the slightest effort to discover the system — it must have the intention to invite the student to look further in that direction and not be content with superficial, vague and arbitrary speculations. For exactly when one does not know the foundations of a thing, it is easy to lose oneself in various speculations, interpreting the text as one thinks fit for the purpose. So it is essential for us to get to know more about this system. Especially when we see that all the time there is a marked regularity to be found in every detail under consideration. We might compare it with the regularity and the systematism one can find in life and in the whole of creation, if only one has sufficient interest to penetrate more deeply into it. If at the very first steps of our examination of the Bible we come across such systematism, the question arises if the Book does not conceal within itself a scheme, a principle exactly as does creation. Hence the question arises if the Bible is not creation itself, only in a different form, in a different quality, i. e. in the word.

It is true, we have so far only demonstrated that there is a certain systematism. We have not yet been able to say much about its significance. And we have also seen that the two schemes, we could draw up of the tales of creation, started from different points of view. In a sense this was apparent, since in the first tale God is introduced under the name of God, and in the second as the Lord God. So there is a different signature as well.

Now we may ask ourselves whether the Bible has come down to us to strike us with its more or less pronounced systematism. It might therewith satisfy all kinds of people eager to know more about principles and schemes and structures; people, who, like mathematicians, delight in finding a system in everything. It might also fascinate people who, proceeding a little further, would try to reveal the thought of antiquity on the why and wherefore of the world with the help of their knowledge of this systematism. And proceeding a little further yet, it might attract people who would discover the relationship of the systematism of the Bible with that of nature and who would then think they had found a key to a further unveiling of nature's secrets. It might make the same deep impression on man as the discovery of the laws of the universe.

All these motives, however, are largely utilitarian; they are useful to man, they give him a little more comfort in the world and a little more joy. And most people long for such things. They are inclined to relate everything to this life and they presume that everything is there or should be there to make life proceed as smoothly as possible. Other things, outside this sphere of snugness should be involved as little as possible, since they only serve to disturb their dream of life. The Bible, however, might also and emphatically be something entirely different. Might it not be also and emphatically, the story told to man about the how and wherefore of this world, the how of life in this world, both in the herefore and the hereafter through all eventual lives and worlds, how man progresses through all this, perchance telling him also *why* he goes like that and what he himself can do or should do. Granted, it is an all-inclusive question. But I express it here because if one were asked to state quite honestly what he would expect of a holy book, coming direct from God, he would be bound to say something along these lines. He would want to be shown a way to know *everything* after all, from beginning to end, that he might be able to offer himself completely, unconditionally, because he would then realize that he did not give himself merely to have this present life proceed satisfactorily – what would it be, measured against eternity – but because it would then be all-inclusive. The man who would dare to demand this, just theoretically, would smile rather shyly, realizing he had demanded a lot.

Yet, without creating an impression of exaggerating, we are entitled to ask ourselves if the Bible because of its systematism – provided this reaches very far and very deep – does not offer irrefutable information to man, concerning the how and wherefore of this world and about the way in which he can meet it all. As stated before, we shall have to inform with life the mechanical character of such systematism. Could not the conceptions which so far we have classed under the heading of emotions, acquire more clarity and character if raised to a very special systematism reflecting the world in its very essence? Just as an action, a kind word, a helping hand, acquire more clarity and character, when we see the person behind it, hear his voice, catch his smile.

To attain knowledge of this more profound systematism, some preparation is necessary. First let us now proceed to get acquainted with the word. This may cause some surprise, yet we shall have to take it literally.

To us – I am not entering into philosophical speculations naturally – the word has become something useful which helps us to contact other people and to make our point of view clear to each other. We learn foreign languages to be able to speak more or less fluently with foreigners, and to understand them and be understood in our turn. There are all sorts of theories on the origin of languages, how they developed and how eventually they degenerated. Nowadays there are also theories, proceeding from the universal doctrine of evolution, explaining how by way of the primitive sounds to warn against danger or to express desire of some sort of food, man began to specify these sounds, group them together into conceptions and transform them. Evolving ever further in this way, man attained to what at present we can consider a language. I shall not busy myself with any of these theories. They originate from a world utterly different from the one I want to describe here.

I shall here discuss the word as it comes down to us through the Bible and I shall apply the same method as in the other speculations: I shall let the Bible speak for *itself* without involving my own or other people's theories.

The word in the Bible – and as I stated in the preface, I shall discuss the Old Testament exclusively – is originally in Hebrew. When I mentioned the fact that throughout the ages, as long as the Bible has been known to us historically, the text has been left unaltered, so that clearly omitted letters or redundant letters were consistently omitted or left standing respectively, I meant the original text, of course.

One might rightly ask if that original text really is so important, when we have such exact and scientifically correct translations. For the contents can be translated quite well, and the translations sometimes even are very powerful. I do not want to rouse any misgivings as to the usefulness of good translations. However, the original text is indispensable for our deeper examination. I shall explain this with the help of a few considerations of the word in the Bible. But first I must resort to an example from another domain to make clear what a word in biblical Hebrew is and why it should remain unaltered, if its character is not to be lost altogether.

For instance, when we speak about water, the conception is clear enough for daily use in our intercourse with other people. It will not be misunderstood. Everybody understands we mean a liquid. It becomes a little more difficult when we have to make a distinction between the three physical stages of water: water as ice, as a liquid, and as steam or vapour. In the first instance water is a solid, in the second a liquid, in the third a gas. It becomes even more difficult, if a microscopic little creature were to give us an explanation of water, an example given by Maeterlinck in one of his books. Suppose a creature like that living on a leaf, were to notice water in the form of a dew-drop, lying on the leaf. It would come to a definition like this: water is spherical, solid, impermeable matter which lifts at a certain temperature. If, however human beings and that microscopic little creature on the leaf — supposing it were equipped with a mind like ours — should examine water more closely, they would finally discover that water, *whether* in the physical state of ice or a liquid or a gas, whether apparently permeable or impermeable, always has the same structure, i.e. It is composed of two atoms of hydrogen and one of oxygen. If we were then to define water as H_2O, no misapprehension would be possible; the small creature on the leaf and the grammar-schoolboy, on seeing vapour would understand they meant the same thing when expressing it as H_2O. Presuming for convenience sake that H_2O is the most exact formula for water.

The formula of H_2O is not only qualitative, it does not only state the presence of hydrogen and oxygen, it is also quantitative, giving a ratio of 2 to 1; two atoms of hydrogen to one of oxygen. If, however, we should go on analysing the water, we would end up with a purely quantitative formula, in which hydrogen and oxygen would have a common denominator, and there would only be a numerical distinction between hydrogen and oxygen. This would finally be the most exact formula. How are we to explain the qualitative differences between hydrogen and oxygen to that microscopic little creature? How would it understand what we mean when we write H or say hydrogen? However, if people are merely to represent a quantum either through a number of taps or a number of sticks, there is no question any longer of their understanding each other's language. In that case something which presents itself to us in a picture, is defined in numerical proportions, unconnected with the picture, leaving undetermined how we look at the picture and judge of it.

It is possible for us, as set forth above, to analyse substances as water and reduce them to a quantitative conception, but we cannot do the same with conceptions such as knowledge, life, love, faith, etc. They cannot be analysed in laboratories and reduced to quantitative formulae.

Now the word in the Bible *is* such a quantitative conception. And the quantitative mode of expression does not restrict itself to substances like water, gold, carbon, meat, blood, etc., but is applicable just as well to conceptions such as knowledge, life, faith, etc.

I am well aware that this is a very strange conception concerning language and the word. But the reader will find by and by that this is not a conception put forward at random, just to spring something new on him, when so much has already been said about the language of the Bible, but that this conception contains its proof in itself. And it will not be difficult to learn to understand the fundamentals of this conception and its application in practice.

The first question to be asked at this juncture is: where are those numbers in which the biblical conceptions can be expressed quantitatively? Do we not see merely letters, also in the Hebrew words of the Bible? The answer is very simple: the things we take to be letters are primarily numbers and it is only because as numbers they have got a numerical order, that they also become letters with all the consequences thereof in regard to the formation of sounds and images.

The language the Bible uses – and this is one of the remarkable things about the Bible – gives a quantitative representation of everything, and with it the purest possible expression. An image can rouse a certain feeling, it can be viewed or valued differently; feelings are very difficult to describe. Nevertheless the images and the feelings described must be included. They, too, have a very important place. But in order to come to a pure, finely shaded understanding, one needs this quantitative structure of the word too. Language in Hebrew is also called 'safa', which is at the same time the word for 'shore, bank'. For language indeed forms the boundary-line between two worlds: our own world where everything is expressed in terms of space-time, and another world entirely different from ours. The best approach to that other world – let us for practical purposes call it the real world, since it is not divided and extended in space-time – is that which in *our* world must be expressed as a proportion, as a juxtaposition of 'a more' and 'a lesser'. It cannot be expressed any other way in space-time. That which we observe here as a proportion, a quantitative term, therefore is our nearest approach to the real world. It forms the bridge from this world of space-time to the real world. As soon as the quantitative is transformed into words representing sound-proportions and images or feelings, which after all can only acquire form in this world because they call forth specific proportions, we get farther removed from that boundary between the two worlds which is formed by this specific language. It is true that the effect of the words as sounds, as spoken language, is after all similar to that of the quantitative proportions written down as letters, because the difference between the letters expresses itself in the difference of sounds and thus also expresses quantitative proportions. Therein lies the power of the spoken word. Certain proportions are given a specific form, are materialized through the pronouncing of words. Similarly the proportions, embodied in written form would through this concretizing of the form, through this materialization in writing – which is connected with the quantitative significance of every letter– contain power, if indeed it is with the word as I have explained it here.

But as soon as the word is nothing except a description of an image, or of a feeling, a sentiment, it loses this perceptible relationship with the quantitative which brought it up to the boundary-line between this space-time world and the world of the real. So, if one insists on regarding a word of the Bible merely as a description of an image, when the word cow merely creates the image of a cow, and the word house merely the image of a house, if, for instance, revenge is only regarded as that which one feels oneself when imagining revenge, then in that case one has divested the word of the Bible of its power, of its deeper sense. One has returned the word into a mere image. And as everybody knows, the Bible does not like the making of images.

If one is willing to accept this conception of language it implies: that one must rank language as something primary; that language is not man-made, not developed out of nothing, out of inarticulate animal sounds, but that sound has come to man as a datum, just as life came to him as a datum, just as he found the universe and the earth as a datum. Language was given 'ready' to man. These propositions will of course have to be clearly proved in the following pages.

So letters are first and foremost numbers representing proportions, and only in the second place letters by means of which sounds can be formed in this world. It will perhaps be urged that I am stating things the other way round. 'For,' people will say, 'it is a well-known thing, that in antiquity letters – hence also Hebrew letters – were given a numerical value. Because,' it will be further argued, 'people had not yet got separate symbols to represent numbers and therefore they took the letter-characters. And from them ensued this juggling with numbers, which was erroneously identified with Kabbala.' Kabbala means ancient lore, tradition, and as such has nothing to do with all this tomfoolery with numbers.

Yet we have to presume that primarily letters are numbers, proportions. I might explain my point of view by asking a question, a very simple question, but a fundamental one. How is it we know that in the alphabet alpha comes before betha, gamma before delta? Because alpha begins with an 'a' and betha with a 'b'? But how can it be proved that 'a' should come before 'b'? The answer is just as simple: because a, i. e. alpha or in Hebrew aleph, is primarily 1 and *that is why* it comes first. The 'one' is the original state, it is the initial state. And since betha, in Hebrew beth, is primarily 2, betha comes after alpha. The 2 represents a phase, a state which comes after the 1. And as gamma is primarily 3, gamma comes after betha. Thus it is with the whole series of the letters. The letters express proportions, they are numbers. And since there is a numerical order in multiplicity, there is also a sequence in letters.

So there was not a committee deciding that aleph was to come before beth; neither was it our primitive ancestors, equipped with economic standards, who thought that aleph – in Hebrew aleph means 'head of a cow' – should come before beth – in Hebrew beth is a house – because a cow was supposed to be more important than a house. It was not like this at all; it was the order of the numbers which gave the letters their sequence.

That the 'one' was represented by 'the head of a cow', the 'two' by a house has to do with the knowledge how a certain state in the real world crystallizes into form in space and time. Since that knowledge did exist – we shall refer to it by and by with further examples – numbers were given names in the world of forms which they still represent. The 'one' has a form different from the 'four' and 'four' differs from 'forty'.

So, if actually, as will be demonstrated further down, the quantitative proportion is the primary factor in language, i.e. that which comes first, that which is nearest the essence of things, then it is only logical that letters are primarily numbers and that they have acquired what we call alphabetical sequence on the strength of their numerical order. It was the numerical order also which determined the forms and the names of the letters.

When I use the word 'primary' in these speculations, it is not meant as strictly primary in temporal sequence. So I do not imply that first there were only numbers and that afterwards these numbers served as letters, leading via combinations of them to speech and afterwards to writing. With primary in this connection I only mean: 'fundamental in principle'. The essential thing about the letter is the fact that it expresses a proportion. That it can besides be used for speaking and writing does not alter its essential function as expressor of proportions. In this connection it is significant that the Hebrew words for book, telling, counting and number, have the same root: s-p-r. Is not there a connection between the word 'tell' and 'tale', a 'number' in English, erzählen with zahlen in German, etc.?

This is not the place to expatiate on Hebrew letters. Suffice it to state here that the names of the letters which have come down to us in the West via the Greek alphabet are originally Hebrew names. Some people maintain they are Phoenician names. It does not matter; at any rate the names of the Hebrew letters which gave the non-Grecian names to Greek letters, mean something in Hebrew. I have already stated that aleph means 'head of a cow', beth means 'house'; thus gimmel, the third letter, means 'camel', daleth, the fourth letter means 'door', etc. In Greek alpha does not mean anything, neither do betha, gamma, delta. Greek tradition has it that a certain Kadmos taught them these letters. Now Kadmos actually means somebody coming from Kedem, viz. from the Orient; it also means 'formerly', 'originally'.

So the letters of the Bible and their names are still the foundation of our present-day alphabet.

As we shall have to consider the letters especially in their primary sense, hence as numbers, the reader need not worry about the fact he knows no Hebrew. As I promised, I shall frame the speculations in this book so as to make them easy to follow. Of course one who does know Hebrew will be able to check things more easily for himself and increase his knowledge of other facts.

I shall now first give the letters of the Hebrew alphabet, together with their names, in my spelling, and with their meaning as a number. With the help of this tabulation, which the reader had better copy and keep with him as he reads on, we shall now revert to the subject where we left off, viz. the second tale of creation. The letters are:

1 =	aleph	30 =	lamed
2 =	beth	40 =	mem
3 =	gimmel	50 =	nun
4 =	daleth	60 =	samech
5 =	hee	70 =	ayin
6 =	waw	80 =	peh or phe
7 =	zayin	90 =	tsade
8 =	cheth	100 =	kof
9 =	teth	200 =	resh
10 =	jod	300 =	shin or sin
20 =	kaf	400 =	taf

I shall not write the words, which are going to be mentioned, in Hebrew characters, but simply give them with the names of the characters used and/or their meaning as a number.

The letters of the Hebrew alphabet are consonants. It is these consonants that form the structure of the word. The vowels are conceived along with them. In later times, exclusively as an aid to those who had not got a sufficient command of the language, determinants were added in the form of lines or dots over, under or beside the letters. They have, however, no real significance. Of course a difference in vowels added can change the meaning of the word as an image. But the structure of the word remains unaltered. Certain consonants are voiceless in themselves, which also applies to 'aleph' and in a lesser degree to 'ayin'. So they only acquire voice and colour from the vowels known to accompany them, hence conceived along with them.

The jod and the waw sometimes occur as a mere vowel. In that case the jod is an 'i', and the waw 'o' or 'u'. For our purpose it is, however, sufficient to confine ourselves to the structure of the word as it is *written* and as it occurs in the Bible.

2
The Secret of the Word

Returning to the diagram of the events in the second tale of creation on page 33 and looking at the word used in the Bible for the 'mist' arising to water the earth (Gen. 2:6), we notice that the word 'ed', spelled aleph-daleth (1–4) is used. (When writing down the word in numbers, I link up the letters with a horizontal line. It is not a minus-sign, but only indicates that these letters together form the word.)

The 'mist' which watered the earth is placed on the right at the top of our diagram. We have already pointed out that the place on the right at the top corresponds with the place on the right at the bottom, where it says that a river went out of Eden to water the garden. For indeed, both have to do with water and watering; one with watering the earth, the other with watering the garden. In the systematism of the first tale of creation we saw that the acts of creation in the first triad of days confirmed those in the second, that the acts of creation in the second triad contained a kind of elaboration, a kind of development of that which was stated in the corresponding place in the first triad. I beg to remind the reader of the 'light' on the right at the top in the first triad and the light-bearers, sun, moon and stars, in the place on the right at the bottom in the second triad.

In what way is this correlation expressed in the system of the second tale of creation, now that we have discovered that the essential nature of 'mist' – apart from the image possibly existing within us – can be rendered as the proportion 1–4? Why, this correlation has suddenly become much more interesting. For unimportant, as it was to us until now, since we did not understand its purport, the river which is to water the Garden of Eden appears 'to part and become into four heads', hence the proportion 1–4.

For a man to whom mist is just mist, and to whom even the Hebrew word for mist, 'ed', is just mist, fails to grasp the correlation existing between mist and the fact that the single river forks out into *four* streams. As far as such a reader is concerned, it might just as well have been five or seven. He might even have added a fine comment on the significance of the 'holy number seven' in Paradise, if the river had forked out into seven heads.

We are here shown even more clearly the effect of the principle that the second triad represents a further development, another stage of the first triad.

That which in the first triad still bore the principle 1–4, hidden within itself, is concretized, condensed, materialized (so to speak) in the second triad. This principle expresses itself as the necessary forking out into 'four' of something which started as 'one'.

It is advisable here to remember the principle, active in the first tale of creation, where indeed out of the 1 developed the 4 of the 4 words of creation in the first triad of days.

The four rivers, which are later on described in greater detail in the second tale, are not first and foremost geographical conceptions – even though like everything which develops into an image, they may be that also –they mean much more than that. Firstly they make it clear how the 4 expresses itself once it becomes concrete. But let us also consider the left side of the scheme into which we are now trying to penetrate a little deeper.

There we perceive man is being made. Again it is difficult to see the why and wherefore. Why just in this place? And why was it so essential for that mist first to arise? What correlation is there between this mist arising and the formation of man? Can it be the primitive conception that water fertilizes and forms an element, indispensible to the existence of man?

Here again the essential reality of the word can show us what actually happens. Man in Hebrew is Adam and it is written aleph-daleth-mem (1–4–40). So we see the 1–4 cropping up here too, but this time in a different development. The 40, which is the 4 in a different quality, in a different plane we might say, attaches itself to the 1–4 proportion and thus evidently calls forth that being: man.

It is quite easy to see that there is a logical sequence of the necessity of the mist and the formation of man afterwards. For the mist appears to have something essential, expressing itself as the principle 1–4. And man is a development, an elaboration of it in a special direction, he is 1–4–40. Thus there actually is a correlation between that mist and man, a correlation which cannot possibly be established, if one were merely to consider mist and man as images. Every argument would then be artificial and far-fetched. It is only in their essence that the correlation does exist. The image, as a matter of fact, is misleading, and whoever does not know the essence cannot help getting off the track.

As far as the body is concerned, man is moulded out of earth. The Hebrew word for earth, the face of the earth, the surface of the earth, 'adamah', is also closely related to 'adam', the word for man. And the word 'face of the earth' also has this 1–4 as its principle, its essence. Adamah, as a matter of fact, is written aleph-daleth-mem-hee, (1–4–40–5). So it too is a further elaboration of this 1–4 principle.

Now that we have taken a cursory glance at this aspect of language, it would be a good idea to show a little more about it in this connection. Quite a different view from that of the modern philologists, in fact. Merely one example by way of illustration. This is not the place for a disquisition on language.

We saw that a man has 1–4–40 as his essential formula. Now truth is 'emeth', spelled aleph-mem-taf (1–40–400). So in the formulation of language, the expression in proportions, there is a certain correlation between man and truth. The 40 and 400 are likewise determined by the four in another plane. Which means that man and truth have the same structure with a difference in level. Man 1–4–40, truth 1–40–400. It also points to the meaning of the conception 'mist', 1–4. Which means that there is a close correspondence between the conception truth and this 1–4. If for instance the 1 should be left out in the word for man, there would only remain daleth-mem, 4–40, which is the word for blood. We might look at it this way: 'blood' connected with the 1 becomes 'man'. Without the 1 it is merely the formula for blood.

If we do the same thing to the word for 'truth', leaving out the 1, owing to which only mem-taf remains, we read 'meth', which is the word for death.

So we see that being linked up with the 1 can change the word essentially. Man without the 1 is merely blood; truth without the initial 1 means 'death'. And since the words for man and truth in their structure show a mere difference in level, there is also a correlation to be seen between man with the 1 as life and man without the one as death.

From these examples also appears the significance of the 1, the undivided, all embracing 'one'. Being linked up with it or no radically changes the situation.

In order not to create the impression that the whole language is built up on this (1–4)-principle, I shall take a single example from a different realm, again merely by way of illustration, without further pretentions, after which we shall revert to the subject of this chapter.

It is an example in which the relationship clearly appears in sentiment. At the same time one will see that proportions, reduced to units, are the determinant factor. That such proportions do occur in decades or centuples shows a difference in level rather than a difference in essence. The decades and centuples merely indicate certain shades of meaning, which one can think of as 'the same thing but on a different level'.

As an example I take the word for serpent, a disagreeable biblical creature. Serpent in Hebrew is nachash, spelled nun-cheth-shin (50–8–300). The word for fall or to fall is nophal, spelled nun-phe-lamed (50–80–30).

In the structure 5–8–3 we clearly see the correlation between serpent and fall. Falling is dropping down from a higher level and landing on a lower level. The word for that aspect of the soul, which is considered closely connected with the animal body, is nephesh, spelled nun-phe-shin (50–80–300). Again the same structure, the same essence. This nephesh is considered to be the animal soul, related to the senses, bodily feelings, etc., in contradistinction to what might be called the divine soul in man, which is called neshamah and has a different structure.

So, what we see is a correlation between serpent (50–8–300), fall (50–80–30) and animal soul (50–80–300).

That which in our feelings we consider correlated — in contradistinction with, for instance, 'mist' and 'man', where our feelings leave us in the lurch — appears to be pointedly stressed in speech.

The structure, which here served as an example, the 5–8–3, can also occur in a different sequence. Sometimes we see a connection, sometimes we do not, though that does not imply that there is none.

For instance, the word for vine, which occurs frequently in the Bible, is gephen, spelled gimmel-phe-nun (3–80–50). So here the structure is reversed. That there must be, or at least *can* be a connection, we know from the intoxication, caused by wine. In this case we may state that the building-bricks are identical, but that they have been reversed. Remember that these few examples, given in a very special way, are merely meant to illustrate the principle. There are of course in reality a great many variations and other phenomena. If a person is very fond of violets, for instance, he should not be disappointed to see roses, tulips and thousands of other flowers and all sorts of grasses and ferns besides, and be prepared not to find violets only, however much he has come to love them. The beauty of the world lies in this very variety of things and conditions, which together bring harmony, which together give us the sense of a totality which is good. Similarly there is very much more to be found in language besides the principle employed here by way of illustration. Now let us return to the (1–4)-principle, we have discovered.

The 'mist' – 'ed' introduces a most remarkable principle in the world. In fact this (1–4)-essence appears to imbue all the rest, just as mist, as a phenomenon, as an image, moistens and drenches the earth. Over and over again we shall recognize this (1–4)-principle in the pattern of the world. In a sense it is like the essence, seeking expression, projecting itself in all the surrounding planes, in all surrounding spheres. We saw how this (1–4)-principle expresses itself in man, who is 1–4–40.

But in a different way this (1–4)-structure is also to be recognized even in the bodily crystallization of man. I merely refer to the hand of man with the thumb which can be opposed as 1 to any of the 4 fingers; the hand, which is so characteristic of man. Or, as people used to look upon the body in former times, divided by the joints according to this (1–4)-structure. The head as 1 over against the 4 parts of the rest of the body: the trunk as far down as the hip-joint, the upper legs down to the knee-joint, the lower legs down to the ankles and finally the foot. The joints too appear to have been formed according to that pattern. This (1–4)-principle can be found back in man in a good many other places and in different ways. It is impossible, though, to expatiate on the subject. Now that we have examined in detail the columns on the right and on the left we shall have to pay some attention to the central column of the diagram. I shall choose the item we shall frequently need in our further discussions and shall therefore repeatedly come across, viz. that of the two trees in the midst of the garden, the tree of life and the tree of the knowledge of good and evil. They play a decisive part in the central column. In the upper part of the diagram the creation of the trees is mentioned, in the lower part there is the command that man may freely eat of every tree of the garden except of the tree of the knowledge of good and evil.

These trees are rather vexing to the 'scientific investigator'. They are so utterly unscientific, so primitive, so rooted in those uncivilized times when people adored trees and ascribed specific powers to them. However concrete they may be, it is even hard to take them as subject for a sermon. In their concrete form they are so unreal, so utterly strange. And however much one may try to penetrate into their eventual phenomenal form, they give no definite answer to any questions, let alone sense to the whole story. If we honestly want to know what the Bible tells and what it means, it is very hard to accept the trees, which challenge us to come to a decision. Now let us closely examine these trees with the help of the language of the Bible, which expresses the real nature, the essence of things. We shall then discover that this wonderful language reaches ever greater depths and that it fits marvellously into the systematism, which the Bible shows in the tale and which we have already drawn the reader's attention to. A systematism which also hides this (1–4)-principle within itself.

The tree of life in Hebrew is called ets hachajim and it is spelled ayin-tsade (which is the word for tree) and hee-cheth-yod-yod-mem (for the phrase 'of life'). In numbers it is (70–90 5–8–10–10–40). The tree of the knowledge of good and of evil is in Hebrew, (as the Bible calls it) ets hadaäth tob wera, spelled ayin-tsade ('tree)' and hee-daleth-ayin-taf (of the knowledge) teth-waw-beth ('good') and waw-resh-ayin ('and evil'). In numbers it is (70–90 5–4–70–400 9–6–2 6–200–70).

We are now in the central column, the column of duality. Therefore we have here the two trees opposite each other, and a little lower down the statement that it is not good that the man should be alone, and next the formation of the woman, who is placed opposite him as a second, forming a duality with him. The central column is also the column of the child which partakes of the father as well as of the mother. Hence the qualities in the central column are not those of the column on the right exclusively, or the left exclusively. They are mixed up and not recognizable at a cursory glance. Just as little as one can distinguish from the outward appearance of the child what it has in common with its father and what with its mother. Speaking in terms of chemistry it is not a mixture, but a compound. That is why the (1–4)-principle will express itself in the central column differently from the right and the left columns. The principle will be there, but hidden, mixed up. Armed with this knowledge we shall have to examine the nature of those two trees. Their elements, their building-bricks, however, will have to reveal that (1–4)-principle.

When we examine the building-bricks of the tree of life, when we measure the weight of the proportion, so to speak – doing this along the lines of an ancient and well-known technique – we shall see that this tree of life contains 70+90+5+8+10+10+40=233 building-bricks, which form the sum total of the conception 'tree of life', as described above.

I shall not enter more deeply into this number 233, since it would divert us from our subject. But I shall now also check the building-bricks of the conception 'tree of the knowledge of good and evil', which as described above contains 70+90+5+4+70+400+9+6+2+6+200+70=932.

And suddenly we see how the right hand and left hand columns have yet put their stamp on the central column, how a miracle is here expressed in a very remarkable way. That which was 1–4 in the columns on the right and the left, expresses itself, here in our example also, in the total structure of the tree of life as compared with the total structure of the tree of the knowledge of good and evil. For 233, the number of the total structure of the tree of life, is to 932, the number of the total structure of the tree of the knowledge of good and evil, as ... 1:4. So, here too the pattern of 1–4 is perceptible. The mist has actually watered the ground of the earth, for *everything* which follows appears to bear this stamp.

At the same time we see something wonderful in the way in which this pattern reveals itself. Not *in* the tree of life is the (1–4)-structure perceptible, not in the tree of the knowledge of good and evil either, but it has revealed itself in an altogether unexpected way. It has revealed itself by specifying *what* the tree of life is, and *what* the tree of the knowledge of good and evil is. For now we see that the tree of life is the 1, over against the tree of knowledge of good and evil as the 4.

Just as in the lower part of the right hand column the conception mist, the 1–4, has revealed itself in the appearance of the one river, forking out into 4 streams, thus making 1–4, so also in the central column the tree of life now appears to represent the 1 of the fundamental (1–4)-conception and the tree of the knowledge of good and bad appears to represent the 4.

Maybe the observant reader will now understand the significance of the 1 in the structure of the words man and truth, which we gave as an example. In leaving out the 1 in the word man, which is (1–4–40), there only remained blood (4–40). And leaving out the 1 in the word truth, which is (1–40–400), there remained the word death (40–400). If one knows that the 1 is that which in the central column expresses itself as the tree of life, one will understand what omission of it will entail.

The central column both in the first diagram of the first tale of creation and in the second of the second tale of creation, is the place where the man is, resp. is ultimately, as man and woman. The central column has a very special meaning, representing our situation in this world, between left and right, ever standing between two conceptions which are each other's contrast or complement. That which finds expression in the central column is what man such as he is, can see. And that is why man in the further part of the tale is faced with the tree of the knowledge of good and bad, and not for instance with the four rivers of the right hand column, which apparently show forth the same principle and with which he is involved in a different way.

So we can now understand the 1 as expression of the tree of life and the 4 as that of the tree of the knowledge of good and evil. Maybe these two trees are now beginning to acquire a little more reality to us and perhaps the (1–4)-principle is therefore getting more alive.

If now we proceed to make a scheme of the second tale of creation — which was selected as an example to elaborate a somewhat more profound reflection in its initial progress — as we have discovered it valid for all the elements we have been discussing, we shall get the following picture:

```
man                                                              mist
1–4–40                                                           1–4
                    tree of life                          1
                    tree of knowledge of good and evil    4
man in the garden                                                river
1–4–40                                                           1–4
in regard to the tree   1
and the tree            4
                    commandment to man (1–4–40)
                    not to eat from the tree 4,
                    now that he is facing tree 1
                    and tree 4
```

It looked as if it was going to be more complicated, but we see now that the scheme has become much simpler and also much more intelligible. At least mechanically so. Language apparently can work wonders, it proves to be able to bring us nearer to the essence of things, if only we view it in the way it has come to us. This is the place to sound a note of warning.

The reader, more or less struck with the results acquired through using language in its more real form, viz. as a quantitative mode of expression, might feel induced to write down all sorts of words from the Bible in the same manner as I have done, to make schemes with columns on the right, on the left and in the centre, in order to count up the structural building-bricks in the words of the central column, or eventually those of the other columns, etc.

He would in that case behave like the young grammar-schoolboy who, having attended the first experiments in chemistry, now wants to experiment on his own. I really must warn against it. For, in all probability, when experimenting on one's own without substantial knowledge of the matter, one will not find anything sensible and give it up in disappointment, disbelieving that there are any correlations anyway, forgetful of the convincing results one has already seen. Or one will, like so many others, lose oneself in absurdities, bordering on the insane, juggling with numbers without any logical coherence. For, as I remarked in connection with another example, there are not only violets or roses among plants. There are so many other kinds and one might be disappointed if, looking for roses, one did not find a single one in wide fields. One has first to find out where to look for roses, where for daisies, where for edelweiss. Besides there are lots of grass and herbs. They too have their significance, their place, their beauty even. And together they create the image of the great harmony. If in this domain one wants to know more, it is open to the resolute. As far as *mental* effort is concerned, one need not sacrifice more to the study of it than one is prepared to sacrifice to the study of any branch of science, or trade or profession. However, not less either. Here too incompetence is dangerous.

I must also point at the widespread inclination to juggle with numbers. I hope the reader has realized that the manner in which I have here dealt with numbers, is utterly serious and straight. If we want to find truth we must be straight with ourselves to start with. We have to view our material with an open mind and critically ask ourselves why we do it this way and not otherwise, whether it is logically justified, whether it is not in contradiction with another procedure we followed first, etc. The approach should be similar to the manner in which we face a scientific problem, when we are properly at work; preferably without vague hypotheses with which anything can be proved, if one exploits this vagueness for all it is worth. I might put it this way: respect and love of the subject — the subject in this case embracing the whole of life, the meaning of existence — should preclude in advance any dishonest approach from indolence, or from an urge to impress other people or to find solace.

Therefore I must declare that I absolutely disapprove of juggling with numbers, which is often perpetrated under the guise of Kabbala. Any operation with numbers should find its origin in a distinct principle and this principle should ever remain effective. If one were to cast up, deduct and multiply numbers at random, just to get a certain result, it is either deceit or extreme foolishness. As often as not it is not exactly normal and by no means bright individuals who dabble in this game of numbers. That so many people should believe in it, well, one is apt to believe in vague theories which promise somewhat to sweeten the bitterness of life.

In the well-known publications of the would-be serious Kabbala, in which some sort of mystical science of numbers is applied, it is difficult to discover any system in the operation of numbers, which is clearly stated and can consistently be stuck to. There may sometimes be interesting coincidences, but one very soon wonders what purpose they serve and what they lead to. Occasionally they may be used as a nice parable. But manifestly all these things lack system as far as the science of numbers is concerned. And all this in spite of the fact that there *is* a definite systematism to be found in the doctrine of the Sephiroth and the view of life, based on this science of numbers and other principles ensuing from serious Kabbala. Probably they are remnants of an ancient lore, concerning the nature of language and the nature of things, in which the real knowledge has got lost and only a vague remembrance of certain techniques remains. And since people could attach great value to these techniques, at the time when the essence of them was known, there is still something left of that veil of sanctity and knowledge of the mystery, the secret, and it was passed on, largely or altogether erroneously to the students of what is at present accepted as Kabbala. Veiling oneself in clouds of mystery, often unconsciously, serves the purpose of concealing vagueness and indistinctness. That which can actually be considered 'secret', has its own method of veiling itself.

All the more reason for me to take care and continue as exact and precise as possible and stick to fundamental principles. Anyway, the serious reader will have realized that the permeation with the (1–4)-principle – even in the short passage in which I discussed it, from the mist to the rivers, from the mist to man, and thence to the tree of life and the tree of the knowledge of good and evil – is not far-fetched and *cannot* be sheer coincidence. It does not even require mathematical proof that coincidence is ruled out. The principle is too pronounced in its effect all through. And when, in the course of these reflections the reader will meet with it time and again, he will come to realize that there is a marvellous law, a systematism, as in creation itself, in the universe itself, in life.

Scientifically speaking we can say about creation that it took milliards of years to develop. Has the Bible with its language also come forth through milliards of years of selecting, developing, etc? And if this cannot be so, then how has this pre-eminent thing found its way into the Bible; and I confine myself to the short passage I have discussed, since I cannot now refer to what is still to come further down? What author could invent words in this way and make compounds of them, at the same time constructing the story into which they fit, so that mist is exactly 1–4, and man 1–4–40, and the proportion of the tree of life, as the totality of the complicated structure of that word, to the totality of the still more complicated structure of the tree of the knowledge of good and evil, is 1 to 4, so that here again the (1–4)-principle obtains! Indeed those words were already in existence when the Bible was written down by man. How then could these words fit into the tale and show this (1–4)-structure?

And what author of the Bible could give the words for serpent, fall and animal soul such a structure that they should be related, both in their structure and in the story? For those words, too, existed. And how is it that if the 1 is left out of the structure of the word 'man' or the related word 'truth', the words are at once deprived of life?

When we begin to realize this, it will gradually dawn on us that there is something very extraordinary about the Bible. When we become aware of these things we shall understand how it is that not a tittle or iota could be altered in the Bible, i. e. in the original text. For then the whole structure would collapse and nothing be left indeed but a mere 'story'.

Supposing for the sake of argument, the original language of the Bible were English and instead of 'the tree of *the* knowledge' we were to write 'the tree of knowledge'. It would not make any real difference to the language or the image. But the structure would have been spoiled. There would not be the exact ratio 1–4 any longer, only 'approximately'. And with it the whole thing would collapse. One will now begin to understand what it would mean if letters were actually omitted, or if there were any surplus letters. In the phrases in question, the nature of certain things expresses itself in a different way, and this different way fits into the structure of the whole. Just as a man with a hump and a man without limbs fit into the structure of the whole, even if it should not please us, when we do not know the whole and judge only from the image which happens to present itself.

There is therefore sense too in the sequence of an enumeration in the Bible. When in the Bible the peoples of Canaan are enumerated now in this sequence, now in that, or the sons of Jacob are enumerated now this way, now the other, it is not a caprice just for a change to pay another tribe the honour of ranking higher in the list, but it is done because it fits into the structure.

One might also ask oneself the question why the 'ten plagues' in Egypt should he enumerated in that very sequence and why they were such marked plagues (Exodus 7–11). We are already beginning to understand a little of the relativity of the material image, of the phenomenon, and we know just a little about the significance of the word itself which represents the real. But then, have these ten plagues also a systematism, do the names of these plagues mean anything in the systematism?

To bring a little about them into prominence by way of illustration of the significance of the systematism in the sequence of events and the structure of the words, I shall subject the plagues in the central column of our scheme to a closer examination. As we already know from the scheme of the tale of creation, the central column is formed by the third of every cycle of three. In the case of the ten plagues there are three cycles of three, the tenth plague taking up a special position.

Thus the central column is occupied by the third, sixth and ninth plague. The third plague is 'flies', the sixth is 'boils', the ninth is 'darkness'. Of an interrelation between flies, boils and darkness nothing can be found with the best intentions. So the image itself does not bring us any further.

But here too an interrelationship comes forward, if the word denoting the names of the plagues is given *the correct place in the scheme*. For the words denoting the names of the plagues do not in themselves say anything about an eventual interrelationship. The name of the third plague in Hebrew is spelled kaf-nun, (20–50–40). The sixth plague is called 'shgin', shin-cheth-nun (300–8–50). The ninth is 'choshech', spelled cheth-shin-kaf (8–300–20).

Placed in the sequence of the ten plagues these three do not show any relationship. However, when they take their correct places in the scheme a very marked interrelationship presents itself all of a sudden, proving how they form a whole, how they are intertwined in their structures.

The scheme of the plagues — leaving the tenth out for convenience sake — is as follows:

2nd plague		1st plague
	3rd plague: 20–50–40	
5th plague		4th plague
	6th plague: 300–8–50	
8th plague		7th plague
	9th plague: 8–300–20	

Since I intended merely to examine the plagues in the central column, the names of the plagues in the right hand and left hand columns have been left out. They do not matter here just now. The plagues of the central column, however, show something rather remarkable with which they affirm the significance of this scheme and also stress the marvellousness of the word.

For, if we take the first letter of each of the plagues in the central column, reading upwards, we get the word 8–300–20. Which is the word for the last plague in the scheme, choshech, the name of the ninth plague. Now taking the middle letter of each of the three plagues in the central column, again reading upwards we get the word 300–80–50. Which is the word for the middle plague in this scheme. And when finally we do the same with the last letter of each of the three plagues in the central column, we get the word 20–50–40, which is the word for the first plague of the central column.

The names of these three plagues of the central column are evidently framed so as to include each other, so as to form a whole. And that implies that the systematism of the cycle of three is imperative.

In the central column is found:

3rd plague	→	20	–	50	–	40
6th plague	→	300	–	8	–	50
9th plague	→	8	–	300	–	20
		↑		↑		↑
		9th plague		6th plague		3rd plague

So there is a fixed structure with a fixed place for every component. There is an interrelationship which cannot be broken through. Here again one is apt to ask how this can be, how an author can write a story about plagues together with the names of those plagues and at the same time accomplish the fact that those names, taken up in that scheme should show that very interrelationship, that they cannot but take up that very place, so as to fit together and form themselves anew, thus being present twice, firstly in their own place and then again through their interrelationship with the two other plagues in the same scheme but in a different triad. So that the duality of the third place should even express itself in this manner: a duality in the central column, which indeed always gives a dual character to the phenomena.

It is the same interrelationship, the same coherence which we also find in the material expression of creation. We cannot remove elementary building-bricks from matter without causing it to lose its character. We can change the *image* of matter, we can take more of it or less, we can expose it to high temperatures or low, we can describe it any odd way. But we cannot affect its essential structure. Thus without doing harm to the Bible as a whole – at the worst we should harm ourselves or other people – we might interpret the meaning of the plagues in diverse ways, we might approve or disapprove of them, but we cannot eliminate a letter or change its place. We cannot apply a systematism different from that which evidently is the systematism which the Bible in its tale gives of the world. Would we endeavour from aesthetic or moral considerations to change the systematism of the periodical system of the elements? Or would we alter the orbits of the planets or their distances from the sun, because it fits our purpose or because we think it is not so important to know what these orbits and distances are and we need not be so exact with them, that it is mere hair-splitting to maintain that those orbits are so accurately fixed and that all this fits into one big whole, into one harmony?

Apparently the Bible in its composition, in its structure, shows the same wonderful coherence and law which by protracted study of natural science has also been found in nature.

Establishing this fact about the Bible and ever discovering more profound and more surprising relationships, would in itself accord the Book an outstanding place. To begin with it could not be the outcome of human thought any more than nature or the universe. No man, nor the whole of humanity either, could even in millions of years be able to create the systematism of the language of the Bible and moreover fit it all into the scheme of sequence and story as appears from the (1–4)-principle, transpiring on all sides even in the conceptions of the 'tree of life' and the 'tree of the knowledge of good and evil'. This fact in itself bespeaks such a profound and inimitable causality, it is only comparable to the same phenomenon in life and in the universe.

Still apart from all this marvellousness, the Bible is a great deal more. For, whereas nature and the universe can only impress us, make us realize that there is a great omnipotence, a great transcendent creator who yet determines every detail, the Bible gives us besides, in the same imposing and surprising manner, the story of individual, human life which is in itself a universe and is as important as the creation of the universe. The Bible gives the story of man in this life and in this world and in other worlds, gives us the sense of life and especially the criteria to know how to measure life and things that we may be able to appreciate them afterwards. The Bible is there for man, is given to man and looks upon man as the centre of life and the world. And with the same impressive systematism with which the Bible was built up, it relates to man why he exists and why the world exists, tells him the way he has to go and the purpose of it all, tells him about the very thing he is ever trying to find and which he thinks is a 'secret'.

This is what we shall deal with in the following pages. We shall see that the alleged mechanical aspect, resembling physical principles is suddenly inspired with life. That they are not merely interesting principles like the (1–4)-principle, etc., but that these principles at the same time contain the standards of life, of behaviour, for observing and gauging things. Those principles will be inspired with life and become human.

The Bible would not come up to the requirements of holiness, if it were a book concurrent with daily life, good enough to read in once in a while or to study in after the fatigues of the day or the week, to draw comfort and peace or good bourgeois morals from. The Bible must he life itself, inspiring us any single moment in any condition.

3
In the Beginning

Many people of good will are baffled by many ideas they find in the Bible about the good life. We shall not conjecture here about the origin of these ideas. They are generally to the effect that man goes about pretty helplessly in this valley of tears; that sound punishment is awaiting him in the hereafter, although often enough he does not know what he is to do here, and why, so as to steer clear of those punishments.

To the religious reader of the Bible it must often seem that the Supreme Being takes a malicious pleasure in keeping man ignorant of all sorts of things, and in indicating a good many other things but vaguely – but keeping His final accounts with meticulous precision. Many religious people go about full of fear, doing all sorts of things diligently in the hope that these are in accord with the will of the Creator, even though they may not understand, or only vaguely through various symbolisms, just why the Creator should wish human beings to perform these acts. Why, they may ask themselves, should an omnipotent God require these acts at the hand of man, and why these particular ones and not any other? But they perform them all the same, thereby hoping to propitiate Him. The parson and priest's normal gloomy sternness, their black garb, their accusing finger raised in wrath all add to this threatening character of the Creator. Fortunately such notions as love and grace are also still abroad, although here again people hold strange views.

On the modern reader, on the other hand, threats of hell and perdition which cannot be subjected to scientific demonstration fail to make any impression; equally he cannot believe the promise of heaven to come which cannot be demonstrated either. Too much of what he has learnt and observed is in conflict with these notions. And those who are supposed to be the guardians and expounders of the Bible all too often abandon religious territory under the fire of scientific doubt; at best, they are on the defensive. The teachers of religion could give in only because they, too, had lost the knowledge of the miracle which the Bible really is; even they no longer knew the real purport of the Bible. Even they came to consider the Bible a primitive, ancient document of historic origin. In consequence, they accepted science and the scientific attitude as a legitimate approach to the Book. They relinquished the basic tenet that the Bible must be all-inclusive – or else crumble away into insignificance.

In trying to adapt themselves as well as the Bible to scientific thought, they robbed the Bible of its very foundation: the fact of its revelation.

The temptation is indeed great. Science has proved itself able to provide all the amenities of man's material existence — we pass over here in silence the many drawbacks it produces at the same time. But owing to its starting point science can have relevance only to man's material existence on earth. This has resulted in a kind of vacuum in most people regarding what used to be termed 'wisdom' by the ancients — the science of the whence and why and the meaning of man's life and the universe, of ultimate justice and injustice, of balance. As man was concentrating his energies on the world of the senses, aided by his scientific discoveries, his ideas of justice and injustice, of good and evil also became tinged with the general utilitarianism. The world and 'progress' came to serve as standards of values. Scientists were not interested in discussing ideas of heaven, pink or blue, or winged angels. What else could these vague notions be but solace in times of stress for people who needed such comfort? In this view religion was not far removed from alcohol and its effects, or from the dreams induced by opium.

I do not insist, neither have I maintained that all people think or act in this way. There are still others of course, who know or feel how things are and live accordingly. But it cannot be denied that many people either do not have any ideas about these things at all, or very distorted, exaggeratedly fearful, or exaggeratedly jubilant conceptions; arisen from perfectly comprehensible psychological reactions, or in consequence of a gradual development during many generations.

I am not going to occupy myself with all these ideas and conceptions. I merely want to try and make clear what the Bible tells us about the purpose of creation and the sense of existence. With it all other conceptions will be done full justice.

As from the foregoing we know something, albeit very little, about the nature of the language of the Bible, we can now avail ourselves of it. Otherwise we would be hard driven to make things sound convincing.

The Bible starts with the well-known word 'in the beginning'. To understand words properly in the image or feeling they call up, we must, as we have already experienced, know something about their real structure.

The word 'in the beginning', in Hebrew bereshit, spelled beth-resh-aleph-shin-yod-taf, has something special in its structure. Firstly, not only does the word begin with the letter beth, 2, as it does in the Bible also, but this letter beth is written bigger than the other letters. It has nothing to do with the fact it is the first letter of the Bible and that it would therefore be printed as a capital, as is often the case in books, when the initial letter of a chapter is printed in a conspicuous size and sometimes even beautifully decorated. For there are a few more letters in the Bible — especially in the Pentateuch — written in big type or in small, sometimes found at random in the middle of a text. Besides, when the Bible gives such an exact structure, one cannot write one letter arbitrarily in big type because it is supposed to look beautiful or distinguished, and for *the* same reason write other letters in a different way, either small or upside down, etc. When the letters of this initial word bereshit are written in numbers, we get 2–200–1–300–10–400.

The capital 2 will strike us even more forcibly, if we remember our first approach of the first tale of creation. For it was there we recognized, that creation was in reality a formation-of-duals. (To show the relationship with numbers-letters more clearly, I shall also use numbers in the text since they can make it easier to see the context.)

Beginning with heaven and earth as the initial dual, continuing via light and darkness down to all details. Thereby expressing itself in the duality of the first and second triads, in the dual character of the third day, the child of the father and mother. Also expressing itself in the fact of there being a second tale of creation, containing the duality of the tree of life as opposed to the tree of the knowledge of good and evil, and likewise expressing itself in the duality of the (1–4)-principle; the 'mist' going up to water the earth.

The capital 2 indicates that everything coming after it, is determined by this 2. Until something else crops up, ushered in by another beginning. It also means that with this 2 the second part commences; that previously there was the 1, an undivided, all-inclusive, state of harmony in unity.

So the capital 2 signifies that the story coming now is a story of duality, determined by the 2. And this 2 is imaged by the words heaven-earth, light-darkness, man-woman, etc.

If we reflect more deeply – and in this direction many people even without any knowledge of the Bible, have reflected deeply, because life itself induced them – we shall see that, indeed, *everything* in our world is determined by this duality. Everything is measured by us on a measuring-rod on which one extreme registers an estimation opposed to that of the other. Without these two extremes we cannot, indeed, measure or assess anything. These extremes may be called 0 and ∞, life and death, soul and body, man and beast, or big and small, good and bad, etc. They determine all our thought and appraisal. Our reasoning, our logic, our conceptions of causality, all these are determined by the existence of this 2. Where the Bible-story begins, there this dual world begins. We might also put it like this: The Bible represents the world in the 2.

We might ask ourselves how it is the Bible does not state the fact explicitly in this way, why the Bible confines itself to rendering a story on objects and beasts, on rather exterior facts concerning human beings. Even if it appears easy to draw the inference, yet one would like the Bible to be a little clearer regarding these facts. We have so far only been concerned with the existence of a duality, of contrasting things, by means of which we measure and appraise things. But if, apart from this, we are also faced with questions of life and death, of existence after death then, as practice has it, it may be more difficult to draw conclusions when there is nothing but a tale in images, with hardly any indication in the tale itself how to interpret these images. One might not unjustly ask questions about the rather materialistic views of life which the Bible seems to show forth. For all the promises uttered in the Bible point towards this earth.

For instance, the people of Israel in the Bible are promised a land, and after a great deal of stir and agitation they get it, and folks will live there in peace and sit under the vine- and the figtree. Quite attractive and rural and all that, but then what? Die sooner or later, of course, according to the notion 'and if they have not died since, they are still alive'. This life under the vine-and the figtree may be very peaceful and everybody may even live to be a hundred and twenty or even more, but do what we will there remains the all-important question *'then what?'* The Eternities before and after life on this earth dominate man far more than he is ready to admit. For he will also have to admit that here he is faced with an immense and fearful unknown.

Besides, this promised land of Israel proves geographically to be rather limited in extent. What happens to all mankind? Is the Bible a book for a specific nation, or according to another interpretation, for a specific church or group of churches? If indeed the enervating drama which the Bible also tells us of mankind, is merely to eventuate in this social and climatologic certainty, we should not resent people remarking: 'so what', or others saying that all this has a rather old-fashioned, primitive, materialistic tinge. Also that, armed with more knowledge one might just as well and with better reason, start building up a sound, modern world, not merely living under the vine- and figtree — with a surplus population at that — but in sensibly built districts with roomy well-lit houses, fitted with all the modern amenities. And that we should not restrict ourselves to looking after the well-being of the people who received the land Kanaan in a promise but of all the nations all over the world. Indeed this sounds more liberal-minded and just, and that is why it attracts many people.

But then, what about the Bible? *IS* the story truly like that?

And now I am reverting again to the things I mentioned before about the word, about the language.

The word in the language of the Bible — only there and nowhere else worth mentioning — contains within itself that which is really the essence of the phenomenal form in this world. This essence expresses itself in matter also. The material phenomenon can be considered a kind of crystallization or condensation of the essence, an expression of it, as it simply cannot help presenting itself when appearing in this world. If one looks at the expression in matter only, i. e. at the image, without any knowledge of its essence, if one forms opinions after those observations of the image, it is generally very hard to understand relationships, to fathom the sense of things. One perceives exterior causalities which may be delusive and in fact one has no idea of the real causalities. This is the very core of that warning not to cling to images, not to make images.

Through them one repudiates, one avoids, coming face to face with the essence of things.

Now, as pointed out above, the Bible is a reflection of the world in the '2'. A '2' which starts with the duality heaven-earth. So it expresses things in matter also, but not exclusively in matter. For the Bible uses the word for this expression in matter, and the word at the same time gives the essence of the thing. In the terminology of the (1–4)-principle, expressing itself in the tree of life as 1 to the 4 of the tree of knowledge of good and evil. The Bible expresses both, the 1 and the 4 simultaneously, just as we saw it in the passage discussed above, in the 'ed', the 'mist', the 1–4, watering the earth. The essence of the word, that which represents the 1 in the principle, is that which is expressed in words as the tree of life; and the material image in which this essence finds its expression, is the 4 in the principle, that which is called the tree of the knowledge of good and evil. The attentive reader may have a premonition now concerning the command not to eat from the tree of the knowledge of good and evil. A command, therefore, not to absorb the images of things, for thus he debars himself from the tree of life. Thus also shutting off the possibility to absorb the essence of things from the words. By and by I shall treat in greater detail the so-called tale of paradise with the two trees at the centre.

The Bible, as rendering of the world in the '2' at the same time gives the images of things. I hope presently to disclose a little more concerning the purpose of all this. At any rate the Bible does not purpose to lead man into temptation with those images and punish him afterwards. It should be quite clear that it would not only be unjust but also entirely wrong to judge the Bible by the light of those images only, i.e. by the light of the story as it is. Then, indeed, one could not help drawing conclusions like materialism, primitivity, etc., which I mentioned above.

If one were to say that there is nothing to be found in the Bible about life in the hereafter, about thoughts concerning the purpose of life, basing that opinion on the Bible-story in its images, one is absolutely right, although one inflicts a gross injustice on the Bible by merely wanting to judge it by the light of those images. For image can only express itself in this world, it is a condensation in matter. It is foolish to demand that an image, a materialization, a crystallization in matter, as a perceptible image should relate things about the hereafter, or disclose the sense of life, when that sense does not pertain to this life on earth only and to this matter only. And that is exactly why there is that bridge of the word, the biblical word, which tells us what is the essence of the image. It enables us actually to penetrate into other worlds, actually to learn to know the purpose of life. And therefore we shall have to adhere to that way. Only then shall we see what wonderful relationships there are, how the purpose of creation and the purpose of life give import to our whole existence.

We shall have to decode the images all the time into their essence; unite them with their essence. Then *they* too will acquire sense.

Why does the Bible only make use of images obviously pertaining to a certain period in antiquity and why does the Bible, obviously again, give a historic tale also taking place in antiquity? Sheep, cattle, camels, slaves, tents, gods, they pertain to antiquity. The Bible does not mention radio, nuclear energy, aeroplanes, trade unions, democracy, and the UN, it does not deal with the great migration of the nations, the discovery of the Americas, any more than with the world wars and Auschwitz. If the Bible has that all-inclusive character, why does it not speak about those things, why does it restrict itself to ancient Egypt which has long since ceased to exist, to ancient Kanaan or Babel? So that all kinds of would-be prophets availing themselves of inevitable vagueness — which an image-story as such is bound to contain, since it is merely the phenomenal form of reality — felt called upon to interpret diverse passages of the Bible so that the end of the world or any other great event could be announced time and again without ever coming to pass. This kind of text-conjurers have not been very lucky in their assertions as far as realization is concerned, any more than the conjurers with numbers, though they have often been surprised at their large following; an eloquent testimony to the deep desire which does exist to understand a little more about the background of the events.

But then, why did the Bible choose those very images from antiquity and that historic tale obviously pertaining to antiquity, if it insists on bearing the stamp of eternity?

Well then, the same answer, given to the foregoing, is apposite here, just as the essence of things crystallizes in matter and forms the images which fill our space, so also, does it crystallize in the events, forming the images which fill our time. For space and time are inseparable in the world of images.

Then why exactly that period in antiquity and not a longer or later period? It is like this: As a being when crystallizing itself in matter, assumes certain proportions therein, and has completed his work of materialization when this process of crystallization has reached completion, similarly does the crystallization of events in time create proportions in time, and as soon as this process of crystallization has been completed, the work of materialization in time is likewise completed.

The process of crystallization in time, which set in with creation, in this world also created various proportions, forms in time — which, as we shall see, similarly show an amazing order and regularity and systematism — and which were completed, fulfilled in the time which the Bible actually describes. *That* is what makes that time so important and it makes the events at that time important too. And that is the only reason why the Bible is eternally operative, what we might style 'holy'; not because of a kind of evolutionistic pattern-character, 'to derive instruction from'. In the temporal story in the Bible it is told how the essence crystallizes in time, just as in the image-story it is told how it crystallizes in matter and in space. Therefore the proportions in the temporal story are important, for they come forth from the essence.

So when the temporal story deals with that special period, it merely means that we can infer from it *how* this essence expressed itself in time and that it expressed itself in time then and there for the first time; that it was *created*. We shall have to decode the slaves and tents just as well as Egypt and Babel and unite it with the essence in order to have a standard for our actions, for the things of the present and the future. The happenings in the remote past, detached from this essence, are devoid of interest to us now. At best they may rouse a measure of archeologic- or historic interest, on behalf of which it is, indeed, misused. In that case there is no sense in trying to understand the Bible and the purpose of life and the world.

Therefore we must not detach the temporal story from the essence which the Bible lays down in its words. Just as we must not detach the images the Bible gives of men and beasts from the essence of the word. For just as we shall then get an image-story in which it is difficult to see any sense and we run the risk to reduce it to nonsense, similarly we must not detach the events in time from the essence. For then we shall get temporal images, another species of idols, which, detached from their essence, are difficult to fit in and which will repeatedly lead to misconceptions and foolishness. Essence and form should ever remain closely united. So we shall constantly have to decode spatial and temporal images into their essence.

We shall now return to our capital '2' with which the Bible begins and with which it expresses, as the stamp of the real, that this is a world of duality. And after the foregoing elucidation of the meaning of the biblical mode of expression in spatial and temporal images, we may now more readily understand why we have to continue decoding the images into the word and unite the two to a complete whole, just as the 1-4 manifests itself as a whole. The '1' by itself or '4' by itself convey no sense for this world. This world as the world of the '2' unites the 1 and the '4' into a harmonious whole, to what we know as the '1'–4. Essence and phenomenon, being and becoming, form a unity.

The '2' is made by God. For: in the beginning God created 'heaven and earth', thus making the 2, which now proceeds to reveal itself in everything. To start with, the earth contains this duality everywhere in itself and on itself. The earth is desolate and void – and this is not just playing with words, but it has absolute sense – darkness was upon the face of the deep, again a duality; and the Spirit of God moved upon the face of the waters, another duality. This duality is now a fact, and when God begins to say the ten words of creation it proceeds as light and darkness, etc.

This duality emanates from God who made it upon the creation of heaven and earth. Before that there was oneness. From the 1, i. e. God the all-inclusive, God makes the 2. So there is a path 1→2. As the 'first' father there is God in action when He makes the 1–2. With it He is the father of creation. Everything that further on and later on is father, is such, in accordance with the selfsame principle proceeding from the 1, the all-inclusive, creating something by causing it to live and remaining united with it, just as, the 1–2 *together* form the word father. (Hebr. ab: aleph–beth). The 2 detached from the 1, or the 1 detached from the 2, causes the conception father to cease to exist.

Mother in Hebrew 'em', spelled aleph-mem, in numbers 1–40. Here we see that the mother is the next phase; for from the 2 comes forth the 4 as its farthest development has been explained above, and in the plane of the decimals this 4 becomes 40. The word mother includes the 1–4, albeit the 4 is in a different plane. The conception mother only gets into another plane when the man and the woman have to leave the Garden of Eden after having eaten from the tree of the knowledge, i.e. after they had got into a different world. We shall by and by revert to this changing of world and of plane.

Because before man was formed, the Lord God caused something different from this 1–40 to come forth as life-condition; at this juncture it was the mist going up to water the earth; so in that case it was the 1–4, instead of the 1–40, which came afterwards.

As a further illustration of the word in this connection: son in Hebrew is 'ben', spelled beth-nun, in numbers 2–50, and daughter is 'bath', spelled beth-taf, in numbers 2–400.

From this we see that son and daughter start as the 2, in contradistinction to father and mother who start as the 1. About the meaning of 50 as the second letter in the son and the 400 as the second letter in the daughter I shall be more explicit later on. By that time the reader will readily understand what these letters convey in those two words. I do not enter into this now, because an explanation *at this moment* would interrupt the story too long. What matters here is that there is a relationship between creation and the creator as father and the words for father and mother and also the typical difference between them and the words for son and daughter.

Now the 2 develops into the 4 – with which the 2 has completed itself, fulfilled itself – because after the coming forth of duality the 4 becomes the power inherent in the 2. With the 4 has been attained the utmost of that which the essence of the 2 brings with it for itself. So this is the principle of the formula 1–4 and that is why the unit of three days of creation also has the 4 as maximum for the number of acts of creation. With it the root-cycle is completed.

We have also seen that the existence of the 4, the furthest development of the 2, includes the presence of 10 different situations and that they express themselves in the 10 words of creation.

In the course of the days of creation the differentiation, i.e. duality expressing itself in ever new forms, is seen to continue and eventuate in the number of plants on the third day, of the stellar world on the fourth, and of the beasts on the fifth and sixth days; in the phenomena of this world ever bearing the stamp of duality, of male – female, but going deeper, ever deeper, into the smallest particles of matter, until they present themselves as a borderland where we think we still perceive that duality in the positive and the negative as the nucleus of the atom and the orbs round the nucleus and finally in the nucleus itself, all this expressing itself everywhere.

Now, this course through multiplicity is suddenly arrested in the second part of the sixth day. For here it is that man stands as one being, all alone facing the vast multiplicity around him. Just as God was alone until the moment He faced multiplicity which He caused to emanate. As the Bible expresses it in the words: 'And God created man in His own image, after His likeness.'

The oneness of man as opposed to the development into ever greater multiplicity is a striking break in that development. Even in principle man is made in a different way, for God says emphatically: 'in Our image, after Our likeness.'

Therefore there is present in man all that which previous to him expressed itself separately in the multiplicity of phenomena. And that is the real sense of man's dominion of all the beasts that are under his sway. What has been translated as 'have dominion' is in Hebrew in that text 'redoo' which really means 'have *under* one'. It also means 'descend' and so it means man descending into the world of multiplicity.

In man everything preceding is present, he has everything under him, he is a kind of terminus where the various threads which from the starting point diverged into ever more ramifications, converge again.

We might represent it in a drawing like this

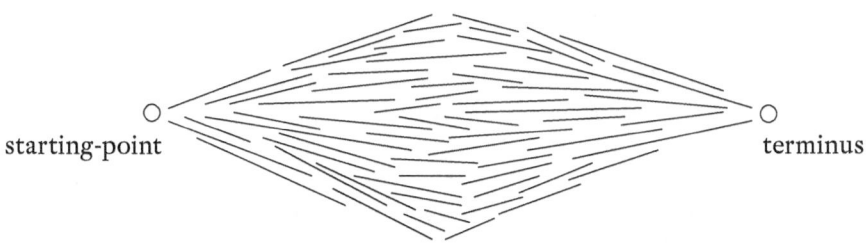

The terminus is an image, a likeness of the starting-point. The starting-point, God before starting creation, has made 'man' in His image and after His likeness, with which creation is complete.

Hence creation is not completed with the great multiplicity but with the coming of man as unity. Man, who as we shall see more circumstantially later on, is male-female, androgyne in one.

Returning to the 'initial' word in the Bible, the word 'in the beginning', the word 2–200–1–300–10–400, we see it is built up of a complex of six parts. The word for 'creating' is in Hebrew 'bara', spelled 2–200–1. And since word in its real form, in its proportion-form, expresses what it is in reality, we shall now examine this real form of the word 'to create' more closely.

The word 'to create' begins with the 2, since creating is essentially identical with the making of the 2, the making of the contrast and the multiplicity which itself is contrasted with the unity of the beginning. That is why the Bible starts with the capital, determinant '2'.

This principle of the '2' penetrates into other planes, it is differentiated there into multiplicity. The highest plane of the 2 to be expressed in matter, is the 2 in the plane of the centuples, hence 200. So the 2 has not completed itself with itself up to the 4, but it has expressed itself in the other planes even as the 2 with the potence, it is true, to become 4, however, as we shall see, not availing itself of this potentiality.

So the word 'to create', 'bara', contains the expression of the 2, the principle of creating, in the plane of the greatest differentiation of the 2, i. e. in the 200. But the word to create is not rounded off with it. The 200 in that word is followed by the 1. Which means that creation is not completed until the 1 has emerged from the many again. Hence 'creation' means: make the 2 which involves multiplicity, which, however, returns to the unity existing before creation, before the 2 was made.

This word 'to create' we also find in the image of creation: beginning with the duality of heaven and earth which God made, proceeding through the great multiplicity of creatures, of things created in heaven and on earth and finally ending up in the oneness of man. Again we see that a word when considered from its essence, contains within itself the structure which expands, puts its stamp on the imaged events, expressed in the world in terms of space-time.

And also we see that even in the structure of the initial word of the Bible, 'in the beginning' this development is outlined, fixed. They are the first three letters, the first three numbers of the Bible and they give the structure 2–200–1. Even these three contain the fact that from the capital 2 will come forth the multiplicity of the 200, but that it will return to the 1. That the world is not going to be lost in ever greater differentiation, in multiplicity developing ever further, but that it will return to the starting-point preceding creation, hence to the 1.

On this point just this little comment on language, on the word, which now claims our attention.

We saw that the word 1–2, the 2 emerging from the 1, also means father, since that which in our image presents itself as father, contains within itself that essential causation of a duality. Now the word 2–1, indicating the return of the 2 to the 1, is the word 'come'. Coming is a gathering in, attaining an end, a goal, in an image it may eventually be a temporary goal. But at any rate conveying the intention to attain something and also containing within itself the attainment, the arrival, the coming.

In the structure of the world it is a return to the original situation, a kind of coming home again.

It is like the story of the prince who left home and wandered through the whole world till he returned to the house of his father. For that is the image of the world-story, that with the coming of the 2 the journey is starting, the son goes into the world, a long way from where he started, towards that which in the Bible is indicated as the '200', finally to return again to the father, to the 1 in whose image and after whose likeness he was made.

So the conception 'creating' includes structurally, as its law, that after making a great multiplicity to the farthest extreme, there is also the return to the 1, to the origin, to the creator. So this is the meaning of the word create in its essence, expressed as 2–200–1.

Man as image and likeness of God, after the unfolding of creation into its ever expanding multiplicity, is this 1. He is alone, one, just as God in the beginning is alone, is one.

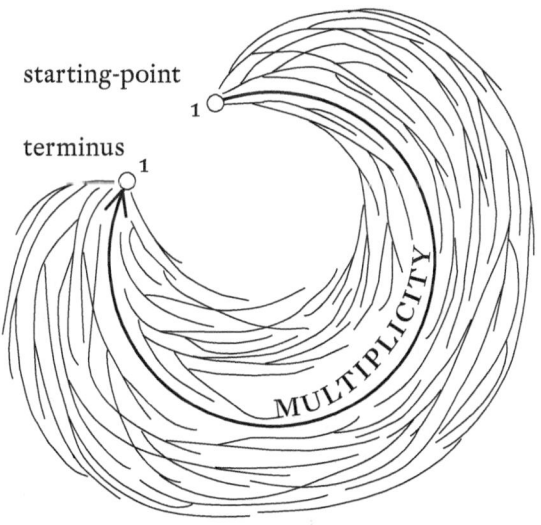

This could be made quite clear in a sketch and this drawing merely serves to express the idea outlined above. It is a specific elaboration of the drawing on page 63 of the way starting from the 1 as the beginning, via multiplicity to the 1 as terminus.

In our mind it is a contradiction that the 1 of the beginning should also be found at the other extreme where, although it is the end, everything is just as it was in the beginning. This viewpoint is the result of what previously we called 'the condition of duality'; it is the manner in which man has been looking at life and the universe ever since the beginning, since the coming of the 2. The mind knows nothing outside duality, contrast; proceeding from this contrast we measure and estimate all things. Our mind knows life and death, good and evil, great and small, diametrically opposed, the one concept at the one extreme, the other at the other extreme of the scale. We simply cannot conceive things differently in this world of space-time. It is the imprint of the capital 2, ingrained in our thought and judgement. To our conception, something moving ever faster away from the origin towards ever increasing multiplicity cannot, logically, turn back upon itself at the farthest point, to reach its starting point over again.

And yet there is this great astonishing fact stated: 'And God said, Let us make man in Our image, after Our likeness,' (Gen. 1:26) This 'us' is indeed not a sort of pluralis majestatis. According to ancient lore this 'us' refers to 'all creation', to everything created before, from the angels down to the lowest creatures on earth, including everything. That God should suddenly manifest himself in a different way and should interfere, does not fit in with 'the line of evolution'.

According to evolution, to the contrary, everything should proceed regularly, and the way of creation, indeed, demonstrates it. Via the world of beasts there comes forth an ever-growing sense of individuality, an ever-increasing urge to emancipate from what looks like dull obedience to natural law, as it is perceptible in inorganic life, in plants and the stellar world of respectively the second, third and fourth day of creation. Man as the summit of this development could emancipate still further and would along this line – as the theory of evolution has it – evolve ever farther away from the point of origin. He would be able to frame his own life according to his own standards and his own ratio. And emancipating completely from his bonds with the origin, he might build up a life of his own, utilizing the world thereto, subordinating everything to his purposes, based on a keen intellect. Such is the logical consequence of the development of creation from the beginning into the enormous multiplicity it shows forth in the end. A multiplicity which also developed an experience-intellect which acquired a particular sense and intuitive feeling in regard to all kinds of facets of the material world, i.e. knowing, feeling how to use them all in behalf of that consistent purpose in view: subjugating the world to man in behalf of an ever-expanding evolution.

All this is contained in the 2–200 bit of our 'formula' of evolution. Man, however, in his volition to emancipate from every bond with his origin, the 1, wants to develop the 2 further still, wants to make it into the 4, or on the plane of the centuples attain the farthest end, the 400, the last letter of the alphabet, expressing the extreme development in matter.

The multiplicity of the 2 and the 200, however, does not come to man in order to be developed into the 4 and the 400, but to be restored to the 1. Side by side with it there is the alternative, the possibility for man to proceed along the path of further development, beyond the 200. We shall have to discuss the consequences thereof in the following chapters. They are also expressed in this initial word of the Bible in the three letters of that word, the letters 300–10–400.

It is on account of this very alternative that there is the basic formula, the principle of creation, as expressed in the word 2–200–1, implying that creation somehow obeys the law of the return to the origin.

Man, however, in his urge to emancipate further and still further from the origin, is not alive to this principle of creation which implies as its law the final 1, the result so different for all man's evolutionistic, logic reasoning. And this final 1 is the result of God's ordaining the line of evolution to move entirely differently with the let us', with the let the great multiplicity and divergence and alienation from the origin' create man, who like God is one, all alone facing multiplicity.

Since man, in his stage of 2–200 fails to see this clearly, since man when reasoning in accordance with observation, can only see himself at the other extreme of evolution, so distant and so busy developing himself and others ever further, that he tends more and more to eliminate and forget God at the other extreme of the beginning, therefore creation to man's mind is still a phenomenon as he also supposes to observe it in what he calls the expanding universe, a kind of explosion into multiplicity and into alienation from the starting-point. Like this:

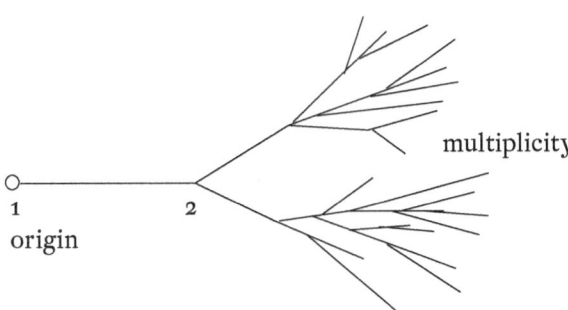

And then he can only visualize himself in an entirely different quality, as a god able to do everything himself, dominating nature and her forces, standing at the other extreme, far removed from what he considers the primitive, underdeveloped beginning. Then in this great multiplicity and its ensuing power he orders everything and the world also, he regulates his own life and that of other people, in accordance with standards which in the course of his evolution he has learned to avail himself of to the best of his ability and to his own advantage. The sketch would then be:

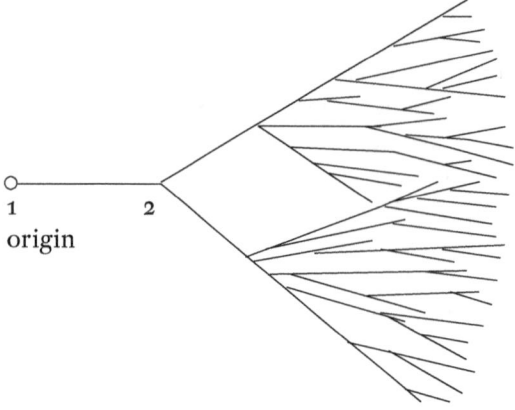

Mankind in its totality, directing everything in accordance with its own plans and decisions, like an independent deity.

That is why we should understand the word 'creating' in its complete sense, viz. that it causes itself to return; whether one wants to or not, whether it coincides with one's plans or not, one returns to the 1. And that is why there is an essentially different development.

Whereas observation indicates that one is ever moving further away, this expansion, as already laid down in the principle of creation (2–200–1), has in it the reversal which takes place right from the beginning: 'in the beginning'. Hence the diagram in which the path is represented as a circle, a path which in reality has existed from the initial word in the Bible, but which man, still caught in the 2–200 phase, *cannot* visualize, a path running counter to his observation and the ratiocination built up thereon.

For the sake of simplicity I shall from now on represent this evolution by a mere circle, emerging from the 1 and returning to the 1 in man as image and likeness of God, standing with God. The sketch will thus be:

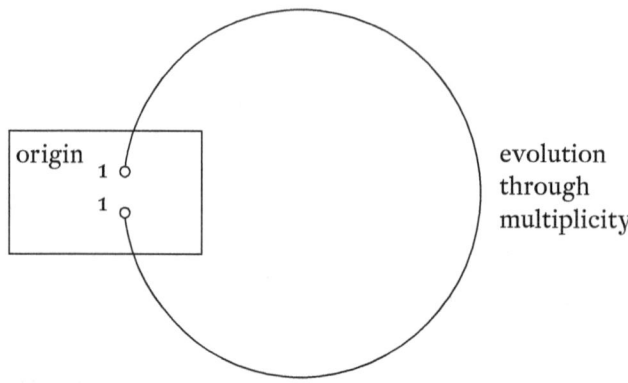

This diagram is merely to be considered as a diagram, as a representation which makes it easier to understand things.

The evolution into multiplicity can also be represented by a number of rings encircling a nucleus which is the origin. The veiling of the nucleus is a process ever going on in the time of evolution. In ancient mystic representations this image is often used, and the veils are called the sheaths around the nucleus, around the origin. In Hebrew these sheaths are called 'klippoth'. The further multiplicity evolves, the more the light of the nucleus gets dimmed, so *this* too is merely an image to express the path into multiplicity.

In this ancient mysticism there occurs also another manner of representation which is known as the doctrine of the Sephiroth. I shall not go into the details of this doctrine. It is a specific way of representing the path of creation and the world. The origin, the supreme sephira is called kether, meaning the crown. It is the crown of God. Kether is unity, the oneness from which springs duality and from which spring all the other Sephiroth. The last of them is called 'malchuth', i. e. kingdom. The malchuth-sephira as a matter of fact is this world. For here in this world the kingdom will eventually be given back to God, to kether; will the unity of 'kether-malchuth' be established. The malchuth-sephira too stands alone, at the *end* of evolution, just as the kether-sephira does at the *beginning*. And the union of these two solitary Sephiroth is the coming together, the encounter of the 1 of the origin and the 1 of the terminus. There evolution has returned to the origin, there the Kingdom is God's again.

Now the word of the Bible proceeds. So far we have been looking at the former part of it, the part 2–200–1. It is followed by 300–10–400.

We have already seen that the first word through its structure causes the rest to come about, how it forms the pattern for the further events. For with the coming of man as solitary being as 'after God's image did He create him' we have watched the path of the 2–200–1. It is man as he exists in the second tale of creation until the final phase of that tale, as 'adam' as solitary man. It is not until the end of that phase after all sorts of events experienced by man as a solitary being, that the woman comes, formed by the Lord God, after He had taken a 'rib' from the man. Then there are two people, the 'man' and the 'woman' with whom all sorts of things are now going to happen. Everybody knows the story and that of the serpent which follows; one can read it in chapters 2 and 3 of Genesis.

In the first tale of creation all this is put much more concisely. Almost unnoticed by the inattentive reader it says in Gen. 1:27: 'So God created man in His own image; in the image of God created He him; male and female created He them.'

Now if we study this verse more closely, we do not do so to be able to prove that in holding some doctrine we are right and others are wrong. For we have now seen from various examples that every letter has its fixed place in the system and that, moreover, the system has a very exact structure in which every shade has its meaning. So, if we look more closely, it is not an arbitrarily applied exactitude in regard to a single text because it is convenient to us, but it is an exactitude which simply *has* to be applied in every exact and serious examination. It is only through close attention that a system will be found, a structure discovered and unexpected relationships will come to light.

The above quotation about the creation of man contains two parts which are remarkable in a certain respect, first it says: 'in the image of God created He *him*' and following it 'male and female created He *them*'. Obviously there is first one being, hence the singular *him*, then after it has been said that there are male and female, the plural form *them* is rightly used. So this denotes a system, running parallel to the second tale of creation, where similarly man is first created as one being and only then, in the next phase, separated into male and female.

But this system proves to have its origin in the initial word itself, that remarkable word 'in the beginning'. For there we saw the whole course of creation expressed in the shortest form possible, in number only. The way 2–200–1 which led to the coming of man as the 1, terminating the way.

But the oneness of man proves impermanent. In the first tale of creation there is the brief statement that after the creation of man there is a new phase in which man becomes male and female, a plural, and in the second tale of creation after a more elaborate story there is the creation of woman who then forms a duality with the man.

That the story actually is not finished with the coming of man as a unit over against the oneness of God, also appears from the initial word 'bereshit'. This goes on after the 2–200–1; for another bit is still to come. In the nucleus-formula — if we may consider this initial word as the determining factor which imposes its structure on the rest — there is yet the 300–10–400 to follow: running parallel with the statement of the 'male-female' in the first tale of creation and the elaboration of it in the second tale of creation, after the Lord God had stated that it was not good 'that the man should be alone'.

Obviously there is a system here, too, and it is beginning to take shape for us. A system starting from a very small perceptible nucleus which in fact contains everything realizing itself in what may be called an initial orb or initial plane — the image we form about it may be anything we like — an initial orb even at this juncture expressing itself in images, which, however, are rather summary in regard to a second orb which tells the same story in a greater number of more detailed images.

We might outline it as follows:

The initial word as the core for the rest of the story	2–200–1–300–10–400	
the first tale of creation as the first orb round the core	multiplicity, coming forth from the creation of the 2, eventuating in the great multiplicity. But subsequently returning to 1 again on the coming of man	The unit man becomes male and female; in the first tale of creation this is followed by the 9th and 10th word of creation
The 2nd tale of creation as a second, much wider circle round the core and the first circle	multiplicity, coming forth from creation, now according to the principle of the 1–4 with man in the Garden of Eden, as one being, with a duty to perform there	The man does not remain alone, he gets the woman, after which comes the story of the serpent, the sending forth from paradise, etc.

That the Bible, of which we have thus seen a few very striking examples of exactitude and systems fitting in with each other, should without any apparent reason repeat a story in partly different words and different images, can hardly be incidental or arbitrary. To the contrary, we now even see that this story is present as the very root in the initial word, and that there is obviously yet another entirely different system in the Bible. A system running through the whole story and giving a structure to time, telling us about the same thing in different situations, in subsequent ages or worlds. Implying that in its mode of expression in one world in contradistinction to that in another world, there is again a certain system, with a definite structure.

What is focused in the sequence 300–10–400, is enacted in the first tale of creation from the moment man appears as a duality and proceeds through the part where God speaks the 9th and 10th word of creation, the words on fruitfulness and food. In the second tale of creation begins the part where God says that it is not good 'that man should be alone', upon which the woman is made and after which comes the story of the serpent and the sending forth from paradise. And the observant reader will in this 300–10–400 have recognized the parallel to the story of the man and the woman as it is related in the tales of creation. For was not 3 the number of man and the 4 that of woman, and do these numbers not face each other here as the 300 and the 400?

Just as I have pursued the former part of the word 'in the beginning', bereshit, in the first tale of creation, so I shall pursue the latter part of that word in the second tale of creation. Of course it might be treated in continuation of the first tale of creation and I shall constantly refer to it, but in the course of my story, which after all can only be an introduction into a new domain, I want to consider various other aspects of the Bible. And as I have started to go a little deeper into the second tale of creation and as the so-called tale of the serpent will also play an important part in the further expositions, I shall now pick out the second orb round the core, to tell a little more about *this* systematism.

4

The Miracle of the Name

In the second tale of creation there is a certain amount of liveliness in the events around the man. As soon as he faces the woman taken out of him, there is the meeting with the serpent, the eating of the tree of the knowledge of good and evil, the hiding from the Presence, subsequently the conversation with God and the sending forth from Paradise. And this activity continues in the story of Cain and Abel and goes on until the end.

We have seen a very specific structure dominating the second tale of creation, the so-called (1–4)-principle. As *second* story it has, as has also been discussed, the character of water. We have likewise seen that the number 4 is typical for things female and that the female corresponds with the left side of the system of the first tale of creation, hence with the side of the water.

The Hebrew word for water is 'mayim' spelled 40–10–40. The word for sea is 'yam' spelled 10–40. In either word is to be found the (1–4)-structure thus ever indicating the water-character of the second tale of creation.

In the second tale of creation the world clearly tends towards the side of water, the female side, the left side, hence the side where water as 10–40–10 was found even in the first tale of creation.

So obviously the second tale of creation, as is apparent here too, enacts itself in a different kind of world. We shall presently see that this is also the reason why in the first tale of creation 'God' is the creator, whereas in the second story we read about 'the Lord God'.

The shifting of the scene from a world where light and the 2 play the important part, to a world with 'water' and the 4 as its determinant forces, has yet another effect. From ordinary observation we know that light and everything that falls within the scope of this conception, has a great velocity as compared to water which has the very opposite. That which governs earthly duration is mere inertia as compared to the unearthly velocity of light. This inertia expressing itself through the structure of the 1–4 and through that of water, therefore – it could not be otherwise, our system again bears it out – is always seen in the Bible as 'duration'.

For the servitude in Egypt lasts 400 years, the journey across the desert 40 years, Moses lingered on Mount Sinai for 40 days, David reigned 40 years, as regards the Flood the 40 days are mentioned a few times, Elijah is in the desert during 40 days. Indeed the word for water is also the name of the Hebrew letter 40. Always the 40 or 400 prove to express something of long duration. In fact infinitely long. For is not 4 the furthest development of the number 2 in the root-cycle? The second tale of creation therefore has this 'water' and the corresponding character of slowness of time. It is the story with the character of the left hand side of the system, which is the side of the water. Hence also the female character. And is not the second tale of creation also determined by the woman? First the detailed information why and how she came. And then, when she is there, she takes the initiative. The story with the serpent is the story of the *woman* with the serpent. The man eats, quite passively, that which the woman offers him.

The reader will remember that the Patriarch of the left hand side of the system, Isaac, had this passive character. That Rebekah, his wife, in fact, performed the determining actions, such as causing the blessing to be given to Jacob, and later on sending Jacob to Laban. I am again pointing this out in this place just to show how the system persists in its very details. As soon as there is a story determined by 'water', like the second tale of creation, which is determined by mist, the woman comes into prominence without fail and the man is passive. Isaac, in the order of systematism taking the second place, on the left, is characterized by a water-story, as we have seen, and has that passivity. The women in the Bible are also always found near the well, watering their cattle. Thus does Abraham's servant find Rebekah for a wife to Isaac; thus does Jacob later on find Rachel, and Moses his wife Zippora. Ever the woman near the water. Now that the pieces of information are growing in number and will increasingly all the time I find it impossible to keep referring to this marvellous system tallying and fitting in everywhere. So I hope the reader entering into the development of the tale, as if it were a detective story, will jot down for himself the facts which have been mentioned before and which will ever fit into the further development of the system.

Since I have started discussing the nature of time with reference to the (1–4)-principle, it will be necessary for us to enter into a special aspect of the second tale of creation. The second tale of creation which has that very character of time, as a matter of fact, always speaks of the 'Lord God', whereas the first tale merely speaks of 'God'. It goes without saying that this distinction must mean something fundamental.

When one begins dimly to understand the wonder of this structure one ceases to take serious such theories as the existence of different authors supposed to have each in their own manner written a bit of the Bible, one having a God who was called God, the other recognizing a God who bore the name of Lord, sometimes mixing up the two names on account of their utter ignorance of the nature of the Bible. Such theories lift the Bible into the sphere of ambitious priest-castes and similar counterfeits of life in modern science and politics.

The word we translate as God in Hebrew is 'Elohim'. The word as can be seen from the ending in 'im', is a plural. Nevertheless it is the name of God who is seen as an absolute unity. It is God who includes all, and from whom emanates creation; creation with the nature of multiplicity, with the structure of the six days of creation.

The creation on the first day begins with the word of God: 'Let there be light'. With it creation is set going. And this light determines the character. The first tale of creation is enacted so 'swiftly' because light dominates. In circumstances utterly incomparable to the circumstances of an inert world, a water-world. It is – to use an image borrowed from modern science– just as if in a nucleus a process is enacted with enormous swiftness which, projected on outer orbs present, takes up space owing to the vastness of the orbs and has 'duration'. The process is expanded in those orbs, divided into enormous distances. One can conceive it by thinking of concentric circles round a nucleus.

In this nucleus everything moves with lightning speed, and things are enacted in a sphere where our conceptions of time do not obtain. Hence the apparent fear of man in the Bible to 'see God'. The coming into contact with this world of concentration of incomparable swiftness, would consume man in less than no time. If God as such should enter into communication with man such as he is, there would be, at least according to man's feelings and reasonings, no chance for him to remain in this world as man.

I beg leave to point at the people of Israel's fear of the ineffable when God descended on Mount Sinai and as such spoke to mankind. To man such a thing cannot be. Nevertheless this moment comes in the Bible.

In this manner does the world come about in the first tale of creation; in this swift and concentrated manner.

Now in the second tale of creation God comes as the Lord God. And this second tale of creation has the character of water, beginning with the 'mist', continuing with the rivers. It is of the nature of inertia, of earthly time and duration.

All this is henceforth determined by what is expressed in the name of 'Lord God'. This name is spelled in Hebrew yod-hee-waw-hee. This name is not pronounced that way, because in pronouncing this proportion, or writing it down in the original Hebrew letters, one would create something of eminent force and power which one is not allowed to use for phenomenal proportions. Only in very special circumstances and in a very special place may this name be uttered, according to ancient lore. If one has already sensed a little of the power and significance of the word, of the miracle of the word, from what could so far be said and demonstrated about it, one will readily understand that one can actually transpose a proportion in sound or in original, real writing which as such can carry with it very special effects. We shall revert to it when we discuss the tree of the knowledge, which was not to be 'used' either. To take an example from modern, daily life, a man would think twice before going about with radium in his pocket, or putting it on his bureau, because he would *know* it was dangerous for him. But from sheer ignorance one does very often transgress other commandments and thinks it merely 'old-fashioned' or 'primitive' not to 'dare' pronounce the name of God.

However, we can and may, for the sake of understanding the wonder of the Bible, speak about this name and see what particular aspects are implied in it. And we may also mention the numbers which form this name. These numbers are in accordance with the letters 10–5–6–5. In this way the name Lord is expressed, and in Hebrew also the expression 'Adonai' is used, meaning 'Lord', but one does not pronounce the name as it is written in reality. But now let us look at the secret of this name. It contains 4 letters, at once reminding us of the 4 with which the second tale of creation is marked, and of the 4 which, as 40 and 400, always expresses itself as 'time of this world'.

The proportion 10–5–6–5 at first sight does not convey anything to us. We shall soon see, however, what remarkable proportion it is, and how this proportion is expressed in a really bewildering manner in the Bible-story.

In the serious kabbala, not in the dilettantic, a great deal of attention is paid to this name, naturally. Knowledge of this name – in Hebrew 'shem' – gives deep insight and confers great power. A 'baal-shem' is a man, who is possessed of this knowledge. In this book we cannot, of course, enter into the details of this very specific knowledge. Moreover it is largely dependent on qualities different from intellectual understanding by itself, hence one cannot write about this knowledge. At best it may be transmitted from teacher to pupil.

But I will mention here that the kabbala also analyses the quantitative proportions. The sum-total of the composing elements is 10+5+6+5=26. The kabbala, however, calculates the full value for each of the four letters, i.e. the value of the name of the letters in question, when written full length. The first letter is the 'jod' spelled jod-waw-daleth, 10–6–4, so its full value is 20. In the same way the second letter the 'hee', according to its orthography is he-jod, 15, the third letter 'waw', spelled waw-jod-waw, 22 and the fourth letter again glee' is 15. (Through varying the orthography of the 'Flee' and the 'wavy' the kabbala arrives at other expressions of this name Lord. I am not entering, however, into these considerations.)

Thus the full value is then 20+15+22+15=72. Now this 72, according to a manner of calculating applied in kabbala, this 72 also lies concealed in the structure of the 10–5–6–5. For if one causes this name to develop from the first letter to the second, then to the third and finally to all four of them, one gets:

		sum-total
1st letter	10	10
1st letter and 2nd letter	10–5	15
1st, 2nd and 3rd letter	10–5–6	21
1st, 2nd, 3rd and 4th letter	10–5–6–5	26
		72

So if one adds up the four situations the sum-total is also 72. It is the identical value of the letters of the name when written in full length. This number 72 plays an important part in the kabbala. It is mentioned as the 'shem-ayin-teeth', which means: 'the name-72', and, indeed, 72 different names are known, each of which has a certain meaning and power. Thus there is a 'shem-42' and a 'shem-63'.

It is doubtful whether there are people nowadays who are still in possession of the 'name' in the manner which actually gives the deeper insight in events and confers remarkable powers on man. Doubtlessly in the so-called circles of initiates there is a good deal of juggling with these things and people trifle with it vaguely and mysteriously, but the real knowledge is lost. And as I said before, it is not merely an intellectual affair.

We shall treat of this 'name' here also in accordance with ancient tradition. But, true to our intentions, we shall do so without any vagueness. The first approach, indeed, should always satisfy our sound common sense. It is not until one has acquired an immense amount of preliminary knowledge, that one can enter the field of mystery. Mystery, by the way, is not identical with 'mysteriousness' or vagueness. It is a different kind of knowledge, which does not merely involve the mind but the complete man.

The name Lord at our first approach proves to reveal very remarkable aspects. We shall even see it is this name which puts its mark on the whole of the biblical story. The story of the Bible up to the revelation of God on Mount Sinai (Ex. 19 and 20) according to tradition – and the correctness of it will be self-evident in the course of the argument – forms a cycle in itself. With the revelation on Mount Sinai a path is closed off which began in Paradise when man ate from the tree of the knowledge and started his journey through the world. It was a long way, essentially bearing the stamp of the way of mankind throughout the ages, towards a new world.

The revelation has it that God returned to earth again, that the condition of the beginning was restored, that the powers of the serpent which had caused the long way, were eliminated. We shall presently revert to these conceptions. For the moment let it suffice that with the descent of God on Mount Sinai a cycle has been rounded off at its roots, a state of unity has been restored. In this descent on Mount Sinai – as we shall see by and by this infers a descent into form – was disclosed the sense of existence, the sense as it is also expressed in the words of the Bible and more especially in the root-story of the Bible, the Pentateuch.

Now the period, as figured out in the Bible, from the second tale of creation up to the revelation on Mount Sinai, i. e. the period of time of the whole way in its essence, is subdivided into four parts by tradition. These four parts are distinguished by the fact that the opening words 'ele toldoth' occur four times in the Pentateuch. Translated it means 'these are the births' and it really means that the story is now going to deal with the history, or rather the historic development of a specific race. It also means that which was born from the unity at the beginning, that which emanated from it.

It is rather striking that there should be mentioned exactly four such 'historic developments'. Four, no more. Again this number, which indicates the farthest possibility in development. The Bible distinguishes between 'births', *toldoth*, directly connected with a preceding story, and those not connected with what precedes. The link between the two parts is made in Hebrew by the letter 'waw', 6. 'Waw' in translation means *hook,* a hook linking up two parts. For the letters in Hebrew have names agreeing with their meaning. And since the letter *waw* connects things, it is also called *hook*. Indeed, we shall see that the six days of creation as a 'six' as a 'hook', similarly join together two conditions: the 1 preceding creation, via the 6 of the days of creation, with the 1 of the terminus.

Now there are 'historic developments' beginning with the *wow*, which are not called 'ele toldoth', but 'we-ele-toldoth'. This 'we', i.e. the 'waw' preceding the word, is translated by 'and'. For this 'and' also joins together two things, which, without it, would stand apart. The connection by means of the *waw*, however, is much stronger and more fundamental. The waw actually joins, and the absence of the *waw* means that there is *no* connection.

Now we know enough of the structure of the Bible, after the few examples I have been able to give, to understand that a letter, a number, is there in that place, because it *has* to be there, that it is not any poetical caprice which insists that the word 'and' must be used, or that it might easily be done without occasionally or substituted by another term for a change. So when it says in the Bible 'these are the births' and not 'and these are the births', it is not an arbitrary variation in the text of the story.

So there are *four* parts, separated from each other by this 'ele toldoth'. A striking fact again that there should be four and that the point of issue is development, events in time. And even more striking is the fact that the word for birth or development 'toled', spelled taf-lamed-daleth, 400–30–4, has the same structure, only written in inverse order, as the word daleth, which is the name of the letter 4. Daleth is spelled 4–30–400. And *daleth,* 4, means 'door'. It is, indeed, the door through which one can enter or leave the house, the 'beth', i.e. the letter 2. The *beth* as house is the 2 of creation. With creation was made the house of the world, in which everything is enacted. That house is the '2' of creation. Through the daleth, 4, the door, we can grow away, leave the house. But one can also, after some absence, develop back to the origin, enter the house again. The door represents the alternative in the world of the '2', in the world as the house.

So it is not surprising, only astounding to see how everything fits in, that the 4 is the door for motion and that therefore there are also 4 birth-stories, development- or motion-stories which indicate in the structure of time what the door represents in the world of sensory perception, i.e. entering or leaving the house, the 'two'. When leaving the house, surrendering oneself to multiplicity, detaching oneself from unity with the father, and on entering returning to unity, to the origin, to the father.

We have not nearly reached the end yet of stating remarkable coherences. The first tale of creation, the tale of the six days of creation, the tale which tells of the birth of the world, its entire development within the inner orb round the core, that tale expresses itself in exactly 434 words. Which is the number of the word 'birth' and of the number daleth, the number 4 (400+30+4=434 and 4+30+400=434).

And this is likewise the 4 of the four constituent parts of the name 'Lord' and of the four 'birth-stories', it is the 4 of the four acts of creation, and it is the 4 representing the extreme possibility. It is also the 4 of the (1–4)-structure, of the tree of the knowledge, of the standard of time which is ever measured by this 4 in the 40 and the 400. The 4 obviously is a very important aspect of the expression of reality in this world. It is also apparent that the Bible which contains within itself these prodigious combinations of all conceptions of the 4, is something real, also existing outside its phenomenal form in this world.

An old tradition expresses it thus: 'God looked in the Thora – i.e. the Pentateuch – and in accordance with it He created the world.' This pronouncement means that we should look upon the Bible as something supernatural, and that this world is considered an imprint of the Bible, an expression of it made by God in space and time, in which the conceptions space and time should be taken in a very wide sense. Likewise stating that the space-time structure of the world and that of the Bible are closely related.

So the four 'birth-stories' are tales which lead to the expression of the reality of the Bible – of that which is with God according to the above quoted tradition – in the happenings in the world until the moment in those happenings when this Bible with all its expression comes to light, becomes perceptible. Then the whole way has in essence fulfilled itself in this world. We shall presently deal with these aspects in greater detail. For that purpose we shall have to examine the four birth-stories more closely.

The first 'birth', the first 'ele toldoth', the Bible gives at the beginning of the second tale of creation. The translation merely says: 'this is the story', and to a translation, since it cannot possibly transmit the wonder of the essence of the word, it makes little difference whether the same words are translated in this way or in that. For a translation is a more intense imaging even than the story in the original language when one merely reads it as a story. I shall therefore in the further enumeration of the four *ele toldoth* take no notice of what the translation has made of it. It is a fact that in the Hebrew text the words *ele toldoth* are used and that these four texts are the only ones where they occur.

The second 'birth', the second *ele toldoth* is mentioned in Gen. 6:9. It is the story of Noah. The third ele toldoth is found in Gen. 11:10. It deals with the generations of Shem. And the fourth and last time the 'ele toldoth' is found is in Gen. 37:2. That is where the story of Jacob begins.

We have already seen that the 4 really includes the 10 different situations.

Thus the 4 *ele toldoth* should also contain 10 toldoth in all. Just as the 4 acts of creation of the first cycle contain the 10 acts in all. Indeed we see this systematism confirmed here too. The 4 ele toldoth have given shape to 6 *we-ele toldoth* so that all in all there are actually 10 birth-stories; 4 of which form the main part and 6 which exist in the background linked up with other stories. These 6 *we-ele toldoth* which I shall not deal with in this hook are found resp. in Gen. 10:1, Gen. 11:27, Gen. 25:12, Gen. 25:19, Gen. 36:1, and Gen. 36:9 in the Hebrew text, that is: the translations, needless to say, are not literal either and they often render the phrase in different wording. Thus there are 6 *we-ele toldoth* till the moment the 4 *ele toldoth* come to expression. These 4 carry the other 6 with them, owing to which the 10 are formed, again in accordance with the structure of the real and of the 6 proceeding from them, as it were. For the 4 has the 3 + 2 + 1 = 6 for its background.

Now let us examine these 4 *ele toldoth* more closely. These 4 parts give the whole development; with these 'four' a cycle is closed, as was the case with the 'four' of the 4 acts of creation in the first cycle of the 3 days of creation. But here we see something very special which comes to the fore in this very connection. For here we see how this 'four' has in it the *manner* in which reality expresses itself in time.

The name Lord, as we saw, contains four letters, 10–5–6–5. So there are 4 proportions indicated in this name. Now the 4 birth-stories prove to be built in exactly the same proportions. So it is in fact the name Lord, this name which must not be uttered, which establishes how the development of the generations will he in time. Their path through history has the structure of the name of Lord; this 'name' determines the development. Thus the first part of the 4 into which the story up to the revelation on Mount Sinai is divided by these 4 'ele toldoth', has the number 10 for its measure, like the first letter of the name Lord, for in this first part are mentioned exactly 10 generations. It can he verified in the text of the Bible (Gen. 5). These 10 generations are:

1. Adam
2. Seth
3. Enos
4. Cainan
5. Mahalaleël
6. Jared
7. Enoch
8. Methuselah
9. Lamech
10. Noah

So we see that the enumeration of the generations, with their names and ages – which we cannot deal with in this connection – is not a haphazard historic statement to impress us with those high ages or to help us to decode the names on excavated potsherds, but that obviously something entirely different is given *first and foremost,* viz. an insight in the structure of the world, in the development of the world in time, which development is closely hound up with the name Lord. Then the second part with the story of the second 'ele toldoth', the story of Noah, in accordance with the second letter of the name Lord, which is 5, contains 5 generations, again easily checked in the text (Gen. 10:21–25). These 5 generations are given for the generation of Shem, since it is only this generation in the Bible which is continued, which goes on serving as standard:

1. Shem
2. Arpachshad
3. Shelah
4. Heber
5. Peleg

There is now the 5 of the second letter of the name Lord. With Peleg (Gen. 10:25) it is specially mentioned that in his days the earth was divided; so there is something special going on. The word Peleg in Hebrew also means splitting, cleaving into parts, cutting up. No children of Peleg's are mentioned here, his brother Joktan's children are mentioned, but the latter is not mentioned any more in the continuation of the generations. These generations continue with Peleg's children, who are not mentioned, however, until the next part, in the next 'ele toldoth'.

Now follows the third part and it will have to correspond with the third component of the name Lord, with the letter 6. This letter, as we have seen, is the connecting letter, the 'waw', the hook which links on all that comes to what precedes.

Whoever is convinced that the Bible is just as much a creation of God as is life, as is the world, will doubtless say that this is a matter of course, that in such a case the miracle *must* work even in all so-called subsidiary matters, that all details must be pervaded by it, and here we see that the third part not only contains 6 generations, but that it also hooks into the preceding part and therefore repeats the former generations, which were mentioned in the second part, but that it does so on purpose to bring forward what is new. In the third part the next 6 generations are given after having hooked in as far back as Shem, repeating the generations up to Peleg. But this time obviously in quite a different plane, Joktan is not even mentioned any more, whereas Peleg's descendants are. So here we have (Gen. 11:10–27 ff in the next chapters dealing with Abraham and Isaac down to the fourth 'ele toldoth'):

1. Rehoe
2. Serug
3. Nahor
4. Terah
5. Abraham
6. Isaac

So this third part continues up to and including Isaac, and the fourth part begins with Jacob. This fourth part, in accordance with the fourth letter of the name Lord, has 5 generations. The fifth generation is that which gets the revelation on Mount Sinai, where God tells Moses (Ex. 6:1–2) that He had not been known under the name of Lord, so far. It is the generation in which there is the important turning-point, where in the Bible— i. e. the Pentateuch — the whole story of what was before and what was to come, is revealed, is seen, and can be heard and read; wherein that becomes perceptible in the world, which at the same time contains the whole story of the world in space-time. For those 5 generations are taken the generations which lead up to Moses. Besides the enumeration of the names of these generations, that of their ages is also continued. This communication of the ages — some people may remark that they are not very interesting, but we shall presently see how fascinating they really are — is only continued as regards the generations from Adam to Moses, mentioned below. For the generation of Moses, there is the event of the revelation. These 5 generations are (Gen. 37 and Ex. 6:15–19):

1. Jacob
2. Levi
3. Kehath
4. Amram
5. Moses

So we have stated something very particular. Let us recapitulate: the name Lord, with the 4 letters 10–5–6–5 appears to express itself comprehensively in the 4 parts of the story up to the revelation, to the point in the root-story where the ultimate condition is reached, in which God restores the unity of the beginning when the circle is closed again. And the expression is such that the generations enumerated in the Bible prove to have the same system in those 4 parts as the name Lord. The Bible up to the revelation gives 26 generations, i. e. the sum-total of the letters of the name Lord. And the story divides those 26 generations into 4 distinctly separated groups, which division produces the same quantitative proportion as that of the name Lord, i. e. 10, 5, 6, 5 generations.

So the name Lord proves to be the pattern for the division of these 26 generations. We might put it like this: the Lord descends into this world with His name and because of it the name of the Lord expresses itself in these 26 generations. The name Lord puts its stamp on time, and thus gives sense and significance to history, to events; it-forms the structure of the events.

Whoever begins to grasp this, will not busy himself overmuch with historic proofs for these generations. Then it is a strange kind of curiosity. These generations are first and foremost mentioned to serve a different purpose something of much wider scope. They show that all ages, however far back, bear a definite stamp, the stamp of the Lord; that nothing ever happens accidentally, that everything is measured by standards not of this world, but with the measure of the name of the Lord.

The Bible first and foremost tells us something entirely different from an archaeologic or prehistoric tale in these generations. It tells us that life in time is formed in a very definite manner, that it has been marked by God. And then it tells us that what happens, the sequence of events, takes place in accordance with a very special systematism, predestined by the fact that the Lord, as God, accompanies man in time. And when we begin to realize this, then these generations suddenly are much closer to us. For they prove to bear with them the communication that the Lord speaks in history, that the tale of the generations is His name, that the generations come and go, into a predestined way, a way which is of the same essence as the name of the Lord.

Whether it was a hundred thousand years ago in our chronology or five thousand years, what does it matter. That we are so eager to know the number of years, at least approximately, is because we hope to understand a little more of the secret of the word, of the sense of existence. But when the secret of the world proves to be disclosed to us in a more direct way, when it proves not to be mysteriously shrouded as if it were a malicious game to trick us, as people have come to think, then our interest will he roused by this miracle, which will then prove to unveil to us the sense of existence. The Bible indeed speaks to us about the sense of existence, that is why it was given to the world. It was not given us as a source of historic data, as a collection of more or less primitive tales, more or less acceptable, more or less impressive, it gives us information as a father would give information to his children, *how* the world is and why it is so and what is the sense of it all and why it is particularly, unsurpassably good. A father will not be able to say this about the whole world, because he did not make it himself and therefore is not responsible for it either. But a father *can* tell us how the things are which *he* has made for us, the house that *he* built and furnished, the education *he* gives us. Now when the maker of a world tells us like a father *how* He made it and why, and why it is good, it is not a story which is kept a secret lest we should lay hold of it. At best it can he kept a secret to those who will not understand, who will misunderstand and eventually abuse it. For such there is as we shall see by and by, a kind of automatic clasp to the book. They do not even know how to unclasp it. But otherwise it is just a revelation, i. e. information to all people to let them know why they are here, what is their path, what is their destination.

Once we know, we shall also know at once how to deal with our era and will not speculate on the problem whether a day of creation is a day or a milliard years. Then we will he able to deal with those years quite normally.

So we see from that story about the 26 generations who bear the mark of the Lord, the mark 10–5–6–5, that the name Lord is something very special. And this will make us understand why in the second tale of creation God appears as the Lord God.

Before returning to the second tale of creation, something has yet to be said about this name 'Lord'.

The number 26 comes into prominence in yet another place and in a very remarkable manner. The first letter, the aleph, 1, is in its outward form built up – and considering the whole systematism in the tale and in the word *that* is not accidental either – out of two jods reflecting each other, two 'tens' reflecting each other, with a 'waw', 6, as the mirror.

The 'aleph', 1, thus looks like this:

$$\begin{array}{c}10\\6\\10\end{array}$$

or in Hebrew — and this conveys little or nothing to the reader who knows no Hebrew —

This specific structure, this form, of the letter or the number 1 is entirely in accordance with the structure which we shall go on seeing all the time.

The Lord, who is 'one', expresses Himself in the 26 generations, in time as a 'whole' up to the revelation. He expresses Himself in 4 parts, in 26 generations but is yet the 1. It is like the letter which stands before the capital 2 of 'in the beginning', before duality appeared in the world. This means that even in the 1 — i.e. the 1 which precedes the differentiation into the 2, the 1 which does not know any other thing outside itself — is included that 26 which will expand in the story of the 26 generations. It is even included in the 1, and after the 1 has made creation, has made the 2, God as Lord, in His quality as Lord, accompanies creation, the world. Until the world at the end of the 26 generations sees Him and can see the sense of it all.

Now that we have been able to see a little of the nature of the name of the Lord, how He expresses Himself in the 26 generations of the Bible, how these generations which form the expression of the name Lord in time are also checked as to their number in years, how the pattern of this name 'Lord', 10–5–6–5, stamps itself on these generations and now that we have also seen how the conception 'one', the number represented by the aleph, also contains this 26 within itself, which from the moment of differentiation of the 1 into the 2 expresses itself in time, we shall now proceed to examine this name from another side, or rather from inside.

Now that we have learned to see the 'waw' as the hook, the connecting number — just as the creation of the 6 days itself forms a connection between two conditions, connecting the preceding condition to the next — therefore we can read the name 10,5 'and', 5. The 2 fives also make 10, but they have been split up and are linked up by that 'hook'. That the 1 in fact consists of 2 tens has been demonstrated in the form of the aleph, which indeed consists of 2 jods, 2 tens with a six as a kind of mirror in between.

Now if we examine more closely this principle of 'ten splitting up into two fives', there appears to be nothing except the 1 dividing itself into two parts, hence the making of the 2, as we saw it when discussing the tale of creation. Thus we see:

$$\frac{10}{5\quad 5} \quad \begin{array}{l}\text{undivided}\\ \text{divided into two parts}\end{array}$$

So it proves to be what we have learned to regard as the principle of creation, the making of the 2. But it is a making of 2 which also includes as principle that the 2 are at once reunited into the 1. The 6, which is the 'and', the 'hook' giving the quantitative proportion 5–6–5, connects the two fives into unity. The '2' is not a permanent thing, a permanent division, but it is at once united again into a unity, owing to which the 26 which forms the name 'Lord', has become a unity of two tens, one up above which is undivided, and one down below which is divided but which has all the same become a unity again.

As it was involved in the word create that the 2, via the multiplicity of the 200, was to become 1 again, thus the name of the Lord contains this principle in itself. But now, since He is before creation, all-inclusive from the very beginning, there is first the 1 dividing itself into 2, then to return to the 1, i.e. connecting the 2 again and making them again into 1.

Thus we see how one thing fits into another. Creation, once it is made, is the 2, and it expands into multiplicity, finally in obedience to the law of the concept of creation, to return to the 1. The creator as 1, as the 'One' makes creation, the 2, which is reunited into the 1. The name Lord, 10–5–6–5, tells us this, tells us about the ten which divides itself into two fives, which are again united to 'one', to the original 'ten'. Hence the principle of 1–2–1. And finally we see in history, in the story of the Bible as it proceeds in time, how this principle expresses itself. And the story itself, so far, on account of its image-building structure not yet explained any further, in its purport similarly eventuates into the 'one', into revelation, into mankind's finding God again, into emancipation from bondage. The path of the story similarly develops via duality, via deviation from the principle of unity, via a removal from the origin. Until the moment when one seems farthest removed, until the moment when the sense of being lost has attained its acme and everything seems utterly hopeless, there yet comes altogether unexpectedly the help and release, and God is seen in the revelation of the sense of existence.

This name 'Lord' which involves a revelation in the world in an accompaniment and determining of time, which puts its stamp on the succession of the generations and the events; which through that very stamp irrevocably leads the development back to unity, to the unison of the opposites, is therefore given in tradition that name of God which expresses God's goodness, compassion, love. It is the love of God towards creation, towards the world, the world He accompanies, the world which He puts His mark on, owing to which it must, according to law, attain its purpose, its destination. The world marked with this sign, *cannot* get lost. *This* is what this structure tells us. The name of God in his quality of 'Elohim', i.e. the name which is translated as 'God', and which in the first tale of creation we see as the only name, whereas in the second tale of creation God appears as Lord God, this name 'Elohim' tells us, according to tradition, about God in His quality of righteousness. Righteous in the sense of 'maintaining harmony', the harmony of unity which supports the world. Even tradition has it that this world with man, as he is here, could not survive after duality leading to multiplicity had been made, if God were only to appear in His quality of strict vindicator of harmony. For in that case every step removing us farther from the origin, moving away from God, would cause God to appear as sustainer of harmony in order to undo this removal, plucking the dissenter away as a disturbing element in the world. But God in His quality of goodness and love, accompanying the world, knowing why the world was made like this, what purpose man's weakness serves, knowing the whole way, starting from unity, going through multiplicity and finally returning to that unity, leads man through time, as root-story in the Bible expressing itself in that way of the 26 generations who because of it bear that mark of the Lord, of God in His mercy. God in *that* quality leads man back to unity, leads him home. And *that* also is told in the story of the Bible, just as its structure, its essence implies. Now that we have learned to recognize all this about the meaning of the names 'Lord' and 'God', let us return to our discussion of the 2nd tale of creation. For only with the knowledge we have acquired, shall we be able to understand this story a little better and with it the principle of all creation and the world.

5
Male and Female *

The structure of time, the expression of the 26 generations, from creation up to the revelation of its purpose, the Bible becoming manifest in the world, reflects itself in the name Lord. And this name expresses itself in the four parts of the story up to the revelation. The name of four letters and these four parts, like everything else measured with the four, contain the expression in matter, in space and time. The four, likewise, is the number of the female, the female which makes material to grow, to come forth. The mother of things.

In the second tale of creation with the (1–4)-principle as its determining factor, the female plays the important part, and the name Lord, too, appears there simultaneously. For as soon as man comes into prominence with the centre of gravity on the female side, the matter-forming side, he is accompanied by the Lord God in His quality of loving compassion.

In this second tale of creation, as contrasted with the first, we see that man is formed on the left side of the scheme as the second event, after the 'mist' which went up. Whereas in the first tale of creation man is created in God's image and after His likeness, in the second tale of creation we hear that man is formed of the dust of the ground, into which the Lord God breathed the 'breath of life'.

It is not until later on, in the Garden of Eden, when man's purpose in life is revealed to him, embracing the direction to eat freely from all the trees in the garden *except* the tree of the knowledge, that we see him appearing in the systematism of the story, i.e. in its central column.

He enters that central column together with an alternative, with duality, which, as we have seen, fits into this central column.

Firstly there is in the central column the duality of the two trees, the tree of life and the tree of the knowledge, and below it in the same central column there is the duality of the alternative: the possibility *either* to eat or *not* to eat from it. The non-eating involves non-absorption of that which is the essence of the tree of the knowledge of good and evil. This tree is what we have recognized as the essence of duality.

---

*After having in the foregoing reproduced the numbers in the form of figures to emphasize the quantitative proportions, I shall henceforward stick to the generally accepted mode of expression to avail myself of figures only when strictly necessary. From now on I shall again write 'one' and 'two' in the text, and no longer 1 and 2 unless it should he necessary.

It is the duality with which God created the world. Duality, which had as its consequence the bringing forth of multiplicity, the great diversity. In contrast to which God created man, to eliminate this duality. Man who in his life, his thought and his action was to break through this duality, to restore the 'one', the harmony preceding this making of duality. Man, indeed, was *not* to continue duality, his coming was intended to abolish the contrast. That is why man was not supposed to absorb that which represented the power and the principle of this duality, crystallizing in an image as the tree of the knowledge of good and evil. Only God had used that power to create and that power was to remain with God to sustain life in multiplicity here. This power was not made to be used by man to the contrary, it is the power which destroys the purpose of the creation of man. The power of man would, to the contrary, he the reversal, the turning hack, the desisting from abusing the power of duality, which brings forth multiplicity, and the turning to his purpose: the integration of everything to the harmony of primeval beginning.

The obvious question is: Why does God play such a game? Why does He first make duality afterwards persuading man under exceedingly difficult circumstances *not* to make the 'two' himself also, but to the contrary re-establish the 'one'? So the question is why God did *not* let the 'one' exist from the beginning, thus avoiding all the complications which seem to accumulate now. After the foregoing we can however anticipate the answer more or less.

As we have seen from the form of the aleph, of the 'one', it consists of a duality which rests serenely in itself, which is in balance. The 'jod' is the smallest letter as far as form is concerned. This letter indicates that there is matter, just enough to make it perceptible, no more. There is no expansion of this matter. And the aleph consists exactly of balance, harmony; it is a reflection of two such 'jods', as we have seen in the Hebrew form.

Hence unity is a duality whose components are each other's reflection, and are at rest. Since this unity, as is indicated by the *jod*, the *ten*, the highest figure developed from the four, contains everything and all this is in harmony, it is the condition of supreme bliss: all-inclusive, having nothing excluded, and all this in complete harmony. To give this greatest, highest bliss, to creation and notably to man is, as the story of the Bible informs us in its structure, the purpose behind all creation.

For God divides this unity into two parts, separating the one jod, the one ten, from the other, just as the name 'Lord' makes clear to us. For what purpose? That the detached ten, essentially participating in the great unity, — in which the two 'jods', the two 'tens', form the aleph, the 'one' — might feel the desire cropping up to become 'one' again with its counterpart, the ten, with which it originally formed that great unity.

This desire for integration would involve that the two separated parts would want to grow towards each other. The jod above would yearn for the jod below, and the one below yearn for the one above. It would be like a game of love, as the Song of Solomon depicts it. It is the great happiness which lies in the knowledge of belonging together and seeking each other, sometimes coming to grief in this search, but this failure merely heightens the desire and raises the expectation of happiness to dizzy heights, once the partners have found each other.

Until the two have found each other and are merged in immense happiness, the happiness of unity and the realization that this unity at the same time involves the knowledge of eternally being at-one, an uninterrupted, never diminishing, everlasting unity at its culmination-point.

That creation, and notably man, might participate in *this* happiness of unity, creation has been made by God, the 'two' has been made. This becoming one involves the becoming one of all opposites, and the bliss of unity is among other things, also that of knowing that everything appearing here as duality in the form of for instance life and death, good and bad, justice and injustice, right and wrong, wealth and poverty, health and disease, publicity and secrecy, can similarly become one, and that it is this becoming-one with all other things which gives this great happiness. A happiness which is so much the greater after the separation which called up the sorrow of being subjected to all these opposites. A sorrow which caused the desire for unity, for understanding and realizing the purpose of things, and through which one would finally perceive that not only was this grief on account of the contrast life and death dissolved, but that it had simultaneously become bliss ineffable, because they would prove together to form the harmony which brings with it supreme joy and happiness.

God made the world from sheer desire to give creation that which He experienced uninterruptedly, which even to Him is the bliss of harmony, embracing all in serenity and satisfaction.

And for that reason, in this immense desire to give joy and happiness, God expresses Himself in this world as the 'Lord', as that which gave the world the duality through which man could come 'forth; coming forth from the all-inclusive, primeval unity, in order to accompany the world on the way of this duality back to unity, to taste with the world that supreme bliss, the bliss of unity.

And there where man, misunderstanding the purpose of this duality in which he was placed, would want to proceed ever farther away from the origin, there the quality of love and compassion of the name 'Lord' would nevertheless lead him back to unity, notwithstanding the fact that the path of man includes such an alienation. Such is the secret of God as 'Lord' accompanying creation.

Thus God made the ten below, expressing itself in the ten words of creation of the first tale of creation. Thus man stood below with everything around him, opposite to the ten above. In this way was man made in the image of God, after God's likeness, having the 'one' within himself, male and female as one being. With the two sides in one, as the old tales have it: with the two countenances. Thus:

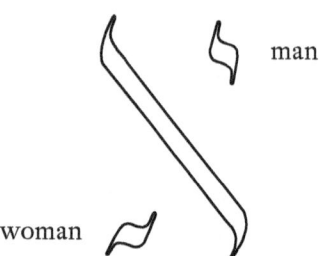

And then the Lord God said that it was not good that man should be alone, alone over against God and that he needed a help over against himself, facing him, as he himself faced God. For man standing as 'one' facing God, cannot realize the purpose of creation. He is not aware of the sorrow and forlornness of multiplicity which yearns to be emancipated, which desires to be led back to the origin. The multiplicity created on purpose to make man experience the bliss of unity.

Something had to be placed below opposite him, divorced from himself, taken from him, that he might experience the desire to be one with it again. If duality should come forth within himself, if he were to experience the sorrow of duality himself, then he would realize what separation, what contrast was and also what unity, abolition of separation and contrast implied. He would at the same time realize what God experiences having caused within Himself the divorce in order to make creation possible to make duality a reality.

Through the experience of his own separateness, his own sorrow, man would begin to grasp the purpose of duality. He would then also understand the world, the sorrow and the forlornness of multiplicity, which yearns just as much for the serenity and the harmony of unity.

And for that reason did the Lord God make from man below, from the 'ten' below, the two fives, the two halves, the male part and the female part. In man himself did the duality of separation express itself.

In the dualism male-female in man lies embedded the dualism in all that affects man. Man himself now got divorced. And his desire to have unity restored would make him realize the desire for unity in all planes, all qualities, up to unity with God. This divorce of man into male and female might be represented as follows in the image of the aleph:

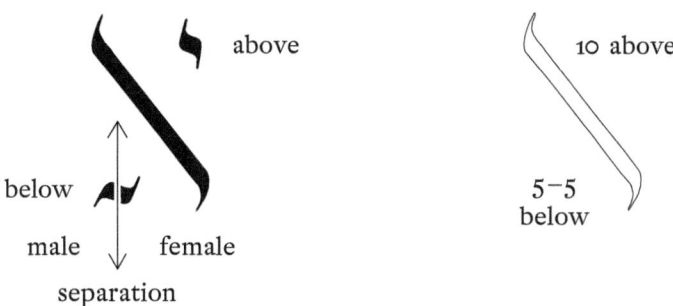

Then 'ten' below was divided into two fives, into two halves. One half kept the nature of the original whole just as the ten above, even after creation, notwithstanding the divorce, kept the nature of the original unity. And the other half got the nature of the creation made by God, the creation which God made out of Himself. For indeed, woman was split off from the unity 'man', just as God split off creation from Himself. She stands over against man, just as the whole of creation, as 'woman', stands over against God.

Before the Lord God made woman, He formed all the beasts on the face of the earth and brought them to the man. The man, then still 'one', male and female in one, was not aware of the sorrow of separateness expressing itself in the appearance of all that lives. Life, meeting man in order to be united by him with that from which it was divorced when duality was achieved, was not understood by man. He himself was not aware of the sorrow and despair of the separateness, of the contrast.

Thus man gave the beasts, i. e. life as it presented itself before real man came, a destination here below, a 'name', a 'place' here below. Name and indication of a place have the same structure in Hebrew, viz. shin-mem, 300–40. Tradition expresses it thus, that man committed adultery with beasts. Contact with other life, indeed, without any desire to unite it with the 'above', with the origin, with that from which it was originally divorced, without any desire to know the purpose of that life, not even to realize that everything *must* have some purpose, thus having this contact directed towards an earthly goal, a utility-goal, such a contact is called 'adultery'.

Therefore the Lord God changed the condition for man, too. The 'tardema'—the deep sleep that comes over him – also means '*descend*'. Man descended into another world, got into a different state. In that lower state he was split up in two. One of his sides stood facing him as a separate being. Man himself now was a duality also. And such in the most expanded sense of the word. The contrast in all things now burned in him as well. The word 'rib' here is most misleading. It rather means one of the characteristics of man, one of the sides or aspects he has, which is now built into something separate.

The word used here for side, translated as 'rib', with a chance of creating a misunderstanding, is 'tselah' in Hebrew, spelled tsade-lamed-ayin, in numbers

90–30–70. The word for image is 'tselem', tsade-lamed-mem, 90–30–40. And the word with which they are both connected is 'tsel', shadow, tsade-lamed, 90–30.

When we look at this word 'side' from the standpoint of its real structure, we shall see that it will he better understood when we translate it as 'facet' or as 'aspect' or 'quality'.

So from man is taken that side, which as the female side formed the unity, the harmony with the male side in him.

And for that which was taken away, there came the 'flesh' instead. As the text has it: the 'Lord God' filled the open space and closed it with flesh.

In that world where man himself is split up in two, where his oneness as man is only a moiety, where – to revert to our systematism – the ten is divided into two fives, there that which here appears as flesh is the same as that which there – in that other world where man was still 'one' – was the place of the female. The place of the flesh is therefore the place of the female. And since flesh is the physical – man in his earthly appearance is called the creature of 'flesh and blood', in Hebrew 'basar wedam' – the body of man is the expression of the female side.

In man, before this division into male-female, body and soul are 'one' in another quality. The body has not yet an independent development. After this division into male-female, into separate beings, there comes simultaneously the body as a separate something, endowed with a life of its own. The fact of the separate female is identical with the fact of the separate body.

This splitting up into male and female took place because man did not view the world, life, material things according to their nature, did not integrate them with the source. That is why man landed in a lower world, a world in which, owing to this attitude, the body leads an existence of its own. Just as woman now stands apart from man.

About this separate body man says he knows and feels it is *his,* that it is part of his nature. Just as he knows and feels about the woman who stands apart from him that she pertains to him, that they ought to have been one being together. In man has arisen the need to become one with that which he now feels and knows as a part of himself and which he now experiences as something taken from him. He suffers on account of that division and his mind is set on making this division undone, on becoming one again with that other thing which actually pertains to him. This suffering, this severance, has come over him because, when still one he had omitted to lead back to the source that which had already been divided.

So now man, too, got the pattern 10–5. He now got conscious of himself as 'half', and so he seeks the other 'half'. He seeks the other 5 to reunite himself with it back to the original 10. And since, together with this severance, his body has also arisen as something separate, he is aware of duality in everything. For now he knows that the body may also fall away from him. Now he realizes what severance means, what duality means. Now he also understands the contrast of good and bad, of right and wrong, etc. And now he can realize what reunion, what unity means.

Now as soon as man appears in this new condition, as separate man and separate woman, there is the meeting with the 'serpent'. The condition of the man separate and the woman separate means, as we have seen, that also the essential nature of man – which may be called his soul – no longer forms an indissoluble, harmonic unity with the body, but that the body can go its own way.

Now that body gets into contact with the serpent. As regards the serpent, too, we have to try and penetrate from the image to its real significance. The serpent is called 'the subtlest of all beasts'. The conception 'beasts' – as has been discussed in the scheme of creation – is the biological condition for the life of man. So the conception 'beast' is also something related to physical life. In contrast with the conception 'woman', however, it is that part which still pertains to the duality of creation. It is the farthest point of creation before the unit man appeared. A unit man containing both the male and the female. The bodily part of man which pertains to the 'beast' cannot be counted to pertain to the essence of man. It is that in man which has in it the power of development, the power which is bent on forming multiplicity, ever proceeding unceasingly. It might eventually be called the instinctive animal in man, that which acts as a natural force. Whereas the physical represented by the conception 'woman', is the human body with its senses and the human power of combination based on it. The part of the body which in the sphynx has the animal-form, i.e. the nether part with its procreative passion, the blind urge to continue developing, is the animal side. The part of the body which includes the senses and the power of perception is the female side of it. The male side of it is that which enables man to pursue the real and grasp it; that which aims at the unity of the restoration of harmony with God. There exists in this world the contact between the animal principle, expressing itself as striving after development, multiplicity, 'record-breaking', and the female principle, i.e. the power of perception and the power of combination to build on those perceptions, to give form to life.

The form, laid down in the 'beast' that it may develop ever further, is the force of duality with which creation was made. It has found its greatest development in the 'beast'. At the stage of man this force of development would already have been so great that it would have outreached itself and could not have turned back unless the principle of the 1–2–1, of the return, had been inserted in creation. This principle was inserted in man through the 'divine breath' that was breathed into him, the 'neshama', which we might translate as 'divine soul'. This it is that makes man the image, the likeness of God.

Man in this condition, as we have already described in great detail, does not see the world in its duality, at any rate he does not realize the sorrow of separateness, to the contrary duality serves the purpose of his joy, intellectual and material; he commits 'adultery' with it. Thus man is brought into the condition in which he himself is also separated; the image of God becomes body and soul separately, male and female separately. The body is free to go its own way and the soul will suffer on account of the body's getting astray.

Now man's body is the 'beast' one stage further perfected. It balances continually on the edge of the plane whence there is no return. That is the reason why the force of development — imaged as 'the subtlest of all beasts' — seeks to come into contact with this enormous potentiality in order to achieve an outburst of growth, development. If it succeeds in convincing *that* body of the grandeur of the possibilities of development, this force will have gained the victory. The 'beast' acts according to its inherent nature. It has in it the forces of development. And the tangent-plane between beast and man is the body, as expressed by the female principle. It takes place in the second tale of creation, with the 'female' as the perceptible expression of man, with the human body taking the initiative. When the 'female' acts, then in this world the 'male' simply and naturally joins in.

Now the serpent as the supreme, the furthest developed expression of the 'beast' opens the dialogue with the 'female', with the human body in possession of its senses, its perception, its power of combination. And the body responds to the serpent's reasoning. It sees that it is a *good* thing to operate the forces of development itself, to take development into its own hands. And when man does so with his perception and the experience based thereon and the possibilities of combination it means that for this life on earth man does it thoroughly. There is not the schizophrenic condition of joining the world on the one hand and turning to God on the other. The Bible tells us even in this initial chapter that when the 'female' eats, the 'male eats with her' quite naturally. If one were to think it is *not* so, it is merely wishful thinking and then even the outer harmony of man will be disturbed, then he will he split up in the abnormal sense, then he will be what is called schizophrenic.

The serpent has something to offer to man. The serpent is the physical Messiah, one might say. It offers the kingdom of this world, the kingdom of endless development. That in doing so it acts contrary to the principle of creation which implies a return to the starting-point, implies attention turned away from development and directed towards the origin, induces strain, posits the alternative. Just as the sphynx did. It has been pointed out that the word for serpent in Hebrew *nachash,* spelled 50–8–300, has as its total 358. And that is also the sum-total of the components of the word Messiah, in Hebrew *mashiach,* spelled 40–300–10–8. So Serpent and Messiah have the same sum-total of components; they have, in a sense, the same value in essence. The serpent is the Redeemer on the opposite side, proposes emancipation in advising to set to work by oneself, to take development in one's own hands. In its dialogue with the 'female' it has the advantage of offering a tangible deliverance according to the standards of this world. Whereas the return to the origin implies accepting the existence of a world of different standards. *That* is the serpent's subtlety that it acts as the Redeemer.

Whatever for? The answer is: it actually places man where he considers himself lost. The path of the serpent leads to catastrophe. Man sees everything he has built up crashing down: his life and the world. And he sees at the same time, as if by magic, that through those other standards, not trusted and turned down by him, he finds himself home all of a sudden, at the starting-point: that it was not *himself* who achieved it, but that his liberation was prepared, according to entirely different standards, according to the principle implied in creation. It is the same principle which in the Pentateuch effects the exodus from Egypt. The bondage could not come to an end, things seemed to have got to a hopeless stage. Development had gone all wrong. And yet it happened. People seem lost. The word lose or lost in Hebrew is abed, spelled 1–2–4. It has in its structure the development from the 'one' to the 'two', but instead of the return to the 'one' there is the further development of the 'two' to its highest perfection, to the 'four'. Now this development is identical with 'getting lost'.

And here we touch on one of the essential points in the image the Bible gives of the world. The development of creation, from the 'one' to the 'two' and from the 'two' to 'multiplicity', brings the principle 'four' into prominence and this implies that with it, indeed, all gets lost.

Therefore the bondage in Egypt which lasted 400 years was a bondage which according to natural law should never have come to an end. God in His love and mercy had conceived unity as the ground plan and purpose of creation, and in His quality of righteous preserver of harmony had implied the return to the 'one' in the structure of creation, as the purpose thereof, and it is only God's interference which effects liberation.

The power of the 'two' is so great and indeed, has been made purposely so great, that it might extend over all things, set its mark on all things: that *everything* might taste the bliss of reunion. This bliss is the greater since it comes after the recognition of one's being lost in development and the sudden discovery of an entirely different power whose existence one had never suspected and which fulfils things just when one had ceased to believe and given up hope. In every plane anew it is the same feeling which comes over a man who knows he is dying and sees his body decaying, yet beyond the threshold where he has relinquished everything, suddenly perceives, that there is something else, that not only is there no death, but that there is a life very much better than he could ever have imagined. A life embracing so very much more, a life in which nothing can get lost, and in which everything supposed to be lost is restored more completely than he had ever known it.

The biblical story teaches us that the purpose of life lies not in intellectual achievement, not in work done here for wages, but that the purpose of it all is the surprise to find that everything was arranged for good in advance, that one has only to see it. And for that reason was the Bible given, that one *might see!!*

In the Garden of Eden in the second tale of creation, man had only to follow one way, 'eat' everything, from every tree, i.e. with the exception of the tree of the knowledge of good and evil.

'Eating' is yet another image. It means essentially that man makes everything he 'eats' one with himself. It means therefore that everything in the world should be man's concern; first and foremost by taking things in, and going out towards them, he should get interested in them, find out their sense, want to know their nature, thereby integrating them with himself.

Only the tree of the knowledge of good and evil he was not to absorb. The essence which the tree of knowledge expresses is exactly what man should not absorb, should not integrate himself with. For that essence meant the development which creation had achieved. And man was to accept this creation as a datum and lead it integrally back to the origin by recognizing, by wanting to recognize, in everything its very nature, its very essence. In *that* sense he would just *have* to eat everything. But he was *not* to eat in the sense of the principle of the tree of knowledge.

Connection with the tree of knowledge also means connection with the image. And not eating from the tree of knowledge implies *not* judging from perception, from the image, from the outward appearances. It implies judging from the essence, and with *such* judgement coincides the union with the origin, with the 'one'.

The word 'eat' in Hebrew is 'achol', spelled 1–20–30. It also means to finish, to perfect. The part 20–30 means 'everything; all'. And this word linked up with the 1 therefore also means uniting everything with reality. What is physically expressed as taking up food which will form one with us, implies the nature of the conception 'eating', of that word 1–20–30, i.e. that one integrates with oneself those things which one really 'eats'. And the purpose of it is that one should eat 'everything', that one should integrate *everything, all,* with the 1.

Man's eating, i.e. the eating by the man and the woman, from the tree of knowledge brings them their death and the expulsion from the world where they lived.

Let us consider this story a little more seriously. It is one of the subjects we do not know how to handle. The things taking place seem rather primitive and the punishment drastic. The punishment, indeed, would extend to the present day. Now what is the story?

Man is placed in a world which is developing, which *must* develop in the direction of multiplicity. On his way he is also divided into male and female, i.e. into 'soul' or essence and body. This body is faced with the subtle world which is conscious of its force of multiplicity, the forces of development which aim at moving ever further away from the origin. The world at first is even brought in a condition in which the side of 'water', the side of the body, is predominant. In this world of physical predominance all the action takes place.

And now that it has happened, now that all the conditions have been prepared, man is punished. Indeed, it is a story which creates the impression that man is lured into a trap nicely set for him.

Others again put all the blame on the first man. It is because of his eating that death has come over the world. And he is covered with reproaches and people think they would have acted more wisely, if they had been in the same condition. Thus giving the primitive ancestor a testimonial of incompetence. Hence one rather refrains from applying the 'honour thy father and thy mother' to that pristine very first father.

In reality the relations are entirely different from what such interpretations would suggest. We have already found the principle that to the contrary God made the world so as to give man supreme happiness. *Not* to bring him to a fall through a subtle combination and to punish him and his descendants most mercilessly for thousands of years.

Besides, if the Bible really is a revelation, a communication from God how the world is throughout time and all the planes, then this attitude of the first man has also been predestined, just as many more things apparently are predestined. Then what about man's guilt?

Indeed, the Bible is the story which tells how the world is. Criticism of the behaviour of primitive man therefore is equivalent with criticism of the fact that there are night and day in nature. God made nature, the universe, and God also made the Bible. So if the Bible tells us that primitive man eats from the tree of the knowledge then the Bible tells us how it is, how the world is made. And when the Bible tells us in what way Jacob took away the blessing from Esau, this too is a communication how the world *is*. We are not concerned first and foremost with a story about certain people living in times more or less probable, in which all sorts of frailties and virtues are related about those people. But it is a communication *how* God has made the world and how it expresses itself, condenses, crystallizes in the happenings in time.

Once we have seen how things crystallize in the happenings in time, we are able to conclude from it how they will *always* crystallize in the happenings of every time. On the coming forth of creation, duality came into the world. This duality we have learned to recognize as the power which achieves development. With duality there ensued the contrast. And it is through this very contrast that development could take place. It is the sine qua non to development.

Contrast brings with it that over against life here stands death. One simply cannot see things differently, once one has come to live through the perception of and the sustenance by these forces of development. To the man who has absorbed duality, life and death are opposites not to be reconciled. Indeed to him they never can be reconciled.

On the other hand to the man who has *not* absorbed duality, there is in reality no contrast between the conceptions of life and death. To him life means appearing into this world but being rooted in the origin. And he will unite everything in this life with that origin. And then death simply means withdrawing from this world, going back to the origin, returning 'home'.

Thus it is with the sending forth from Paradise. The Garden of Eden is the world in which one can live, if one does *not* absorb the force of duality. As soon as one has absorbed this force of duality, that world gets lost. One sees different things, one does not even perceive the whole world of the Garden of Eden any more.

As the story has it: man's eyes get opened. By then man will view things with these physical eyes, he will see their images. And he will then see his 'nakedness' also. He will perceive that in absorbing duality within himself, he has lost power over himself. That the body often goes its own way, a way he cannot any more prevent it from going. This is the consequence of the absorbing of the force of duality. That which one ought to master, goes its own sweet way. And that is why man hides himself from the presence of God. He presumes he can loosen himself from God. For he knows in his essential nature that he has turned the wrong way, a way where he refuses to be faced with God, because he knows he will then have to be ashamed of himself, since he then stands in opposition to his inner nature, in opposition to the purpose of his coming into this world.

Thus man finally enters another world. The way to Paradise is closed to him. By an entirely different way, the way through time, a long, long way he will return there.

It is at this juncture that the way of the 26 generations through the world is starting. And at the end of that way there is God again, and the purpose of everything is clearly perceptible, the purpose of things is revealed. And with it one has returned to the origin. For indeed, knowing the purpose of things means being already united with the origin. And that is the sense of the story in the Bible; that is how the Bible puts it. Whoever is ready to take it in seriously will come to know the purpose of life, hence he will be united with the origin. With the Bible was restored the way to the tree of life, the way which was blocked after the absorption of the forces of the tree of the knowledge of good and evil. I have here, very concisely and one-sidedly, sketched the development which the second tale of creation proceeds to give. All these items I hope to work out in greater detail. For further study of this chapter the above sketch suffices.

The reader will remember that in the tale of creation we followed up that part which is expressed by the term 'in the beginning' in the quantitative proportion 2–200–1 and that the part 300–10–400 remained undiscussed. Now this part 300–10–400 enacts itself in what we discussed above. Remember how the conception 'man' is rendered by the 3, and the conception 'woman' by the 4. In this part 300–10–400 male and female stand apart opposite each other. In one of the planes of multiplicity, that of the centuples, the greatest development the word allows of and which apparently exists. In this connection I shall not go more fully into the meaning of the 10 between the 300 of the male and the 400 of the female. Male and female now have to reunite unto the oneness they formed originally. And with this reintegration they have to bring the whole of creation back to the origin; and together with creation he reintegrated with the origin.

This union of the man as 300 and the woman as 400 would result in the 'child' as 500 in the same way we saw it happen when the 3 and the 4 and the 5, after squaring formed the $3^2 + 4^2 = 5^2$.

Now this 500 is a supramundane number. For the numbers which render the proportions of this world, do not go beyond 400. Not because people in those days could not count any further, or that there was not enough imagination to expand the alphabet any further, but because the 400 is the furthest development.

The 4 as the furthest development in the root-cycle, produces the 10, and together with the ten it achieves the 400.

As a matter of fact 400 is without end. It is the number which stands for servitude, a servitude from which, logically reasoning by the standards of this world, no emancipation is to be expected. But from it comes liberation as a breaking through the normal, through the logical.

The sign of the 400 in ancient Hebrew writing – not in that of the Bible – is the cross, which, indeed, was known as the sign of suffering. Hence expressing the same as the 400, a rendering of the protracted, apparently eternal suffering in servitude. So the last letter of the word 'in the beginning', the word 'bereshit', is 400. And the final part of the tale of creation we have pursued, indicates: suffering, death, expulsion. In fact, if we go through the tale of the Bible, as far as the Old Testament is concerned, the end of the story is the destruction of the temple and the exile.

Mention is made of a return, rather vaguely, but it proves to be a mere reflection of a real return. In many respects it is an unsatisfactory return. As if in another much lower world. And those who had known the first temple with all its wonders and all its glory could not, as the Bible has it, find consolation in the second. For the world did not proceed in such a way that the Bible could jubilantly relate how glorious and wonderful things were going to be.

It is true that all this has been prophesied. The prophets speak of great times to come, a wonderful future when everything will be good and peaceful. But all this is yet to come. As far as the Bible pictures reality, i. e. history fulfilled, it ends in death and exile. There is no fulfilment in time of an apotheosis of happiness, of life eternal. One way or another man does not seem able to attain it, he 'fails', just as the first man failed in the Garden of Eden, hence had to undergo expulsion and death.

So there is a strong parallelism between this first story, the root-story in the beginning of Genesis, and the further development as related in the Bible. Here too there appears to exist a definite systematism. The first story of man in the Garden of Eden, and the story of the Bible in all its phases has the same development. A development which ends in the 400 of suffering, of being plunged in servitude which has the character of endlessness just as the number 400 as highest number-and-image expresses it in reality. For beyond the 400 nothing exists.

What comes beyond the 400, beyond that furthest development to be expressed in material form, cannot exist in this world. Just as we should not be able to understand what might be beyond the infinity of the universe, since the universe indeed embraces everything. We might argue that there is a curve of the universe, but what might be beyond defeats our imagination.

The material world ends with the letter 'taf', the last of the 22 letters which offer the whole range of expression, of crystallization, in the material world. If one tries to realize these things and begins to understand that the Bible has a language of its own and a very particular mode of expressing itself, one will understand that the ancient science of the Bible, the ancient mode of expression, relying on the knowledge of the world of the Bible, gives the measure of 500 as the distance between heaven and earth. For the 500 cannot be used as a mode of expression for things material.

The 500 cannot possibly express anything material, it lies beyond the letters which exhaust the whole range of modes of expression. There is no letter for the 500. The very last letter is the 400, expressing servitude, expulsion, death, the extreme end of things expressible.

The ancients have also measured the size of the tree of life. That size is ... 500 years. Again of course not in the measures of our world. For our world does not know anything beyond the 400. This 500 as measure indicates that one will *not* be able to embrace the tree of life in this world since this is to end with the 400. It simply does not fit in with our world, owing to its measure.

But this 500 will come true some time. That is what the prophets tell us, but not for the 'near future', not for *this* world. This 500 will come true when the 300 of the male and the 400 of the female have fulfilled themselves and have integrated into a unity which produces the 'child', so when the $300^2 + 400^2$ make the 500^2.

It will be — if we translate the image into other planes as well — when time is over and body and soul will once more form such a unity that a new man arises. Of course this also includes that when all contrasts have combined to a harmonious unity.

And it will also be — we shall revert to this story by and by — when what the Bible calls 'the house of Joseph' is united again with 'the house of Judah'. For we shall see, as a matter of course, that the pattern of what we call male and female, soul and body, is likewise stamped on these two houses. Thus the prophet Ezekiel sees the resurrection of the bones — considered dead for all eternity — coming to pass when the house of Joseph and the house of Judah have melted into 'one'.

And this 500 will then be fulfilled when the *whole* time is fulfilled. When God gives man the words 'be ye fruitful and multiply' (Gen. 1:28) He gives him this way to completion, to heaven. For in Hebrew the 'be ye fruitful and multiply' as expressed in words is 'pru urebu' in letters peh-resh-waw and waw-resh-beth-waw, and in numbers 80–200–6 and 6–200–2–6 with as the sum-total of the component parts ... 500!

So this 'be ye fruitful and multiply' is the way through time which — and the structure implies it *here* too — leads quite naturally to this 500. Just as the word 'create', 'bara' implies the final emerging into the 'one', just as the name 'Lord' implies the reintegration of the two separated parts. Separated, that is, in order to grant man the supreme happiness of finding and experiencing reintegration.

And the way leading all through the biblical story gives this 500. For when with the Patriarch Abraham for the first time in this world, the power breaks through to reverse the way of evolution back to its origin, it is in the tale of years in the Bible — which we shall revert to in a chapter by itself — exactly 500 years removed from the revelation of God and God's promise to the world, i.e. the event described as that of Mount Sinai.

It is a way which leads beyond this world, beyond this life. This world and this life end *here* with the 400 which is the last letter which permits of expression. But the Bible proves in yet another way to embrace this way to the 500, this way to heaven, the way which evidently includes the whole tree of life. Which way to the prophets is the source of their revelations from another world.

6
The Bounds of this World

This way beyond the 400 is mentioned in a very special manner in the Bible. The first mention of this passing beyond the 400, this going further, we can find even in the first tale of creation, in the so-called root-story. It is the seventh day, the Sabbath.

For *that* is the real meaning of the Sabbath, that this day leads beyond, that it proceeds to give shape to a new world.

Let us first return to the duality, that dual character, expressing itself in the creation of the six days. There we saw duality also expressing itself in the two triads, in the appearance of two triads as each other's counterpart.

As the origin of creation, of the making of duality, God stands as the 'one', embracing all in harmony. Just as the shape of the first letter, the aleph, expresses it in the two 'jods' reflecting, balancing each other. As such is viewed the sphere of the origin; the world with God, a world of various facets, aspects, it is true, but in harmony with these facets, in unity.

From that origin emanates creation, expressing itself as duality so that the two parts seeking and finally finding each other, shall in this search and in this finding and integrating into a new unity, experience the ineffable bliss which none but God knows.

The state of duality finds its expression and also its furthest extent in the duality of the two triads of the six days of creation. Over against this duality of the two triads there is the seventh day, as unity again. This seventh day, about which it says in Gen. 2:2, 2:3 that God blessed and hallowed it, is unity again. For the sake of a comprehensive view of the structure, let us make yet another scheme of the situation (see below). Of the seventh day it is said that God rested on that day and that He blessed and hallowed it. Three facets which now express themselves also as a unity in this seventh day. No longer as a right side and a left side apart from each other, but as oneness in this day of unity.

On the seventh day unity is also restored between male, expressing itself as the 300 and female, expressing itself as the 400.

For the word Sabbath in Hebrew is Shabbath, spelled shin-beth-taf, hence in numbers 300–2–400. So here we find again the 300 and 400 in question, the 300 and the 400 which we came across as the latter part of the word In the beginning'. Again, in order not to deviate too far from the subject in hand, I cannot enter here into the meaning of the 2 standing in between the 300 and the 400. In its structure the Sabbath has that which integrates duality into unity.

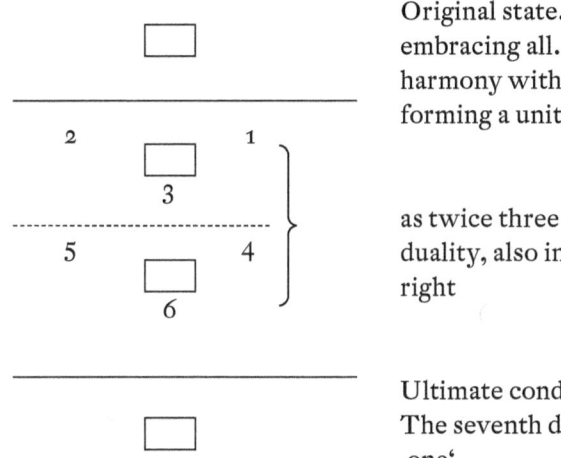

Original state. The ‚one', the ‚aleph' embracing all. Duality is there in harmony with the connecting third forming a unity.

as twice three days, expressing itself in duality, also in the contrast of left and right

Ultimate condition.
The seventh day, leading back to the ‚one'.

Let us mention, but again not expatiate on, the relationship between the word 'shabbath' and the word for 'return', i.e. 'shab' spelled shin-beth, in numbers 300–2; and also the relationship in structure with the word for seven, sheba, spelled shin-beth-ayin, in numbers 300–2–70. And also that with the word for satiety, satisfaction, which is 'seba', spelled sin-beth-ayin, hence again 300–2–70. So there is a great resemblance in nature, in the word, between 'seven' and 'satiety'. For, indeed, on the seventh day does this satisfaction *come*, does the fulfilment come in the reunion. To bring forward another relationship, existing in the word, I should like to point out that the word for 'hunger', the opposite to satiety, in Hebrew is 'raäb', spelled resh-ayin-beth, 200–70–2. As sum-total of the components— indeed the same as that of the word for satiety, with the only difference that in the latter there is 200 and in the former 300 — we find 200+70+2=272. The sum-total of the components of the word satiety, as we can verify above, is 300+2+70=372. This difference of a 100, of the 10 which has fulfilled itself, is indeed the entire way through the 10, just as, for instance, the ten acts of creation in the tale of creation, which in multiplicity are also imbued with the true essence of the 100. In this connection we should besides mention the relationship between the word 'hunger' and 'fecundate', either of them with the components 200 and 2 and 70. Indeed, the word for 'four' has the same components (1–200–2–70): the four which will ultimately lead to the completing of creation, which will then pass on into the Sabbath. Like the word fecundate which casts the seed that will cause the birth of things new, the new world. Time and again it will be seen that the language of the Bible, the word expressing the essential, brings into prominence those marvellous relationships, that it reveals them properly.

The combination of the 'shin' and the 'taf', the 300 and the 400 are seen in yet another way appearing as the foundation of the world coming now.

When later on a son is born to the first man, who is to bring to completion the way without an ending via Cain and Abel, his name is Sheth, spelled shin-taf, again this 300–400. For from this Sheth, this 300–400, this bond of the male and the female everything is coming now. It is thence the 'child' will finally come. And here again we see a systematism pervading all.

Tradition has it that the place of the Holy of Holies in the biblical temple of Jerusalem was defined by a specific stone, the 'Eben Shetijah'. This stone or rock was supposed to be the spot whence the world had started to develop. In a manner of speaking it is the 'navel' of the world; the foundation-stone. This is the reason why *this* very place is the Holy of Holies, because it represents the origin as expressed in this world. In that spot there was the connection with God, the essential origin of all things. Now the Hebrew word for this stone 'shetijah' is spelled shin-taf-jod-hee, 300–400–10–5. Again this combination of the 300 and 400 in the very spot which forms the foundation of this world.

It will besides have been noticed that this 300–400 as the foundation for the world which brings unity, has 700 as sum-total of the components, just as the 3 and the 4 as the determining components for the structure of the three days of creation – three days of creation and four acts of creation – similarly form the 7 which has the innate faculty of leading to a seventh day in which the 3 and 4 can come to completion, thus forming the 5, the 'child'.

And so the story of the integration of the 300 and 400 is the story of the seventh day. As the completed 300 plus the completed 400 they form the purpose in view of the seventh day. As the $300^2 + 400^2$ they do indeed, make the 500^2, the way after all to another world. So the seventh day is characterized by the fact that integration will take place therein. It is the day of the male and the female meeting in every plane. In Jewish practice of life the night of the Sabbath is the appropriate night for the man meeting the woman.

Just as male and female are expressed in the conceptions 3 and 4, ensuing from the systematism which the Bible gives for the world, this forming together a new world, that of the 5, or as we have also seen that of the 500 which represents something supramundane or extramundane – the distance between earth and heaven, or the circumference of the tree of life – thus in language there is something very special to be read in a direct way about the unity of the male and the female. The word for 'male and female' in the Bible, for instance where in the first tale of creation it says 'male and female created He them' is 'zachar unekeba' spelled zayin-kaf-resh for 'man' and waw-nun-kof-beth-hee for 'and woman', in numbers 7–20–200–6–50–100–2–5, with the sum-total of 390 for the component parts.

And the word for heaven is 'sha mayim', spelled shin-mem-jod-mem, 300–40–10–40, with similarly the sum-total of 390. So we see that the structure of the language of the Bible, one way or another, in the combination of the two conceptions male-female, always stresses this supramundane or extramundane: the distance between earth and heaven and the word heaven itself.

On the seventh day these two conceptions meet. Then is fulfilled what the Song of Solomon expresses as the quest and the finding of each other, of the man and the woman, who are separate from each other, just as God, in creation, made this separation within Himself also. They are separated from each other, these two halves, but they know and feel that they belong together, that at one time they were together. Thus in Jewish practice of life it is the custom to read the Song of Solomon at the beginning of the seventh day.

They suffer under the separation, but in the end they come together. And it is the male and the female in every plane. Not merely in its expression in mankind as man and woman. It is just as much seeking one another and finding one another in a regained harmony of body and soul, of God and the world, of life and death, of the sense of good and of evil, of every contrast which continues to hurt as long as it has not yet been reunited into oneness.

On that seventh day is achieved this reunion of all things which previously formed a contrast with each other. That is why in Jewish daily life the Sabbath begins with a duality of, for instance, the two loaves, the two candles, which duality is brought to unity by the Sabbath's hallowing. The way of the Sabbath is, as it says in the first tale of creation, the way of blessing and hallowing by God.

The principle of keeping a day of rest on the Sabbath has nothing to do with the utilitarian purport the modern world tends to endow it with: that one should be allowed a breathing interval after a week's exertions, so that one may take part in the process of production with renewed vigour after the Sabbath.

The principle of the Sabbath is exactly as the Bible has it, that God had completed the world, that everything was finished. This is strongly emphasized in the image of the word. At the end of the sixth day the world was completed and God saw that it was very good. This means that nothing new could be done on the seventh day. Development is complete, so now there is nothing left except the task of integrating, the reunion of everything as it had gone on developing until then, with the source of origin. Every creative act, at least every act essentially meant to be creative, is a negation of the fact that with creation God had completed the world, is an urge to develop things further, an urge to go beyond the goal which God ever sets man in creation. Continuing the development is tantamount to a statement that the world is *not yet* good and that it must necessarily be improved by man. It is the statement that unless man interferes much shall go wrong. *This* is the reality about the desecration of the Sabbath.

What *should* be done on the Sabbath is what is meant with hallowing the Sabbath. In Dutch as well as in English and in German the world 'hallow' embraces the conception of making whole, healing, healing a crack, a break.

The Sabbath is for man to bring the separate parts together, to unite the opposites. In our terminology: to remake the 'one'.

All man's work and thought should aim at this. Only then will he be able ultimately to accomplish reintegration. For indeed, this is man's duty. If we bring before us again the diagram on page 68 with man at the two extremes having the divine soul of the origin within himself as his essence and on the opposite end the most perfected animal body, the most evolved expression in matter of the force of duality, the separating force which makes multiplicity, we shall see anew that the integration in this world will have to be effected in man. Man has, so to speak, the starting-point and the terminus within himself, and all that lies in between depends on his willingness to connect these two points. Indeed that is what man was made for, that is the purpose of his life. For it is just because the integration of all things is effected in him, that he experiences the immense bliss, the indescribable happiness which this reunion, this integration brings with it. And this is the bliss of the seventh day.

The man, however, who thinks that it is up to him to cause the world to evolve still further on the seventh day, is the one who goes the reverse direction, who declines the chance to unite the two extremes, to reunite what was separated in the beginning. It is what we expressed as the 'temptation' by the serpent who makes his appearance as the 'earthly' Messiah and points out the possibilities to reach Paradise by way of the earth. A way leading – we might say in obedience to natural law or in obedience to the law of creation since that way exists already in the Bible and expresses itself in everything as the pattern of the Bible – to the fear of death, as contrasted with life, and to expulsion instead. Expulsion in our plane means constant unrest and dissatisfaction.

Now what exactly is the seventh day in this world? We can read in the Bible how each of the six days of creation ends in 'and the evening and the morning were' followed by the number of the day completed therewith. And this goes on up to and including the sixth day. About the seventh day, however, it is *not* stated that it is ended. Now it may be objected that it is likely to have been forgotten, or even that continuing the same formula was getting rather dreary. Besides it may be remarked that, even though the Bible should have forgotten to state the end of the seventh day, this omission has been superseded by the facts, and that meanwhile many more days have passed, even in our own lives. And that the seventh day of the Bible has long since closed off.

Yet it is not so. We have seen that every letter in the Bible fits exactly into its text; that in a marvellous way all these texts form a system in which sequence, words and letters used, quantitative proportions, structures, etc. are just as accurately determined as the smallest particles of matter or the stars in their worlds.

And that it is therefore impossible in such a creation for things to be arbitrarily mentioned or omitted. Hence the fact that this seventh day in the Bible, in contradistinction with the six previous days, does not end, must indicate that in the root-story of the first tale of creation, this seventh day actually was *not* closed. That this day in the root-story still continues, hence that, projected on our plane revolving round the root-story, this conception 'seventh day' is also ever continuing.

Though the subject of judging time in the Bible will be discussed in detail in a following chapter, I should like to make a brief remark here concerning the seventh day.

A day in the Bible is not a day of our perception, neither is it a thousand years or a milliard years. A day in the Bible expresses the nature of a day. In the world of the essence, in that root-world, it is that which projected here into our world expresses itself as the phenomenon which we perceive as 'day'. Just as difficult as it is to recognize in the phenomenon we perceive as 'mist', the (1–4)-principle which proves so marvellously persistent everywhere, just as difficult it is to compare a day in our perception to the essential reality 'day' in the world of the Bible.

Hence it is rather a puerile game, showing grave misunderstanding of the purpose of the Bible, when people start arguing about the length of the days of creation and compare them with all kinds of archeological observations. They are entirely non-comparable units.

All the same the biblical day *has* something to do with the day of our observation. It indicates the reality of the day, it being evening and it being morning, so the duality of it, and the closing off of a cycle by the day. And also in using the day as a standard by which to measure the proportion to a week, a month, a year, etc. For the pattern of the measure of time of creation, of the Bible, also expresses itself in our world, with *our* measure of time. And with the help of this measure of time which stamps itself as a pattern on things, a pattern produced here by that which we perceive as sun, moon, planets, stars, we can read off the crystallization of the Bible in time, the Lord's accompanying the world into history.

That is why the seventh day always has that particular significance in our world, because in our matter, in our time, in our world-of-multiplicity, that day is an expression of the essential event which takes place on the seventh day, viz. the integration, the reunion of the divorced parts, of the break; the realization and recognition into every detail that the world, as it is made, is good and is finished and that it is *not* for us to 'develop' that world with our means, but that to the contrary it is for us to bring the opposites together, to heal the break. And that the seventh day is a real day, especially blessed and hallowed by God and that our life in this world should be lived accordingly.

In our world-of-multiplicity there have been ever so many seventh days. The seventh day of the root of the first tale of creation, expresses itself in all these seventh days; all these seventh days have received the hallmark of that seventh day of creation.

Day in Hebrew is 'yom', spelled jod-waw-mem, 10–6–40. Here again we see the (1–4)- principle, in the decades, with the 'waw', the 6, as connecting link. So we see that the reality of 'day' is a relationship of the two opposite principles of the 1 and the 4. The day does effect the relationship, for the day is an expression of time, and time, indeed, effects the relationship. As we saw in the 'be fruitful and multiply', which in course of time covers the way of the 500, which connects heaven and earth, which goes beyond the 400, hence also links up 4 and 1 unto 5, or 40 and 10 unto 50.

Now in that root-story, that most essential story, the Bible tells us how the world is made, what is its way and what its purpose. And that way leads across the six days to the seventh day. And the purpose is that on the seventh day is dissolved this divorce, this duality which made us suffer; that there is the bliss of having found what one sought all the time, that one has found the way which connects everything with the origin in a direct way.

The day which in the first tale of creation is the seventh day, is in reality not completed there; it continues to project itself into our world as the 'day in which we live now'. And the integration effected in the end by that day is our way through this world. This way – if it is to be in agreement with that purpose of the integration with which that seventh day was to be completed – is nothing but the effecting of this integration with life and through life. Through man's actions and thought, through his interest, his intention, he will have to reunite, bring back to the origin everything that in the course of evolution got divorced from the origin, and that embraces practically everything in the world. *Then* man will feel not only satisfied, but he will even experience the greatest possible happiness.

Indeed, what man performs in his life *is* nothing different. The only thing is that *he* thinks that this reunion, this integration is to be attained along a way representing a further development, a further growth of the material world. He pursues a way as if creation is *not* yet complete, as if he and his descendants should attain this through study, sacrifice, reorganization, etc. It is the way of the world presenting itself as redeemer, that which has been told in the tale of the serpent, which has the same sum total of components as the Messiah.

But even along *that* way it is man's concern – his wrong determination notwithstanding – to attain unity, to integrate the opposites. And so he will always experience joy when he has discovered something; it is the joy of finding back things lost. He wants to find the secret of life, of the soul, of society. And he wants to find it through observing everything, by looking through microscopes or telescopes, by counting men and their produce, by observing them in their behaviour and in their thought. It is the way which – like the story of the serpent – begins with the discovery that 'the tree of the knowledge was good for food and that it was pleasant to the eyes, and a tree to be desired to make one wise' (Gen. 3:6).

Man *really* ever desires this reunion. And when he does not know which way to turn, since the way he followed gave him moral qualms instead of happiness, he feels thoroughly miserable and plunges into forgetfulness. Man's striving to lead this world to a goal where the opposites are dissolved, where rule peace and happiness, is characteristic of him. The only thing is that the ways may differ. There is the way leading through the tree of knowledge of good and evil, and there is the way *avoiding* that tree. However, the purpose always is to heal the break one experiences, to reintegrate the things one undergoes as a divorce.

And *this* seventh day is still in progress. That is why the solar system functions so as to have four times seven days and the fifth time it has only just begun, it is *just* in progress when there is a new moon again, a new form.

And maybe there is also some relationship with what we think we perceive in the periodicity of the elements. I purposely say 'maybe', because an argument based on sensory perceptions should never be considered as a foundation or a proof. But with the necessary discretion one might make use of it as an indication in a certain direction. As a matter of fact this periodic system of elements, as we know it from chemistry, also has seven horizontal rows, where the seventh gives the same impression of incompleteness, of very volatile elements. Just as if the elements in this row have not yet found their way in this world to become a permanent reality. A striking feature in this periodic system is the fact that the first row consists of two elements, called hydrogen and helium. It is like the 'two' as foundation for matter.

And another striking feature is that the atomic weights of the two elements of the first row show the proportion of 1:4; i.e. the same proportion of the tales of creation, the 'two' containing within themselves the 1–4.

So it is possible that this pattern of the 'two' and of the 1–4 has been retraced in the systematism of nature. If this should be the case, it might indicate that in the research of matter we have come within close proximity of essential proportions. This does not imply that one will actually be able to penetrate into the essence of things along that path, or that one will find the master key to disclose all secrets. This, as we shall have ample opportunity to see, is decidedly out of the question. The key to understanding can only be obtained from the expression of creation in the word. In the word everything is present so as to enable one to see and understand it in his lifetime. But it is quite possible one should occasionally come near the real on one's journey though this labyrinthine phenomenal world. And because of it one will feel tempted to continue the journey in that way. It forms part of the dialogue between the saviour 'serpent' and the 'female', the body with its faculty of perception, during which one ever thinks: 'now I know, now I've got it', after which, however, another long, long way looms up ahead, again leading almost to the goal, but again showing a new way one has yet to go.

The seventh day is the day which is still completing itself. To us it is this entire world which we know. Because it is our world, it presents itself to us as infinite. In fact, one cannot logically think of a beginning or of an ending. In space, too, it appears as endless. It is our world, our day, our 10–6–40, as the connecting link between the 10 and the 40.

The character of infinity which this world shows, also expresses itself in the spherical shape. The sphere is an expression in matter of that which in this matter appears as infinite. One is, so to speak, caught up in it, one constantly revolves back to the same point.

It is difficult to realize that there might exist anything outside a sphere with an infinite radius, although a sphere implies the possibility of something existing outside. Even when viewed as a cross-section of another world, the sphere is this one perceived here, and as such it gives the impression of infinity. So there is no sense in measuring where it begins or where it ends. It would mean juggling about with milliards of years, hence it would be futile to project man and human history on it. And it is, of course, just as impossible to measure years of biblical chronology with the help of this sphere. The spherical world will always have to reply that there is something wrong with those standards, since everything within its compass seems much longer.

The world of creation, of the six days, lies in a different plane. It cannot be attained with the standards our spherical world supplies.

As second phenomenon, coming after creation in the six days, this seventh day therefore has the character of things second, hence also of that which is expressed in the second tale of creation. It runs parallel with the 'water'-character, which began with the 'mist'. The mist which is 1–4, and the water, as we saw, is 40–10–40. And the sea in Hebrew is 'iam' spelled jod-mem, 10–40. And the time-measure of the day as basis of chronology is 10–6–40.

Also it is sluggish time which comes with water, it is duration, having the character of that which to us also makes its appearance as mist or water, viz. everlasting repetition, great unchanging multiplicity giving the impression, if one lives in it, that nothing exists outside.

Water, in the systematism of the first tale of creation on the left side, therefore imparts that character of the left hand side to the world of the second tale of creation, i.e. the character of the 'female', of the form. For, as the second tale of creation starts: *nothing* can appear in *this* world as long as there is no water. Everything was present elsewhere, but it could find no expression in this world, because the water-character had first to find its form. And that is why the 'mist' went up and everything then got stamped with that 1–4 pattern.

And everything as told in the first tale of creation, now found expression in the second tale anew, but *this time* it was the expression of this special water-world, the world stamped with the 1–4.

Thus everything happening in those six days expresses itself in the second tale until the moment when after eating from the tree of knowledge, man hears the decree from the 'Lord God' that he must leave the Garden of Eden to reach another world. With it ends the sixth day and on coming into the world *outside* Paradise, man enters the seventh day. And the story developing from now onwards is the story of the seventh day, with embryonic indications of a proceeding beyond the seventh day, but ever with the consciousness of this seventh day exclusively. On the seventh day, ever in action man proceeds unto reintegration. As it is expressed in the first tale of creation 'in order to do', in Hebrew 'laäsoth', derived from the word 'to do'. This seventh day is made 'for to do'. Translated literally this third verse of the second chapter of Genesis, says: 'that God created for to do', or 'for to be done'. The seventh day is present for the very purpose that man shall join, shall unite the two extremes. And this is only possible if he is 'active' here, if in doing actions he involves his body in this process of reintegration. All man's actions in this life, since they must be accomplished with the help of the body, with matter, have to unite it with the divine part which man has in himself also, thus achieving unity between the two extremes. That is what man was given his body for and all the things of this world. That he might recognize all things presenting themselves to him as divorced from the origin, and that he might reintegrate it all with the origin. Thus bringing everything to its destination, redeeming things from being divorced and in doing so, bestowing the happiness of reunion, himself also tasting this bliss in each of his actions.

Thus, after the expulsion in the second tale of creation, when entering upon the seventh day, man has to 'act' on this seventh day, till the soil. We saw that the word for earth was 1–4–40–5, the word for man being 1–4–40. The letter 5 at the end of a word indicates that the word is female. It expresses itself thus, because the single 5 has to be joined unto its counterpart, the other 5, so that the 5–6–5 be achieved. It is a 5 informed with affinity, with the urge to be fulfilled, with the craving for fulfilment. Just as a woman craves to be joined unto the man; just as everything, having that nature, yearns for completion that it may form a unity with its counterpart.

So the earth is like the woman waiting for the man. It is the unredeemed side waiting for the deliverance through man, who can join it unto its counterpart thus giving it the peace of harmony which one ever yearned for, but failed to realize.

Man entering upon the seventh day, will be faced as the male with the world as the female, and through his action he will reintegrate the world with its origin.

Man was taken from this earth as a body, just as a child comes from the mother. And now he will again stand as the unity of this body with the God-given divine soul, the 'neshamah' facing that earth, facing the female not yet delivered, and through busying himself with it, working with it, he will reunite it with the origin. He will accomplish that union – just remember our diagram – because it flows through him since he is the only one in this world that has both the divine essence and the body. That is the reason why tradition calls this world 'the world of action', in Hebrew 'Olam Assia'.

In the systematism of the tradition therefore this world is seen as the fourth, in the same way that the place of the seventh day was indicated in a scheme (p.103). The scheme which expressed the growing of the duality of the twice three days, emanating from the unity of God and resulting in the seventh day which was to restore unity.

That first world is called in tradition 'Olam Atsiluth', which means 'the world which is near by' and with 'near by' is meant near to God. In the Sephiroth-systematism it is the world above which was placed 'kether', the crown, and which world was considered to consist of a harmony of various possibilities of insight, expressed in Hebrew as 'chochmah', 'binah' and 'daäth'. The harmony of this triad is looked upon as creation being present in the world with God, in the knowledge and the insight of the purpose and of the way of creation.

The second world, that of the first triad of days, was called 'Olam Briah', translated as 'the world of creation'. The third, that of the second triad of days, was called the 'Olam Yetsirah', the world of formation, of form-development. And finally the fourth, that of the seventh day, there were the Sephira 'Malchuth', the 'Kingdom' finds itself, is called 'Olam Assiah', the world of action, of 'doing'.

So man comes from the third of these four worlds. This third world still belongs to an entirely different sphere, it is the sphere of the days of creation. Man comes into the fourth world, that of the seventh day which is to accomplish the reunion. This fourth world is also the world which is to join the two fives of the name Lord, the world which is to bring the 5–6–5. It is like the latter 5 of that name, which will now be able to hook on to the former 5, which has come from the origin when the divorce was accomplished. In the fourth world the latter 5, man, through his 'be-ness', through his 'doing, his acting' will unite with the former five, from which he was divorced in the beginning.

This union of the seventh day with the previous world is of course also retraced in the word of the Bible. The Bible shows how God Himself unites these two worlds: that of the six days and that of the seventh day. For it is the name of God as the Lord which unites these two worlds, which achieves this union we have been discussing above.

Indeed, the name Lord as is the case in several other texts in the Bible, is in a wonderful way inserted in and stamped on the structure of the story of the transit from the sixth day to the seventh.

The last two words of the six days, in fact, are: 'the sixth day'. In Hebrew it is 'yom hashishi', spelled jod-waw-mem and hee-shin-shin-jod. In number 10–6–40 and 5–300–300–10.

The initial words introducing the seventh day are: 'thus the heavens were finished, etc.', in Hebrew the initial two words, thus translated into the five mentioned above are, 'wayechulu hashamayim', meaning literally 'and there were finished the heavens', and spelled waw-jod-kaf-lamed-waw and hee-shin-mem-jod-mem, hence in numbers resp. 6–10–20–30–6 and 5–300–40–10–40.

We here see the stamp of the pattern of the name 'Lord' presenting itself in a very particular manner. For the last two words of the six days, with which those six days are rounded off, have as their beginning, as we can see resp. a 10 and a 5, so 10–5; and the initial two words introducing the seventh day have as their beginning resp. a 6 and a 5, so 6–5. With it, therefore, the name Lord, the 10–5–6–5, unites the sixth and the seventh day, the 10–5 representing the sixth day and the 6–5 the seventh day.

Man in this world is not forsaken, cut away from his origin, but it is the Lord who goes with him from one world to the other and who through this union with that which proceeded, lays the foundation for the ultimate reintegration of all things.

The union through the name Lord, stamped across the boundary line, relates in reality *what* it is that accomplishes that union. It relates that it has been established in the very structure of the world that the union between this world and that of creation is effected by God Himself.

The sixth day which ends in the 10–5, pertains to the Olam Yetshirah the third world; the seventh day, beginning with the 6–5 is the fourth world, the Olam Assiah. Thus here again we see how the male 3 and the female 4 are united. And He who actually effects this union is the Lord who has stamped His name on this union in the very structure of creation. The integration of the contrast male-female in all phenomena is the very purpose of the seventh day. And this integration is an incontestable fact since the Lord appears in the structure just where a sharp cut boundary-line seems to present itself.

The 10–5 coming from the sixth day is that with which man in this world of the seventh day is faced. This world of the seventh day has the hall-mark of the 6–5 with which the seventh day begins in the root-tale. That which man 'does' on the seventh day is joining this 6–5 to the 10–5 presenting itself to him from the previous world, from the previous day. Thus he reintegrates the two sides to the 10–5–6–5.

Man on the seventh day – just remember the left-hand character of the seventh day and the water-character – stands like the woman who, as the Song of Solomon has it, strives after union with God, with the reality which is with God.

Man faces the world as the male that is to deliver it; to God he is as the female waiting for deliverance. It is the character of duality, of the two extremes, which finds its expression here as well.

7
The Coming World is Beyond Our Boundaries

We have repeatedly mentioned the 'five' of this world. We have seen that this 'five' means half of what there was originally, as viewed from this world. The origin here embraces the whole series of potentialities which can be expressed in proportions up to and including the 'ten'. It is the 'ten' which completes the sequence of numbers of the decimal system. It is also the ten of the name Lord. And this 'five' would have to join the five, unite with the 'five' which is divorced from it, thus completing once more the 'ten' of this world. Thus likewise completing the name 10–5–6–5.

But we have also seen that in fact 'five' is a number, pointing beyond the principles of this world's furthest possible development. For we recognized the 'four' as the furthest possible development. Indeed, with this 'four' the root-cycle was completed. What came after, was merely an elaboration, a deeper pondering on the 'four'. Up to and including the 'ten', the 'four' asserted itself.

All the following numbers, viewed in this way, are there in consequence of the 'four'. They have no existence of their own, as the 'four' has it. The 'five' which comes next to the 'four', forms part of the 'four', just as the 'one', viewed in this manner, forms part of the 'four' and is not identical with the 'one' preceding everything and embracing all.

As 'four' is the number furthest developed, there is no other number to be expressed in form beyond the 400, beyond the 'taf' as the final letter.

Hence there is no 'five' with an independent place, a place of its own, comparable with the places of the 'one', 'two', 'three' and 'four'. Therefore we saw that the conception 'five hundred' expressed something alive beyond this world. It stands for a conception incompatible with this world, like for instance the distance from the earth to heaven. Heaven is 'imperceptible' in this world. Our sensory organs can perceive an infinite universe, it is true. Heaven, however, is of a different order, it is not to be measured or approached with the standards of this world which do not extend beyond the 'four', or in the plane of centuples beyond the 'four hundred'.

The world of the myriads, too, is closed to our expression of numerical proportions. The word thousand is 'eleph', spelled as 'aleph', i.e. like the 'one'. With the thousand we revert to the 'one'.

We can count beyond this, of course, and it is equally a matter of course that people continued counting on. The number of men of twenty years old and over twenty was counted in the desert and amounted to six hundred thousand and odd. But in essence, when one has reached the one thousand as thought-consequence the ultimate potentiality of expression, viz. the four-hundred, (400+300+200+100 = 1,000) one has covered all the potentialities of expression. The ten-thousand, for instance, is called 'rebaba' spelled 200–2–2–5, so in proportions it is again the duality moreover ending in '5', thus indicating its female character. The ten thousand is distinctly expressed as something derived, having the nature of duality and of the female.

So, if the 'four' is the number which in this world expresses itself in the embracing of all creation as far as matter is concerned, there is no room left for the 'five' in that respect. The 'five' therefore belongs to a different category. As we saw at the outset of our reflections, this 'four' is looked upon as containing the 4 elements with which everything is made. For that reason they did not make people count beyond 'four' in the school of Pythagoras. And for the same reason the 40 days, the 40 years or the 400 years are expression of the furthest-removed, the ultimate, as measured by the standards of this world. For it is really not for nothing that the Bible does persistently revert to the 40 and the 400.

Thus the word for 'always', meaning that which embraces all time, the ever, and always, for all time, in Hebrew is 'tamid', spelled 400–40–10–4. Again we see how the conception, emotional value and structure of the word are determined by this all-pervading systematism. The conception 'ever' *cannot but* contain the 4 on all levels.

Now if we realize this, the word 'mist', the 1–4, acquires a special significance for us. For the sum-total of its components is 5. But to our world this 5 is essentially 1 and 4. In our world the foundation of the 5 is only possible as the juxtaposition of the 'one' and the 'four'. The 'one' as the all-embracing, undivided 'one', and the 'four' as the 'all' in matter.

Thus man contains within himself the 'one' with the Divine soul, the 'neshamah', and the 'four' with the perfected physical mechanism. And since it pertains to the pattern of creation and therefore hallmarks everything, the 'one' finds a form in physical man too, namely, as we saw before, in the head, as the place where in reality all the other bodily functions are present. The head is that place in the body whence everything is directed. So it is the expression in physical form of that which essentially is the 'one'. When we point upwards, meaning to point towards heaven, it does not mean that heaven is the space overhead, but that in essence the conception 'above' contains the 'one' and the conception 'below' contains the 'four'.

Now we have also seen that the 'one' expresses itself in the conception 'tree of life' and the 'four' in the conception 'tree of the knowledge of good and evil'. So the tree of knowledge is that which is everywhere expressed in the 'four', it is this world in its material phenomenal form, in its endless multiplicity. And the tree of life is that which expresses itself in the 'one', undivided as yet, the all-embracing 'one'. They are opposed to each other as the body and the soul in man. And the 'five' can only be formed here by uniting this world, which expresses itself as the 'four' with what expresses itself here in the 'one', hence with what we call the 'word of God'. In no other way can the 'five' be formed here, except as the integration of the 'one' and the 'four'.

The 'five' which we know from the name 'Lord' is the integrated 1–4. Not until these two form a unity, is the 'five' of this world completed and can it unite with its counterpart 'five', thus forming the 5–6–5 with which the name Lord is completed here on earth.

This means that the 'five' is certainly to be attained here, but not until all that goes to make the 'four', the world of matter, is united with the 'one' of God.

Just as man in his body forms a unity of the 'one', the head, with the 'four', the rest of the body, so also is real life possible only if the 'one' of God is united with the 'four' of the world.

Failing the 'one', there is no life, then there is death, as we saw for instance when discussing the words for 'man' and 'truth'. The 'one' bestows life and is therefore the tree of life.

The 'four' without the 'one' means a development of the body without the head. It is a dead body. It is like this with every endeavour to understand the world without the 'one'. That is why the way the serpent wanted man to go is the way which, according to the law of creation, must lead to death. For that reason does God say that eating from the tree of knowledge leads to death.

And whoever goes this way has simultaneously blocked the way to the 'one'. The way towards the tree of life, as the Bible has it, is barred to those that try to find the solution of all problems and their ultimate happiness along the way turned towards the forces of development of the world.

Thus it is that the 'five' is really the number which ought to express this world but it cannot do so until it unites the 'four' of the world with the 'one' of God. We also saw that the 'five' could be achieved by man fulfilling himself in the 'three' and woman fulfilling herself in the 'four'. For thus would come the 'five' as the child.

It expresses the same thing as the uniting of the 'one' and the 'four'. The 'one' as the soul and the 'four' as the body, but for that reason also the 'one' as the man and the 'four' as the woman. So it implies the integration of all opposites.

This principle of the 'five' can also be illustrated with a fragment from the second tale of creation. In it we shall again see that the structure fits completely in every detail.

The second tale of creation begins with the words: 'this is the story of heaven and earth when they were created'. I do not intend to enter more deeply into every word of this passage. But I must point out something special in this connection. The words 'when they were created', as we learn from our perusal, refers to the creation of heaven and earth. In Hebrew the phrase 'when they were created' is rendered in one word, viz. behibaram, spelled beth-hee-beth-resh-aleph-mem, 2–5–2–200–1–40. One also recognizes in it the word bara, 2–200–1.

Now the peculiar thing is that the 'hee', the 5, is not written in normal size, like the other letters, but that this 'hee' is written in very small type. We have already seen that the 'beth' of the word in the beginning', the initial word of the Bible, in contradistinction to the other letters, is written as a very big capital.

It goes without saying that this rendering in 'small' type of the 5 here, has the same significance in principle as the rendering in 'big' type of the 2 with which the Bible begins. The 'hee' in question is a letter in the middle of a word and it is most striking suddenly to come across such a dwarfish letter among normal-sized ones.

The individual character of this 5 in that very place causes this passage traditionally to be read thus: 'with the 5 did He create them'. The 'be' of the word 'behibaram' we are discussing here, means 'with' and the 'hee' after it, owing to its individual character, is an expression in itself, and so it says: 'with a hee'. 'Baram' means 'created He them'.

If the Bible with every letter in every text is taken as an expression of the great harmony of creation where similarly everything has its fixed place and definite form, then one should try to understand such deviation from normal procedure as this small 'hee' shows, in the emphasis with which it is presented. Approached in this way, the text reads: 'with a "hee" created He them'. Mind, with a conspicuously small 'hee' created He them.

Now that we understand a little more of the significance of the 'five' and the factual impossibility to express this 'five' here in earthly things, we can somehow appreciate what is stated here. The world was indeed created with the 'five' as 'one', the world in fact contains the five within itself. The 1–4 in creation actually *is* the 5. The only thing is that it is still veiled, it cannot express itself distinctly yet. That is why this 5, this 'hee' is written in such small type. It still has to come into prominence, it is embryonic as yet, it has as yet got to realize itself.

Again we see what a marvel the Bible is in its veriest details, how in every particle is expressed what God purposed with creation, how He made man and how He made the world. And at the same time we see how the systematism, the principle, is ever the same. That indeed it is one simple story that is being told; in all its simplicity, however, so all-pervading, so all-embracing, that for that very reason it has grandeur. It is not the complicatedness of higher mathematics, of nuclear physics. It is simple, it can be quite clear to everybody, yet in its penetration it is so grand. In connection with the preceding, I should like to point at the change which the name of Abraham underwent.

In Genesis 17:5 the name of Abram is changed by God into Abraham. Because Abraham had found the way to God, the way in agreement with the principle of creation, and therefore God made a 'covenant' with him. The covenant implied what is called circumcision. In practice it means the removal of part of the prepuce. It forms a kind of covering of the place whence the semen comes. When that which sheathes, veils things, is restricted, is partly removed and for the rest curtailed, it means that the physical, the sensory is restrained and that the essential, the inner reality, is liberated. This inner reality finds its expression in the physical because in the place whence is to come the succession of generations, the covering disappears, is restrained. It is the place, indeed, where begins the way of the 'be ye fruitful and multiply', as we have seen, of the 500, of that which physically is inconsistent. Everyone born into that 'covenant' of the restraint of things material, is therefore brought in harmony with this principle even physically, in the mode of expression of this world.

When Abraham attains this union with God, in restraining the physical, the mundane, God tells him how such a life finds expression in the body of man. For the body is a crystallization, a condensation of the real in matter. The body is not something apart from the real. Things take place simultaneously in the physical and in the real. And for that reason does God change the name of Abram into Abraham. The expression in the name, in the formula, also changes on account of it.

The name Abram in Hebrew is aleph-beth-resh-mem, 1–2–200–40. So what happens is the insertion of a 'hee', a 5, in the name. It is this very 'five' which ensues when the physical is restrained, because one has joined the 'four' to the 'one', because the 1–4 has become a unity and with it achieves something factually considered impossible on earth. We see this 'five' is of extreme significance for creation and for the existence of man, and that therefore it always becomes prominent in a special way.

If, moreover, we examine more closely the two words discussed above, we shall notice another peculiarity. The word 'behibaram' spelled with the 'hee' in small type, is written 2–5–2–200–1–40, and the name Abram 1–2–200–40, and Abraham, with the 5 added, 1–2–200–5–40.

We see the same components occurring in the words 'with the "hee" created He them' and 'Abraham'. The small-type 'hee' being absent in the word Abram, but appearing as a normal 'hee' in Abraham. Hibaram (for the sake of simplicity I leave out the word 'with', the 'be') is 5–2–200–1–40; Abram has the components 2–200–1–40 and Abraham has 5–2–200–1–40. For the sake of convenience I have here written the components of the words Abram and Abraham in the same sequence as those of the word 'hibaram', 'with the "hee" created He them'.

Therefore it is pointed out in tradition that in reality it says 'beabraham', when one reads the word 'be-hibaram'. The structure expressing itself in the components, the expression in numbers, is closely related.

So it means that heaven and earth had been created for the sake of the coming of Abraham the man who had taken the way to God according to the principles of creation. The new name of Abraham was to be found already in the structure of this word '*behibaram*', with which is expressed the creation of heaven and earth. And that name was contained in it in the manner in which it was going to be achieved. First without the 5, afterwards with the 5, and therefore with the small 'hee', the more or less embryonic 'hee'.

Thus the 5 and consequently the 500 are of extreme significance. So far we have come across the 5 and the 500, but not yet with the 50. I had to wait with it until we had got so far. For in discussing this conception 'fifty' we shall come upon yet another marvel which the structure of the Bible, and that of the word, hence that of number, shows us.

The seventh day in the first tale of creation is not finished. In this world, the world of 'doing', of 'action', Olam Assiah, this seventh day is completed. When this seventh day is completed, it means that it has completed itself with itself, with the highest measure for that world of the seven, i.e. in seven times seven. Then there is consequently, the 49 as the extreme boundary of this world. And then the eighth day begins, as the new day, starting with the 50.

Again we see that the 'five' expresses a world beyond this world. Just as the 500 is non-existent in this world, so also is the 50 of a different quality. And both of them are like the 5 which can only express itself here as 1–4.

So here we see *how* this 50 ensues, namely when this world, this seventh day, is completed. As long as the seventh day continues to exist, the world is on its way to integration, which indeed can be effected during this seventh day. The new world, however, begins beyond, begins with the 50 and *that* is the eighth day.

We shall recurrently come across this eighth day in that sense in the Bible. In the sense of a new world, with which all bygones are bygones. The transition to that new world, indeed, is like a transition from one world to the other.

The coincidence of the seventh day completed in the 49, and the beginning of the eighth day in the 50, is not just coincidence. It connects this seventh day with the fulfilment, with the new day marked by the 'five'

Just as the 3 and the 4, as the 3^2 and the 4^2, make the 5^2, so also do the 3 and the 4 as the 7 in the 7^2 mark the boundary with the 50. It is a most extraordinary quality, this structure of the word and the number.

That a new world begins with the 50, we can see all through the Bible. A few examples will suffice. They will, however, demonstrate sufficiently how the marvellous structure of the Bible expresses itself therein too.

The word for son which we discussed in one of the previous chapters in order to point to the beginning with the 'beth', the 'two' of something created, in contrast with the words for father and mother, which begin with the 'one', is 'ben' spelled beth-nun, 2–50.

I had to postpone discussing the number 50, since we had not yet discussed the seventh day, which when completed, inaugurates the 50 as the beginning of the eighth day. Now, however, we see what the word 'son' implies; it is that which the father 'ab', 1–2, together with the mother, 'em', 1–40, give to this world. And what they give, begins with the duality with which it is created for father and mother, and it has as its purpose in view exactly that 50, this passing beyond the seventh day and the attaining of the new world, of a completely different world.

The daughter, 'bath', beth-taf, 2–400, merely attains the boundary of this world. The son, however, goes beyond and enters the other world. This also means, as viewed on another plane, that the female side, the physical, the left hand side, *cannot* get beyond this world. But that the male side, the soul, the root, *does* enter the new world. With the physical is meant what in this world expresses itself as body, form. It is a way of expression in *this* world, pertaining exclusively to *this* world. In another world it would express itself differently, in a way which also passes beyond the 400, beyond the 'tar'.

The masculine, however, that which, when viewed in these proportions, stands as the 'one' facing the 'four' of the feminine, contains everything within itself and it *does* progress towards the next world. Just as the tree of life – which is to the tree of knowledge as 'one' to 'four' – gives the measure of 500, hence also containing everything, both the 'one' *and* the 'four'. Thus the 'one' also embraces the 'four', and therefore is able to create anywhere any kind of body-formation.

It is easy now to understand what is meant with 'stone'. That which in essence represents the principle of stone, when it crystallizes in matter, takes on the quality of material stone. It is therefore something permanent, something persistent throughout time. Just as the essential principle of the 1–4 on appearing in matter has the quality of 'mist'. Now stone is 'eben', spelled aleph-beth-nun, 1–2–50. So it has within itself that which in human relationship is expressed as father, the 1–2, and the son, the 2–50. Hence the stone accompanies all the way, from the origin, across the differentiation into duality, to the 50 of the coming new world, beyond the seventh day.

So this gives a different sense considering stones in the Bible a pillar, an altar or the 'stone'-tablets of the Sinai, the stone 'shetijah' which we discussed above in connection with the 300–400 now gets a very special meaning, as does also 'the stone which the builders refused, is become the head stone of the corner' (Psalm 118:22).

The word for build is 'boneh', spelled beth-nun-hee, 2–50–5. This 'hee', 5, is an ending and does not belong to the root of the verb. That word, too, has the 2–50, hence the same structure as the word for son. And building is essentially bringing the world of creation, of duality, to the coming new world of the 50, of the eighth day. Just as one builds by means of the son, and experiences the new world through him. Thus we can, albeit from merely one point of view, understand a little better the fact that it was not David who could build the house of God, but that it was his son Solomon who was allowed to do so (2 Sam. 7). For in the counting of the generations David is the seventh generation – after the

26 generations which there be unto Sinai — and Solomon is the eighth. In the seventh day there is not the place yet for the *established* house. Not until the eighth day does it come; the son building it.

Between the exodus from Egypt — a story we hope to discuss at greater length — and the revelation of Mount Sinai there are exactly 49 days. The 50th day is the revelation of God. This, too, is embedded in the structure of the tale of the Bible, in a coming world, not in the seventh day. It is true, the latter days of the period of the 'seventh day' are devoted to the preparations of the coming of that new world. That new world itself, however, is different; in that new world, in the 50th day God appears, God reveals Himself. Then has the unity in the 26th generation become a fact.

We also observe it in the so-called regulation of slavery. *This* point, too, I hope to discuss in greater detail in another chapter. For just as 'mist' is an expression of the (1–4)-principle, and 'stone' of the (1–2–50)-principle, so also is 'slave' an expression in this world of something we simply have to learn and see in its essence.

We should not allow ourselves to be deceived by the image of 'slave' any more than by the images of 'mist' or 'stone'. A slave is the expression in matter and in human organization-form of the principle that a human being is not completely free or sometimes not free at all in his actions. It is seen daily with many people. Viewed from the standpoint of reality it is not essential whether such a person has a subordinate social position or that he belongs to the governing classes. Humanly speaking unfree are those that somehow or other are caught up in the material world. In the form of living in a whirl of sensations or in the form of being unable to think except through sensory perception. We shall revert to the subject by and by.

Now such a 'slave' can get free in the seventh year. Just as, viewed from the principle of creation, man having got beyond through eating from the tree of knowledge — as the tale of creation has it — can be delivered on that seventh day, the day of the Sabbath. If man is *bent* on having his freedom, *bent* on freeing himself from the consequences of eating from the tree of the knowledge, he can do so. The seventh day is blessed and hallowed by God for that purpose, i. e. It has been endowed with a very special quality for that purpose. Even if man should have acted differently before in going the way of the serpent, even if he should on account of it have got bound, attached to matter, on that seventh day he can emancipate himself. That is the power of this world, which was made with the principle of creation, which finally emerges in integration. The world has this power of integration within itself.

On another level this enacts itself with the 'slave' in the seventh year. The slave can be emancipated in the seventh year. The man, attached to matter can emancipate himself in this seventh day, in this world.

If, however, he should feel so much attached to this condition of being bound, as to insist on continuing to be tied to the master who owns him, in spite of the seventh day; as to refuse to relinquish the wife the master gave him and the children born to him, just as a man can feel so much attached to all things material of this world and its prospects as to *refuse* to relinquish them, then something peculiar will happen to that slave. Then – as we can read in Exodus 21:1–6 – he will be led to the door and his master shall bore his ear through with an awl, and the slave shall serve his master 'for ever'.

A strange story, and many 'educated' people will wave it aside as a cruel ancient custom. These wavers-aside happen to be image-worshippers and they fail to see the real.

We have seen that the word for door, 'daleth', is the word for the fourth letter, hence for the 4. And when we take the Hebrew word for 'awl' with which the slave's ear was to be bored, we find it is 'martsea', spelled mem-resh-tsade-ayin, 40–200–90–70. The sum-total of the components of this word is 40+200+90+70=400. The word 'ear', in Hebrew 'ozen', too, gives interesting information when we study it in its real structure. It is a pity I cannot go into it at this juncture, since we have yet to learn all sorts of things, undiscussed so far. We shall come across it further down.

It will be sufficient, though, to consider the typical facts which bring about that 'eternal' slavery. For here we see proportions we have learned something about, both the 4 and the 400, the two numbers expressing 'this world', the 400 especially expressing the suffering, the slavery, in this world. The 4 of the 'door' causes him to enter the world of slavery. The door 'daleth', as we have seen, has the same structure as the word 'birth', 'development' which indeed is related to the conception 'four'. Through that 'door' is 'slavery' born for ever, it develops across the door.

Again we see that the word contains within itself the secret of reality. Not in the image as it is. It might take an infinite time for us to attain reality through the image, after having lost our way and erred in our judgement every so often. We should not even have the means of control to find out whether we were erring or no. But with the wonder of the word we realize at once what certain things are, what they express.

So the slave has to serve 'forever', 'eternally'. There is no misunderstanding the fact.

Nevertheless this 'forever' proves to have a measure. In the discussion of the year of the jubilee in Leviticus 25:8, 9, 10, we read that in the *fiftieth* year 'liberty shall be proclaimed throughout the land unto all the inhabitants thereof'. Then will the slaves also return, everyone 'unto his possession and unto his family'. Also those who in the seventh year had refused to be free, now go away all the same. The 'forever' simply means as long as the seventh day lasts. And at the worst it takes seven times seven, i.e. 49. With the 50th, however, there is another world, so this 'forever' appears to have had significance merely for that world of the seventh day which seemed endless, 'eternal'.

The word eternal, 'olam', which also means 'world' and thus expresses the infinite in space-time, has for its root the word 'ol', which means 'yoke'. In our world the meaning of 'eternal' has the character of a yoke. It implies servitude to the world; being bound to matter, hence the exhortation to free oneself from the yoke.

But on the eighth day, when the 50th has begun, there is a new world, there is for everybody a return to his origin, as it is expressed in the image; a return to his possession which is restored to him, and to his family whither he returns.

Again we see the 50 coming into prominence as the new world and again emphatically as that which comes after the seven. For it literally says there are 'seven times seven years, so that the days of the seven sabbaths of years make forty-nine years'. Followed by the words 'thou shalt hallow the fiftieth year ...'

We have again seen, in a different plane, that the 50 as conclusion of the world of the seventh day makes its appearance as the beginning of an entirely new world. A very clear example is that of the journey of biblical Israel through the desert.

In a detailed explanation of this story further down we shall see that this journey across the desert is a representation of the seventh day. The seventh-day principle crystallized, condensed in the space-time event of the journey through the wilderness. The Bible tells us in this story of the desert how the essential finds its expression in the happenings in the world and how it puts its stamp on that time when for the first time *this* happening penetrated as far down as this our world for its expression.

That it has to do with the seventh day, we can see for instance from the fact that the taxing of the population, of the men past twenty, yielded a number of 600,000 odd, viz. 603,500 and 601,730, a number entering the 700,000, i.e. a seventh cycle (Numbers 1:46 & 26:51).

Moreover, as the seventh day it is the period in which one can 'do' the seventh day, namely by uniting it with the 'one', by turning away from duality, which at the end of the previous day one had received within oneself through eating from the tree of the knowledge. The whole of the seventh day is the day of the alternative to man: on that day man can go the way to union, or he remains bound to the world which the serpent had offered him as a means of attainment. As we have just seen about the 'slave' he can obtain the seventh day and freedom, but he also can get so much attached to his master as to desist from that freedom and then he remains a slave.

This journey across the desert, like the seventh day, is the way of the alternative, either turning away from duality, the divorce which brought suffering, and opt for the 'one', or remaining attached to duality. So the way through the desert can, like the seventh day, become the way to the 'one', turning away from the 'two', in every respect, in every plane.

Now the word in the Bible for Egypt, where one is the servant, hence where there is suffering, is 'Mitsrayim', spelled mem-tsade-resh-jod-mem, 40–90–200–10–40.

The word 'Mitsrayim' is a very typical word, it indicates 'duality'. The ending '-ayim' representing a dual. Thus, for instance the two legs are called 'rag*layim*', the two hands 'yad*ayim*', the two eyes 'en*ayim*', the two ears 'ozn*ayim*'. It is the dual of the word 'Mitsr', just as 'yad*ayim*' is the dual of the word 'yad', hand.

Now that word 'Mitsr' contains as its root the word 'tsar', spelled tsade-resh, which refers to form as well as to sorrow and oppression. So the word Mitsrayim means 'the form in the dual', or 'the dual form' and also 'the sorrow of the dual' or 'the sorrow in duality', 'the oppression in duality'.

With it the word indicates what Egypt really means in the biblical story. It is the crystallization in time, and the expression in a specific place in that time, of that which essentially means the suffering in duality, being caught up in the duality of the world, and the inability to free oneself, not knowing how to get out of it.

Whereas Canaan is the promised land, where another world is to begin, where the end-in-view is attained. A land with entirely different standards. There unity will be restored, the unity which one had known before landing in Egypt.

From the story of the word one can see that 'the formation' of man and of the world of which the second tale of creation ever speaks in contradistinction with 'creation' as it is used in the first tale of creation, is also to be retraced in the word for Egypt.

For the word for forming, as used in the second tale of creation, with the root 'tsr' goes back on the same word which forms the root of the word Egypt, i. e. Mitsrayim. And in the second tale of creation this 'formation' also ended in the coming of suffering. Man in that world of form, Olam Yetsira, eats the fruit of the tree of the knowledge and because of it falls into great suffering. It is the tree of duality, of good and evil, from which he eats and which brings with it that sorrow. Just as Egypt is the land of 'duality', *Mitsrayim*, with the suffering owing to that duality there.

So there is the parallel even in the name, 'mitsrayim' and the formation, the 'tsr' in the world of the second tale of creation. And either of them implies form and suffering. And both of them end in an exodus from that world.

There is still more, running parallel, and it is even possible to indicate it at the first reading.

The second tale of creation is a story of the side of the water, it is a story in which the female plays the decisive part. One need merely point at the significance of the 'river' there from Pharaoh's dream, up to and including the throwing of the children into the river and the plagues in connection with the river. A typical world of water. And again the decisive actions of the women in that world. From the two midwives, Moses' sister on the lookout and Moses' mother hiding the babe and later on fostering it, to the daughter of Pharaoh who saved it and kept it alive. It will always be seen, as soon as it is a case of formation, making form, it is a story of the left side, water plays a part in it and women as well. Moses, the deliverer of that world, bears a name meaning 'taken from the water', 'derived from the water'. So it is with him the exodus takes place from that world of the water (Exod. 2:10).

But do not let us stray too far from the subject in hand. For I shall have to revert to the story of Egypt further down. What I wanted to point out here is the dual character of the name of Egypt and the relationship between this dual character and suffering, with at the end the exodus which when viewed from the side of Egypt was an expulsion, just as the Bible has it. And that it runs parallel with man's coming from the sixth day into the seventh day, the seventh-day-world.

Then the way begins from the land of bondage, from suffering, to the promised land where everything will be good. Such a journey is always marked by the alternative. People often yearn for Egypt, people yet love the world of duality and therefore continue wandering about in the wilderness, die there and remain there 'forever'. But the journey goes on none the less, a return to Egypt is precluded, that way is cut off. Whoever yearns to go back, remains bound 'forever' in that desert-world. The image of the 'desert' should likewise be looked upon as an expression of something real.

The desert is the world one passes through. It is nothing in itself, it is barren and inhospitable. It is not meant for people to remain in. One travels through the wilderness as one travels through time. Just like time, so does the desert lead to a new world, to the promised land. Time does not allow of a return. But whoever yearns back to the world of development, of strong growth, of sensation through matter, of being submerged in intoxication, is like the slave who desists from freedom in that seventh day and therefore continues a slave 'forever'. All the same, the way goes on and finally ends up in another world.

The journey across the desert is something endless. For that journey takes 40 years. In the plane of decades it is the longest time possible. Properly speaking 'forever' for this seventh day; seeming just as endless as the 400 years of servitude in Egypt. One simply cannot see the end of it, because there is nothing to go beyond the 4 or 40 or 400 in this world of form. So it is like that journey in the seventh day, this journey of the 'world-of-the-two', the world of the opposites and of suffering in consequence, towards the 'world-of-the one', the world of ultimate harmony, of peace, and of abiding in peace everlasting.

The representation and the more profound consideration of the word taught us as much. But the same can, of course, be found back in the essence of the word, in the quantitative proportions of the word, in the quantitative value of the components.

The word for Egypt, Mitsrayim, is spelled 40–90–200–10–40. The sum total of the components is 380.

The word for Canaan is spelled kaf-nun-ayin-nun, so in numbers 20–50–70–50, with a sum total of the components of 190.

Now that we know a little more of this wonderful systematism, of this interlocking of image and word and of proportion in the word, it is only natural for us to see that this transition from the 'world-of-the-two' to the 'world-of-the-one' also finds its expression in the essence of the word. One should rather say: *just because* it is like that in the essence of the word, therefore it must come to expression in the form of the word, in the image in space and in the event in time.

For indeed we see that the proportion Egypt-Canaan is 380:190, hence exactly 2:1 again.

The journey from Egypt to Canaan *is* the way from the 'two' to the 'one'. The essence of the word, where the word borders on the other world, informs us of the fact.

Again we can ask: *who* is it that has been able *thus* to form that word, before there was a story, that the structure of the word and that of the story should tally? Or was the story there *anyway together with* the word, before this world, even outside it, beyond it, before it could express itself here in this way? The answer inevitably must be in the affirmative, since it is out of the question, anyway, that *both* the word *and* the story could have been formed like this by mankind even after millions of years, and since coincidence, in such overwhelming quantity that it has become the normal condition, no longer is coincidence, but must be called law.

It goes without saying that this transition from duality to unity expresses itself in many respects in this story. I shall give one more example. When the exodus from Egypt takes place, Moses is eighty years old. The journey across the desert takes forty years. Again we have the same proportion. The period from Moses' birth *to* the exodus is eighty years, twice the time Moses spends in the desert, which is forty years. Moses as the leader on that journey from the 'two' to the 'one', even in the structure of his own lifetime shows this proportion of 2 : 1.

Of course one must not cling too much to the image in such a story or concentrate on an eventual proof of the historic event. That historic event *took* place, since in its essence this event was present already and this reality in the Bible-story also put its mark on this world. *That* is the proof of the reality of the event. That, however, our manner of viewing history cannot make things tally, is a subject more closely to be discussed in one of the following chapters.

Now this journey across the desert is essentially the transition of the world in 'duality' to the world which has united the counterparts in harmony. It is what in the root-story is the essence of the seventh day. Hence reaching the land which is the promised world, is what we have learned to regard as the eighth day.

And again we see a seemingly unimportant facet shedding light. He that effects this transition to the new world, who leads biblical Israel across the border is, as is well known from the Bible-story (otherwise one should read it, at the end of Deuteronomy and the opening chapters of Joshua) a new figure, called Joshua, the son of Nun.

And again it is the word which informs us of what actually happens. For the word 'Nun', apart from its translation as 'fish' which in fact fits in completely with the structure, is nothing but what the letter 'nun' denotes, namely ... 50.

Joshua the leader to the new world is the 'ben nun', the son of the nun, of the 50, hence — as we have repeatedly seen in connection with the 50 — of that which is the entrance into the eighth day.

Again, how marvellously does everything fit together. The journey across the desert as the seventh day, as the journey from the 'world-of-the-two' with its suffering, towards the 'world-of-the-one' with its peace and harmony, which eventuates in that new world, the new day which follows, the eighth day. And at the same time he that effects this transition of the seventh day to the eighth, bears the name of 'son of the fifty', son of the eighth day.

The Bible, however, in the Pentateuch, the part which makes its appearance as root-passage over against the whole complex, winds up with the seventh day, i.e. with the end of the seventh day. And it merely relates that this Joshua ben Nun was going to lead the transition to the other world.

Even Moses only saw the 'promised land', that coming world, from afar and did not enter it in the Bible-story which describes this world, this world which has as its highest number the 4 or the 40 or the 400. Only Joshua, as son of the 50, the next number, was to set foot in that land. But in that root-story even he does not enter it.

The root-story finishes towards the end of the seventh day, as it does in the very heart of that root-story itself, as it also does in the first tale of creation. That seventh day is not completed there either. And at the end of Pentateuch there is merely the statement that Joshua, the son of the 'fifty' was to round it off, cross the border and occupy the new world.

The story in Pentateuch winds up with the death of Moses and mourning because of it as a fact, with merely the prospect of what Joshua, the son of Nun, would do; just as the story of the whole of the Bible ends with the exile, death, and again the bare statement that there would be a new world and the appearance on this seventh day of the man who was to be the leader in the new world, who was to put his mark on the new world which is the eighth day.

His appearance, even in this seventh day, sets into relief the coming realization of the eighth day, of the new world. But that eighth day cannot be measured by the standards of this world, since they do not go beyond the 4. That is why the eighth day cannot in this world become that reality which the seventh day stands for. And therefore the story always finishes towards the end of the seventh day, which end, as indeed it represents leaving one world and entering another, looks rather disastrous when measured by the standards of the seventh day itself. These standards all point to a perishing, a disintegration, briefly: an ending.

Since the complete pattern according to which God made the world is stamped on this world, the eighth day and that which follows, up to and including the tenth, are present therein. It is just as much present in it as the preceding days are stamped on this world. The preceding days likewise find expression in this seventh day. They can all be measured with the formal standards, the material standards which we find in this seventh day by means of the word. They get there with the characteristics of this seventh day. The characteristics of that which is round, which is transient. The days yet to come, when expressed by standards of matter, by this transient character of matter, also adopt a certain 'volatile' quality here. They pass by together with this transient form of realization. Since they are expressed in unstable matter, they adopt an unstable character in this phenomenal form. Thus the pattern-stamp of all that is to come, of all that has not yet become real, passes together with the seventh day.

But the stamp of the pattern *is* there, just as well as the pattern-stamp of all that preceded. Everything which makes its appearance here bears this stamp. It is a hallmark that worlds have been and worlds will be and that this stamp of God remains forever. Thus the seventh day bears that stamp, even though everything is expressed in a reality which is merely the reality of the seventh day. The reality of the coming from a 'world-of-the-two' and the moving towards the 'world-of-the-one', with at the end the certainty of passing into the new day.

Therefore in the story of the book Joshua the eighth day does not begin as a reality, but there is only the story *what* that eighth day, as expressed in terms of this world of the seventh day, looks like. If the eighth day was to have appeared as a reality, even the first tale of creation should have mentioned 'and the evening and the morning were the seventh day', and it would have had to give expression to the eighth day *there* as well. And *in that case* the story of Pentateuch would have continued and Joshua would have entered Canaan even in Pentateuch. However all this is not there, and for that reason the eighth day can only be expressed in terms of this reality of the seventh day.

If one reads the story of Pentateuch according to its essential nature and understands it in that sense — detached from the images which the words call up for our world — the entire story of the reality of the days to come is actually found present in it. This wonderful entirety of the Bible is essentially present in every reality, in every 'day', hence also in the coming worlds. For the coming worlds, too, it is the source of the wonder and of man's yearning to be with God. Only the words are differently expressed there, hence the images are seen and understood differently. The extraordinary thing, however, is that the words remain identical. For indeed they are the entire creation, of all worlds and of all times and the wonderful thing is that in all worlds they arouse the same joy and gladness as they do in this. That is why tradition has it that those people who have already left this world and abide in 'paradise', consider reading the Thora, i.e. Pentateuch their greatest joy.

Since the pattern-stamp of the eighth day is present in the matter of the seventh day — albeit carried onwards by the volatile character of this seventh day — we can also see what this eighth day is in reality. Here, too a few examples will serve the purpose.

In connection with the name Abraham I have already said a few words on circumcision. As it says in the Bible it is accomplished on the eighth day after birth, after this union of Abraham with God.

The new man of the eighth day, owing to his coming to 'integration' in this world of the seventh day, is already divested of the obscuring physical sheath. The core, the essence of the new man, is freer, even though the physical still exists. One of the details of circumcision, for instance is the so-called 'pria' which means that the surrounding prepuce is not wholly removed, but that part of it is left and folded back to set the centre free. This part which is folded back, is a continuation of the veiling, the physical, the material, but no longer in the manner of the seventh day of hiding the centre, but to the contrary leaving the centre free.

Eighth-day man is circumcised. Thus Joshua (vide Joshua 5) caused biblical Israel to be circumcised in Gilgal. For indeed, the eighth day had come. Man in the eighth day has a different quality. A quality which, according to ancient lore, was not attainable during the seventh day.

On the journey across the desert, according to tradition, circumcision would have been deadly. Only three of the four elements would have been fulfilled. The fourth, the bodily element, represented by the point of the compass 'north', had not yet fulfilled itself, hence circumcision could not be accomplished without causing the death of the person circumcised. Another example is seen in the rules concerning impurity. Of course they too have a significance altogether different from the utilitarian sense demanded by the hygienic principles of society, so that a man may devote himself undisturbedly to the so-called pleasures of this world. I cannot possibly enter here into the complicated rules on purity and impurity. Briefly it amounts to this that man is so strongly attracted by the forces of this world, the forces of duality as we called them, the forces of development, that he is bound, enslaved, becomes unclean. In the world of matter, for instance, on coming upon a dead body, he may get into such a state as to lose faith in man's ever coming to life again; he may see injustice and unfairness in man's fate, think that there is evidently nothing but coincidence and arbitrariness when a person *dies* in spite of his having lived a clean and decent life and his recovery having been earnestly prayed for, whereas wicked people and unbelievers live on merrily. Thus there are many encounters which drive man to the crucial point and cause a change in his mode of living while yet in this world. And the principle of impurity also implies that ever since the eating of the fruit of the tree of the knowledge, the whole world has shared in this impurity and has started a definite course towards purification. It is, for instance, the way of the 26 generations up to the revelation, the way through the 4 'toldoth', through the 4 parts, just as all creation also passes through the 4 worlds; the condition of 'duality'.

Now this principle of impurity imparts to us that it lasts seven days and that at the end of the seventh day when in the evening the eighth day commences, impurity ceases to be.

So this is, indeed, what the eighth day brings with it, as we saw in our reflections above: the ultimate emancipation from oppression, even from the alternative, from duality, from divorce.

In this process of purification the third day, i. e. the day rounding off the first cycle of three, plays a special part, as a kind of condition for ultimate purity after the seventh day (vide Numbers 19:12). We shall revert to the point in a later chapter and again notice how the systematism of the structure makes itself felt in the veriest details.

We also come across the eighth day in our discussion of the Sabbatical year (Lev. 25). There we see that the produce of the sixth year is used for that year itself, and for the seventh year, as also for the eighth year. The seventh year the land, the earth, too must 'rest'. Even there, even in that plane, must be realized this single purpose of the seventh day, viz. ceasing to busy oneself with the development of the earth, of the world, ceasing to make it 'new', to 'improve' it, but only to occupy oneself with its 'reintegration'. Man in all his thought and action should concentrate on this single purpose which implies the emancipation of everything that is separated, the emancipation which reunites. No other fruits should he desire but these.

And his material foundation, his material existence, is insured by the structure of the world which God made such that whatever comes forth from the sixth day, whatever has been made on the sixth day, does not only serve as a basis for the sixth day, but also ensures the existence of the seventh day. The world of the seventh day lives by the grace of that which God made for it in the sixth day; *that* is its existence. It cannot alter it, and if it should try to alter it all the same, it will end in failure, it gets lost together with man who is bent on this alteration on the seventh day. I merely refer to the story of the 'manna' and 'gathering firewood', without expatiating on the subject just yet (resp. Exodus 16, more especially verse 27, and Numbers 15:32–36).

Not until the eighth year is the earth tilled again, not until then, led by the seventh day to a new world, which appears in a new form, can one devote oneself to the earth, to the world. It has now resumed its unity and there is no longer any danger of turning towards the earthly part of duality, of separation. Man by then is a 'five', the 'one' and the 'four' having been integrated all through. If he is *now* to occupy himself with the 'four', this 'four' has become integrated with the principle of the 'one' facing it. By now body and soul are 'one', the opposites are dissolved. In the eighth year something new is sown. However, one still 'eats' of the sixth year, as the Bible tells us loco citato. On the eighth day, too, that which God made on the sixth day, serves as the basis for existence. Although the world assumes a new aspect, and in a sense man appears in a different form, yet there is still this drawing on what was created in the sixth day. Only that which begins with the nine is different. For in the ninth year one has the produce of the eighth, of what the new man made on earth and with the world.

Which is another facet of the eighth expressing itself in this world of the seventh day.

In a very special way we see this structure turning up again in the systematism shown by the sons of Jacob. The seventh son is Gad. The very name is typical, as it is spelled, gimmel-daleth, 3–4.

So that which we found to be the very principle of the seventh day, the male and female facing each other that they might be reintegrated, as it is also expressed in the structure of the tale of creation with the 3 and the 4, constitutes the name of the seventh son of Jacob.

And this name means (vide Genesis 30:11) 'happiness has come', hence what is characteristic of the seventh day, as its potential fulfilment. And when Jacob gives his sons his blessing, he says about Gad (Genesis 49:19) 'a troop shall overcome him; but he shall overcome at the last'. It is the onslaught of the forces of development on the seventh day, which onslaught can, however, not be successful, because the seventh day *must* lead to the end in view: union. It is the power of God's blessing and hallowing this seventh day. Moses' blessing of Gad implies the same thing (Deut. 33:20–21). And Gad is the tribe which goes in advance to conquer the 'land' for the other tribes. This seventh day paves the way for all that is to come, it is the shock-troop for the others (Numbers 32 and Joshua 22). Moreover Gad has seven sons, so here again, after the place and the name, this seven is brought forward (Gen. 46:16).

Now the eighth son is Asher. And promptly we see the character of the eighth day revealing itself. I cannot here expatiate on *all* aspects, it would carry us too far. But Leah's words at the birth of Asher 'Happy am I, for the daughters will call me blessed', give expression to it.

When Jacob gives Asher his blessing, we notice something very special. For he says 'his bread shall be fat and he shall yield royal dainties' (Gen. 49:20). This fat is also emphasized in the blessing of Moses (Deut. 33:24) 'let him dip his foot in oil'.

In behalf of this discourse, necessarily brief, I shall only point at the mention of the 'royal dainties', the 'fat' and the 'oil' where Asher is concerned.

The eighth day is the world where the king, foreseen in the seventh day, does appear, he that shall build the solid house, as we have discussed it above, at the building of Solomon's temple, the temple which David could not yet build, but about which he had been told that his son would be able to build it.

It is also the king who is to come after this world and who in tradition is called 'the anointed king', in Hebrew the 'Messiah'. Messiah means 'anointed', 'Mashiach', spelled mem-shin-jod-cheth, or in numbers 40–300–10–8.

Asher, indeed, with his blessing, is the source for this anointment. From Asher comes the oil for this anointment. And with Asher come the palmy days, the great abundance. The new world with its unlimited abundance, just because it had already become 'one'.

So in the passage on Asher this oil is emphasized. And this oil is characteristic of the name of the king of the new world, of the king who was to accomplish the transition of the seventh day to the eighth. As we saw in Pentateuch that Joshua was the king who was to lead biblical Israel from the world of the 'journey across the desert' to the coming new world.

When we have come to realize this from the verbal story, we shall see again it is astonishingly confirmed at our closer consideration of the essence of the word. The word for oil, as it is also used in the story of Asher, the eighth son of Jacob, is 'shemen', spelled shin-mem-nun. And the word for 'eight' has exactly the same root, also shin-mem-nun; the word for eight is 'shmonah', spelled shin-mem-nun-hee, so with the feminine ending 'hee', both words have the numerical root 300–40–50. And both refer to Asher, the eighth son. 'Shemen' as image of oil, yet hiding the eight in the word, and 'eight' as order of sequence, which in its turn has 'shemen' for its root. Is there a stronger and more striking coherence to be constructed than presents itself to us here anew? In the passage, in the image, and in the structure of the word?

In parenthesis I should like to point at the connection between this word 'shemen', oil, written 300–40–50, and the word for heaven, 'shamayim', written 300–40–10–40. Both with a sum-total of 390.

That 'oil' should be used for anointing is not because oil is useful and is good for nourishment of the body and is a mark of comfortable circumstances, but especially because there is an essential connection between 'oil' as a phenomenon here and the conception 'heaven' as it presents itself to us. The king is anointed by 'heaven' and the image for it is exactly that which appears here as 'oil'. Our view of things has become rather externalized, earthy, hence oil to us is merely something earthy. And we are apt to forget that every single thing is an expression of something real and that we can find that reality when we know the word. The word has been given to us for that purpose.

The word for heaven 'shamayim' can also be seen as the dual form, the 'ayim'-form of 'sham'; as we have already seen how 'ayim' occurs in everything which exists in duality, in pairs.

'Shamayim' taken in that sense is double 'sham' and 'sham' really means 'there', a definite place. We know 'place' here as a sign of the presence of duality. A place is expression for the fact that there is an alternative. One is here in this place, hence not in another place. That other place is proof positive that there is a contrast. In the word for heaven, however, is expressed the simultaneous presence of the alternative in both places. That which makes itself unpleasantly felt here, in contradistinction is present there in unity. Thus the word shamayim is also looked upon as a contraction of the words esh(fire) and mayim(water) therewith expressing the possible presence of the contrasts in the same place, at the same time.

Just as the 'aleph', as pristine form of the name' Lord', unites the two 'jods' in a harmony in which duality is reflected. Just as the two 'cherubim' on the arc in the tabernacle are each other's reflection and in their duality show the tranquillity in the heart of hearts, the harmony there (Exod. 25:18–21). They stand like the two 'jods' in the 'aleph' opposite each other, as each other's reflection and at rest.

It is the same principle as that of 'heaven' which also shows duality at rest. Therefore heaven is the place where God lives. The place where is present the original unity which caused the making of the two, which caused duality to emanate.

From *that* place, with the structure of heaven, the king has been anointed and it is *that* which makes of him something special. *This* oil is no longer known. Oil nowadays is only known as an article of consumption which in consequence of a vaguely remembered tradition is still used for 'anointing'. As soon as oil shall be known in its real nature, there will be a king again who shall be anointed by heaven.

In yet another place is found this connection between oil and the eighth day. It is the event known as the story of the Maccabees. Briefly the point of the story is that the oil in the temple had been defiled by idolatry. There was only sufficient left for one day's service. And it would take eight days to make new oil. For oil *is* eight, oil does not come until the eighth day!

When idolatry was cast out from the temple on the initiative of the Masmonites and a new beginning was going to be made, it appeared, as we have seen, that there was enough oil left for one single day. But this small quantity of oil proved miraculously sufficient to give light for the complete eight days until the new oil was ready.

This story among other things stresses that this specific oil which lights the temple has the quality of breaking the law of nature as soon as the temple is cleansed of idolatrous service and people start making new oil. Then that oil will spread light throughout the seven days till the eighth day. After which the new world can commence celebrating in the temple with the new oil for lighting. The temple to be understood, as we shall see further on, as the substance of this world.

I need not pursue this story of the Maccabees, but I want to point at coherences also occurring in stories which are indirectly related to the central theme.

The race which took the initiative for the action of renewal, radically breaking with ancient customs, was called the race of the Hasmonites. The word is Chashmonaim, spelled cheth-shin-mem-nun-aleph-jod-mem, in numbers 8–300–40–50–1–10–40. And the root of this word is again 300–40–50, the same root found in the words 'oil' and 'eight'. And the story of those 'Chashmonaim' *is* a story of oil *and* eight days. The Jewish feast celebrated on the ground of this story, the Channooka, meaning 'renewal', is celebrated with *oil* which is *burned* during eight days. The feast of the oil, as contrasted with all other feasts, continues for eight days. It is the same oil of Asher, the eighth son of Jacob. And the name Chashmonaim, known here as Hasmonites, has the eight for its root.

And this structure and this place of the eight and of the eighth will be found everywhere, even in its subtlest details.

I can only adduce very few examples in order not to stray too far from the subject, which aims at leading the reader through many more new domains.

But I should like to give one more example drawn from the practice of Jewish life, though this book is not meant to be a description of Jewish life. This facet, however, may throw some light on the knowledge which people in ancient times had of this structure and how that knowledge was adapted to the practice of daily life.

This daily practice enters upon the seventh day with great joy, with much light and abundance. After the latter part of the sixth day with the encounter with the serpent and the eating from the tree of knowledge at the summit of development and power, after the expulsion, on that ground, from that world of Paradise, the seventh day is a proof that God brings man into a new world, into a new life and in that seventh day will lead him to integration.

In fact, the seventh day starts as early as the latter part of the sixth day. A part in which the encounter with the serpent begins to show its destructive consequences and where the greatest danger threatens man, is absorbed by the Sabbath which starts a good hour earlier than it should.

In that latter part of the sixth day highly evolved matter even threatens to adopt forms which might cause matter to emancipate away from its origin.

Tradition among other things has it that certain 'spirits' might permanently have expressed themselves in matter, unless God had rounded off the sixth day in that respect. The power of duality created by God Himself had so vastly increased, nay it *had* to increase so as to embrace all, that none but God could suppress and restrain it. It had swollen to infinite multiplicity with the immense power of multiplicity. It is at this point where the physical acquires such power, that the world of the sixth day comes to an end. An end which God infixed in it under the law of creation. We shall come upon this critical point later on when discussing the so-called Flood and the tale of 'Egypt'. There, too, does the end of the sixth day appear, that summit of material power. An end, entirely unexpected, incredible when it is told, like a break in a continuity already felt as enforced by law. There again an interference in development and the end of a world, of a 'day'.

But after that sense of destruction which tradition also communicates about the first man, Adam, there is the surprise of man's insight that the new world, the new day, restores to him all that he had lost in the former world, the former life, owing to his too intensive preoccupation with matter, with the world of matter.

That is, according to tradition, why Adam thought that the world was being destroyed when he had to leave the world of Paradise, till he found that the very opposite was the case, that a new world had arisen with a new purpose, which was to lead back everything to the condition of unity. On the ground of that story it is said that at that moment Adam could recite the 92nd Psalm for the Sabbath-day.

Of course such a story is beyond every historic causality, a horror to continuity-historians. But here again is expressed a typical aspect of the Bible and of the world which lives with the Bible. The conception time as we know it in our world, does not apply to the Bible. One of the principles for rightly understanding the Bible is therefore expressed as 'een moekdam oe-meochar ba-tora', i. e. 'there is neither before nor after in the Thora'. We shall examine this principle more closely in a following chapter. At any rate it is not illogical in the world of the Bible to ascribe the recital of the 92nd Psalm to Adam. Even though it is rather strange to our sense of causality in time.

The 150 Psalms can be subdivided into ten groups of fifteen, in accordance with the ten as result of the structure of creation with the four elements. According to this division the sixth part ends with the 90th Psalm. In the projection of the 'days' the end of the sixth day is rendered with the 90th Psalm. It says in that Psalm that life can number some seventy or eighty years. With the 91st Psalm the seventh day sets in, the seventh group of fifteen. This Psalm tells us about the way from one world to another. It gives the feeling that God is the leader on that way and guards all. With the next Psalm, the 92nd, there is the certainty of the new world of the seventh day.

The ancient knowledge of this structure is traced back to the custom of accompanying a dead man at his burial with this 91st Psalm. For it is also a transition from this world to another. And even when one goes on a journey, has a change of environment, or when one goes to bed, which is likewise going from one world to another, an expression in this world of the pattern of death, it is this 91st Psalm which is recited with the last verse of the 90th Psalm as its opening part. For the sixth day is bound up with the seventh, as we saw from the connection formed by the name of the Lord, the 10–5 forming the final part of the sixth day and the 6–5 forming the beginning of the seventh day. And similarly by the fact that the final part of the sixth day is related in 'duration' to the beginning of the seventh day. Thus we see how this knowledge of the structure of the world expressed itself also in its very details in the practice of daily life.

So the seventh day begins a little earlier 'on principle', and proves to be a redemption, an emancipation. In that seventh day the male is reunited to the female; in that seventh day the human being as man receives this world in its attractive form of the seventh day, as the bride, and he goes out to meet her to receive her with joy. For the purpose of this seventh day is this integration of man and the world of the seventh day. The purpose is for man to take that world to himself, to deliver it and reunite it with its origin: that same world which before the seventh day had been a stumbling-block to him in the sixth day, because it was still developing, still growing, and had reached the summit of development. But the world in the form in which it is *now* led to man, and man in the form of the seventh day in which he *now* approaches the world, makes it possible that their reunion is effected. As long as man does not desecrate this seventh day in his desire for rapprochement, as he had it in the sixth day. In our terminology of the desert-story it means that man in this seventh day, in his journey to the Promised Land, must not yearn back for Egypt, the world of duality, of contrast, of development.

Thus man travels through the seventh day and with it he is a pioneer marching towards the new world.

But the end of the seventh day is veiled in quiet, in the atmosphere of the end of a world; tradition has it that towards the end of the Sabbath there was the moment when Moses, the leader throughout the seventh day, took leave of the world and died. It is also the moment when another 'seventh', King David, died.

In that atmosphere of the end of the world, when a world disappears to make place for a new world, already foretold, just as Joshua will come after Moses, and after David will come Solomon; in that atmosphere in which according to tradition the wars of Gog and Magog are fought, there is stillness and moderation. In that atmosphere people speak about the secret of the world, about the meaning of things.

And then, when the previous day has gone by, when it has completely passed and it is pitch dark, the eighth day comes. A new light is lit. And then the time of the prophet Elijah is come; he comes to announce the new king, and then there is a new meal, that of the everlasting king David, who is the anointed, i.e. the meal of King Messiah with which the eighth day is ushered in. Again with rejoicing, because the new world has come.

Thus we see that the story of the sixth, seventh and eighth day likewise found expression in the practice of daily life. Daily life of Judaism in principle purposes to be itself the pattern of the Bible and through it to experience the Bible. Therefore, like creation and also like creation in the word of the Bible, it is pervaded by the same pattern through which in its veriest details, again in conformity with life and with creation, everything becomes an expression of life as it is essentially made for man and for the world.

Daily life of Judaism therefore is *not* a copy of the image-story of the Bible, but to the contrary of the essential story, of the story as it is given by the *word*.

In ancient lore, ipso facto, a great deal is said about the eighth day. And naturally the whole story of the eighth son of Jacob, Asher, takes its place therein. These traditions are based on the knowledge of the essential structure and therefore it is they that make it possible for us to read the Bible at all. They form an important part of what may be called oral tradition. This oral tradition gives us, when we read the word, the indication how to find the systematism and how to understand the structure. It is only through this tradition we can learn to know how marvellous the Bible is. Seeking for oneself, making schemes and graphics oneself, one cannot help realizing very quickly that one is hopelessly entangled without any indication how to find one's way through the labyrinth. And the extraordinary thing is that once one has followed the directions of tradition, the same marvels appear to unfold themselves as those one can see in the written Bible, in the word of the Bible.

Now in this complex of traditions are found communications about Asher, the eighth son. I shall select only one which deals with the daughter of Asher, called Serah (Gen. 46:17). Tradition has it that Serah is the messenger of glad tidings. She gives the joy of finding back, the glad surprise of the arrival of the unexpected.

When the brothers of Joseph come back from Egypt, after Joseph had made himself known to them, Serah, the daughter of Asher is the first to learn about it, and it is she who hastens to Jacob to tell him the glad news. It is Serah who tells him what is considered impossible, that 'Joseph is alive'. And with it she gives Jacob a new lease of life. She brings the glad news after the long separation between Jacob and Joseph, between the brothers, who sold him to Egypt, and Joseph. She is the herald of reunion, of the new unity.

Now one of the aspects of the 'anointed', of the Messiah, of the King of the eighth day, is that the structure of the word 'anoint' and the structure of the word 'joy' contain the same components. Anoint, from which the word 'anointed', 'Messiah', is formed, is 'mashach', spelled mem-shin-cheth, 40–300–8. And giving joy is 'sameach', spelled sin-mem-cheth, 300–40–8.

So in this structure is to be found the relationship between the Messiah, the King of the new world, and giving joy, rejoicing.

For our daily life, which indeed is an expression of the substance, giving joy and rejoicing therefore are the condition for showing in this life the pattern of the new world, of that 'eighth day'. He that is cheerful, ever in a mood of certainty that whatever is, is best, and that things will be understood in their relationship and purpose, lays the foundation for that integration, not only in the utilitarian sense of a balanced life, of preventing gastric ulcers, heart-disease, or any kind of managers' diseases, but in the profounder and wider form of experiencing and knowing for a certainty that there is an eternally good and harmonious world, yielding joy in every respect.

Therefore there is also the insight in this practice of life, that people full of joy and cheerfulness – in the right sense, as alert persons and not with the licentiousness of people caught in a whirl of excitement – are good people, imbued with knowledge of redemption, of integration. And that is why 'sour' people, 'gloomy' people can never redeem others, for they threaten with hell and damnation and they know all about the refined and horrid torments which a so-called God avails Himself of to punish His creatures, punish them for things concerning which He has moreover never clearly stated how to withstand them, and which numerous churches and denominations are continually wrangling about.

These gloomy people know nothing of that cheerfulness that things will come right after *all!* They do not feel that urge to tell people that things are good just the same, for they have not that inner conviction that God has made everything to gladden creation with.

And therefore Serah is said to carry the message of reunion, the message which, in good reason, should rouse misgivings. But she hastens ahead to bring the glad news even before the others who actually should have carried the message, because they had been witnessess of that reunion. And this reunion is the greatest happiness, it gives one the taste of that which God ever has within Himself, this oneness, the harmony of never being separated any more, since one has experienced how this unity has its root in everything.

The separation from Joseph — a story we shall revert to by and by — has lasted 22 years, as can be computed from the Bible. After those 22 years there follows this reunion, and it is Serah, the daughter of the eighth, who has proclaimed this reunion and because of it has resuscitated and gladdened Jacob who had suffered so much from this separation.

So it is the union, as it also takes place after this world, after this seventh day, between body and soul, as it does between all things previously opposites. It is the reunion of the eighth day. Hence in ancient lore there is this appearance of Serah, the daughter of Asher, the eighth.

But we can view it in yet another way. Joseph had been separated from Jacob for 22 years. These 22 years are looked upon as years of exile in matter, in being sent out into the crystallization-form in this world.

For the 22 are the 22 possibilities the alphabet supplies, the alphabet of the Bible which, as we have seen in the table of letters, consists of 22 variations. The first is the aleph, the 'one', the last is the taf, the 400. Together there are 22 letters, yielding the 22 possibilities of expression. As long as a thing is incorporated in these 22 letters, it is in exile, it can be separated by the image from its origin. When the 22 have been left behind, one gets — to use our well-known terminology — beyond the 400, the farthest possibility of expression of this world. For after it comes the 500, for which there is no letter available in this world, no possibility of expression; it is the 500 of the next world, of the eighth day.

And the extraordinary thing about this relationship is also that the extreme completion of the conception 22, the 222, gives 484, on the borderline between the 400 and 500. For the 23 as 232 gives 529, which is beyond the 500.

That the 22nd letter is the 400, the farthest possibility of expression in the world of matter; that moreover the 22 itself just manages to reach that boundary between the world of the 400 and that of the 500; that after the 22 there is the reunion, the integration after the separation in the story of Joseph; and that

Asher plays a part in the proclamation of the reunion; all this is so intimately blended and so coherent with this structure elsewhere that we can state once more we have come across one of the many wonders of this structure.

This Serah, daughter of Asher, also plays a part, a few hundred years 'later', towards the end of the servitude in Egypt: characteristically again where an emancipation is at hand.

I would advise historians not to frown on this historical enormity. For how on earth could Serah live so long, they might rightly ask. But all this is enacted in a world altogether different from that of the historians. These historians must ipso facto continue revolving in this round world constructed by their perception, and in such a world such a thing is not possible, at least not just to be stated without more ado. But we shall revert to the subject of time-reckoning in the Bible by and by.

So Serah is in Egypt at the end of the period of bondage and she is then the wise woman who, whenever anybody constitutes himself as the deliverer from bondage, is always asked the question whether this man is the true deliverer. For is not Serah the one who knows how deliverance comes, since she is a daughter of the 'eighth'?

And ever again Serah has to answer that all those who presume they are deliverers, are not the genuine ones. She ever inquires after their motives and their statements. And these motives are not the true ones. Until Moses comes and utters the 'pakod jifkod', the 'God will surely visit you' (Gen. 50:24) literally translated 'God will surely think of you, remember you', which Joseph before his death gave as his message for the new time which was to come after the end of the book of Genesis.

Serah recognizes in him the deliverer who relies on God's interference, on the certainty that God is sure to come and bring a new world.

Thus it is the daughter of Asher, the eighth, who knows the right way of deliverance, and proclaims this deliverance anew. Not the deliverance because the end had been computed, or because people thought the time had come for bondage to end, or because people presumed there had been enough suffering. The motive is that God will interfere, because God thinks the time is come.

And thus we see in the rest of the story of deliverance from bondage in Egypt a noticeable passivity of the people to be delivered, who are even bidden 'to remain indoors', go about their jobs at home while the Lord will pass through the world and destroy that world and overtly arrange the exodus in detail Himself.

This is the deliverance which Serah points out as the real, for this deliverance has the characteristics of the coming of a new world, of a new day. So, according to ancient lore Serah lived to be very old. She also tells that she has lived so long, because she is the deliverer of good tidings. Besides, the eighth actually live to be old. The eighth in the generations from Adam, i.e. from the first decade of generations, also lived longer than any other. It is Methuselah, the eighth in the order of precedence. He lived to see all the world of the ten generations going down in the Flood.

His father Enoch, the seventh in rank of the generations, like the seventh day, had something very particular. 'And Enoch walked with God, and he was not, for God took him' (Gen. 5:24). There was not an ordinary ending, as with all the other generations. He did not 'die', as the others, he was only taken by God, in his 365th year, much younger than all the others, and curiously at the number of the solar year which characterizes the seventh day of the world.

With that 'seventh' there is always something peculiar when people pass away. But this is not the place to enter into it more deeply.

I should like to wind up this passage with one more characteristic trait of Asher as the eighth. For then we shall have, in my opinion, given due consideration to the seventh and eighth day.

In Genesis 30:14–17 we can read how Reuben, the eldest son of Jacob, went into the fields in the days of the wheat-harvest and found the so-called mandrakes, which he brought to his mother Leah and Rachel acquired them from her, thus leaving Jacob to her.

Surely a strange situation for him that reads this story as an image-story. A kind of transaction, with the husband as passive object, between two rivalling women.

It is impossible exhaustively to treat this story which contains as many surprises as all the other stories in the Bible. Surprises which give us a picture of how the world is made and why it was made like that.

I should like to expatiate here on merely a few aspects of the story, especially those which might throw a clear light on the moment of the happenings.

For this story is enacted as a striking intermezzo at the enumeration of the births of the eleven sons and the one daughter of Jacob, as it is given in chapters 29 and 30 of the book Genesis.

At the very moment when the eighth son, Asher, is born, there is this intermezzo of the so-called mandrakes, love-apples, 'doudaim' as they are called in Hebrew. In no other place is the enumeration of the births interrupted. So this is a special place, where something new is beginning. And that place is where the eighth comes. Moreover as time of action is stated the time of the wheat-harvest. This, too, is a very special time; it is identical with that of Pentecost.

Easter is the time when people 'begin to put the sickle to the corn' (Deut. 16:9) and seven weeks later, when harvest is reaped (Deut. 16:10 and Lev. 23:10–11) there is the feast of weeks, the 50th day after Easter. The tale of Ruth is also enacted at that time. So among the Jews the tale of Ruth is traditionally read at Pentecost.

The time of harvest-home therefore is the time of the so-called 50th day, as we have seen, the time of the world which comes after the 49 days, after the completed seven, the seven which has fulfilled itself with itself. And in our story this 50th day comes immediately after the birth of Asher.

The seven weeks between Easter and Pentecost are the weeks of reaping the wheat. On the 49th day the crops are cut, the harvest is stored up. Looked at from this world, man is cut off from the earth in this period of seven weeks, just as he is cut off from the earth in the seventh day of the world. It is the loosening of the bonds with the earth, which starts at Easter.

We shall see by and by what connection there is in essence between wheat, as the first of the seven fruit, according to the systematism of the Bible, and the phenomenon man with the body as it developed after his eating of the tree of the knowledge.

In another plane the exodus, the emancipation from servitude in Egypt, is identical with the reaping of the grain which is then also being cut off from the earth.

It is also characteristic of the seventh day this ever being cut off from the bonds with the earth and stored up somewhere else for a specific purpose. In the image of the botanical world and in the relationship between men and plants it is thus expressed as man, the higher being, cutting the grain for everybody's good.

None the less this being cut off and removed from the earth, in a certain sense causes grief. The purpose of this cutting off is not known throughout the seven weeks. It is like the contrast between life and death, obtaining in this world of the seventh day. People witness this passing away from the earth, yet are ignorant about the why and wherefore.

And that is why tradition has given these seven weeks the hallmark of sadness, grief. During these seven weeks between Easter and Pentecost according to Jewish practice of life, hence in agreement with the structure of the world, there ought not to be any special rejoicing.

Even though one knows oneself emancipated at Easter, although one has entered upon the seventh day which will lead to integration, one also sees death as one's companion on the way. And one is merely *on one's way* to integration, to reconciling things, one does not *know* as yet, even though one hopes and trusts and believes that things have now definitely taken a turn for the better. This period of the seven weeks, of the 49 days, is 'numbered'. Usage has it that from the start it is fixed every day what day of the week and what week it is. For instance, 'today it is the thirty-third day, it is four weeks and five days'. For all this world of the seventh day is a world of proportions. Things in this world can only express themselves as proportions, as a more or a lesser on the measuring-staff, as an ever changing configuration in space-time. Nothing remains stable, everything flows out, according to the standard of this 7×7.

The 33rd day in this period of seven weeks plays an important part in ancient lore. On this 33rd day rejoicing *is* possible, and in the subsequent sixteen days the sadness is considerably mitigated.

Again we see the structure of the way coming into prominence. In the period of 49 days, as a matter of fact, exactly two-thirds of the way have been covered on the 33rd day and after it comes the last third. So on the 33rd day the stretch covered is two to one to the part yet to come from the 33rd up to and including the 49th day. Again it is the proportion 2:1 which characterizes the 33rd day.

Until the 33rd day duality still obtains, after the 33rd day unity looms up. It is just as with the 120 years of Moses' life, where we saw that there was servitude till his 80th year, and the non-appearance of the redeemer, whereas *after* the 80th year until the 120th, there was the emancipation and the journey across the desert. As far as the boundaries of Canaan. Likewise a proportion of 2:1.

Similarly there is in the seventh day, in this world, a structure of 2:1. Two parts still entirely oppressed by ignorance and suffering and the third part as 'one' which realizes the way to revelation, the part in which one knows one is travelling towards the Promised Land.

In ancient lore it is represented in a statement that till the 33rd day the pupils of a great sage, Akiba, passed away, but that on the 33rd day this passing away of the sage's pupils ceased. Just as death actually ceases to be after duality has dissolved and unity been achieved.

Tradition expresses this fact in the sage Akiba. On that point, when a person makes ready to pass from the 'two' to the 'one', death must cease to be for the pupils of that sage.

This point is something constantly to be repeated in the structure of daily life. *Not* the historical fact that some two-thousand years ago an 'epidemic' ceased to rage.

People must have an undue sense of nationalism if they insist on commemorating a purely historical fact with so much emphasis as this 33rd day is commemorated. In the meantime a large number of far more serious epidemics and other forms of arbitrary slaughter have come over the Jews, and these, too, have come to an end.

The point is that we should realize that death ceases among the sage's pupils, when they have passed beyond the 'two' and entered the 'one'. In the period of the 'two' there was the strong contrast, the great contradiction. On passing into the 'one' there is reconciliation, there is understanding. And that is what, according to tradition, this sage bestowed on his pupils after the period of death.

But the cutting and reaping continues till it definitely stops at the end of the 49th day. That day the gleanings of the harvest are left in the fields, it is the remainder which there will be in the world when the cutting off of man as fruit of the earth will also have come to an end.

These gleanings are a biblical establishment. The Bible has it that when a field is harvested, there must be a remainder, gleanings. If a man does that in his practice of life in any domain where he appropriates something to himself, then in his own life he abides by the structure which the Bible gives to the world. Then he lives up to the Bible and his expression is in harmony with the expression God gave to creation in matter. Then there exists unity between the substance and the phenomenon.

On the 49th day there is the final harvesting. And then, on the 50th day God appears on Mount Sinai, there is the revelation of God's words. Then there is the recognition of the purpose of everything, then God appears down here in this world. The old world, the world of the seventh day, has completed itself in the 49th day, and now on the fiftieth day begins the new world.

And at that moment in time, when the crops have been harvested and the eighth son, Asher, has just been born, there is the break in the enumeration of the births of the children of Jacob. At the very birth of the eighth, indeed, harvesting is finished and people are returning home from the fields.

Again we notice the relationship between the various realms which belong together, according to the systematism of the Bible. And again this emphasis on the transition from this world to the next. This intermezzo exists on account of the very significance of that transition. Reuben brings the 'doedaim', a fruit which is the expression of a certain substance. This substance expresses itself in the sense that this fruit causes an attraction and a merging between the male and the female. An integrating of that which so far had expressed itself as a contrast.

So it is a striking concurrence again. Exactly when the seventh day is completed, that is brought as something found, which brings together, which 'unites' the male and the female.

In the world of the seventh day the joining of male and female, i.e. of every contrast, finds expression in the word 'arissa' which means 'betrothal'. The couple know they are destined for each other, but they also know that the actual being together will not take place until a later stage, the marriage. And that marriage is in the subsequent world. This world is merely the preparation for it, it is the way to union, on which through the promise of being for each other, the couple renounce all thoughts and actions which might do harm to that promise. It is the way of the seventh day, the way preparatory to that union, leading to the borders of Canaan in the assurance that Canaan will be entered. And that future marriage between the man and the woman is like the marriage of all things still present in this world as duality, but because of the promise, knowing that there will be a marriage some time, and therefore ready to prepare for this coming event. Similarly the relationship of body and soul in this world is that of being betrothed and it is not until the coming world that there will be the marriage, the definite union.

At this juncture there are the 'mandrakes' which will bring about the union of the man and the woman. The name 'doedaim' is spelled 4–6–4–1–10–40. It is the plural form of 'doed', 4–6–4. The word doed also means beloved. And it has the same structure as the name David, similarly spelled 4–6–4.

In the Song of Solomon, in which indeed is expressed this searching and yearning of the man and the woman, these 'doedaim' also play a part. What comes at the end in the Song of Solomon, the actual union, is accomplished in the eighth day.

That is why in Jewish tradition the Song of Solomon, besides being read during the weekly transition from the sixth day to the seventh, hence on Friday night, is read at Easter, at the advent of the seventh day, when the craving for unity between the man and the woman is becoming apparent. They begin their quest of each other. It is the way through this world, the world in which man tries to bridge the opposites, tries to understand the purpose of life and therewith proves to be ripe for marriage, for yearning after unity.

And on the 50th day after the exodus from Egypt, after that transition from the sixth day to the seventh, it is Pentecost, the eighth day with the revelation of the purpose of life.

The cutting of the grain is finished and the book Ruth is 'read'. For therein it is stated that at the end of the harvesting the woman who remained solitary, is found by the man. Boaz takes Ruth to be his wife and from this union is born Obed, from whom is born Issai and then David. The story of the 50th day tells how David comes, the parent of the Messiah.

For Pentecost, the 50th day is exactly the time of the new King, the Messiah, of the king anointed with 'oil' which has the structure of 'heaven'. The 50th day inaugurates the eighth cycle, the seven times seven are over.

This bringing into prominence at Pentecost the phenomenon David as the ancestor of the Messiah is similarly stated by our systematism. For the eighth day *is* the day of the Messiah. And the Messiah comes because the man has found the woman again. The woman who came from afar, returned and was united with the man.

This, in fact, is the relationship between the name of David and these mandrakes, either with the root 4–6–4. And that is why these doedaim make their appearance when the reaping is done.

About these 'doedaim' it says in ancient lore that they have the shape of a human being, that they are hidden *within* the earth like a root, and that anyone who uproots them will die in consequence.

In the case of Rueben who brought the 'doedaim' with him, it is related that his ass had been tied to a bush, and that the animal while pulling itself free had dragged forth the root and that it then lay dead by the side of it, when Reuben came. In this way Rueben was able to bring these 'doedaim' along with him.

This apparently childish story, too, has to be understood in the light of the knowledge of the structure of the world. These stories all of them express the relationship between things in the form of images. But then one has to connect these images again with their substance in the same way as it is done in the Bible.

Tradition always expresses itself in these images. Via the knowledge of the word these images offer the formulae which hide the substance. And it is the same formulae which the Bible makes use of. Whoever stops at the image, will of course get a rather strange conception of things and he will assuredly not grasp the meaning of the story. To such a man it will look like childish sport.

But if one knows that the images have a very special purpose, that, if correctly formulated at least, they will at all times enable us to translate them into their substance, then we shall take these images very seriously as a specific mode of expression.

For that reason there is often this utterly incomprehensible detail of image, the enumeration of rather infantile trivialities. The same phenomenon is seen in mythology and in fairy-tales which partly find their origin in a world which possessed knowledge of these things.

The image even is a very good basis for formulating. An 'ass', for instance, cannot be misunderstood as an image. A longwinded definition or a scanty one would no longer be understood in other times with different modes of thought-expression. The form of things in this world does not change in the course of the whole world-period.

And therefore this form is the best mode of expression; starting from the assumption, though, that one realizes that the image of the form is the expression of something real, something essential; that one knows the bridge of the word and can always translate the image back into the essential. In the same way we shall have to consider the story of the doedaim and Reuben's ass. The story tells us that the person who wants to remove this integrating force from this world, shall die. That this unifying and integrating in the new world can only be attained through death. In another way it is impossible.

It is man who all through the seventh day is still covered with earth, is hidden from view. Bringing this man to view is the condition sine qua non for joining the contrasts, for the union of that which is expressed in principle as the man and the woman. This calling forth, however, is identical with causing death.

Now in this story it is the ass who meets death, not Reuben himself, although it is Reuben who acquires the doedaim. The ass is the image, the expression in matter of that which in its substance is the bearer of the burden in this world. The ass, as indeed is still well known in everyday parlance, is the body which in this world bears man, which gives man the possiblity of expression here in this world.

The word for ass is 'chamor', spelled cheth-mem-resh, 8–40–200. As far as structure is concerned it is the same word as loam, 'chemer', which is also the expression for earthly matter, and for the body. Similarly, 8–40–200. The sum-total of the components is 248, a total which we repeatedly come across elsewhere. We saw it in the principle 'hibaram'– 'when they were created', in the opening of the second tale of creation. And it was the same number which formed the name Abraham. Even viewed from that side it is a mode of expression, a phenomenon in this world.

The number 248, however, is also used in ancient lore to indicate the number of parts of the human skeleton. Of that which bears man through this world.

Thus it is the basis for producing visible man in this world. Just as does 'chemer', loam, the matter of this earth.

In ancient lore the number of 'positive' actions which man has to perform to build his existence in this world, is also divided into 248 parts. These 248 proceed from statements made in the Bible and handed on as such by ancient lore with its knowledge of the structure of the Bible and that of the world. In fulfilling this 248 as much as possible in his life, man would bring his existence into harmony with the structure of the world as it has been revealed by the Bible, and therewith give sense to his existence in the great totality.

Over against these 248 things which man has to do in his life, there are the 365 which he has to avoid, the 'negative' actions.

Through this complex of positive and negative actions which all the time present an alternative of either doing things or no, leaving off things or no, man can effect the connection between the world of duality and the origin. Thus he fulfills the purpose of his existence. According to tradition the purpose of existence finds expression also in his body in the 248 parts of the skeleton, and the 365 parts of the body of 'flesh'. These parts, 613 all in all, alien altogether to anatomy which is based on perception, and can never be reconciled to it, render the pattern of the Bible in the phenomenon man, and also in the way to his destination. Man's acting in regard to the ever-present alternative, determines whether he follows that way or no.

The 248 positive actions, the activities, are called the male aspect, crystallized in man's body in the skeleton which bears and causes motion, whereas the 365 'negative', the passive, actions represent the female aspect, expressed in the body as the 'flesh'-aspect, which did come, indeed to fill the place of the woman.

Now if a person in his life of action, in his course through the happenings, actually lives in this way, he likewise builds up a life with his actions, a life in a more real plane than that expressed in his physical aspect and which because of it, effects more real living, through his being engaged with the world, effecting the connection between the opposites, between substance and phenomenon, between soul and body, between the man and the woman.

The complete man has a body and a soul; the body as the phenomenon in this world, the soul as the substance. Now this duality expresses itself in the body too, has put its stamp on it. And the skeleton is the expression of that which in complete man is the soul, and the 'flesh' is the expression of what the body is in man in his totality. Hence the skeleton is the male part and the 'flesh' the female part of the body. The whole body in this world is to the soul as the female part is to the male part of total man. In this world with its female character man expresses himself with his female aspect, the body. And in its potentialities of growth and in its development, this body in its turn runs parallel to the beast.

Leaving behind the body, leaving behind that which caused man to move, and act here, cannot be expressed differently in the plane of the images of this world; it is expressed there as dismounting or leaving the beast behind, or the death of this mount. In principle it is also taking off the shoes made of leather. In brief, it is getting off the animal's back as one's seat in this world. In mounting the beast, man makes his appearance in this world of matter.

Another mode of expression which amounts to the same thing is covering oneself with clothes. Just as the outer covering is the sheath veiling the substance, the nucleus, just as the woman envelops the man, just as the body encloses the soul, thus the clothes envelop man. Everything 'outside' is parallel to the body, and everything 'inside' in the pattern, corresponds with the soul.

Taking off or changing clothes therefore is a discarding or changing of a form of life, of appearing in life. Doing these things in this life is equal to an essential change in one's phenomenal form. And when in a transition of periods or worlds, the Bible wants to express leaving behind a body or the acquisition of a new body, it cannot in this plane of crystallization be expressed any other way except as dismounting the animal or taking off of one's clothes.

This way of expressing things in these images shows that real man, the essential, cannot be changed. It is merely man's way of expressing himself which changes from one condition to the next, from world to world.

Producing the 'doedaim' from the earth, to take them along to the other world therefore brings with it the death of Reuben's 'ass'. The body as it existed in the world of the seventh day, dies. Indeed, this dying is the characteristic thing about existence in that world of the seventh day. For every moment does the body change, does a condition die, never to return. And this death of the body is at the same time the drawing forth of a new substance from the earth which in the coming world will unite the man and woman, like all other opposites.

Reuben himself, however, passes just as he is from the seventh day into the eighth. Nothing about him changes any more. We shall by and by revert to this course through the days and the worlds.

This new man, therefore, is the man of the 'doedaim' and he joins the man and the woman together. Just as the Messiah, the son of David — with the same root 4–6–4 as the 'doedaim' — effects the unity of the contrasts, extending this to *all* things which are separated from each other. The 'fours' on either side are joined together by the 'six', the hook.

The word 'doed', 4–6–4, as beloved, also means 'dod', 'uncle'. And it is curious to see how in the Bible the principle of the beloved is expressed in the place taken by the 'uncle'. It is as if the place of the woman that has to be emancipated is on a lower level. Just as the earth lies lower than heaven, and man is lower than God. Similarly in the systematism of the patriarchs and matriarchs the female is alway below the male.

Even with the first man, the woman is one degree further removed in development. She came forth from a unity of male and female which existed initially, after which the female was taken out of the male. And this female returns to the male out of whom it was in reality taken. Thus even there the man is the 'clod', the 'uncle', of the woman; even there he stands one level closer to the origin than the woman.

With the patriarchs, in whom the principle of the proportion male-female is expressed, we notice the same thing. In the graphic down below it is clearly to be seen.

We have now seen from various sides that the structure of the Bible recognizes these seventh and eighth days as a sequence of different worlds. At the same time it has become clear from diverse examples how this structure pervades the veriest details, how the pattern of this structure puts its stamp on all parts. We have also seen this story constantly turning up, this story of the transition from one world to the next, from one day to the next, demonstrating itself throughout, even unto the structure of the words and the very names of things, like for instance the 'doedaim'. So this is the right moment to say a word on the manner in which the Bible expresses these transitions in its chronology. It will be yet another opportunity to allow the miracles hidden therein, to penetrate to our consciousness.

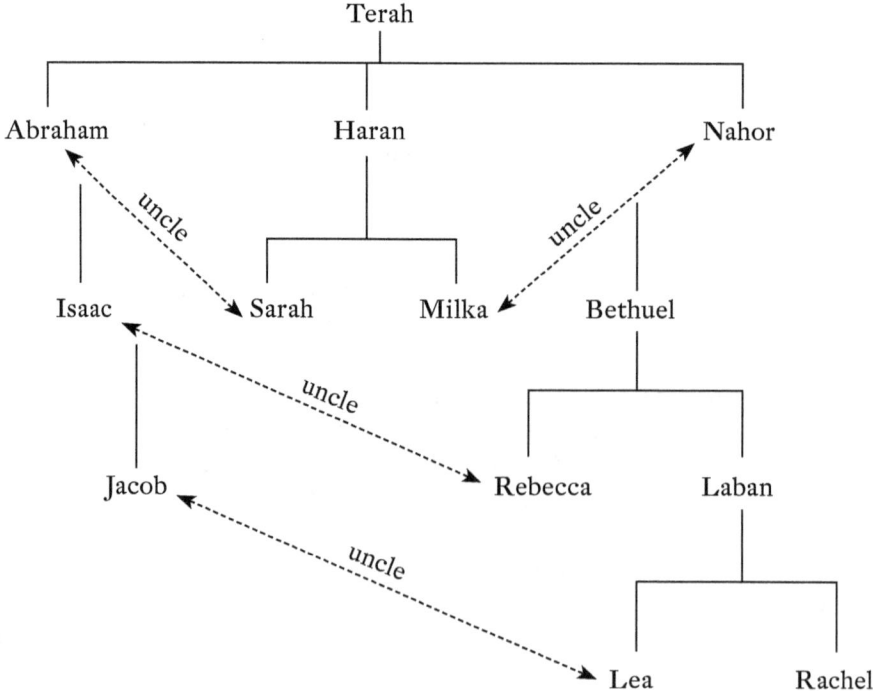

8
The Chronology of the Bible

There are as serious misconceptions about the chronology of the Bible as about a great number of other aspects of the Book. Although a great deal in this field thrusts itself on the reader to be taken seriously, people pass lightly over it and then remark superciliously that 'all this cannot be so, anyway'.

One of the modern misconceptions — modern in the sense of pertaining to these latter centuries — consists in looking on the Bible as a kind of history book, relating events especially of the national history of the Jewish people. That these events prove in many respects not to tally with each other, and worse than that, cannot literally tally with reality, is rather painful. But all kinds of excuses have been made in connection with the age of the Bible, mistakes liable to have crept in, in course of time, and the natural childlike exaggerations perpetrated by primitive ancestors. What was left, was quite worthwhile yet, and if one was not too critically disposed, the principle events might in broad outline be considered fairly correct. All the same there is quite a lot that does not tally; and certainly not, if one would care to take the details seriously too.

After all the things we have discovered in the foregoing about the structure of the Bible, the question arises if the Bible, also in regard to its chronology, does not contain a great deal besides the historic account of a certain nation, however interesting this may be in itself.

If the substance of creation were expressed by God in the Bible in terms of historicity also, then the years or days in the Bible would have to render that real structure.

And as we have already seen in the foregoing, there is this crystallization in time, just as it exists in the word; and in the image in space. Therefore biblical chronology must render something different from a tale about the historical development of a people in antiquity. The fact that the Bible is still taken so seriously by millions of people shows that they realize that it is not only that, but that the Bible is infinitely more.

Historically the Bible is not incorrect either. The only thing is that the standards by which the Bible are to be measured are emphatically not our space-time standards. If they were, they would lose themselves in endlessness or they would create confusion in adding up dissimilar things.

One of the very first facts which strike us when we consider the Bible in its historical account, is that the Bible evidently neglects to join periods of time together, in stating for instance that King David was born in such and such a year after creation or that Joshua occupied Canaan in such and such a year after creation. It is not even mentioned in what year the great Flood took place, although the year is easily to be computed from the text.

Whereas in other fields numbers are mentioned in scrupulous detail and there are a great many added up for the benefit of the reader, till he is bored to death, the Bible omits doing so with evident principled stubbornness where years are concerned. So there is something rather special about this adding up of years.

The longest period of time the Bible mentions is the age of Methuselah, namely 969 years. Nowhere do we find the number one thousand, let alone any number beyond one thousand. And those periods of the first decade of generations are very long indeed, as compared with the subsequent periods with their shorter lifetimes.

The longest period found in Pentateuch after this first decade of generations, ending with Noah, is the statement that Shem lived five hundred years after his son Arpachshad had been begotten. And after this the statement that the servitude in Egypt had lasted 430 years. And in the later books of the Bible there is the statement that the temple was built 480 years after the exodus from Egypt, which is the longest period mentioned.

A striking fact is for instance that when the kings of Judah and Israel are mentioned, it is always stated how long they reigned, but not how long their dynasty lasted or how long it was after the building of the temple or after the disruption of the kingdom.

If certain events in time are to be localized, for instance the appearance of certain prophets, it is merely stated: in such and such a year of such and such a king. How comfortable it would have been to the historians, if there had been the statement 'in such and such a year after Adam', or after Noe, or after Abraham. But no, to the contrary, when even a child might add it up by himself – it is true there would be some difficulties on the way – it is evidently omitted on *principle*. Even in those places where there are no difficulties whatsoever and adding up would have been a small matter.

Obviously the Bible thus means to state that adding up periods of time cannot be done without more ado, because in specific cases – i.e. the cases when the Bible itself does not add up things – one would add up dissimilar entities. Something like, 12 chairs and 3 tables make 15; 15 what? Not 15 chairs, nor 15 tables either. One might say: 15 pieces of furniture. Surely, in *that* sense one might probably also add up the years. Provided one connects the conception 'year' with the standard pertaining to it and does not continually make use of one and the same standard.

Obviously there is *not* a continuity in time such as we imagine. For this reason the Bible *cannot* add up the years in that sense. Adding up presupposes the existence of a continuity.

We cannot fit together the years of the Bible without more ado, even though a year on earth has to do with the earth's revolution round the sun. Something else proves to crystallize in time as well, and that is the reason why the periods of time *cannot* be strung together and measured over the whole length by one and the same standard. The longest period of comparable years is less than a thousand years. And *these* thousand years cannot be compared to any other thousand years anywhere else in the Bible, or with a hundred years or with ten years elsewhere.

The events mentioned in the Bible also show that something is simultaneously changing in the universe, and with it in the standards of time.

The Great Flood, apart from all other consequences, proves radically to change the aspect of the world, according to the story in the Bible. It is just as if the whole universe became different. The same thing might be stated about the passage in Joshua, where the sun is supposed to have stood still. If one is to take the statement seriously at all and not to wave it aside as a 'primitive exaggeration', it implies that something entirely new, something entirely different was coming. And that in the images of this world it simply had to be expressed in *that* way. The same holds good in the case of Hezekiah in his disease when the shadow moved backwards ten degrees. Here again a statement about a modification in the universe.

More circumstantially and in greater detail are these modifications in the aspect of time expressed in ancient lore. We see from it that ancient lore considers it rather self-evident that the aspects of the world and of time should repeatedly be modified and that therefore the periods of time do not form a continuum.

Thus ancient lore says for instance, that after the eating of the tree of knowledge a star was removed from the universe, owing to which there was a complete change in the proportions, in the standards on earth. The same thing is stated about the time of the Flood, when two stars were removed on account of which that very 'Flood' could submerge the earth.

More clearly still does tradition speak when it states that the 'distance' between heaven and earth kept changing. Always when certain events take place in the Bible which change the face of the earth, it is related how heaven comes nearer or moves away, dependent on the nature of the event. And this implies of course an entirely different valuation of the standard of time. It goes without saying that astronomically speaking this is a horror. But the Bible knows no continuity in this astronomy either. Admittedly, to the world as it appears to us *now*, applies the astronomical aspect we know at present, at least as much as observation allows us to. And to this our world applies the continuity of this chronology as the astronomical complex of the moment presents it to us.

The Bible, however, quite deliberately breaks through this continuity and emphatically tells us a story of *dis*continuity. A story which enacts itself in different planes, a story taking place in different worlds, although somehow or other this earth evidently is the place of action.

To prevent all misunderstanding: with 'world' I do not mean our globe as it appears to us now, and with 'other worlds' I do not mean Mars or Venus for instance, but with 'world' I mean the situation which *now* presents itself to us as reality, and with 'other worlds' those situations which differ from this present reality.

The world we know at present is a world with phenomena valid to it exclusively, according to this point of view. In this our world of the present, it is impossible for instance for angels to go about, for God to speak to people in the way it evidently *was* possible at other periods of time, according to the Bible As well as according to ancient lore and the mythologies of non-biblical origin.

Tradition even goes so far in this separation of periods of time as to consider it impossible for instance to have in our present world a temple with the temple-service pertaining to it as it is described in the Bible.

Owing to all sorts of circumstances this world has changed in position and relationship in regard to heaven, and because of it, it is *different*. Sacrifices in this world would simply mean slaughterings of beasts and there would be no sense in them. Therefore they are impossible now.

That is why ancient lore speaks of the coming of a new world with a new 'King', the Messiah, after which all relationships would alter and people would see and understand things differently again. And *then* sacrifices would acquire an entirely different aspect and they would be considered normal, necessary, nay even right, as pertaining to life.

Thus the Bible tells us for instance that sacrifices were impossible in Egypt and that they could only be brought in the desert, beyond Egypt. We shall revert to this in our, rather summary, discussion of the tale of Egypt and the sacrifices. The fact that 'bringing sacrifice' was out of the question in Egypt, points to a certain structure of life there, on account of which sacrifices there would indeed be 'something gruesome'.

All during the servitude in Egypt God does not appear either. Only at the very end, when redemption has commenced, does God come; and after this, in the 'desert', God is perceptible all day, and every day. Egypt, according to the biblical story, is a world utterly different from the world before and after, where God appears repeatedly and where sacrifices obviously are a very good thing.

The world, as we know it *now*, is entirely different, and only the image together with the word, which can depict the substance, enables us to find out what life is like in different situations, with different relationships, and gives us an opportunity to learn to know the purpose of life through comparison of man's progress across these different worlds.

Now, if one were to add up the years of the Bible with the years of our reality of the moment, and argue that the world has shown a continual development these 5,700 years and odd since creation, one is just as much at variance with the statement of the Bible as when maintaining that milliards of years have passed in a continuum since creation.

One should rather argue that bringing into account the discontinuity of the biblical story, in calculating the incomparability of the various periods in regard to the circumstances, more than 5,700 years have actually passed since creation, years which in the diverse periods are a measure for entirely different things. And if we assume — altogether hypothetically too — that a continuum has obtained throughout, then indeed the history of the world cannot be measured, and milliards of years would merely denote that, to all intents and purposes, it is practically infinite to our present-day understanding. Just as in the universe the impression is created of its having existed for millions of light-years.

As soon as the idea of continuous development gets a grip on us, space and time indeed become 'round'; infinite to our mind.

But since the Bible quite distinctly states no continuity in time, there is no sense in discussing historicity according to *our* view of time, according to *our* aspect of the world, of biblical events, from the moment of God's appearance on earth and the creation in six days.

The biblical story also expresses itself in the world in its present aspect, in its present relationship to heaven; it also crystallizes in the world as it is now. And since this world — we shall revert to it again — has the nature of globular infinity, the biblical events also express themselves in that sense. It might be compared to the reflection of a thing in a mirror which, owing to its concavity, gives the image something terribly elongated. But then it is that the aspect of this world and observation in this world will reflect that which the world has within it as mirror-formula.

It is not our intention to look at the Bible through this mirror. We want to look at the Bible as it offers *itself.* The Bible itself tells us and again it is repeated and underlined in the traditions which 'translate' and specify the Bible for us, that there is discontinuity, that the various periods are to be looked upon as separate phenomena side by side; that they are like separate worlds side by side with each other.

Man, too, and all things created progressed through that discontinuity. In essence man remained the same, just as a year essentially remained the same. It is only the images of the various periods which cannot be compared. One simply cannot portray in present-day reality how certain events took place in another reality. It is only through the word that those events taken from various periods are joined together. If one should try to picture the images of such different periods, one would get unreal results. It is very much as if one were to see spirits appearing during a spiritistic seance. Things of the past belonging to such different periods cannot materialize in our world. Therefore one should let it alone, and restrain one's curiosity to see it *all the same.* It is only through the word that we can have contact with them, and it will then be a most vital and stimulating contact. It will inspire *our* phenomenon with life. It is this *progress* through the various situations, through the various worlds the Bible speaks of, not the length of years, measured throughout all those periods. The Bible purposely does not speak of it. The years there have a different meaning. As soon as we know this meaning, we can certainly add up the years. For then they will not represent a historical development, but will be an expression of the manner in which God causes the substance of creation to crystallize in time.

So there is no sense in examining, let us say, the journey across the desert from the standpoint of our world of continuity, the world which allowed the conception of evolution to come into prominence. It is quite likely it exists somewhere in some corner or other in utterly distorted proportions because of the curve of our mirror. But it will also show a totally different relationship – distorted also – with other events, and it will also act strangely in regard to the conception of continuity and the doctrine of evolution. In them, among other things, there is no room for a 'column of fire' and a 'column of smoke' with which God appears; in them is no room for those 'forty years' of the journey, nor is there room for that multitude of many millions travelling through the desert. In the atmosphere of the doctrine of continuity and the doctrine of evolution there is at best room for a kind of migration of nomadic tribes under the leadership of a powerful and intelligent super-sheikh acting as law-giver who, like the sensible man, he was, borrowed a great deal from the knowledge and practices of established, well-educated neighbouring nations. Quite rightly, too.

So there is no sense in analysing the behaviour of anybody special in the Bible from the point of view of our world. For everything would in that case look strange and at any rate one would get quite a wrong picture.

The Bible wants to tell us *how* the essential expresses itself in time, and therefore one has to take the temporal story of the Bible as such a crystallization of the essential. It is only through connecting the biblical events in time with the essence – and the Bible gives plenty of opportunity for through the word and the systematism – that they will acquire significance. Only then does the Bible show how things really are, how the world is made and what the special events lead to. They lead to certain things because there is the law of creation which has hallmarked everything. A law, based on the principle that all things, divorced for the sake of creation, are to unite again in the source of origin, a principle which in the terminology of our emotions expresses itself in such conceptions as 'goodness', 'mercy', because reunion is ultimately bound to come, in spite of man's thoughts and actions being often differently directed.

When one is deeply conscious of the fact that the Bible must not be read as if it were a history book in which side by side with harsh and cruel things we come across preaching of morals and public spirit one can try and find out what is *actually* meant with this chronology often indicated very minutely, down to the very days of a specific month. And maybe it will then be clear what is really meant with the periods of longer duration, as long as they are not measured by *our* vision of time.

From the foregoing we know that time was measured by the standard of the 'four'. We have seen that the 40 days, the 40 years and the 400 years intend to render something very definite, and the 5, the 50 and the 500 are expressive of a new world. Not, because there were no other means of expression, but obviously because the 'four' has to do with the reality of the conception: 'very far away and very great' for this our world.

A distance of 'four cubits' is considered a real distance. Obviously such a distance of four cubits would in *our* standards amount to a separation-breech, a partition in the real. If a milligram of some distance or other, or a few degrees rising or falling of body temperature can be lethal, it is just as possible that a certain distance in matter expresses marked alterations in things real, even though in our plane we have not yet been able to prove by means of our causality-doctrine whether it is so and whether it is possible.

Thus ancient lore tells us casually, and of course contrary to our knowledge based on observation, that the land Canaan has a length of 400 parsa (a certain measure) and a width of 400 parsa. That a man can cover 10 parsa a day and would therefore need 40 days to traverse the land in one direction. Quite obviously something entirely different is meant from the geographically charted land on the Eastern shores of the Mediterranean. And that people were so naïve as to accept these measures as geographically satisfactory even in *those* days is just as little to be believed.

Thus the outer walls of the temple, i.e. the surrounding walls, are stated to measure 500 cubits in length and similarly in width.

The 400 of the land and the 500 of the central supra-mondial place must surely give us food for thought now that we know a little more about the numbers 400 and 500.

The bold assumption in tradition that the whole nation, i.e. millions of people, could be assembled in that one place, inside the temple-territory, within those 500 cubits, and that, though they were thronging the place, there yet was enough room when all of them bent down, defies all sense of proportion in this world, so much so that one can either speak of chauvinistic exaggeration or, supposing one knows more about this far-reaching systematism, one must realize that here are mentioned measurements of an entirely different world, a world which cannot be measured by our standards.

Now when this same tradition has it, for instance, that at the translation of the Bible into Greek, the earth leaped away 400 parsa again, one can of course shrug one's scientific shoulders at it, but then one only wilfully ignores this 400. Obviously the world is measured by different standards and it is seen in a different plane. In a plane where completely different standards obtain.

We shall see further on that the waters of the Flood rose 15 cubits over 'the mountains' while those moutains themselves appear to be 15 cubits high too, the ark, mark you, being 30 cubits high. Considering the impressiveness of the systematism, in the tale of the Flood, it cannot be waved aside as a naïve representation of some kind of troglodytes. Many there are who would be glad to take *that* aspect of the stories in this way, to get over their alarm that there might be a world after all, different from the one we perceive and which we are so eager to subdue.

When ancient lore for instance has it that King Solomon was king of the whole world, that he understood the language of beasts, etc., again we are not faced with nationalistic exaggeration, but it fits in exactly with the real systematism. It merely shows that the Bible is *not* a history book of a small nation, that the tale merely expresses itself in the history of one nation – which in itself is something very special – but that it renders the purpose of all life, life's happenings throughout the worlds, far beyond our conceptions of space-time. And because of it the Bible is so very important, world-embracing, life-embracing. With it the Bible suddenly is different from a book for 'edification', for educating to honest, quiet people, a useful constituent of the affluent state.

For the affluent state is not the goal of life, the purpose of man in this world, but life itself is man's purpose, the meaning of life plus the meaning of death.

And now I have come to the fundamental question: is the Bible a reference-guide for this life, a kind of recipe-book, a king of 'book on etiquette'; is the Bible a book 'to get away from things', just as people like to go camping in a tent to have a breathing-interval from 'status'-hunting; does the Bible give us strength to fight the battle of life with an eye on a future in a 'better world'? Is the Bible a book to comfort us when the world, to our mind, has dealt with us disproportionately harshly; is it a book for 'quiet hours'?

Or is the Bible something entirely different? May it not be, *after all*, the communication from God – and none but God could make it – to all people about their whole life? Not only about life here – these 70 or 100 and odd years – but reaching far beyond, embracing much more, really embracing all man's life. The whence, how, whither, and especially the purpose of it all.

Why, what would be the good of a reference-guide for our society, when one has to leave it *all the same*? Supposing all technical improvements were to guarantee man an average life of 150 years, even so the time would come when he would have to pass away. Then what? Man is quite willing to believe things will come all right, but nobody can tell him anything about it. Would God have placed man here in this world with all its harshness and cruelty – as far as history goes back it always was just as harsh and cruel – did God mean to tell man that he must die, because a rather vague, historically not quite acceptable, ancestor with whom he does not feel he has anything to do whatsoever, had sinned one day, and would God then have left man to his own devices? For all that rosy-pink and sky-blue tales about a heaven full of angels do *not* originate from the Bible, most assuredly *not*. Has one to believe all kinds of people, specialized in tending comfort, who tell us that everything will come all right? But how do they know? And how do those that threaten us with hell and damnation know all about it? The Bible never mentions it. It is mere man-made deduction and man-made construction. Well, the Bible *is* something different. The Bible *definitely* is the communication from God to men how things are; it is *not* just a book for this life; it is a communication for all lives, before and after this world, and before and after this life, and it has the same attraction in all worlds. Because it exists in all worlds.

Tradition for instance expresses it like this, that in the other world, too, taking up the Bible gives the greatest joy to man there.

As has been mentioned, the Bible expresses in images of this world *how* this course is through the worlds and the lives. For instance 'man leaving Egypt' is an expression in the images of *this* world how it is when he passes away from a life, from the world. Why he passes out of the world, what he came into the world for, whither he is bound, and how things are over there. All this is expressed in images of this world. For with our qualities in this life we could not even see another mode of expression, nor understand it, even *if* we were to see it. It would be even more alien than the pink and the sky-blue and the jolly little angels with their downy wings; it would all be beyond the scope of our perceptivity.

And these images are expressed in words which build the bridge for understanding another world in which we can find the essence of the story. And these images are also fitted into a systematism in space – time which similarly leads us to that substance, through which we discover the identity, the parallelism, between the systematism of the word and that of the events.

Just as a good father is eager to tell his child how everything is, why it is so, and wants to save his child from all fright and horror of the unknown.

People talk a lot about the God of Love, but assign to Him qualities of arbitrariness and sadism which they would indignantly refute for themselves. For they are loving fathers themselves. They like to teach others, even strangers, just because one feels the need of telling others how things are.

The Bible definitely tells us how life goes on. It is up to us to translate the images in which the tale must express itself in this world into terms of reality. And *then* one does no longer need any images, for by then one has built up within oneself something entirely different. Something not to be expressed in images, and often not even in words.

When you receive a present, carefully wrapped up, you do not confine yourself to observing you take it for granted that it is a fine present, only to put it away unopened in a cupboard. The joy both of the receiver and the giver lies in unwrapping and admiring the present, the discovery of ever new facets, of ever more unsuspected surprises. In a similar way does the joy about the gift, which the Bible is, arise as soon as it is unveiled, and the many miracles are perceived radiating forth continually from this present. It would be most unkind and unfeeling if you were to nod at the giver and say you take it for granted that it is very fine.

Now this communication by the Bible should be quite exact; just as clear or rather much clearer than the things we can perceive in nature on which we have built up our sciences. It must not be so as to allow all kinds of speculations to be based on it, that for instance anybody can pick out a text at random and draw from it exactly *that* which suits him at a certain moment. Neither should it be so as to allow of any conjuring tricks likewise adapted to the occasion.

Therefore the story of life must have the same exact structure as those which we indicated with a few examples in the foregoing, bearing on the structure of the world as it was effected through creation. The tale of time has been given to mankind just as exact as that of the contents of the events and it can form the foundation for our implicit faith in the purpose of life, for our entire thought and action.

Of course we shall have to learn from this tale that the images are the mode of expression for this space-time world. Here too we shall have to make an effort to penetrate more deeply into the essence of things.

One of the things which will readily strike us is the fact that there are in the Bible so many aspects which, although expressed in images pertaining to this life, do not occur in our life or have a secondary place in it. For example the stories about angels, prophets speaking with God, God making His appearance, the existence of sacrifices or the improbable ages of people. Why this abundance of communications which play no part in our present-day existence? The same question is often asked about the organization of the world itself and that of nature. Here too side by side with particularly useful phenomena there are a good number which make us wonder what purpose they serve, whether nature did not make a mistake here, or that it continued developing in a direction, obviously useless at present, merely because long ago that development might have been necessary. One wonders why there is this immense waste of seed in nature, when only a very small part of it comes to life; why certain organs still exist which may at one time have had their use, but which have long since ceased to be useful and now have a rather disturbing effect; one may wonder why there are barren deserts and zones of unbearable heat or unbearable cold. Similarly one is justified in wondering why there is so much apparent cruelty in nature and so much pain and suffering. And the same applies to the world of men. If everything is really meant for the best, why is there so much injustice, why club-law, and the law of the jungle, why all those diseases, why all those monsters, why gloomy inscrutable death which with mechanical regularity collects its daily ration. And that all this should continue good deeds and prayers notwithstanding. That there is obviously little connection, if one is without prejudice, between personal conduct and belief on the one hand and personal destiny on the other.

In either case our questions result from the fact that we relate everything exclusively to our world and to our standards. According to views which have grown in us through certain events, fully to be discussed by and by, everything is expected to have its use for this world so as to be noticeable to our perception. If things are outside the scope of the usefulness for our world, we are apt to reject them as essentially impossible or at least as erroneous and useless. In fact, we could ourselves write a more useful and much more scientific Bible and, if possessed of sufficient technical ability, we would build a more useful and efficient world, at least we would transform the existing world into one which functioned a great deal better.

When on the one hand the Bible actually deals with things which do not exist here or which are utterly useless to our world — such as for instance animal sacrifices — and on the other hand there are things in nature which seem to us almost pointless wastage, and which are opposed to our standards of justice and order, we might feel justified in asking the question if there is sense in it *after all,* and if it *is* possible after all, if only one were to include other standards, other worlds and other lives as well in one's considerations.

May not those angels, those sacrifices, etc. have some sense after all and be normal in other lives (planes of consciousness) of that selfsame man of whom the Bible speaks, and may not this so-called wasted seed, this life, often so unnecessarily brief, this being saddled with useless or even aggravating organs, have a great deal of sense, after all, for other planes where all this exists as well, and may it not be so that all these seemingly useless things are merely an expression of those other planes *in this our world?* An expression which, just because it is beyond the proportions normal to this world, directs our attention to the reality of other qualities, other potentialities.

One of the important influences on this life here on earth is that very certainty of death. The only certainty about which we further know nothing whatsoever. Except our knowledge based on perception which cannot but draw the inference of our complete disappearance. And even spiritistic experimenting does not get beyond an oppressive probability of a meagre and rather uncanny existence after death.

It is this very abyss of death which causes man to turn to utilizing this life definitely and intensively, which utilizing also implies man's banishing the very thought of death from his consciousness, thus playing an utterly unreal game. For we know that death *does* exist and that we do everything to forget it quickly when it comes near. And this game of 'a world which is a sufficiency unto itself', is unsatisfactory. Man knows it quite well and at set intervals he smashes it up.

Now man often draws the Bible within this game. The Bible is supposed to tell us how to gain a seat in heaven, if we live respectably in this world, or in hell if we do not. And also that God joined the game by covering a great deal with the cloak of charity, after having first confronted man with all sorts of unsoluble problems, unprepared. It is the 'utility'-idea which imposes such an interpretation and such a meaning on the Bible.

The Bible, however, is something vastly different, the Bible is a creation more grand than that which we perceive in nature and in the universe. And this Bible, this creation, including all times and all worlds, has been bestowed on man to serve as a foundation for his knowledge of the purpose of life.

It is astonishing how in course of time people have come to view all this in the wrong way.

We have for instance the expression 'the fear of God', and again 'the awful' deeds of God. When we take the word 'fear' of God, for instance, in Hebrew we have 'jirath', in the expression 'jirath shamayim', i.e. 'fear of heaven' or 'jirath adonai' or 'fear of the Lord'.

Now this word for fear has the same root as the word for 'see', spelled jod-resh-aleph, 10–200–1. And the word translated as 'awful' i.e. 'nora', spelled nun-resh-aleph, 50–200–1, is derived from the same root. So what is really meant and what man is urged to do, is not trembling before a fickle, vindictive power, but merely to be willing to *perceive* God and heaven and be impressed by the grandeur, the profound depth, the coherence, thus to come to cherish a feeling of reverence and immense bliss. As it says in the Bible (Deut. 6:5) 'Thou shalt love the Lord thy God will all thy heart, and with all shy soul and with all thy might'. For it is only through learning to know the miracle of the world, of the life of the Bible, it is only through *this* that can arise the love which God seeks in order to make man abolish divorcing heaven and earth, thus to bestow on man the greatest possible good.

Man is eager to act as a guide on a journey through things wonderful. It may be things intellectual or a journey through lovely scenery. Man is eager to point out to his fellow-travellers everything beautiful and he is happy with their interest. That is what can make teaching so attractive.

God has made heaven and earth and He has laid the purpose of it all in a communication, a revelation which He has given to man, to understand everything about Him, to see how wonderfully everything has been arranged down to the smallest details, why it is so and whither it leads.

Wanting to find out how things are and why everything is just as it is, is an affair without end, as infinite as creation in space-time. Viewing this creation through the Bible is the work of a lifetime here and it gives bliss infinite, as infinite as creation appears to be.

For this reason has God made it all, and all this He has laid down in a wondrous way, in a miracle even greater than creation itself, in that Book, in that story of the world. That it may be seen, that it may be taken in within the scope of one life, even while in this world.

Now, if there were such a thing to be seen, enabling one to understand, it would be an offence not to want to take notice of it. A man acting as guide through lovely scenery, would feel uncomfortable, if his fellow-travellers paid more attention to crossword-puzzles than to the beautiful things he pointed out to them. A teacher demonstrating the wonders of chemistry would resent it, if his pupils happened to be absorbed in strips during his lesson.

Yet large numbers of people maintain quietly they do not feel any need of this Book. They think the Bible interesting as a vestige of antiquity which can be analysed and unrolled like a 'Dead-Sea'-scroll or unwrapped like a mummy, declaring offhandedly and with great learning that this or that does not tally with this, that or the other. Or one considers the Bible quite acceptable to a certain extent as a manual for excavations, and people have the joy of the research-worker when they can point out that such and such a place has indeed existed, really and truly, and that potsherds of ancient household utensils have been found. Mind you: 'found' by so and so himself. Others again enjoy comparing biblical morals – such as they elicit from the Book – with the morals in other countries of antiquity, and they, too, feel immensely happy and honoured when they find identical or non-identical things. Others again get excited when by the light of some passage torn from its context they can prove that the end of the world has *actually* come, or that one must not do this, that, or the other, but something else instead. But *none* of these people know the Bible as the communication from God how the world is made by Him and why it is made thus, and all these people even disregard the fact that it *might* be like that.

All these people are lacking in 'jirath', willingness to see, to be impressed by God. It is they *themselves* who want to impress. They want to impress themselves, if nobody else. Next there is another group, that of the respectable, discreet people. They maintain they want to believe. Indeed, there are such who have a childlike innocence of spirit, so utterly untainted by this world of multiplicity as to live in real unity with the origin.

But do not let us be deceived. This kind does not grow on every hedge. Most people, the vast majority of people, who maintain they want to believe, only this or that nothing else, prove to be interested in all sorts of things besides. They study biology for instance in every detail, or psychology or sociology, they study economics, mathematics, physics, nuclear physics, they study all branches of technicology, or they make themselves proficient in breeding all kinds of cattle, or in various branches of sports and games, they go in for hobbies, they go in for business-transactions, sailing, yachting, holiday-trips, and in all these fields – each one in his own – they are very, very much interested in all details. They are immensely interested in politics or in society-life, and do not consider any sacrifice too much in that field. There is only one thing they believe in: God.

Maybe many of them do not realize it is an unconscious excuse for their grudge of spending time on it, for their fear of not-understanding things, because what penetrated to them as explanation seemed so vague, so illogical and so primitive, or because even the clergy got absorbed – and stimulated and even admired that absorption in others – in secular sciences and activities.

But in fact it comes to this: one simply does not feel interested in the things God most emphatically and circumstantially has to tell the world. It is just as if God and His communication is left alone, because people are so much occupied with other things. People just cannot be bothered.

However, the abundance of communications in the Bible, their profundity, their surprising interrelationships, all this has *not* been made to be *ignored*.

One may rightly maintain that it is not necessary for individual man to see the Amazonian jungle, or to gaze at the earth from a height of a hundred kilometres, however grand such things may be. But the Bible *has* been given to man, in the language of man, and therefore it demands to be seen and to be taken seriously. And it has for its purpose that on account of this imposing depth and abundance, man shall find the contact with God in the same way, i. e. going deeply into all details of life and embracing all life. The Bible is not a social instrument to stimulate production, to help the national income to grow, and to help to attain all this through a moral and ethical injection once a week.

Life cannot be trifled with. It is terribly serious; it reaches beyond death. And one cannot flatter oneself with the illusion that things will turn out all right, that one is too tired and that one has to work so very hard to maintain one's social position.

Faith is based on this 'jirath adonai', on this 'fear of the Lord', i. e. on this seeing what God is and what God tells about Himself and about the world, about creation, about man.

For never will man come to real belief through nuclear physics or biology or psychology. Even though he may imagine so. Man is apt to be lazy, when it is a question of believing. The Creator showed one way towards knowledge and to act on the strength of that knowledge and arrange life accordingly. Along this path man can have the right relationship with God, the relationship which is so gruesomely translated by 'fear' and is often sensed in that way, and which really is nothing but this sublime *seeing* of God; just as God *Himself* affords us to.

On such seeing does a very powerful faith and a very great confidence unfold. It is such seeing that shows the way to the mystery.

This 'seeing' does *not* lead to what many people expect via gnosis, namely to some kind of magic; to a desire to constrain nature and man. It is exactly those other ways of knowledge, of cognizance which is a better translation of gnosis, the ways we call scientific, which notwithstanding all protestations of humility on the part of insignificant man in the immense universe, lead to a desire to constrain nature and men; lead to a magic which, to excuse ourselves, we call by a new word: technology.

The 'seeing' of God, which God enables man to effect through the Bible, forms the basis for faith and confidence and thus the starting-point for right action.

It seemed necessary to discuss these problems more circumstantially here. For the structure we discovered in the world of the Bible and which we are going to avail ourselves of throughout the book, has this 'jirath' for its foundation: seeing God and His miracles. And this structure will prove to be the place where we can also see and understand how life in this world must be lived, because life here is part and parcel of all-embracing life of man, which life starts from the source of origin and returns thereto.

For it is merely a logic based on more than this earthly life alone, which can tell man how things are and why they are thus, and why he should do certain things and omit doing other things.

And in order to approach this path through the worlds, as it is described by the Bible, in the same way as we approached the structure of creation in the preceding chapter, we shall penetrate a little more deeply into the way in which the Bible presents its chronology.

One of the striking things in the structure of time is the fact that the period from the birth of Isaac to the exodus from Egypt, as stated in another passage, is 400 years. And that, counted from the moment of the birth of Abraham there are consequently 500 years. The length of Abraham's life up to the birth of Isaac is one hundred over against the 400 after it. So there is the (1–4)-proportion in this structure of time too. And the duration from the birth of Abraham is 500 which we have come across as the measure for a non-earthly distance.

But before entering into the question of the 400 and 500, which, indeed, we have already mentioned in another place, we shall have to say a word on these calculations. For if one reads the Bible and connects the various periods with each other and adds them up one will get the following table of years; it is a short schedule in which I merely include the most important dates to mark the distance:

	Flood	1656
birth of	Abraham	1948
birth of	Isaac	2048
birth of	Jacob	2108
Jacob to	Egypt	2238
death of	Jacob	2255
death of	Joseph	2309

Herewith, in fact, does the book Genesis end; we find a statement in Exodus, it is true, that the sojourn of the children of Israel in Egypt had lasted 430 years, and that God had told Abraham that his children would be oppressed in a foreign land 400 years, that they would not return from bondage until the fourth generation and that therefore three generations would live in oppression. In other texts the sojourn in Egypt is also mentioned as 400 years.

So here we have a kind of 'technical' difficulty. For, if we should want to reckon the 400 or 430 years' suppression from the moment Jacob travelled to Egypt, we should arrive at the 'year' 2638 or 2668 for the exodus from Egypt.

Now it is not very logical, in connection with the story, to have the bondage start at the time when Joseph still is king. It would be more logical to have this bondage start after Joseph's death. For from the story it appears that Joseph was honoured till his death. Joseph's death is in 2309. So the bondage would have lasted till 2709 or 2739.

But if we draw up such a computation, we get into a fearful conflict with another computation. In Exodus 6:13–26 a list of generations is given of the names of the ancestors of Moses who at the moment of the exodus itself was, as stated, 80 years old. In that list of generations Kehath is mentioned as Moses' grandfather. And Kehath's number of years is given 133. This Kehath was present among the 70 souls who came to Egypt with Jacob in 2238 (Gen. 46:11). Let us take the extreme limit — not very likely, indeed — that Kehath had just been born at the time. Then he would have died in 2371 (2238 + 133). The list of generations mentioned in Exodus gives Amram as the son of Kehath, hence as the father of Moses. According to the Bible he lived to be 137. To meet the critic half-way and protract the period, let us take for granted the highly improbable case that Amram was born in the year his father Kehath died, hence in 2371, then Amram would have died in 2371 + 137 = 2508. And again taking the improbable for granted, let us suppose Moses was born in the year his father died, in 2508. Then the exodus from Egypt would have taken place in 2588, when Moses was 80 years old, which is a great deal earlier than the most improbable early date of 2638 and very much earlier than the more rational date of 2739.

So things do not tally here. Would not the Bible itself be aware of this? Would it possess that all-permeating structure of interrelationship between word, number and systematism, yet overlook this contradiction which is even clear to a child: this mention of 430 years for the sojourn of the children of Israel (Exod. 12:40–41) and at the same time giving a list of generations a few chapters earlier, which at once disproves this statement of the 430 years?

Once we have seen how minute the Bible is — we need only call to mind the example given of the (1–4)-principle — and that it has a certain structure, extending on all sides and in the veriest details, then this simple computation which does not tally, is bound to mean something too. For the 400 years in Egypt are stubbornly reiterated — and again why this deviation of 30 to make it 430 in this text of Exodus? — and just as distinctly, as if with the intention to have it verified, ages are given of the generations during this period, showing that it is *impossible* anyway, *out of the question altogether* that they were in Egypt for 400 years.

This is one of the cases where we can plainly see that it is impossible to add up periods of time with the years mentioned in the story. We have to view these periods in a different way. It shows that we have to take the 400 as 'the extreme in duration', as gauged by the standards of this world. And that this 430 has a special message for us and that it does not merely imply 'a different reading'.

The sojourn in Egypt, as tradition keeps reiterating on that point, in regard to its duration, is indicated by the word 'descends', which is used when Jacob and his people journey to Egypt in 2238. In Hebrew the word 'rdoe', spelled resh-daleth-waw, 200–4–6.

Owing to the geographic position, the phenomenon of Egypt's lying lower, the descent into Egypt is a pictural expression, an image of a real condition. This real condition is like the descent on earth at creation; and the journey from Egypt to Canaan is called 'ascent'. We have already seen that the numerical proportions of the word Canaan is to Mitsrayim (Egypt) as 1:2. So the journey from Canaan to Egypt is like going from the state of unity, of all-embracing harmony, to a condition of duality, of suffering in duality, of suffering in being compressed, exiled, into the form of the earth.

As we shall see when discussing the story of Joseph, going down to Egypt is an expression in the tale of events which is identical with sending man down to this earth. Leaving Canaan in whatever form Canaan may present itself, ever runs parallel somehow to leaving some expression of the 'one' for an expression of 'duality'. In Jewish tradition therefore, living in the land which on our earth is the crystallization of what in essence is the 'state of oneness', is considered something uncommon. Especially so, if one leads a 'life of unity' oneself, if in everything one does connects the things of this world with the origin, if one wants to know the purpose of life, thus reuniting everything just as in that very place the force of unity has been expressed ever since creation. Just as in the human body the nucleus crystallizes in one place, within the brain, within the head, and the life of the form in another place, the heart, etc. And if in that place of 'unity' one lives a life of duality, a life of multiplicity, then there is disharmony and it is just as if that place ejects man, just as the inhabitants who lived there previously the Canaanites, and the other nations, were ejected; just as the Bible tells about biblical Israel which can live there only when itself leads a life which in its expression is a 'uniting'. The time when the Canaanite lived there was the time when the world had not yet attained 'reunion'. This did not come to pass until the 26th generation with which the name 'Lord' came to fulfilment on earth. As long as God allowed the world to continue in duality, for the very reason of causing the 'one' to arise again at the mutal retrieving of the divorced parts, so long did the seven peoples live in that land, like the seven days of the world, serving multiplicity. All that time it was only Abraham, and after him Isaac and Jacob, who knew that when the 'one' should be fulfilled, the force of multiplicity of these seven peoples would come to an end, and then man would live as an integrated being in that place which on earth is the expression of this 'unity'. Therefore this person knows he shall acquire that place, when the time of duality shall be 'fulfilled', i.e. when the time of the integration of man shall also be fulfilled in the world of divorce, of multiplicity. And to make sure this integration, the Lord God descended along with man into that world, in order definitely to effect this unity with the 26 generations. Leaving that place of 'unity' is similarly expressed in the earthly form, as something which is not good. It always is a descent into that which expressed itself in the world as duality.

And herewith happens the same thing which happened at creation, when the world descended from the state of 'oneness' to the condition of divorce, of form, of suffering, of duality.

Therefore does God say to Jacob when the latter leaves Canaan to go down to Egypt, that He will come with him in his descent and return with him in his descent and return with him when he 'ascends' again from Egypt to Canaan (Gen. 46:4).

In the image, in the expression of the substance on earth, there is also an above and a below. Just as our head is up above in the body and the trunk is below, so also the world of duality is below and the world of oneness is above. It expresses itself in the geographical statement just as much as in the biological condition of man.

So the Lord God accompanies man into Egypt, just as the Lord God accompanies man into creation, until reunion has become a fact. Accompanying man into creation took place, as we have seen, in the form of the 26 generations, with the same structure of division into four parts as those in the name of God as the Lord God, i.e. as 10–5–6–5.

So we see that when this place is attained in the story which then reveals itself in the temporal structure in a different period, the same principal things do happen. If there is a journey from the 'one' to the 'two', then there is the Lord God accompanying man into the 'two', in order to lead man back again to the 'one'.

This descending, 'rdoe' written 200–4–6 is determined by the structure and the 'weight' of the components of the word. Just as the tree of life proved to be 'one' to 'four' to the tree of the knowledge which then was 'four', and just as 'mist' was defined as 1–4, with the total-weight of 'five'.

The descent here as a word is 200–4–6, with a sum-total of 210. And now the period of the sojourn in Egypt, in that world of duality, proves to be exactly 210. The sojourn of the children of Israel who came down with Jacob to Egypt, lasted exactly 210 years, the duration of the components of the word 'descent'. The time in Egypt measured by this standard of the *word*, lasted from 2238 when the descent took place, to 2448 the moment the exodus commences, i.e. the ascent back to the 'one'.

And ancient lore, ipso facto familiar with this 210 as duration of the sojourn, states that of these 210 years there were only 86 years of real bondage, i.e. from six years before the birth of Moses, viz. from the moment Miriam was born.

Rather amazing how suddenly the very structure comes into prominence again which we already came across in the tale of creation. For the 86 in regard to the 430 which the Bible mentions as the duration of the bondage, shows a very definite proportion. It implies, in fact, that of those 430 years merely 86 were spent in 'real bondage', hence 430−86 = 344 years were 'something different'. And these two facets of bondage, the actual bondage of 86 and the other of 344, indeed form again the structure 1–4.

What do the other years stand for? They are there, and they prove to form the 'four' to the 'one' of real, hard slavery, where the Bible in Exodus mentions that Pharaoh is going to take measures against the people who had first come as guests. Pharaoh who had indeed forgotten what Joseph had done for Egypt.

Since the exodus appears to be in 2448, the 400 years begin in 2048, the year Isaac was born. And when we make it 430 years, the commencement is in 2018.

It goes without saying that the 400 and 430 are not contradictory versions, they have their significance in the whole. We shall presently see that they represent a most important principle and that on account of it very special aspects of the biblical story come into prominence.

Ancient lore has it – and it is from this sort of details we can infer how tradition is based on *that* knowledge of the Bible which bestows on the Book that marvellous depth and shows those numerous coherences – that in that very year 2018 when Abraham was 70 years old, the word of the Lord came to him that his descendants would be strangers for 400 years in a land that was not theirs, that they would be slaves and be afflicted (Gen. 15:1–21). It is the tale of Abram's sacrifice, when he divided the beasts in the midst, but he did not divide the birds. And when the Lord God promises him that the land Canaan, which originally is 'one', shall ultimately be bestowed on man, man who as Abraham was to unite the world with God, Abram asks; 'whereby shall I know that I shall inherit it?'. In Hebrew 'whereby shall I know' is 'bama eda'.

If we want to know how a thing shall come to pass, we shall see that it goes out from 'oneness', via division, the making of the two, and back again to oneness. That on the way there is the fear of ruin and destruction, but that everything returns to the 'one', that everything comes right after all. As the Lord God says to Abram on that occasion also that 'the fourth generation' will come back.

I do not intend to enter more deeply into the details of that special sacrifice brought there by Abram, as directed by the Lord God. But I want to point at one facet of it. There are, in fact, four species of creatures, birds, heifers, goats and rams. Among them, the birds were *not* divided in the midst, the others were. In a diagram it looks like this:

```
                    ☐         complete turtlodove

          ☐                   ☐  divided heifer

          ☐                   ☐  divided goat

          ☐                   ☐  divided ram

                    ☐         young pigeon
```

The young pigeon and the turtledove are of the same kind. The only difference is that the young pigeon is a later phenomenal form of the turtledove. We see that the diagram of the sacrifice is a rendering of the scheme of creation. The undivided 'one' as the beginning, as point of origin, after which there is the division into two.

The first division into two is that in the world of God, in Olam Atsiloeth. It is a division which does not make its appearance into our world as yet, but which, according to ancient lore represents the duality which God made in His world and which subsequently took shape in creation. Olam Atsiloeth is the world crowned by 'Kether', the crown of God, as the Kabbala expresses it.

Then comes the world of the first triad of days and that of the second triad of days, also divided, and finally the world of the seventh day again as 'one' and again of the same quality as the origin, as Kether, the crown of God.

So Abram is told what creation is like, how the world is made. And here, in this crystallization of that specific period of time, we are told how it expresses itself in the life of man.

Time in duality is shown to be a fearful time, a consuming time; dense darkness and a smoking furnace, a burning lamp passing between the pieces of duality. A bird of prey prepares to settle on the carcasses, but Abram chases it away.

It is the world of duality which, however, eventuates in oneness. For the fourth generation returns. The fourth is the undivided bird again. Just as one descends from Canaan, the 'one', descending into Egypt, the 'two', so there is the bird which is 'one' and there are the pieces which are divided in the midst, which are 'two'. Thus the fourth returns again to Canaan, for after the three divided pieces following upon the one whole, there comes as the fourth an undivided whole, the 'young pigeon'. The fourth world comes back to unity, the world of the seventh day attains the 'one'. Thus does Abram see the course of the world and thus does he see servitude in the world of duality, the world of the opposites. And from that moment, when Abram *knows* about this servitude, do the 430 years begin.

The structure of the word for 'bodily soul', which makes its appearance here as life, i.e. the 'nefesh', is, as we have seen: 50–80–300. The sum-total is also 430. For as soon as life comes to expression in this 'nefesh', there is the consciousness of servitude.

One of the cities, built by the children of Israel in Egypt, is called by the Bible 'Raämses', spelled resh-ayim-mem-samech-samech, 200–70–40–60–60, with a sum-total of again 430.

When the children of Israel leave Egypt, their first stage (Exod. 12:37) is that from Raämses (Rameses) to Succoth. Raämses has as sum-total of its components 430. Sukkoth (Succoth) is spelled samech-kaf-taf, 60–20–400. Sum-total 480. This first stage is one stage removed from this life, it covers a distance of 430–480, which makes 50. This first stage bears the stamp, the pattern, expressive of a passing from this world into another, the passing beyond

49, the completed seven, and the coming into the 50, there where the eight begins. Leaving Raämes, with its value of 430, and mentioning in that very text (Exod. 12:40) the fact of the 430 years in Egypt, is in itself a proof of the significance of this connection. And mentioning Succoth as destination in that very verse, also points out in the difference of 50 what is the meaning of this exodus. Raämses is the place built to store the abundance of Egypt, the storing away of which abundance brings with it the great suffering for the children of Israel who are aware of life's other destiny. And the 430 is at the same time the value of the word 'nefesh', being imprisoned in the expression of the body which reigns supreme, which afflicts, which has tied itself to the forces of development.

Servitude in Egypt in its essence is this servitude which originates with the coming of the 'bodily soul'. In that world of duality one has in fact to build up this bodily life (this physical life). *That* in reality is servitude. And that is what one is liberated from.

Servitude starts with the arrival of Abraham's descendants. For these descendants there is this servitude. To Abraham it is merely a communication, only a *'knowing'*. Abraham knows that when Isaac is born to him, it is the beginning of the servitude of 400 years which the Lord God had spoken of, and which Abraham had known about all those 30 years of waiting for Isaac. With the coming of Isaac begins that infinitely long earthly period of the '400', of the extreme possibility of expression, of the letter 'taf'.

With the commencement of that hard servitude, of the final 86 years, the 'one' over against the 'four', does the exodus virtually start. It is the beginning of the end. On earth it is expressed in a most 'violent' time. For the standards on earth measure everything in an earthly direction. The earth, indeed, is their starting-point. Thus the liberation from Egypt is accomplished through the so-called 'ten plagues'. These 'ten' are opposed to the 'ten' of the words of creation with which God created the world. And they are opposed to the 'ten' of the words with which God created the structure of 'unifying' man, at the revelation of the Bible on Mount Sinai. With the 'ten', the consequence of the 'four', does God create the new. And similarly does He also create the liberation from duality with the 'ten'. But Egypt esteems this liberation from duality as its own end and therefore Egypt quite logically has a most negative opinion about these ten 'plagues'. They are the pangs of birth which torment the body of the mother in order to relinquish the new.

Biblical Israel, living in Goshen – the name literally means 'close to' Egypt, but not *in* Egypt – did not suffer from the plagues, as the Bible has it. It is only to Egypt which as duality wants to keep its hold on man, that these events are plagues. Duality is opposed to relinquishment of its world, it fears the coming of the world of the 'one'.

In the 400 also there is this structure of the 'one' and the 'four' opposed to each other. Indeed, 80 years before the exodus, Moses the redeemer, is born;

so that there are 320 years beyond these 80. The 80 as 'one' stands for the time the redeemer is already present in that servitude without anybody realizing it as yet. At the time when the redeemer is already alive, suffering is most profound. Before the redeemer was born, as it is expressed in the tale of Egypt, suffering was more or less bearable. It was not until the time when his birth was nigh, according to ancient lore, that Pharaoh ordained that all the male children should be thrown into the water. For Pharaoh had been told that the redeemer was to be born about that time. And to prevent it, this measure was taken, showing even in the historic, outer tale, that it is impossible to try and resist the coming integration. In spite of all measures taken to kill that redeemer at the outset, it is Pharaoh's daughter who takes up the babe and even has it reared in the house of Pharaoh. So here again there is the (1–4)-structure with the 80 years from the birth of Moses to the exodus, and the 320, the 4 × 80 of the preceding period, over against it.

We see how this 400 and the 430 state exactly what this servitude is in fact; either number having the (1–4)-structure. Servitude has been there ever since the moment when there was this knowledge of having to pass through duality on earth. And throughout the time there is danger and fear. Even Isaac is born a stranger in a world which one day, in the far future, will be his. Jacob's life, too, even to a greater extent, is that of a foreigner, fleeing full of cares, hunted. *He*, too, knows that this world will be his. Like man on this earth who feels and knows that the world as it is *now*, does not belong to real man; but that the time will come when he, as man, *can* live in peace and surety in the world. Not because he will be able to improve or develop the world, but because the world has been created and in substance already been promised to man, and when all things shall be fulfilled, when union shall be completed, God shall lead him back to this world in 'an incredible way'.

The word for 'live' in this sense is 'gar' in Hebrew, spelled gimmel-resh and it is the same word as 'ger', stranger. In *this* way must man live in the world. Knowing himself for a stranger, because he lives in the 400 years which started with man's coming into this world and which will end when the exodus from this world takes place.

And those 400 years are even there, when man is not yet directly submitted to the fierce yoke of duality, the yoke which comes at the end of time. The 400 begins with man's coming into the world, where he cannot feel at home. It is *this* man that belongs to Abraham's descendants.

This servitude virtually begins before the 400 years, when there is the knowledge that the 400 shall come, even before the 400 has appeared on this earth. Just as in Abram's sacrifice the division in the midst has been made in the place where it already exists in thought, in knowledge, even in 'Olam Atsiloeth', in the world which is still entirely with God.

The Sephiroth in this Olam Atsiloeth are called 'chochma' and 'binah' in the Kabbala, expressions taken from the atmosphere of the 'knowledge', often translated as 'wisdom' and 'insight'. They show that it is the world which has to do with the 'knowledge', before creation itself appears in this world.

It is for this reason that servitude extends beyond this world itself. It has its roots elsewhere, even before the 400 makes its appearance here. And that is why this servitude in the 400 – present already in the four acts of creation in the three days of creation – is a decisive factor for this world and the whole story of the world virtually turns around this getting into servitude, servitude proper, and redemption from it, on the way to a new world.

Once one has more or less grasped this fundamental interference of the 400 and the 430 in the whole story, one will also realize why this 400 or 430 cannot without more ado be added to the 2238 when Jacob descends into Egypt. The Bible, indeed, is something entirely different from and infinitely more than a history-book, cut to the measure of our idea of years.

If one wants to reckon in years, in years with circumstances and conditions different from *our* years, the word 'rdu' tells us how that reckoning is.

One will also understand more or less that it is impossible to connect at random any divergent periods of time. On the other hand one does find a correlation in years between the moment the temple is built under Solomon and the exodus from Egypt. For the 480 mentioned in that text (1 Kings 6:1) is related to a comparable world. But one can never correlate that period to the years in Egypt, or to the years in the world before that. And if one should want to do so, one would have to supply a different standard altogether.

After this necessary expatiation with the example of the '400', which somehow taught us *how* to estimate the years and periods of time in the Bible, now let us return to our argument.

We see that it is 500 years from the birth of Abraham to the exodus from Egypt, from 1948–2448, and that the 400 begins at the birth of Isaac. So here again there is the (1–4)-structure. The moment of the birth of Abraham and of Isaac fixed the moment of the exodus, at least according to biblical standards. We have also seen how this 400 itself shows the (1–4)-structure, like the 430. This (1–4) proves to put its mark everywhere, and it is always the 'one' which is the great force forming the bridge with the other world, which is ever the 'fifth', which always fulfils the 'five'.

I propose to examine one facet of this biblical chronology, since it will in a sense form a keystone for reflections discussed in the preceding chapters, and will ever play a part in the following too. It is moreover a very special facet which will again bring forward the amazing structure of the Bible, also in regard to time.

When discussing the name Lord, we saw how it expressed itself in the period of the 26 generations, from creation to the revelation on Mount Sinai, how it gave the pattern of the 10–5–6–5 to the structure of time.

The principle of this name is that the second 'ten' divides itself into two fives. The two fives form the male and female sides in this world, that which expresses itself here as contrasts, though like the man and the woman it has come forth from the same whole. It is the opposites: body and soul; life and death; good and bad; etc.

And the purpose of this division into two is accomplishing union. A union which was definitely to be established, since it bore the pattern of the name Lord God, the name which also indicates on what principle this union will take place namely the quality of goodness, the will of God to give joy, bliss. The Bible says that this union is effected essentially at the revelation on Mount Sinai, when God reveals Himself and the purpose of everything becomes clear in that revelation.

The first part of this name Lord God, is the name 'Jah', in which in fact the first part of the story is told (this name is found in 'halleluyah', which means 'praise the Lord', 'praise Jah'.) This name 'Jah', also used as a separate name, is the first part of the unuttered name of 'Lord', formed by the letters 10–5.

In the story of the 26 generations we see that with the 15th generation when the part 10–5 of the name Lord is completed, 'the earth is divided', literally 'split'. In the very name 'Peleg' of the 15th generation, meaning 'divide', 'split', it is indicated that something is divided, split. Here also it is the name 'Lord' which is split into the first part 'Yah' and the next part which will show an affinity to bind itself to that first part.

For this first part, indeed, contains one half of the 'ten' which was split into two parts at the division. *That* first part has the 10–5 and the other 5 will have to be united with it to make the second 10 complete again. That other 5 seeks this very union, just as the woman seeks the man, just as we seek the opposite of everything, finally to discover the unity of things again. Just as man desperately seeks to unite life and death into an intelligible unity.

As long as the division exists, however, as long as the 10–5 stands by itself, death will stand by itself and life will stand by itself, and the world will suffer under this division which, when ended, will give the greatest happiness.

It is Abraham who together with Isaac effects the union with the other 'five' in the structure of the 26 generations, and it is the generation of Jacob up to and including Moses which informs the second 'five' with life. That which is called the 'merit of the fathers' connects these two parts, the two fives.

The Bible as a whole – and here again as most of the time when I use the generally more intelligible word Bible, I mean Pentateuch – similarly is to be united with the world and with life. *This* union, too, shows the same structure and accomplishes oneness.

That is why at the commencement of this chapter on chronology and the measuring of time I put such emphasis on eagerness to *see* and *accept* the Bible. The Bible presents itself with all its fullness, its splendour, extending in every direction, to be taken in the right way, so that man can become 'one' with it. For this very reason the Bible wants man to cherish it within himself, to have it ever with him as a standard; the Bible wants man to take it seriously as a wonderful thing in itself; that man shall not look down on it as an object to be analysed with his brilliant mind, and declare that one thing is indeed quite worthwhile but the other is not; that this here is a primitive outburst of a vindictive god and *that* is such another addition of a grasping priestcast, etc; coming to the final conclusion that the Bible is quite useful and is on many points borne out by the science of history.

The Bible demands to be taken in dead earnest. As something independent. As something *not* originating from erudites, although it has indeed to do with spirit and mind. That one shall look on it as something really originating from another world; as something miraculous, which it shows with so much control and at the same time with such continuous challenge.

The Bible demands to be united with man's thought and with man's life. So that reunion of all things, of the whole world, can take place at all times. For the Bible contains a systematism which communicates *that* too.

Indeed, if one adds up the years — done simply enough, since the data lie about handy in the text — one will see that the Flood came when Noah was 600 years old, 1656 after creation. We are not now discussing the quality of the years. But since the Bible gives them together as one whole, they can be added up together without any objections, as long as one does not draw any conclusions in connection with *our* years and *our* chronology. For the Bible there have passed 1,656 years since creation when the Flood comes.

Now the second part of the name Lord God begins with the 'ele toldoth' of Shem, when the enumeration begins of the six connecting generations which grasp back like a hook, which hook into things preceding. This 'ele toldoth' of Shem, the third in the series of four, begins with Gen. 11:10, and as it says there 'two years after the Flood'. So that makes 1,658.

The second 'ele toldoth' gives no chronology, it merely gives the names of the generations. The chronology, started in the first birth-story, is not continued until the third 'ele toldoth'. So when the third story begins, the two preceding ones can be considered closed. And that means that the name 'Yah', 10–5, is completed also.

The story of Pentateuch continues until just before the entrance into Canaan, with Joshua. It ends with the death of Moses and the thirty days of the people's mourning thereafter. The fortieth year of the journey across the desert has almost, but not quite, been completed.

About the Flood it says that it takes place, not at the beginning of the year but 'in the second month on the seventeenth day of the month'.

With these specially given details of days, at the end of Pentateuch as well as at the beginning of Joshua and in the story of the Flood in Genesis, we come to another most amazing conclusion in regard to the whole structure of time in the Bible. For the time on which are based the first two 'birth-stories', in which the 10–5 story is told, appears to be in a definite proportion to the time described after it, which contains the rest of the Pentateuch-story.

THE CHRONOLOGY OF THE BIBLE 173

For the time of the first two 'birth-stories' embraces 1,658 years plus a number of days, and the time from that moment to the end of Pentateuch contains 829 years plus a number of days. And the remarkable thing about it is that the period which comes after the 1,658 is half of the period of 1,655. Again they show the proportion of 2:1. It is the proportion in which is expressed the way-back from duality to oneness. A proportion which we have also found in the value of the letters of Egypt over against Canaan which similarly was the ascent from the 'world of duality' to the 'world of oneness'. And it is the development of creation which similarly implies that after the 'making of duality' in the two triads of days of creation there comes the union in the seventh day.

It is really amazing that even in the structure of time there is the impress of this pattern. All people's ages and periods of events added together prove to show this remarkable structure, they form part of a great and very distinct development. It is just as if the Bible insists on stating in *every* happening: 'the important thing is this evolution from the "two" to the "one". And this evolution is *sure* to come. The world is made with it; be not impatient and do not try to attain unity in your own way.'

Again the Bible shows the deep interrelationship even between all the phenomena one can perceive in the Book. In the word, in the names, in the systematism, in the structure of time, everywhere does this same pattern prove to obtain. It is a structure as utterly beyond man's ability as that of life or of the universe. The only thing is that it is present in greater concentration in the Bible; in a form to be viewed comprehensively and understood within a lifetime; to be experienced by man.

Even if one should not be familiar with the argumentation about the four birth-stories, even then it will hit one in the eye that the chronology after the Flood continues in a year precisely at two-thirds of the whole duration of Pentateuch. So that year lies at a point of time which determines the proportion 2:1. This in itself brings the structure 2–1 into prominence, a structure which equals the conception 10–5. And this proportion of 2–1 is an established fact, even without any further argumentation. It can be found at once by anybody ready to make a serious study of the Bible and the chronology as it is also given by ancient lore.

One facet of this 2–1 proportion should be examined more closely. The attentive reader will have noticed it for himself. Where in creation the seventh day represents the 'one' over against the 'two' of the preceding six days, this 'one' is nothing but an earthly 'one' waiting for reunion with the 'one' above. In the expression of the Sephiroth it implies that the Sephira Malchuth is waiting for reunion with the Sephira Kether above. The 'one' below is nothing but a preparation of man and the world for the return, the reunion with above, with the source of origin. In itself it is not complete yet.

There will be no completion until the 'one' below has united with the 'one' above. Only then will the condition have been attained in which the 'ten' below can be in harmony with the 'ten' above, both reflecting each other like the two 'jods' in the letter 'aleph' and like the two cherubs on the mercy-seat of the ark.

In the name 10–5–6–5 it means that the latter five does not stand apart from the former five, but that it has found the intermediate six as the link to get united to the former five, therewith making the name 10–5–6–5 'whole' again, 'hallowing' it. For not until then will the 10–5–6–5, as also in the expression in the world, be the condition of harmony between the two tens, the ten above and the ten below. This happens when the two fives are united.

When the new world comes after the Flood, it is the world after the first decade of generations, hence also after the 10 of the 10–5–6–5. So it is the world of the second 'ten' which here presents itself as one five opposite another five, which when reunited will be able to form the whole ten below. And as soon as it has become 'complete' this ten will be in harmony with the former ten. There is disharmony just because the second ten was divided into two fives.

This reunion of the two fives is the reunion in this world and that is the purpose of this world. It is the integration of all polarities, of all contrasts, of all opposites.

So man is faced in this world with the 10–5, which in words implies that the 'five' of it seeks union with the other 'five', so that harmony may be achieved. The 2–1 means that the 'one' of this world does not represent the ultimate completeness as yet, but that it merely creates the condition for union with the 'one' above. The 'one' seeks union with its reverse that it may complete harmony.

When biblical Israel comes to Canaan, it is liberated from the duality of Egypt, it is true, it is free from suffering in duality, so it is returning to unity, but this unity demands integration with that other unity, with that of God. Only then will there be the harmony like that of the two *jods* in the *aleph* and that of the two *cherubs* on the mercy-seat of the ark. It is a covenant which is at the same time borne out by the historic covenant with the 'merit of the fathers', to whom Canaan was promised.

Creation is the way of the 'one' before creation, through the 'two' of creation, to the 'one' of the ultimate goal, which 'one' is opposed to the 'one' before creation. Only then can the name become 'complete', when the union of the former 'one' with the latter 'one' has been effected.

The same idea is rendered by the name 10–5–6–5. The condition before creation is that of the 'aleph', the two 'jods' reflecting each other; creation is creating the two fives from one of the 'jods', and the condition at the end is the union of those two fives which through that reunion restore the balance, the harmony to the former 'ten'. On account of the creation of the two 'fives', the former 'ten' also lost its own reflection, also lost its own harmony.

This former 'ten' owing to the loss of harmony went along, as it is called 'into exile' that it might regain its harmony with the reunion of the two fives.

This condition of the exile of the original 'one' which divides itself into two, is also expressed by the occupation of Canaan by the seven peoples. Only when the 'one' is reached again after the exodus from Egypt and the occupation of Canaan, the end of the seven peoples has come also. By then the seventh day has been completed, the forty years of the desert have come to an end, and the eighth day commences. On this eighth day there is the expulsion of the seven peoples and in that eighth day the 'one' of Canaan can be united again with the 'one' of the past, the 'one' previous to the descent from Canaan into Egypt. The 1–2–1 of the principle of creation, as we see, is also expressed in the way Canaan-Egypt-Canaan.

Thus the condition of the patriarchs in Canaan is the expression of the 'one' before creation, the suffering in Egypt is the expression of the suffering through duality which came along with creation, and the return to Canaan is again the 'one' of the ultimate goal of creation. And that 'one' has to be united with the 'one' before Egypt, the 'one' of the Canaan of the patriarchs. Only *then* will the occupation of Canaan serve any purpose, for only then will there be the restoration of harmony throughout the world, the harmony of the original undivided 'one'. On the way Canaan-Egypt-Canaan the connection must be accomplished with the 'patriarchs', with the 'origin'.

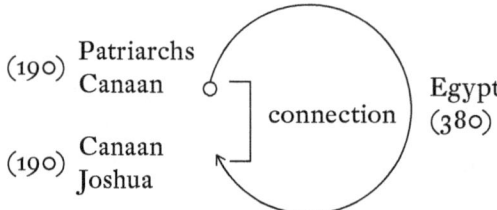

The 10–5 of the name 'Yah' is at the same time the way from the 'two' to the 'one'. But we now understand that this 'one' has sense only when united with the 'one' before creation, the 'one' of God. This means that the name 10–5 merely creates the condition for the other five of the name 10–5–6–5, to unite with the 'five' of the 10–5. Attaining the 'one' after the 2–1 only means that with it the condition has been created to reunite with the 'one' before duality.

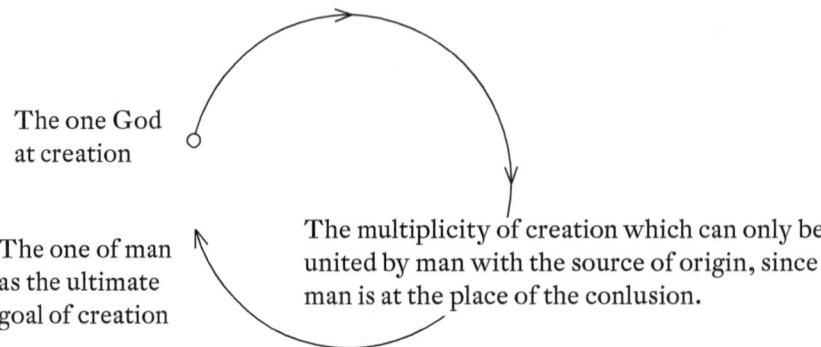

It is the same image we used at the creation of man, who indeed was 'one' over against the 'two' of creation, just as God was 'one' over against creation (see scheme above). Here, too, the two 'ones' face each other and the purpose of creation is the union of the two 'ones' to the original harmony.

Ever again we shall see that the way 2–1 is completed only when it faces the 1–2 of creation. Thus 1–2–1 turns into the original harmony.

In its *structure of time* Pentateuch as a whole does not give anything beyond this 10–5, the 'Yah' of the name Lord God. For there is the 1,658 opposite the 829, as already explained, the 2 opposite the 1. It is the structure of the 10–5, of the name 'Yah'.

In the *story* of Pentateuch on the other hand, it says how the ultimate 'one' is achieved, how, in essence, everything is accomplished with the 26 generations, so that at the hand of this root-pattern it will be fulfilled always and everywhere. According to the proportions of Pentateuch with which all creation took place, the fulfilment of the story is present in its root. This root fulfilled, will inexorably determine the course of development in the surrounding zones.

However, just as the story of ultimate union is completed in its root, so this root expresses in its structure of time that it appears in the process of time only as 10–5, as the part which is still waiting for the reunion. With it Pentateuch establishes that on man depends the realization of the integration in that which to us manifests as time. Will man unite with the 10–5, thus forming the 6–5 and completing the 10–5–6–5, or will he *not* take that way? So man is faced with the 10–5 in the form of Pentateuch. He ever faces the 10–5 either to unite it with life, with the world, or not. Man learns from the Bible how his life is permeated with the pattern of creation. He learns from it how he himself is faced with the 10–5, and how in his life he can complete the 10–5–6–5 by uniting his 'five' with the other 'five', thus driving out the Canaanite and restoring the original harmony.

That is why the Bible has this strong affinity, this disposition to attract, and why it presents itself as such. The Bible insists on being read, studied, understood, for in that way will the union with it be effected.

The Bible with the 10–5 as its structure of time, as it is lived, experienced in the world, is united with man and through him with the world. In this way does the 6–5 grow in the life of man, and similarly in that of the whole world, and thus the name 10–5–6–5 is completed. The Bible, as is apparent here again, is not a history book. It is the root, the starting-point for life. It is the 'one' at the one end, the end where God is when He makes creation, and where are the patriarchs also. It is the 'one' which yearns to be united with the 'one' of the other end, with man who in his world in this seventh day has reached the 'one', who is ready to enter the land Canaan in the eighth day. It is the Sephira Kether seeking union with the Sephira Malchuth.

This form of 2–1, or of 10–5, in fact is the form 11 as well. There is a 'whole time', the time up to the 1,658, and there is a 'half time', the time of the 829.

And this 'whole time' and 'half time' get their fulfilment through that other 'half', which is there at the starting-point which is the origin and which will bestow peace and balance and serenity on the 'whole'.

This other 'half' in fact also expresses itself in the period of time when biblical Israel, according to the chronology of the Bible, is in Canaan. The presence of Israel in Canaan is manifested there in the form of this world of the seventh day, just as it will be a permanent reality in the eighth day. For, if we add this 'half time' of 829 to the moment of entering into Canaan, namely to 2,488, we prove to be in the period of the fall of the Realm of Judah, when Babylonian captivity began and the temple as an image on earth of another world of different qualities was going to be destroyed. It is even seen how this 'halving' ever comes into prominence in chronology. For if we take the 829 years as a whole over against that which is still to come, we shall see that in the middle of that period of 829 there is the lifetime of King David, who essentially is the fulfilment of the promise of the anointed king whose son was to build the permanent house.

1658
———
the period of the initial two 'ele toldoth'

829
———
the ½, leading to the reaching of Canaan,
to the bounds of the 8th day

414/15
———
the ½ again leading to the reaching of the bounds
of the 8th day, in this case to King David and
the birth of the son who was to build the temple,
the permanent house.

According to the time-reckoning of the Bible the following data obtain:

1658	– beginning of the third 'ele toldoth'
2488	– end of the journey across the desert and entrance into Canaan
2885–2925	– reign of King David
2928	– beginning of the building of the temple
3319–3338	– the period of the Babylonian captivity, ending in the destruction of the temple.

The 'half' over against the 'whole' is a principal standard, always to be found back in the structure. Always the 'half' is as the 'one' over against the 'two' of the 'whole'.

Similarly the height of the ark in the tabernacle is 1½ cubits, like the periods of 1½. And *on top of* those 1½ cubits there is the mercy-seat with the cherubs. For it is there, over those 1½ cubits that the union is effected with the 'half' above. There, in that place, according to the Bible, does God appear and therewith bestows significance on the 'ark', bestows on it the harmony of the whole.

Within the ark, within the 1½ cubits, are the stone tables and is confined the story of Pentateuch. The story with the 10–5 as time-structure and the datum of pattern of the 10–5–6–5 in the root-story. The root-story stands as a model for *every* story which is to evolve in time. That is why it is given in its first fulfilment. *Every* story starts from the 10–5 and unites it with the 6–5. So that in every story the 10–5–6–5 forms the pattern.

This 1½ in the Bible is determined in time by the standard of the 1658. At this point begins the 'ele toldoth' of Shem, which is going to effect the union of the 'five' below with the 'five' above. Every life and every event down here begins at this point. Every life stands for duality and wants to unite the opposites. That is the way of life in this world.

For this 1658 proves to be the 10 for the whole time-structure of Pentateuch, whereas the further story of Pentateuch forms the 5, owing to which the whole complex of Pentateuch takes the form of the 10–5.

As *standard* therefore there is the 10–5, the 'Yah' for the whole of Pentateuch. For with this 1658, the 10–5 *itself* for the *story* of Pentateuch, the story of the 26 generations, time is now measured. This 1658 occurs 1½ times, as the 'Yah' in structure. It is for this reason that Pentateuch is said to be written with the name 'Yah'.

This special knowledge which points the way to the secret, expresses itself among other things in the way in which from remote times the scroll with the Pentateuch has been written. Rules are laid down as a matter of fact, in what place in the written scroll of Pentateuch a new column had to start anyway, and this rule is called 'be-Yah-shmo', which, translated, is 'with His name Yah'.

Now the first column of course begins with the 'beth' of the word 'in the beginning' 'bereshith'. A following column which has to be there at any rate, irrespective of other columns which one can make oneself, begins with the letter 'jod' of 'Yah', the next column with the 'hee' of the word 'Yah', then a column with the 'shin' of the word 'shmo', after which there are columns beginning respectively with the letters 'mem' and 'waw' of the word 'shmo'.

In this way these fixed initial letters of the columns form the expression: 'with His name Yah', which means that the scroll of Pentateuch in writing has got the hallmark of this name 'Yah'. Hence Pentateuch to us is the 10–5 which has to be united by us, by our life, with the 6–5.

This clearly shows that people knew about this structure in the Bible, that knowledge was based on these things. That they have for the greater part been forgotten by most people does not alter the greatness of the fact. This forgetting merely shows how far the world has strayed from the original knowledge.

Thus the Bible is one side of life, written with the name 'Yah', and man's thought and action are the other side. In uniting with the Bible he links the 6–5 to the 10–5 which already exists, and thus he forms the name of the Lord. *That* is the purpose of life, a purpose extending far beyond this life here. With it there arises in man the knowledge that he was made to have the good which he desperately searches for in everything, but owing to the hopeless endlessness of things, he feels like an unnecessary cog in the wheel, gives it up and seeks the intoxicating whirl of enjoyment in which a sham-world is created, whether aroused through narcotics or the manifold potentialities of social life. All these are efforts to escape the awful sense one does not *know*, that nobody even *can* know, that in fact it is all without hope, that one only knows one thing for certain, death, and that one does not want to think overmuch of it. It is the situation of man after eating of the tree of the knowledge, when he hides from God.

After finding this 10–5, this name 'Yah' in the structure of time and the simultaneous revelation that the name Lord God is already completed in that root-story, that the 10–5–6–5 is already fulfilled in it, 'learning', from the Bible acquires a special significance.

What is told there as a story, what is completed there as the way in the 26 generations forming the name of Lord God, all this presents itself in time as 'one side' to be fulfilled by life. Life forms the other side and finally forms a unity with it. And then it will also be completed in time, fulfilled in the time *here*. This is the purpose of life.

So the communications in the Bible have significance for our life in time. However, not as 'example' or as 'lesson from the past' or as 'indication how far we have progressed in civilization since those primitive ages', but as a statement how the situations always *are*. That we are ever faced with these situations, because they always come to us in the form of the 10–5 and get their fulfilment in life. Life, which will unite the other 'five' with it, by which the original unity will be formed anew.

PART TWO

Expanding

9
The Story of the Two Trees

What is the significance of the systematism, discovered in the preceding part for the whole story of the Bible? As already pointed out by means of a few examples, it is also found in the separate stories. Now what is its purpose for each separate story and what is the relationship between the story and the structure contained in it?

We shall try to answer these questions with the aid of a few examples taken from the biblical story.

The Bible embraces more than just this life. Expressed in the images of this world, it points out the course through the whole of life, a life which neither begins here nor ends here. All the stages in the course of life through other 'worlds' find their expression in the Bible in images, in forms, which in their outward appearance represent a crystallization of the substance in our space-time world.

Therefore the Bible should be followed closely and every story should be seen and understood in its essence. Indeed this is what can be done in this life. Within the limited scope of one book, which moreover introduces a subject practically unknown, owing to which a great deal of space had to be devoted to explanations about the method of approach, it is impossible for us thus to pursue the subject fully. I shall, however, endeavour to discuss some of the important aspects. In the end an impression may be formed which does justice to the Bible.

Keeping to the order of sequence in its main outline, let us first of all approach the so-called Story of Paradise again, although largely from a different direction this time. In order to avoid needless repetition, I shall have to take it for granted that the reader is now fairly familiar with a great deal of what we discussed in Part One. For the moment let us forget the images, both those of the story – since we generally interpret images in the wrong way and consequently react to them wrongly – and those which have come to us through paintings, films, edifying books, etc., and let us try and follow the story and see how it essentially presents itself.

In the world man appears as the man and the woman. This is a way of expressing things in material form originating from the same principle as that which describes body and soul as facing each other.

The woman is, as it were, the outer covering of the man, just as she is the flesh which fills up her place in the whole of man. In Jeremiah 31:22 it is put like this: 'a woman shall compass a man'. The word for 'female' in Hebrew is 'nekebah', spelt nun-kof-beth-hee, and that word is derived from 'nakeeb', which means 'hole', 'hollow', or 'pit'. And this 'hole' is supposed to be filled up by the man. A hole without this filling, without this nucleus in it, is supposed to be 'unfilled' or 'unfulfilled'. It has not found its destination or fulfilment. From it originates the sentiment that a women by herself is no good.

Of course organically, too, in the expression of the women in the human body this 'hole' is determinant for the conception 'woman'. This 'hole' makes of her the bearer of life, when she has been fulfilled by man.

In another respect also the female always compasses the male. It compasses a being which then finds itself as if inside a house. Thus the soul as the male aspect is lodged in the body as the female aspect. In the systematism of the Bible, the female side, as we have seen, is the left side. 'Left' in Hebrew is 'smol', spelt sin-mem-aleph-lamed, 300–40–1–30. And a word for garment, veiling, sheathing, is 'simla', sin-mem-lamed-hee, 300–40–30–5. 'Left' and garment have the same stucture, the same root. For, indeed, the left veils, compasses, sheathes, clothes. It is for the female to compass, to cover.

There is yet another word which, according to its pronunciation has the same root, which similarly throws a clear light on this left aspect. It is the word 'Samael', that which is sometimes called 'the destroying angel' or the 'angel of death'. The word is spelt samech-mem-aleph-lamed, 60–40–1–30. It is pronounced like the word for garment and the word for left, the only thing is that the 'sin' is exchanged for the 'samech'. In pronunciation it is the same and actually the 'sin' is identical with the 'samech'.

In this connection I should like to refer to the word for poison, 'sam', spelt samech-mem, which is related to Samael. So 'samech' and 'sin' have the same pronunciation, and they are often used the one for the other. The letter 'sin', which like 'shin' is 300, is distinguished in pronunciation from the 'shin', because it takes the sound of the 'samech'. In handwriting it is often indicated by a dot on the *left* above the letter, if it is a 'sin' and on the right above the letter if it is a 'shin'. It is done like this because in reality the 'sin' is the left side of the 'shin'. The tale of the Shibboleth or Sibboleth, in Judges, with the tribe of Benjamin, has something to do with these aspects of left and right of the 'shin'.

Thus there is a strong relationship between these words for garment, left, Samael, poison. It shows that the phenomena on the left side have a very specific character. The relationship between these various phenomena is therefore fairly easy to discover through the medium of the word of the Bible.

That is why knowledge of the word and its contexts in ancient lore is the basis for statements on life. For example: an image which seems rather futile and childish to the layman is to be found in one of the ancient sources, where it says, 'the serpent was of the size of a camel and Samael was mounted on it'. Indeed, to a man who clings to this image and even wants to make a drawing of it, it would seem an expression of a childish mind which these ancient sages must have had.

Yet the image expresses great wisdom. This image in itself might induce one to write a book on metaphysics about it. I could not, even at the expense of many pages, give more than a superficial description of the intention of the sage who handed down this wisdom – as it is called – from Mount Sinai.

Camel in Hebrew is *gammel*, 3–40–30, the word which is also used for the letter 'three', *gimmel*.

The camel which Samael is mounted on is the 'gimmel', the 'three' the 'third'. This 'third' has the special nature of duality, of the dual. In that third place is found the dual: Jacob-Esau and also the dual: tree of life – tree of knowledge.

In its phenomenal form the camel likewise shows this duality, for instance, in the two humps and also in the fact that in the systematism of the animal world it is called 'the creature that chews the cud but does not divide the hoof' (Lev. 11:4). Besides, the letter gimmel is the only letter whose foot is divided.

On that very duality is mounted Samael, the power of the left side, the power of destruction. For with that very duality he is able to tempt man to follow his way; give voice to the opposites and rouse man to the desire of eliminating the contrast himself by means of standards he has made himself; and show the world the multiplicity, the ever-growing greater and vaster development, records, etc. It is *he* who is mounted on duality, *he* that is the force of duality. And of course he is death also. For duality implies that life faces death. As the power of the left side, he determines duality. He leads duality to further veilings, he makes the nucleus more and more invisible. He emphasizes the female, that which compasses the nucleus. The story is quite clear, and, considering all that I have already said about the structure of the Bible, it is intelligible and acceptable.

The question remains, however: why *that* image exactly? What is the meaning of that image?

By means of this one example I shall show here a little more of the meaning of such images. The story mentions a 'great' camel, a great 'gimmel'. In the arithmetic of ancient lore gimmel is meant not only in its outward value as 'three', but in its complete value as gimmel, hence of the word 'gimmel', as it is built up with the three letters gimmel-mem-lamed, 3–40–30. For the second letter, mem, it means mem-mem, 40–40, and for the third letter, the lamed, it is lamed-mem-daleth, 30–40–4. The sum total of the 'great' word 'gimmel' therefore is (3+40+30)+(40+40)+(30+40+4)=227.

Now it is on that great gimmel that Samael is mounted, spelt samech-mem-aleph-lamed 60–40–1–30, with a sum total of 131. If indeed we allow the 131 to be mounted on the 227, hence 131 + 227, we find 358 as the result of their being together. And the number 358, as we have found, is the number of the serpent, of 'nachash', nun-cheth-shin, 50–8–300. The serpent, the 358, is indeed the 131, mounted on the great camel, on the 227.

So we see that these images spring from the knowledge of the substance of them; that they are not used by a playful, childish mind. These images are expressions in familiar terms of formulae which indeed render the substance of things. Now the remarkable thing in this image is, moreover, that the 'great' camel appears to have 227 as the sum total of the component parts. This 227, like the 358 of the serpent, is also a well-known 'total' weight, which has a specific meaning especially in this place.

As a matter of fact, the word for 'male', 'zachar', spelt zajin-kaf-resh, 7–20–200, has this 227 as sum total of the component parts. By understanding the substance of the word, i.e. through its quantitative components, we have penetrated more profoundly into the real meaning of the serpent.

For it is the Samael, the power of the left side, which is seated on the male, which makes use of the male as its mount, as its pied-a-terre. When the male, i.e. the soul, allows itself to be mounted by the power of the left side, the power of the compassing, the covering, the surface, the exterior, then that is the serpent.

The 'gimmel' itself as the 'third', hiding duality within itself, as 'great' gimmel, is the male aspect of that duality.

This implies at the same time that the 'gimmel', the third, has got to free itself from the influence of the left side. This left side, as we saw, is second in the systematism of sequence. And the bond between this second and the third is not good; it hides danger within itself. Therefore every day in the tale of creation is connected with the next by the expression 'God saw that it was good', except at the connection between the second and third days, where it is absent. That is why in Jacob's blessing of his sons (Gen. 49:5–7) the second and the third, Simeon and Levi, are mentioned together for the very reason of eliminating this combination. In their association, as it was manifested in the story of Dinah and the Shechemites (Gen. 34), which we shall not enter into here, they work mischief. And therefore we see that as soon as Levi had cut himself loose from this bond with the 'second', the 'left hand side', he becomes the great leader in the redemption, on the way from the 'two' to the 'one'. And Simeon was also the one who shared the fall of Baal Peor (Num. 25) when Phinehas, of Levi, took action against Simeon and killed the leader of the apostasy. A distinct aloofness on the part of the 'third' in regard to the 'second'.

Joseph too, separates Simeon from the others (Gen. 42:24) and keeps him in Egypt; it is the left side, that which forms the material basis for things to come; that which announced itself at the first appearance of Joseph's brethren in Egypt; that which is held in Eygpt.

Now that we touch upon the sons of Jacob, let us point to the *name* of Simeon, which is derived from the root of the word 'hear', whereas the name of Reuben, the first son, is derived from the root 'see'. On the right side of the systematism there is this seeing, which has to do with velocity, with light, whereas on the left side, the second place, there is hearing, which is slower, just as the side of water is the inert side as contrasted with the velocity of the side of light.

In that world there is the man with the soul and body. The body is the left side, the female; it encompasses the soul. And this body is made aware of the world by the serpent, by Samael mounted on the male aspect of duality. On becoming aware of the world it develops its senses. It has eyes, ears, a nose, it can combine perceptions. And it can draw conclusions. It contains within itself, as received with creation, the awareness or at least the sense not to bestow itself on the forces which develop the world still further, moving away from the origin, building upon the experiences drawn from the perceptions; but aware that it must serve as starting point for uniting the opposites, for the return to the origin. That is what the body bears within itself instinctively, so to speak; this yearning to be united with the origin, this yearning to be safe in its knowledge concerning the origin. But it ever finds the glamour of development facing it with the promise of a goal where man is free and strong, in control of the universe, living in peace through his own power and the knowledge he has built up himself. Development, however, was the consequence of duality, brought by God into the world and directed by God to its externe consequence so that in bringing the divorced parts together, man might taste the happiness and joy of the integation. Development itself, the making of duality therefore is to God as the tree of knowledge, the tree of duality. God made development for man's sake. Only in standing by God or against God can man develop also.

Development forms part of the principle of the creator, and whoever develops things alongside God, destroys the purpose, the design of creation. Whoever develops things usurps the place of God, and this is most tempting. Man, in fact, is constantly faced with these forces of development; the world is full of them.

For it is also the power which caused the body to come forth and continues to develop the body. And the body knows that a great deal can be attained with the power. It is the power which accomplished this precious body and the glamorous world. It is ever seen and felt in its activity. It allures man to continue along that way. Is not everything exceptionally beautiful and attractive?

All this, however, is creation; everything has been already made. Every man individually suddenly comes into the world and then faces everything; he even faces his body which grows and develops through that power of creation. And he feels like a king in his realm and he wants consciously to continue his further development, taking things in hand himself now, putting all his strength at stake.

The body has come with all this strength and it can sense *how* it has come.

From practically nothing, from a speck of dust perhaps; it has developed to this amazing complexity. In this way does the body argue with its organs as it awakes to this consciousness. And this argument is right, from the physical point of view.

The senses produce standards from the numerous perceptions. These standards show a law active in the events. And they show one can get a long way with the help of these standards. One can rule the world with it through biology, chemistry, medicine, psychology, economics, etc. And one sees that one can change the world. The appearance of the world is indeed changing.

And in the end one fails to understand how it was that God said man was not to eat from this tree. It seems to be the foolishness, the jealousy of a primitive God, which is opposed to this development. An old-fashioned, jealous God. For one can *see* the results, surely; life is getting easier and more comfortable, development is speeding up. There is an increase of material, in fact there is an excess of material. One can hardly cope with it. But one makes appliances and thinks out methods to sort out, systematize, compute things for the body, and in this way one gains more power and ever more power.

With all this material, one can set up new standards again, how one is to live and behave in order to speed up this development even more. There are standards by which to adapt oneself to society, to science. Our judgement is getting flexible, for the standards keep changing. There is utilitarianism and opportunism.

And when one has eaten from the tree of knowledge, one becomes aware of something very special, something unexpected. For one's eyes are opened.

Was man blind before? How could he 'dress' and 'keep' the garden, and how could he see the tree at all and perceive that 'it was good to look at'?

Really, this opening of the eyes is something most extraordinary. Whoever starts using his senses to observe the world in her powers of development will perceive that it is getting easier and easier all the time. The eyes actually *are* opened: planes whose existence we had barely suspected, new dimensions open out before us.

The younger generations appear to grasp without the slightest difficulty all sorts of techniques which their seniors found quite strange and hard to acquire. The world bears down upon man. New experiences accelerate towards him. The scope of man's abilities grows ever wider.

Everything suddenly seems so simple that one is surprised at the blindness of former generations. How could they have failed to discover all this long ago? People are surprised at their ancestors, but they forget that they should be surprised at themselves, at their own enormous expansion.

With the opening of these our physical eyes, the other eyes were closed. Ancient lore has it that man before partaking of this fruit could survey the whole world from one end to the other in the twinkling of an eye, and view the whole of time from beginning to end. It is *these* eyes that were closed. Whereas, previously, man could see all things simultaneously, could see through spacetime in all its contexts and with an all-embracing insight, he now sees multiplicity. He sees everything divided into moments and places where he happens to be at the time. The total vision became obscured, and began to flow in a stream of pictures, a small fraction being lit up clearly and the rest left in utter darkness. Endless multiplicity began to oppress man, giving him a sense of there being no beginning and no end.

Man now got buried under this multiplicity, under the details. He had to specialize if he was to understand anything at all; he had no time to encompass the whole; the details claimed his attention more and more. And he still does not see the end of it; on the contrary, other and newer aspects are opening up all the time, more details increasingly crop up, promising more and more power and knowledge, and never any end to it. With the prospect of more studies, more research work, further details, as a 'necessary nuisance', both as regards the infinitely small and the infinitely vast. Then, when the eyes have opened after the eating from the tree, standing amidst this endless multiplicity which whispers to him on all sides that he, as man, is really very powerful, very clever, he suddenly discovers that he is ... naked. That all life, all this hurrying, all this developing is so utterly senseless and illusory.

The man is ashamed before the woman, and the woman is ashamed before the man. The body is ashamed of the soul, and the soul is ashamed of the body. For the body is aware all at once that it has actually nothing whatsoever to offer; that everything about itself is mere illusion, show; that it can only present one side, and that is has to take jealous care to hide that immense, surrounding blackness, that side of death. And the soul is ashamed of the body, that it has allowed itself to be led by the body, and on account of it it has without more ado accepted what the body handed on as the fruit of its encounter with the world. Indeed the man has allowed himself to be mounted by the left side, by Samael, and now he, too, is ashamed of himself. Both body and soul are aware of their nakedness. In reality they have nothing to offer. There is merely a 'hangover'.

The word for naked, 'arum', ayin-resh-waw-mem, 70–200–6–40, is exactly the same word as that for 'subtle', the word which is also used in regard to the serpent. For if one is what one pretends to be, if there is no contrast, no contradiction, there is no reason for feeling ashamed. There is shame when a man is unable to express what essentially he feels he is. It is the confrontation with the fact that substance and appearance are at variance with each other. In case of subtlety, wiliness, one is consciously at variance; man was passively, unintentionally so. In the case of subtlety one 'uses make-up' to help one confront the world, and intimidate others with impressive show. Deep down in his heart man knows that he is merely 'showing off', and if he would only reflect he would recognize it.

Man perceives as a matter of fact he does not control the material world at all. He merely imagined that he did, preferring not to see his limitations. For, whatever he may do, injustice and death keep looming up and remind him of the folly of his course.

Then man makes himself aprons of fig leaves to cover his shame. Let us examine this image. In the Bible fruits are also arranged according to a definite systematism, which ipso facto finds its origin in the Bible itself (Deut. 8:8). The Bible mentions seven 'fruits'. The first four are corn, barley, the vine, and the fig. Next come the pomegranate, the olive, and the date, the last of which produces honey. Of course these fruits are an expression for something real, but it is impossible to enter more deeply into these things in this book. Suffice it to state here that the fig is the fourth fruit. So it takes up the place of that which is expressed as 'four'. And tradition has it that the tree of knowledge was this tree of the fourth fruit. Indeed the tree of knowledge is to the tree of life as 'four' to 'one'.

Man wants to cover up his nakedness with materials from that tree itself, derived from the argument of that tree of duality, of multiplicity. That which had given him the feeling of nakedness, namely his scientific observation, his arguing according to the things he 'saw', that was what he tried to avail himself of to cover up that nakedness.

Ancient lore has it that man for all that continued to feel naked. It was merely 'aprons' he could make for himself; a great deal still remained uncovered. Afterwards this was also his excuse before God as to why he had hidden himself. He was ashamed of his nakedness before God.

For the tree of knowledge cannot yield enough material for man really to cover up that nakedness; there are too many deficiencies and one cannot get rid of the feeling of being naked.

When man begins to perceive that he is naked, he goes and hides himself. He hides from God before Whom he is now well aware of having taken the wrong turning. A turning which did not lead to the goal; a turning at variance with the purpose of creation and the purpose of life. It was a way which held out to him the prospect of becoming a God *himself,* independent, powerful, irremovable. He now knows he has not dressed and kept the garden, that he has not achieved harmony there; to the contrary, he has through his choice of way made the gap wider. He had interfered with the purpose of the whole and he too had changed because of it, a new propensity had arisen in him which made him see things only in great multiplicity which had blinded him and robbed him of his perspicacity, his encompassing vision.

God had told him to eat from *all* the trees, except from the tree of the knowledge of good and evil, because that tree had the power of duality, implying the power of making duality which in its turn implied the force of development, moving ever further away from the source of origin, hence ever emphasizing duality more and more. To fulfil the puposeof life man would have to go the opposite way, back from multiplicity to unity. In connecting and reuniting lay the purpose of his existence and that was what constituted his happiness.

Making duality, hence making 'development', creating 'distance' between source of origin and point of development attained, was the visible work of God's creation. And if man, too were to make multiplicity, were to develop everything 'further', driven by a strange desire of being a god, a desire fed by the 'serpent' clinging to his body, he would do exactly as God did with creation. And then he would feel himself to be lord. The same power God had used to make this visible world, man would then avail himself of. The serpent had been right when it had stated that man would then be like God. This urge to imitate God, this desire to pretend to be God, is part and parcel of the illusory world one builds up for oneself. It is the force of development – remember it implies an ever further removal from the origin, even though one does not like to look at it that way – which man has within himself, and which has formed him, and faces him with the alternative: continuing along the way of duality on which he finds himself in this life in order thus to find happiness, the secret of the purpose of life, or uniting everything with the source of origin, reuniting everything with God. If he chooses the way of development, he chooses his own standards, he puts himself in the place of God; if he takes the way of reunion with the source of origin, then he applies the standards of the Lord God, those which the Lord God gave him for that very purpose in His revelation of the purpose of creation and of existence.

The purpose of the world – according to the Bible – is not further development. The world *is* complete as it is, it simply has to be united, just as it is, with the source of origin. For that purpose man has to take in everything of this world, eat everything; life is a grand 'meal', the world offers the food, thus to bring back everything to the source, through man, who himself is bound to do so on account of his being specifically created in the likeness of God. And to reunite all this he should *not* develop further – for in the six days everything had been completed – and therefore he was to leave alone that force with which God has imbued the world to develop it so far.

With it man would recognize that the world such as God had given him was good and that it need not be helped any further in its development. For that reason his task consisted in keeping and dressing that garden – as ancient lore has it – and protecting it against the attacks of the beasts, who like the serpent had the force of development within themselves, on purpose to have it bridled by man – that is why man got the power to control the beasts – and to bring things back and unite them with the origin. The beasts might attack the garden, just as in the end the subtlest and most developed beast did make the attack.

Man would have had to do his work in that garden in a very specific way. His service would be to reintegrate everything with the source of origin through his understanding of the purpose thereof. Tradition expresses it in this way, that man 'would learn the Bible', i.e. that he would unite everything with the words which God had given him concerning the world. And protecting, the second task of man, would have consisted in beating off the attacks of multiplicity. His task, therefore, was to direct everything in his life of action towards integration with the origin and not to allow himself to be tempted by the enticements of multiplicity. Of all trees he was to eat, thus to unite them with the origin.

Now eating in Hebrew is 'achol', aleph-kaf-lamed, 1–20–30. The word also means completing, fulfilling. The part 'chol' means 'all'. And uniting the 'all' with the 'one' placed before it, implies that *then* it is completed. Hence taking up anything for this purpose, means eating, digesting, as well as completing, fulfilling.

If a thing is *not* taken up to be completed, it is 'taref', which means 'tearing to pieces', hence reducing to many parts, to multiplicity. Exactly the opposite of 'eating', fulfilling, completing. The 'beast' tears up, makes multiplicity. Man, on the contrary, eats, integrates.

Eating is considered a special action, quite beyond our modern utilism. Our conception of 'utility' allows man to eat to be healthy, to enjoy food. Eating, as viewed by the Bible, sets a purpose to both aspects, implying the integration of the world. Just as all things are united with the origin through man's thought and understanding, so they have to be united in their material expression with man's expression in matter. Thus union with the source of origin is possible even in the extreme development of creation, in that which is farthest removed from the origin, in matter. Man, who in himself has *both* the extreme development of the physical, of the material, and at the same time that which binds him to God, the divine soul, is here on earth for the very purpose to let everything pass through him in thought, in understanding, assimilation, treatment.

And for man to be able to do *that,* God had told him *how* the world is and what it is for and what all things mean. Lest he should judge from the standpoint of his body, of his senses. For unless man is firmly united with what is called divine soul, *Neshamah,* this very body as extreme, material development, will merely show him the external, the forces of development, and nothing else.

Thus man has to unite everything in the Garden of Eden with the source of origin, through himself. That was what he was brought there for, *that* was the purpose of his existence there. This integration of all things with the source, this reunion, gives the greatest satisfaction. *Thus* should eating be understood. Every other way of eating on the part of man, while turned away from the origin, is senseless, useless eating. It may even become 'tearing to pieces', making multiplicity.

The word 'chol', 20–30, the word which means 'all', has 50 as its sum-total. 'All' also means that it is '50', beyond the seventh day, that which we have learned to know as the beginning of the eighth day. What in the seventh day becomes together to be reunited, shows itself in fulfilment on the eighth day. There it is full, there it is 'all'.

Man, who had taken within himself the tree of the knowledge, had followed the way of further development, the way which was to form ever increasing multiplicity. And with this force of development within himself, man became aware of his nakedness, the senselessness in reality of the way which was now opening up to him. He made an effort to cover up that nakedness with material derived from this 'way of development'. But this material proved inadequate. It might at best remove the worst feeling of shame for the exterior. Before God, however, he knew himself to be naked, and therefore he now began to hide himself. This hiding always takes place, if one goes the way of development, of multiplicity. One hides oneself in life. One plunges into multiplicity, both mentally and physically. Both the man and the woman hide themselves. They get submerged in the world.

Until God calls them. God's call is heard in the word 'where are thou', in Hebrew 'ajeka', spelt aleph-jot-kaf-hee, 1–10–20–5. Ancient lore points out that this structure of 1–10–20–5 is identical with the word 'how' with which the lamentations begin, in the 'how dost thou sit solitary …'

It means that the call of God is heard when everything has crashed down about man. When he knows he is forsaken by all that he had relied on, when he has reached the end of a world and the end of a life.

It is then that communion with God comes to be. The man then points to the woman, to the body God had given him, that it was *that* which had driven him to go that way. And the woman, i.e. the body, points to the serpent, to the world with its aspect of growth, its force of development, which had created the impression that that was the direction to be taken and that it would be good. In spite of the constant inner awareness that one should not take that way.

When man has eaten from the tree of knowledge, he is not aware of any guilt within himself, but it is always 'the woman thou gavest me', this body, weak and easily tempted. To man it is God who is really to blame, because He made the world and man so that man could be led to do these things.

Then comes the weakening of these forces of enticement. The serpent is deprived of its feet, the 'two' (and then in fact the four) on which it can stand in the world.

Foot in Hebrew is 'regel', spelt resh-gimmel-lamed, 200–3–30. Now we see something remarkable here. The measure of the tree of life and that of the tree of knowledge was 233, *once* 233 for the tree of life and *four* times 233 for the tree of knowledge. In the tree of life, it means standing on the 'one'; just as it says in ancient lore that the angels are standing on 'one', the two feet touching, as man should also stand before God. The story in ancient lore subtly adds: 'for as soon as man moves his feet away from each other, if ever so slightly, the serpent crawls in between and bites him on the heel.'

Bringing the feet together physically, is bringing the body in harmony with the essential, where the two pillars on which everything seems to be based, are brought together in union.

The serpent, i.e. the world in its subtlest material development, stood on the 'four'. Based on the 'four', on the four elements, the four as the basis of the whole world, as it appears to us in fact, it aspired very high. Being based on the 'four', the serpent was clear and distinct, the building up could be distinguished. This 4× 'foot', this 4×233 is the 932, the sum-total, the value of the tree of the knowledge of good and evil.

This means, in other words, that with the serpent the power of duality of creation could be seen clearly and distinctly and could be used. There were, in fact, no secrets attached to it; everything was open.

But then things begin to change. The world as it then exists and one period of life upon it comes to an end.

The serpent loses its attractiveness. The subtlety in its mode of expression is taken away from it. It no longer masquerades, but shows itself just as it is. The force of development in itself now is nothing, it is merely a vile creature, eating 'dust'. Dust in Hebrew is 'afar', 70–80–200. This dust, with the sum-total of 350, is the image of infinite multiplicity.

The serpent has no distinct contact with the world; its feet are gone. There is no clear basis any longer. There is a kind of continuity, a roundness, a vagueness of distinction in the base, some sort of insolubility.

And it expresses itself 'vilely', where there cannot be an expression of things important to man.

Besides, the serpent expresses itself in its bite, having a poison which can be lethal. We can by this time realize that coming into touch with this world spells mortal danger to man, and there will be mutual hostility.

As soon as this world begins to rear its head, man will have to crush it. If not, that head will bite him where he is based on this world and then man will be destroyed. He will *have* to recognize the hostility, he will ever have to realize the danger to his existence from the part of this world which likes to present itself as enticing. What was first offered to him as his choice, as an indication not to accept the world in this way, will now express itself physically as well. If he does accept it, he will be bitten by it and therefore he will be more on his guard against it.

The serpent will have to crawl on its belly, devoid of legs. Writhing round, expressing what it is, the circle, roundness, which people can get entangled in, thinking it infinite, whereas it is merely a finite circle.

Belly is 'gachon', gimel-cheth-nun, 3–8–50. It has the same components, only partly in a different plane from serpent 'nachash', which is 50–8–300.

The woman, too, is weakened in her power. The body will perceive that passing from one world into another, as a result of man's having admitted the force of duality within himself, is a bitter thing. Now that man has received the tree of knowledge within himself, he has received duality, hence multiplicity. He himself would now get into multiplicity. The numerous generations, spread hither and thither, would in their entirety form mankind. They would hurt each other in not fitting together, because of the broken harmony, through contrasts cropping up on matters of priniciple, everywhere and always.

Man was now to continue life by way of the generations, compelled thereto by the force of duality he had assimilated. Through that force multiplicity will enter into everything consistently, also in man's own existence. And this passing from generation to generation, from world to world, would be a matter of suffering and pain to the body too – in order that it might rouse the desire for liberation from that condition, the desire for a world which would be permanent. Man would henceforward yearn – even physically – that the world should be one again, integrated. Now that physically too he had got the imprint of the transition from one world into the next, he would make an effort to terminate it. He would not consider it a joy any longer; he would recognize its many disadvantages. And the woman would desire the man, and he would dominate her. After this communion with God, after this hiding and this shame, the body would be freed from the force which made it act so independently. The body would henceforward have something to turn it more towards the soul, the divine soul. And having gone through it all, it would he dominated by the soul.

And man himself was told he would now find out how difficult the course through the world would he. Until he should have found things, they would cause him a lot of trouble and in the end he would see it was mere 'thorns and thistles'. The passage of the earth would he hard and not at all attractive. And that which was implied by the tree of knowledge, death as the other extreme of life, was henceforward to be man's share as well. He would share in the life of multiplicity, since he wanted to see everything in multiplicity. Death, too would drive him to strive, *body and soul,* after reunion, unity in everything, so that the bitterness, the gloom, the incomprehensibility of death, might come to an end simultaneously. Everything proclaiming 'messianism' and coming from the world of perception, of the senses, now gets the damper of limitation, of harshness of death. And all this expresses itself to its extreme consequence in the physical body, so that hence might arise the aversion to further development, and a desire instead for union with the origin, for reflection on the reason for existence, the significance of all that happens.

Then God replaced the aprons made of material from the tree of knowledge with garments made by God Himself. For nakedness had been very poorly covered with those aprons. After having attained this new situation, man acquired coats of skins. Let us dwell a moment on this word 'skin'. 'Skin' in Hebrew is 'or', spelt 70–6–200. It really means 'hide', but it can also be translated as 'skin'. In pronunciation this word 'or' is the same as the word 'or' which means 'light', only this latter word is spelt 1–6–200. The difference is that the aleph of the word for 'light' has been replaced by the ayin. The 1 has been replaced by the 70. And this has its meaning. We have already seen how the 'one' of the origin, the all-inclusive 'one', divided itself into the seven days, i. e. the six days of creation and this seventh day. The 'seven' therefore is an expression of the 'one' in this world. Moreover, in this seventh day one has come nearer unity again, and the beginning of the 'eighth' day restores the 'one'.

This 'seven', into which the world is divided in the root-story expresses itself as 'seventy' in the next plane, the plane of Decades. That is why we always see the 'seventy' appearing as an expression of multiplicity in the human relationships of this world. Just as forty and four hundred are an expression of multiplicity in the space-time principle of this world.

There are 70 nations, descended from Noah (Gen. 10) and there are the 70 children of Jacob, travelling down to Egypt; there are the 70 elders of the people in the journey across the desert. Tradition mentions 70 languages and 70 sciences. It is an expression of the appearance of multiplicity in this seventh day; it does not imply that in the phenomenal appearance of this world there are no numbers higher than 'seventy' to describe things. But as an expression of the essence of this seventh day in regard to man, the seventy is a principle.

Thus in the seventh day the 'aleph' of the beginning is replaced by the ayin, the 70, hence all things get a different aspect. The garment of 'light' man wears, before he eats from the tree of knowledge, is extinguished, so to speak. The physical eyes open to another light, a light broken in multiplicity. Man does not survey things at a glance, but he sees things broken up into bits; it would take an infinite time in an infinite space for him to see *eveything* again.

The garment of light which was extinguished meant man's very shame. Man saw that the limitation he had acquired now did not fit in with his destination which was to be all-embracing. His lost power, a power he possessed before – and which he himself and everything about him knew belonged to him – made him feel ashamed. And therefore he made the aprons, the shabby coverings.

But now God made him another garment. He now got the hide, the skin, the sheath, of a 'beast'. Especially in those places where the fall of man was most strongly emphasized. The head got hair on it, it also came to grow round the eyes which wanted 'to see', the arms which wanted to do things with the world, the fruitfulness which wanted to find physical expression, in multiplicity; all this acquired the 'coat of skin' in a marked way in those places.

'Hair' is 'saar', spelt sin-ayin-resh, 300–70–200. Spelt with the 300, pronounced as 'shin', hence shaar, it means 'gate'. So it is the place which gives the connection, inwards and outwards. But with the 'left hand' sin it acquires a different character, the character of the strong, the bodily, the female, briefly, the 'left hand side' of our systematism.

Now this 'coat of skin' covered the contrast between man's character of eternity and his broken appearance of the present. In conformity therewith does man continue to cover himself up. For even in *that* body is expressed what actually happened. And it is especially the places indicating this fall which man covers up.

And then there is man's removal from the world where he had lived. That world is now closed to him; there is no return by that road any more. Man had to leave that world where, according to ancient lore, all this had enacted itself in an unconscionably short time, according to our conception of time. At the end of the sixth day, at the end of Friday afternoon. The closer to the origin, however, the more 'rapidly' does time uncoil things, i.e. the more there happens in what to our conception is a very brief space of time. And the further removed from the origin, the longer time seems to last, in spite of a great number of events, taking place at every moment of time.

And man had to leave that world, because otherwise he would also have eaten from the tree of life, which in fact had been destined for him as one of the trees from which he would ever have to eat. But, with multiplicity within himself, this assimilation of the tree of life would have given man the opportunity of continuing the work of development of multiplicity unto all eternity, without even accomplishing any purpose. There would have been no return any more. The line of development would simply continue. The curve, the return to the source of origin would not be achieved. The purpose of creation, that very bliss of 'coming home' would be eliminated.

Ancient lore has it that God created many worlds even before this, but that He had 'destroyed' them again, because they all shot away from the origin and wanted to develop even further. Until God decided to accompany this world *Himself* in His quality of 'Lord God', that He might bring it home again without fail.

That is why among other things ancient lore mentions 974 earlier worlds. The remarkable thing is that there should remain those 26, to make up the 1000, and these 26 render the number of the name 'Lord God' and of the 26 generations.

Now shooting away of the world into infinity never to return again to the origin is prevented in *this* world. Whoever carries the tree of knowledge within himself, is 'automatically' cut off from the tree of life. For otherwise such a one would indeed become 'like a god', he would be able to continue unfolding matter uninterruptedly and never come back. It would be a complete detachment, a complete emancipation of material development from its source of origin. As an independent godhead it would move throughout eternity, equipped with the force of duality bestowed by God on the world to cause it to arise; thus in its breaking away leaving God no choice but eliminating it, destroying it.

But now, in this creation, where the same thing enacts itself all the time according to this pattern, where all the time matter, the world, is tempting man to develop it further, where it rouses in him the idea that he himself may become a godhead in availing himself of matter as the building-brick to build up his eternal happiness – the serpent uses that motive – in this creation something different has been laid down. Always, when this development arises, and it will come time and again, then that other force will come into action, God's force which pulls back, which causes the curve to arise, which does not admit of uncurbed further development. Then this force comes into action weakening matter in its power of attraction depriving the serpent of its feet, which bestow death on man.

The tree of life can only be taken by those who have *not* eaten from the tree of knowledge, hence by those who have not identified themselves with the forces of development to lead the world by way of material development to a human ideal, by those who do *not* measure the world with the standards of their senses.

The Bible is called by ancient lore – and such not as a mere 'image', but as a reality – the tree of life. Whoever knows the Bible, *knows* eternity. But in its essence the Bible is close to those who simultaneously want to take the tree of knowledge, or have already taken of it. In that case one may read the Bible, one may see the various images of the story, but one will not be able to penetrate to the essence of the Bible. The way to the tree of knowledge, too, is then closed off.

We are now coming to an important principle. *What* exactly was man to do in the Garden of Eden? What does it mean – Garden of Eden? And what are those trees? I am sure many people wonder a lot about those trees. People are perfectly willing to ponder on the essence by way of an image, but that it should be exactly those trees I shall try make things as clear as possible in a few words.

Now what was man supposed to do in the Garden of Eden? Considering the principle of creation, the principle of the 1–2–1, he was to bring everything around him, as it presented itself to him in that duality, back to unity right through himself, through man himself. But he was to leave alone the force which made the duality in which he found everything; tempted though he might be by the attraction of this creative force through which God had created everything and which expressed itself on all sides, he was not allowed to appropriate this force to do likewise and become a creator of this world like God.

The work in the Garden of Eden is described as 'obed' and 'shomer', literally 'working' and 'preserving'. Man, therefore, has a task where it is not *himself* that is the lord, the head, but where he follows the directions, the instructions from a master who has given him this task to perform.

This 'working' or 'tending' or 'dressing' is not service given to an inconstant and harsh lord, but it implies that one has to do things trusting to the rightness of the result. It can also be done from love, from attachment, from self-surrender to somebody else, since one trusts, takes for granted that that which the other imposes, is absolutely good.

Reducing duality to 'unity' in this world is based on the principle that it is done in the belief and faith that the lord who gave the instructions knew things well and meant well and that the outcome was bound to be very good. The basis of this integration therefore is not a previous determination *why* one is going to do it like that – for instance, because one has noticed for oneself that things will yield good results, since one has computed things for oneself and reasoned them out and planned them accordingly. It is not that one has previously proved to oneself that one was to gain eternal bliss that way. To the contrary, it is purely because God said the result would be good, if one did things that way; just because one trusts in God, has faith in God.

For it is here as it is with the reflection in a mirror. As God made the world to bestow on man the greatest bliss on his way to reunion, all for nothing, only because God created him to let him experience the good, therefore on the part of man there is a similar relationship, a following of the way indicated by God, without first calculating whether or not that way is good for him, whether there might not be a better way, which man in his *own* interests had better go. Just as God gives the way to 'man', 'for nothing', similarly man should go 'for nothing'.

If man were first to calculate and weigh things, and find the proof that the way was really good, then it would have been *man's* way; then he would have done things for his own benefit, not for God. Therefore God made man go a way which gave man a certain passivity, an attitude first to accept what God presents as good and only then to find out what it led to. So it is related to the foundation which creation is established on, the basis of mutual love and affection.

In the structure of the word, belief or faith, 'emunah', is aleph-mem-nun-hee, 1–40–50–5. The root is aleph mem-nun, 1–40–50. It is the same word used when one says 'amen', which also literally means 'I believe that'.

We remember that the structure of the word 'truth' is 1–40–400. It is the connection of expressions 'furthest removed' in this world, the 40 and the 400, with the 1. So it is that which we can *prove* here as being true.

The word belief, or faith, however, is a higher form of the word 'demonstrable truth'. Instead of the 1–40–400, it has the 1–40–50; hence it ends with what we learned to know as realization in the next world, the next day. Belief, faith, therefore passes beyond this world to the eighth day, connects it with this world. It is of an order, different from demonstrable truth; its proof is more certain, more profound.

Thus the word for man 'adam', as we have seen, is 1–4–40. The word for lord, however, also for Lord God, pronounced differently from the way it is written, is 1–4–50. Hence again that relationship with the next world, with a world higher than this. Mankind living in the Garden of Eden, attaining the tree of life, is *not* merely an intellectual affair. The condition is the attitude of willingness to accept the way of God, without first judging for ourselves whether this way fits in with our conceptions and whether there is not another way of our own which might yield better results. The fact that, after one has taken the decision to go the way of God, because one trusts that that way will be good, there is abundant proof and much more besides, together with profound intellectual joy and much more besides, is a different matter. In fact, one who undertakes to dress and keep the garden after God's instructions, knows it quite well. He is even aware of such knowledge more profoundly than the man, who thinks he can reach the goal by the standards of development, can possible have any suspicion of.

But whoever, before accepting the tree of life, the Bible, wants to take the way of the world in order to reach the tree of life along *that* road, i.e. whoever wants to build things himself with the help of his intellect, with his 'true' standards, will be faced with the effect of the law of creation, that he has thus cut off the way to the tree of life. He will never reach it and besides, in his individual life he will soon leave the world where the tree of life is present, and he will move into another plane, into the world weakened by God and typified by what God did to the serpent, the woman, the man and the earth, when the tree of knowledge had been plucked from. It is comparable with an automatic security. As soon as the argument of the serpent has taken root in man and he has taken the forces of development as instruments for the rest of his life, this becomes operative.

Since essentially every man – as it is told in the Bible in the root-story of Adam – owing to the fact that he has a body and must use it to live, eats in *that* place in his life from the tree of knowledge, therefore every man on account of *this* body is subject to death.

Tradition mentions that it ceases with the 26th generation in the Bible, i.e. the generation present at the revelation. At that moment, as an unexpected gift of God, the tree of life is restored. It is the word of God, as expressed in the Bible and made known to man. In accepting that and in not accepting the tree of knowledge, man regains the life of the Origin. As long, however, as this seventh day lasts in this world, as long as the promised land, the coming world has not been attained, man still finds his expression in this body too, and is subject to death. At that time, however, not as one getting lost, a thing he prefers not to think about, but with the cognisance that death is a transition to another world, an emancipation from bondage to duality, back to the origin, back to that very 'Garden of Eden'.

Now what is the purpose of death, after man has eaten from the tree of knowledge? One has to accustom oneself no longer to consider God as a stern punisher. God *must* love mankind better – men *must* be nearer and dearer to Him as their creator, since He made them completely – than parents love their children, whom they made only partly, whom they did not make as they are and down to the tiniest details. If God gives death to man, then there must be a distinct purpose for it, for man's benefit. Now that man has assimilated the principle of the tree of knowledge within himself, and wants to measure and weigh and observe everything, since he cannot behave any other way, there is yet one possibility left to him to put that faith and belief in God, which he should have shown in the Garden of Eden, by doing what God recommended, *confident* that that would be right. This possibility of putting faith in God lies in the fact that man in this life and in this world should do the things which God presents as good to him in the Bible, without demanding to see the results here and now, thus showing he obeys all the same, knowing that God purposes well with the world and creation and man himself.

Death has become the point, all knowledge of the world fails to fathom. For in spite of all parapsychology which can merely contribute to increasing the horror of death, behind that point there is only something unknown and unaccountable to *knowledge*. But to faith and belief, to every individual in his own way, there is often a much greater certainty beyond the point of death than demonstrable knowledge could ever indicate. Thus the possibility remained for man for his part to give an act of emotion, an assurance of faith 'for nothing' in exchange for the bliss of the re-union which God offered man at creation.

This moment of eating of the tree of knowledge, hence bringing death into this world, according to tradition is expressed in the first tale of creation in the final words of the sixth day, namely where it says in the Bible that God saw that it was 'very good', all that He had made. The word for 'very' which is used here instead of the word 'good' at the end of all the other days is 'mend' in Hebrew, spelt mem-aleph-daleth, 40–1–4. The word for 'death' is 'maweth', spelt mem-wau-taf, 40–6–400. At the end of the sixth day, when man has eaten from the tree of knowledge, and death has come for him, tradition has the passage '*tob maweth*', 'death is good', instead of '*tob meod*', 'very good', since the structure of letters in both expressions shows close affinity. It is read thus, because with death, the possibility was restored to man, in spite of his contact with the tree of knowledge – existing already on account of the presence of the body – to live *all the same* and in living consciously to show that he is confident everything will come right. A confidence which the tree of knowledge had no answer for. For that tree of knowledge would have had to give a very negative and a very horrible answer.

Attaining the goal is not an intellectual affair to the effect that man paves his way led by the intellect. On the other hand it is not an affair either which enacts itself outside the intellect or is even opposed to the intellect. The intellect, as one of the agencies through which man can experience his grandeur still more profoundly, through which he can experience things all the more consciously, even plays an important part. 'Dressing the garden' is no stupid, obtuse labour, only to be performed by a creature uninterested in intellectual matters. For indeed we have already seen that what God gave unto man as the tree of life, as revelation, as His greatest and very first creation, is something which should be assimilated by man with great interest and real insight, something with which he should be occupied night and day in everything he does. So it absolutely is not a thing man can wave away negligently, to return to the order of the day afterwards.

The immense difference with what we consider as intellectual labour, however, is that we should first accept the Bible as a serious thing, of the same order as creation itself, and then ponder on what might be the pupose of *our* life and *our* world according to the Bible. Looking at the Bible in that way, we shall see how it opens up to us a world so profound, so full of miracles and so full of certainties that we feel sure we have found the tree of life therewith.

The difference in our ordinary intellectual approach to things lies in the fact that we are accustomed first to create standards according to our observations of the world, in agreement with our arguments, then to measure everything, also as regards the destination of man and of the world, and consequently to mould or remould things.

So what one does is to take one's own observations, one's own logic as fundamental, with it to probe heaven, the eternal, thus to build up one's vision of life. But according to the Bible this is the very way of the tree of knowledge, *even* if one is condescending enough to accept the Bible as a most important hook. It is not for us, it is not for the world to determine whether the Bible is important. Since it is a creation, the Bible must be fundamental, and come to us as such, and it is only by means of the Bible that we should build our view of life and let our actions be determined. That is what is meant by 'dressing' the garden; one should be able to accept things from a loftier point of view.

What one accepts is not *contrary* to everything one sees and can understand. It is not an obscure, and complicated belief in magic, with all kinds of unintelligible and repugnant things. It is like that only when one 'merely believes'. But if one accepts it seriously, as coming from a higher world, the miracles will reveal themselves; then those things I am trying to point out in this book as special contexts, as marvellous profundities, are yet the very first approach, an orientation at the gate of a very remarkable palace. This acceptance of the Bible as coming from a higher world is readily confirmed by the numerous wonderful relationships one will find, by the very special structure, pointing out the connection between the profound structure of life and of creation.

So it certainly is something to be approached with great intellectual interest. Every man received the intellect at creation, the more intensely to experience the joy of probing the purpose of life, of all creation. Consciously or unconsciously eliminating the intellect is mutilating man in one of the very aspects of his likeness to God. And often this elimination of the intellect is an evasion to excuse to oneself one's lack of interest in these things. People then use their intellect all the more energetically for other, so called worldly affairs. The difference merely lies in the starting-point. One should not take oneself for a god, one should not consider one's own experiences, one's own standards as decisive criteria. One should start with the attitude of being willing to accept something which *cannot* possibly derive from human beings, because its composition is too grand, its structure too profound, too distinctly pre-mundane and pre-human.

It evidently is a very difficult matter. For one is perfectly ready to accept things from other people, or even to admit that no man knows or can do it yet, but that it is sure to be found by future, more erudite generations. For then it remains connected with the species man, to which one belongs oneself, and then it will exclude the presence of a higher power, regulating and surveying everything to the veriest details.

Now one may eventually be ready to accept God as the original creator or as the power that created the universe and preserves it. But this world and this life one had rather decide on for oneself, one wants to have things under one's own control; one had rather not have anything higher than man. Therefore one argues God away from these details. They are then called too trivial, too niggling for Him.

But the Bible shows how God gave every letter in it a very definite place either directly, or indirectly through guiding the hand of the man who wrote it down. Every single detail in the Bible, even the smallest, proves to have been arranged, put in its appropriate place. Thus every little detail in life is purposeful, agreeing with the structure of the world, with the structure of life.

So one must not create a contrast between intellect and faith. The contrast is that between having the intellect operate with its own standards derived from observation and experience, or having the intellect operate with standards which one has first to draw from another creation, which expresses itself through the word, it is true, but will then promptly open up a new world to us, a world which, besides a number of other things, affords an intense, intellectual joy, because of its phenomenal systematism, its balanced completeness, fitting all component parts into one great harmony.

It is *not* the right way, if — as many people do and have done — we should accept the Bible as something special, and subsequently interpret it by various standards, often adapted to definite purposes. Then again 'I and mine' would be the determinant and not the 'dressing' in the 'Garden of Eden', i.e. accepting the method supplied by the Creator of the garden.

For these interpretations of one's own merely serve one's own purposes, however good their intentions may often be. They cannot but be arbitrary or be based on a superficial systematism, for none can create a systematism which can hold its ground throughout, down to the structure of the word.

Therefore only an interpretation entirely built up on the systematism of the Bible itself can be consistent and at the same time mentally acceptable and even strengthening our faith. And such an interpretation, based on the systematism of the Bible, has to draw its standards for such systematism for the Bible itself. Without knowledge of *these* standards and of *that* systematism it would be a meaningless and rather dangerous labour to 'give an exegesis' of the Bible. 'What standards are we to use and why only in this way and not otherwise?' one may ask. It may be compared with talking about stars and their orbits, the coherence between orbits and times of revolution without first acquainting oneself with the systematism which the astronomy of this creation of the universe has to proclaim.

This is one of the reasons why in the first part of this book I tried to give the reader some conception of a systematism, a structure present in the Bible.

Only on the basis of such systematism and structure, drawn from the Bible *itself*, can an exegesis of the Bible also be logically acceptable. People should not complain of opposition offered in various circles to 'preachments' from the Bible, when these groups realize how arbitrary the interpretations of certain texts are, which often imply criticism of personages in the Bible, with the wise conclusion that we are now farther advanced and better people and would not *dream* of doing such and such a thing. One should really feel heartily glad that there are many left yet who are *willing* to take the Bible seriously and do not tolerate other people to wrench and tear the texts of the Bible arbitrarily to make them fit in with their special 'school', hence at variance with other 'schools'.

If the 'predications' were based on the structure of the Bible itself, not to be misunderstood by anybody because of its penetration into the smallest details, one could only accept or give the impression of wanting to evade the *facts*. But in that case it would be no longer a vague question of texts here or texts there, sometimes interpreted this way, sometimes that.

The great difficulty is not to point out the profound structure of the Bible; the difficulty lies in the fact that man often prefers going the way of the tree of knowledge.

Man wants to fix the standards himself, there is something which whispers to him that he can be a god himself; that he himself can rule the world, life, perhaps even the universe; control things; introduce things for the benefit of *this* world. He is inclined to try out this possibility first and therefore to reject in advance the possibility of something existing in the word something not subject to development, growth, something which evidently must originate from another world, if indeed it is to possess this sweeping and profound systematism; he will reject this possibility, since it would imply an interference in the very details of everything in life.

For this would imply that human interference through 'planning', 'politics', etc. is merely childish make-believe to imagine one really has power.

That is why many people will reject this 'service' in advance; they will *refuse* to seek their standards elsewhere instead of in themselves and they will prefer from the outset to follow the way of the tree of knowledge. With all the consequences thereof, and also with one that closes off the way to the tree of life. For then these people will lose the faculty of seeing any other way at all. The way to the tree of life will then be closed off on account of the danger it might be, if assimilated by those who already have in themselves the force of duality, of making multiplicity.

It is a remarkable fact that people are ready to accept they are descended from puny, primitive creatures, that a doctrine of evolution was created implying that, although mankind has not yet achieved a great deal, it is bound to be considerable in the far future, as long as everything is left to man, as long as no other great knowledge, all-encompassing knowledge, anywhere else need he accepted. It is remarkable, yet remember, it is human. The Bible gives this structure to man in the very beginning.

The story of the tree which was 'good for food, and pleasant for the eyes and a tree to be desired to make one wise', therefore implies a great deal, if one ponders on the meaning which the structure of the biblical story reveals. The only thing is that one should ever watch carefully whether the translations into conceptions which one applies, do actually follow from the structure of the word and the systematism. We have meticulously done so in the foregoing, by means of all that has already been stated by us about the story.

Now where do we stand as regards the images used in this story; the 'garden', 'Eden', the 'trees'?

In the foregoing something has been said about the significance of the images as expressions in matter of things essential. All the same there remains the question whether there cannot be a more logical connection, some visible connection, between these modes of expression and the substance.

There is such a connection indeed; the only thing is that modern man has largely lost his vision of this coherence. To him phenomena have become things of a certain 'utility'; he has come to look upon them in connection with their greater or lesser utility in his life in this world. He uses them and merely thinks of them in relation to their use.

When he finds occasionally that earlier generations looked on things differently, he has a word ready with which to sweep away these views of long ago – 'formerly people saw things in their magic context'. Since magic is something unscientific, which does not fit into the system he has built up for himself of the world, it is 'primitive', hence dated, stupid. In doing so he forgets that *his* magic too has formulae, that it merely uses things in a different way. His magic is chemistry, physics, biology, with magical instruments like microcopes, etc., to analyse matter from which things have been built up.

Indeed it is better in our times not to step into eventual techniques of former times, into their 'magic' approach to things. Suffice it to say that people saw things differently, used things differently, since they had knowledge, understanding of what there was behind such a thing. It is sufficient for modern man to realize that 'images', the phenomena of things essential, may be approached very differently from the way we generally do today.

For there is a connection between the phenomena and the essence, although this connection often is very difficult of find. The only more direct and exact connection is that of the word, just as the Bible uses it. But if we stop to think of the 'ed', the mist, which was to rise up before man and all the rest could make their appearance in this phenomenal world, this left-hand world, then we are justified in asking ourselves what connection there is between 'mist' and 'man'. A connection which is bound to exist with the structure of the words 1–4 and 1–4–40. The 40 which in man comes after the 1–4 of the mist is, as it were, the concretizing, the further materializing.

The conception 'mist' — it need not be watery vapour exclusively — indicates in the image that the initial appearance resembled something we might call gaseous, that this was the first sign of assuming form in this world, when it already existed essentially in another world which was of an altogether different quality. The second tale of creation expresses it thus: that it simply could not pierce through here, as long as a definite basic structure had not been achieved for this world. This basic structure had to do with water, rain, and it expressed itself initially in this gaseous form. Once *it* was there, the rest which already existed in substance in another world could acquire a form *here* too.

This image is intelligible to our understanding albeit at the risk of many misconceptions. It shows us that the world in its phenomenal form, as the second tale of creation gives it, did *not* find its base in wild rocky formations, but that something very light, almost ethereal, invisible, became the base, later on to pass into heavier matter.

However, reasoning, even along this way, and making use of the images, is very difficult. One is so apt to make use of those images for *oneself*, then to act further by means of the experiences one gathers therewith.

For those images *can*, if properly understood, yield forces to man which give him power and knowledge in this world. *That* was the idolatry of olden times. It is identical with what our sciences do *nowadays*, only along a different line. It is the desire to control the world with the help of exhaustive knowledge of matter and its phenomena.

The struggle against idolatry in the Bible, therefore, is not a struggle against man's ignorance and primitivity, a battle which was to lose its significance as soon as man had 'developed' a little more, and started studying modern science and technology. That is one of many foolish conceits of modern man who imagines himself to be so much wiser and 'more advanced' than his ancestors.

The struggle against idolatry in the Bible is the struggle against the desire to use the image, the exterior form of the world, in order to acquire power over the world through knowledge of it; the desire to feel oneself to be the lord and to try to get man to stake all his resources on this path. It is a path which deviates from man's real purpose, which leads him to multiplicity instead of leading him to the reintegration of all things with the origin.

For these reasons it is so dangerous to attach *this* significance to these images. It is the way of the tree of knowledge, it is indeed the way which is the measuring of the world with the self-made standards built up from observation, and using the world to support constructions thus built by oneself.

It is for this reason one should transfer the image directly to the word, to the essence and realize that one should set the image free through integrating it with its essence.

Looked at in this way, the image of a 'garden', as the Garden of Eden is expressed, is a place where grow all kinds of plants. In Hebrew the word is 'gan', gimmel-nun, 3–50, and it really just means 'garden'. A garden is the place where plants grow, develop. One sees things growing out of practically 'nothing', like a seed, growing to full maturity. Such is the image.

The word is built up of the initial 3 and the final 50. The 'three' implies a duality. And indeed that garden proves to express this duality in the image. The duality of the two 'trees', the tree of knowledge and the tree of life as the centre, in the midst of the 'garden'. So, as soon as we consider the word after its substance, in its relationship with the structure of the biblical story, we promptly notice an emphasis different from what we would see, if we merely occupied ourselves with the image of the 'garden'. It is therefore, for the very reason that 'garden' has the 3 as its determining initial digit, that the image of the Bible, which indeed is based on the essence of the word, puts that sudden emphasis on the two different trees in the garden.

And the word for 'garden' has for its ending the 'nun', 50. The 50 which ever has the very special nature of being beyond the 49, beyond the world of the seventh day, which points to the coming world of the eighth day.

Expressed in words, 'garden' essentially means: the duality of the world which has its destiny to pass into the coming world and there, as we already know from the structure of the whole, to become 'one' again, a unity.

And man's labour in the garden is to take care that that coming world, the fruit of what was fostered here, is attained, and he will experience himself the bliss of this attainment.

This garden of the biblical story of the beginning, lies in 'Eden'. This too is a word with a specific meaning, with a specific significance. In common parlance it has acquired a pleasant emotional value, so it is used as a name for hotels pretending they can send grilled pigeons flying into the mouths of their guests.

The word 'Eden' is spelt ayin-daleth-nun, 70–4–50. Fortunately it is not translated except sometimes as Paradise, which however, is not a translation, but merely the use of a different word for garden namely, 'pardes', spelt peh-resh-daleth-samech, 80–200–4–60.

The word Eden is built up from two typical numbers of multiplicity. The 70 as multiplicity in man, as we have already seen, as multiplicity expressed in the division into the seven days of the world, and the 4 as number of the furthest development, the number serving as base for the 40 and the 400, hence also for the 10, and the 100, and the 1,000. And then again the word Eden also ends in the 50 of the coming world, of the coming eighth day, the day beyond this completed seventh day, beyond the 49.

Together this 70 and 4 form a very special combination. Among other things they also mean 'witness', a person who sees something and knows it, who can give witness. This combination of 70–4 also means 'towards', the way towards a certain goal, or destination.

In either case the word expresses a presence in its full extent, in the 70 as highest number, and in the 4 as highest number in a different quality. A witness should on principle know to its full extent that which he gives witness of; he must not make combinations or conclusions himself. He should know that which he says as a witness, completely from alpha to omega, hence as 70 and 4. The word 'to' similarly indicates that one has covered the whole way, the whole 70, every detail of the appearance into the seventh day, and the whole 4, all that as principle indicates the furthest possibility.

Moreover this 70–4 expresses that it is the 'mist', the 'ed', the 1–4 of the beginning, but now expressed in every single part pertaining to the phenomenal form, as it was to appear in the seventh day.

So Eden is the passing of this world of multiplicity into the future world of the 50, into the world of the eighth day. But in the conception 'Eden' this passing is completed also, just as *in the image of a 'garden'*, the fruits are already there, at least they can be there, for otherwise it is not a garden hut just an odd hit of ground which might eventually be a wilderness as well.

In 'Eden' multiplicity is inherent in unity. And in the Garden of Eden duality is specially cultivated by man to bring it to unity and to preserve, and keep it on the way to unity. On the conception 'preserving' I wrote previously, and so I refer there.

Both 'gan', the garden, and Eden are places of duality, resp. multiplicity, which in that world are at the same time in unity, integrated. The 'nun' at the end indicates that they are at the same time in the eighth day, in the world-to-come.

So there is a synthesis there which to us is incomprehensible: there is multiplicity, there is the way to unity, yet unity itself is already attained. To our minds there can only be a journey to unity or unity attained. In that world, however, the two opposites are at one. It is as in the original 'one', in which the opposites are united in harmony. Just as in the 'aleph', in which both 'jots' are present in harmony.

That this 'ayin' and 'daleth', 70 and 4 of 'Eden' have a special significance as expressions of 'multiplicity' which are led to oneness is evident from the following:

In Deuteronomy (6:4) occurs the well-known pronouncement which in translation is, 'Hear, O Israel, the Lord our God is one God.'

It implies in words that the Lord God – God in His quality of accompanying mankind in history, a coming along with mankind expressive of God's compassion with creation, His love of it – to us is God, and that God as Lord God just because of His special quality of going with the world and putting His mark on this world, is not yet seen by many as oneness, *cannot* yet be beheld as such on account of the many opposites coming to expression in the development of history, on account of much unrighteousness, cruelty, ignorance, but that none the less it should be known that He is 'one', that everything *does* tally and everything *is* good. God as the Lord God, in the development of time, in the course of the 26 generations is 'one'. Although He seems to reveal Himself in time, in evolution, in a great variety on the way to revelation, *yet* at the same time He is 'one'. To see that much is meant with the statement made in this text.

In the words of the Bible in the original language there is something remarkable to see in the text. In this sentence again two letters have been written in capitals, just as for instance the 'beth', the 'two' of the word 'bereshith', in the beginning. And those two letters written in capitals are these very letters which we discussed just now, viz. the 70 and the 4, the 'ayin' and the 'daleth', the letters 'Ed' of 'Eden'.

That here in this very place, and only here, they are written in capitals, gives that significance to the statement in words, mentioned, namely that the Lord God indeed may appear to the world as multiplicity, as manifest 70 and manifest 4, but that one should know none the less He is 'one'. That in all happenings and in all things one should see their context, their emerging from the 'one'. That ultimately what seemed multiplicity, either in the world of men with for instance the 70 peoples embracing 'all' nations in this world, or in the space-time world expressed in the 4 as furthest development, will become 'one'. Thus the 70–4 in 'capitals' is connected with the world-to-come, with the coming day, and ipso facto becomes 'Eden'. In seeing, understanding, realizing this even *here* in this world, one changes multiplicity into 'unity'.

Though I do not intend to discuss in this book the structure of the ancient Jewish practice of life on this basis of knowledge and cognition of the Bible, I should like in this connection to mention by way of illustration that in the daily pronouncement of three passages from the Pentateuch in consequence of the statement that the capital 'Ed', can already be Eden here, if one sees the Lord God and knows Him as 'one', this 'one' will consciously permeate every detail and integrate the whole into 'one'.

These three passages, well known as 'Kriath Shma' (Deut. 6:4–9; Deut. 11:13–21; Num. 15:37–41) contain the biblical statement that people should be constantly engaged with the Bible; then, the statement of the relationship between life in this world and that of eternity, and finally not to judge on observation and standards of one's own, but accepting the standards which God reveals to men. They are contextual, they are an extension of the principle in the opening words that in fact the 70–4 in 'capitals', multiplicity here, must yet be seen as 'one'. These three passages end with the word 'truth', 'emeth', stating that one bears witness to it, just as the 70–4 in capitals bears witness. And after the first line has been pronounced, the pronouncement is added of a few words, of ancient usage, with which the name of the Lord is further specified.

At any rate, this entire whole, based on the statement of 'oneness' in this world of multiplicity and of the way in which this statement can be realized, experienced, contains exactly 1,000 letters, hence that which is again the 'one', again written as the 'aleph', the 'one', but now pronounced as 'eleph'. It is the 10, not only of this world in its fulfilment of 10^2, but in a higher degree of fulfilment, viz. that of 10^3.

This 1,000, as 'one' of a higher order – and again this is not mere coincidence, but it is another expression of the very secret of proportions – also implies twice the conception 500. We have already seen that this 500 is the expression of a measure representing the distance from this world to the world-to-come, also from the earth to heaven. The conception 1,000, therefore, is also the realization, yearned for by mankind throughout all time, of the mutual connection of this world and the next, of earth and heaven. It means that God hears him and answers him. And this is the very meaning of the words of these passages, forming one whole. For those words tell us about the manner in which this connection is effected and how it works. The opposite movement here means the harmony as it always exists in the 'one'. And because of the fact that in this passage there is unity of the image of the word and its substance, manifesting in this 1,000, it has such a profound significance.

The distance, too, between heaven and earth is measured with this measure of the 500. The 500 always bridges the unbridgeable. The 1,000 of the 'Kriath Shma' expresses in images of our world how this bridging is effected from either side and how the connection endures. The significance of imbuing these words with life is fostered by the essence with the secret of this 1,000, of this especial 'one'.

I propose to confine myself to this single example, and to point out how in ancient times the practice of life was built up on the basis of that knowledge. It was not society aiming at utility on the part of the prophets who did the work, no aiming at binding a nation together through giving them special customs, it was not a question of an ambitious 'caste of priests'. It always indicates in the smallest details the sublime and profound vision of the purpose of life, the purpose of all existence. Compared with it all considerations of utility, either hygienic or psychic are of a much lower order.

I shall now pass on to the discussion of the conception 'tree' we have so often came across in the tree of life and the tree of knowledge. Since we have already discussed the 'garden' as an image, the image for 'tree' is easier to explain.

A tree as a phenomenon in this world is a thing growing out of an originally obscure beginning, practically invisible, and which in its growth and development comes to yield fruits which in their turn permit of a new beginning apart from the original tree. Trees form part of the entirety of the 'garden' where this development can take place controlled and aided by man.

The garden in its word-structure contains duality expressing itself in the word, in the 'gimmel', the 'three', the number of duality. In the story this duality is expressed in the fact that there are *two* trees coming into prominence: the tree of life and the tree of knowledge.

We also saw that the conception 'garden', 'gan', 3–50, implies that duality is eliminated by the '50', by the passing into or the presence of the world to come, the world of the eighth day. In the conception Eden this passing into unity was also implied.

Both conceptions, 'garden' as well as 'Eden' therefore present duality, multiplicity on the side of growth, development; and on the other hand, because of the 'nun' at the end, there is 'unity' again. It is a contrast which must exist for us, since we do not know anything which is still duality or multiplicity in a stage of development, yet which simultaneously is already 'one', complete, finished, in the next world as fruit of the previous world.

We do not know this condition, because we have actually been expelled from 'Eden', and from that 'garden' of Eden. To us the '50' is yet to come, after the end of this world, after the end of growth and development. To us the number denoting the end is still the 40, the 'mem'.

What is expressed in the conceptions 'garden' and 'Eden' is enacted with the tree as something separate. For the garden and Eden are determined by the presence of 'trees', and particularly, in accordance with the structure of the word 'garden', by two trees: one of which, the tree of life, distinctly has the character of 'unity', while the other, the tree of the knowledge of good and evil, obviously has the character of duality, of multiplicity.

Now the statement about the trees are the first occurring in the Bible which denote life arising. This initial life expresses itself in plants and, as mentioned especially, in trees.

And this first expression of life proves to be a life of development, of growth. It has a specific purpose running parallel with development, viz. the forming of seed and fruits for a new life. So this is the first expression of life. Life, in its image obviously has to show growth; it is not, like water or earth, something which presents itself as invariable in its image. So the phenomenon of life is growth, development.

Now one will wonder where in the first tale of creation are we told about those two trees which in the second tale of creation prove to be of such preponderant significance? For they should appear in the first tale as well, and this appearance should be very distinct there as well, considering the significance this duality has in the world. In both tales of creation this expression of life in the world of plants takes the third place. But in the image of the first tale of creation there seems to be nothing, at least at first sight, about these two special trees, the tree of life and the tree of knowledge.

None the less they are there, and even in such a way that we learn much better to understand the conceptions tree of life and tree of knowledge, which occur later on. But to perceive them one should understand a little of the language of the Bible.

In the translation we can read, in the first story of creation, that on the third day, at the creation of the trees, God said, 'Let the earth bring forth grass, the herb yielding seed, and the fruit tree yielding fruit after his kind whose seed is in itself, upon the earth; and it was so. And the earth brought forth grass, and herb yielding seed after his kind and the tree yielding fruit, whose seed was in itself, after his kind. And God saw that it was good.'

We shall restrict ourselves to the trees in this text and skip a number of things which are in themselves interesting.

Our translation, laboriously plodding along and trying to follow the text in its imagery, tells us that God said that there should be '*fruit trees* yielding fruit after their kind' whose seed was in themselves; whereas the earth did not produce *this,* but merely '*trees* yielding fruit after their kind, whose seed was in themselves.' A very slight difference, it is true, and to the pictorial story this difference is of negligible significnce and people will probably overlook it in reading.

But since we know that every letter in the Bible has its place in the great whole and that that place is definite and is a determining factor to effect complete harmony in the world, we shall have to ask ourselves here too why there is this difference. By now we have, let us hope, got rid of the thought that 'the poet wanted to use other words for a change.'

As to that, the discrepancy is more conspicuous in the Hebrew text. Granted that it is not easy to express it clearly in translation, if a translation is at all able to create a reasonably intelligible image.

In the Hebrew text we read that God says: let there come 'ets pri ose pri', yet there came *not that,* but only 'ets ose pri'. So a word drops out, when we are told what the earth did after God had said what was to come. Literally translated it is as follows: God said there was to come 'tree that is fruit and makes fruit', whereas there only came 'tree that makes fruit'. Biblical Hebrew, on account of the fact that it is also the expression of the substance of things, is very brief, and one always has to fill in a lot oneself, to get the story across.

Now, if we give literal translation of this text concerning the trees, we read that God said that there was to be: 'tree fruit makes fruit', whereas that was not what came, but only 'tree makes fruit'.

Indeed there is at once a duality here, a contrast, and we shall see that this contrast here is a determining factor for the appearance of the tree of life and of the tree of the knowledge of good and evil. At the same time the character of these two kinds of 'trees' will become more distinct.

What the earth brings forth, 'the tree that makes fruit', is what to our minds is normal. There is a development which in the end yields the fruit, the goal. What God asks is, in fact, impossible in our 'imagination', for God wanted 'tree which is already fruit', hence attainment, and 'which at the same time makes fruit'. To our minds this contains a contradiction. A thing that is making fruit, has no fruit yet, and what has fruit, is already at its goal; it cannot be trying to reach that goal. So to us it is: either one has reached the goal and in that case one need not grow towards that goal, or one is growing towards it and then one has *not yet* reached the goal.

So the earth makes that which we think 'normal' as the principle of development. Something develops from a very small, infinitesimal beginning; it grows towards something, creates ever new situation. It gives the tension, the expectation, hope and despair, and finally after that long journey full of adventures it reaches its destination. It is thus, we know, development in everything. A child develops from the embryonic stage into a human being, and then it grows to full maturity.

If one wants to examine something, wants to learn to know it, then knowledge grows gradually. For that purpose we have schools, universities, etc. The criterion of development towards a certain goal is also that one looks forward so much to reaching that goal that one is often in despair on the way, yet clinging to hope. But nobody knows whether the goal will be reached and nobody knows whether things will be as one imagines them to be.

From the picture of the first expression in this life which is 'growth', 'development', hence from the image of the tree, one sees a certain systematism in that development. The tree which first gathers, concentrating everything in its trunk, with tremendous energy finally breaks out into a multitude of branches and leaves. It is not until that great multitude of branches and leaves has appeared and especially when the time has come to shed the leaves, that the fruit comes forth.

The word for tree, 'ets', ayin-tsade, 70–90, in sound is closely related to the word for time, 'eth', ayin-taf, 70–400. The final letters, tsade and taf resp., 90 and 400, are in a remarkable relationship to each other, for the 400 is 4.44 times 90. But do not let us again stray away from our subject and let it suffice for the scope of this book to state the close relationship in the pronunciation of the words.

Time, in fact, has the same force of development which we detected in the tree. The fact of 'development' as such implies that there just be 'time', and in this way too does one see the close relationship between 'tree' as first expression of a development in the world, and 'time' which is inherent in this phenomenon of 'development'.

That is why there is a close relationship between the phenomenon 'tree' and that with which 'time' makes the development. That the tree does develop in the manner described above is caused by the fact that time causes every development to happen that way. A development therefore, expressed in an explosion of multiplicity towards the end of time. A multiplicity which leads to the weakness of the one leaf which is left, but which also implies that then the fruit will come, the goal, that which in the world of the tree expresses itself as the new world, the new life.

On this form of expression of time in our world were based the 'prophecies' of the weak time of the end, a time of decline, but also a time in which the new fruit ripens. Thus we ever see in the story of the Bible a period ending in great multiplicity, abundance and exuberance, and at the same time a great weakness of the human race. And we also notice how the new period, like a fruit detaching itself, proceeds from that weakness and explosion into multiplicity of the end.

Easy as it is to conceive this earthly picture of growth and development, so it is correspondingly difficult to depict the situation pronounced by God of 'goal attained and at the same time growing towards that goal'. It simply does not exist in any earthly form. Here it is that we get to the decisive point of difference between these two situations.

The 'tree which is fruit *and* makes fruit' indeed is that which is present in the original 'oneness'. It is the union of what in this world can only exist as duality, as separate and opposite things.

In 'unity', all-embracing unity, the conception time is present in such a manner that the goal is present, so that one can rejoice in beholding the goal attained, which is there as a reality. But side by side with it there is in this all-embracing unity the element of growth and development as well. This growth and development indeed are the way to the goal, the way to reunion. And that way gives great joy, if one not only knows the goal which will be reached, but at the same time conceives it as a reality. The way to reunion, to the attainment of the goal, however, often is a way of great suffering, of despair and much disappointment, if one does not know anything about the goal, does not know whether it will be attained.

That which God said was to come to the world, was this condition of goal already attained, with at the same time the sense of joy within oneself of witnessing the reunion. That is what the world of Eden was indeed. It contained multiplicity, the 70 and the 4, but also the 50, the condition of the world-to-come where the goal had been realized already. It is the Paradise of many stories of antiquity, which, although often rather distorted, have persisted until our times. Just think of the 'land of Cockaigne' where roast pigeons fly into one's mouth. One has not got all the toil of preparation, the fear of non-having, of failure, which arise from being unsure of whether the aim in view is the real goal.

Earth, however, did not do as God told her. Hence tradition has it that after the eating of the tree of knowledge, earth too was 'cursed' – let us say, in agreement with what has been set forth about the 'punishment' for the serpent, the woman and the man –'weakened' in its force of duality.

Earth in fact cannot give anything except growth, development. Earth had already been made as multiplicity, and, through man, earth with all that had come forth from her would indeed be brought back to her origin. For that which has come into prominence in the first story of creation about duality on the third day is the duality expressing itself also in that of the tree of life over against the tree of knowledge.

The condition God pronounced, the condition of 'Eden', the condition of having multiplicity, yet being already complete in unity, that is the tree of life. Which, therefore, has the measure of 500, the measure inconsistent with this world. This condition implies the reunion of the opposites, and at the same time the way towards reunion.

The condition the earth *had* to bring forth was that of only one side of it, viz. that of the way towards that goal. Hence the condition of the 400 as furthest measure.

And facing this duality in the 'garden', in the 3–50, the place of duality, since the 3 has that duality and therefore promptly brings it forward in the first tale of creation, man has it as his duty to leave alone the tree of duality in that 'garden'. Duality arose because earth had to produce it in obedience to the law of creation. Earth had been created in duality for the very purpose of creating multiplicity, that man might reintegrate this multiplicity into unity and thus participate in the bliss of going towards unity.

If man were to partake of the tree of duality, i. e. of time as development, he *himself* would get the character of duality. For development implies the continual contrast of the existing condition and the purpose in view. Whoever goes this way gets this duality within himself and he is no longer able to bring all the rest to unity from himself, like a creature that has unity within himself.

Man comes into that world of Eden, the world of 'both multiplicity and oneness' to make complete whatever is in duality there, *all* trees, all the possibilities of time, all phenomena in time, all that grows and develops, to 'eat' it all, i. e. complete it all, unite it with himself, thus to bring all things to God, to the origin, through himself, since he had been created a oneness. Thus man would experience the immense bliss of integration and also his own reunion.

Man would then *know* for what purpose he was brought into the world. For the tree of life was there too and was meant to be eaten from. Man would therewith know the purpose of God, he would, as it is expressed in the condition of Eden, of the 70–4–50, see the goal as a reality and also journey towards that goal. He would know neither fear nor despair, uncertainty nor vagueness, he would ever clearly see the goal, he would already bear it within himself in all its splendour, and besides, he would participate in the glory of integration, where that goal ever fulfils itself, how harmony is ever effected again.

For the tree of life *does* contain within itself this purpose, which is one of its components. Knowing the purpose, continually enjoying the splendour of harmony, the bliss of being, man would also experience this more sublime growth, the harmony of that reunion.

Life would no longer be a puzzle which man would finally learn to solve after a great deal of misery, taught by the numerous lashes of trial-and-error. Life was set forth quite plainly and distinctly. He would only have to eat from the tree of life.

One thing, however, man would have to do: he would have to accept that there was a knowledge, outside himself, extant previous to him, bestowed on him as a finished product. Now this is the point where man becomes rebellious.

Sensing reality within himself, which tells him he is a summit of development, that he is on the verge of breaking loose from the origin in order to lead development onwards as a supreme being, man prefers this second course. He is tempted thereto by the world which also suspects this in man; man being the summit of development, on the verge of breaking loose and shooting off, away from the origin, feeling free from the origin's power of attraction. Man himself is then the god of further development. And everything in the world points it out to him, shouts it in his ears, just as the 'serpent' does to the woman, the body, the senses of man.

This is not a wicked game with man either. To the contrary, man is brought to this extremity that he may have the full experience of integration, that he may thus bring everything back to the origin, so that creation may come to full enfoldment.

And man is not set down nonchalantly in that farthest domain, it being left to his choice either to return or to go to perdition. For just as in Eden the tree of life was placed in the midst, for man to partake of it to know what was the purpose of the 'service' in the garden, so also through the fulfilment of the root-story in the Bible, the story written with the the name 'Yah', the 10–5, the tree of life, is present at all time and within every man.

This tree of life was indeed given as the fruit of development, when the tree of knowledge, the 'tree which makes fruit', had actually made that fruit, in the 26th generation, as revelation of the purpose of the world and of existence. And this revelation, as fruit at the end of a development when biblical Israel was cut loose from the bond with the world of duality of Egypt, has ever remained with man in *his* world, as tree of life.

In that revelation, expressed in the words of the Bible in its root-story, it is indeed stated how the world is made, why it is made like that, what for, what is the place of man and all other creatures there. But besides all this, revelation contains the fruit, the goal, and points the way to the goal, shows how the goal is reached. It is indeed 'the tree which is fruit and makes fruit' and it stands in the midst of the world. Whoever partakes of the tree, has the development towards this goal, which is this world, but besides and simultaneously he possesses within himself that fruit, that goal. Which is the world-to-come. Then he lives in Eden, in the 70–4 of *this* world, the world which forms the way, which is the time of the development, of the growth; *and* simultaneously in the 50, which completes the 70–4–50, in the other world. He has *both* the growth towards the goal, and the goal itself.

Whoever refuses to accept this possibility, because in seeing the world and encountering the world he has come to consider himself a summit of growth with the possibility of further development and detachment from the source of origin, to view the origin merely as the place where his material expression commences, goes the way of the 'tree that makes fruit'. He, too, reaches the fruit. But on his way he will experience a great many things, for the very reason that he does not know the goal, does not know whether he is on the right way, and does not even know whether there is goal. He will go through many conflicts in his discussions with others concerning the correctness of the way and goal, bitter conflicts as often as not, with bloodshed, with immense grief and sorrow.

For the earth, which produced the tree of knowledge, the 'tree that makes fruit' awakens in man a similar manner of thought and vision. Man will see the world, himself and everything about him as a phenomenon subject to development, to evolution. He cannot help it, once it has got into him. The only thing he can do, and that is the most remarkable thing about these endlessly recurring cycles of time, the only thing he can do is to give up this way, return to the beginning and take the other way, that of the tree of life.

But in that case he has radically to give up the way he has gone: he has, so to speak, to kill himself on that way. For a compromise is out of the question. The Bible says that man when he has eaten from the tree of knowledge, must die. He cannot eat from the tree of knowledge and then go and find out what the tree of life tastes like. These are cosmic facts, facts of creation, which man cannot alter any more than the place of the sun in the solar system. However, man can stop on the way at any time and return to take the other way, the way of the tree of life. With his return all the evil of the first way is eliminated, the evil of the way of the tree of knowledge, which man was *not* to travel.

In the way of the tree of life, with the revelation, man has united the opposites within himself, eliminated the contrast. He knows the fruit, he knows the goal and he experiences the reunion in a completely different way from those who do *not* know that goal, who always fix a goal before them, give it up again or, if they have attained it, have to look for another goal, since that which was attained proves after all not to be the ultimate goal.

With the tree of life the contrast between life and death is also eliminated. Life then is the development towards the fruit, towards that other life. Death merely means 'being in the other world'. Indeed, whoever merely knows that one possibility, i. e. of the 'tree which makes fruit', 'life', which is development to him means all. If there is no tree any more which is making fruit, then there is nothing left any more. To dispel his apprehensions he may argue that this development will continue somewhere else, that man shall continue to improve there all the time, but he is quite well aware within himself — for after all he is human — that this is mere fabrication, building further on this continual making 'fruit' on that endless journey of making fruit. The man, who has accepted revelation with the standards of revelation itself, the standards that God laid down in revelation, this man looks upon 'death' as the fruit in the world to come, and he knows that the 'tree which is fruit and makes fruit' represents death in the part 'tree which is fruit' and represents life in part 'which makes fruit'. To him what is called death is another world already well known to him; it is the condition of that world. And he knows that there he has that part expressed as 'which makes fruit', hence also the development of life. He has simultaneously the world to come and this world; he has 'Eden'.

The Bible itself has that character of the 'tree which is fruit and which makes fruit'. In its story it tells us the whole development of the 26 generations till the fruit comes with the revelation. Therewith it tells us how everything *is*. The Bible gives it, a fruit in diverse layers, from the core in the centre, with the various layers surrounding it, up to and including the skin which gives the outside of the story. As such the Bible is the fruit. It indicates how the name Lord God is expressed in the 10–5–6–5 of the 26 generations.

And at the same time the Bible is the part that 'makes fruit'. For its structure of time is that of the 'Yah', of the name 10–5 which causes the 6–5 to grow in order to unite itself therewith. But, because it is also fruit itself, the 10–5–6–5 in the story of how the fruit of the revelation, of the appearance of God in the world is effected, we also know how one is to approach that fruit and what it contains. Indeed it is again the revelation of God therein. One knows it in the 10–5–6–5 of the 26 generations and one experiences it in the 6–5 which will evolve unto reunion with the 10–5.

That death comes to those in this world who have partaken of the tree of life, is the very phenomenon of this world of the seventh day. This world is transient, it is like the journey across the desert, it runs out into its ending, the eighth day. Everything in this world continually changes its aspect, just as one moves from one place to the other during the journey across the desert, until eventually everything has gone by. One enters the eighth day in a new form. It is also like the seven weeks between Easter and Pentecost, as depicted above, between the exodus from Egypt and the revelation of God. The reader will remember how in those seven weeks the corn was cut from the earth and that therefore there is sadness. At the revelation one realizes what it was all for; then it is the 50th day, the new world.

To those who have the tree of life, who know the revelation, who already have within themselves the goal of life, death does not alter any principle of life. They already know the world which comes as the fruit of this world. And they know the aspect of this seventh day, in which everything is unstable, transitional, since it is the day when one leaves this world for another, with which integration becomes a fact at the same time.

Thus the story of the happenings in Paradise has given rise to a number of reflections. One realizes, however, that there remains plenty of room for elaboration in our own life. We see how the structure of the 1–4 of the mist persisted in the tree of life and the tree of knowledge, how the duality of these trees arose from the dual character of the third day in which they appeared, how it expresses itself in the 'garden' as a phenomenon of that third day and of Eden on that day. Moreover, one could perceive how even in the first tale of creation this duality comes to expression with the creation of the trees and how this very mode of expression made us realize even better what the tree of life really was and what the tree of the knowledge actually implied.

We also saw how the principles 'three' and 'seventy' and 'four' played a part there and how they made it quite clear what certain names and words meant.

All this I have all the more emphatically thrown into relief to show that 'studying' the Bible must be a very exact affair, veracious first and foremost, open to understanding and that it must not be an interpretation here and an interpretation there, in accordance with certain theories drawn up for oneself, often based on complete absence of knowledge of language, structure, and systematism of the Bible. For if one does things like *that,* anything is possible. Then the Bible loses its dignity and becomes a mere source for quotations, as one thinks fit in certain situations, giving interpretations of one's own.

We should realize that that is the very reason why the Bible has lost so many people of integrity (upright people) as its adherents, or even that an approach is greatly hampered. Veracious people dislike loose contentions, sanctioned by an appeal to holiness. Intuitively they want to see these most important things built up on a structure which permeates all life, clearly and distinctly. So clearly that it is just this glorious light that irradiates them and convinces them of the holiness of all.

Our society has come to suffer from the many obscurities, the strange arbitrariness with which people handle the Bible. That is why society has looked elsewhere for certainties, however without being able to find them. However clever or subtle their expositions may be, people will never be able to furnish certainties. One will perceive all the time that the aim one pursued was not *the* aim, and one will follow another, similar way, with yet another aim.

One will have the development just as the tree has it, as time has it. Ending in an explosion of multiplicity and weakness. This will also characterize the end of this world. Ever having to go on specializing, ever hankering after intoxication, changing scenery, drugging, all this is a sign of a world approaching its end.

In that way came the end of the world of Eden. The way to the tree of life is attained in *duration.* It is expressed as the Lord God accompanying the 26 generations, with at the end the certainty of the fruit, the new world. We shall briefly try to follow this way, as the Bible sets it out. It is the way of man through the world, and the way of the world through duration. Whoever has assimilated the tree of life, will see the glory of this way.

For the others it is a way of terrible shocks, of the coming and going of worlds and of lives. In its tragedy this way is unique. Greater but also more sublime suffering is unimaginable.

It is the suffering of the farthest extreme where man does not realize it is God who draws back everything unto Himself. They merely know and experience the moment, they are attached to the moment, just as the tree which makes fruit also merely knows ever-changing situations, changing from second to second, yet trying to hold on to them because it does not know why they are changing. Man wants to hold them in his grip, and if it is not possible in any other way, he must have photographs.

But everything does move onward; God does draw everything back unto Himself. The man who does not know this for a fact becomes sentimental. He is so attached to the moment, he wants to stop growth. The tragedy is immense indeed, and the suffering indescribable.

But both tragedy and suffering set man free from this attachment to the world, both lead him at the end of this life to communion with God. And if he is to follow the way, through those numerous worlds, through the 26 generations, then he will, like Adam, realize that it is God in His quality of Lord God who goes with him.

But on that way too the attraction of the world, the force of gravitation of matter is immense. One desires to return to it all the time. Man always finds himself at the extreme point facing the alternative. Why all this? Whatever for? It is this further way which I now propose to discuss briefly, using the Bible to provide the standard of judgement.

10
Cain's Death

The first story we come across in the new world is that of Cain and Abel. The story is quite well known; it is found in Gen. 4:1–26. It is not enacted between man and woman, but between two of their descendants, one of whom is older than the other.

Beginning with this story of Cain and Abel, the Bible is seen systematically to allow the elder son, who should manifestly have the best rights, to be ousted by the younger brother who is elected to take the foremost place, as we see it happen in the case of younger ones such as Jacob, Joseph, Perez, Moses, David.

What is the meaning of this order of sequence? We can rediscover the systematism of the sequence in the tale of creation discussed above. There we find that heaven is mentioned first in creation, before the earth. And that at the creation of man in the first tale of creation, man is 'one' at first, androgyne, male and female, and afterwards divided into two beings, the man and the woman separately.

In the second tale of creation, the tale of water, the tale of the left hand side, we see a reversal of the sequence. In Gen. 2:4 we read: 'These are the generations of the heavens and of the earth when they were created, in the day that the Lord God made the earth and the heavens.' After suddenly conferring precedence to the earth, the story continues with the earth in its watery character. Light and the heavenly bodies are not even mentioned. It is water, beginning with the *ed*, the mist, which determines the further course of the story.

And when man makes his appearance, almost in consequence, as we have seen, of the 1–4, the 'mist', there is first his body and afterwards God breathes the 'neshamah', the divine soul, into his nostrils. Again earth preceding the heavens.

In the phenomenon on earth, this world that is, the body is expressed as the first, and the soul – I shall for the sake of brevity use the word soul, and I point out that in this case the 'neshamah' is meant – as the second. This body expressing itself as the first, was that aspect of man which was made into the female. And this female aspect, like the body and the earth, assumed in a sense the right of primogeniture, (the birth-right): it entered into a dialogue with the world and gave the passive male aspect the fruit of the tree of the knowledge to eat.

Now in this story of Cain and Abel it is Cain who makes his appearance into the world as the first. So he stands there where the body was created as the first and afterwards took the lead as the female.

The word 'first-born' – meaning that which is first to make its appearance in this world – is 'bechor', spelt beth-kaf-resh, 2–20–200. The word shows distinctly that that which appears as first in this dual-world, bears the unmistakable structure of the 'two'. The word leaves no doubt as to that. The first-born here is essentially the second. What makes its appearance afterwards, as conclusion, as finishing touch, is the soul which gives meaning to what appeared first.

After the first meeting of the man and the woman in Eden, hence of soul and body, there is, however, in the next phase an extraordinary rivalry. Both, body and soul, expressing themselves here in this world in the crystallization of this story as Cain and Abel, bring a sacrifice to God.

The word sacrifice must first be explained here, since it rouses an entirely false mental image in many people.

Sacrifice in Hebrew is 'korban', spelt kof-resh-beth-nun, 100–200–2–50. It means literally 'approach' or 'bring nearer'. And as the word is used on principle in the relationship between man and God, or a higher power recognized as such by man, it therefore means man approaching God or bringing something of man nearer to God. In a sense it aims at attaining an integration, a union between man and God.

And that which man brings to God as 'korban' is his earthly existence, his phenomenal form here, which was divorced from the origin at creation for the very purpose of reuniting itself with that origin.

Man's earthly existence expresses itself in his body. And that body is the extreme development in the material world, it is the 'best', the most valuable 'beast'. Man called his wife, i.e. that which became the body, Eve (Gen. 3:20); in Hebrew it is 'Chawa', spelt cheth-waw-hee, 8–6–5. And this word has a certain identity with the word for 'beast', chaya. With Eve – the name which arose after partaking of the tree of knowledge – the woman on account of her mortal body, becomes the mother of all the coming generations. This breaking of unity into mulitplicity was to carry on life in multiplicity by means of this body. Bringing the world nearer to God expresses itself in bringing one's own earthly existence nearer to God. And the substance of this earthly existence finds its expression in those animals which are called 'sacrificial beasts'. As regards his body, man is indeed a further evolution of the beast.

For that very reason he must not allow this body to develop any further; he is to use the best of it, his greatest force, to bring it nearer to God, to connect it again with its origin.

In essence the beast and the body of man are on the same level. In the differentiation into the multiplicity of the phenomena in this world, the beasts have adopted various forms, deviating more or less from the phenomenal form of man. In certain animals, for instance those that among other things have the horn as characteristic in their phenomenal form — horn in Hebrew is 'keren', spelt kof-resh-nun, 100–200–50 — the relationship as regards their substance and that of the body of man, is most pronounced. By this relationship is not meant a biological relationship, which of course may be present, but a relationship in the substance of things, in another world.

The 'korban' in fact cannot be brought in the world in which we live now. At least not in the form in which the Bible describes it. Only when the world enters into a different relationship with heaven, and consequently man will know and feel again the relationship between the substance of things and their phenomena in this world, will there be that connection again between the phenomenal form of certain animals here and the human body, owing to which certain actions in regard to the animal in this world will essentially cause changes in the proportions between the body of man and the source of origin.

It goes without saying that all this presupposes complete knowledge on the part of man of that happening and, moreover, his complete participation in the purpose of the happening. If not, it would deteriorate into a foolish technique, an attempt at magic, to accomplish by way of certain actions, certain reactions useful for our life on earth. If it comes to *that*, it is mere idolatry, i.e. service aiming at results useful for the further development of material existence. But that is the very opposite to reunion with the source of origin. Idolatry in antiquity purpose to promote the development of earthly existence with the help of a certain technique. Biblical sacrifice — which I propose to deal with at greater length — aims at making the body and earthly existence take a turn in their development, and thereby bring them from this extreme alienation back to the source of origin.

Thus there is in Cain and Abel the *will* to turn to God, to come nearer, to bring their earthly existence nearer. To give purpose to existence. Cain's business is 'service to the earth'. In translation this has simply become 'tiller of the ground'. Cain is 'obed adama', tiller of the ground. Of the earth which had produced that very tree of the knowledge, the 'tree that makes fruit'. Cain occupies himself with these forces of development. And his 'korban', that which he brings nearer, also pertains to these things. He brings 'of the fruit of the ground' as an offering. Ancient lore says that he brought what happened to fall into his hands, what he happened to come across. Not the very best; nor the worst. He brought what was determined by the earth, what development offered him at the moment.

It is, indeed, characteristic of what the body wants to bring nearer. Not itself; no, not that, never. We shall see by and by how in Egypt — which is also to biblical Israel as body to soul — bringing beasts as 'korban' is considered out of the question altogether. The beast is the body itself and *that* is what the body neither will nor *can* bring. The body wants to be here, wants to go on developing.

Yet in a certain phase of its development it feels the need of contact with its creator, and then it avails itself of the occasion as it arises, but never of the substance.

The body as product of the earth merely knows momentary situations, it is ever on its way, ever developing. It is the 'tree which makes fruit'. That is why it cannot offer anything except the very phase of development which presents itself. It most assuredly has time to spare for God, it is certainly willing to pay due regard to God. But never to the extent of endangering the development, the further growth of the body. This would indeed be against its law of creation. The body *must* maintain itself.

Abel, on the other hand, is a shepherd: he leads and controls the animals just as the soul wants to lead the body. The soul cannot serve the forces of development. It originates from the world where opposites do not exist. To the soul the fruit is there already and development is a thing quite well known. Abel, the soul, the latter the younger son, leads the body. Whither? The answer is quite distinct: 'to bring it nearer to God, to bring it as "Korban".' The sacrifice of Abel is the 'first born', i.e. that which in this world is the force of the physical breaking through to make its appearance as force of development, that which is the earthly of the body. And of the 'fat' did Abel bring the 'korban'.

Fat in its image is all that is best, all that is farthest developed. The word for 'fat' is 'cheleb', spelt cheth-lamed-beth, 8–30–2. The sum total of the components is 40. So it is what is physically furthest, highest, worthiest.

So Abel did what the soul, if it is uninhibited, will do quite naturally, i.e. take the best of the body, that which on earth appears as principal part of it, to bring it to God, to reunite it, therewith bringing everything, including the rest.

For the body too arises from the origin. Thus also came the female part of the man, who originally appeared here as 'one'.

And the purpose of creation is that reunion of what was separated, to be accomplished by man as purpose of his existence, to bring body and soul together again, the male and the female, thus uniting everything belonging to the world with the source of its origin again.

If man brings all his existence, his pied-a-terre here, nearer to God, then God goes out to meet man and his 'korban'. It *is* accepted, since it gives indeed that which was farthest removed and because of it exercises the strongest attraction on man to become a god himself. Thus God 'had respect', as it says in the translation, to the 'korban' of Abel, God accepted it. Ancient lore has it that a flame from heaven took it on high.

What the body itself wants to bring nearer, however, *cannot* be of a quality to fulfil the purpose of creation. The body can merely bring something of lower development, if it is not to eliminate its own existence. What can serve as 'korban' is only the extreme development, that which has to be united with the origin, therewith to close the whole circle.

It may serve our purpose to make this situation clearer with the help of the diagram we made use of before, of the development rendered as a circle to be closed by man (vide diagram on this page).

So it is not a reproach addressed to Cain, that he did not bring of his best. Cain brought what he *could* bring. The body is not capable of more. Besides, the body does not know the principle of reuniting everything with the origin, it is not even aware any more of that origin. At best it can feel it has to do with something else besides growth and development.

The story shows that the body *itself* can never bring that korban. It cannot unite anything with the origin, because itself merely belongs to the side of development, of the 'tree that makes fruit'.

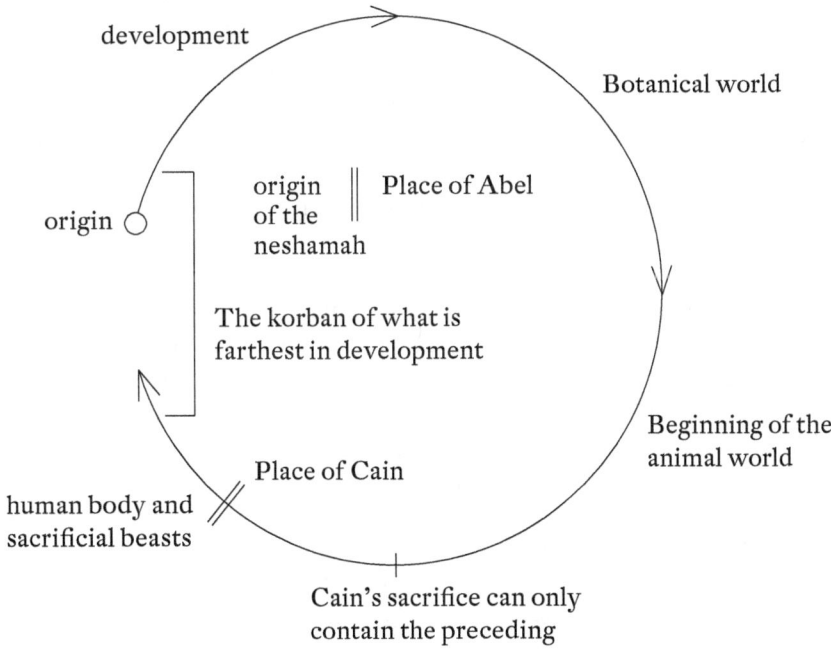

It is only Abel, the soul, who can bring the korban. And this korban is that very body. It does not imply *killing* the body, as we shall see by and by. It only means turning the body towards an entirely different goal, towards a goal the body itself cannot even understand.

That is what the soul came into man for, at the creation of man, that it might reunite the body with the origin. And that is why Abel came after Cain, to reunite the body with the origin.

The body, however, experiencing this situation, feels that it is at variance with what itself observes to be the world. The body observes development, further growth. It fails to see that that way does not bring nearer to God. And when it sees that an entirely different way must be followed, a way which stops the body in its development; it feels it to be contradictory with its bodily logic. The body with its developed machinery of senses, and thought based on experience, becomes rebellious. It refuses to accept a way which has to stop this development, it feels itself fenced in in the world which it had entered as its ruler, being the highest developed.

Then there is the dialogue with God. At that very moment the body feels this wrath surging up. And God points out the danger of the way to the body. In our world it cannot be a dialogue in words. In our world the dialogue is carried on in images and happenings.

For instance, there may be wars, in spite of the further development of man's material abilities. Wars, more cruel and bloody than in times when people were not so highly developed. The chances are that man, in spite of that development, feels less comfortable; more agitated, more afraid, weaker, in poorer health. He may see his family life breaking up, his children probably seeking their benefit elsewhere and sneering at the older generation.

All this may be God's answer to the body's wrath, that the material way does *not* lead to God, that God 'has no respect for it'. Through the events God shows man the possibility to reflect on the purpose of his existence here. Whether this is really identical with that which he conjures up before his eyes, with his mind directed towards development. And through the events God points out to him the danger of proceeding along that way.

If, God's interference notwithstanding, God's words and warning voice notwithstanding, the body yet continues on its way, the decisive moment will come when it kills Abel. The body, if it refuses to listen but insists on developing along the course adopted, encounters the soul at the crucial moment. At this encounter it silences the soul, rules it out. It refuses any longer to take into account any phenomena coming from another world except the 'scientific' observations it has made *itself*. All the rest is waved aside as unscientific, is rejected. What does not benefit the body, all physical life, that part of life which in common parlance is called 'life', is disregarded. If the soul can be employed for the benefit of life, for instance in making people more 'normal', more ready to co-operate in the system of economy, technology, society, then psychology is something useful, it has made itself subservient to that grand purpose. If theology is ready to give people diversion for a few hours of 'relaxation', and especially when it is ready to follow the way of science, of evolution, from the evil primitive start to an ever improving and especially a more benevolent society, it will also be accepted.

'The voice of thy brother's blood crieth to me from the ground,' God says to Cain. The soul has not only been killed, it has been made subservient, it is employed by the forces of development.

This is indeed the way which opens up to us, if, at the crucial moment, after God's admonitions in the happenings in time, one does not turn back. When Cain has killed Abel, there ensues in Cain the great fear and feeling of guilt. He no longer sees a way out, in fact he only sees death, which he, the body, as something which only knows growth and further development, holds in abhorrence.

Cain gets a rather strange 'punishment' for his deed. In fact, he is *not* going to be killed. He becomes a 'fugitive and a vagabond' and 'when he tillest the ground, it shall not henceforth yield unto him her strength.'

When the first man had merely eaten from 'the tree of knowledge', death was the result, whereas when Cain commits *murder*, he is protected, by a special mark too, lest anyone finding him should kill him.

What happens to Cain, the body, after it has killed the soul, has drenched the earth with his brother's blood? The expression 'fugitive and vagabond' in Hebrew is 'na wenad', spelt nun-ayin and waw-nun-daleth, 50–70 and 6–50–4.

What strikes us at first sight in this expression, as soon as we consider it in its essence, is the proportion of the sums-total of the components. The first word has 50+70=120 as sum-total; the second has 6+50+4=60; and the proportion is exactly 2:1.

So this implies that even Cain, even the body, shall go the way to 'oneness', shall be made ready for 'integration'. *That* is the substance of this expression. It is like the way from Egypt to Canaan, which indeed, is also a way from 'duality' to 'unity'.

But now we see that the significance of the image contains something entirely different. Not the guidance of God, perceptible every day as it was in the desert when practically every step was manifestly guided by God – God ever present in the expressions 'pillar of cloud' or 'pillar of fire' – but now wandering and straying about, like a fugitive and a vagabond, not knowing what the morrow will bring to him, let alone in a future farther ahead. So it is exactly the way we know already from the story of the tree of knowledge which in its substance proves to be the 'tree which makes fruit'. This tree which makes fruit without knowing what the fruit is, whether there will be any fruit or what it will be like. It is that which we described as the great tragedy and the immense suffering of man on his way towards the goal without ANY knowledge of the goal.

There too, with the tree of knowledge, it was the way of the body, the way of development, of constant change, of growth. And about Cain who in the systematism has the place of the body we hear the same story. But this time still more earthy, still more in terms of this world.

In the story of the tree that makes fruit we still had to try to explain with the help of our imagination what it implies: making fruit without knowing what that fruit may be. Here, in the story of Cain, it is specified more clearly what it is. Just as in the second triad of days of creation, there is a clearer specification of what was done by God in the first triad of the days of creation.

In the story of Cain as the body we see what is the way, if one partakes of the tree of knowledge. It means that one kills the soul. The way to the tree of life is cut off. And it means that one goes the way in a tragic frame of mind towards the goal God has marked out, knowing and feeling oneself as a 'fugitive and a vagabond' from one period of time to another, from one theory to the next, through wars, revolutions, injustices, because one neither knows the purpose of it all, nor what one is aiming at.

The way of the 'two' to the 'one' is again 'the tree that makes fruit'. But since the soul has been 'killed', since the connection with the tree of life has been cut off by the body, this way leads towards the goal with the sentiment of being a 'fugitive and a vagabond'.

And the ground does not yield all her fruit unto Cain, the body that is, of which the story of Cain is an expression. Literally it says in the Bible that the earth will not yield all her strength to Cain. Just as after man's eating of the tree of knowledge, the strength of the earth, its attraction on man diminishes, so again with Cain, where the body is fenced in, drawn back after having done the utmost the body *can* do about its development.

It is as it were an aspect of being a fugitive and a vagabond. For the earth which brought a strong feeling of optimism along with its temptation of development, suddenly shows it cannot at all develop in the right sense any longer. We see degeneration, weakness, neuroses. There is culture-pessimism. People feel disappointed, yet keep on hoping, since they know no other way. Thus they go on and on, fugitives and vagabonds, not aware that in substance the proportion 2:1 exists, *even* in this condition of 'fugitive and vagabond'.

Like the body, Cain is afraid of death, because death implies radically bringing development to a standstill, when it was taken for granted that it was ever to continue. Therefore the body refuses to think of death, just as Egypt *refuses* to discuss an exodus of the children of Israel. The body shuts off death to a plane which it had rather not mention. The body thinks death something unfair, unreasonable. It had much rather go on and on evolving itself for ages and ages, falling and rising up again, until it had reached a world in which science and technology could not be improved upon, since they had reached their highest level. Death might in that case not come until man had reached the age of 200, or maybe 300! And there would be peace and people would have leisure for their hobbies, guided by clever psychologists and sociologists. Along these lines does the body think more or less. And tacitly it is taken for granted that on *that* level a new goal, a new ideal will be found. For life in the body without an ideal to aim at, with an ideal already attained, is inconceivable. And that there would he death behind it all, with that great emptiness and the profound question, '*then, what*', the body had much rather not discuss.

Therefore at the stage of his having killed Abel and God's pronouncement of the way towards the goal as 'a fugitive and a vagabond', when God warns him that the earth with its temptation of development will disappoint him, Cain's deep concern is 'what to do about death'. For animal nature gives life, but kills as well. How is the body to live in this condition?

Now that the strength of the earth has diminished, it also means that the body's vital strength has weakened. As with Adam, here too death comes as an expression of this deterioration of strength. Death disrupts development; death in spite of man himself leads him back to the origin. Just as the circle, the return to the origin, is essentially inherent in creation, so it now expresses itself in every man's life. Development *cannot* continue to an unlimited extent. At a certain point it stops and everything turns back. Thus it is with individual man and thus it is, in an analogous, wider circle, with all mankind. For all mankind, too, there are times coming and times going. There too there is a return. It is the law of creation with its 1–2–1 principle.

This journey through time and worlds will likewise be that of 'the fugitive and vagabond'. The body which has killed the soul, or made it subservient to the earth, which comes to the same thing – the blood crieth from the ground – this body also passes on through time without knowing the how and wherefore.

It is this complete nescience which is the tragedy of the body. The doctrine of development proves to be at fault, it does not come true, and since there is no soul any more than there is a tree of life to explain the how and wherefore, the body feels lost, and it similarly goes through time and the worlds as 'a fugitive and a vagabond'.

Thus God sets a mark upon Cain, lest anyone finding him should kill him. The body gets something through which it can forget death, suppress the thought of it. Life all about the body will make it forget death, though death is ever hovering about.

What is this mark? We see a very special line of development looming up now, which has caused many readers of the biblical story of images to wonder when Cain's 'punishment' was to come.

Development, indeed, implies that Cain's descendants shall expand enormously in the sphere of what we would call culture and technology. Cain himself, together with his son Enoch, becomes a city-builder. A city – in our modern times we are quite well aware of it – is a concentration of people, a merging of human strength. In a city one is apt to forget there is anything beside the existence of the sham-world of development created there; the city creates the very conditions for forgetting it all; it does that quite unintentionally. The normal pursuits in a city are those aiming at the further refinement of material potentialities. It is not being occupied with matter which is wrong, but being so occupied with the set purpose of making material life stronger, richer, more powerful.

Our contact with matter should be so as to make us want every time to experience the purpose of matter, what it means in the great cosmic whole. The individuality of the man who gets engaged with matter, with everything concerning this world, can either liberate it or not.

There is, for instance, a story about one of the ancient Jewish sages who was a shoemaker. With every stitch with which he sewed the top-part to the sole, he connected heaven and earth. Everything man does should by the very fact he is occupied with it, and constantly thinks of the reunion of heaven and earth, also be reunited with its origin.

The Bible implicitly desires man to be occupied with the world. That is what the multiplicity of creation was made for: for the very purpose of man's coming into contact with it, being attracted by it, so that, driven by his own desire to learn the purpose of life, to be integrated with the source of origin, he should unite it all with that origin.

But if man does *not* think of the origin, but merely of further development in order to keep ahead in the nations' race for material welfare, then he will remove everything he contacts, further from the origin, along with himself. Man in his religious denomination may consider himself 'orthodox' or not, the very fact he *can*, without suffering deeply on account of it, be interested in the research into matter, into the material phenomenon, on purpose to make the world more comfortable, to develop sciences still further for the sake of their technical application, shows that he has eaten from the tree of knowledge and that going along that way he has been cut off from the tree of life. So primarily it is man's disposition which is decisive for his character, not the doctrine or the society which he adheres to. Which, of course, does not mean that if the disposition is right, there is not a definite practice of life pertaining to it, founded on the Bible in every detail. In the thought and action of his daily man should develop the same structure God gave to the Bible.

Now let us return to the city Cain built. This story of the city shows how the Bible regards the sequence of time. For, if we were even for a moment to look at it from the historical point of view, then who is supposed to live there? Where would the people be to do that? But here again we are concerned with the expression of the substance in this world, and the substance reveals that as soon as the body has done what we read about Cain, one of the first signs of its trying to safeguard itself against the contacts with death, is to build the city.

In the Bible the city everywhere is the sign of idolatry, of disposition towards a further 'useful' development of the earth. Jerusalem, as the one exception, takes a different place altogether, owing to the fact that there the temple was built with everything which made of biblical Jerusalem a specific phenomenon. It is like the strong body with all the forces of development, guided however by the soul and in harmony with it: the starting-point of creation and the purpose of creation.

And when the city is there, then in the seventh generation, reckoned from Cain, there comes exactly what we know as culture and technology, in that very society of men who seek the city, who regard the city as a concentration of power and strength. Then there is the Jubal, of music, the Tubal-Cain, artificer of brass and iron. It is only Jubal who lives in tents and in the vicinity of the herds, as the saying is.

Cain's punishment is this flight from death into all the domains called – quite characteristically, culture, arts, technology. It is always considered a great merit when one has attained it.

Considering all this, what about Cain's being called a 'fugitive and a vagabond' and the 'ground becoming weaker'? Does it not seem to be at variance therewith? Is not the city a settling and establishing in safety, is not the fact of our stressing music as an expression of art and metallurgy as an expression of technology, the very opposite of the life of 'a fugitive and a vagabond'? Does not the earth prove able to offer all sorts of good things, in contradistinction with God's pronouncement on Cain? Is it not, to the contrary, a great reward ultimately conferred on Cain after his murder of Abel?

It is essential for us to understand the story of Cain properly, and not try to run away from the consequences, as Cain did. The story is quite clear about Cain being 'punished' after his killing of Abel, about his being a fugitive and a vagabond, and the earth not yielding her strength to him any more. His fear of death and his running away from death is even part and parcel of that punishment. Cain sees the potential murderer everywhere. And God somehow even excludes the possibility of death owing to which this wandering and straying about becomes more horrible and agonizing. It is a very hard thing, and even though we know that Cain, too, will eventually reach his goal, the way thither, a long long way, is a very harsh fate.

And then we see all this working out in city-building, arts, technology, briefly in what we call culture, development. This development in urbanization, in art, technology, etc., proceeding from the killing of the soul, is it not then a punishment after all? Would not this after all be what is implied by being a 'fugitive and a vagabond', and the earth growing weak? Is not all this an escape from death, a waving aside of the image of death? Is not the mark Cain got exactly *this* image of life?

In the Hebrew words for 'fugitive and vagabond', 'na wenad', which, as we saw, show the proportion 2:1, there is yet another remarkable thing to notice. As stated above, these words are spelt 50–70 and 6–50–4.

Here again we see the letters 'ayin' and 'daleth', 70 and 4, which we have already come across in the word 'Eden'. Not as initial letters running into the 'nun', the 50 of the new world, but this time as an ending, as a conclusion. The starting-point here is that very 50, for Cain comes from the world of unity, the world where he still was with Abel, and now he gets into the world of multiplicity, into the 70 as multiplicity in man, into this seventh day, and into the multiplicity of the 4, that of the world in space-time. It is essentially the reverse of Eden. Moreover it is divided. After having thus eliminated the soul, the body finds itself in the multiplicity of the 70 and that of the 4, without any prospect, without seeing any inclusion into anything else. Here it ends in merging into an infinite multiplicity, in an extreme removal from the origin. *That* is what bestows despair on this 'wandering and straying about', this being a 'fugitive and a vagabond'. Although the way ultimately *does* end in 'one', as its essence shows in its quantitative formula. He that takes this way, however, is not aware of it. To him the way ends in his merging in infinite multiplicity.

And that *is* the way of the city-builder, it is the way of the creator of culture and technology, after the deed of Cain. This way is indeed expressed as an explosion into multiplicity, as an eruption, just as we have seen it in the image of the tree which, like time, has in the end the great multiplicity as well as the great weakness. And then the fruit also comes to maturity.

But the way leading thither is a way of bitterness. And life in that culture is a hard and lonely life. It is a flight from a reality, from a world which indeed knows the purpose of things, because one is afraid of facing death. And to the man who has killed the soul, death certainly *is* agonizing. For the body in itself *cannot* accept death; it ever wants to run away from it, and rightly so.

So the culture of the generations of Cain is the answer to the killing, the elimination of the soul. The world knows this story of Cain in another version; there it is called the story of Faustus. Faustus wants to possess this world; he wants to fathom it along the way of matter, with worldly standards. And promptly he is faced with the devil who claims the man's soul as his due. As soon as man has actually promised his soul to the devil, there is his marvellous unfolding in knowledge and power. He is then a party to the culture of Cain. Yet on that way he brings misery and anxiety everywhere; he is a 'fugitive and a vagabond' all the same.

The world has known this theme a long time. Whoever wants to have this world, must sell his soul to the devil.

The end of Cain's story is most touching. People are generally at a loss to understand such expressions as 'vengeance shall be taken on him sevenfold' and the 'seventy and sevenfold', in connection with the killing of Cain (Gen. 4:15) and the words of Lamech (Gen. 4:23–24).

I shall not enter more deeply into the numerous other possibilities by working out in detail these communications through the formation of the words and their contexts in the structure of things. One might write volumes on these things alone. And if I am yet to discuss a few other aspects illustrated by other stories in the Bible, I must not dwell too long on one single story. But I should like to say a few words on the tradition concerning Cain's death.

Ancient lore, in fact, says that Cain was killed by Lamech. It happened this way. Lamech, the sixth generation after Cain, was already very old but he yet insisted on going hunting. To track down the beasts and show him where they were he took along his son Tubal-Cain, the technician, the metal-worker. Tubal-Cain spotted the horns of a beast behind a bush and pointed them out to Lamech. Lamech who could not see very well on account of his old age, went in the direction his son had indicated, and shot. When he went to collect the quarry, he saw he had killed his ancestor, Cain, and that Tubal-Cain had mistaken his ancestor Cain for a beast. In his rage and despair at having killed

Cain, Lamech beat his hands together and destroyed his son who had brought him to this act between his bare hands.

Tubal-Cain is the seventh generation after Cain. This is where the world of Cain ends; it does not go beyond the 'seven'. This body does not get beyond the seventh day.

The last generation takes its ancestor for a beast. And that is the cause that man, who in reality arises from the sixth day which still knew the world in another quality — the mark of the 'six', indeed stamps things with the pattern which pertains to the 'six', wherever it may appear — that this man of the sixth day kills his ancestor owing to the information given by his form of expression in the seventh day. Upon which in his bitterness he also kills the man of the seventh day who had given him this foolish information.

This story, like everything in tradition, is based on a profound knowledge of the meaning of the Bible, on the structure of development, on the formation of the word. I shall here merely refer to the coherence of this story with the whole story of Cain to show how even thousands of years ago certain situations in the world — whenever and wherever they present themselves — always have the same structure and how they have all been described in the Bible in their essence and development is expressive of the whole of creation.

The body itself does not get beyond the seventh day. On that seventh day it is killed because the last generation takes it for a beast. Cain's horn which was visible, the horn which also plays a part in the appearance of the beasts of sacrifice, was an indication to Tubal-Cain, the last generation, of the extreme development of Cain's body. We shall yet have to discuss this horn, the 'keren', with the sum-total of the components of 350. For the moment let us accept it as a sign of the phenomenal form of the body.

The world of Cain is the world of the body. And this body, taken in itself, is aware of nothing except development, growth, like the 'tree that makes fruit'. And this development finds a most characteristic ending.

The hunter is he that hunts the beast. It means that to him it is a joy that the beast hides from him, runs away from him, that he can show he is more intelligent, higher in development, by catching the beast all the same. It is this sensation of the hunt that man enjoys. Once the beast is caught, he generally leaves it to his huntsmen to transport it. He himself, however, will continue the hunt. In order to experience again the sensation of the hunt and so on. The hunter, in fact, has no specific end in view. When he has caught one beast, there are so many others, and he will go on hunting as long as he lives.

Hunting is also represented by the man desiring to catch the woman. The woman tries to hide. And it is this very desire to hide on the part of the woman that provokes the man and makes a hunter of him.

This image, as it was used in antiquity, with the woman as the beast running way and the man as the hunter, is an expression of the reality of the behaviour of matter, of the world, as soon as man treads the way of the tree of knowledge, the 'tree that makes fruit'. He is ever on his way, too; he wants to catch what is ever slipping away, ever moving, hiding, but he finds all the time that he is not satisfied. In fact he is not sure when he will have reached *that* which is to give him complete satisfaction, without a break. Always there will be other beasts, not yet caught, to entice him to new hunting experiences.

Thus in his desire to catch the material world — the female side of the world — man thinks he will find something marvellous, if he manages to catch exactly *that* which he is hunting at the moment. He will then lose sight of all proportions, for indeed he is hunting. Thus everybody tries to pursue this female side of the world and catch exactly what he is hunting for at the moment. One man thinks the circulation of the blood in the tail of tadpoles rewards his hunting and he merely sees this field, another man thinks 'it' is attained with his method of reducing the petrol-consumption of a motor by 5%.

With all of them it is the way of the 'tree that makes fruit', the way of the 'fugitive and vagabond'.

Once a man has started hunting, he is ever more attracted by it. It is characteristic of the contact with the tree of knowledge, the 'tree that makes fruit', that whoever indulges in that contact will get into the sway of a power of attraction with considerable acceleration. The earth attracts him, just as it expresses itself also in material gravity.

Hunting is just such another expression of the escape into the world, of wanting to hide in the world. Just as the first man did after eating from the tree of knowledge, and as Cain did in his building up of the Cain-culture. It is an urge to get drugged, to get intoxicated.

Whoever starts the habit of getting intoxicated, of drugging, will find that he cannot do without it. Whoever starts hunting will find that he cannot do without that. He considers it *the* thing in life. Thus it is with all things material in the world; at any given moment, they present themselves as the most important thing. The moment one has got it, the emotion passes quickly and one casts about for a new object to hunt. Just as one reaches for another cigarette.

The great hunters in the Bible therefore are also the great idolaters. They are, like for instance Nimrod and Esau, those who have chosen the way of the earth and have become enormously powerful in that way. They are always diametrically opposed to man as God created him and as God ultimately will have him again.

That is why there is such a hunter in the generation of Cain too. Once the world-culture has been built by physical man, after the elimination of the soul, that culture also implies hunting: looking for a goal which promises satisfaction, but which, when attained, merely shows another goal and one has to try to reach it anew. Man is ever on the way, ever in motion, dynamic, developing himself and others, and he always sees the way continuing in front of him: there is indeed no attainable goal which is satisfactory in every respect.

The hunter Lamech goes accompanied by his son Tubal-Cain. We saw how in the structure of the Bible the sixth and seventh days are also conjoined. Thus hunting, in their search after a goal, they got to the point when they took their ancestor for a beast. They did not know that *this* was what the hunt would lead to. And with the discovery they destroyed both their material origin and their goal. First and last went to destruction because of it. Development led to one's recognizing the beast as one's origin. And that was the end of that world. In the seventh generation, just as in the seventh day, does this clash come. The sevenfold avenging for Cain is this journey through the seven days of matter. The seventy and seven of Lamech is this bringing of the seven too into the world, in the next plane, that of the seventy. This world of Cain comes to an end. It is the end of an entire world.

11
Sons of the Gods

The first mention in the Bible of a period of time after the six days of creation and the seventh day is that of the 130 years of Adam when he got another son, Sheth (Gen. 5:1–3).

This number also occurs in other texts. Moses, for instance, was born 130 years after the descent of Jacob and his family into Egypt.

When, after the exodus from Egypt, the revelation takes place, it occurs on Mount Sinai, spelt samech-jot-nun-jot, 60–10–50–10, with a sum-total of components of 130 also. With the coming of 130 into space-time, something very unusual is achieved.

130 is the expression of the number 13 in the plane of the decades. The word for 'one', 'echad', as a matter of fact has the value of 13. It is spelt aleph-cheth-daleth, 1–8–4.

So with 13 is achieved a unity. The 13 is beyond the 12 which is still of this world; just as the 500 is beyond the 400. The 12 is the combination of the 3 and the 4, both unfulfilled as yet. They form the 7 when juxtaposed, and the 12 when combined. But both the 7 and the 12 wait for completeness, in the 8 and in the 13.

Thus the sons of Jacob were meant to be 13 in number. On account of the act of Reuben (Gen. 35:22) they remain 12 for the time being. Reuben, who as tradition has it, of course knew about this 12 and 13, hence also realized that the sons of Jacob would only be complete with the coming of the thirteenth, did not see how this thirteenth was to come into being now that Rachel had passed away. The more so since Jacob, in his opinion, did not follow the course which was to lead to the coming of the thirteenth in the right place. That is why he interfered in the course of events in order to accomplish through this interference the coming of the thirteenth in the right place. So it was a well-meant interference, inspired by knowledge of the purpose in view. It is the attitude of the man who knows that something is to come in a certain manner and now sees everything going differently. He thinks he is doing the right thing in turning the course of events into the right direction. Caused by human anxiety that things might go wrong otherwise. It is this human rashness which Jacob therefore reproaches his first-born with, the first appearance of it on earth (Gen. 49:4). It is the same tendency in man to support development, to send it into the right direction, it is the same rashness one also finds in the story of Uzza (2 Samuel 6:6–10) who reached out to support the ark when it threatened to fall. Man's life and work should be directed at other things than interference with history. Even if one knows one purpose well, it is not man's way. Interference is the way of development. I merely mention these aspects here; I cannot possibly refer to them more deeply in this place. Indeed, we shall come across them in a different way in our account.

Owing to this act of Reuben, the sons of Jacob remained 'twelve in number' as it is emphatically mentioned in Gen. 35:22. And with these twelve there is first enacted an event in time, a bodily event; the coming of the numerous generations of Esau and the kings of Edom. And in the end the thirteenth tribe of Jacob does come after all, in the right place, namely because Joseph is divided into two by his sons Ephraim and Manasseh, born in Egypt. The number of 'tribes' of Jacob thus becomes thirteen yet, and the thirteenth did indeed come from Rachel. The world actually emerges where it should. The only thing is that the way in which it happens is often different from what man expects when observing the course of events. It is one of the things man should not do, he must not be anxious on account of developments which seem to proceed differently from what he would feel warranted to expect. Man is very limited in his observations and he has not the slightest idea of what is enacted on the other side of the events. Therefore the Bible points to this aspect in the world. The '13' is bound to come, one need not worry about it. It may come in a way different from what one expects, but it will at any rate come in a better and grander way than one *could* possibly imagine.

So 'thirteen' is a unity, it is an expression of the word 'one' and 130 is this point, this unity, in the plane of decads. Beyond 'time'; beyond the 'twelve', it is achieved.

Thus a new world arises on the 130 of Adam. Sheth comes in Abel's stead. This new man comes again in the likeness of God, as a man with a divine soul, that is.

And this new man lives for ten generations, whereas the man of Cain, of the body exclusively, lived for seven generations.

The names, that is to say the expression in 'the formula' of these seven generations and the ten, are related to each other, as appears from the corrupted names in the orthography of translations from original Hebrew texts. The physical man of the seven generations is related to the complete man of the ten generations. The difference in names exactly indicates the difference between the expression in the world of the physical man and that in the world of the complete man. However, I do not propose to enter upon a description of these seven generations here.

When Noah comes, i.e. the tenth generation, there occurs a great change in the world. The earth which had weakened all the time after the eating from the tree of knowledge, regains an enormous power towards the end. The world goes through a period of immense development at the end. Tradition records many details about it. People regain power over the earth which puts her great forces of development at their disposal. Thus, for instance, it is narrated that man who before Noah possessed closed hands with the fingers all grown together, from the appearance of Noah opened his thumb opposite the four fingers. The potentiality of knowledge concerning the structure of the world was revealed. It was a time of richness and abundance. And we see that 'it came to pass when men began to multiply on the face of the earth, and daughters were born unto them' (Gen. 6:1). It is another expression in the Bible about the coming of an end, a conclusion of a world. Here, in fact comes the end of the first 'toldoth', the first of the four birth-stories. And towards the end there is the great multiplicity, that explosion into multiplicity we have already discussed in connection with the image of the tree as an expression of the phenomenon time.

Excessive multiplicity finds its expression in men on earth in the births of daughters. The female, as we have seen time and again, in our criteria, is the expression of that which in the man is his body, and that which in the world is matter. At the end of time especially the expansion of matter is characteristic. It is then released in all its possibilities of development. And in man there is the emphasis on the body. *That* is born unto him in abundance.

I here refer to the story of the bondage in Egypt where Pharaoh had the sons thrown into the water, but emphatically allowed the daughters to live. For the world of duality is anxious to have matter, is fond of these forces of development. Men, as expression of the soul, are killed, are thrown into the colourless, character-destroying water, therein to perish. They are not supposed to stand out as personalities, they must be levelled down, covered by the gliding masses of waters.

With the daughters, however, Egypt, as tradition has it, could commit adultery. It is adultery to use matter, the body, for wrong purposes. For the body should be united to the soul, thus to form the complete, integrated man. If, however, man should divert the body from that purpose, he commits adultery with it. It is left to itself and delivered up to the lust of development, of intoxication; to the woman is denied the unifying man. Man abuses her for the sake of worldly gain.

Let me point out here that the daughter, the woman, is not looked upon as something inferior. There is a current idea that in the Bible woman was treated as a slave, as an inferior creature. Just as it is pointed out that with certain nations the birth of a daughter is considered unimportant, whereas the birth of a son is considered a blessing.

To begin with, there is an equal balance between the births of sons and the births of daughters. The balance is slightly in favour of sons, but this is soon offset, and very often at a riper age the balance is reversed in favour of the number of women. Maybe this expresses the essential principle that at the beginning, at creation, the soul is accorded slight preponderance, whereas later on, as the world develops, matter and things physical rather gain the ascendancy. But by and large the number of men equals that of women, just as there is a balance between soul and body.

Now the body is destined to unite with the soul, just as matter must be united with the source of origin, just as man must seek union with God.

At the integration of body and soul, of matter and the source of origin, of man and God, the body, matter and man are meant to relinquish the world in which they live and accept the criteria of unity, of the world whence they originate and whither their conscious or unconscious desire was directed all the time throughout their separation.

The woman, taken from the man in the same way, yearns for a return to the condition of unity. She, too, yearns for the world where harmony obtains, where opposites are eliminated, where man and woman each take up an essential place in the great whole.

The woman must not and should not be held in contempt or oppressed by the man. It would mean that the soul does not see any purpose in the body except oppressing, stifling it. That is not what God made creation for. God created matter in all its beauty and variety, in all its strength and seductiveness to hallow it, to unify it in its veriest details into a harmony with man, for the purpose of this harmony thus regaining its place in the great harmony with God. Whoever disdains the woman, virtually rejects the whole purpose of creation. It means that he sets himself up as a superior deity carping at people about him and tyrannizing over them.

Therefore the woman, like all of God's creation, should be held in esteem and treated with respect. The man, indeed, should behold in the woman that which enables him to accomplish integration. As the Bible puts it, (Gen. 2:18) 'ezer kenegdo', translated literally 'a help opposite him', a help, a mate for him, i. e. the possibility to achieve the reunion of all creation with God. At this reunion the woman has a task just as important as man. She has to employ her personality so that the goal, reunion of creation with God, can be attained.

Through misapprehension of the purpose of creation, through the erroneous idea, well known to us by now, that the world must go on developing according to criteria built up on experience and observation an entirely lopsided vision has cropped up concerning the place of the woman in this world.

People have come to look upon the Bible as a book which also has its place in this current of evolution, in the current of the 'tree that makes fruit'. That place ipso facto comes at least a few thousand years earlier than the place the world takes now. From the evolutionists' standpoint, therefore, the Bible is primitive, uncouth, in many fields not nearly as wise as we are ourselves, let alone our descendants, the future generations.

And since, according to these evolutionists the Bible is a history book with, among other things, descriptions of society, these society-descriptions must similarly be old-fashioned, primitive, rather uncouth. And since woman seems to come off rather badly there, *that* too should be amended in the sense of greater development.

The Bible, however, does not describe any form of society anywhere in history; the Bible uses the society-form of the time when God's pattern of creation expressed itself in the world, so as to formulate by means of those images in that type of society what is the substance of creation and of the world.

And then the Bible insists that one should see to it that matter does not race on in development, that it should not be left to itself, that it is inclined to fall into multiplicity, to attach itself more to men. The Bible then tells us matter is meant to co-operate to get the fruit, to attain the goal. Man can have more forms for his own, just as God can have more worlds, just as a nucleus can have more spheres.

The Bible tells us how the world *is*. And it is only when one understands this well that one can build up one's practice of life, based on that structure and applied to our world. The Bible is not a recipe-book or cookery-book to learn by means of examples how to set about things, how, to behave. This would imply a complete misunderstanding of the Bible. In that case one might say — which indeed people do — that if David did so and so, one is free to do likewise, that since Jacob had done this or that or the other, one would not be so very bad really if one did the same things. One might for instance deduce from it that it is not really wicked to wipe out one's defeated enemies, since God supposedly commanded biblical Israel to do that. Then one will also come to the 'eve for an eve', etc.

Neither does the Bible tell us in its story how to treat women, nor how women should behave. Only in understanding how the world is made, what its structure is, how time evolves, to what purpose it has all been made, what is the place of everything, only then could one state how life in this world might be built up, so that it would in every detail agree with the structure God gave to the world.

And then one will realize that the 'eye for an eye' *must* not be applied at all, that it is merely an indication of how God maintains the balance, the great harmony, but that man has a place all by himself and is not even allowed to take those decisions. In the discussion of the principles of the administering of justice further on in this book I hope to return to the subject.

The treatment of woman and her behaviour cannot become clear either until one understands the purpose of the Bible. Then one will see that woman should be treated with profound regard, and also what is her place in life.

The foundation for that arrangement is the principle that matter, as creation made by God, must be led back by man to its source of origin. And as a human being woman has the same duty towards matter as man. That woman has another characteristic besides, that she is the expression of matter in the compound of man, lays on her a number of very special, personal duties.

For instance, woman is not at all excluded from social life, as it is recorded in detail in oral tradition. She could, if she wanted, pursue any employment, any profession; as a human being she has the same rank and status as man. If, however, in connection with her personality, she had rather not pursue certain callings or commit certain actions, it is up to her own personal decision, the milieu in which she lives, the influence such a conduct might or might not exercise on others.

It is just as silly to maintain that according to the Bible woman should content herself with an inferior position as it would be to state that according to the Bible the 'eye for an eye' should be applied. The immense complex of ancient lore which pertains to the Bible just as this world pertains to heaven and which, so to speak, is an expression of heaven in this world, shows in fact that woman has a place in this world equal to man.

The purpose of woman's coming into this world is the reunion of the male and female principles in everything. A reunion which is prepared in this world in the seventh day, like a betrothal and which is completed in the eighth day, in the world-to-come.

On that foundation did mankind also know the principle of the betrothal before marriage. It was not a utilistic arrangement; it was something made in this way in accordance with this structure of reunion.

The word for 'male betrothed' is 'chatan' in Hebrew, spelt cheth-taf-nun, 8–400–50. This word has initially the 8–400, the cheth, the eighth letter. And as conclusion the nun, 50, the letter we know as the expression of the eighth day, of the world-to-come. So the word is composed of the 'eighth' as beginning and ending. It shows that the destination of the betrothed is the eighth day.

The word for 'female betrothed' is 'kalla', spelt kaf-lamed-hee, 20–30–5. Here we have to do with a feminine form, hence with a 'hee', a '5' as ending. It is the 'hee' which occurs at the end of every feminine word, expressing the female 'five' waiting for the 'male five' to be integrated into unity.

Thus this 'kalla' has as its root the 20–30, the word 'all' which, as we saw before, also expresses the 50, which is the next day, the eighth day, the condition after the completion of the seventh day in the seven times seven. It is the 50th day which brings the revelation after the emancipation from bondage in the world of opposites, Egypt.

Facing each other are the betrothed who found each other in the seventh day, and both have in the structure of the world the 'eight' as something strongly stressed. For in the eighth day lies their destination, as it was already expressed in their appearance in the seventh day. The word for marriage indeed is 'chathana', spelt cheth-taf-nun-hee, 8–400–50–5. It is a form of the word chathan, or one might also put it thus, the word for male betrothed is a form of the word marriage. And both words contain the 'cheth', the 'eight', and the 'nun', the 'fifty'.

That is why from olden times there has been the custom that the woman is led seven times round the man at the wedding performance, and the custom of the seven days feasting after the wedding. For in the seven did they come together. The eighth day leaves them together, alone, and then the union is consummated. In all this the woman is not only a partner of equal standing in the whole, she is indispensable. As is indicated by the bride being led seven times round the betrothed as the centre, she is matter encompassing the centre and it is only through their being together that the world can exist.

Now when towards the end of time man multiplies, when the great multiplicity comes, the daughters are born. By that time the physical is greatly stressed, the emphasis is on matter. Ancient lore has it that these numerous 'women' came forth from the generation of Cain, the maker of matter, the maker-of-the-Cain-culture. From this culture does the great expansion of matter result.

And the sons of God took them wives all which they chose (Gen. 6:2). These sons of God are men, made in God's image and after God's likeness, as it is recorded about the generation of Sheth. Of Sheth, who came instead of Abel, the soul ousted by Cain (Gen. 4:25).

At the end of time, man with his divine soul will feel attracted by matter. That great multiplicity means a great temptation. The ease with which matter now yields everything, offers itself, leads man to turning towards matter, away from his purpose.

Nature's beauty, her strength have man in their grip. It is, as in the story of Paradise, the man who accepts the fruit from the woman, and eats it. The union of the soul and the body proves to draw the soul towards matter through the great strength and beauty of the development of matter. The soul is unable itself to withstand this power of attraction. To the contrary the soul has given its own enormous potential to matter, and 'there were giants in the earth', the immense concentration of matter, fructified by super-mundane forces. Men of renown came; man sought a name for *himself* and a place in this world to settle in. It was his purpose now that he should lead this world with his divine power. He saw himself acquiring a hold on the world, on the universe, he saw that there were practically no barriers left. Matter had tempted him thereto, it had found the way to grip man.

And at this decisive moment God determines to put an end to this world. It is the same situation as on that last moment in the sixth day of creation. The woman had seduced man to eat from the tree of knowledge and God decided to put an end to the world in which man lived, the world of the sixth day, and to bring man into another world, into the world of the seventh day. Man himself would not be able to unite the body with the origin. If it were left to man's devices, he would with the body as his leader stray ever farther away from the source of origin. He would form giants of matter and power and he would feel like a god himself, he would establish his own name and never give a thought to the name of God and to the meaning, the purpose of creation.

For that reason did God take man away from the world at the end of the sixth day, did God manifestly take the lead and break off the development of the body and of matter. To emancipate man from it, to reduce matter to a weaker form, spread about time, lest it should fall on man in its previous concentration. In the seventh day matter would be more restrained. The seventh day is a day of 'rest'. Matter's force of development will also come to rest in the pattern of the seventh day. But for God's interference, as already established in creation, the reunion could never be achieved. God had to cause the line to curve back, the line which was going to move ever further away from the origin. The word 'create' for this world has therefore as its final letter, as its ending, the 'one'. For this world creation had already got this character of roundness; the curve is inherent to the conception 'create' in this world.

Just as the story of Paradise, as root-story, is enacted at the end of the sixth day, thus we see the end of the world-story at the end of the first 'toldoth', of the first of the four parts, enacted at the end of Noah's six-hundredth year (Gen. 5:32 and Gen. 7:11).

The new world which is beginning now, has the criterion of Noah, in which everything will he expressed now; the seventh day; it is the seventh 'hundred' of Noah.

In this way came the end of the first world, the first part of the four worlds, of the four 'toldoth', in the systematism of the root-story. Again it was an explosion of the strength of matter, which had overwhelmed man. The woman, turned adrift, standing alone by herself in the world, drawn into dialogue with the serpent, had tempted the man. The daughters of men had seduced the sons of God. The daughters of men came forth from the Cain-culture. The Cain-culture cropped up because Cain had killed the soul, eliminated it, placed it in the service of the earth.

The story was now 'more elaborate' than in the root-story, the second tale of creation, and *still* more elaborate than in the first tale of creation. It tells, however, the same thing. The pattern is analogous. There is merely a change in background. It is enacted in a wider circle, in a layer further removed from the core of the fruit, moving more slowly, one might say, in a more detailed fashion. But the structure is the same; matter proves too strong; man realizes he cannot restrain it and sees that God has established creation so as to enable man yet to reach the goal, through God's intervention. Adam thought that the world was destroyed when he was removed from the sixth day, when the dark night came. Until he found that the world had not perished, but that a new world, a new day had come. Upon which, as ancient lore tells us with such depth of meaning, he recited the Psalm of the Sabbath, the 92nd Psalm. The new day was a new life and Adam saw that indeed it was very good what God had done.

Here too with Noah, does the new world come, again in the transition from the sixth day to the seventh, this time as the sixth and seventh 'hundred' of Noah. The structure is the same, the background against which the story is enacted, has changed. One might ask the question, why this repetition? To what purpose? Indeed, why this repetition in such a fundamental story in which every word and letter is weighed, as the story of the Bible?

The repetition is apparent in the structure, it is true, but the story most certainly takes a new course.

For the first time there appears a man who now provides an exception to the rule in this destruction of the world. This time there is a man with a group pertaining to him, passing consciously from one world into the next. It is the story of Noah, 'a just man and perfect in his generations, and Noah walked with God' (Gen. 6:9).

There is something new now in the structure of *time*. A new element is coming to expression. This new element arises from the fact that now begins the *second* of the four 'toldoth', the story which in the structure of time is signed with the letter 'five' of the name Lord God.

In the expression of the name Lord God in time, the first 'ten' has gone by, has slid past; now the first 'five' of the 10–5–6–5 is coming. Another vital experience of the structure, a condensation, a crystallization in another medium.

The description of this cystallization, expressing itself as the story of Noah and the Great Flood will be the subject of the next chapter.

12
The Word Carries Life through Time

Before the old world perishes, when God has decreed to grant the world 120 years yet till the destruction, He shows Noah how to get to the new world (Gen. 6:5–22).

God tells Noah to make an ark, He even furnishes him with all kinds of details for the manner in which to build it, as too its measurements. The command to build the ark, as ancient lore records, comes at a moment when God sees man tending more and more towards the earth, 120 years before the great Flood, that is. This command from God to start building as early as that, served the purpose of making people see what Noah was doing that they might ask him why he was doing it, what it was meant for, this ark, on dry land, in the middle of the country.

The 120 years, in ancient lore, are the measure of every individual life, in the time-reckoning of this world. Every individual life 'principle' covers 120 years. Just as an infinite period of time is measured with the number 400, and an all-embracing multiplicity in human life is expressed by 70. We have already seen that 130 is the measure of 'reunion', beyond the 120, that is, finding expression in another world.

It implies that the ark is *also* built from the moment of birth of every individual man, so that every man may throughout his life see Noah building his ark; then to inquire after the purpose of it all.

A longer life than those 120 years allotted to him as essential measure would dispose man in favour of the earthly forces, towards the earthly body in its development; 'evil', i.e. development tending away from the origin, would attract man overmuch and draw him away from his destination.

These 120 years, when occurring in another 'history', cannot be compared with the ages of the first decade of generations, nor with those of the five generations, now at hand. It is only Moses, the composer of the Pentateuch, who has these 120 years as his measure of life. So one should regard the 120 years as an absolute criterion for *life* of man on earth.

They represent a curtailment as regards the 130 years which have already transgressed the bounds of another world. And this curtailment takes place so that death may bend the life of man, giving it the curve in his course through the worlds to lead him back to the origin. If man were to get past these '120', he would be lost and never return, owing to the attraction of the forces of development.

Now what is this ark which is to bear Noah and his family together with representatives of all that lives to another world, a new world?

The world, going to be destroyed, is that of the sixth hundred of the time of Noah, of the sixth day, that is, here in the expression of *this* toldoth, and the ark will bear Noah across to the life in his seventh hundred, i.e. to the seventh day. The story tells us how the transition is from the sixth to the seventh, expressed in the terms of this 'history'.

Ark is 'teba' in Hebrew, spelt taf-Beth-hee, 400–2–5. 'Teba' also means 'word'.

The measurements of the ark are 300 cubits in length, 50 in breadth and 30 in height. Spelt in letters these numbers are respectively shin (300), nun (50), and lamed (30). These three letters also form the components of the word 'lashon', which means 'language'. Lashon is spelt lamed-shin-nun, 30–300–50. So the measurements of the ark, which itself means 'word', yield the term 'language'.

Here again we have found something most extraordinary. Something devised to carry life from one world to another, itself is called 'word', and the measurements given of it form the word 'language'.

It is not very difficult to find the meaning of what the Bible tells us here. It simply means that that which carries life from one world to another is the word and the language. Is not the Bible itself the same? For indeed, it is 'word' and 'language'. Does it not carry life in the word and in the language from one world into another?

Life, as the story has it, is wrapped up in the word which has the criteria of 'language', it remains preserved therein during the transition from one world into another, and it is again informed with life on earth in the new world.

This transition of life from one world into another, as we express it in the images and phenomena of this world, is very much as if one carries something into a ship, and when everything else around it is covered with water and perishes as individuality, all that is carried into the ship remains in existence. It is in this sense that God stamps on this space-time world the pattern of the transition of man and of all other life on earth, from one world to another, at the stage when the first 'ten' of the 10–5–6–5 has passed.

But the Bible gives this image in such a way, thus expressed in the word, that through it one can see *how* this transition takes place really and why it takes place.

The attraction of the forces of development exercised on man is so great that everything dominated by these forces, loses its individuality in this world. Everything is covered by the waters, made invisible, killed as an individual being. That man, however, who has not surrendered to these forces, but has built at the word all his life with the criteria God has given him, since he knows that the purpose of life is seeking union with the source of origin, the return thither where the opposites turn into harmony, that man and all that is his will be saved and pass into another world. The bridge between this world and the other is the 'teba', the 'word', and this 'teba' has the measures of the 'language', the 'tongue'.

In this way life passes over, and in this way, through the word and through language can we follow it and remain united with it. The story here tells us how this transition takes place and how one can from this world join the transition with the help of the word.

The Hebrew word for 'Flood' is 'mabul', mem-beth-waw-lamed, 40–2–6–30. It implies among other things 'commingling' in the sense of being thrown together in disorder and confusion. The word 'Babel' is connected with it.

This commingling takes place because the waters under the firmament and the waters above the firmament overflow their bounds and commingle. On the second day of creation God had made the division between the waters below, which became the earth, and the waters above which became the firmament. Through this division individual life in the third day and the following days became possible. With this 'mabul', however, this division is eliminated again and individual life, as it was able to express itself, is simultaneously destroyed with it.

It is the 'one' recapturing its undivided condition on the left hand side of the systematism, on the side of water. Through it everything which existed because of that very duality, loses the basis of its existence. It is simply wiped out from existence.

Let me point at a similar situation: the Egyptians perishing in the waters covering them, when biblical Israel, like Noah, gets safely across. Moses also got into a 'teba' and thus was saved in the water. And the passing into the promised land, the world-to-come, with Joshua, takes place through the water that creates a safe passage, through the river 'Jordan'.

Water, in Hebrew 'mayim', as mentioned before, mem-jot-mem, 40–10–40, has the structure of the 'mem', which letter has the name of 'water'. So *Mem* is that which flows, moves. Water and the letter mem thus indicate the conception 'time' which similarly is 'flowing', in motion, and which on account of its inexorable motion onwards similarly wipes out the individuality of the moment. Being drowned in the water and being drowned in time are virtually the same thing. Ever moving 'mem' expresses flowing, continuous flowing. That is why time is always measured with this *mem*, the 40, or with the 400. The connection between time and water, one might say, exists through the 'mem', the 40. Time is measured with the *mem*, with water.

The old-Hebrew glyph for the 'mem' therefore is 〰 a sign of wave motion. This wave motion expresses itself materially in water, but every phenomenon in time, perceived materially, expresses itself similarly as wave motion. Just think of sound-waves, light-waves.

Out of this ancient glyph 〰 for the 'mem' ultimately developed our letter M, via Greek script. So with 'mem' is meant the word 'water', and the ancient glyph for 'mem' therefore gives the image of water.

Similarly we saw that this world, coming into existence in form, was based on the 'ed', the 'mist'; that the principle of 'water' had to exist, to enable this world to express itself in the phenomenon of space-time. This is quite evident in the second tale of creation, as we have already amply discussed. That is the very reason why we called this world the world of the left hand side, the world built on water, because water appears in the systematism of creation on the second day, on the left hand side.

The passage through this world is very much like passing through water, hence – remember the *mem*, the 40, as measure for time – a passage through time.

And lest we should he drowned in water and in time, God gave us the 'teba', the 'word', which carries us like a ship through the water so that we can preserve our personality. Or rather, God causes the waters to dry up, causes time to stop, so that man may continue to live as a personality.

Remember the passage through the sea after the exodus from Egypt, or the passage through the river Jordan which fell dry at the entry into Canaan (Joshua 3).

Proceeding through the seventh day therefore as a whole is like proceeding through time and similarly like proceeding through water. For that reason the journey across the desert is a journey of 40 years hence of the number of *mem*, and for that reason Noah has the 'teba', the 'word', to be able to proceed through the water. Therefore water is the sine qua non in the desert and Moses is ever concerned with water on this journey. And even his non-entering Canaan is a consequence of this 'water'.

We might put it like this: man proceeds through this seventh day like a ship through the water, at least if he knows the 'word'. And he runs the risk of perishing in the water, if he has not got the word. The word which can preserve him from getting lost in the mass, in multiplicity. We have seen how the exodus from Egypt was marked by the beginning of the seventh 'hundred thousand' in the census of the population and how also with Noah at the exodus from his world, his seventh 'hundred' begins. This is not the place to enter more deeply into the question that there we were concerned with numbers of masses, whereas here it is numbers in time; any more than we can enter into the difference that now they are counting in hundreds, now in thousands. For our purpose, giving an introduction into the thought and vision of the Bible, these shades of difference need not be taken into account. We should then have to enter too much into details which would make this book too bulky.

So man proceeds through this seventh day as if in a ship, if he is at all to attain the other side of that day. This ship is the 'word' God gave to Noah, which He made him build at during these 120 years.

The old-Hebrew glyph for the 'zayin', the 'seven' therefore is:

It is the image of a ship with the oar to get into motion. In this case too, the glyph via Greek script, has passed into the modern alphabet. It is the sign of the Z (i.e. of Zayin). Many glyphs were rendered in mirror-writing, and the Z too has come down to us like that.

So we see that even the glyphs for the letters express these views. To us an M or a Z is something useful, we can form words with them, as we wish. We even try to make language and script efficient, that we may derive as much joy of this world as possible and in the easiest way. Owing to this we have completely lost every contact with the substance of things through language. Now the 'ark' carries man through this high-tide, this flood of time, carries him through that world in which everything is destroyed by this explosion of time. An explosion which causes all individuality to cease to exist. An explosion because both above and below such multiplicity is created that the personality *cannot* but perish in that mass.

It also shows how this body, when it has entered this life, will ultimately perish, if one should take the way of the daughters of men oneself; and that it is only Noah, living in the midst of such a world, who remains himself, because all his life he has built at the 'teba', at the 'word'. According to the standards God gave him.

At the moment the Flood came, Noah was 600 years old. The 120 years when he built at the 'teba' again are 'one' to 'four' to the 480 previous years. It is in this 'one' that man builds the word and understands the language. For this 'one' is the tree of life, expressing the Bible, to the 'four' of the tree of knowledge, the tree that makes fruit. Here again we see the proportion 1–4 coming forward, and again it tells us about the fundamental structure of creation.

Into the ark enter Noah and his three sons, each with his wife. So there is present a quadruplicity – one might call it the extreme potentiality – and this quadruplicity is bilateral, it is male and female.

Of all live beings the male and the female specimens come into the 'teba'. The word contains the two opposite sides of everything. In the word they remain divorced; as a duality they come into the word.

The ark also has the three parts out of which the word is built up and the sentence too is built up. The three letters of the word 'ark' form the root, the three parts of the sentence make it into one whole. Just as, indeed, every argument contains the two parts which through synthesis are composed into an intelligible whole. Just as creation too is built up with the cycle of the three days.

About the 'teba' it is said besides that 'in a cubit shall it be finished above' (Gen. 6:16). This expression at first sight is not very clear, especially in translation. It means, however – and ancient lore ipso facto affirms it – that the ark tapered off towards the top, and that at the top it measured one cubit in length and one in width. Which means that the 'teba' has the form of a truncated pyramid. The upper 'stone' has been omitted 'on purpose'.

Although I cannot here expatiate on ancient Egypt's knowledge of life, it may be rather interesting to point at this aspect of the pyramid. The 'ark' is the form in which life passes from one world to another. The pyramid with the same structure as the ark was also meant for the transition of a very special people from one world into another. The ship, too, which in other Egyptian expressions is used as a means of transition from one life to another, points in that direction.

The ark with its measurements as the pyramid, contains a great many marvellous communications, expressed in the numbers of its measurements. It herewith shows that it is indeed the word and the language of the Bible in all its aspects. But since it would carry us too far into other fields, I must drop this most interesting subject.

On the other hand I should like here to enter into the behaviour of this ark during the Flood. In this way too a great deal will be elucidated about the character of the ark. And then we shall also have returned to the course of our story and come across things with which we are fairly familiar by now.

The story of the Flood, the 'mabul', to the reader is a rather strange and confusing story, with all its data, water-levels, etc. Let us try to consider this story seriously as well and not wave aside the communications as orginating from a primitive manner of expression about some inundation or other in ancient Babel. The story is briefly as follows: the Flood comes 'after seven days' and in the first instance it lasts 40 days. The beginning of the 40 days falls 'in the second month, in the seventeenth day of the second month' (Gen. 7 and 8).

I have here to interrupt the argument. This 17th of the second month as a communication should really intrigue us. Why this specification?

There is something very uncommon about this 'seventeenth'. For if we look a little more closely, we see that the Flood takes place in the year 1656, i.e. in the 17th hundred since creation, counted with biblical criteria, of course. Besides, we see that Joseph was sold to Egypt (Gen. 37:2) when he was seventeen. The 'molten calf' – as can he computed from the text, since it was 40 days after the revelation – was made on the seventeenth day of the fourth month. According to ancient lore, Moses, when he fled from Egypt, was seventeen years old.

So there actually is something about this number 'seventeen'. It is always used when a world, a period, is drawing to a close and a new one is beginning. For wherever we come across this 'seventeen' there is an end of something and it all seems very bitter and hard, and there comes a new situation. The great Flood is a bitter thing, so is the sale of Joseph. Similarly, Moses being compelled to flee from Egypt, where he had been brought up as a prince. At the 'molten calf' the stone tables were smashed, hence a world is broken up. But all the time we see how a very good new world arises after that bitter destruction.

After the Flood come Abraham and the other Patriarchs. It all proves to turn out right. When Joseph descends into Egypt, it proves to be all to the good; he becomes a king there and he looks after the well-being of this brothers. What was to come went into fulfilment and it was wonderfully well fulfilled. Because Moses had to flee from Egypt, he got to Mount Horeb and there he met God. It is true, the broken tables inaugurated an exile, but with a redemption the more sublime for all that. The 'seventeen' marks an ending, and it is hard, but there arises a new world which is more sublime and glorious than the previous one.

Now this number 'seventeen' also occurs in the first tale of creation, to wit where in this tale too one situation ceases and another begins. The number 'seventeen' is there to mark the principle of transition. And for that reason does it come into prominence in the pattern whenever a transition takes place. This number 'seventeen' in the first tale of creation is, in fact, the word 'good' which ever occurs when one day of creation ends and God is going to make a new day; when it says in the Bible, 'and God saw that it was "*good*".'

For the word 'good' in Hebrew is 'tob', spelt teth-waw-beth, 9–6–2. The sum-total of the components is 17. In number it says there: 'and God saw that it was 17'. In the first tale of creation too every day a world ends with '17', and after it there begins a new one.

At the same time we learn from it that viewing it from the standpoint of the complete design of creation, God calls such an ending 'good'. Wherever occurs such a transition and this in the story appears to express itself as very bitter, hard and sorrowful, and where this 'seventeen' plays a part, it is evident that, viewed from the design of creation, from the purpose of discovering the origin again, it is 'good' all the same. As the story indicates too, when one reads on. Only to one who is merely aware of the moment, the one who eats of the 'tree that makes fruit', it is a grievous affair. He merely sees the destruction and knows nothing about the coming world. He does not know the 'word', hence he does not know the word 'good' either, which bestows on this transition its 'value', its significance, its meaning.

To the man who knows the tree of life, who is not cut off from it, because he did not eat from the tree of knowledge and did not refuse to take the way back, such a transition is indeed stamped with the hallmark 'good'. It is only the man who ate from the tree of knowledge that will regard the transition as suffering and destruction.

The end of the sixth day of creation is marked with the word 5 'very good', 'tob meod'. I have already pointed out that the word 'very', 'meod', is spelt 40–1–4, and that in its structure it shows a relationship with the word 'dead' which is 40–6–400, the word 'meth' 40–400 is more often used for something dead, while the word 40–6–400 'maweth' is used for death.

The words 'very good', as stated before, are read in tradition as 'death is good', pointing at that transition from the sixth world to the seventh, which takes place through death, and which yet is good. Thus the tale of the Flood is this transition from the sixth day to the seventh, expressing itself here as the age of Noah who is just 600 years old when the Flood is rising, and who has just entered his seventh hundred. And this transition is a 'death' too. But here we see how Noah and his family in reality continue alive, for the very reason that Noah had built the ark, the 'word', with the criteria God had given him. And because of it he passes over from one world to the other 'alive', and this transition is 'very good', there where he really is, 'death is good'. And this transition is marked by the number 17; it begins on the 17th of the second month.

Thus the Flood, the 'Mabul', begins in this sign of the 'seventeen', both as regards the century and the day of the month.

We see that from the 17th day of the second month it continues raining for forty days. According to the computation of months as applied by the Bible, this lasts until the 28th day of the third month.

After which 'the waters prevailed upon the earth an hundred and fifty days'. And at the end of those 150 days the waters decreased. In the seventh month after the 'Flood' had begun — the Flood had already lasted 40 days plus 150 days, and we have then got to the seventh month after the beginning — again on the 17th of that month, the ark stuck on Mount Ararat. As the Flood had begun in the second month, it is now the ninth month of the year.

The months as the Bible takes them are reckoned as periods of 29½ days. Before the beginning of the Flood, the Bible mentions God waited yet seven days (Gen. 7:4). One of the explanations for it is that after the 120 years God yet waited seven days to see whether people would not *after all* turn away from their adoration of multiplicity. For God had made Noah build the teba all those 120 years, the 'word' which with its heavenly criteria had been given as a present to the world, that men might see it and marvel at it.

Then they would ask questions, and from these questions and answers they might draw the conclusion that the course they had followed so far, was wrong, that that course had never been purposed by creation. Man, as created after God's likeness, would have to choose the way himself, would of his own accord have to bestow the love on God and choose the way leading towards God. On this point only the decision lay with man. All the rest had been prepared by God in His plan to reunite everything with the source of origin. To 'turn the heart of the fathers to the children and the heart of the children to their fathers' (Malachi 4:6). According to ancient lore Noah pointed out to men the impending end of man. Man's life would not outlast 120 years, a lifetime in this world. Then what?

Noah pointed out to them how one would then continue to live with one's full individuality beyond this life here, if one were to consider this 'word' with its divine criteria as one's home.

But the world merely laughed at him. In the first instance they refused to hear about an ending. Such a thing was non-existent in their code of life; it was downright indecent to use the word. Just as they would not hear about any individual death, they refused to believe in the destruction of a period, let alone a whole world.

They did not want to hear about the destruction of the individual in the multiplicity of masses, in the 'city'-culture of Cain's world, and they built and added to it, unconcerned, although on the other hand they could perceive everything quite well. Neither did they want to hear about the end of a complete era, in which a complete period goes to destruction, is submerged into oblivion. And with it a complete world.

Ancient lore has it that just before these final seven days Methuselah died. He was the 8th after Adam, and like everything signed with the 'eight', with the 'fat' of the 'eight', he outlived every other man. People had seen how this rich, 'fat' world of Methuselah had gone down, how

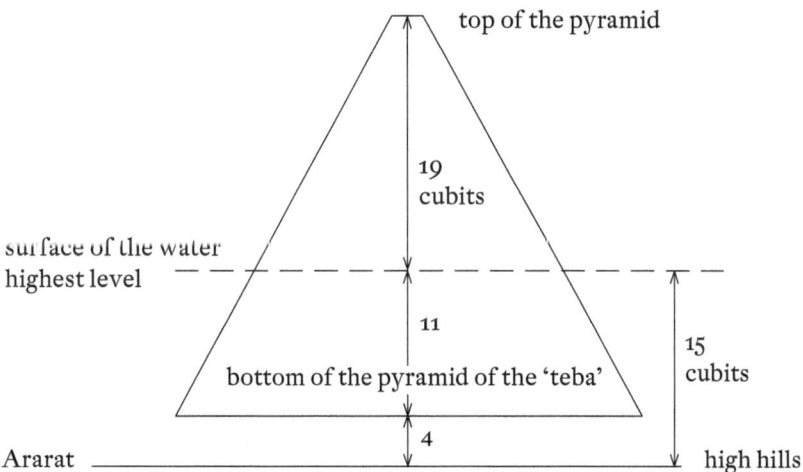

there actually was an end of the unfoldment into multiplicity. With Methuselah's death the 120 years were past. Yet God added the seven days in which people mourned for the passing away of Methuselah, next to Noah the last survivor of the ten generations. The shock of Methuselah's passing away might cause people to retrace their steps, as yet to inquire after the purpose of life, to turn to Noah after all.

But even now people refused to believe it. They simply *could* not believe it, it was utterly beyond all that one had always thought about and with which one had always occupied oneself.

And when they had refused to pay regard to all these intimations about the end, *after* the seven days the way to the 'teba' was cut off. When they experienced the end themselves and saw the world being destroyed, many there were, according to ancient lore, who would as yet try and escape into the 'teba'. But now the way was cut off; 'beasts' blocked up the entrance. That with which one had ever acted the wrong way, the world of the forces of development, now obstructed the way to the word and to salvation.

These seven days are for that very reason emphatically mentioned as a period preceeding the Flood.

Until the moment the teba strikes Mount *Ararat* there are four phases:

1. The seven days before the Mabul, when people were aware of the approaching end.
2. The 40 days, from the 17/II – 28/III
3. The 150 days, from the 28/III – 1/IX
4. The 16 days, when the water starts decreasing, till the teba rests on Mount Ararat, 1/IX– 17/IX

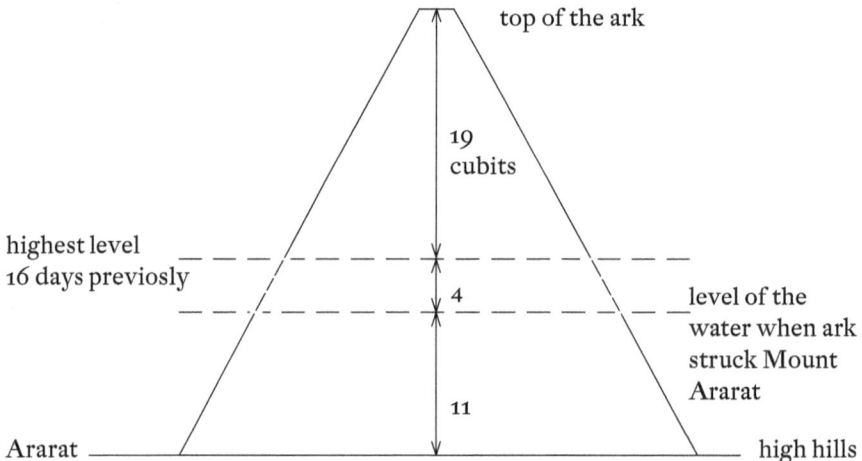

On the 17th day of the 9th month, owing to the abating of the water for the past 16 days, the ark strikes Mount Ararat. At the end of this fourth phase there is a renewed contact with the earth, with something individual. Whereas previously everything was covered, hidden by water.

The water continues decreasing, also after the ark has struck Mount Ararat on the 17/IX, and consequently on the 1st day of the tenth month (Gen. 8:5) the tops of the hills are seen.

This 'tenth month' is not the tenth month of our calendar, but the tenth month after the beginning of the Flood. And since it began in the second month, according to the calendar it is the 1st day of the eleventh month. The period from the ark's striking Mount Ararat and running aground, to the hilltops' getting visible therefore is:

5. 17/IX – 1/XI

It says in the Bible that at the highest level of the Flood the water had risen 15 cubits over the 'hilltops' (Gen. 7:20). So when these hills got visible on the 1st day of the eleventh month, the water had been decreasing for 60 days, from 1/IX up to and including 1/XI. In these 60 days the water had decreased 15 cubits. The 15 cubits, the water had risen over the hills, were gone in those 60 days.

Again we see a proportion familiar to us. In 60 days 15 cubits; this makes one cubit in 4 days. It is the proportion 1–4 which proves to express itself here again. And the word for cubit, 'ama', 1–40–5, in which the 5 merely is the feminine ending, similarly has this 1–4 structure. That which measures, which is used as a criterion, itself is marked with this 1–4.

From these measures which the Bible gives us, we can find various other proportions. For when the water decreased in a proportion of 1 cubit in 4 days – and does not the context drive us to regard the 'cubit' as something different from the measurement we are familiar with? – it means that when after the 16 days' decreasing of the water the ark reached Mount Ararat, the water must have fallen four cubits in those 16 days. And this implies that at the highest level of the water the bottom of the ark was merely 4 cubits over Mount Ararat. As the water was then 15 cubits over the hills, it means that the ark lay 11 cubits deep in the water. The ark was 30 cubits in height. Of those 30 cubits, 11 were in the water and 19 above it.

The situation therefore was as shown in the drawing on page 253. And at the moment the ark struck Mount Ararat, the situation was as is shown in the drawing on page 254.

After the hills had become visible, i.e. after the water had been decreasing for 60 days we get new periods of time mentioned: another 40 days, after which Noah opened the 'window' (Gen. 8:6) and then, after various details about the raven and the dove to which we shall revert again, there is the statement that in the 601st year of Noah, in the first month, on the first day of that month, the waters were dried up, that the earth itself was visible but still drenched with water (Gen. 8:13). And finally, on the seventh and twentieth day of the second month, was the earth dried, and Noah and all that were his went forth from the ark.

Now let us again arrange these statements and associate them with the preceding statements in the five phases mentioned previously.

The 5th phase ended on the 1/XI. When Noah, after the hilltops have become visible, waits another 40 days before opening the window, the 6th phase is that of waiting until the water shall decrease still further. Now, how much does it decrease in those 40 days? Again 10 cubits, since every 4 days it decreases 1 cubit. That makes, when reckoned from the 1/XI, 40 days, so that the calendar then gives 10/XII.

After this we have to wait till the 1/I, before the earth can be seen, which means another 20 days.

All in all it is 40+20 days until the earth can be seen. In those 60 days the water has decreased 15 cubits, i.e. again 1 cubit in 4 days. When the water was still 5 cubits high, after the 40 days with the decrease of 10 cubits on a total of 15 cubits at the beginning of the 40 days, Noah opened the 'window' and began sending forth the raven and the dove.

Let us arrange things a little more conveniently in a scheme, beginning with the 6th phase, after the hills have become visible.

6. Noah waits 40 days after the hills have become visible, 1/XI – 10/XII.
7. Noah opens the window and sends forth:
   1 the raven
   2 ⎫
   3 ⎬ the dove, three times
   4 ⎭

This period embraces 20 days; on the 21st day the dove found a place to rest on and did not return any more 10/XII – 1/I. In the 60 days from 1/XI – 1/I, from the moment the tops of the high hills were getting visible to the moment the earth became visible, the water decreased 15 cubits. Which means that the 'high hills' were also 15 cubits high. And that at its highest level the water was as high again as those high mountains: for at its highest level the water was 15 cubits over these mountains. From this we see that we must not blindly confuse the standards which the Bible uses with those of our perception. The Bible expresses the substance, hence the measures, even if used for our world, are not those of our perception.

So now we see that the water at its highest level was 30 cubits high, while the highest hills were 15 cubits high, hence half of the total height.

And when we draw the position of the ark at the highest level of the Flood, we get the following picture.

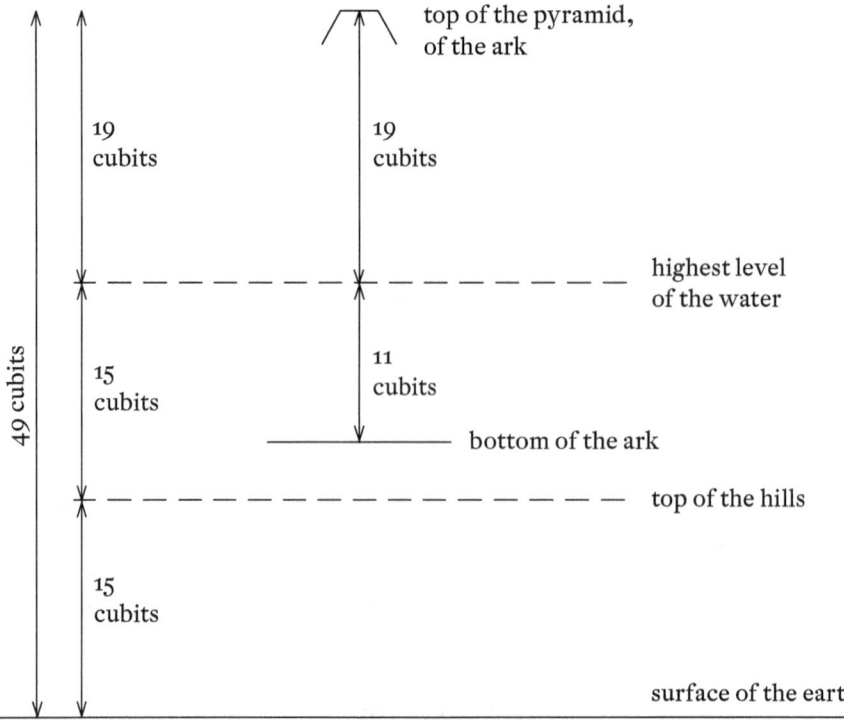

And then we find that the whole story of the Flood, the 'Mabul', is enacted within 49 cubits. That it exactly covers all this seventh day in its entire completion. And the *teba* had indeed been given to get through this seventh day!

Now we realize why the pyramid has a flattened surface. The 'missing stone' would, in fact, reach up into the 50th, and the 50th is beyond the material form of expression which this world of the seventh day knows. The pyramid might have ended in a point at that height of 30 cubits. But in that case everything would have been closed off. Now however the form of the pyramid presupposes a continuation invisible to us, it is true, since it points into another world; however, it emphatically exists as a continuation. It may he put like this, that the viability in the ark depends on this invisible top.

The top-part in detail, therefore, offers this outline:

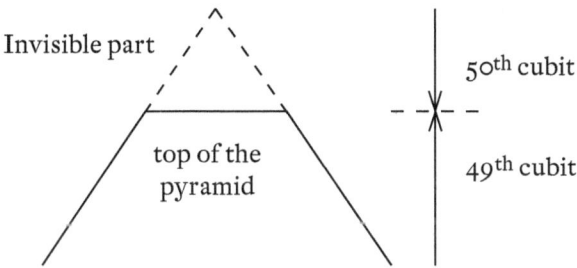

In the total 'height' of the tale of the Flood we clearly recognize the structure which we were fairly familiar with from the foregoing.

It shows that at the entrance to the seventh day – for, as we have already seen, the Flood begins, when the seventh hundred of Noah begins – the story of this seventh day is outlined. Things come to the worst in the seventh day when the water has risen to a level as high again as solid non-flowing matter. With the 30, the 2 × 15 has been attained. It cannot get beyond this 'twice'.

In the word '*create*' the extreme development is also this 'two'. For indeed it embraces all the rest of multiplicity. At that point everything is swallowed up by time, by water. At *that* point the word reaches as high as the top, to the boundary of the other world.

And at that point the teba is 4 cubits removed from solid matter. The complete 4 of development, included in the 2, is then completed. So here again there is a boundary; things cannot get beyond this either.

At that point when things are at their worst, when there is the greatest danger of complete destruction, also for Noah – ancient lore gives us details about it – the *teba* reaches as high as the 50th cubit; the word, so to speak, touching the other world.

And at that moment when the 'teba' of Noah, his word, reaches the boundary of the other world, when he has in his word approached God as nearly as possible, there is this, 'and God remembered Noah' (Gen. 8:1).

And then the water decreases and a new situation arises when the 'teba' strikes the highest tops of the earth, of solid matter. It also means that the word is again associated with non-fluid matter. Although everything is still covered with water, there is this, invisible but tangible, contact.

This situation, when the water has decreased 4 cubits, again on the 17th of a month, seven months after the beginning of the Flood, is identical with the coming of a new world. For between the 17/II and the 17/IX seven full months have elapsed. At the beginning of the 8th month there is the contact between the 'teba' and solid matter. Now the 'word' descends on the 'hill', gets into contact with the world. Just as God descended on Mount Sinai with the 'word' at the end of the seven weeks after the exodus from Egypt, at the beginning of the 8th week.

Now what is the situation like in our schematic representation? The following change has taken place, as compared with the situation drawn in the previous diagram:

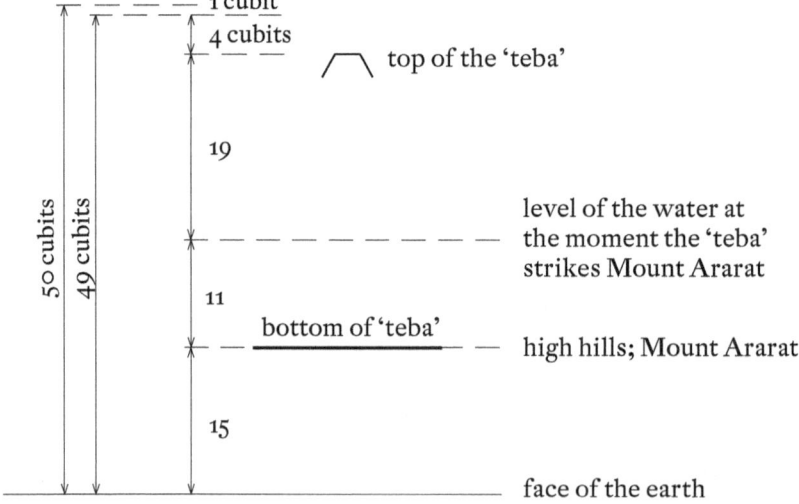

Again we see something very uncommon, which specially emphasizes the 'argument' of God's appearance on the 8th day, and the 'teba' striking the 'mountain'.

For the water which had decreased 4 cubits after its highest level of 30 cubits, has now reached a level of 26 cubits. And these 26 cubits are divided into two parts. One part is the 15 cubits of the 'mountain'; the other part is the 11 cubits of the 'teba' which, indeed, was 11 cubits deep in the water, and which now with these 11 cubits 'draught of water' strikes the mountain.

And these 26, divided into 15 and 11, into 10–5 and 6–5, are indeed the 26 of the name Lord God, as we have seen it making its appearance several times now. He appears here too as giver of measure, as expression of the purpose of the whole.

The moment the 'teba', the 'word' contacts non-fluid matter, the 'mountain', at that moment does God appear in His quality of Lord God in the measurements of the 'teba' and those of the Flood. Which happens after the seven complete months, when the 8th is just starting.

So here we see expressed in measures how this name Lord God appears, as soon as the 'word' with the measure 6–5 attains matter with measure 10–5. The 10–5, as Yah, is waiting for this contact with the 6–5, as we have amply discussed. And as soon as this contact has been made, the name Lord is completed. And this contact is ever expressed as a situation of 'beyond the seventh day', as a situation with which the eighth day begins.

This situation has arisen, because the ark has moved through the four worlds, the four cubits. This course across the four cubits is the course of the seventh day. Ancient lore indeed acknowledges for this seventh day the 4 Kingdoms and the 4 Exiles, through which the world must pass to reach the 8th day. During the seventh month in this tale of the Flood, the ark penetrates through the four cubits. Thus the course during this seventh day-of-the-world is the course through those four worlds.

During the Flood and especially at the highest level of the Flood, the ark was rocked to and fro, and, as ancient lore has it, everything threatened to perish *within* the ark as well. The word was cast to and fro, lost every hold in such a manner that what it embraced was in so insecure a position, that at the extreme moment God made the waters recede and abate. It was the situation when the water had attained the dual measure of the hills, of solid matter, the situation in which the 'two' was completed. But now, at the end of the seventh month, the mountain is struck, contact is made and thus at the same time the name Lord God as 10–5–6–5 is integrated, after it had previously been divided into the two parts 10–5 and 6–5, divorced by these 4 cubits which had yet to be covered, before those two parts could be reunited. It is the same situation here of the coming together of the 10–5 with the 6–5 to form the complete name Lord God, as we saw it in the first tale of creation, at the transition from the sixth to the seventh day.

Thus we saw that the whole period of the 'Five Books' similarly formed the 10–5, demanding union throughout life with the 6–5. This principle indeed contains the secret of creation and of life. And therefore it expresses itself in this place too, in the 'Flood'. For here, too, the point at issue is to accomplish union.

A great deal more can be said about this Mabul-story. But I shall content myself with pointing at a single aspect, connected with the foregoing.

When the hills have become visible, we see the period of 60 days subdivided into the '40 days' waiting', when the window of the teba is opened, and the 20 days thereafter, when Noah sends forth the raven and the dove from the teba. Again there is this point 2/3, the point indicating the proportion 2–1, as the beginning of a new phase. All through the 'two' there is the waiting, there is passivity; when the 'one' has arrived, there is Noah's activity. The window is opened, and thus, when the 'two' is past and the 'one' begins there is the possibility of looking out from the teba, to look from the word into the world, to make contact with the world through the word. Once the contact is established, there will also be the sending forth of the raven and the dove.

In this connection I should like to point at the relationship between the Hebrew word for window, 'chalon', 8–30–50, and dream, which is 'chalom', 8–30–40. The two words are merely distinguished in that 'window' has 50 as an ending and 'dream' has 40 as such. In a dream one can also look into another world, but the view is still clouded by the time of the 40, of the *mem*. With the window there is the 50, making the connection with the other world, the eighth day. Through the window one can see clearly; in the dream only veiled, obscured through time, one sees things expressed in the proportions of this world in which one lives and one can only translate things with great difficulty. As soon as the 40 has become 50, however, expressing the situation of the next world, the view is clear and distinct.

In this part of the 'one', of the 60 days, Noah sends forth the raven and the dove. I cannot expatiate on the details of this story. Let it suffice to point out that the raven, which was sent first, can also be regarded as the expression of the body, and the dove as that of the soul, which is thus sent forth into the world as the second phase.

The raven keeps flying to and fro, it cannot attain any message or goal. The dove, even in the expression in the image, has this characteristic that it ever returns to its origin. The soul returns and brings with it the message, until it has found its firm place in this world too. And with it begins the new world. Noah removes the covering of the teba. The way up, into the 50th cubit, lies open; the connection is definitely made.

The message brought back by the dove after it had been sent forth the second time, is the olive leaf. Now the olive is the sixth fruit in the systematism of the seven fruits. Ancient lore points out that it is a bitter fruit. The soul which is sent into the world on the sixth day at the creation of man, knows that there is a bitter way, a hard way. But, as ancient lore has it, the dove accepts this way full of love. For of this fruit of the sixth day, after the soul has gone through the process of buffets and blows, the oil is made, the *shemen,* i.e. with the hallmark of the eighth day – remember the connection between shemen and shmona, *eight* – which oil is the token of the coronation of the redeemer of the eighth day, the Messiah. The Messiah is anointed with the oil, pressed from the fruit of the sixth day. It is this message the soul brings to the teba, to the word. And after this message, the third time it returns to the earth – it is the fourth sending out after the first of the raven – it finds the firm place on earth; then there is the definite connection which is expressed in the teba in the removal of the covering.

It is the 1st day of the first month of the new year, the 601st year of Noah. This day is the first of the new year. According to the calendar it is the day of the creation of man, the biblical New Year's Day. In another plane it is the first day of the new year when biblical Israel is emancipated from the duality in Egypt to set out on the way to the 'one' in Canaan. The Jewish calendar as a matter of fact, begins on 1st Tishri, the day of the creation of man, as well as on 1st Nissan, the day God decrees that a new time-reckoning is introduced through redemption from duality, from Egypt. Both statements have the same content; the difference lies in the plane of realization. But since both define man and the world, both are used. On 1st Nissan one starts counting the months, on 1st Tishri the years.

Noah waits another 56 days in the ark, before leaving it on God's instruction and going out into the world. From the word now goes forth life, spreading all over the world. It is then the 27th day of the month. All in all Noah has been in the ark from the 17th day of the second month in the one year till the 27th day of the second month the next year. As the lunar year reckons with months of slightly over 29½ days, and numbers 355 days in all, Noah's staving ten days more then the lunar year in the teba, means that he had been in it exactly 365 days, i.e. the days of the solar year. These extra ten days, from the 17th of the second month is the 27th of the second month therefore means that there is a transition from a lunar-year era to a solar year era. The lunar era is connected with the left hand side of the world, the water-character. This water-character had now come to an end, the water had dried up and another world began. A world in which the stable sun was going to constitute the time-reckoning, was going to take it over from the ever changing fluid moon which was subject to phases. The moon which is ever disappearing to reappear again. The moon which characterized the nocturnal world. Thus there is a new time-reckoning, that which, after the water has dried up, no longer knows the lunar condition of flowing, coming and going, of growth and decline, but now reckoning with the stable, invariable sun.

Thus the Mabul-story tells us about the transition of one world to another, indicating the proportions of the way in which this transition takes place. It is a transition which represents an emancipation from a night-situation and a transition into a new situation, a day-situation. So this story occurs in the universe of the word. This universe lives and tells us of the purpose of things, it reveals the way of man in its every detail.

13
How Time is Measured

After the Flood the story turns to this world again. It has told us what the end of the ten generations was like; the 10 of the 10–5–6–5 has been left behind, the 5 is going to begin. And the whole story, the whole structure will now be expressed in this 5. The 10 is divided into two, and everything seems split up into two, everything showing its opposite. As it is expressed in Gen. 8:22 there is now 'seed-time and harvest, cold and heat, summer and winter, day and night'. Even the ages of the five generations now coming, appear to be practically halved. This cutting-in-two, this placing of the two halves opposite each other, just as the two fives of the 10–5–6–5 will now face each other, also expressed itself in the ring, which now becomes the token of a never-ending world. The bow, the curve, becomes the token (Gen. 9:13). In the circle no end seems possible.

The story will now express itself in the 5, just as in the preceding it was expressed in the 10. The expression in the 5 will not end in destruction, for it now finds the other 5 over against itself, and they are to reunite, they will again form the 'one'. Once there has been this perishing, this destruction, the further way is a return to the origin. After the expulsion from Paradise, at the end of the sixth day, there is only the way back, in the seventh day. In the seventh day the two face each other to be reunited. It is expressed also in this story. The Flood, in another plane, runs parallel to the expulsion from Paradise. Both are the end of a 'sixth'. We shall again come across the end of the 'sixth'. It will then no longer have the signature of the 10, but of the 5–6–5. Every ending will now mean a way to reunion. The ending with the *Mabul* gives the general structure of an ending, showing what is destroyed and what remains and at the same time *how* the transition from this world to another is accomplished.

As regards the first ending in the structure of the 10–5–6–5 the point of time in the Bible when that ending takes place and the new world begins, also gives the standard for measuring this biblical time. I should like to say a few words about it, for it is a very important and profound topic. In the scope of this book with its introductory character I can only point out a few external aspects.

To the attentive reader, however, they will form a direction for correct understanding of the time structure in the Bible.

After the Flood Noah lives 350 years. After the six times one hundred till the

Flood, there are now 3½ times one hundred. In the life of Noah, when his seventh hundred begins, there comes a time which is signed with the 3½. As the transition from the sixth to the seventh hundred of Noah runs parallel with the transition of the sixth day of creation to the seventh, this 3½ is also significant as a criterion for our seventh day of the world.

To the world this transition takes place in the year 1656, when the Flood begins, when the old world is left, and in 1657 when the new world is entered. In 1658, as we have seen, the second part of the four 'ele toldoth' begins to be enumerated.

In the story of time in the Pentateuch we see how this transition from the sixth to the seventh is expressed in the life of Noah. Time is measured on him. The 3½ therefore which is given as measure of the life of Noah *after* the Flood at the same time gives import to the moment of the transition, to the phase of 1656–1657–1658.

This is shown in a most unusual way indeed. Noah as the builder of the teha, of the word, is also used by the Bible as the builder of the word in time. Via Noah we can build the bridge of the structure of the word to the structure of time.

Let me explain. The name Noah is spelt Nun-cheth, 50–8. This name is associated with comforting and with resting. Just as Noah's life indeed speaks of the comfort of man's not being destroyed. The name Noah has as sum-total of the components 58. This 58 essentially expresses what can be uttered in words and sentiments about 'comforting' and about the certainty of coming into a new world after the destruction of an old world. This 58 in reality is the measure with which that transition of the sixth day to the seventh is measured and which becomes the time-measure for the seventh. Until later on, with the eighth a new time-reckoning will begin. Mind the context – again not an accidental one – between the year 1656 as the last year of the old world, signed with the 6; the year 1657 as the transition to the new world, with the 7, and the year 1658 with the 8, when the new time-reckoning of the 'ele toldoth' of Shem begins.

The principle 'Noah', the 58, is emphatically expressed in the pattern of the time of creation. It marks this seventh day.

For if we take the 3½ of Noah's life in this seventh day as measure for the proportion with which time is expressed at that moment of transition, we shall see that this 3½ times 1656/1657 makes exactly 5,800. And 58 is indeed the value of the components of the name Noah. The name Noah and the world which begins with him at the transition of the sixth to the seventh prove to be closely related.

This 3½ times, in relation to the moment of this determining transition, yields the name of Noah, the name built up on the conception 'comforting'.

It means this: what in Noah's life is expressed as 3½ times a hundred as measure for its duration in the seventh day, as length of time, expresses itself for the world as a whole as 3½ times the time with which people calculate at this moment. That this manner of measuring time is correct, is proved by the fact that in doing so one gets the name of Noah again, in centuples now.

This 3½ — referred to likewise in Daniel 12:7, as 'time, times, (= double time) and a half,' which together also form the 3½ in fact — is found in many texts. It always indicates the measure of the world as it expressers itself after the halving of the ten, after the transition from the sixth day to the seventh. It ever expresses the structure of time during which the matter of this world appears in the seventh day of the world. The time when reunion is in readiness that it may be realized in a new world, in the eighth day.

We have already come across part of this 3½. For indeed in the story of the Pentateuch we saw that the structure of time had the character of 'a time' and 'a half time', i.e. of 1½ together. There too, the 1656/1657/1658 played a part as criterion. The 1½ times that time pointed in fact to the duration of the whole story of the Pentateuch. And now we find that this 1½ has side by side with it the conception 'double time', i.e. the 2, through which arises the measure for the whole of the seventh day, the measure 3½. This 2 of the 'double time' in reality is the 2 of the world which is coupled to the 1½ of the root-story of the Pentateuch. The 2 of the world in fact represents a real measure. It is again the 4 facing the 3. The 4 × half time over against the 3 × half time. The 2 of the world is in this 4 like the woman who wants to attach herself to the 1½ of the Pentateuch, to the 3 of the man. When the world unites with the Bible, this 3½ will be visible; then the measure will be understood. The 2 of the 'double time' of the world is long time, round time, endless time, which, coupled to the 1½ of the root-story renders the 3½ manifest as measure for the whole of the seventh day. So there are 7 'half times', 7 periods like that which from entering into the world after the Flood led to entering into the world of Canaan, the world beyond the seventh day, i.e. the world of the eighth day. This 'half time' therefore is the progress through the seventh day, the beginning of which is expressed in the story of Noah and the end thereof in the story of the desert on the borders of Canaan, when Moses, the leader, dies.

Of these 7 'half times' there are 3 which form the Story of Pentateuch, of the nucleus. These three are determining, formative. Therefore this proportion is also valid for the principle of 'becoming clean'. Clean and unclean are not hygienic, biological conceptions, of course, but in the first instance they imply the attitude of man in regard to life, to the world. Whoever sees death in this world, is unclean. And he remains unclean seven days. Vide Numbers 19:11–12. Just as death made man unclean after his eating from the tree of knowledge, and man only becomes clean after the seventh day of the world, in the eighth day. The eighth day in which comes the revelation on Mount Sinai.

In the text of Numbers, mentioned above, we see however, that man should purify himself even on the third day, that he might be clean on the seventh day. This means that whoever does not purify in the third 'half time', whoever is not united in the third 'half time' with the emancipation from Egypt pertaining to that time, and with the revelation given to man; whoever does not then go all the way to the borders of Canaan, cannot become clean at the end of the seven days. The seven days derive their sense through the events of the third day.

The 'seven' in the world of this seventh day expresses itself in the seven of the 7 × (half time), the seven times of the period between 1656/58–2488 of biblical time-reckoning. The seventh day only acquires its import through the contact every person must have with the happenings in that part which has the signature of the 6–5 over against the 10–5. Everyone must have gone through the experience of this 'third', all the happenings of the 'third'. Only then will one he clean after the seven days, i.e. free from death. The 3½ has significance as emancipatory measure, if revelation coincides with 3/7. The 4 of the 4 'half times' must unite with the 3 of the 3 'half times'. The woman with the man. Thus there will be the child on the eighth day.

This 3½, according to the structure of the biblical story; brings the 58. The structures of time and of the word are interwoven here. The 3½ of the time of Noah, with the 1657 of the moment of transition from the 10 to the 5–6–5, the moment stamped with the happening of Noah and the teba, give the word Noah. The 3½ forms the bridge from the time-structure to the word-structure.

I should like to give here a few examples of these relationships. Thus, for instance, the word for 'dust', that with which the body of man is made (Gen. 3:19) is 'aphar', 70–80–200. The sum-total is 350, i.e. the 3½ in the plane centuples. It indicates that physical existence is concerned with this 3½.

The word for 'horn', characterizing the 'sacrificial beasts' which are connected with the human body – as also the animals of the first, second and tenth places in the expression of the Zodiac – is 'keren', 100–200–50; similarly 350, the 3½ in centuples.

In Jewish practice of life, which is based on the Bible and on tradition connected with the Bible, this horn is used as the instrument which is blown on the first two days of the new year, when man makes his appearance in this world as live being. Through this horn the life-breath is blown into the body, which therewith adopts the time-structure of the 3½. It is also blown on the tenth day of the year, the day on which the root-cycle of the ten has completed itself as that which first appears in the year. This tenth day in the fiftieth year is the day of emancipation, of the return of everything to the origin (Lev. 25:8–13). This fiftieth year is also determined by the measure of the 3½. With the 3½ is determined the beginning of the new year, as also the end, the tenth day and the fiftieth year.

Now this horn has the name 'shofar', 300–80–200. The sum-total of the name of the horn, which itself is 350, is ... 580.

The relationship, here again, between the 3½ and the 58 (for convenience sake let us neglect decads and centuples, and merely take notice of the determining numbers) shows how profound these relationships are. Especially so, if one takes into consideration the significance of horn and shofar and the times when they are employed.

The new year, according to the biblical calendar, begins on the first day of the seventh month. Just as the 'seventh' of Noah is determined by the 3½ and the 58, there is similarly the 3½ of the horn with the 58 of the shofar for the entrance into the seventh month, which at the same time expresses the fact that the world is in the seventh phase. And this 3½ and 58 similarly determine the whole structure of this seventh day of the world. The 3½ as measure for the seventh day also comes to expression in the 35 words with which the tale of creation renders the seventh day.

The tone of the shofar blowing the assembly, the tone which makes 'one', is called '*tekia*', 400–100–10–70, with again the sum-total of 58. For with the 58 the time of the seventh day is past, and then there is the reunion of the eighth day.

The 58 indeed is the essential measure determining this world of the seventh day. Just as the 40 and the 400 are operative as measures absolute, like the 50 and the 500, thus the time-measure for the physical body, for the formal expression of the seventh day, is this 58.

That is why the Pentateuch, the root-story leading to the boundary of the eighth day, contains 5,845 verses. These 5,845 are connected with the nucleus of this root-story, i.e. with the first tale of creation, of which they are an expression in the form of the seventh day. The creation of the six days is expressed in 1,671 letters. Now every letter is related to 3½ verses of the tale, completing itself round this inner nucleus. For 3½ × 1,671 makes 5,848. I herewith give merely the rough calculations, for indeed the finer, more detailed ones would carry us too far. The reader will, however, have noticed for himself that 1,671 is quite close to the 1656/1658 of the moment in the time of the world with which the factor 3½ is linked up. The finer calculations, in fact, take into account the slight differences which here show a deviation of 1%. For our purpose let it suffice to sense the connection existing between the 1656/1657 and the 58 via the 3½. And the 58 renders the complete story. Beyond the 58, as viewed from the measure of this world, one has got beyond the Pentateuch, into another world.

When Jacob gives Esau this world of the body (Gen. 32:13–15) – we shall revert to this story further on – he gives him 580 beasts. Now we already know the beast as expressive of the physical body, and we shall also see how Esau is the expression for the physical body. In fact Jacob gives Esau the whole duration of this world.

And Esau gets Seir, 300–70–10–200, again 580 (Gen. 36:8) as his dwelling-place.

The 58 as such, and as 580 and also as 5,800, ever proves to be the measure of the duration of things material.

The 3½ as standard for the time-structure in this seventh day thus plays an important part in many texts. Let me point out the word for 'year', which is 'shana', spelt 300–50–5, the final 5 merely being a feminine ending. The year as criterion for the entrance into a new cycle, which somehow is connected with the previous year, is similarly determined by this 3½. Besides the word 'shana' is connected with the conception 'change'. So it means exactly what the 3½ implies, namely that with the 3½ something changes fundamentally, whereas other aspects such as the return of the seasons remain unaltered.

We have also seen that the conception 'eating' implies the linking up of the 50 with the 1, thus expressing that the essential significance of eating and digesting is that 'all', in Hebrew 'kol', the 50 in the word 'eating', is bound to the 1. It therefore is a condition expressing through this 1 and the 50, that what is eaten or digested enters the condition of the eighth day.

The word for 'mouth', where the eating starts, is the letter 'peh' which means mouth and has the numerical value of 80. Similarly the word, which leaves the mouth, comes from a world of the eighth day. For indeed even though people do not realize it, substance and image are bound up in unity in the word.

That with which the process of eating is set going, the teeth, is called 'shen', spelt 300–50, again the 3½. These 3½ prepare the food for the rest of the process; everything has at any rate to pass through this 3½.

As for the teeth, they consist of four different component parts the incisors, canines, molars, and wisdom-teeth. And these four component parts each occur four times in the mouth. So the 3½ and the 4 are also united in the conception 'tooth'.

By means of these examples I meant to show that the 3½ forms a subdivision of the great structure which puts its stamp on all creation just as well as the various other proportions we have already met with. And I also want to point out that this structure expresses itself in everything: in the word, in time, as well as in the human body. The human body naturally is also an expression of all creation. It was similarly made in the image and after the likeness of God. Therefore everything in creation, as it is revealed in the Bible, expresses itself in man. We saw it when discussing the 1–4 principle, and we have now come across an example in which the 3½, the 4 and the 8 find their logical expression in quite natural places. Biblical anatomy, ipso facto, is entirely different from that based on sense-perception.

To return to our argument, we saw the 3½ and the 58 as determining factors for the time-structure. These indications of the time-measure do not imply that one can now start computations to calculate 'the end'.

Although the Bible shows implicitly that with the 58, the 3½ × 1,657, something very unusual has been attained, one should realize this does not imply that these years coincide with the years of our present phenomenal form. The time-reckoning of the Bible, side by side with the structural mechanical momentum, undoubtedly present also, is in the first instance determined by the divine and the human elements. Although the divine and the human essentially have a measure also, it will never do to try to express this essence in merely mechanistic time and duration. It would be very much like eating from the tree of knowledge to determine the time of the universe. The serpent likes to pretend it can have 'times' computed with the standards of our mechanistic times. And therewith tempts people to follow its way, a way which ultimately leads nowhere.

The Bible gives many good, very clear indications how to judge time as seen from the human standpoint with the criteria God put in the Bible. With the help of *those* criteria one can very well determine *where* one is in time. And 'the end' in that case depends on the relationship of man to God rather than on the mechanical termination of astronomical time. In the Bible, sun, moon and stars 'live' because the Bible describes their substance. And *if* they live, it implies that they are not tied to a mechanical ending, but that God can give them other instructions.

It has often been attempted by great and wise men to calculate the moment when 'the end' would be. Sometimes by means of a single text, or a play upon words, just as if God with the Bible had given man a kind of riddle to try to find out when this silly game of hide-and-seek would come to an end. Time and again it was proved they had one and all erred in their judgement. There merely remains the surprise at the phenomenon of how small-minded great and wise men often can be. The image as conception in space, and time as conception in astronomy, amount to the same thing. People no longer have an idea of the substance, they no longer know the miracle of the word.

Whoever knows the sublime structure of the Bible at all, will realize that the measure of time must be included in the whole structure, and that it does not depend on the mere coincidence of one text or of one image. That very structure indicates in everything that it is man and his attitude in the world that can make the balance of the end or no. If he *fails* to do it, God will yet bring the world back to unity, back to its origin. It will in that case he the progress of the 'fugitive and vagabond' of Cain, who also went from duality to unity. Those who proceed along this path, cannot however 'compute' the end, for the very reason that they are 'fugitives and vagabonds' and every employ utterly useless criteria.

The 58, or 5,800 of the end, is a human criterion built up on the conception 'solace' and the conception 'grace'. In its substance it is completed indeed to the 58. And for those that can approach the substance because they did *not* eat from the tree of knowledge, this 58 most certainly has a special, concrete significance which can be measured.

In this way it is possible to calculate from the structure of the Bible 'where' a certain time lies, and also where 'the end' is. These are humane rather than mechanical calculations.

In the course of our reflections we shall moreover find an opportunity to give clearer indications with more data 'where we stand now in time' and 'where is the time of the end'. A word to the wise is enough.

14
The Eye and the Ear of the Servant

After the Flood Noah became 'a man of the earth' — the translation says 'husbandman', which does not make much difference to the outward appearance of the story. But 'man of the earth' means that now he began also to pay attention to the material appearance, just as Cain had done.

And Noah planted a vineyard, drank of the wine, and was drunken and he was uncovered within his tent (Gen. 9:20–21).

The vineyard which occurs rather frequently in the Bible, in Hebrew is 'kerem', 20–200–40. The sum-total of the letters is 260, so it is connected with the 26 which we learned to know for instance in the 26 generations, of the whole period until the Revelation.

In 'kerem' therefore is expressed that which moves through time in this world, the motive of the 26.

But at the same time it expresses that one should be very cautious with the fruit. He that 'hallows' the fruit, unites it with the substance; he that understands why God made the world into this vineyard, will indeed be able to live in this world as the vineyard and see the purpose thereof. He that uses the fruit for himself, however, to get enjoyment of the earth, will get drunken. He gets intoxicated with the earth, he loses sight of the real proportions, animalizes himself and rather makes himself ridiculous as man. Just because in him becomes conspicuous that way which is incompatible with man. His outward appearance demonstrates what it is like when one gets intoxicated with the earth. It is beautiful, yet demoniac, it is something that leads to gaiety for a short while, but immediately afterwards makes people lose all sense of proportion. Thus it is when for the sake of earthly pleasure and enjoyment, one gathers the fruit of the world.

Whoever accepts intoxication, in fact uncovers himself. It was in this way the first man became aware that he was 'naked', after he had eaten from the tree of knowledge. That which had not been evident, the bodily side of man, now becomes his form of expression. Man reveals himself as something physical, as an intelligent well-developed 'animal'.

And then Ham sees him. Ham sees that nakedness, because he uses his eyes, because he uses his senses so as to draw his conclusions. When some time afterwards Shem and Japheth come, they do the opposite thing. They purposely go in backwards, they do not avail themselves of sense-perception and they cover the nakedness which had appeared on man's following the way of the tree of knowledge, with the garment, the covering, just as God had given man the coat of skins, after the intoxication man had gone through when he had taken from the 'tree that makes fruit'. In consequence of this attitude, Shem and Japheth get a blessing, union with the origin, with God, and Ham is made their servant.

This story, at the beginning of the new world, shows the same pattern of the beginning, as we saw it in the story of Paradise and that of Cain.

Since Noah had taken in the forces of development through drinking wine as an earthly enjoyment, nakedness revealed itself in him. He showed what the earth can show, viz. progress, growth from the puny creature at the beginning of evolution, via the whole animal kingdom, to man as the extreme point of development. Whoever, like Ham, looks with the eyes, perceives with the senses and argues from that point of view, sees that nakedness, sees that man is a higher developed, biological creature. Ham sees it – and as tradition has it – he tells Shem and Japheth denigratingly what he has discovered about his father and about his descent.

Indeed, whoever perceives with his senses, comes to the conclusion that everything preceding must be inferior to him. That it is primitive, dull, cruel. And he will come to the conclusion that the primordial ancestors cannot have been but troglodytes, club-swinging despots, clan-tyrants, prize-fighters with low foreheads and stooping gait. And who observes well, may yet discover that there are links which ancestors have in common with our present-day apes, and, who knows, may reach even further back. After all, the human embryo starts its life in the matrix as a creature on the brink of animal- and plant-life, and again passes, quite perceptibly, through the development of many millions of years.

And for such it is very hard to feel any respect for older generations. Speaking from one's own, high, well-developed standpoint, one can at best say that those ancestors had not tackled things so very clumsily, but by and large they had been far inferior to modern man.

Whoever '*looks*' at the origin, *cannot but* see progress. The eye and the other senses, plus thought based on it, cannot help leading to some doctrine of evolution.

This logically implies that all things preceding must have been primitive, that people at present know more at any rate, and that the future will yield much more yet as result of the progress of development. Social welfare, hygiene, technology, science, all this will continue to develop. For perceiving the 'father', the previous one, will make this incumbent on us as a compelling consequence. And if we are honest in our argument, we shall have to accept this consequence.

This attitude implies that one cannot help being rather sceptical about the advice given by the older generation. *How* can the older generation know things better, since we ourselves are grown-up now? Did they know all the recent editions of our text-books, did they realize the very existence of sciences we are pursuing now? And is the world as they handed it over to us such a habitable, harmonious world? Thus there continually arises rebellion on the part of every rising generation against the former.

In the same way do we look at the Bible. It is an indisputable fact that the book dates from antiquity. This at once implies a certain attitude in the modern observer. He can discuss it like a clever, erudite master, point out the good things in it, explain away the contradictions, forgive the perceptibly primitive expressions. It appeals to him to try to find out with the spade or with the help of modern instruments in how far certain things tally with theories advanced by present-day, highly-evolved science. And it has become an agreeable pastime to demonstrate that indeed there is quite a lot which does not deviate too much. For instance, that the Bible really has a definite, concrete, material background, rooted in history. That certain places actually existed, certain names prove not to be imaginary. Of course, thoughts, life, cannot be dug up. But that is not necessary at all. For are not our highly evolved, human ideas the best criterion to judge the thoughts of the Bible by? It looks very much as if people were judging some child's construction and pointing out the places where the child had not done things so badly either. Anyhow it is tacitly understood that our well developed knowledge of sociology, psychology, economics, etc. reaches farther and incomparably deeper. For the sake of an unaccountable feeling of veneration, or whatever one likes to call it, a few general pronouncements are accepted, such as loving one's neighbour, non-stealing, etc. They are useful anyway for modern society to develop without friction.

For that reason, according to ancient lore, Ham spoke rather denigratingly about his father, about his origin. Ham could not help speaking like that, since he had judged with the senses, with the body. Matter cannot yield another point of view.

Altogether different is the attitude of Shem and Japheth. They purposely refuse to look, they dismiss sense-perception quite deliberately; indeed, they are anxious to cover up this revelation of earthly development. Their reasoning and their progress are entirely different. So, when on awakening Noah perceives the attitude of his sons, he gives his blessing to Shem and Japheth. He thanks the Lord God, the God of Shem. For he realizes that it is only because Shem knows the Lord, he has been able to act like that. And to Japheth who had followed Shem, he gives the blessing of expansion over the world and further contact with Shem.

But Ham is 'cursed' in Canaan his fourth son. Even when Ham looks at his father's nakedness, he is called 'the father of Canaan'. For it is in this fourth son that is revealed the power and will to such perception.

Thus is Canaan made a 'servant' to his two brothers. What we have seen here is again man facing the tree of knowledge, the force of physical development. Even in the world after the Flood man experiences this confrontation.

Man is now divided into Shem, Ham, and Japheth. They are facing their terrestrial origin.

One man, Ham, the father of Canaan, accepts this terrestrial origin, studies it and is 'cursed'. The two others, Shem and Japheth, however, turn their backs on this terrestrial origin.

In Noah, the man who had learned to build with God's criteria; who, in a world carried away by the rapid waters of progress, had built on at the word, an aspect comes to expression now which can deliberately leave alone the tree of knowledge, which *refuses* to eat of it. Another aspect of his, however, does take of the tree.

Noah who, in spite of his origin, had as 'husbandman' yielded to the intoxication of the earth, and had got stupefied by the forces of the earth, revealed to them that tree of knowledge. It was only Ham who took of it; the other two declined to do so.

The drunkenness of Noah is the development of the body at the beginning of the seventh day. It is the datum of the body with which every man appears in this world. One can observe this body and through it find all that pertains to the body; one can also be observed oneself in this body. The growth of the new world brings with it the alternative of observing or non-observing. In this alternative Shem and Japheth are diametrically opposed to Ham. Noah's drunkenness is not so much a 'wrong act' of his. It is the statement that the world has then come into the phase of the seventh day, into the phase of this life, that is; that the body owing to its appearance here and its growth, is getting into this state of intoxication, an intoxication from which one has to wake up; from which Noah does wake up in fact. In its appearance, in its growth, in its development, the physical body like the tree of the knowledge which then, ipso facto, it gives expression to, offers the alternatives of taking up this development or letting it pass. And now the strength of Noah, who had built the *teba* in the previous day, is continued in Shem and Japheth. Especially in Shem this knowledge of the *teba*, of the word, is carried on it leads on to the patriarchs and to the entrance into the eighth day.

Thus a new development is coming. In the first 'five' split off from the original 'ten' of the 10–5–6–5, the seed manifest itself which proves that in Noah there is a man who will *not* take of this 'tree that makes fruit'. And that is why Noah praises God, since he has realized it. Noah himself woke up from his drunkenness and realized the danger of turning towards the earth. He had experienced what it brought with it and retraced his steps. And from this new awakening, which this revelation brought to Noah, he praised the Lord God of Shem, owing to Whom Shem had not taken of the tree of the knowledge. Shem knew the name of the Lord God and was consecrated thereby. With it the new world had begun. A seed which was going to develop further, had been passed on to the generation of Shem. And Japheth who had progressed along this way with Shem, also received the blessing to 'enlarge in this world'.

But for Ham there was servitude. Ancient lore has it that in reality it was Ham's youngest son, Canaan, who had perceived Noah in that state, and he had told Ham. Ham had done nothing to mend it and had even spoken disparagingly about it with the others. And that is why there is this emphasis on Ham's fourth son, Canaan.

Canaan's servitude implies that Canaan was to be dependent on the doings of his masters, Shem and Japheth, in all things. It is the same situation again with the woman who was made dependent on man, after eating of the tree of knowledge, although or rather just because the man on account of her had eaten of the fruit too. It is the same dependence into which the body has got in regard to the soul.

The servant is to the master as the body is to the soul. After the world and man have passed from the 'ten' to the first 'five', even as the 1 at creation passes into the two counterparts of the 2, in the new world, a 'man', the 'soul', asserts himself, who does not take from the tree of knowledge. Even though Ham, the body, hands it to him.

Even though in man is still present this part which eats from the tree, there is another part as well, a new part of the foundation, where the soul does not take from the tree. The influence of the power of attraction of the origin which causes the curve, is here beginning to assert itself. A special branch is developing on the tree, with specific qualities, fed by this attitude of Shem and Japheth.

And therefore the part which is the force of development of the body, is now destined to be subordinate to that which does not take from the tree of knowledge. This means that if man does not take from the tree of knowledge, the body's force of development becomes his servant. That man is then become the master of the forces of development of the body.

When therefore we read in the Bible about the Canaanite servant it means that the body with its forces of development, with its earthy character, will always remain the servant of the soul, of the man who wants to become one with God on his path of life. It means that this part of the body will never get free to assault man with its forces of development.

On the other hand, the servant who comes from biblical Israel, because he has deviated from the right path and has consequently got into a position of subservience, is like the erring man who can turn back again. He may possibly have deviated through a misconception of his destination, owing to which he lapsed into appropriating what did not belong to him, in any domain whatsoever.

On account of these doings he may get into a position towards the others like that of the erring body towards the soul. But the exile in the bodily condition, in the condition of subservience, merely lasted six years; in the seventh year he could regain freedom, just as everything pertaining to man can regain freedom in the seventh day, in this world.

We have already seen in discussing this situation that man in the seventh year can prefer to remain with his master. He had got attached to the condition of being bound to the earth, he misjudged the relationships, he assigned values which did not exist. In that case such a man, as we saw, remained a servant till the year of the jubilee, till the fiftieth year. Till the cycle of the seven times seven had run out, till that seventh day had completed itself.

We also saw how the master then led him to the doorpost and pierced his ear with an awl. And I pointed out in that place, that the door is the image of the fourth letter and the awl has the sum total of 400 in its component letters, thus indicating the 'eternal' duration of the 4 and the 400.

I could not then and there discuss the fact of the piercing of the ear. This is possible now after the story of Noah.

Ear is 'ozen', 1–7–50. That makes 58 in all. It shows that this duration of 'endlessness', as expressed in the 400 and in the seventh day completing itself as seven times seven, is also found *in that which pertains to the human body,* the 58. here we have one of the numerous places where the 58 appears as criterion for the period man lives in the body in this world. The 4 and the 400 and the 58 all three of them are standards of time, and all three of them indicate that it will take all the time until this world, this seventh day has come to an end. 'Eternal' a man of this world would call it.

The structure of the word '*ozen*' moreover shows that the ear is there to unite this seventh day with the 'one', that hearing should he the hearing of this union. And that, just as it is the case with other human organs, it is intended to bring man within the clasp of the 50, which the word ends with, in the 50 of the eighth day.

The word for 'eye' is 'ayin', spelt 70–10–50. It is at the same time the letter '70', as we can see from the table of letters. With the eye one can perceive multiplicity in things human, the 70. The structure of the word has the same components as the word 'ear', only in a different plane. There is also the seven and the 1, and here too there is this uniting of outward things, that which we see, with the substance, the 1, that the clasping within the 50 of the eighth day may be accomplished. The sum total of the word 'eye' is 130. And we have also seen that this 130 is unity beyond this world of the 120. So, if one does not merely see superficial things with the eye, not merely the 70, but if one penetrates to the essence, it means that the eye leads to the 130, to the 1. Just as the ear leads to the coming of the next day in another standard of time, to the 58.

Man has got his senses that he may unite them with the coming world, not to cling with them to this world. It is exactly through man's decision that he can, with his senses and with all the organs, direct himself to the goal for which he has entered into this world.

So the servant in the Bible is something entirely different from that which in the image of earthly society is meant with slave. The biblical conception reaches much further and deeper.

Therefore the Bible must never be regarded merely as an image, as a historic tale. For then one measures the Bible with the criteria of the earth, of the 'tree that makes fruit'. And then the law of creation is brought into operation so that one understand the Bible. The world and man have been made such that as soon as man takes the way of the tree of knowledge, i.e. the way of judging with earthly, sensory criteria, the path to the tree of life is automatically closed off.

One cannot then understand the Bible, it remains a closed book. It is therefore wrong to analyse the biblical figures 'in the times in which they lived', and to try to picture them in wide-flowing garments, walking on sandals, their heads covered with turbans or any other 'Oriental' headdress. That is merely desecration of the Bible. The Bible was not given to us to make close-ups of. Nor was it given to us to make a mental picture of personages in a certain period of time.

The Bible is the expression of the substance of the world, as it has found expression in mankind ever since its existence, to the end of the cycle which contains the pattern in its very heart. Therefore there is 'nothing new under the sun'.

Besides, the Bible is the form of expression as God uses it, as God sees it in conformity with the substance. And the only thing we have got to do is always to bring back to the substance this manner of expressing things in the forms of this world. Just as we have to bring everything of this world of form, of our life, back to the substance. Whatever we may be occupied with, we have to try to follow this path to the origin, to the essential. This path one has to go with an open mind, straight forward, full of joy. In every detail of life one can go this way through right understanding and right action.

Therefore it is so very important to see such subjects as the 'servant' in the Bible in their true significance. The Bible is not concerned with an investigation in the historic developments and the social circumstances of those 'servants'. To be sure, there have been servants and I am not certain whether they have felt happier or unhappier than the bulk of humanity at present. There have always been people, however, who could not for themselves determine their fate, as regards discovering the purpose of life and the way which gives purpose to life, and whose fate in this respect was determined by others or by circumstances. These people may have been workmen, peasants, labourers, but also great businessmen, millionaires, ministers, kings, research-workers, both men and women. Among them there are people, dependent on fate – in fact, the majority of them – and there are independent ones.

Now the Bible expresses this dependence in the social form existing when the essential for the first time crystallized into the happenings in this world, in space-time. This social form is an image and it is the only possible image, as soon as one wants to express in images of the world and of humanity what the relationships are essentially. One should take the direct way from the image back to the essential. It is not the images which are the gods. Those images are subservient to man, he can make them and destroy them. Whoever sticks to these images, is an image-worshipper, an idolater.

The Canaanite servant is therefore that in the body which is the expression of the forces of development. Now these forces have weakened again in this second world, that of the 'toldoth' of Noah; they have been made subservient to the man who does *not* take of the 'tree that makes fruit'. And that is why this man is protected now, he cannot any more go through the experience of this destruction which has concretrized itself in the other part of the basis, at the end of the sixth day. It is the protection again which the seventh day affords.

This Canaanite servant has nothing to do with the 'coloured man' as slave. Moreover, the Canaanite, also seen historically, in the first instance is not a dark-skinned person, but white. The other descendants of Ham, too, are white. The ancient Egyptian descends from Ham; so does Nimrod, and none of them are coloured people. Besides, in our world it is no longer possible to state who descends from whom, any more than it is possible to measure biblical times with our criteria.

Since the end of the biblical times, as given in the Old Testament, it does no longer apply in the practice of Judaism that the Ammonite or the Moabite are not admitted into the community: simply because the world has become entirely different and we cannot and must not point out, even theoretically, which derives from Ammon and which from Moab. For these conceptions have acquired an altogether different value nowadays.

Thus modern Egypt or modern Greece cannot be associated with biblical Egypt or biblical Greece. From *this* standpoint the Bible cannot be used as a historic source either. The wisdom of the tradition of Jewish practice has made this identification of biblical nations with those of the present day almost impossible, in allotting an altogether different place to important nations like Ammon, Moab and Egypt, wherever they may live. In this physical sense nobody could be excluded from the community. The change of the world after the time which gives expression to the biblical story, does not only give a different standard of time to the world, but at the same time another geographic and ethnograpic aspect.

And the servant, pertaining to biblical Israel, i. e. the stray, should be treated with respect. For he pertains to the nucleus, to divine man, He should be treated well and worthily and be shown the possibilities of emancipation in the seventh year, i. e. in this world. For in the pattern of the seventh world, of this our world, he may indeed get emancipated. Such is the aspect of servitude as given by the Bible.

Those who, like Ham and Canaan, want to perceive their origin and discover the purpose of their existence along the way of sense-perception and the argumentation based thereon, will indisputably become servants. They will become 'earthy', progress in the material sense, like Cain and his culture, of which they are a parallel. In the eyes of the world they may belong to the Great Powers and to the leaders thereof. The fact in itself that they progress along that way of wanting to know and to regard their origin in this manner, stamps them as subservient. They progress and do not know whither. They make plans to attain things, but fate leads them on different paths. They even think they are masters and free, but they are 'indirect', they are deprived of the link with the real, motory power.

It is thus the Bible characterizes the servant; it is man who with the aid of sensory perception tries to discover the secret of life and of the world. *That* was what Ham and Canaan did. And it was exactly what the woman did with the serpent in the Garden of Eden and it was exactly what Cain did.

The stories of Paradise, Cain, and that of Ham and Canaan are interrelated; they reflect the same situation. The story of Paradise is enacted in the root-story of the second tale of creation; the tale of Cain is the expression of it in this world, in the first of its four stages, of its four 'toldoth'. And the story of Ham and Canaan is the expression of it in the second of the four 'toldoth'. The theme is the same; but there are various details now in different relationships. The man in the story of Paradise ate; the soul took what the body offered it. Abel, in the Cain-story, is killed. In his stead there is now the man Sheth, and from Sheth there is finally Noah who, just because he derives from the side of Abel, in spite of the terrible decline of his time, sticks to the right course and builds the 'teba' after God's instructions.

And now, in the story of Noah, the other side becomes even more predominant. Now there are Shem and Japheth who deliberately leave the tree of knowledge alone. Over against the 'curse', the weakening of Canaan, there is a 'blessing', the eternalizing of a man as expression of the certainty of the return to unity.

In the story we see that Ham and Canaan, as far as outward appearances are concerned, are anything but servants. Egypt and Canaan are the masters; the world belongs to them. And the children of Shem live among them as strangers. Nevertheless the Bible tells how the life of the children of Shem, of the Patriarchs, determines the fate of those that to all intents and purposes, live as masters.

In the world, things material seem to give the lead. All the same it is a different power that gives the lead. Things material are the Canaanite servant.

The physical, this place of the forces of development, occupies the origin, the 'land', the coming world, to the very end. Canaan is lord to the end. For duality still obtains in the origin, as long as the two fives have not been united. Just as Canaan remained in the land, just as biblical Israel journeyed across the desert, and the 'two' were not yet reunited into the 'one'. Not until the 'one' has been achieved, will the force of development of the body be restrained, and will the other force, that of oneness restored, take possession of the land of the origin. From the very heart, from that land of the origin, this power of unity will then radiate harmony forth to all the surrounding spheres. The restoration of the 'one' in the nucleus signifies the end of the progress through the seventh day. Then there will be the king of the eighth day.

15
Destruction in Multiplicity

At the end of this second 'birth-story', of this 'toldoth' of Noah there is, just as at every end, another explosion into multiplicity. The story is told in Gen. 11:9. The earth passes through another period of great prosperity. Tradition gives countless characteristic details about that pinnacle of development. In this story, again is found the same wealth of relationships, the same depths of structure.

People have one aspiration; they speak one language. It is the language of Shem, expressing with the thing its substance as well. It similarly is the language in which God gave the Bible for the very reason that the words of that language, together with the image, rendered the substance of the image. This language was given to the first man, as he was also give life and the world, and this language, according to ancient lore, had been handed on via Noah to his children.

Unity in mankind's aspiration lay in people's proposing with the help of the forces of the earth and with matter in all its phenomenal expressions ranging from fire to stone, again to build 'the city', where they might occupy themselves intensively with this life so as to forget everything else; and together with that town they purposed to build a tower whose top was to reach into heaven.

Ancient lore furnishes us with further details of this aspiration. People purposed to expand this life on earth and make it take root in 'heaven'. They wanted to conquer heaven so as to make life on earth more secure, more agreeable, more constant. And all this they thought they could reach with the help of the forces of matter and the results of sensory perception and the argumentation therewith.

The mighty results of material development at the end of every epoch, of every world, the knowledge of the essence of things and the unamimity as regards the goal they were aiming at, had given mankind enormous power and great self-assurance. There was no war, so that people could in unison strive after their object in view.

Again we see how towards the end of a world the power of material development is such as to convince people of their unlimited possibilities. Again it is the situation in which the serpent presents itself as the Messiah. And it is the situation in which the sons of God turn to the daughters of men in order to achieve gigantic progress with them.

People thought they could press the forces of heaven into the service of earthly development. According to ancient lore for instance, 'arrows' were shot at the sky which took a long time to reach a certain goal there, before returning to the earth.

Building-stones for the conquest of heaven had to be conveyed from ever greater distances. It took a year to get such a 'stone' to the place of destination. And when such a 'stone' miscarried and dropped down, it was mourned for more than any man who had died. For that stone constituted part of the great world-plan to conquer heaven and place it in the service of earth's development.

And all people had to co-operate in the execution of this plan: there were 600,000 of them.

Again this number 600,000, which we also come across at the exodus from Egypt. In both these texts it stands for 'all' at the end of the sixth phase, when the destruction of the world is nigh. Just think of the end of the sixth day in Paradise, the 600 years of Noah, when the Flood comes and puts an end to the world.

When a world ends, the number six makes its appearance in the essential, because every ending has the signature of the sixth day ending up in the eating from the tree of knowledge. It ever is an ending in consequence of taking the way of development, of the hope of the fulfilment of promises held out by the forces of development. It ever ends in multiplicity, material power, intoxication. Whenever this development ensues, it is stamped with this number six. Thus there is a tradition that this world was to exist 6,000 years, that the Messiah would then come and lead the world into the seventh day. These 6,000 years here are not the years of our phenomenal form either, any more than the 600,000 represent numbers of our phenomenal form. The 6,000 years merely means that this our world of development – if indeed this development should take such a flight that it would run parallel with the essential situation at the end of the sixth day in Paradise or at the end of the epoch which was destroyed by the Mabul – would then essentially get the mark of the six and that it would at that point have existed 6,000 years. Our world's ending would at the same time imply that a saviour would lead the survivors into the seventh day.

The end of the seventh day has an entirely different aspect. There is no explosion into multiplicity there, and it is preceded by the exodus from Egypt. This implies that the end of the seventh day merely exists for those that have left the world of duality and in their lives follow the way to reunion. They are those that have subjected themselves to the purification of the 'third day'; on the 'third half time', which implies the exodus from duality, the way to Mount Sinai, the journey to the 'one'. It is only they that reach the seventh day and it is only they that are cleansed of death at the end of the seventh day and the beginning of the eighth day. The end of the seventh day is marked by silence, by the revelation of the mystery of the world and of life. The sign is a.o. the 58 and the 3½, as discussed above. At the end of the sixth day these 600,000 formed a long chain and if a man in his chain fell down, nobody heeded him, for the great purpose did not allow of worrying about any individual dropping down for the sake of progress on the way of progress. The process had to be carried on and he was soon forgotten. Another who happened to come after him simply took his place. Everything had to go on uninterruptedly on that way towards the conquest of heaven. Thus one man handed on the building-stones to the other, till they had reached people at the top.

This development, peaceful, unanimous, directed at making life on this earth more secure, similarly ended in catastrophe, as viewed from the earthly standpoint. It says in the story that man has not come into this world to order his life in this way. It is not the welfare state, insured all-in, full of technical developments that is man's purpose and the world's. Man came into this world to unite all that he should meet here with God, with an entirely different world. He was, indeed, to avoid the development of this world in the sense championed by the generation of the tower-builders. He was to see that, if things had come to such a development, it was a sure sign of 'punishment', of 'going astray', of 'approaching destruction'. That was why God had told him in the Bible about this pattern, about this structure of the world.

It is difficult, once one has set foot on this way of progress, to see the unreasonableness of it all. To the contrary, one thinks one is doing a good thing in promoting this progress on earth, one often thinks one is helping mankind that way. It is not that it is bad to help mankind; only it is not good, if one thinks one can do it in following a way which leads to mankind's destruction. It is for this very reason that the Bible states with clear emphasis that there always is the inclination to take this way, because matter and its power of growth continue to exercise an enormous attraction on man. And the Bible tells us why it is like this. It is like this because man is faced with matter exactly in its extreme and highest development. Matter comes to man at a stage, when as 'serpent' it has the same letter-value as the word 'Messiah'.

And indeed the Bible insists that man can prove his great love and faith in God, in rejecting *that* emancipation and in choosing the way less materialistic, less glamorous, less epoch-making, the simple way to God. Then this power of affection in man would face the power of affection in God and union would come to pass, yielding man 'all', the 'tree that *is* fruit *and* makes fruit', all in one, this world and the other world in *one*. God's power of love towards man is gratuitous. Man has not done anything, *could* not have done anything to deserve it. To give man even here, at this point, the supreme good, God places him in the situation where simply in faith, in belief he chooses God, where he cannot expect anything perceptible from God, and where he leaves alone the greatly attractive world with its promises of spectacular results, with the 'serpent' as saviour.

The progress of man in the direction of the unfolding of the material forces in the end comes to catastrophe. For God has made creation with a power inherent in it, through which at the point of the strongest material development, a curve is made. At the zenith of development, at the end of the sixth day, God had the day end with the words 'it was very good', which for this world expressed itself as destruction, as an expulsion of man from Paradise, to make him as yet go the way back to the origin in the seventh day, this time accompanied by God as the Lord God.

Thus there arises this situation at the end of the generation of the tower-builders.

The unity of their aspirations and the unity of their language is broken. All of a sudden people have different aims and purposes and they no longer understand each other. What had given man the enormous impetus, his unity, his knowledge of the substance of things in a way not be misapprehended, had driven him, just as in the previous 'toldoth' to take possession of the earth, to exploit it further yet in its seductive possibilities of development, taking things into his own hands like a deity, and with this profound knowledge of the essence of things to employ heaven itself for stimulating the forces of material progress.

But just as the 'Mabul' came in the previous part, this getting drowned, submerged, in uniformity, in all-absorbing time, in waters killing the personality, here too there arises confusion, 'Babel'. The contact with the essence of things is lost, the knowledge of the secret of language is lost. Everything now gets halved because of it and the image which appears, to man's mind is dissociated from its substance.

All languages are 'halved', except the language of the Bible. Their images no longer are associated with the substance. Because of it a great variety of opinions can arise. Everybody can now interpret the image and the happenings in a different way. People do not know what they are after, and do not even see clearly how to tackle things in order to realize what they think they want.

Again it is the weakening of human power. Again man is protected against his seductive surroundings. His basis on earth is narrowed down, the duration of his presence here is made shorter. The law of creation with the predestined return to the source of origin expresses itself in life.

The stories which have come down to us by way of tradition enter profoundly into the various details of the consequences of this situation. They tell us how great numbers, a large part of humanity, perished in the catastrophe arising on earth, when God put an end to this way of reaching heaven with the means of earthly progress, the way of the tree of the knowledge. The world acquired an altogether different aspect; there virtually came a new world. Mankind settled down on earth in an altogether new way. The power of mankind's unity and of its knowledge of the essence of things got lost.

In tradition this happening is called 'Haflaga', related to the word 'Peleg', the name of the fifth generation after Shem. 'Peleg' in fact means splitting up and the generation got that name because in that epoch everything in the world was split up.

The 10–5–6–5 got split up into 10–5 and 6–5; in all things the image got detached from the substance; the ages of the generations were split — after Peleg they got halved; the death-rate was high; the body was detached from the soul; the dwelling-places of men got split up; they were weakened and got spread about; and even the 'tower', the way to attain heaven, the essence of things, with earthly criteria and earthly means, got split up.

Everything again shows the pattern of the destruction of a world. Yet here again there is a survival. At the Mabul we saw how Noah survived with the 'word'. This time it is through Shem who had refused to eat from the tree of knowledge, that life continues.

PART THREE

The Curve

16
Facing the Others

The 'Haflaga', the splitting-up, takes place in 1996. One can calculate it by means of people's ages in the Bible. In 1996 Peleg dies at an age which is merely half of the ages of the previous generations, it is 'split'. It is 340 years after the Flood. This number as sum-total, also covers the meaning of the word, 'Shem'. For Shem is spelt shin-mem, 300–40.

Shem means 'name', or rather, knowledge of the essence, of the real name. It was because of this knowledge that Shem was not tempted by the forces of progress, the 'tree that makes fruit'. This knowledge of the 'name' caused him to live on beyond this happening, just as Noah lived on with the 'word' beyond Mabul.

Shem is not perturbed by this 'Haflaga'. In fact, Shem and his fourth generation, Heber, are fully aware of the purpose of life, their attitude and practice of life are adjusted to their knowledge of the essential.

So 'Shem' means 'name'. 'Heber', spelt 70–2–200, means 'from the other side', 'from beyond'.

Now the way of man towards God, as ancient lore also proves with ample evidence, is pointed by Shem and Heber; Shem who knows the name of God, hence the meaning and purpose of life, and Heber, as fourth generation, making the connection with the 'other world', with the 'beyond', the 'other side of this life'.

That is why the Bible gives Israel the name of 'Ibrim', Hebrews after this Heber, hence the coming from the 'other side', in opposition to this world, being different from it, not pertaining to this world. And the language of the Bible, Hebrew, also means 'from another world', coming to us from the other side, the beyond.

This principle of this side and the beyond, ipso facto, expresses itself in other fields as well. In the second tale of creation, for instance, the river of the Garden of Eden forked into four heads. For the moment we shall deal with only two of these rivers, the first and the fourth.

The first river is the Pishon. According to ancient lore this river Pishon finds its expression on earth as the river Nile. The fourth river is the Euphrates. The world with all its happenings is enacted in the basin of the four rivers, just as life enacts itself in the four 'toldoth', or in the four 'elements'. Thus there also are the four 'worlds', known to the Kabbala, and already mentioned before. Thus ancient lore knows the four 'exiles' as four incorporations. An exile is an incorporation in a form, becoming a body.

These four rivers are over against the 'one' river, just as the 1–4 appears in all things, everywhere. With the four rivers, therefore, this whole world, expressing itself in the 'four', is bounded. For the 'four' is in essence the principle of the greatest earthly number.

When the Bible indicates the bounds of the 'land', the promised land of the future, it speaks about the land, stretching from the river of Egypt to the river Euphrates, from the first river to the fourth. The 'land' embraces 'everything' from end to end, the whole world, or even beyond, the four worlds. When, for instance, ancient lore speaks of King Solomon who reigned over the whole world, this is meant in the same sense: his territory was encompassed by the four 'rivers', passed through the four streams.

That these rivers run a different course geographically – how on earth could rivers encompass a whole world in a geographical sense? – that the Nile, for instance, comes from the South and the Euphrates from the North and that they cannot possibly originate from the same source, the one main river on this earth, is exactly what we should *not* concern ourselves with. Assuredly, the phenomenal form on earth, as a kind of crosscut of a higher dimensional world, does not represent the essential. Sometimes we shall be able to see the connection with the space-time phenomenon, very often the image will not show the connection, but, to the contrary, cause us to conjecture the very opposite. If one wants to know the essence of things, one will have to go the way of the Bible, 'not seeking after your own heart, and your own eyes' (Numbers 15.39). The criteria of the world have been given in the Bible. Our senses, and our physical desire to learn to know the world through these senses, through ourselves, that is, merely deflect us from this essence.

Our senses and our argumentation established thereon, merely lead to a round world, to a structure of the world which is different from that of the Bible. Granted that the round world is correct as far as the world of the senses is concerned; the real world, however, has the four corners, the opposite of roundness; the real world has the (1–4)-structure, has the 400 and the 500 as measures.

Now the 'Ibri', the Hebrew, comes from the other side, from the 'beyond' of the four rivers. Geographically speaking, one might say, he comes from the other side of the Euphrates, of the fourth river, from beyond the fourth which is the outermost bound of the world. *Heber,* the fourth generation, comes from beyond the fourth river.

Therefore the 'Ibri' is ever different from this world, and in a sense, ever in conflict with it.

Tradition has it that Abraham and Issac were educated in the school of Shem and Heber, and that Jacob, too, was a pupil of Heber.

At the time of the 'Haflaga', there is this deliberate way of Shem and Heber in contrast with the world. Abraham was already born then. He is 48 at the time. In *his* era the splitting-up is at the end of the seventh day, at the approach of the 49.

Ancient lore gives an enormous variety of details about Abraham's youth and vicissitudes of life, until the moment he comes into prominence in the story of the Bible. All the communications of ancient lore imply that even previous to his birth, Abraham was considered by the world as a danger to the progress of the world, as it was then at the pinnacle of its development. People knew that if this seed came to life, it would greatly endanger the development of the world.

And from his birth Abraham is in conflict with the world, as represented in the king, the great hunter, Nimrod. For Nimrod knows and senses that Abraham has no faith in the forces of development of the earth, and he is aware that this mere lack of faith spells danger. It is a different power, from a different world, with other standards. And Nimrod and all his counsellors somehow know that the other world with its different criteria is the real leader of their world. Nimrod, begotten by Kush, so descending from Ham, knows that he is the servant to that other world, once and for all. Therefore the other world is a vexation to him, it spoils the illusion of his game. The game he plays to pretend he is lord of the world.

Not only does Abraham belong to a different world, he *shows* he does. According to ancient lore, he proved that all this service to the earth was mere vanity. He smashed up the gods people worshipped, the gods they had made for themselves, showing that they had been made with human standards, that they were products of human reasoning and construction.

He held up to ridicule the game of the world played so seriously, he put all the self-importance in the place where such sporting belonged.

Because of this attitude he became an outcast, and had to leave his country and his neighbourhood. Nimrod had repeatedly tried to kill him, but in this respect, too, Abraham proved to belong to another world. Whatever they undertook – going as far as to throw him into a lime-pit – contrary to all laws of matter, Abraham remained alive. Matter can be destroyed, the substance Abraham, coming from another world, cannot be injured by the methods of the king, the hunter Nimrod.

Thus at the end of the world which goes down with the 'Haflaga', there is this Abraham fixed into it, like a hook from the other world. When the third phase is to begin, the third 'ele toldoth', this Abraham already exists. The third 'ele toldoth' is the *waw*, the 6 of the 10–5–6–5. This 6, like a hook, joins the first 'five' to the latter 'five'. It accomplishes the union of the opposites.

Together with Shem and Heber, Abraham forms a bridge to the new world. Even though a world comes to an end, even though life is divided, those that draw their life from beyond this world, continue to live. This Haflaga does not affect them, because they themselves are alien to it, gazing as if from another world at this chaos of over-estimation and radically erroneous judgement of matter and of this world.

God had removed Abraham from the world of Nimrod, the hunter. Abraham, owing to his attitude in that world, had moved away to its bounds, to Charan. Beyond that boundary his father Terah could not go. God removed Abraham from a world in which everything was familiar to him, and sent him to a new world. Abraham was 75 at the time.

Expressed in the criteria of this world, it might be a 'dying', a passing-over into a new world. Indeed some stories of ancient lore do point to this facet. To life as a whole, however, it does not express itself in the sense which dying has to life on earth. Life exchanges one place for another, and it says in the Bible, that to these people it is like travelling into another country. Terah cannot reach that other country, and he remains in Charan. He cannot tear himself away from it.

The world which Abraham enters now is the land which at that moment is occupied by Canaan. It is the land which here expresses the world of the origin and at the same time the world of the future, when harmony shall he restored, when reunion shall be completed. Now, however in the phase when the world is in duality, this duality finds expression there as well.

In our terminology: when the 'ten below', the 5–6–5, is split off from the 'ten above', the first letter of the 10–5–6–5, there is duality *everywhere*. Ancient lore expresses it thus: God went with creation into duality, went with it into captivity.

In this other world, the original world of unity, God points out to Abraham how one day Abraham's descendants shall live again in this world, embracing all in unity and harmony. It is a wonderful, new world including the tree of life, the tree which *is* fruit and *makes* fruit. In this world man can actually live when he has passed the phase of duality, when the time of the Canaanite in the land of unity is past.

Abraham also has Lot with him, the son of his brother Haran. According to ancient lore this Haran, like Abraham, suffered Nimrod to cast him into the fire, but that he was burnt. For Haran had seen that Abraham was saved and did not get burnt. When he saw this, he determined to follow Abraham and not Nimrod. Before that moment he had been in doubt, in an inner conflict. But when he saw the reward, the success of Abraham's way, he resolved to go that way … and was burnt. For whoever follows this way, '*knowing*' it is worth while, *knowing* it bestows immortality, is lacking in the principal motive for reunion with God, i. e. faith, implicit belief, although everything seems entirely different, the very opposite. Haran was not to see his reward until after the utter consternation of getting burnt all the same. There, at *that* moment, when everything turned out entirely differently from what he had calculated and expected, he might show that he loved God, not for the reward of immortality.

From Haran is begotten Lot, and ancient lore describes him as the serpentine part of man, most highly developed in the material sense. Since the complete man Abraham journeys to the other world, that lowest part 'Lot' accompanies him.

After God had promised Abraham this world of Canaan for the future, for what was to come after him, Abraham arrived at the spot between Bethel and Hai (Gen. 12:8).

I must here interrupt the story consider the names and places mentioned. If with the names Bethel and Hai we were to state that Abraham was somewhere 'in some place in the world', the meaning of the datum of *those very* names would escape us altogether. Or maybe it would satisfy our historic curiosity, or give historians an occasion to thresh out thoroughly whether those places had actually existed, where they were situated, and especially how small they were in fact.

The names of the places and the substance of the word of those names of course *are* most significant. It is for us to be eager to know what God intimates to us with the Bible, not what we have to remark about it.

The name Bethel is spelt beth-jot-taf-aleph-lamed, 2–10–400–1–30, it means 'house of God', and its sum-total is $2+10+400+1+30=443$.

The name Hai, actually ha-ai, is spelt hee-ayin-jot, 5–70–10, with the sum-total of 85.

Abraham settles down between Bethel and Hai. The distance in the essence of the words, between Bethel and Hai is $443-85=358$. This 358 we know already as the number with the sum-total of the components of the word 'Messiah'. Hence the measure of the distance between Bethel and Hai is this word 'Messiah'. In the story of Gen. 12:7–8, it says that the Lord appeared unto Abraham and said: ' "Unto thy seed will I give this land." And there built he an altar to the Lord who had appeared to him. And he removed from thence unto a mountain on the east of Beth-el, and pitched his tent, having Beth-el on the west and Hai on the east; and there he built an altar unto the Lord and called upon the name of the Lord.'

When God gives Abraham that land, the coming world, destined for the seed of Abraham, then Abraham journeys to that place which also represents that coming time, the place with the number of the Messiah. For with it is determined this journeying and settling after the communication of the coming world.

Abraham now settles down between those two places. Which means that on either side there is a distance of 179; for twice 179 makes 358.

Now this number 179 also indicates a certain condition. The 'Garden of Eden', the 'gan be Eden' is gimmel-nun-beth-ayin-daleth-nun, $3+50+2+70+4+50=179$. In that coming world, in fact, this place of settlement is indeed the Garden of Eden, and there one lives indeed near the tree of life. And under the vine and the fig-tree, which there pertain to us as a matter of course as the tree of knowledge now that we have the tree of life.

The statement in one of the stories in ancient lore that Abraham on the journey from Charan arrived in 'the other world' and in the 'Garden of Eden' is based on this knowledge of the names or the places and of the knowledge of the structure of the Bible. Indeed, after this life of deriding and smashing-up of those gods in the likeness of man, Abraham gets into the coming world, at the place which is the Garden of Eden, and on the way which is the way of the Messiah. It goes without saying one should approach every place and every name as also every image in the story of the Bible in such a manner. I can, however, within the narrow limits of this introduction, hardly do more than point to an occasional example; an example which moreover must he intelligible considering the limited knowledge of the structure of the Bible, I have been able to impart to the reader in this book which is small in proportion to the immense mass of material.

All the same there may be one or two examples in his area of place-names worth mentioning here. Jacob also calls a place Bethel (Gen. 28:19). It had first been called Luz, according to the Bible. Is this a geographical orientation? Again for the benefit of later seekers with their spades? In that spot Jacob beheld the ladder. The top reached to heaven and God had also told him that this 'land' was destined for his seed. We know Bethel has the sum-total of 443. Luz is spelt lamed-waw-zayin, 30–6–7. Pronounced as number Luz is 43. So what Jacob did was adding 400 to the ancient name. With this happening of beholding the ladder with its top reaching heaven and everything taking place on it the way of the 400, this period of the servitude of the world, the era of the four worlds, had come to an end. For *that* reason the two names are mentioned. The substance, as expressed in the quantitative proportion, and the image of the word are interrelated. The addition of the 400 made of Luz the 'House of God'.

Let me round this off with just one more example. The name Bethlehem is sufficiently well known. It means 'house of the bread'. Now bread is the finished product of wheat, 'chita'. As already mentioned in a previous chapter wheat is considered another level of the fig-tree, the tree of knowledge. For wheat in the systematism of fruit, is the first, the fig is the fourth, and we know that, just like the first and the fourth days of creation, here too the first is placed over the fourth in the systematism. As the story of the tree of knowledge was enacted in the second triad of days, it is there that the fig-tree is mentioned. However, viewed from the biological point of view, it is of course an unintelligible and illogical projection of the original wheat.

Owing to the fall after the eating of the tree of knowledge this wheat which participated in the fall acquired the character of the 'tree that makes fruit'. Since then, after the season of the growing and ripening of the corn, there is the harvesting and the threshing to divide the grain from the chaff, then the grinding, the mixing with water, the kneading and baking before the finished product, the 'bread', appears. In the situation of the tree of life, the final product is already present, the bread, so to speak, is hanging on the tree.

Here, however, there is the long and hard road before that final product is there; fire and water enter into the affair, it is uphill-work. It is a way full of heartbreaking struggle and strife.

The word for bread is 'lechem', 30–8–40. And the word for 'war', 'milchama', mem-lamed-cheth-mem-hee, 40–30–8–40–5, has the word 'lechem' as its root. Not because wars are carried on for economic reasons – as people are nowadays inclined to say in their utilistic and materialistic conception of the world – but because strife, war, ensue from the eating from the tree of knowledge, owing to which this tree has now acquired the form of wheat. This implies that in this world everything can only be achieved after laborious growth and development, and also that the corn as a first phenomenon of this principle of growth has to go through a great number of harsh manipulations, such as mowing, dying, threshing, grinding, etc. before the goal is attained.

It is the way of the 'tree that makes fruit', which is expressed in the process from wheat to bread, owing to which there will be war, duality and strife to the very end, to the baking of the bread.

Now in Bethlehem, in the 'house of the bread', of the final product of the wheat, hence when progress has come to an end, Ruth comes to Boaz, and the foundation is laid for the birth of David, the anointed king who himself was born in Bethlehem too, who even derives his name from it. And it is at the same time the place where the whole Messianic generation finds its origin.

Even the structual story, with the place in the structure taken by wheat, by the tree that makes fruit, the significance of the Messiah as terminus of the way of this world, makes it intelligible that the place the Messianic generation comes from, has this name. Bread, as completion of wheat, indicates that the way of the world is completed. In bread all this is expressed, hence the profound significance bread has for the life of man. Of course I do not mean the so-called significance because of calories and vitamins. Bread unites man with the essence of things and brings the end of the way near to him. And Bethlehem, as house of bread, according to the structure of the Bible, is the place whence the Messiah comes.

But the word Bethlehem, in the essence of the word, tells us even more; it confirms again in the striking way we have got familiar with, what the structure already imparts so amazingly and emphatically.

The word Bethlehem is spelt beth-jot-taf-lamed-cheth-mem, 2–10–400–30–8–40. So it has the value of $2+10+400+30+8+40=490$. And is not that, indeed, the boundary for the coming of the 500, since it is the seven times seven in the plane of the decade; it is the end of the seventh day, the place of the transition of the seventh day to the eighth, from this world to the next.

David is the seventh generation, as we have seen; he is the father of the eighth, which builds the solid house of God in this world. In the Bible in the book Samuel, it says that David as king comes from Bethlehem, from the place where the way of the seventh day is completed, where the wheat becomes bread.

17
The Incredible

Abraham learns that he shall be multiplied, and that it will be in that coming world. But according to the law of nature it is unintelligible. How can the life of this world exist in the coming world? Everything in this world, whichever way one looks at it, shows it is impossible. One can accept that anything following logically, consequently from this life, can be its continuation. One gets older here, ever older, one's strength decays, days go by and are forgotten, thoughts crop up and disappear, there are dreams, desires; all this goes by. Then how does man get into that promised world, and what will he be like?

Abraham would indeed have been quite satisfied, if his son Ishmael could stand for that future. Ishmael at least followed consequently from earthly development (Gen. 17:18).

The name Ishmael in the Bible is written Jishmael, jot-shin-mem-ayin-aleph-lamed, 10–300–40–70–1–30, with a sum-total of 451. Abram begot him on Hagar, the Egyptian; from the body which came from this world of opposites, from this world of duality. Abram, as he was still called at the time, is spelt aleph-beth-resh-mem, 1–2–200–40, with a sum-total of 243. Hagar is spelt 5–3–200=208. That Abram and Hagar, as 243 and 208, should consequently have Ishmael, the 451, is logical from the earthly point of view, for 243 + 208 makes 451. But the coming future, embracing everything this life had procured, everything with a permanent character besides, is utterly beyond the imaginable.

When Abraham reminds God of his being without issue; of the impossibility of producing a future such as God had held out to him; of the contradiction between the potentially possible and this promise for the future, Abraham maintains that from the earthly point of view only the Damascene Eliezer could represent the future. Eliezer hails from Damascus, 'Dameshek', daleth-mem-shin-kof, 4–40–300–100, sum-total 444. The heir will be this world of the 'four' in all planes, nothing else.

Just as the child in this world is a continuation of life, so also is the coming life in reality like a child of this life. And the dialogue God has with Abraham deals with this life-to-come, which God had shown to Abraham, after which Abraham had gone to that place between Bethel and Hai. The vital question is whether his own life of the moment, plus the life that had gone by, and that which is yet to ensue from him on this earth can actually be in the coming world. Everything this world shows to man, seems to be at variance with it.

In Gen. 15:5 it says in the Bible that God brought Abraham forth abroad. According to ancient lore this is the diverting of Abraham's glance from the laws of nature and the phenomena of this world. God supposedly told Abraham to give up the habit of measuring the future with the earthly space-time standards. Just as we are unable to count the terrestrially and sensorily perceptible worlds about us, since we know that space is infinite and that there are countless worlds in space which we can merely have a suspicion of, so we have to realize that the future, which moreover pertains to a different plane, cannot be computed with these standards. God suggests Abraham's giving up these earthly space-time criteria.

Again it is the confrontation with the tree of knowledge. Like every creature possessing the human soul, Abraham too had stated that the coming world did not tally somehow with the earthly criteria. And he had tried to penetrate deeper with subtle earthly standards. And he had discovered the proof that what God had told him was impossible. This is the point where man might eat from the tree of knowledge, where he might take progress into his own hands to create a picture of the future for himself, a construction which would definitely be logical, a complex of theories about God and the hereafter, in accordance with human standards.

And at this juncture God speaks with Abraham and points out to him the limitations of this course, and, as tradition has it, brings him forth, abroad, away from this kind of thought.

And another victory is gained on the seductiveness of this world for Abraham trusted the criteria God had revealed to him would eliminate the contradiction that there should actually exist a possibility of time flowing and yet standing still. As it says in the Bible: 'And he believed in the Lord, and He counted it to him for righteousness.'

Now that Abraham takes this course, the way to the tree of life is open to him. And therefore he does see the whole development now as it will enact itself, all those four hundred years, and the fourth generation which march out. It is the complex of Gen. 15 which we have already discussed, the part where Abraham beholds the order of the world in the three divided parts, with at either end the 'undivided' birds, the doves.

Abraham does not take from the tree of knowledge and for that very reason he acquires an insight into this world, the tree that is fruit and makes fruit.

Isaac comes when virtually none can believe it any more. The name Isaac therefore means something like 'absurd (to believe it)', absurd (to have faith in it, build on it) 'it is laughable'.

For indeed, the coming world appears when all hope is past, when every possibility of it has proved utterly out of the question. In the reckoning of Abraham's life there is then the '100 years', the 'ten' as the consequence of the 'four' has fulfilled itself completely. It has proved so utterly impossible that from this life might yet ensue the future, every single experience has proved it so definitely and absolutely, that anybody eventually hearing it announced cannot help but burst out laughing. The contrast between possibility and reality is *too* great.

Isaac does not come until Abraham is circumcised. Not until the covering sheath, the downright earthy, is removed, can the future so far considered impossible, penetrate.

For Ishmael, logically the earthly successor to Abraham's life, circumcision comes in the 13th year. When the 'twelve' of time has been left behind, when the 'thirteen', the word, 'one', has come. Such a man first passes through this whole life, expressing himself, as we have already discussed, in the 'twelve', and only beyond this life comes the removal of the covering, which hides the nucleus, the folding back of the remainder.

When Abraham has accomplished this circumcision on himself, he awaits the guests. He is desirous to receive 'knowledge' from God; he is prepared to receive it as an honoured guest. He waits for the guests at the entrance of his dwelling, lest they should pass by unseen. Because he is thus waiting deferentially for that which is coming from beyond his world, this 'future' assumes the form of messengers from God, and it is God Himself speaking through them.

And these guests tell him that in the next cycle of the year this succession will come in the person of the son thus far considered an impossibility. But at the same time they foretell the destruction of Sodom.

Sodom is the world where Lot had gone. We have already seen that Lot is considered by tradition to be the human body in its quality of extreme development, following after Abraham. After a certain time Lot had separated from Abraham and settled down in Sodom. I shall not enter into the motives and other details, because they are unnecessary for the purpose of our story.

Sodom is the world of material progress. It is the world of duality. In ancient lore it is mentioned as quality of Sodom, as characteristic of that duality, that people acted on the principle of 'mine is mine, and thine is thine' in Sodom. It is characteristic of a world in its aspect of: 'everybody to his own', or 'mind your own business and don't meddle with other people's; it will only lead you into a mess.' It is the world of 'sound' social egoism, considered so healthy in the struggle for life. At the same time it implies the impossibility of reconciling the opposites. 'Mine' is incompatible with 'thine', and duality remains.

Therefore Sodom does not accept anything from outside. What cannot be measured with the criteria of this world of Sodom, must be rejected. It simply is not there. Sodom belongs to the Sodomites, and outside-criteria have no business there. Whoever is occupied with receiving guests from beyond that world, is considered 'out of bounds' by Sodom. To Sodom 'reunion' is identical with death, and he that receives guests demonstrates an inclination towards union with another world, a world which Sodom proclaims does not exist.

Thus tradition has it that a girl in Sodom, caught in such an act, in defiance of the spirit of Sodom, was smeared all over with honey and laid down in the open so that the bees might come and kill her with their stings. It is a Sodomite demonstration of what union is in their opinion and in regard to their existence. The honey of the bees attracts the bees themselves. They want to reunite with this honey. But to man it is lethal, man undergoes this reunion as a fearful sorrow accompanied by terrible pain, and through it ceases to exist for that world of Sodom.

Now Lot lived in that world. But Lot had lived with Abraham, had as subdivision of the body formed the whole with Abraham. And this being together of the physical with the man Abraham had emancipated it, had bestowed faculties and qualities upon it, which had effected a change. This is also one of the facets of the purpose of our contact with things of the world. Owing to the fact they have been contacted by us, looked at, operated with by us, these things undergo a change in their essence, if there exists in us that will-power to relate everything to the source of origin. That is what we meet with things for. It is in that sense that Lot had accepted in himself Abraham's conception of what is called hospitality. It is that which makes us long for the guest, the message from outside ourselves, because everything which comes as a guest has something within itself of the divine which comes down to this world, that the world may reunite with it. Thus the soul is the guest in the body.

Taking in a guest therefore expresses the desire for integration. Of course with this is meant a hospitality which pays the guest the honour of sincere joy at his arrival, when the criteria of the guest are respected and his world is welcome to enter with him. Therefore ancient lore emphasizes as a quality of the good man, as contrasted with the man of Sodom, that he sticks to the principle: 'mine is thine and thine is thine'.

Thus does Lot receive guests in defiance of the spirit of Sodom. And Lot is saved from destruction. People in Sodom refuse to believe in the destruction of their flourishing world. It would be utterly incompatible with all perceptions concerning the continuity of development.

From Lot after all comes Ruth, from Lot's son Moab. And Ruth becomes an ancestress of the Messianic generation. The forces of development of the human body in contact with the man who through his way of living unites them with the origin, partipate in the building up of the generation of the Messiah.

The world of Sodom goes under. Lot could not imagine any world outside it, in spite of Abraham being so near. This world, however, blinds people with its deceptiveness and so they cannot understand how there could be anything outside.

Abraham has reached the limit of time, also in himself. He is now 99 years old; he has almost passed through the whole range of possibilities of the 'ten'. Thus there is first a destruction, coinciding with the removal of the sheath which covers the nucleus, coinciding with the circumcision, before the new world comes. The world of duality, of the forces of development of matter, perishes.

The coming of the new world is so unbelievable, so utterly unlikely, one always feels like 'laughing at it'.

Tradition has it that Isaac closely resembles Abraham. So much so one could take the one for the other. Indeed that is exactly what the coming life is: it is as like to this life as two peas. It is purely a continuation, yet entirely new. It is like the tree that is fruit and makes fruit.

The circumcision of Isaac takes place on the eighth day. In its phenomenal form in the world of the seventh day, after seven days life in duality, in the chrysalis of matter, this new world on the eighth day has the emancipation from the chrysalis, yet it does not perish. The covering skin is only restricted and folded back so as to show forth the nucleus on the eighth day.

It is the situation which the world will experience on the eighth day. It is therefore an old Jewish custom at the circumcision to put a chair ready for the prophet Elijah, for he announces the coming of the Messiah on the eighth day. The coming of Isaac in this world of the seventh day therefore is an indication that the life of the eighth day will actually come. The stamp of the pattern God gave to the world, impressed on the phenomenal appearance of the seventh day: that the eighth day is sure to come, how it will come, and how life in the eighth day will be. The imprint is there on the phenomena of the seventh day, and one can read from it what its structure is, one can translate it into the forms of the eighth day.

18
The Offering and Paradise

In Isaac's life the story of his so-called offering plays an important part. This story, too, often proves to be a source of confusion.

When the new life flourishes in Isaac, the one that came although it was unbelievable, it is suddenly demanded by God; He wants to take it back. Even in the surface story it is a most dramatic event. God had given Abraham the promise of this one and only son and had finally fulfilled it, and now God asks Abraham to give Him this son back again. There is a distinct inconsistency in all this, and the inconsistency is very much stressed in the story. For indeed, the world was to be Isaac's, and now this same Isaac is to leave this world at God's direction (Gen. 22).

It is the same contradiction man feels throughout life. On the one hand there is the promise and the inner conviction that there is a future life, on the other hand a man's life is getting a little closer to death every day. And every day one wonders what about that promise, and that dim inner faith? But one *has* to go on; time just draws one a bit further every day.

The way leads to the land Moria, the place of origin of the world; whence everything came forth; unknown to life here; not to be argued about; everything returning thither again. In spite of the promise that one shall have life, even the life of this world, forever.

On that way Abraham takes the ass and 'two boys', and when on the third day he can see the place from afar, he leaves the ass and the two 'boys' behind and proceeds alone with Isaac.

According to ancient lore those two boys were Eliezer and Ishmael. After Ishmael had been driven away with his mother Hagar, he had just returned to Abraham, and according to ancient lore he remained with Abraham ever since. His mother, Hagar, according to ancient lore, also returned, and under the name of Keturah became Abraham's wife again. But we shall leave this topic out of account here.

This leaving behind of the 'two boys' at that specific point, when the goal, the origin is coming into view, throws some added light on the meaning of the relationships in the Bible.

The place Moria, the origin of the world, as it expresses itself in matter in the form of this earth, is the same place as that where ultimately the temple comes.

The Bible considers that place as the 'navel' of the world. The stone 'shetiva', about which I have given some information, is the centre of this place.

Moria, as the word, is related to 'teaching', 'tuition'. Just as the word 'Thorah' too, means 'teaching', 'doctrine'. It is the doctrine, the knowledge, which imparts to us how the world is and how life is, why it is so, and what is the purpose of it. So the name Moria means that learning, insight, understanding goes forth from this place which is the origin of the world. Whoever derives his knowledge from *that* place, has the real knowledge, he understands the purpose of the world, the purpose of creation. For this spot is origin and goal of everything. In this place, even if it should become visible in this world, the laws of nature obtaining in the rest of the world do not apply, as ancient lore tells us by means of a great many examples. Conceptions such as space, etc., have an entirely different meaning there. It is the place on earth where the laws of the 'one' obtain.

The particular thing about the temple in this world was therefore that everything was enacted concentratedly and at the same time clearly and distinctly in *that* place, in a small space, whereas in the space-time world it unrolled itself complicatedly, confusedly in duration. So the temple meant the presence of another world here on earth; a world where things were clear and distinct, where every action had an entirely different effect from similar actions outside this place. That is why an 'offering', a 'korban' could only be brought *there*. Because in a way that place was at the same time here on earth and in heaven. Bringing a sacrificial animal *hither* implied bringing the earthly body. Because in essence the animal and the body are united. Bringing an animal as an offering anywhere else on earth therefore was not only purposeless, but altogether wrong and therefore 'prohibited'.

Only in this place where the 'one' obtained i. e. the condition of all-inclusiveness, did image and form coincide with being, with the essence. The animal when brought *thither*, at once communed with the essence, contacted the essence. People's disposition to bring their 'offerings' in 'high places', outside the temple, throughout the land, means that they point out other situations as 'the nucleus' as the origin. It means that they *determine for themselves* what is the nucleus and the origin and that they do not accept the origin which God has made and shown to man as such.

So this place Moria is the origin of things; it is the 'one' which is and which is all-embracing. Therefore Abraham leaves behind all these that served him in the world of 'duality', as soon as he becomes aware of the 'one'. The 'two boys', the duality accompanying him which he first also regarded as his future – he had mentioned both Eliezer and Ishmael as his eventual, logical heirs – he now leaves behind; together with the ass, i.e. that which had carried him through the world.

It is a situation analogous to earthly death. In that case, too, the duality of this world is left behind together with the body one was 'mounted' on.

But at this moment, seeing the place of the 'one', Abraham also knows he shall return with Isaac, even though he does not yet realize how. The aspect, the percipience of 'oneness' even at a distance, at the very border of this world and the other, yields the knowledge that it will be *good* anyhow.

When he has ultimately got there, Abraham prepares everything for the offering, and that even now implies that he will have to relinquish Isaac, his future, his further life in the world whence he came. An animal, brought as a 'korban', has its four feet bound together. That is one of the important acts. For the body which is put in readiness to come nearer to God, is first to bind its multiplicity, its quadruplicity, to 'one'. This is the first act. A man who still lives in multiplicity, who suffers himself to be led by the senses, *cannot* come nearer, he cannot bring that 'korban'.

Then the jugular artery of the sacrificial animal is cut. The circulation of the blood, i.e. the circle incessantly functioning in life which virtually is the foundation for physical life, is interfered with. That which kept man incarcerated within the circle of this world, is cut through; what had given him the impression that this world is all; that what he had thought about it was indeed all that existed; that everything was brought to a finish here; that it was round; it is the circle that is cut through, and subject to the purpose of the 'korban', the blood is carried to the place of the ark, the holy of holies, the origin of everything, there where the stone 'shetiya' is; or it is taken to the altar – on which, in fact, the animal was not slaughtered, for it was slaughtered on the north side opposite the altar – and sprinkled or poured on the four sides of it. The blood which, according to the Bible, is the bearer of the 'nefesh', the animal-soul or the physical soul, here in this place-of-'oneness', in this place where image and substance coincide, is united with the real origin, with the purpose of life, with the purpose of existence. If this is performed with the image of the 'animal' in that place of 'oneness', then man living in this world, experiences the 'coming nearer to God'. And he returns to life in this world.

Of course all this is only to the purpose, if indeed there *is* such a place in this world; and if one knows what one is doing there, and has as one's purpose in life to come nearer to God and unite with God, then this purpose in that particular place will assume the form of the acts as described so accurately in the Bible and in ancient lore. For in that place the act and the purpose coincide, as also the image and the substance thereof.

Now Abraham performs this act of binding on Isaac. Isaac's hands and feet are fastened together, the 'four' are bound into 'one'. But when the knife is held ready to cut through the circle in Isaac *too*, at the very moment when the earthly life is going to be severed, God shows Abraham the animal, which at this juncture takes over the function of the body. In that place of the origin, of 'unity', where everything is in its proper place, where all proportions, all relationships are clear and distinct, there it becomes evident that death merely means that an animal put in readiness goes to its destination, that owing to this union with man, it is also liberated from the line of development directed at infinitude. The animal, because of its substituting the human body, arrives at the origin together with man; it is emancipated from animalhood. The animal, as it says in tradition, has been in readiness ever since creation. Even from creation everything has been thus ordained that the body can continue to live, that it returns alive, that in this way, moreover, the animal attains union with man.

This knowledge Abraham only acquires, with Isaac, when he has gone all the way to Moria and has given evidence in that place of his readiness to give up *everything* in this life, even his future life in this world. Not until one looks on this life as something one also desires to render up to God, eventually never to have it back in any future – although on the other hand one knows in an unaccountable way which does not tally with the facts, that there *will* be a future life *somehow* – not until then does one become aware that life as such continues, that it does come back. And that in the structure of creation, visible only to him that has gone this way like Abraham and has reached this place of the origin of everything, where image and substance coincide, that even there, as if attended to by a very good father, everything has been in readiness from the beginning, owing to which man *naturally* keeps alive and will certainly come back to this world. But then, why was it all made so difficult for Abraham? Why was not everything straightaway told him clearly and distinctly? Again, the same answer: so that man may attain reunion with God at a divine level, equipped with the same faculties and characteristics God gave him at creation; that he may know that reunion comes because he, man, has shown great faith in God, great affection and immense interest. That he is *not* placed in a world as a robot, and taken back again, without any purpose, without sentiment, as if he were droning his lessons. That is why God gave man the 'neshamah', the divine soul that he might, inspired by the divine within, make his appearance in the sphere of the divine, showing implicit faith, showing 'jirath shamayin', interest in God and His creation. Thus will man actually become the image of God, dispensing the same acts from a supramundane sphere. He will then be like the one jot in the aleph which is the reflection of the other.

This faith is something which goes to extreme lengths, because this life is single and embraces everything. Therefore faith should embrace *all* to the extreme limit. Man should be ready to give up this life and future life, although God has promised him both, if the way God desires him to go seems to be at variance with that promise. Even though something seems wrong about the promises, if it is the way God points to him, man has to go it, confident that it will prove right, since it it God, who makes and arranges everything even to its very smallest detail.

The point at issue is that man knows that the way he goes in life is the way to Moria, where he shall learn and become aware what everything is for, and that he knows that he can only go that way if he is ready to accept the visible path to old age and death, to decay and disappearance. That he is ready to go this way which points to death in spite of God's promise of life eternal also in this world, knowing that in this way he rises beyond this world, that in doing so he performs actions which pertain to another world.

Tradition gives many details about this way of Abraham with Isaac. For this situation existed even in Paradise. There, too, man was free to follow the way of worldly progress, the way of the 'tree that makes fruit', for man learns directly through the senses, and if he makes no mistakes, and is intelligent and ingenious enough, results will logically follow after exertion and sacrifice. Why, one needs, in that case, not accept things from God first, afterwards to discover, eventually, God has done things well. One can *oneself* be a god, fix standards for oneself, decide for oneself on life and death, on development or stagnation.

It is for this reason, according to ancient lore, when they were on their way to Moria, Satan advanced towards them. The word Satan really means 'disturber', i.e. he disturbs man on his way to God, he always wants man to go the way of the world, he shows the advantages of the way of the world, just as the serpent did. The words for Satan and the serpent are closely related, for that matter, but I cannot here expatiate on the manner of that relationship. Satan is spelt sin-teth-nun, 300–9–50; and the serpent, as we know, is 50–8–300. Satan has the sum-total of 359, the serpent has 358. But do not let us here enter into the details of the assessment of the words. To my mind the relationship is quite evident from the facts mentioned.

So Satan advanced towards them and reasoned quite logically with them. He pointed out that there must be a mistake, a misunderstanding somewhere, that it simply could not be that on the one hand God should make the promise and on the other hand break it. When Abraham and Isaac made no comment on these logical arguments, but pointed at God's clear words which could not be misunderstood, that God surely knew what He was doing, that He had things firmly in hand, that life evidently had to take that course and that they were sure to see on Mount Moria why things had to take that course, Satan adopted another line to prevent them from going to Moria.

He caused a river to come in their way which they would be unable to cross. Circumstances were made so as to prevent man from going that way. Very often it is material or economic conditions, or professional or home conditions which make it difficult, which very soon furnish one with a motive for not going that way, to choose the way of the world instead and first to build up a good position, or first to undertake an intensive study of one of the many branches of science, or first to establish one's social status more firmly.

Although the water reached to their lips, Abraham and Isaac went on and finally Satan had to give it up. It was very much the same dialogue as that in Paradise between the serpent and the woman. This time, however, there is a break-through and the law ceases to operate. That which had at first to split up to create this world, now has to reunite. This time there is the third of the 'ele toldoth', this time there is already the 6 of the 6–5; the way now leads to reunion. According to tradition, Isaac, when he was taken to Moria, was 37 years old. This 37 also means that the phase of the 'six' was over; the 36 had just been passed; and that Isaac had now entered the seventh. As principle of the seventh, indeed, there always is this way to reunion.

Sarah was 90 years old, when Isaac was born, and she died when she was 127. So the 37 years of Isaac's age coincide with Sarah's death. An old world disappears at one's entrance into the seventh day.

In tradition this story of Isaac at Mount Moria is called the 'Akeda', the 'binding', the 'fastening'. For this 'binding' of the 'four' into the 'one' is the essential fact of the whole event. This very going to Mount Moria, going into that paradox, is a binding of the 'four' unto the 'one'. It is the *refusal* to accept a worldly logic, circumstances, pretence; it is a distinct disposition to do as God asks; afterwards to hear and learn on Mount Moria what the purpose of it is. In Moria, in the place of the 'one', where image and essence coincide, therefore the *act* in the image is this binding of the 'four' unto the 'one'.

The word 'Akeda' is spelt ayin-kof-daleth-hee, 70–100–4–5. The sum-total of the components is 179. And as we saw before, when Abraham settled in the place between Bethel and Hai, this 179 is the value of the word 'Gan-be-Eden', Garden of Eden, hence of Paradise. What happened with Isaac, this binding of the 'four' unto the 'one', therefore is identical with entering Paradise. In binding together the 'four' of the world and making it into 'one', man indeed has entered the condition of Paradise, and has the tree of life which is to the tree of knowledge as 'one' is to 'four'. Moria, where this binding-together ever takes place in essence, and where the animals for the 'korban' are similarly bound like that, therefore is also the place which has the measures of the tree of life, i.e. the place which has the 500 for its measure. It is, as described above, the place of the temple which with this measure of the 500 proved not to be of this world, which can merely count to 400. Therefore ancient lore says that the 'Akeda' of Isaac actually translated him into Paradise, that he sojourned in Paradise, as if after a 'death', and afterwards returned to this life. This story of ancient lore also tells us that Isaac indeed died at Moria and afterwards as one risen-from-death, after having been in Paradise and having seen the roots of existence, the purpose of things, returned to this world again.

I mention this version on purpose to show how the Bible and ancient lore, the 'oral doctrine', which was given simultaneously with the Bible, speak of death and life, life and death, as quite normal conditions, one following after the other, just as the days of the week, the months of the year follow one after the other. That the Bible is assuredly not a book for this life exclusively, but that it is at the same time the book for the journey through all lives, in all worlds, and that this journey is looked upon as a very common affair. And finally that the stories only acquire meaning, and the expressions of the substance in the word get their significance, only if one sees them as such.

19
The Twins

Jacob and Esau are twins, Esau being the first-born. After Abraham and Isaac, they are the third in the sequence of the Patriarchs. We have already pointed out how the dual character comes into prominence in the 'third' in systematism. We have also seen, in the tale of Cain and Abel that the one appearing first in this world, is an expression of the physical, just as in the tale of creation there first was the body, and the soul was added as the younger one.

Therefore the relationship Jacob-Esau with all the stories pertaining to it is at the same time an expression of the relationship soul-body.

In the systematism of the Patriarchs Isaac is the second. The place of Isaac as the second, automatically associates him with the structure of that which happened in the second day of creation. It also implies that the place of Isaac is analogous to that of the second tale of creation, which indeed functions as second in the sequence of things. That is why the place of Isaac is characterized as the place on the left, hence also as the place of that which expresses itself as 'water'. Isaac comes into conflict with Abimelech on account of the wells (Gen. 26:16–33). There are 'four' of them again, since they also express the significance of the four worlds, the four elements, briefly of everything that on account of its substance has to unite with the 'four'.

Owing to his position on the left, the place of water, and also of the woman, there is a certain affinity to the physical. In the second tale of creation, given under circumstances characteristic of Isaac, water therefore plays an important part, as also does the woman, and similarly the body and the serpent. In that second tale of creation it says how man came, as a body formed from dust, to which God finally added the 'neshamah'.

Through this relationship of the place on the left and the physical, Esau makes his appearance emphatically as the physical body, and there is a certain affinity on the part of Isaac with Esau. It is analogous to the affinity God has towards the body of man which in the second story of creation He made first.

In the second tale of creation is expressed in the forms and images of our world, how the body as the woman is convinced by the serpent that it should choose the way of development and that because of it, this voting for development and progress on the part of the body takes up the central place of the things happening.

The relation between male and female facing the world's forces of development as expressed in the form of the 'serpent' can be regarded as the two aspects of man, that of the soul, the neshamah, and that of the body, which essentially form a unity as contrasted with the forces of progress of the 'tree that makes fruit', at whose root the serpent lies coiled.

In the tale of Paradise, the root-story, the body takes the way indicated by the serpent as 'Messiah'. Because of it the woman becomes 'the mother of all that lives', which means that the body too is endowed with the forces of development which now also express themselves as the progress, the growth of man during his life and all through the generations, towards the goal, the fruit which will make its appearance at the end as the last link in the chain of development.

This happening expresses itself in the body in the appearance of the sex organs. They are therefore the place which acquired form in man because the body chose the way of the serpent. That the body chose this way in the beginning has to do with the principle of creation which purposed to lead man to the very extreme of development, that his return might embrace all the possibilities of the infinite diversity of creation. With the consequence that man might from this extreme point go the whole way of reunion, and just because of this alienation from the source of origin go in utter faith in the rightness of the criteria which from that distance he can no longer discern.

In the beginning there *is* a dividing into two, a splitting-up, and man was meant to obey in his body this law of creation, made by God. That is why ancient lore has it that among the 'offerings' on the day of the new moon (Numbers 28:15) also 'one kid of the goats shall be offered for a sin-offering unto the Lord beside the continual burnt-offering and his drink-offering'. So it is 'a sin-offering unto the Lord'. And ancient lore maintains that God desires to have this sin-offering brought for *Him,* because He has made the world essentially so that new moons have to appear. The moon, on the left, opposite the sun, has the place of the woman, of the body of man.

Originally, according to tradition, the moon was the same size at the sun, they were the two great lights. In their duality they formed a harmony, just as in the letter 'one', in the aleph, the two jots are present in harmony.

But the moon came to God and wanted a difference, it wanted to be the bigger of the two. That there should be a duality without a contrast, a duality forming a harmony, did not suit the moon. Upon which God made the duality with the contrast, namely 'the greater light to rule the day and the lesser light to rule the night' (Gen. 1:16).

God then said that there would indeed be a difference and that that which had induced the difference was to be the sign of the night. It would at the same time be the lesser one, the dependent one. The light which had found satisfaction in harmony would remain the greater one and be the sign for the day, and it would essentially contain within itself the light for the day and the night.

The lesser light, as sign for the night, would therefore indicate the substance of night. The substance of night, therefore, is the ever changing form of the moon. Coming forth from the apparent void, it would wax and wane until it had obtained its fullest form. Nothing can grow here beyond the circle. Then it would wane and finally disappear into the void, whence it had also come forth.

This waxing, this growth and development, would be the sign for the world as 'night'. That night-world would give its light indirectly, the source of light perceived would not be the original. Besides, it would be characterized by waxing, by continual, flowing change of form. And this waxing would ever begin from an apparent 'void' and wane again into an apparent 'void'.

Such would also be the life in the world-of-night. It would ever renew itself, it would ever come and go. Life in the world-of-day, however, would remain constant, would issue forth owing to the original light, and never disappear.

That the moon should have got 'rebellious', God says, finds its cause in the fact that God made the world with the 'two', that even in the beginning God divided light from darkness. Therefore the moon *could not help* acting like that in the next world, in the second triad of days, i.e. in the world of form, and because of it there also came the 'tree that makes fruit', and that was why there was the serpent with that tree; the serpent representing that very force-of-duality made my God Himself. This force-of-duality had to operate till the world had reached its furthest point of development, so that the return to the origin might indeed embrace all potentialities imaginable.

Now, owing to the fact that woman had accepted the contact with the serpent, in the sixth day, on the way of creation, the way of creation's expanding and extending to its farthest extreme, as was in keeping with it, so that the 'tree that makes fruit' had to come forth, and the moon had to arise as light for the world-of-night, therefore in keeping with the completion of duality, woman, hence the human body also, acquired this character of the world-of-night with the moon as sign thereof. Hence also the contact of woman with the 'tree that makes fruit'. Thus woman in her appearance obtained that expression of the substance which is represented by 'the tree that makes fruit'. Thus, like the moon, woman has her periods, which indeed correspond with the phases of the moon. And together with it, the form acquires this development in periods, in coming and going. Just as the moon comes and goes, so in this world of night there is the imprint that everything pertaining to the body comes and goes, is born and dies. And the source which gives life to the body, to the form, is not seen any more than the sun is seen at night.

This principle of physical life ever expresses itself in the coming of the new moon. It is a life which ever leads to death again. And that is why, according to tradition, God demands that special sin offering for Himself, because God Himself originated this course of life and death at creation, in that He caused this duality to emanate from His unity in the very principle of creation.

The offering is a kid of the goat. In the systematism of the zodiacal constellations we find this kid of the goat, the 'gedi', gimmel-daleth-jot, 3–4–10, as the tenth constellation. Duality, as can be seen in the systematism of creation, leads via the three and the four of the three days of creation with the four words of creation to the 'ten' as its extreme development, also expressing itself in the ten words of creation.

The offering, i.e. the 'bringing nearer to God' of the kid of the goat, actually is the reuniting of this extreme development, this furthest expansion, with the origin, with the 'one'. Through it, it is brought back to God, and the purpose of this creation will have been completed to its farthest extent, and then the farthest, embracing all the rest, is restored to God.

Since the kid of the goat in its systematism has come up for discussion, I should like to point out how to approach from this point of view the strongly emphasized injunction that 'this kid of the goat shall not be seethed in his mother's milk' (Exod. 23:19). That which has already reached the farthest development, the tenth place, must not be further developed, it must not be commingled with that which *is* an expression of further development, of new growth, of new formation. Milk is that; it comes from the mother just when she has brought forth new life; it expresses the forming of generations. That is why milk in Hebrew is 'chalab', cheth-lamed-beth, 8–30–2, so with a sum-total of 40. Again we see how the logical significance and the essential structure of the word coincide. For indeed 40 is exactly what in our proportions expresses a great length of time, the endless course through the time of this world. And this farthest development, this 'ten', must not be connected again with the force of development of the '40'.

Through knowledge of this principle the 'oral doctrine', tradition, has for the Jewish practice of life severed everything which is expressive of that furthest development, the animal body, from that which is the expression of a stimulus growth, milk. Neither in substance nor in phenomenal forms, which indeed are an expression of the essence, may these two be mixed.

The '*gedi*', the kid of the goat, is taken as starting-point, because in the goat this furthest development is predominant in systematism. Beyond the 'tenth' beast there is no other, it is the farthest removed. In fact it means, however, that anything expressing itself as flesh in the form of the sacrificial beasts represents what is farthest removed. It pertains to the extreme of creation. It is related to the extreme potencies of man in his earthly progress.

So the kid of the goat is a phenomenon in animal form of this furthest development. That is the reason why the devil was regarded as a being with horns and bucks' feet. The seducer is at the furthest point of development and therefore has bucks' feet. That in later times, such as the Middle Ages, people principally considered the image and were no longer aware of its context with the substance, and may therefore have gone in for all sorts or monkey-tricks with horns and bucks' feet need not detain us here. They were for the greater part merely reminiscences of primordial knowledge. But as such they are significant.

I also want to point out here that the sacrificial beasts, belonging to the genus 'sheep', 'cattle' and 'goats', in the systematism of the zodiacal constellations take the first, second and tenth places, viz. the 'ram' as expression for the genus 'sheep' coming first; then the 'bull' for the genus 'cattle' and finally 'capricorn' for the 'goats' as the tenth group. They therefore embrace the ten, which is the expression of the development of creation.

The 'ram' comes as bodily substitute for man. Just as we saw the ram suddenly appearing when Isaac was 'bound' at the 'Akeda'.

And the kid of the goat, by another name called 'Seir', the area which was given to Esau, (Gen. 33:16 and 36:8), has as sum-total of its name sin-ayin-jot-resh, 300–70–10–200, the 580 again, which we have also seen as a 'terminus', a finishing point of the development in the expression in matter.

The first-mentioned name for kid of the goat, 'gedi', 3–4–10, ultimately expresses the same thing, we should almost say, of course. For its sum-total of components is 17. And we remember this 17 too as measure for the ending of a world. We saw that in the phrase 'and God saw that it was good', the word 'good' contained the '17', therewith intimating that the end was 'good', that there was a purpose in the transition, that it was not only right, but that it was 'good'. The 17 and the 58 here too are interrelated, just as we saw this relationship in the time-measure of the 3½ and the name of Noah.

At the phase of the new moon there is this sin offering for God, as expressed by the union of the kid of the goat with the origin. For every new moon intimates that development is appearing anew, that the cycle will begin all over again. Until finally the light of the moon is like that of the sun once more and like the still unbroken light of creation, when everything will have returned into the harmony of the great whole (Isaiah 30:26). Then there will no longer be the continual change of the body, the growth and decay, the constant coming and going.

The contact with the serpent and the acceptance of its course of further development, has expressed itself in the body in the appearance of the sex-organs. They give the body that lunar development, that growth and constant renewal. And especially in the woman this lunar character is very clearly expressed in the periods. The embarrassment of normal man in connection with these sex-organs is bound up with his embarrassment in regard to this stamp which indicates that man at his entrance into this world chose the way of the serpent.

We may put it like this: the physical appearance of man expresses that at his coming into the world the contact with the serpent must have taken place, the contact with the forces of development. A contact which *had* to be made at that starting-point, just as the tree of knowledge *had* to come, and the moon *had* to come in contrast with the sun. For creation was made by God as a duality.

20
Blindness and Vision

In ancient lore the conception man is divided into three parts: the male part, which is called 'adam', in the figure of man expressed by the head; the female part called 'eve' and expressed by the trunk; and the part called 'serpent' which finds its expression in the sex organs.

The contact with the 'serpent', with the forces which dispose one towards development, change, desire-to-be-god in this world takes place through the 'woman' who forms the connecting link. So it is the human body which may or may not accomplish this contact with the serpent. Thus woman in Paradise had had this contact; Cain had also taken the way of the serpent and Ham had acted similarly.

In this story of Isaac the woman again plays an important part. For it is the second place in the sequence, it is the place on the left.

The woman who makes her appearance now, is Rebekah, Isaac's wife. And the force of development now facing her, is Esau.

The name Esau implies the conception 'made', 'ready'. It is development at its extreme. It appears here in this perfect form, because everything again expresses itself in the same condition as in the second story of creation; here again it is a 'second' story, that of the second Patriarch, Isaac.

That is why, according to ancient lore, Rebekah in her turn is facing the serpent, like Eve. But this time in a different world, in the seventh day, and in the third 'story', the 'ele toldoth' of Shem, which is to unite the two divided parts, the opposites, to make the complete 10–5–6–5. She is now the wife of Isaac, who had already got the binding of the 'four' into the 'one' through the 'Akeda', and the sign of the removal and the folding back of the material covering, the cutting-off of the material forces of development as represented by the serpent; the sign of the eighth day.

Now Isaac desires to give his blessing to that which is to come. He desires to give it a destination, he desires to determine it. He is the second; and that which is to come i. e. the third will be the completion. The cycle, indeed finds its close in the third. Isaac himself is Abraham's 'future', the promise of further life to him. Therefore Isaac's life appears as the completion of Abraham's on the other side. But both these sides together, the right and the left of life, form the harmony, the reunion in the third which embraces them.

And as the one of the left side, Isaac has a certain affinity to the physical, to that which is developing; to that which makes its appearance as form. It is the same affinity God demonstrated when in the second tale of creation he caused everything to appear in form, caused it to shoot forth from the face of the earth, in an immense, an overwhelming multiplicity and variety. An affinity which made this life in form at all possible.

And the force of development, Esau, his hunter's disposition, fostered this inclination towards becoming form. Jacob was 'domesticated', a man living in tents, but Esau was a cunning hunter, a man of the field (Gen. 25:27).

Jacob was static, a pivot at rest, whereas Esau was ever going round it, in circles, ever moving, ever changing.

We have already seen that the hunter is looked upon as the pursuer of the animal which ever evades him, thus provoking him to further emotion. The animal expressing itself in its four legs which give it speed, is for this reason in our representation of images, the quadruplicity of the world which refuses to be caught and which entices man ever further away, stirring the hunter's lust in him, in which intoxication he forgets everything else.

The woman who through her contact with the serpent acquires these faculties and therefore has these faculties finding expression through her, is the person who, pretending to elude the man, is set on provoking him to pursue her. And the man who takes the offered fruit, feels the hunter's passion stirring within; he forgets everything else and thinks that the world will be gained or lost, according to his catching or failing to catch this woman who provokes him to the pursuit.

The human body, as the expression of the female aspect of man, can also accept this contact with the serpent, and it will likewise obtain this 'poison' from the serpent. This will stir the man to the pursuit of things material, it will rouse the passion in him as he is excited by the desire to catch the 'four' which is making off. The 'four' will ever run off. The 'four' cannot be caught on the path of the hunter. For the way of the 'four' is eternal, endless, infinite for this earth. It leads to the 40 and the 400, the X sign of 'waters infinite' and to the sign of suffering in the servitude of the 400, the sign which in ancient writing is the 'cross'. Whenever one animal, one 'four' has been caught, emotion creates another, just as after one cigarette a man desires the next, after one glass of drink another after one woman another. There is no end to it, the way of the 'four' is the 'extreme' for this world; there is not any 'farther'. And this farthest extreme is grievously far away.

The affinity of the man on the left side of the systematism for things physical, as it also express itself in Isaac's affection for Esau, brings with it certain consequences, according to the story of the Bible and ancient lore.

Man in the second tale of creation is also created on the left side of the systematism, hence on the same side as Isaac. Therefore the expressions in the life of the man are analogous to those of the story of Isaac.

We have already discussed that on the left side the forces of the body are predominant, the forces which also obscure the nucleus, the essence. Man on this left side therefore cannot rightly discern the substance; to him it is clouded. Like Isaac, he is blind. According to ancient lore Isaac's blindness was caused by the idolatry practised by the wives of Esau. These women, in a way, veil the substance by the shadow.

Similarly it is the man placed on the left side, who eats from the 'tree' that makes fruit'. He allows himself to be tempted by appearances; he is blind as to the substance.

This quality of the man on the left side, this disposition to judge from appearances, finds expression in various aspects of the practice of life as it is built up on the knowledge of these things. Let me give one or two examples by way of illustration.

Whereas in the Bible the principle of right is very clearly expressed, as for example in the notorious saying, 'an eye for an eye; a life for a life', or briefly 'he shall be killed', after certain crimes, we see in the practice of justice people do not at all proceed so resolutely; to the contrary, everything is done to avoid this explicit 'eye for an eye' and the killing after these crimes. On the other hand *great* emphasis is laid on the manipulation of witnesses necessary to ascertain the truth about a crime. For these witnesses must observe, see, hear things. Without ascertainment of the truth on the part of witnesses no case can even be brought before the court.

Now we see that it falls to the court to try to prove that the witnesses were not in a position to observe things well. It is just as if they are out to show that human perception is fallacious, that appearances are deceptive. They are out to detect contrariety in the witnesses, indistinctnesses in their observations, inaccuracies in their warnings to the offender, which warnings – containing the statement that offender will be accused and also the punishment awaiting him – are the condition for their ability to bear witness. In the majority of cases such a complexity of conditions must end in proving that the witnesses have failed. That, in fact, human observation is not complete and dependable enough for a pronouncement of sentence. And that is the point.

Now supposing for the sake of argument, the witnesses have come up to all the requirements and that the offender has been proved guilty. Then finally the court has to vote on the statements of the witnesses. If the evidence is indeed incontestable, it implies the court will have to give the verdict 'guilty'. In the case of capital crimes the sentence is not consummated because then the principle holds good that the man who is forsaken by everybody is protected by God.

From all this it appears that they are reluctant to have the definite sentence pronounced by people. They are convinced a guilty man will be found out by God, and that according to the principle of ultimate harmony every deed will meet with its reverse power, its reflection. Man, however, wants to evade a pronouncement based on observation. Man to the contrary is set on proving that this pronouncement is impossible.

Prevention is promoted by the fact of one's getting accused; by the discussion of all the details before the court; by the conviction which, somehow, can be inferred from the evidence.

The aspect of God finding the guilty man and God restoring harmony is a.o. expressed in a characteristic tale in ancient lore, which shows again that judgement, based on man's observation and the combinations built up on it, must necessarily be incomplete.

The story says that Moses one day was resting near a well, behind a bush. He saw a traveller coming up and drinking of the water, losing his purse while he did so. The traveller was not aware of it and went his way. Soon afterwards another traveller arrived, who found the purse and went off. A little later a third traveller arrived, ignorant of what had been enacted previously. In the meantime the first traveller had discovered his loss and hurried back to the well, where found the third man. It was only a short while after the first had lost his purse, and he took it for granted that the man he came upon must have found it. However he denied, and rightly so, any knowledge of the purse. The man who had lost it, got terribly excited, started to fight with the innocent third traveller and killed him, upon which he took to his heels, still without his purse.

Moses, who had observed all this, now turns to God to ask what it all means. He does not understand at all. The first traveller had lost his possessions and now was a homicide as well. The innocent third traveller was killed. And the second had made off with the money he was not entitled to. Moses fails to understand how it can all pass off unpunished. Upon which God reveals the ins and outs. The first traveller had not come honestly by that money, it had originally belonged to the second who found it. And the third deserved death for a terrible crime, at which there had been no witnesses. In this way justice had taken its course after all and harmony had been restored. No human witnesses could have given evidence, since everything had happened in secret. Everything, however, will be put right in its proper time. The guilty man moreover having the opportunity to retrace his steps before God. In that case, too, God knows how to restore the condition of balance, of harmony. These are not human standards. Revenge, in fact, means 're-erection', restoring to balance. And in order to restore *that* balance, one has got to know a good deal more about the causalities of every individual case. And for this one need have other criteria than those known to man.

Thus it is with the principle 'an eye for an eye', etc. Justice and the practice of law rightly take it, on the grounds of tradition, that this implies a complete restoration of balance. But that would imply that the man whose eye will have to be taken away is completely identical to the man whose eye he has taken. Such completely identical people do not exist. People will always show dissimilarity in age, trade, profession, physical or mental disposition, etc. Therefore it is for the courts, by means of these data, to calculate the damage which the ill-treated man has suffered, and which for the offender, when translated into the terms of his life, amounts to missing one eye. What is left 'unavenged', or is eventually 'too much avenged', will be redressed, restored to harmony by God in the course of people's further life.

In every lawsuit there must be two witnesses. Two at least, so that contradiction may arise, because people want to point out, want to create this contrast of the 'two', which determines this world of things perceptible to us.

This is also the reason why 'justice' in the systematism of the Sephiroth is placed on the left side. To us it is obscure. And therefore we also notice that Isaac's judgement was wrong, when he wanted to penetrate to the bottom of things, and that things only came right because Rebekah – the body thus formed by him – all the same passed on to him what was good. The good, which indeed he recognized, when he realized how the whole was built up and what had happened. So man on the left side of the systematism cannot observe correctly and therefore should not base this judgement on that observation. Isaac's eyes were dim (vide Gen. 27), he felt old and he knew not the day of his death. In fact Isaac at that time, according to ancient lore, had reached only two thirds of his years; he had just passed the part of the 'two' and entered upon the part of the 'one' in the (2–1)-development.

But that Isaac felt old and did not know where he was in life was because the 'man' on the left side in reality takes up the place of the woman. It is the place of water, moon, body, development. And man, judging things as a man, is in a weak position there, groping like a blind man; not knowing where he is. He is there at the end of the 'two', the end of 'everything'. The 'one' which comes after this is to him beyond his world which is merely that of the 'two'. That is why he believes that he will die now and he desires to give his blessing before his death. Nevertheless he continues to live, he lives on in the 'one'. In Isaac's life it expresses itself as a life of nearly sixty years yet after this blessing.

But then, how is it that the woman, to the contrary, *does* come to understand the situation and to reject Esau? Should not one expect her to be far more keenly directed towards the forces of development than the man? Was it not the woman in the second tale of creation who went with the serpent and owing to it led man on the way of development? Answering these questions opens the eyes to a new and important principle.

Rebekah in the first place is the wife of Isaac. This puts a stamp on her, it characterizes her. Her actions are determined by the fact that she is bound to the man Isaac. This man Isaac is the man who has lived through the binding of the 'four' to the 'one', who has discerned the other world. It is also the man who is marked with the sign of the covenant with God, which implies that the power of the veiling by matter has decreased in him, a sign which likewise expresses that this man will enter the eighth day of the world, a world in which the forces of development are subservient to the harmony of unity.

So Isaac is a very uncommon man, on that left side. Situations have come to expression in him, which man did not yet show at the creation of the body in the second tale of creation. And that is why his wife, i.e. his body, expresses herself in this third of the four *ele toldoth* differently from the woman, the body, in the second tale of creation. We now see the significance and the purpose of the time-structure in the structure of creation. God's accompanying creation as Lord God, as 10–5–6–5 in time, inspires the structure of creation with life, makes it divine and human, gives it a deeper meaning.

So Rebekah has a husband, possessed of completely different powers and potential from the man who co-operated in giving expression to the arising of duality in creation. It remains ever the same man, for all that; present in essence in the Bible indeed, as it is with God even before creation. Isaac is just as much beyond time as Adam; either of them represents the essence of man. It is merely in the expression in time that Adam is found in a different piece of the line of time from Isaac. That which in time presents itself as development, is a crystallization of that reality, man, who contains within himself every aspect of the *four toldoth,* each aspect giving expression to another part of every individual man himself in his space-time-expression. Thus tradition has it that Isaac was born on New Year's Day, the day on which Adam too was formed.

On the left side of the systematism, man, as we have seen repeatedly, finds expression through the body, through the woman. In this the man is passive. But that which lives in him finds expression in the body. Since Isaac has the binding of the 'four' to the 'one' in himself, since he is essentially prepared not to go the way of development, and since this essence expresses itself in a practice of life which is the crystallization of the essential for the world of the body, i.e. the world of the left side, therefore the body now discerns the danger of the forces of development and rejects the way of Esau and prevents that way from getting the blessing, i.e. its being established as real destination. Because on the eighth day of Isaac's life the covering of matter is removed, weakened, therefore does the body now act in such a sense as to recognize its destination in Jacob, in him who lives in the centre, who is hardly perceptible in this world of the left side, who has not got the notoriety and the emphasis, the pomp and circumstance of things external, of the covering, of Esau.

If man has got that which is set forth in Isaac, he can trust in the behaviour of his body, of his expression in this world of the left side. Then this expression in form will pass on to him what is right, not the tree of the knowledge any longer, not Esau any more, but now the tree of life, Jacob.

This man on the left discovers in his life that he cannot perceive, that he is blind on that point, that he merely sees the exterior, the covering and is disposed to judge accordingly. The essential, the nucleus eludes him in the observation. That is why he turns away from this observation. To his horror he finds that his judgement based on that observation is altogether false. Isaac perceives that he would have blessed Esau, if his wife, his own body, had not made it impossible for him. And he realizes his body does so because in himself the 'four' has been bound unto 'one' and in himself the power of the covering has weakened.

It is not as if one could look upon Isaac as a passive figure, lacking in grit. It only means that man on the left side of the systematism expresses himself as body; that the essential does not perceptibly penetrate into it; that it is emphatically the female side which is active, which appeals to us. But, just as the body acts only in consequence of the soul's attitude, so also does Rebekah act thus, because she is Isaac's wife. The imperceptible, yet recorded forces, active in Isaac, determine the action on the part of Rebekah. This action we see, the forces active in Isaac we know from the story of Isaac, the story of the 'Akeda' and of the covenant with God on the eighth day.

We see from that story that the soul cannot act here except through the body. And that this body acts on account of specific qualities of the soul. On the left side of systematism the soul cannot but express itself in this way. It is covered up, it can merely grope about in this world. It is the world of night, of the moon, of the body, of the woman. The soul cannot but acknowledge that it errs, that it is blind, that there is a thick covering.

Circumstances are black as death, inscrutable. That is why man is placed on this left side, that, recognizing how his observations are inadequate to form a sound judgement, he may gain confidence in other criteria, sensing that there is guidance, even though he cannot assess it with what he observes and draws conclusions from.

Under the circumstances he will long for the end of the night enveloping him, he will long for another world. Besides, he will recognize that the body's acting is of uncommon significance. That the body acts according to the attitude of the soul, and, if that is right, the actions of man in this world will prevent him from eating of the tree of knowledge and will open the way to him to the tree of life. Thus is the situation of the man on the left side, also in this, our world.

21
Life Expresses Itself as Subtlety Facing Subtlety

Isaac desired to bless this world, which had called forth that great multiplicity, the splendour of the phenomena on earth. He could not but bless it, for through its appearance it gave purpose to creation. Now that it was there, man could reunite it with the source of origin, could himself go the way to reunion and take with him what had thus far come to unfoldment in creation.

And he calls Esau, in who this unfoldment had so convincingly come to expression and begs him to go out into the field and catch the running deer. In our terminology of 'hunter' and 'deer' it means that he begged him to catch the 'four' which ever runs farther and farther and wants to run off again. For it is this 'four' which, when caught and bound, gives that delicious taste. This 'four' of the world, of life, prepared and bound by man; this four, having ceased to move, and now taken up by man, is the goal of life. One has caught the moving 'four' and through oneself restored it to God. That which is ever running away, ever developing itself, now is caught in its extreme and brought back.

Esau immediately sets out to catch the deer. Ancient lore, as based on this structure of the Bible and of creation, says that Esau soon perceived the animal he meant to catch. But the deer all the time suffered him to come up quite close, but at the moment he was going to catch it or shoot it, it made off and the emotion of the hunt started anew. Thus the animal lured Esau on across the field in a mighty, exciting chase.

Meanwhile Rebekah, Isaac's wife, his phenomenal form in this world, his bodily expression, in a way, made her appearance. Through the very binding Isaac had been subjected to, she knew that Esau hurrying after the deer was again the serpent, carried away by the hunt, intoxicated with the passion for things material. She knew that this force of development had come into the world together with that quiet Jacob, who had come stealing in like a thief in the night, thus expressing how the soul, too, had smuggled itself into that big, boastful body at creation. And she was aware that man would only get the blessing for the sake of that imperceptible divine essence within.

Therefore in Rebekah was now repeated what had already happened to man at creation. At creation, in the world of the left side, at his appearance here in the second tale of creation, man had also come as a body, as something created out of dust, of that which possessed the forces of development. But hidden within this man, who was really nothing but the material covering, was that principal thing, that which endowed him with life as a human being, that which God had informed the body with, had breathed into it, the divine breath, the 'neshamah'.

Similarly did Rebekah again clothe the man, who made his appearance as Jacob, in the covering of the earth, the garment of development, with the scent of growth. Hidden under the garment was the true man. Only in this way could the man get the blessing in this world. Thus had God established him in this world. Also in that garment of the earth, that he might with it acquire the quality of living perceptibility in this world of the left side. It would be the mask, the animal-mask in which man was to be 'infiltrated' into this world, in order to be able to make his appearance here. In this world of the uttermost, the extreme development. And again did man come here to bring the world back from this extreme point to its creator, its fountain-head. And that is man's phenomenal form here.

Thus tradition has it that the prophet Elijah, the announcer, the messenger of the Messiah, ever appears on earth in the garb of an ordinary man in any definite period of time; not garbed conspicuously, imposingly. For like the prophet Elijah, man is this messenger of the Messiah, the Saviour. Already at his creation he was endowed with this appearance which can express itself at any time as that of the inconspicuous man, hiding within himself, however, the secret of that which is under that garment, under that mask. Just as the prophet Elijah is ever recognized as such, afterwards, when he is gone.

Thus Jacob also comes dressed in that garment of the earth, in that which constitutes the reality of Esau. Jacob *cannot* appear as he is in reality. Man must come covered by the body into this world of the left side, because the body has sense here; it expresses the fact that man shall gather in everything pertaining to the world, to restore it to the source of origin. It is his battledress here.

Rebekah tells him to fetch two kids of the goats. As we have already seen, the kid of the goat is the 'tenth' animal; the animal with which the cycle of the 'ten' is closed. The animal which in the place of the 'sacrificial animals' expresses the extreme development.

That is the reason why the kids of the goats play such an important part in the very important tenth day of the seventh month, the so-called Day of Atonement, of the biblical era. Then they make their appearance under the name of 'Seir', the word for kid of the goat which we discussed in connection with the value of 580. On the tenth day, too, a world is rounded off. Man leaves an old world to enter a new one. It is also the day when in the fiftieth year everything returns to its source of origin (Lev. 16 and 25). Ever does this animal of the tenth zodiacal constellation come into prominence, when the purpose of duality has to be accounted for, atoned for, in a way. It is an answer to the why and wherefore.

With this blessing from Isaac a development is also closed off, an old world ends and a new one begins. In these kids of the goats, the tenth animal, the development of the 'four' is indeed closed off. They need not be 'caught', 'hunted'. They are there ready to be caught by him who knows.

Jacob then receives the blessing, clad in the garment of the body; in the body at its pinnacle of development. And Isaac now senses that duality. For he can feel the hands of Esau, the outward appearance, yet, as he says himself, he hears the voice of Jacob speaking from that form. He hears that which utters the words, which is human.

That voice, mark you, says that what has come to receive the blessing, is the first-born, Esau. The voice of the man that has stolen in, calls itself Esau, after its covering, its garb, its mask. And it is to this duality, the bodily covering together with the man smuggled into it, that Isaac gives his blessing.

Man in this world of the left side can therefore only receive the blessing, if he is accompanied by the forces of development of the body, however alien they maybe to him. He must bring them along. That is how man was created here; he received the body together with the forces of development. He would have to wrestle with them; they would assault him; he would have to flee from them; he would have to leave the world to them for the period of the development, the period we learned to know as expressed in the measure of 58. But ultimately he would conquer them; in the end he would stop development, and he would bring this body, liberated from these forces, along with him to the source of origin, on his way to reunion.

We cannot here enter upon the subject of the blessing from Isaac. Let me only point out that it also has a very uncommon structure, naturally. It consists of 26 words, the number of the name 'Lord', and it is built up of 111 letters, i.e. 111 number-components. And 111 is the number of the word 'aleph', of the 'one', as we have seen. So this blessing establishes something most important, as its structure already shows.

Thus, for instance, the priestly blessing (Numbers 6:24–26) also has a certain structure, namely in the three subsequent stages, respectively 3,5 and 7 words and respectively 15, 20 and 25 letters. It at once reveals a definite intention in the remarkable form of the sequences. The complete priestly blessing besides contains 15 words and 60 letters. Again we see the (1–4)-structure, in which the 'four' of the 60 letters in its development is bound to the 'one' of the 15 words.

All the time during Jacob's preparation for the blessing and during the receiving of the blessing, Esau is passionately chasing the animal which all the time suffers itself almost to be caught, but not quite. But at the very moment Jacob has received the blessing, according to ancient lore, the hunted animal stops in its course and simply suffers itself to be caught. For then, indeed, time has come to an end. By then everything has already enacted itself in a world utterly different from Esau's, in a world within a nucleus; then in that world the 'tenth' animal, the kid of the goat, has been fetched and the blessing has been given and received through it.

It is again the expression of what we discussed in the story of Ham, viz. the essence of servitude. The servant is the indirect one, the dependant. That Esau should catch the animal is not in consequence of the result of his cunningly and well-devised hunt, maybe much admired by himself. That is merely *his* causal reasoning. He is not aware of the powers at work elsewhere, which made him reach his aim at that moment, in his sphere, far removed from the pivot. In the action, without at first realizing it, he was the servant, dependent on a happening elsewhere, which determined everything as regards his developments.

When Esau comes to Isaac with the deer he has caught and prepares it for him, he hears that Jacob has forestalled him. And when Isaac detects this confusion (Gen. 27:33) he 'trembles very exceedingly', he realizes that his opinion of Esau had not penetrated to the very depth of his being; that somebody else had guided his actions and he emphatically leaves the blessing with Jacob. He then pronounces the 'yea, and he shall be blessed'.

And he can only confirm that Esau shall be his brother's servant, since the facts had confirmed that Esau had all the time been dependent on Jacob, been Jacob's servant. The blessing to Esau is characterized by the 'And by thy sword shalt thou live'. The sword which divides everything; brings things to multiplicity; which ever makes its appearance when there are contradictions and contrasts; becomes the characteristic for the forces of material development. They will remain servants, dependent, as long as Jacob indeed represents the place of the nucleus, of the essence. Should Jacob ever relinquish that place then the forces of development will resume their free course. And only at the end, when everything has returned to the fountainhead of origin, will this duality, this opposition between Jacob and Esau cease to be.

So what has happened here is equivalent to subordinating the forces of material development to the essence of man. As long as man obeys his destiny, these forces of development shall not take him off his guard. This surprise-attack achieved by the serpent, when the world was still to develop on its way of duality, now found its counterpart. The world is returning to the source of origin and the forces of development are now subject to man. The woman who, as body, had first passed on the forces of development to man, now to the contrary cuts them off and thus subjects them to man.

Isaac was frightened at his original judgement. He sees that in this world on the left side, appearances are deceptive indeed. That all judgement based on what appears before us in this world, in reality hides the great danger of error within itself. Hence the great caution of justice and the endeavour to refute evidence. For all 'seeing' in this world, all observing, is like Isaac's. It is dim, and it cannot see the substance. And just as Isaac accepted the unpleasant surprise of the facts which yet put everything right, so does justice, placed on the left side, follow in the track of this 'coming right through God's intervention'.

Isaac did not force things either, when he realized that Jacob had got the blessing through subtlety. He recognized the subtlety as a correction of his feeble observation of the substance of things. He realized that in his case the same thing had happened which God had done when He created man; God, too, had hidden the man in an animal body. And Isaac had judged after the outward appearances of the events, after that which had enacted itself perceptibly, measurably.

The purpose of Esua's coming was like the purpose of the creation of the forces of development of matter. At the point of their furthest development they curve back, completely dependent on man who is now their lord. It is actually their purpose now to serve man, to be subservient to man. For man will restore them to their origin, and man will then do that for which creation was made.

Every time, however, development observes that its forces have been curbed, since *this* is not the purpose of the world, that the world has been created for different reasons, there is the tragedy of that ending. Whoever has attached himself to those forces, similarly experiences this tragedy. He will most sentimentally deplore this ending and hate Jacob. It is because like Cain he goes the way towards the goal as a 'fugitive and a vagabond', never knowing what the goal is.

Esau is the expression of these forces of material development. The development which ever creates new situations in which the proportions and relationships change. That is, for instance, why we see Esau's wives changing their places and names. Please compare these names in Gen. 26:34–35; Gen. 28:9; and Gen. 36:2–5. This hopeless confusion of names is not the result of inaccuracies committed by primitive scribes – in that case they might have been corrected – neither is it in consequence of the various sources from which they have been drawn; it simply is a correct indication how the changes take place in course of time in that which is development. Just as the number of data on the generations of Esau in Gen. 36 are nothing but indications of the standards by which to measure these forces of development.

Jacob is 'a plain man, dwelling in tents' (Gen. 25:27). In contrast with Esau, Jacob is not variable, dynamic, or expansive. To him this world is a life he passes through. He recognizes reality, does not close himself off to it by rushing into a whirl of pretence and make-believe. That is why he lives in 'tents'.

Not because those biblical Patriarchs lived like nomads, unaccustomed to civilized houses, like the city-dwellers of the generation of Cain, or those of the generations of the tower-builders, of the 'Haflaga'.

In expressing a reality in its phenomenal form, implying living in tents, the Bible means that this tent-dweller is loosely attached to this world, he knows he cannot yet take root here. For this is not the ultimate world yet.

That was why even the house of God was a 'tent' up to and including the days of David, the seventh in the series of generations after those 26 first root-generations. But with Solomon, the eighth generation, there *is* a house. For *then* it is the ultimate world, then reunion here is become a fact.

That is why the dwelling of the Patriarchs is ever expressed in the word 'gur', which means living like a stranger on this earth. Not until reunion has taken place will man take possession of this earth. For that reason has the Bible expressed the life of man in a form corresponding with the nomad living in tents and ever migrating. And therefore it has expressed the man clinging to this world with its force of development as the city-dweller, lodged not in the tent which can he quickly rolled up and pitched elsewhere, but in the house with its foundations in this earth.

Hence the elaborate statements how the 'tabernacle' for the house of God in this world is constructed, how it is put up and how its parts are taken down again. For the way through this world of duality, of the opposites, to unity, to harmony, is like the journey across the desert which similarly was a moving away from the duality in Egypt to the unity in Canaan. And this journey was characterized by ever putting up and taking down that 'tabernacle' which served as nucleus for the life of man. For everything was grouped into the 'four' groups around this tent. Whoever goes this way to reunion, similarly has this constant change of location. And he knows too that it is God whoever gives the signal for removing, that it is not the development one has planned for oneself or has arranged for oneself.

Thus Jacob is also a tent-dweller who has not yet taken root in this world which is moving towards reunion.

It is in this sense that Esau's selling his birthright to Jacob is enacted, before Jacob received the blessing for which Esau had gone hunting (Gen. 25:29–34). At first sight it is a rather strange story; Esau is tired, he sees that Jacob is preparing a meal; he is eager to have it, and then exchanges his birthright for this food. A rather sinister game with a right evidently considered important as stake.

Here again the old story in tradition sheds light on the meaning of this happening. The dish Jacob was preparing was the so-called funeral meal for the passing away of Abraham. Jacob and Esau were 15 at the time.

According to ancient lore, God took Abraham away from this world before his time, lest he should see the forces of earthly development as they were just then revealing in Esau. Now when Esau came in from the field and asked Jacob what this food was meant for, and heard the reason, he said: 'If a man like Abraham must die, and before his time at that, I do not believe in the justice of God.' It did not tally with his criteria of justice and so he rejected God's justice. Not even remotely guessing that God had taken away Abraham on purpose, that he might behold the incipient development of Esau's hard, earthly way, not from the limited standpoint here, but from another world, all-embracing. With his characteristic cry of the man caught up by the forces of development, 'If God allows this, then God does not exist,' Esau chose the funeral meal. That which was meant for mourning for somebody one had loved and respected on earth, in connection with people's passing away to other worlds, was harsh and unjust, full of arbitrariness.

And therefore he refused to accept the birthright, which demanded of the first-born the 'korban', bringing this life nearer to God. He preferred to live his life to its very end, since he was 'going to die anyway'. He preferred the intoxication of this life of pretence, fancying that one was alive and could take everything into one's own hands, to an approach to a God who had standards different from those one had found for oneself observed in the field, on earth. Even then Esau had given evidence of overflowing with the force of material development. And with it he had excluded himself from the blessing which is exactly meant for the human man, for man deriving life from the divine soul.

Tragic is Esau's desire for a blessing, after he had just voted for the forces of the earth. Ever again do we see mankind on the one hand voting for earthly development, the pride of new inventions, of new conquests in the material domination of the earth, and on the other hand never understanding how it is that the blessing proves to recede ever further and further. One cannot understand how it is that this technical and scientific progress as it is called, goes hand in hand with ever greater discontent and anxiety, with a levelling down of ever more human values, which are then substituted by values of momentary utility, values which, if required, can be modified again. It is the tragedy of man who in the passage of time, frightened as he is at the uncomprehended 'I shall die, anyway', takes the way of Esau, who wanted to measure God's justice with his own standards and refused to see that God Himself gave the criteria thereof.

Jacob, who 'stays at home' and 'lives in tents', knows these standards. As tradition expresses it, 'he learned God's Word at home, and the ways of God with this world, therefrom.' Only he that orders his life accordingly, receives the blessing. He that in this world has scientific ambitions, wants to conquer the earth or space, most assuredly does not get the blessing, as it is set forth in this story of Jacob and Esau.

In accordance with this principle, Jacob, in a further stage, gives Esau this world of matter, gives him (Gen. 32 and 33) the 580 animals, the life of development in this world, when Esau comes 'to meet him, and four hundred men with him.' And he himself goes, 'according as the cattle that goes and the children be able to endure, rejecting going together with Esau. Until he shall meet Esau again in Seir.'

As we saw, the sum-total of Seir is also 580. There, in the end, will be a different confrontation between Jacob and Esau. Ancient lore points out that this will be, as Obadiah 1:21 says, at the end of time. The time of material development, as we saw, is expressed in the Bible with this standard of 58. This time has also been allotted to the development of Esau; then, however, Jacob arrives in Seir and there is an end to the development of material forces.

I cannot expatiate on the details of Jacob's encounter with Esau at the brook Jabbok, and of Jacob's wrestling, within the scope of this book. A few aspects of them will be elucidated in the next chapter.

22
The Reversal

That Jacob became the first-born, to the Bible is not merely a question of eventually giving Jacob more rights of heirship, etc. For that matter, whatever happened after the so-called 'buying' of the birthright, and later on after his receiving Isaac's blessing, does not exactly point to Jacob's obtaining more earthly riches. He had to make his escape, serve Laban, go to Egypt afterwards, while Esau lived quietly as a powerful and well-to-do earthly lord.

The birthright, however, has quite a different meaning for our story and that is why the Bible puts such emphasis on all that happens between Jacob and Esau.

Until the birth of Esau it ever was the physical which appeared first and set the tone. Just as in the second tale of creation the emphasis is also on the physical, on the woman, on the left side of systematism.

With Jacob's desire, however, for obtaining the birthright, is expressed the desire of the soul, of the divine, to make its appearance in this world as something manifest, as the stronger one, as ruling power. It is the desire with which creation has been inspired, to have the earthly forces, which are first expanded, gathered together and then returned to their source of origin. To make this way perceptible, to give prominence to the divine, that is what was given to man as his destination. The expansion of creation, its full unfolding takes place in the second tale of creation, the story of the left side, where everything acquires form and makes its appearance here. That is what the body gets its birthright for, the soul being enshrined in it as an invisible hidden something. Action there goes forth from the woman, the body, and from the forces of development of matter, from the serpent.

Through Abel, who is killed, eliminated; through Noah who arrives safely in a following world; through Shem who averts his face from the path of matter; and then through Abraham and Isaac, the power of the soul is coming into prominence now more and more. The body is already 'circumcised', restrained, the matriarchs resolutely reject the way of the serpent, of material development. And then Jacob comes and fights for the birthright, i. e. the right, even in this world of the left side, the world of phenomena, to have the soul as pre-eminent, with the body annexed to it, forming a unity, and the forces of material development, of the serpent, now distinctly subservient. The body, as Sarah and Rebekah showed in this story, has now identified itself with the duty of the man, of the divine soul, and now forms a unity with the man.

That Jacob should obtain the birthright therefore means that henceforward in the world of the left side the soul appears as the first and the body as the second, the body now being the beloved of the soul, and not the power which binds the soul and makes it subservient to the forces of material development. For indeed with Jacob begins the fourth, the last of the *ele toldoth;* does the second 'five' appear which is now attached to the first 'five' by the 'six' of the *toldoth* of Shem. Now comes the completion, the complete fulfilment of the 10–5–6–5.

Hence in Jacob the emphasis on wrestling for the birthright. Which is now to appear pre-eminent in the world and he the lord?

Jacob comes out conqueror in the struggle. It is the opposite to the situation in the beginning, in Paradise, where the serpent won the battle.

When Jacob at the ford Jabbok (Gen. 32 and 33) is going to encounter Esau anew, he wrestles in the night with a 'man'; and in the end he comes forth from the struggle with a new name, Israel.

This wrestling is a wrestling for the sake of matter. The name of the ford, of the brook, is Jabbok, jot-beth-kof, 10–2–100; and the word for matter 'abbok', aleph-beth-kof, 1–2–100, points in that direction. And the word used for 'wrestle' has the same root; the word 'wrestled' is there 'je-abek', jot-aleph-beth-kof, 10–1–2–100, in which the initial 'jot' denotes the verbal form '*he* wrestled'. Ancient lore says that in this wrestling the dust whirled aloft unto heaven. Hence the name of the brook he forded – the border of a new world which is ever formed by that concentration of 'water', as also of 'time' – implies what will happen in that world; the wrestling, in fact, for matter; for matter in that enormous, suffocating quantity; matter which will choke men.

According to ancient lore, that 'man' was the 'sar' of Esau, Esau's supramundane lord. One might say: the substance, whose expression on earth was Esau. So *before* Jacob shall encounter Esau on earth, the encounter takes place with the latter's substance.

Without entering into the details of this wrestling, which of course contains a great deal about this encounter between Jacob and the substance of Esau, let me point here at the change of the name of Jacob. The name Jacob is spelt 10–70–100–2, with a sum-total of the letters of 182. The new name Israelis spelt 10–300–200–1–30, so 541 in all.

To the old name therefore has been added 541–182 = 359. And this 359 is the number we know already for the word 'Satan'. So the wrestling with the 'lord' of Esau ended in Jacob's taking up into himself that which was Esau's substance, and as such Jacob's opposite; just as in the ultimate harmony both good and bad, life and death, day and night, high and low, will exist in unity, as a harmonic whole. Through this taking up of the substance of that which means 'obstacle', which is the 'interferer', the 'Satan', in a new name, in a new destiny, Esau himself is paralysed. Therefore this 'man' is powerless to give his name after the struggle, and therefore Esau is powerless in the ensuing encounter with Jacob. Originally he had meant to kill him and therefore he had advanced on him with the '400', but now he could merely embrace him.

This word 'and he embraced him' (Gen. 33:4) is specially marked in the text with a dot over each of the letters. Ancient lore says that it is presented like this in the original text, because in reality Esau meant to bite him, just as the serpent bites man, but that he had been rendered powerless by the previous meeting of his substance with Jacob and that this biting now expressed itself as an embrace, in spite of himself. The Hebrew word for embracing and that for biting differ only in one letter, hence in the special punctuation of the word it is expressed that the utterance of embracing ensued from the substance biting, so that a change had taken place.

And now the 400 men of Esau, according to tradition, left him and Esau returned to Seir by himself. Powerless, the forces of development had lost the battle, the course of the world was curving back.

Tradition also sets forth how it was that Jacob had this encounter with the 'lord' of Esau. After Jacob had sent everything he possessed over the brook, he remembered he had left behind a small jug, chipped here and there. He then returned by himself to fetch it. And when he was alone on the other side, there suddenly was this 'man' advancing upon him.

This tradition has called forth a great many explanations. It means among other things that the interest, the affection one has for the inconspicuous as well, for things of practically no importance puts man in this special position. A man appreciates these trifles, because they also have their place, because essentially the significance does not depend on the size of the material phenomenon. One knows that everything has its place in the harmony of the whole. There is nothing important nor unimportant. Everything has its place in the great harmony.

It is not the man of flowery speech that has this decisive encounter with the substance of the forces of development of matter; it is not the man of learned formulae, of analyses, but to the contrary the man with an understanding of things made, things created, even though small and chipped. It is regarded as running parallel to God's sympathy even with the very smallest things in life, with the so-called inconspicuous, the cast-off, just as this whole world as compared with the immensity of all worlds and all lives is like a chipped jug. Owing to this return and consequently being alone, one will get to the plane where things are not in their phenomenal form, but where one meets the substance of things; one is as if in a different world. And then there is the dialogue with the substance. As the 'man' said to Jacob after the wrestling, 'thou hast wrestled with gods and with men.' In turning even to the minutest thing, Jacob arrived at a level where is the substance of things, and where he also came to a dialogue with the force of material development. The translation sometimes refers to a fight with 'God and with men' (Gen. 32:28). According to ancient lore it proves to have been the wrestling with an angel or a 'sar'. The meaning of the story is not that Jacob wrestled with God. When shortly afterwards he meets Esau (Gen. 33:10) Jacob intimates to him that he has seen him 'as though he had seen the face of God', and this is a reference to the previous nocturnal struggle Jacob had with the substance of Esau, which had appeared before him as a god. The word, too, which the Bible uses here for 'wrestled' is not the ordinary word (Gen. 32:28) but the word which expresses a struggle on a higher plane, which is on the level of the 'sar', of the lord. Hence a level where is found the substance of things and they are therefore called 'the gods'. Through his mode of living, as expressed in his care for the small jug which had been left behind, Jacob as a man now found himself in the world where the substance of things finds its expression. And in this struggle now consummated, Jacob confirmed that he could restrain the forces of development even without having to steal into Esau's skin. Now that he was in the plane of the essence of things, Jacob could show himself just as he was, for this was his real world, the world of his soul. It is only when this soul has to express itself in the world of matter that it has to clothe itself in matter, that it has to penetrate deeply and follow difficult paths. In wrestling, however, with the 'sar' of Esau, Jacob faced him squarely and in that struggle and with the new name he was now given, he confirmed the birthright of the soul down here in this world as well, the birthright which seemed to have been obtained down here by tricks and devices because down here the soul has no other possibility of expression except through the body which is subjected to development and growth.

Jacob's birthright effects a complete change in the image of the world. Henceforward the soul is the first-born; it is the soul which ranks first and the body which is to come now is the body that is attached to the soul. The condition of the tree of life obtains, the condition of the 'tree that is fruit and makes fruit'. The part 'which is fruit' now is the soul, and the part attached to it 'which makes fruit' is the body.

Jacob is also called 'whole', 'complete', because in him is again expressed complete harmony. That is why the Bible states that all the sons of Jacob were good. They were different, but together they formed the good all the same. There was not that deviation, as it existed in all the other figures from Cain and Ham to Esau, with the exception of the Patriarchs.

23
The Colours of Time

Now Jacob wanted Rachel for his wife, but Laban the father of Rachel and Leah, first gave him Leah, so he deceived him, and only later on gave him Rachel as well. Laban takes a very special position in the whole story. For indeed he brought duality to Jacob in the form of the two wives. This duality was continued in the children of the two mothers and finally led to the brothers' selling Joseph. And it is this duality which, after Solomon, caused the realm to be split up into two parts. We shall find, however, that this duality, purposely given by Laban to Jacob, leads to reunion among the children of Jacob, for whom the duality made by Laban was really meant to be a new endeavour to rouse to life the material forces of development. The name Laban, 30–2–50, is as it were the masculine form of the 'moon', lebanah, 30–2–50–5, which, as discussed before, had brought duality to the world at creation. This force of duality, as law of creation, comes to expression everywhere. For it is ever the purpose of life to join duality into 'one'. Laban's action in smuggling in the 'two', when Jacob had counted on 'one wife', therefore is that which is ever introduced into life and presents itself to man, that it may be restored through him to the origin in the 'one'.

Thus there now come sons of Leah and her handmaid, as also sons of Rachel and her handmaid. The children of the handmaid are to be considered as children who come 'indirectly' from the mothers, hence connected by a link. The fifth, sixth, seventh and eighth sons are of such an indirect character. The first four are Leah's, and of the latter four two are Leah's and two of Rachel. I merely mention it, but cannot enter more deeply into it here.

Leah has six sons, before Rachel has her first son, Joseph. So he is the seventh of the sons, born directly from Leah and Rachel. At the birth of Benjamin, Rachel's second son and the eighth of the 'direct' children Rachel dies. On the way to Ephrath, which is Bethlehem (Gen. 35:16–20). Again the eighth coming quite close to Bethlehem, which, as we saw, is 'the house of bread', with the sum-total of the border between the seventh and the eighth (the 490).

Now Jacob loved Joseph very dearly. It is like the love of God for the seventh day. And it was like a new world coming. After the ten children of Leah, and Bilhah and Zilpah, there came as the first in a new line, from the specially beloved wife, from Rachel, this child, so long waited for.

Now that Jacob had become the first-born, the same principle obtained in his children that the soul appeared in the first phase and afterwards the body.

But this time a body, pertaining to the tree of life, a body bound up with the soul, into a harmonious whole. It was for this child that Jacob had been waiting, for this new body, which was to show all the characteristics of earthly life yet at the same time completely united with the soul. Therefore there was that strong bond between Jacob and Joseph.

Jacob made a 'coat of many colours' for Joseph (Gen. 37:3). This coat of many colours in Hebrew is called 'ketoneth passim', spelt 20–400–50–400 and 80–60–10–40. Literally it means 'many-coloured' coat or shirt. In tradition, too, it plays a great part.

For it is not only a beautifully coloured and costly garment. That the brothers were jealous of it, is quite possible, human too, but we should realize that the Bible desires to express more than this fact of a rather exaggerated preference of one child to the others.

Ancient lore says that this shirt was made of various pieces sewn together, every piece having a different colour. Now, if we remember that Joseph is the *seventh* son of the two wives together, the son expected so eagerly, the human phenomenon which had been waited for so long, in the same way as God had finished everything in creation when finally He accomplished the objective, the purpose of creation, in making man, then this coat of many colours, described to the minutest detail, must play an important part.

Why, this 'ketoneth passim' is something very special, indeed. It is like this world which was given to man, as it is also expressed in the Bible. The diverse lives and the diverse worlds in which the lives of man are enacted, are given as one whole, joined together. They are distinguished from each other as various pieces of cloth with various colours. But as a covering, as phenomenal form of man, they form the one whole. And therefore the 'coat of many colours' is a gorgeous garment, something very uncommon.

Thus the Bible, too, is one whole. It gives expression in the matter of this world to the various lives in the various worlds. The parts are joined together, the various pieces in their various colours have been sewn together. They are the pieces, a few of which we have been considering cursorily in our story, such as the four 'ele toldoth', the stories of Paradise, of Cain and Abel, of the Great Flood, etc. All the time we have recognized the same structure of the cloth, but every time there was a different colour. Put together they form a gorgeous garment indeed.

It is not as if that coat had just one colour. There is not just this one phenomenal form we know here in this life. This vast entirety has been given as a present to man, to this world with the awareness of other lives and other worlds, which, joined together, form life and the world.

Whoever wants to attribute merely one colour to the coat, proceeds from the assumption that there is continuity in evolution, and looks upon the colour of this life as the only one that counts. But the Bible to the contrary speaks of repeated discontinuity, of ever varying standards. One cannot go on reckoning in terms of grey, when one is moving about in tints of red and passing on to yellow or blue. The reckonings in years do not tally, there is a change of criteria, briefly, we have to adopt another method. But indeed one can understand the whole, if one knows the structure of the material and the significance and the interrelationship of the various colours. Therefore the study should have a completely different orientation.

This break of the continuity is similarly found where Jacob wants to separate his flocks from those of Laban in Gen. 30:25–43. There Jacob, too, takes the beasts with a discontinuous skin, whereas Laban keeps the single-coloured ones. These beasts, expression as we have seen, of the human body, similarly formulate the principle of life in various phases, in various worlds.

Joseph's coat of many colours is of such exquisite beauty owing to its very harmony, its brilliant combination of colours. One should know the whole in all its richness of colour to be able to enjoy the beauty of it. If one represents it as something, single-coloured, uniform, vague, it loses its greatest charm. In Joseph's coat of many colours is expressed what God gave to the world and to man: the tree of life, the Bible, knowledge of all life, knowledge concerning the purpose of life having attained the goal and simultaneously working towards that goal.

It was for that man Jacob had been waiting, to give him this present, and again it is analogous to God's waiting for man in creation, to give His word to that man.

To people, accustomed to regard the world as a growing, developing single-coloured mass of things, this variegation may make the story of the Bible rather strange to follow, while the Bible sets forth so emphatically *how* that story should be read. Because people cannot grasp how it is that the (1–4)-structure comes into prominence everywhere, and everywhere in a different manner again. They do not understand why on all sides there is this confrontation between the soul, the body and the material forces of development, why biblical arithmetic of the 40 and 50 and of the 400 and 500 holds good everywhere, and how it is that duality, multiplicity and reunion play a part ever again.

It is like this because every piece of cloth of this multicoloured coat is something complete in itself, a life in a definite world and because in every one of these pieces the same thing happens according to the same principles, only in a different colour. And this colour in its turn indicates, how these encounters are enacted there. All the same there is real life in these colours, because the encounters with ever the same forces are every time enacted in a different way; even so it is one course towards one definite goal.

Just as the sun rises every day to the world, with the same structure, with the same encounters. And yet there is progress in nature through the seasons till the same point has been reached again. But there is a slight difference, for a year has passed meanwhile. That is why in antiquity the snail-shell, the spiral, was used as an image, as an expression of the mode of development.

It was on account of this coat of many colours that brethren envied Joseph. Thus ancient stories set forth how there was a terrific rebellion in the heavens, when man appeared on earth with all his splendour and all his potentialities.

The angels' protest at the creation of man was conducive to the fact that Satan, in the form of a serpent, caused man to fail in that world of splendour and bliss, and that man ultimately found himself in another world with death as companion on the way.

Thus all the brethren, the elder ones, fall on Joseph and take his glory from him, his 'coat of many colours', tear it up and cast Joseph into a pit. And afterwards he is sold into Egypt, the world of duality, as we have learned to know the name for Egypt, 'Mitsraim'.

To Jacob, Joseph is dead now. The blood of the kid of the goats, the tenth animal with the number 17, as we saw, the 3–4–10, smeared on that which caused Joseph to appear in the world (Gen. 37:31–32), on his coat, and Joseph's age, which also was seventeen (Gen. 37:2) show that here is expressed an ending, a death. Even though in the historic tale of Joseph, in which God expressed this happening, this only meant an entering into a new phase of life, just as in the story of the 'binding' of Isaac, it similarly represented a mere entering into a new condition. That is why one should be able to read the Bible beyond the bounds of the historic tale, the tale as it is in its essence, for which the Bible supplies us with the standards of its systematism and its word.

Now Joseph comes into the world of Egypt, Mitsraim. The story shows that there is more to it besides merely settling down in another country. For as a king, which Joseph became later on, he might surely have found out how things were with his father and his brothers in Canaan, a country of geographically not very far away. That they were mutually ignorant about each other, means that even in the image-story the separation is meant as something radical and definite.

Now in Mitsraim he soon rises to a highly esteemed position with his master Potiphar (Gen. 39). But then follows his encounter with Potiphar's wife. She offers herself to him, but Joseph rejects her. He rejects her for the reason that she is not his, but belongs to his master. The Hebrew text in Gen. 39:6 and in Gen. 39:9 uses the identical words where it is stated that Potiphar left everything in Joseph's hands, except the bread Potiphar ate, and where it is stated that Joseph told the woman that everything about the house was left in his hands, except the *wife* of Potiphar.

It is the same situation as that which man faced in Paradise. Everything had been given into his hands by God, with the exception of that one thing, the tree of knowledge. And we have already discussed how in the systematism of the 'fruit', wheat took the same place in the first triad, which the fig tree as tree of knowledge took in the second triad of the fruit. And we have also seen that therefore bread acquired that very special significance, as it is also expressed in the name Bethlehem.

Again the tree of knowledge is offered to man, the only thing he had been denied. Therefore there is first the statement that only the 'bread' was left to the master; a rather difficult image which the translations are generally at a loss about. The bread which was reserved for the master was therefore this tree of knowledge, the 'tree which makes fruit', and here again it is expressed as the wife who desires to leave her husband, who desires many husbands, who seeks multiplicity. It is this woman 'deviating from the right path', in whom is ever expressed the development which is moving away from the origin, and which makes multiplicity. So that is why the same words are used for the bread being reserved for the master and the wife being reserved for the master; in either case it is the force of development which is reserved to God and which man must not abuse for himself, if he is not to undermine the purpose of his existence, if he is not to ruin himself and the world.

Now Joseph does not take that 'bread'. Tradition has it that at the critical moment he saw appearing before himself, the figure of his father, the father who had conquered Esau, the force of development.

And now the Bible tells us what happens to the man who follows this right path, pointed out by God. The force of development rejected by him, now turns against him, crushes him under her lies, just as the wife of Potiphar simply turns matters upside down and pretends it was Joseph who would have taken her, but could not, because she had lifted her voice. She shows his coat as a token he had been with her. The fact that man has a body, is to serve as proof that he is sure to have sinned with it, that he is sure to have availed himself of the development. And yet she calls him the 'Ibri', the man 'from the other side', he that is a stranger in this world where everybody thinks it normal to attach himself to the forces of development.

Again there is a new phase in the life of Joseph. The garment left behind is the biblical expression of his leaving behind a phenomenal form. The force of material development shows the body of man as a token that man was quite eager for further development, but that it had not allowed him to do so. In reality, however, this man had left that world on purpose *not* to have the contact with this force of development. This very relating of everything to herself in its power of growth, this very measuring of everything from the standpoint of her own imagination, turns the lie into truth to her. Just as the names of the wives of Esau kept changing, according to his position in the development; and just as the phenomenal form of man changes in its growth from a child to an old man; and just as points of view are changed; compromises made; so as to 'adapt oneself to the development' as the saying is. Joseph has to leave this world, forsaken and misapprehended. This is the apparent reward here for his rejection of the forces of development.

After his rejection of Potiphar's wife, Joseph now enters into a new world, a world expressed in the story as a prison. The word actually means 'being bound', not free, because of the fact that one is bound. Towards the end of his going about in that world which is like a condition of death as compared with the previous world, he meets with the 'butler' and the 'baker' (Gen. 40).

It is a fascinating story, the whole tale of Joseph, and the quantity of rather strange information not very intelligible as such perhaps make it even more attractive. And in fact this applies to the whole Bible-story, from the beginning to end. For, just because there is such a wonderful structure in the Bible, because in every detail it is imbued with the principles of life and of creation, therefore there is that harmony which also makes the outer image-story so fascinating. The outer story is based on the marvellous systematism and structure of the substance, and whoever merely reads this outer story undergoes without being aware of it the attraction of this very uncommon structure which expresses the purpose of life, the purpose of the world. So much the greater will the influence be when one sees this structure branching out, when one's eyes are opened to this essence in the Bible.

The butler and the baker represent two extremes. The butler is on the side of 'water' and the baker on the side of 'fire'. Just as at creation the systematism gave the left and the right sides, as also the sides of water and of fire. When, towards the end of the period of imprisonment in Egypt, the new life is approaching, Joseph is faced with these two extremes, which have also descended from a former life into this imprisonment, this condition of being bound.

Besides expressing the extremes of right and left, of 'fire' and of 'water', there is the fact that the baker is concerned with the first 'fruit', wheat, and the butler with the third fruit, the vine. Wheat, originally also the finished loaf of bread, is what we have already learned to know as the tree of the knowledge.

Joseph sees that he who offers this tree of the knowledge is rejected, removed from the earth, loses the contact with the earth. And he sees that the world will be based on the way of the slow left side and its connection with the third place, the place where harmony, reunion can be accomplished.

That is why the butler and the baker, on the strength of this ancient knowledge, are present when the meals begin. A meal in essence, is the expression of the happenings in the world, in the atmosphere of daily life, in the atmosphere of home.

At the meal, man in his world, in his home, takes food, unites it with himself and therefore hallows it. For through the purpose and resolution of his life and of his interest man is meant similarly to carry along to the origin all that he takes to himself. The home of man is his 'two'. For the letter 'two', the 'beth' means 'house'. Man in his home is the world and what he performs in his home is decisive for his human presence on this earth. The meal at home, with the family, and all the preparations preceding it, is the only manner in which man in his world can travel the way to the origin. The 'table' is as it were the altar where the purpose of life gets significance.

In this sense did Jacob together with his house, his family, draw up in battle-array against Esau at the final encounter at the ford Jabbok (Gen. 33:13), himself leading the way, followed by four groups of his four wives with their children. It is the 1–4 of Jacob facing the 400 of Esau.

Thus it is at the exodus from Egypt. When God Himself smites the world of Egypt, those that will be emancipated are seated at table, (Exodus 12); they are not even *allowed* to go out. Outside is God's concern, He shall arrange things as ordained. But within, inside the home, it is man's concern; there it is he that completes the journey.

The meal and the conversation round the meal, therefore, are not an utilistic, well-reasoned matter of vitamins and calories, neither is it something gratifying to the tongue and stomach; the meal is an expression of the transition from one world to the other. Performing action here in this world brings with it a simultaneous change in the substance. For just because he is present in both worlds, on either end of the circle which is to close itself, man is of such significance in his actions. The action joins the one extreme, the physical, to the other extreme, the origin.

Now meals start with a special act, with the bread and the wine. The bread is kept covered and people begin with a blessing on the wine. Covering the bread implies that bread, with which the tree of knowledge began, shall not be allowed in visible presence, to play its part in the opening of the meal with the wine. Not until the wine has been taken, will the blessing of the bread be given and will it be uncovered and eaten. Such is also the commencement of the world with the 'wine' and therefore does the butler return to Pharaoh, whereas the baker does not return to the world any more. The duality butler-baker is halved, and the butler appears as the first. The meal, however, shows that in due course the bread is to appear as well, after having remained covered at first. And the meal is completed with the wine *and* the bread.

The transition to the other world, as set forth at the exodus from Egypt, also takes place in that the meal is taken within the house. Whoever takes this meal, comes from Egypt 'alive'. Whoever does not know this meal, finds his death in Egypt through God. Now remaining alive is expressed in the word 'pesach', which means pass over, God passing over the houses where that meal is taken, whereas death is brought by God into the other houses, into the other dualities.

Now the meaning of the duality of the wine and the bread is identical with this passing over, this *pesach*. For the value of the letters of the word bread, *lechem,* is 30–8–40, making 78, and the value of the word for wine, jayin, is 10–10–50, making 70. Taken together as marks of the meal they make 78 + 70 = 148. Now the word pesach has the letter-value of 80–60–8, so similarly 148. With it the meal at home, with the family, is characterized. In regarding that meal as a hallowing of the world, as man's duty, man comes from one world into the other 'alive'. And has part in the exodus with all the miracles which then will come to expression.

So bread and wine have a very special meaning. And the way people partake of them, as tradition has passed it on from antiquity to our times, in first having the wine, keeping the bread covered awhile, afterwards also eating of the bread, similarly has a profound significance.

Thus it is in this world; after one side of duality has made its appearance here, it is in the course of life joined to the other, so that the two will reunite again. This unity had been disturbed, as it is stated that the butler and the baker had sinned. And thus it is restored in bringing the butler, of the left side, into the world as the first. For it is the world of the left side, the world of water, of the second tale of creation. The world is complete at the moment when the bread is introduced into the meal. It is like the 10–5 again, which is formed first, then to be completed with the 6–5.

24
The Disappearance of Life

Joseph again enters into a new life, when Pharaoh has had his dream (Gen. 41). It is the fourth phase in Joseph's life, the first covering his life until he was sold in his seventeenth year, the second in Potiphar's house and the third in prison.

Pharaoh's dreams come after the return of the butler into the world of Egypt. The dreams are enacted at the waters of the river and with them. The contents are sufficiently familiar to us and we can read them again to refresh our memory.

Briefly it comes to a distinct propounding of duality, of the contrast. The seven fat-fleshed kine and the seven good ears of corn are eaten up by the seven lean-fleshed kine and the seven thin ears and nothing is left. According to earthly standards, this does not tally. And Egypt, Mitsraim, is this very world of duality where the goad sticks because of the ever-existing contrast, where there is suffering for the very reason that this duality cannot be resolved. So Pharaoh's dream also reveals the real foundation of Egypt.

I should like to point out here a few relationships on account of the words used. In everything concerning Egypt we see the form '*Phar*' coming forward. Thus the king is called 'Pharaoh'; the first master of Joseph is called Poti-Phar; Joseph's wife is the daughter of a man called Poti-Pherah. And the kine, playing such an important part in Pharaoh's dream, in Hebrew similarly are called *Phar*. This word *Phar* is related to the word for fruit and fruitfulness, we have already come across, namely, 'pri' or 'pru', meaning 'be ye fruitful'. Also in the name of Ephraim Joseph's son born in Egypt, this '*Phar*' forms the root.

As is quite well known, the 'Phar' as cow, is also the second Zodiacal constellation, the image which the systematism is on the left side, facing the Ram on the right. The constellation is Taurus, i.e. the male aspect of the cow. The left side of Egypt, therefore, is also determined by the river which according to the Bible controls everything in Egypt, which also marks the rhythm of the life of that world of Egypt. In that sense the moon, too, plays an important part in the life of Egypt.

Now this 'Phar' expresses fertility in the world of the left, the world of multiplicity. And the king of Egypt – of the world controlled by the presence of a disharmonic duality, a duality causing sorrow and suffering, as we have learned the word Mitsraim means – has 'Phar'aoh as his name, hence a name bearing growth, fruitfulness in itself. And the other names, indicating definite personages in that world of Egypt, also have the 'Phar' as component part. That these names might eventually have a different meaning in Egyptian, is quite inmaterial here. The Bible uses the events enacted in historical Egypt to express what to it is the essence of that world. And in the language of the Bible in which this essence expresses itself, these names have the meaning given above.

So the kine in Pharaoh's dream express what is the essence of the development of Egypt. And this immediately calls up before us the main problem. For what is the meaning of the seven fat-fleshed cows, when there is nothing left after the lean-fleshed ones have consumed them? The lean-fleshed ones do not grow fat on it, which, in earthly terms, would have been only logical.

It is the question of this world, 'what becomes of life?' One lives here, is full of thoughts, intentions, feelings, actions, hope and despair; and all this passes away. On every level it is observed and in each life. As long as one lives, one is full of activity, as if there would never be an end of life, but the moment it passes away there is nothing, absolutely nothing to be perceived of it any more. The other world seems to be just as empty as before, there is only darkness, ugliness, horror.

Egypt cannot bridge this contrast. Whether life and death are concerned, or good and bad, right and wrong, it is the same thing everywhere. And no earthly wisdom, founded on the criteria of the world of duality can give an answer to it.

Until the butler with the slowness of duration, initially forgetful but later on remembering, brings forward the man from the 'other side', the 'Ibri', who belongs to a different kind of world. He is a stranger to Egypt, but perchance capable of giving the answer. Before the butler returned to the world to fill Pharaoh's glass, Joseph had already given evidence of his uncommon knowledge and wisdom, as he said, bestowed on him by God, to see the structure of the world, to analyse what was vaguely outlined like a dream, and to show what was the meaning of it, how it fitted in with the whole.

Thus does Joseph come as 'Ibri', as 'the other', to Pharaoh. And Joseph unites these two worlds, expressed in terms of opposites. He shows that the 'lean years', death, need not be lean at all, if during one's life one brings everything to bear upon that period. People are rather inclined to forget, to live as long as there is life and to suppress the horrible other thing, as it is called.

But the way Joseph points at is exactly the opposite. All during life everything should be brought to bear upon what is coming, upon those lean years, sure to come. Over against the life of the seventh day there is, in the sense of the world of duality, death of this seventh day.

Now we see that Joseph shows a very specific method to stock supplies for the life in the lean world. He proposes to take up a fifth part of the produce in all these plenteous years for the life thereafter, and lay it up somewhere. This one fifth is not so strange to us any longer. For again it is the 'one' opposite the 'four'. It is not the earthly 20%, but it is 'the one' opposite 'multiplicity', it means that we should gather up the 'one' of everything that exists in this life, that which unites it with the source of origin, that which is the vision of the tree of life. And the 'four', multiplicity, we should simply leave to this existence, for it cannot he taken along; it is like a covering which is left. For this 'four' as 'tree that makes fruit' is indeed included in the 'one' which is the tree which at the same time is fruit and makes fruit, the tree with the circumference of the 500, of the 400+100.

It is only the 'Ibri', he that comes from beyond this world, who knows God, it is only he that can point out this connection. No amount of wisdom of this world will ever attain these things, since the world has not got the standards to reach these conclusions. However much one might observe and examine, from this world can never be drawn this (1–4)-conclusion with its full significance for all situations. Only he that knows God's standards, will be able to bring about this connection between life and death, will be able to bring the opposites to harmony.

Thus does Pharaoh appoint Joseph to be the executor of this plan, he comes next to Pharaoh. Pharaoh himself is essentially that which gives life in this world, it is the power of development. Without Pharaoh the world would he without its nucleus without its source of life. Pharaoh, in a way, is also the god of Egypt. With god is meant here the power which from a different plane gives the world its appearance, just at it is. As the force of development, making multiplicity on the left side, on the '*Phar*'-side that is, Pharaoh at the extreme limit comes into conflict with God's purpose to bring the world back again from that extreme point to its origin; he becomes the serpent, the seducer, and is forced back. But that is the story of Exodus, which we have yet to discuss.

So Joseph is in the world which is determined by the principle of Pharaoh, he is the one who will give purpose to life, who is to guide it from the time of plenty to the years of famine, and who will give life to man even in that time of famine, for the very reason that the 'one' had been gathered up in everything during the years of plenty. Joseph gives the world the knowledge of the standards of the 'one'.

That is why he now gets the name of 'Zafnath Paaneah' and Pharaoh gives him to wife 'Asenath, the daughter of Potipherah, priest of On' (Gen. 41:45).

The name Zafnath Paaneah is spelt 90–80–50–400 80–70–50–8; the sum total of the numbers is 620+208=828.

And this 828 we also found as the 'half time' after the 1656–1657–1658, the period in which the 10–5 was to be completed with the 6–5 ending up in the coming into the promised land on the eighth day.

For indeed that is Joseph's mission now. He will bring the world which is in duality, in which the one 'five' is divorced from the other 'five', back to the reunion of these two 'fives'. And this bringing back in the Bible is measured exactly with the 828–829. Again we see that mission, destination and name coincide with the substance of the word; that every letter proves to have its significance.

About his wife, Asenath, tradition has it that she was the identical wife of Potiphar who had at first desired to seduce him. Her desire to have Joseph even at that time, in her way, is explained from the feeling, the intuition she had that the time would come when she should be united with Joseph.

For the forces of development, of material growth, ultimately fall to man too. For the very reason that he rejected them in the world in which he had to follow the way to reunion. For if man goes the way to the 'one' through first rejecting them, he will find the tree of life, the 'tree that is fruit and makes fruit' and therefore also contains the development within itself as component of a wonderful harmony.

25
This World as Centre of the Universe

Then the years of famine come after the plenteous years. And now the source of life is merely that 'one fifth', that 'one' of the (1–4) which Joseph gathered up in this world. One can only continue to live, if one ever gives of what one still possesses and which has come forth from the plenteous years, from the years of development (Gen. 47:13–26), until finally everything is bound and the (1–4) law becomes the principle for all Egypt. Pharaoh in this phase acknowledges the principle of 'reunion', of judging and treating everything therewith, owing to which Joseph is the manifest lord of the world.

From all sides people were coming towards this world, which began as the duality without harmony, the duality which had no solution for the inherent contrast. But this world had now followed the way of the 'Ibri', of the man from another world, possessing the standards of God. The power of development, Pharaoh, had given the leadership of the world into his hands. Thus it grew into a centre of all the worlds; everybody needed this world, this world with the harmonized duality, to live in. For this world, if it eliminates contrast is indeed the world which closes the circle, and then it embraces everything from beginning to end. Just remember the scheme, representing the circle, at either end of which is man in this world of the extreme development, at the source of origin as the 'one' and at the extreme limit of development, as the 'four', opposite the source of origin.

This is what makes this world so important. It is not the importance on account of the enormous bulk of the terrestrial globe, or on account of the keen intellect of the human brain which detected the means to bridge vast distances. For all this is yet inconceivably small compared with that which man will never be able to survey or attain, whatever means he may apply. The importance, however, becomes clear in the place which the Bible and ancient lore bestow on man. According to the standards of the Bible this world is indeed the centre of the universe, owing to its being able to unite the 'one' with the 'four'. The only thing is that it was never meant to form a picture of it in space-time sense. These criteria have practically nothing in common with the real standards which the Bible gives and which can only be understood by one who also takes up his stand on the other side, who also is willing to be the 'Ibri'. And according to the Bible man in this world is indeed the pivot around which everything turns. Through his unification, everything in this world and other worlds is united with the source of origin; through his deviating from this path, everything disperses everywhere and shoots away from the origin. It is only when measured with these standards the world and man can be regarded as the centre of everything.

That is why in the end the sons of Jacob had to travel along this way to acquire the food to keep alive in the years of famine in Egypt, the world of duality, made into 'one' by Joseph.

As stated before, the difference between 'hunger', 'raab' and 'satiety', 'soba' is this very way through the world.

For hunger is 200–70–2, sum-total 272; and satiety, just as the word for 'seven' is 300–2–70, so 372. And traversing the complete 'ten' is this very way through the world, where reign life and death, and where Joseph had taught how man could live in the period of death and how he had to perceive the (1–4) of everything during this life for that purpose and gather up the 'one' of it in behalf of the period after this life. With it would come the harmony between the opposites. A harmony between life and death, but equally between justice and injustice, between good and bad. In perceiving this 1–4 proportion of everything, and gathering up the 'one' of it, people would be able to grasp the purpose of everything, contrast as such would cease to exist and would pass into a harmony which was life-giving and at the same time giving purpose to life.

26

The Game

This is how the brothers of Joseph came to Egypt, because hunger and famine had come over Canaan. With the duality in this world in which man is situated, this world which makes its appearance as Egypt, harmony is broken up in all worlds. Creation embraces all worlds, all conditions. Everywhere do life and death now stand as opposites. Only in Egypt, which is the expression for this world and this life there is the man who has his source of origin elsewhere, who is an 'Ibri'. And it is only this man that is able to bridge the opposites. That is why all words and all lives are dependent on this world and on this man. It is only for this world and this man there is the potentiality of uniting the 1–4.

Now the brethren are unaware they are standing before Joseph and they see in him a foreign ruler, acting with harsh severity. They also feel that they are treated strangely and unfairly on purpose. And they immediately connect their present fate with their conduct in the past towards Joseph. Among each other they give evidence of regretting their deed. But Joseph who knows who they are carries on the game still further. He orders them (Gen. 42–45) to bring Benjamin with them on their second journey, just to see how they will behave, if Benjamin gets into trouble. Joseph goes to great lengths in that game, he has his cup put into Benjamin's sack, so that he may later on accuse him of theft, and when finally, although nobody could understand how this cup had got into Benjamin's sack, Benjamin is threatened to be taken by him as a bondsman, Judah comes forward and stands before Joseph. Judah had been the one to take the lead when Joseph was sold. Judah belongs to the first-born group of 'four' sons of Leah. Of that first group he is the fourth. The principle that now the soul is the first-horn, crystallizes in Judah. The last group, the crystallization of the conception 'body', is formed by Joseph and Benjamin. Judah has taken upon himself to bring Benjamin safely home again. Now that Benjamin is to stay in Egypt as a bondsman, Judah stands up for him and offers himself as a bondsman instead in order to obtain Benjamin's freedom. When things have come to this pass and the brethren have given up all hope, on the one hand unable to understand what it is the harsh foreign ruler desires from them, on the other hand realizing for themselves that on them was wreaked now what they had done unto Joseph, then Joseph stops the game and makes himself known to them. Then the whole thing is turned for the brethren from the deepest sorrow and despair to an entirely unexpected joy. Not only are they all free, but that ruler of Egypt on whom depended everything, whom they had trembled for so much and whom they simply could not make out, this lord now proves to be their own brother, Joseph. The recognition has reversed everything from fear and despair to joy and happiness.

The story in itself is fascinating enough and one draws from it the satisfaction that on the one hand Joseph's brethren were taught a lesson, while on the other hand peace and unity were restored.

But indeed this story of Joseph contains a great deal more. The Bible does not only state the outward facts about one single, favoured family, but the Bible shows how in these happenings God's plan and God's creation come to expression.

And the Bible, in constantly repeating the same principles in different surroundings, urges us to realize how the world is made and what is the point at issue. And let me repeat, the Bible itself supplies the standards by which to fathom these principles and recognize them everywhere in life and subsequently, of course, gauge things by those standards.

From the time Jacob acquired the birthright, that which came earlier became the expression of the soul, also in his children, and that which came later became the physical. Now, at this stage, however, the physical which was completely bound up with the soul. The children of Leah, therefore, who came earlier, bear this same relationship to the children of Rachel. Now Jacob loved Rachel and then Joseph so dearly, because with them there came a bodily appearance, joined in unity with the soul, in true harmony. That was why Jacob gave Joseph that most uncommon 'coat of many colours'. Rachel accepted the Dudaim from Leah, just because as the younger of the two she stood in that particular relationship to Jacob. From her were born the seventh and eighth sons, or in the complete series, the first and second of the new beginning, after the 'ten'.

Now Judah as the earlier one, cannot accept anything appearing as body to be king, however much it may be bound to the soul, to the origin. And he sells that body into Egypt, into the world of duality, of development, of growth, of the 'Thar'. He tears up the coat of many colours, the 'Ketoneth Passim' which Jacob had purposely given to Joseph: evolution come to harmony.

It is man's argumentation that the soul is near the essence of things, that the physical can never have that importance; it is an argumentation which qualifies all pronouncements of the physical in that direction as pride and false ambition. It is likewise the argumentation of all that comes earlier in creation, of the angels, that that man down there on earth, endowed with that body, simply cannot be the purpose of creation.

So it is the opposite argumentation to that given by the doctrine of evolution. It is also the counter force of evolution. Everything in the origin is good, is holy, and all that develops away from it is always obsessed by this development's pride of power, by that material beauty and is merely temptation and is itself ever ready to be seduced.

By means of this argumentation, Joseph is delivered up to the world of duality to serve there as bondsman, is deprived of the uncommon coat which gives expression to everything in the happenings of the physical body. Just as the Bible similarly expresses everything in the images and forms of the body and not in esoteric, undecipherable formulae. That garment is taken from Joseph, for it cannot be that the body should take up this place.

It is the seed Laban had introduced, which shows up in this argumentation, disturbing the harmony of unity in reality laying the foundation for servitude in Egypt.

Thus that body has a development of its own in an entirely different world, in a world about which man, as Judah, has no conception. It enacts itself as if behind an impenetrable wall, in a world one has no contact with.

Until such time as the Judah-man with his honest faith in the power and significance of the soul, is compelled also to descend from his world and from his life and suddenly finds himself facing that world of the body which he does not understand at all, which in his eyes is unfair, unreasonable, which frightens him out of his senses, a real horror, in which at a given moment he feels utterly giving up all his world, abandoning all hope of ever returning there.

The moment comes when none of the criteria man had been so sure of, tally any more, the criteria he had, mark you, built up on the soul, on the world, which, as he thought, was good, since it was the world of the origin. He had come up to all requirements in this life with the body, had paid his due, had kept his word, he knew that everything on his part had been honourable and true, but evidently there was *nothing* after that descent into Egypt, after this life in spite of all one's good deeds, one would be eaten up, consumed by a dark lord who twisted everything in an evil manner.

In such moments, however, such a man is quite aware that he has done something wrong somewhere. He had accorded a subordinate place to the body, which had been with him like a brother, had descended from the same father, but only been begotten from a different mother, to serve the world of duality as a slave. There it could perform its task, join in the service of the 'Phar', the forces of development, mulitplicity, whether he was enjoying it or no. What did it matter to reality, to the world what the body ate, whether it stood up or lay down, whether it knelt down or walked, as long as it had its bread and games, its enjoyment, its vitamins and calories. The body, of course, had a claim to enjoyment, pleasures. What concern was it of the soul; what did it matter to God; the body is merely the body, dust, it is the bearer of the soul here and that is its function. The body should be in Egypt, the soul of course sojourns in Canaan. Similarly do people talk about ordinary things material and in reality they mean to draw a sharp line of demarcation between it and things sublimely spiritual.

At the moment of the confrontation with a completely new world, with the world which also expresses death, the unreasonable ruler of that world inquires after Benjamin. Now Benjamin derives from the same mother as Joseph. And ancient lore shows that Benjamin is really a kind of projection of Joseph in another plane. Thus tradition points out that the names of the ten sons of Benjamin have a connection with the ten determining events in the life of Joseph. Benjamin is like the remaining half of the original, complete body, the last reminders of Rachel left to Jacob. And now he is to renounce this as well.

It is at that juncture the brethren begin to see that injustice was done to Joseph. That this stream of unintelligible things coming over them has somehow to do with the unjust treatment dealt out to Joseph. It is there that especially Judah sees that there must be something about this body he has completely misunderstood, owing to which he had done it a great wrong. And therefore he now makes himself responsible for Benjamin to his father. Now he is convinced that if he brings Benjamin down into Egypt, everything will somehow come right. Then everything will arrange itself according to the standards which are better understood now.

Benjamin therefore is treated by Joseph with great consideration: he gets five portions, whereas the others merely get one. Benjamin is given the complete 1–4, the supermundane, the supertemporal 'five' whereas the others receive the 'one' of the 1–4, the aspect of the soul, but emphatically not the 'four' of the world, *not* the part of the body, the part that '*makes*' fruit, which has to be united to the part that 'is fruit', in order thus to accomplish the full harmony of the tree of life. With Benjamin and the five parts it is therefore the 'tree that which is fruit and makes fruit', the 'one' *and* the 'four'. It is that which later on will find expression in the story yet to be discussed which tells us that Benjamin got the temple within his domain, also with the super-mundane measures, the measures of the 500.

But now that everything seems very good and there seems to be mutual respect and understanding, there is the terrible blow. The ruler of that world now goes to the extreme limit, he wants to keep Benjamin as a bondsman. Bondsman in Egypt. In the same position in which the brethren had purposely put Joseph. Benjamin, as an expression of Joseph in another plane, is now to be subjected to the same lot as Joseph, according to the behest of this ruler they do not know.

Now Judah protests against it; he had rather sacrifice himself than take Benjamin away from Jacob. Everything seemed so logical at first. If Benjamin was there, everything would be right. But now everything has turned worse than ever.

Judah who had made himself responsible for Benjamin to his father; Judah who had taken under his protection this new body in the world of Canaan, to which Jacob felt so attached, in order to shield it from every injustice; this Judah had rather become a slave himself in the world of duality than surrender the body to it. So there is a complete reversal in Judah. He has now realized what the body means and besides he acts in utter loyalty to his father whom he had promised to take care of that very special, new, and dearly beloved body.

After Judah's regret and remorse about the sale of Joseph and his willingness to revert to the right course in desiring to sacrifice himself for Benjamin, Joseph reveals himself. Then there is the denouement. The terror appears to have been caused by a game played by their own brother. They see it is not an inconstant foreign ruler, arbitrarily afflicting them against all justice and logic, but there is the great surprise that everything was a mere game, that the brethren are facing their own brother, an 'Ibri' like themselves, similarly from the other side, *not* belonging to the world of duality.

According to ancient lore, the brethren do not recognize Joseph because of their wrong attitude at the sale of Joseph. Whoever thinks that the body of man is nothing more than a product of high development and that it therefore belongs to that world of development, of the 'Phar' in Egypt, does not realize what are the motive powers in this world of duality. He that in the images and forms and events in time sees nothing but consequences of evolution; he that refuses to see in it the real, will not have the slightest notion of what is going on inside this world of duality. For he has sold Joseph. Not until one has seen that this is an error, not until one has proved *to the contrary* to set great store by it; to be willing to recognize something very substantial in it, something that should be 'one' with us, something divided by Laban in giving two different mothers for it; not until then shall one recognize Joseph in this world of duality. Then one will see that everything can be understood, because everything is arranged by Joseph. The physical which we rejected as vulgarly material and unimportant, proves to be the motive power of everything and we cannot see that it was all just a 'game', until we have recognized Joseph. He that would not retrace his steps, as the brethren did, and especially Judah did, will remain in that condition of horror and fear, at the incomprehensible chaos which the ruler of the world of duality seems to find delight in creating in order to reverse all the values one was familiar with.

The disposition, expressing itself first in Judah to consider Joseph and his dreams of the future merely as a boastful, material urge to development, and to consign him, the body, to Egypt, to live there as a bondsman, as an 'indirect' one, is a tendency ever present in man. Through connecting itself with the forces of development the body has indeed caused death. It is the stage when the body follows the way of the serpent, of continual growth. Yet this stage also forms the basis for human existence which from that far distance can bring forth the deep conviction that in spite of death and decay perceptible everywhere, yet everything is good. But after this, the body has passed through a great many subsequent stages to the desire to be united with the divine soul, to a rejection of the forces so near by, of what we call the 'serpent'; and the body points to this new existence, the other possibility.

And in every man, at every moment, in every now, these various stages of the body are there simultaneously. That which in the story of the Bible expresses itself as a temporal story, is the ever present 10–5, is the given condition, ever present at any moment. The point at issue is that man should be aware of these various stages and this also depends on his attitude towards creation, an attitude which may range between eagerness to unite with the forces of development and the desire to search for the meaning of things in uniting the opposites, the desire to go to the source of origin.

It is also found in the Song of Solomon, where the woman similarly is the expression for the physical in the world, and where she begs not be rejected because previously she had taken another way, because she is 'black'. And in the Song there is also the dialogue which in the end leads to their finding each other again, to the reunion which had always been desired.

The disposition to reject the body as unimportant, to banish its actions to a world with which one has no dealings, refutes however the very purpose of creation. One should rather ask oneself the question how it is that the physical has acquired such an outstanding place in this world, so that we cannot undertake anything without coming across it. One should really ask oneself why Jacob gave Joseph that 'coat of many colours', why the Bible should set forth that mulitplicity of events in the form of the material covering.

Then one would begin to understand that God has not made this body and everything material as a kind of error which one had better forget as quickly as possible, as something merely to be rejected. All this has been made purposely to put the hallmark of God's creation on the extreme limit, in order to recognize God even in this; to see how in every happening, in every act there is this bond with the fountain-head. Man does not sleep merely to rest, but to see that the ebb and flow in the world similarly expresses itself in sleep and awakening. Just as man wakes up every morning, thus there is the principle of creation that all going to sleep, which in this darkness is considered as being dead, is identical with that going to sleep which is followed by awakening, as long as man exists in this phenomenal form of the world now. Even in the eyes' blinking is expressed this coming and going. Breathing, too, is an expression of the 1–2–1 way of creation. Thus in everything man does and in every form in which he is expressed, there is the hallmark of the origin. So man should realize that because of it, all his actions here have a connection with the origin. Joseph is the specially beloved son of Jacob; Joseph who was as the body and therefore, as it is only said about the matriarchs, 'a goodly person and well favoured' (Gen. 39:6).

Therefore it is not a matter of indifference whether a man sits or stands, whether he is immersed in water or no, whether his body comes into touch with certain things or no. Bodily action is not utilistic, for the sake of society or hygiene, it is not symbolic either, to be reminded of things. Physical action is very direct. Physical action, just as Joseph faces his father, is in direct contact with God, it leads man to God or away from Him. Physical action brings this world into contact with God, as was proved by the actions of the matriarchs, who were united with their husbands, as the body with the soul, and who, as body, rejected the way of the serpent, the way of the forces of development.

Ancient lore has it that when Joseph was sold into Egypt, Jacob lost his character of totality. His name Israel, implying union of the opposites, was lost and it did not return to him until he knew that Joseph was still alive. Without this new body, without Joseph, Jacob the father, too, will be broken.

That is why God has made this multiplicity in the phenomena. So that man with the revelation of the purpose of the world in the Bible should know how this multiplicity in the phenomena is connected with the root, with the essence. The Bible sets it forth in its multiplicity of phenomena and in the manner in which it builds them up after the pattern God gave to the world. And with this knowledge man would be able to face the multiplicity of phenomena about him, only now recognizing the pattern God has woven into them, subsequently bringing to expression that structure and that pattern in his actions in the midst of multiplicity of phenomena, thus uniting them with God. In this way does man bring creation around him together with himself to God. It is on these grounds that tradition has also established for the practice of life what significance the actions of men have in daily life. Subject to the condition, of course, that the body with its sensory perception has not united itself with the forces of development. When people do not turn towards the origin any more but measure and judge everything from the standpoint of their idolatry of the forces of development which suggest to them that they can lead the world and model it after their ideas of evolution; to such people, indeed, the performance of those actions of course is senseless. They are the people about whom the prophets so often cried out that God does not desire the flesh or the fat of the offerings, but that God first and foremost desires the hearts of men. For once man does indeed turn his heart to God, he will also begin to see why every action of his in this life is of such importance; then too will he realize the sense of multiplicity around him and see that God arranged it about him with a very special intent. So that man may bring it through himself to God and therewith see reality.

The significance of the physical, hence of Joseph, I should like to illustrate by means of a very charateristic physical service which the Bible takes very seriously, the so-called sacrificial service.

The Bible deals at great length with the kinds of offerings, entering into detail about bringing them, and it likewise expatiates on the arrangement of the tabernacle and the temple. All this is not an expression of a perfectionist priestly scribe. It is the statement of how man's actions are connected with the origin and outline how they attain to the origin. Every detail is indispensable in that story. Building and design of the tabernacle on the level of this world, according to tradition, are identical with the building and design of all creation.

It is described what the innermost space looks like, if expressed in the material terms of this world.

Thus the temple is also divided into four parts, because the way through the temple is the way through the whole of creation. The entrance is on the east side and man moves from east to west, clockwise. Standing where the Bible expresses its story in the forms of this world, the day begins in the east and goes down in the west.

The outer part of the four divisions in the temple is called the 'Outer Court of the Women'. That which one comes across first, the outside, is the physical, is the plane which in creation is the female. In that court, therefore, was the place of justice. As we saw, justice 'Din', was placed on the left side, the female side. The next part is the 'court of Israel'. For the next stage of the physical is that in which the right of primogeniture was passed on to Jacob who with it could form the unity of soul and body and thus received the name of Israel.

Then comes the third part, called the 'court of the priests'. In that part are brought the offerings; there is also found the altar for the sacrificial beasts.

The fourth part is the 'sacred place'. In that place there is in the temple the 'house', there is found that which is ever covered. This fourth part is subdivided into two parts, as indeed in the nucleus, in the sacred place, duality is present in harmony. The outer division contains three things, i. e. on the north side the so-called table of shewbread, on the south side the candlestick and on the east side the so-called incense-altar. The west side is closed off by the veil, behind which is the second subdivision, the holy of holies. There is merely the ark with the two cherubs mounted on it, which as each other's reflection form the 'one', just as the aleph in its written form also has the two jots as each other's reflection. In the ark are the two tables of the law, which as 'two' form also a unity.

Man does not come into the temple empty-handed. He brings an offering, a 'Korban'. He desires to bring something nearer to God, which is the meaning of the word korban. Whoever comes empty-handed cannot go the way through the temple. This expression means, translated from the nucleus into this world, that one has no chance of treading the path which leads to the substance, the fountain-head, unless one has something earthly, something material to offer to God. For without it there is no admittance, so to speak.

And when a man has a 'korban', something he desires to bring to God, it must be offered wholeheartedly, joyfully. An offering under compulsion is out of the question; in that case it would not be an offering and nothing would happen. Man must bring it of his own accord, with joyous impetus.

For simplicity's sake let us confine ourselves to the 'korban', brought as an 'animal'. With it man brings his physical existence with his physical actions to God. In the nucleus it is expressed as bringing an animal which only there in that place substitutes the body. We saw how at the 'offering' of Isaac, the latter went up *himself,* as a person. Only on Mount Moriah, where later on the temple is to come, at the very last moment an animal appears to be at hand.

Only in the nucleus, in the substance, the body proves to be divided and it is the animal which in this 'korban' finds its destination, gets emancipated from its animal existence, while the man returns as the complete man, just as Isaac returned.

Now the animal brought by man as an offering, must be sound and whole, it must be a goodly and fine animal. When the sick man or the broken man seeks God, it is not a 'korban'. Obviously a man in dire straits catches at a straw; he clings to doctors, solicitors, quacks, etc, maybe even to God. Most assuredly there may eventually ensue that dialogue with God, which may put him on a different track, unless of course he wants to forget everything as quickly as possible when the trouble is passed over, and take up the old ways again as is generally the case.

Being ill and broken down is a thing in itself. Sometimes suffering comes to a man, because God desires to call him back to reality, or because He wants him to ponder on the purpose of existence thus to find his proper course in life.

So the 'korban' has to be a goodly and fine animal. In this life where the animal is not yet available to us, we must be prepared to unite the principal thing in life, the most beautiful thing in life, with God, in order to call up this animal in the nucleus: one's calling, one's business, one's studies, home-life, life in society. Not just the odd hour one is prepared to assign to relaxation, after which quite refreshed to go and do what one considers the principle thing which one would cheerfully give a year of one's life for, or put up with heart-disease or gastric ulcers for; the thing one gets emotional about, worries about night and day to make more rapid 'progress in life'.

With the animal, leading it along by the halter, does the man go forth who full of joy feels impelled to unite the best thing of his existence, everything in fact, with God, in this way does man present himself in the nucleus, in that place Moriah, the place where the substance is seen clothed in earthly form.

Now it is this animal which he leads through the two outer courts into the third, the 'court of the priests'.

I shall first have to say a few words about these priests, for on this subject too there is a good deal of misunderstanding. The priests are of the tribe of Levi, the tribe coming into prominence with Moses and Aaron. The word Levi is related to the conception 'accompany', attaching oneself to a thing and accompanying it. Thus the tribe Levi became the guide during the journey through the desert, the journey from Egypt to Canaan. Moses, in the systematism on the right, under Abraham, that is, as the fourth, and Aaron, in the systematism on the left, as the fifth, under Isaac. Levi makes his appearance as the one who makes the journey from Egypt to Canaan at all possible, from duality to unity, from this world to the next.

Thus, according to tradition, the 'fish' Leviathan is that which as guide accompanies this whole world on to the next. In the third of the three biblical 'feasts', Easter, Pentecost, and the feast of the Tabernacles, the produce of the crops cut between Easter and Pentecost is threshed, the grain is altogether separated from the chaff that it may attain its ultimate destination to be taken as bread by man, and man may thus be taken up by God (vide Lev. 23:33–36, and 39–44; Numbers 29:12–38). During the Feast of the Tabernacles, people remain for seven days in a 'tabernacle', the characteristic of which is that it is a temporal abode, and that its roof should be so loosely arranged, for instance, of leafy twigs, that one can see the sky through it and the stars in the sky. Seven days on end does one live in this temporal abode not yet built on solid ground; just as man until the seventh day of the world has not got the solid house on earth. He lives in the house in which, according to tradition, biblical Israel lived, when it journeyed from Egypt to Canaan. Then, too, it was the way of the seventh day, with the cycle of the seven characterizing the journey across the desert. In the afore-mentioned we saw from various examples how this fact of the seventh day and the journey across the desert coincided. As long as one is on one's way to the promised land, one has no solid house here, and one has ever to be able to see heaven through the roof. In the knowledge that only *there* is the real roof, and that the roof of the earthly abode indeed can shut man from heaven, can make him oblivious of the fact that life has a purpose other than merely seeking protection on this earth.

The eighth day, however– and the feast of the tabernacles is the only one finished off by an eighth day – there is another 'feast'. It is the feast that the seven days are past and the eighth day has come. On that eighth day one leaves the 'tabernacle' and goes within the house. Then the period of migrating from Egypt to Canaan is past, people have reached the coming world. It is only when the crops threshed and the grapes pressed have been gathered, when the grain has come free in everything, only then it is the eighth day, the day immediately following after the seventh. After the seven days of Easter, the getting emancipated from Egypt, from the world of duality, there were still seven weeks required as we have seen, to attain the eighth week, in which there was the Revelation. For the world as a whole we saw the cycle of seven times seven years, until with the year of the jubilee the 'eighth day' begins. But here, after the feast of the tabernacles, the eighth day follows immediately after the seven previous ones. It is the feast *after* Easter and Pentecost in which the wheat harvested is threshed and ready for its final destination. It is then the seventh month after Easter, which is the first month, and Pentecost which is in the third month. Therefore it is customary at the feast of the tabernacles to read the book 'Ecclesiastes', which speaks of the vanity of all earthly things and of the other standards indeed operative.

Tradition has it that the time of the end coincides with the period of the feast of the tabernacles. Then are waged the wars of Gog and Magog. They are the wars of all against all, the struggle for the possession of the world which will not fall to the share of any of them.

The words 'Gog and Magog' are spelt 3–6–3; 6–40–3–6–3. The sum-total of the letters is 70. Indeed, it is the war of the seventy nations, an expression for 'all the nations' among each other. This war is enacted in the plane of the feast of the tabernacles, another or, if one prefers, a 'higher' plane as compared to the two previous ones. In the offerings of the feast of the tabernacles, in Num. 29:12–38 therefore 70 bulls are brought in all, viz.13 on the first day, 12 on the second day, every day one less, until on the seventh day there are only 7. Together it makes 70 for the seven days. The other offerings remain the same in number. It is only that of the bulls which decreases by *one* every day. The bull, as the second animal is the systematism of the Zodical constellations, is the animal on the left side, where is also found the 'Phar', the cow of Egypt. It is the expression of the strong earthly force, the development into multiplicity. The 'goring ox' mentioned by the Bible, is the principle of everything inflicting damage, because it comes from this left side, the side which operates as a force of nature. Now the nations as multiplicity also are in this place and their numbers decrease in the course of the seven days. The 'korban', bringing the bulls nearer to God, therefore is the unifying of this struggle of all against all, with the fountain-head, showing the purpose of the external appearance of the battle.

The names 'Gog' and 'Magog' are related to the word for roof, 'gag'. This struggle of all against all, rightly expressed in the period of the feast of the tabernacles, when the roof has to be so as to allow heaven to be seen through it, is of particular significance for this life. Those that build the solid house even in this world; those that imagine themselves safe here with the material roof overhead, are those that will be in conflict as long as the world lasts, with themselves, with others, in every plane. Everywhere there will be duality, contrast. But their power decreases, just as the power of further development continues decreasing, finally to return to the source of origin. The 'korban' of the other animals in that period, the two rams and the fourteen sheep remains unaltered throughout these seven days. The roof-nations, however, are these Gog and Magog, mutually destroying each other; their power decreases.

Thus the Leviathan is the guide through the world till the eighth day comes.

The Leviathan as 'fish' bears the world. One should not of course visualize it in our space-time world as a gigantic fish with the globe on its back. In another plane it expresses that this seventh day is a world of the water, a world characterized by 'water'. And in this world of the water it is the conception 'Leviathan' – the 'fish' making life in the water possible – which guides this life till the time of drought comes again, when the water is poured out. In this way for instance, should be comprehended the saying: 'The earth is the Lord's, and the fullness thereof; the world, and they that dwell therein. For He hath founded it upon the seas and established it upon the floods', (Ps. 24:1–2). Neither are we allowed to make a mental picture here, as people did even in antiquity, when they began to ignore the substance. We simply cannot draw the earth as a disc, floating in the ocean with fish all around it lifting their heads out of the water.

The world established on the sea is the world built up with the character of water, with the character of the left side. Sea in Hebrew is 'yam', spelt 10–40. The world is built up on this 10–40, on the (1–4)-principle; the principle which as *ed,* as mist in the image, made this water-world possible. It is the principle which also gave expression to duality in the tree of life and in the tree of knowledge. So as soon as people began to draw Leviathan and picture the sea as basis of the world, they showed they had lost their understanding of the substance. Leviathan is not a fish in the sense of such a picture. Leviathan bears this life through the seventh day, just as the ship, the ark, bears life through the 'water' of the seventh day. Till a new world comes, the world of the eighth day.

Then, according to tradition, Leviathan is eaten, his task is fulfilled, and then the tabernacle is made as a house, with the skin of Leviathan. He has led the world to the eighth day; he was the guide through the seventh day, on this way from Egypt to Canaan. Thus the conception Levi is ever 'that which leads man along this way'.

And the priest is a 'Levi' and therefore he accompanies, in an active sense, as guide, on the way from duality to unity.

It is the mission of the priest to arrange the world so as to enable man to bring the 'korban', as it is explicitly expressed in the arrangement in the temple. He has to accompany man on that way.

The word for priest is 'kahen', 20–5–50. It has in its structure the 4–1 – for the 20–5 has the 4×5 and the 1×5 – with the well-known '50' as ending. Indeed, it is the mission of the priest to bring this 4–1 to life. We saw above that the so-called priestly blessing had this (4–1)-proportion in the 15 words with the 60 letters.

In the third court, the court of the priests, man stands at the border of the origin. In front of him is the 'house', containing within, as yet closed-off to him, the secret of the essence. And now comes the task of the priest at the transition from the 'two' to the 'one'. For man has come with the animal and has covered the way as far as the court of the priest. Here the animal is bound, the 'four' is bound to 'one', and then the man who brought it with him, not the priest, has to cut the ring through. We saw, when discussing the 'Akeda' of Isaac what it implies. It is making that which causes man to observe and experience things, i.e. the body, realize that this circle in which it is enclosed must be broken through. That there is a world outside the circle in which the body keeps man imprisoned, a world with different standards, within which the body too can enter once it has broken through this circle. When the body has accomplished this, it can actually even enter into the holy of holies.

This piercing through the circle is demonstrated in the place of the temple, i.e. there where man and animal are present as separate phenomena, when the jugular artery of the animal is cut through. In consequence of it, man enters into his body at the stage when it is free from the attraction exercised by the forces of development. The serpent has been rejected, it is killed. All this man has got to do for himself; the priest merely gives him directions, instructs him, but he cannot do it for him.

Then the blood of the animal, that which in our appearance represents the 'nefesh', the animal soul, comes into contact with the so-called altar of the burnt-offerings which is on the south side of this court of the priests. On the north side the animal, if it belongs to the category of important offerings, is killed, then the blood is brought to the south side and sprinkled on the corners of the altar. In certain cases, which we need not enter upon here, the blood is also brought into the 'house' into the 'sanctum' and by way of exception even into the 'sanctum sanctorum' in the place where is the ark.

Now, what is the significance of the place where the blood of the animal is poured out for the sake of emancipation, i.e. the place of the altar of the burnt-offering? To discuss this I shall now return to the story of Joseph, at the point where Judah came forward to plead for Benjamin before Joseph.

The division of Canaan amongst the sons of Jacob of course has a much deeper significance then that one son should have got more pastures and the other more desert land. I should like to point out just one aspect of that division.

Jerusalem is situated in the land of Benjamin; the temple, too, is in Benjamin. Benjamin as the eighth son of the two mothers, has the place where the world has united again with its origin in the eighth day. From the land of Judah, south of that of Benjamin, a narrow strip however runs through Benjamin's domain up to the place of the altar of the burnt-offerings, the south-eastern corner of which therefore belongs to Judah's area. At this altar it is that Judah and Benjamin meet.

For the blood of the animal, the bodily soul, 'nefesh', contacts the corners of the altar, it contacts the very connection between Judah and Benjamin, it is then on either side of the border and consequently forms the bond.

There where Judah identified himself with Benjamin, was ready to sacrifice himself to the unknown ruler of the world of duality, where was the point of the most terrible chaos in logic and expectations, where obtained the deepest despair, there also suddenly sprang up the greatest surprise, when it became evident that the brethren had feared their own brother, Joseph. That they had got excited and been gripped by extreme fear, because they had not recognized whom they were facing.

But as soon as man has shown in life that he knows the importance of the body, if he does not keep the best of this material life which promises the future, outside the temple, in the world of duality outside, but regards it as the condition, as the foundation for entering into the temple himself, for coming to the essence of things, then, if he cuts through the circle of his own standards, he will come to the site where in the biblical story Judah unites with Benjamin, and then Joseph will be recognized as the giver of life in the world of duality. Then he will realize it is his very own brother, also an' Ibri'.

Similarly does man go through life and he will come to the point where this life is taken from him, where he leaves the world of duality. Then, supposing he has sold Joseph, he will first have a great fright, the terror for a ruler apparently asserting himself against all justice and logic in that land of famine, where he had hoped to get a new lease of life. But if, at this juncture, man realizes that his attitude has been wrong, that he has falsely judged the body and all details and actions in the world, if he feels remorse on account of it to the bottom of his soul, and if he shows in what he now possesses of that body, in Benjamin, how he will stake himself for that, then his eves will be opened, and he will see that all his fear was merely the outcome of a game. A game only he himself could not see through; that it had never been intended to deprive him of that body 'Benjamin', that it had never been intended to keep him as a slave in the world of opposites, but that from the beginning his own brother Joseph had been facing him. That he had only been unable to recognize it as a game, since Joseph to him had meant something entirely different, because he had misjudged Joseph's significance. 'The stone which the builders refused, is become the headstone of the corner', (Ps.118:22); this principle here again has proved to be a reality.

Thus every man, who does not know the meaning of the 'korban' in his life; who does not joyfully bring the 'korban' of the very best; who wants to exclude Joseph from Canaan; who sells him into Egypt; will go this way without understanding; like the 'tree that makes fruit', not knowing where all this leads to, what the fruit will be. He will have to cross a difficult threshold, he will live through a horrible fright, as it is depicted in the story of Joseph, until the moment when he follows the way of Joseph's brethren and recognizes the error, regrets it, and shows that he can act differently. At that moment he will see that it was a game all along, and that from the very first his own brother, whom he had considered so insignificant in this world, had been facing him, and that he had never desired to do him any wrong. The fright had only been the consequence of his own mistaken attitude.

He that knows how to bring the 'korban', lives through it all as with the 'tree that is fruit and makes fruit'. He knows the significance of the body, he knows Joseph, he knows where evolution takes him, he knows the fruit and he experiences the joy of being able to follow this way which by then is become surpassingly beautiful, into the temple, bringing the animal along with him.

Thus the scene of this meeting of Benjamin and Judah in the biblical story is also laid in that site in the world where the animal soul, the 'nefesh' is brought to experience the integration of the children of Rachel and Leah, the integration of body and soul. It is the outcome of the way one went with the body, as a unit, to bring it to God with all it stands for in this world. For in that place, Moriah, when the 'four' have been bound unto the 'one', when the ring of sensory perception which kept man imprisoned has been cut through; in that place where Judah and Benjamin are united, one experiences the integration of body and soul, and then one will know it will last forever.

The fourth stage of the way through the temple will then be free. One can only get there, if in the last stage but one, the animal has been made into a 'korban'. Not until then, after the integration in the spot where Judah and Benjamin similarly are together, will the way be open to understand the other, present in the last stage. Then it is the priest who can go on, the guide on the way from Egypt to Canaan. Just as in the story of the Bible it is only Moses who approaches God on Mount Sinai. And it is in the fourth stage that the essential finds expression. There is the origin. Just as the stone 'Shetiya', the point of origin of the material world, is there as well.

Without entering into the details of the temple, let me mention here that the three objects in the first part of the 'house', i. e. before the veil, are arranged in the manner in which we saw the systematism of the Bible established, viz. in the form of a triangle, pointing downwards.

The table with the shew-bread in the north is a crystallization in form of what in substance is the end of the way of development. Bread is the terminus of the long way of the wheat. In the north therefore the animal was slaughtered, in the former stage, in the third court. The power of the physical, of development, lies in the north. Thus it is that Jeremiah (Jer.1:14) sees that, 'out of the north an evil shall break forth'. The surprise attack with the bodily force, with physical development, comes from the north. For that reason the animal is killed in *that* place, the ring is pierced through in the spot of the most vigorous power and the most stubborn will to push further development of that force. When this has taken place in the third court, the bread is ready in the 'house', in all the twelve places of time.

In the south there is the seven-armed candlestick in which burns the oil specially prepared for it. This candlestick consists of twice three lights with the seventh in the centre. In the south is the side of the soul, facing the side of the body in the north. In the south there is also the altar of the burnt offering, against the corners of which is sprinkled the blood of the animal killed in the north. That blood, too, flows from the body in the direction of the soul. The oil in the candle has been pressed from the olive, the sixth fruit, which in the word '*shemen*' has the structure, as discussed above, of the eighth day. The word for oil and the word for eight have the same structure. That which keeps the soul burning; is the power of the eighth day, of the coming world, which is nourished with the fruit of the sixth day, of the previous world. The candlestick, which crystallizes this seventh day in the place in the nucleus therefore burns with the strength of the past and of the future, connecting these two. This integration is characteristic of the soul in this world. And the blood of the animal the man has brought along is sprinkled on the spot where the union takes place, that of Benjamin and Judah, hence also of body and soul.

In the centre of the systematism of the three, there is the altar of the incense. It is opposite the ark in the holy of holies, in the final part of the 'house'. On this altar of incense – on which no offerings are brought – the fragrance diffuses of various herbs of very specific composition, which naturally we cannot enter into here. Whereas the lights in the candlestick burn only at night, the altar of the incense is used both in the morning and at night, when the lights of the candlestick are extinguished or lit again. So it is only at night that the soul is in the south, facing the body in the north. In the daytime there is the place in the centre, where soul and body are already 'one', and this is expressed in what is practically inexpressible in earthly terms, in the scent of very special kinds of herbs. In this world it cannot yet be realized, and therefore the Bible states that the man who would imitate it in order to assimilate the scent himself, cannot live; it is something pertaining to an entirely different world, where duality has been resolved into unity again.

That is why this special altar is opposite the ark, within the holy of holies. From that place, at that altar, as the scent diffuses, does God appoint the times of meeting with Moses. It is the place of the soul in the world of the day, after this world of the night.

The feasts are also called 'times of congregation', 'moed', 40–6–70–4. It is a combination again with the rather familiar conception 70–4. And it really means a meeting, a concurrence, of something which happens in the substance and that which at a certain moment is also expressed on earth. Thus the seventh day on earth coincides with the seventh day in substance. And thus the *period* of Easter coincides with the *happening* of Easter in the substance, etc. It can also be seen as a kind of point of intersection between the time of this world and that of the world of the substance.

Therefore these days all have their fixed place, stated more explicitly by tradition according to this systematism and structure. For then these times actually do coincide here and in the substance. Otherwise people could push these so-called feast days on to days which are 'more convenient', as it is often represented in these modern, utilistic times, merely adapted to the world and the national income. The 'times of the congregation', however, are fixed, just because they coincide with other times which are not of this world. This coincidence stresses the importance of these times here.

At this altar of the incense this 'coinciding' is made known. In this place of the soul there always is this coinciding. It is alive already in the world of the substance, a world which in this world can merely express itself as fragrance diffused by these 'herbs' so very special they cannot be imitated by man here.

Then, in the final part of the 'house' there is the division with the ark. It is the place of the upper part of the 'one', the place where man, as high-priest, can enter only at one 'moment of congregation' every year. On the tenth day of the seventh month, when man indeed stands on the border of this world and the next, according to this coinciding of terrestrial time with that otherworldly time. To man in this world, if he has actually passed through the other stages, and on the strength of it has become the high-priest the only one in the generation that can be the greatest of all the leaders on the way of the world of duality towards the 'one', it means that he could come there too even beyond that boundary, and remain alive, just as happened with the high-priest, in projection in the temple.

Thus did man move from the outer court, through the other courts, entering alone with the 'korban'. And thus can he attain the origin, where the purpose of everything becomes clear and distinct, even to the holy of holies, closed off from the rest of the world. The only place where only 'one' man can come, embracing all the rest in harmony within himself.

The temple area measures 500×500, so it is the place where the other world projects itself here on this earth of the 400, – for indeed, the land Canaan measures 400×400.

Beyond the holy of holies, in the extreme western part of the temple, there is not anything anymore. The west has no gate. In the west lies the origin. Thence did the world develop outwards, downwards, if you like. There in the west there is another world, the world of Eden. There man has got beyond the 'four' of this world; he has hound the 'four' unto the 'one'.

When man was expelled from Paradise, God set the cherubim there, on the east of the garden, the extreme west to man, who in the earthly time ensuing simultaneously, moved from east to west. There in the west he cannot get any farther in this world. The cherubim of the ark are on the border.

When man moves away from the source of origin, he goes towards the east; in the image of the temple therefore, he follows the way out of the 'house', via the court of the priests to that of Israel and on to that of the women.

Therefore when Cain had killed Abel, he 'went out from the presence of the Lord, and dwelt in the land of Nod, on the east of Eden' (Gen. 4:16). So it was the course outwards, downwards, away from the origin. And then there begins the Cain culture, in the land towards the east.

And when the generation of the tower builders, the Haflaga, journeyed eastwards, (Gen. 11:2), they hit upon the idea of storming heaven with the power of material development. Again this journeying away from the origin, whereas the way to the origin is the way westwards. The land Canaan, too, is occupied starting from the east towards the west.

So the story of Joseph is the story of the surprise concerning the body and its central significance for life. The way through the temple can only be covered with the body; bringing the body nearer is the only possibility to get to the holy of holies to learn to fathom the secret. Only in this way does one fulfil the purpose of creation, bringing the 'extreme' back to the origin.

Now, before concluding the story of Joseph, we shall have to say a few words on the significance of the relationship Judah-Joseph. That there is a very special relationship between Judah and Joseph is apparent from the fact that immediately after the sale of Joseph it is stated that Judah, too, 'went down from his brethren' (Gen. 38:1). In the Hebrew text the same word is used in both cases, namely 'he went down'. And just as Joseph goes through a decisive phase on account of a woman, from whom he gets estranged first, but who later on comes to him after all, Potiphar's wife, so does Judah experience the same thing with Tamar. Judah, too, comes out victorious in this encounter with the woman. In his case because he openly admits that he has failed with Tamar. Just as Joseph gets two sons, Ephraim and Manasseh, so Judah has two of Tamar, viz. Perez and Zerah. Though Manasseh is the older one, Jacob yet accords Ephraim precedence, recognizing in him as he had done in Joseph, the valuable body, the body in which redemption would be won, the body which God had made to make the return possible on the way of the 10–5–6–5, and which could now he integrated with the soul. The same thing is enacted with Judah. Zerah who appears as the first is superseded by Perez, whose name in fact implies this piercing through. Again, I shall not enter into the numerous details of this story of Judah and Tamar, but content myself with pointing at this typical analogy in the fortunes of Judah and Joseph.

Then we see that the two 'spies', the only ones among the twelve refusing to judge the coming world Canaan by the standards of this world, are Caleb of the tribe of Judah and Joshuah of the tribe of Joseph (Num.13 and 14). The spies of that which is to come, had rejected this promised land as measured by the standards of the world whence they came. Logically it was impossible, man would not be able to live there, it was not a place for people of this world. The world of duality with its sorrow and suffering, Egypt, was to be preferred. Only Joshua and Caleb had faith and especially the modesty, rarely found in mankind, to assume that there might he different standards from those which our senses presented and our ratiocination established thereon.

Owing to this faith that God could only purpose well with mankind anyway, they were the only ones who had known Egypt as grown-ups and got alive into Canaan as well.

The first king in the story of the Bible is Saul. He is of the tribe of Benjamin, hence from the side of Joseph. And so there ensues, when Saul is not willing to suppress completely Amalek, the characteristic force of development which ever reveals itself as the Esau force in time, the opposite to David, who is of the tribe of Judah.

I cannot here enter more deeply into this story, I am merely quoting it here to illustrate the relationship Judah-Joseph. Notwithstanding the continual strife between Saul and David, there yet arises the friendship between the son of Saul, Jonathan, and David. This friendship, in this world concealed from others, would be revealed in the future; as Jonathan says, 'the Lord be between me and thee and between my seed and thy seed for ever' (1 Sam. 20:42). Ancient lore on the ground of the 'tomorrow is the new moon' (1 Sam. 20:5–18) has fixed this event, as the condition obtaining immediately before the coming of the new moon, of the world in a new phenomenal form. David fears death, for indeed, the form disappears, one does not know what becomes of it. But then Jonathan binds himself with the promise to save David's life, and act on his behalf at the moment of the change, of the new moon.

The conflict Judah-Joseph in Egypt is therefore similarly expressed in the condition immediately preceding the new moon, when death threatens to be a complete annihilation. Thus Judah stood before Joseph and saw everything he had logically and reasonably built on crashing down about him. It is the condition of death, when there is nothing left of the preceding; it is the condition therefore which is also depicted in the complete disappearance of the moon. The former phase is gone and the new one is not yet known, if life itself is but the expression of one cycle of growth, zenith, waning and ending in nothing. The new is an immense surprise to the man who compasses merely one cycle in this life; he suddenly perceives that everything is entirely different from what he could have imagined; that his fright was the consequence of not having realized what the body was at all, what it meant. Jonathan helps David across this phase of the 'new moon', just as Benjamin and Joseph had done to Judah, David's ancestor.

Let me repeat, the moon in the Bible is the expression of something real, of something which has to do with the body, with growth, development, time. The moon which one sees is merely the sign that there is a moon in substance. The visible moon can, through the word, be translated into the real moon. And the real moon can here be expressed in the forms of the perceptible. If one knows this bridge, one can speak about the moon. As long as one does not know this bridge, does not even know how it exists, one will think that the Bible lets all this be enacted with that moon which revolves around the earth. One will not even realize that this very revolving round the earth is an expression of the character of the 'female', the 'physical', the 'covering', which indeed revolve likewise around the centre.

And then we see Judah and Joseph turning up once more at the dividing of the land after Solomon. Solomon is the expression in the world of the Bible of the coming of David's son, the eighth generation, the eighth day. But since the expression is clothed in the forms of this world of the seventh day the structure of the end of the world is likewise ever present. The transition from this world to the next, but for the exceptions, is effected in the seventh day through death. Not until this seventh day is past, will that transition be a thing of the past. Therefore the expression of the story of Solomon in the world of the seventh day is outlined with the pattern which ends in ruin, and destruction. And resurrection and life eternal are ever merely present in the communications of the prophets, hence as something which is yet to come after this world. The facts themselves, though, end in the seventh day and to man that end has the aspect of death. Thus also ends the kingdom of Solomon. The disposition of the man of this world to make 'multiplicity' is expressed in the story of Solomon a.o. in his taking to wife the woman from Egypt, the world with the force of development of duality, and his taking numerous other women to wife. This disposition pertaining to the body from its origin, brings death with it for mankind in this world. We have already discussed all this several times.

After Solomon there is once more the condition of duality, a new cycle has started. In this condition of duality there is the kingdom of Judah and that of Ephraim, i. e. Joseph, the so-called kingdom of Israel. And these two are often opposed to each other and they have a different development.

The kingdom of Judah has one dynasty ruling it, that of the house of David. The kings of that dynasty are now good, now bad. The kingdom of Israel has not got an established dynasty. There are continually new families, which provide a king. To be brief, *none* of these kings were good.

Now the contrast Joseph-Judah, as it is depicted in 1 Kings 10:11ff and 2 Chron. 10ff forms a period of decline for both kingdoms. In this period is expressed the way to death which man follows when body and soul in him are detached, when they form a duality, a contrast. In that case the body is nothing but a source of misery and idolatry. It ever has the conflict of the generations; ever new kings come and rule Israel from ever different standpoints. There is continual suppression and war, injustice and suffering. Many are the prophets pointing out the error of this way, but nobody heeds them.

The forsaken soul from whom the body has detached itself, on account of a certain attitude in man, who indeed, as it is said about Solomon, went in pursuit of multiplicity –, similarly has a life of its own. It is true it has the house of God in its domain, but it often really is at a loss as to what to do with it. There too idolatry reigns sometimes. Nevertheless, there always is one royal house, and there are several kings who recognize and pursue the good and thus cause others to pursue it. The prophets admonish *this* kingdom as well and they specially point at the importance of reunion.

Of course all this has enacted itself in history as well. But here too, historic events should be seen as an image whose essential structure we have to rediscover. And, since the image shows Judah and Joseph separately, as if disrupted, this essential structure shows that we have to do with the principle which ever confronts body and soul, heaven and earth, man and woman, left and right, in order that they reunite. They came forth from the 'one' and will have to reunite to the 'one'.

With this structure such a story should be measured, if one is to understand the substance of it. And that structure shows how the development of the body is, when that body has detached itself from the soul on account of the actions of the man. That body does not come to rest, and goes to destruction. And this knowledge of the structure leaves it to us to judge what happens to the soul that has no contact any more with the body. It fares rather better, for there is at least the essential unity, expressed in the house of David's ruling; but this soul, too, goes to destruction. The kingdom of Israel is the first to be overcome. All are sent into exile into Assur (2 Kings 17).

And nobody knows what became of them. The biblical story continues to state that some time afterwards the house of Judah is also overcome and all are likewise sent into exile (2 Kings 24,25).

This time, however, there is a difference. Whereas the house of Israel has disappeared and we even do not know what has become of the former inhabitants – they are the mysterious ten tribes about which so many scientific and unscientific conjectures are being launched – the kingdom of Judah as such has disappeared, it is true, but the inhabitants are only too well known in the world. As far as history goes back, i.e. scientific history, the inhabitants of Judah can be retraced in any place in the world.

Here we are faced with something most extraordinary, especially if we keep in mind the structure of the story Judah-Joseph.

The destruction of the kingdom of Israel is rather like the ruin of the body which has detached itself from the soul. That body disappears. Eventually it is resolved in surrounding matter. Anyway nobody can locate the body any more. The body dies first and is the first to leave the place, the world where it lived.

The destruction of the kingdom of Judah is like the passing away of the soul. The soul, too, leaves the place, the world, it has lived in. It remains longer than the body, but eventually it has to go as well. The soul, however, in the other world whither it now goes, remains manifest. It is a reality, even in this world, but it is in captivity here.

Now the return is similar. First there is, as in creation, the return of the body, without a soul, as yet. In the next phase the soul enters the body; the soul which had all that time been waiting for a body in this world.

Thus the Bible has it (Ezekiel 37) that Ezekiel is set by God in a valley full of dry bones. At the word of God the bones began to come to life again. They came together, sinews and flesh came upon them and skin covered them. But there was no spirit yet, no soul in them. Upon which the spirit comes as the second phase. In the text we read the word 'ruach' meaning soul. Soul is rendered by the conceptions 'nefesh' and 'neshamah', which we have already come across, and in this third expression 'ruach'. I shall not enter into the difference between them; as regards nefesh and neshamah, I have already referred to them, as much as the scope of this book permits. This spirit informs the whole with life and thus all the bones stand up and, as the story makes it clear further down, it is a sign of the dead resurrecting from their graves and the coming of new life. And at that resurrection, too, there is first the formation of the lost foundation; the bones, dispersed everywhere, gathered together, whatever the quality, perceptible or imperceptible, they were, form the pied-a-terre and as soon as it has assumed the expression of the man in this world, life is poured into them on four sides. These four sides unite in man and give him renewed life. Thus the side of 'Joseph', the house of Israel, comes to life first, after which, when the soul, the house of Judah, comes into it, they form the new life together.

Even if one should not have been able to give the name of 'Joseph' to the bones as yet, and the name of 'Judah' to the soul, it becomes quite clear in the course of the story immediately after this action as a sign of resurrection from the dead, when God tells Ezekiel to take two pieces of wood and to write 'for Judah' on the one, and on the other 'for Joseph' and to join those two bits of wood together, to make them into the 'one'. And this union implies that which it has come to be as life eternal, as the end of this 37th chapter of Ezekiel tells us.

Just as the union of Judah and Joseph in our story in Egypt, caused new life to come, after the previous experience of despair and fear of death, thus this union of Judah and Joseph in Ezekiel similarly is the principle of resurrection from the dead and the simultaneous coming of the new life which is to remain for all eternity, the life of the 'eighth day', of the coming world. The story of the two sticks with the names of Judah and Joseph has been given together with the story of the bones into which life, the spirit, entered again after they had regained the form of man.

That is why ancient lore has the story of the two 'saviours', one as the son of Joseph and the other as the son of David. And ancient lore has it that first comes the saviour of the house of Joseph, who witnesses the wars of 'Gag and Magog'. So it is the saviour who, as Joseph, appears on the side of the body and carries on the war in this world. And he is followed by the Messiah, who is of the house of Judah, of David.

And this structure is present throughout the Bible. Joshuah is the first in Canaan and he derives from Ephraim, from Joseph; he builds the foundations. Thus there is first King Saul, of the line of Benjamin, hence also of the side of Joseph. But completeness comes with David, of the line of Judah, the lord of the united kingdoms uniting the houses of Joseph and of Judah. For unity is ruled by that which expresses the soul; it is the soul that bestows on the whole that life which indeed causes it to resurrect.

So in the Joseph-Judah story, we are told, as one of the motives throughout the pattern of creation, about the relationship between body and soul, indeed the relationship between all opposites here. It tells us what the world is like under the sway of the opposites and what it will be when the opposites have been eliminated. Through the story we know the situation man is in, when at the end of his life, but also at the end of the time of this world, he is faced with his accuser in the form of that lord of Egypt, how everything is changed beyond the threshold and how a new life sets in with the utterly unexpected surprise that this crossing had only caused fear, because in consequence of one's own life one did not realize who was there facing one.

Although the relationship Judah-Joseph has here principally been set forth as viewed from the relationship soul-body, one should realize that it embraces all planes. The relationship soul-body is a rendering in one plane; in other planes this relationship presents itself under another name. But the same structure holds good and integration develops along the same lines.

People, as mentioned before, have always asked themselves what has become of the 'ten tribes' of the house of Israel. Tradition has answered it.

They are still there, viz. on the other side of the river Sambation, or Sabbath-river. There they live their own lives, a great monarchy with powerful kings. But the river cannot be crossed; such is its character that people are unable to cross it. There will be a time, however, when these ten tribes will come and wage wars to lay the foundation for emancipation, after which the Messiah shall make His appearance and everything will remain good in all eternity.

So the story tells us that the ten tribes live on the other side of the Sabbath-river, hence beyond this world. The Sabbath-river forms the boundary between this world of the seventh day, of the day of the Sabbath, and the territory which is the world of these children of Joseph. From this world people cannot cross that river; it is impossible. Neither can they cross from the other side to this world. However, when the seventh day has passed, when in time the boundary of the Sabbath, of the seventh day, has been crossed, then the river Sambation, the Sabbath river, shall also have been crossed. Then the children of Joseph will come and form the new man, just as the dry bones in the story of Ezekiel did at the command of God. Their king will lead them. Then, for then it is the eighth day, the river can be crossed, then will come the final emancipation, and life eternal. If one realizes what the seventh day means, if one knows about the structure of the world, as the Bible tells it, if one understands what a river is in substance, then one will comprehend the meaning of this story of ancient lore. Then one will know that after the seventh day the children of the kingdom of Joseph will appear again before us, that all the dead bodies will arise and with it, to our utter surprise that the new day is become a fact, that life eternal has begun.

It is then a 'new moon' again. After the darkness of the waning, there comes a new cycle again. In the eighth day, however, the unity of sun and moon will similarly have been restored. Then the moon will be the ever changing form, the part which 'makes fruit' and the sun will be the constant form, the part that 'is fruit'. And sun and moon will be there simultaneously, there will no longer be the contrast night-day, life-death, development – and goal attained. The condition of the tree of life, which is fruit and makes fruit', of the harmony of the opposites, is there.

The story likewise implies that these children of Joseph cannot be looked for in this world. They cannot be sought here any more than the dead who have similarly passed away from this world. As ancient lore has to suppose the terminology of the structure of the Bible to be well known, it can formulate the knowledge of it all very briefly and clearly and accurately. Similarly using the images of this world, knowing that they can be translated into the everyday language of every time. Any formulation of philosophic thought bound to a specific period of time would be difficult to understand or not at all in any other period. The formulation, however, in the structure of the word of the Bible and in the systematism which the Bible contains within itself, can be understood in all times, as long as one has not lost the knowledge about the structure of the world, as the Bible gives it. And that is why, with the loss of this knowledge and the simultaneous penetration of the sensory reflection of everything, people are seen to seek theses ten tribes in this world, of all places. The river Sambation was supposed to lie in Araby or in Afghanistan or somewhere in Africa. People began to view things from the earthly standpoint, i.e. began to see everything 'in development', in 'evolution' and the Bible was used more and more as a source of history; just as well as ancient lore, which with its forms, purposely unearthly, often evaded it with deliberate intent. People simply extrapolated time of biblical time-reckoning and the biblical phenomena into those of our times. And started from the same geography. Not realizing that repeatedly there had been a leap from one plane to the other; that there is discontinuity all the time. Who was there to know about the 'ketoneth passim', the 'garment of many colours' of Joseph?

This development, resulting from people's ever more turning to the tree of knowledge, through which the earthly eyes were opened began thousands of years ago. It was very pronounced at the time of the second temple, lost impetus a little at times, but on the whole it became more and more intensive as time went on. We shake our heads about sinful Solomon; are surprised at David's last words to Solomon; we think very poorly of the conduct of biblical Israel in the desert, after the miracles and good words; and especially our first ancestor, Adam, gets it in the neck. We simply do not realize that the Bible tells us how the world is, how God made it, and that we are faced with this world and that our life has no sense, until we are ready to realize from the Bible what creation is and what is the purpose of our life. The Bible has not been given to us to hear our charitable criticism or otherwise, or to attach our approval or disapproval to. The Bible exists all the same, as does the world, whatever our opinion about it.

Thus the story of the river Sambation has long ceased to find comprehension with the majority of people. It was ascribed to imperfect knowledge of geography in those 'primitive' times, owing to which nations on earth could be done away with in far off continents. And they forget that those who passed on this tradition and finally wrote it down, were not at all interested in geography in this sense. To them, for instance, the land Canaan was 400 by 400 parsa, and that was that. These people were not interested in the moon as territory for colonizing purposes or fields yielding ore. To them the moon was an entity which caused disruption of harmony in the 'one'; caused duality, growth, evolution. What the moon looked like, was not so important. For anyway it was only a very relative picture bound to the possibilities of crystallization in our space-time world.

The body of man they knew from the description of the 'offerings' and from the substance of animals and the parts of them which were brought along by man for the'korban' on his way to the source of origin.

Thus in the *Merkabah*-story, the so-called vision in the initial chapter of Ezekiel, there are three kinds of animals with man, standing before 'God's throne', i.e. in the substance. Animals and men have a very special interrelationship in the substance.

But mankind lost this kind of knowledge more and more. People did not know the starting points of the argumentations any more. Thus people began to look at the sun and moon, started to examine minerals, analyse bodies, draw geographical and astronomic maps and charts, started on a way without end, taking it all quite seriously, too. The spoil-sports fared very much as did Abraham with Nimrod; again just as ancient lore passes it on.

There is also a story in tradition about the king David. It tells us that death simply could not overtake him, because David was ever engrossed in the Bible. And when one is occupied with it, death loses its grip on man. Then death blew like a wind through the leaves of the garden and David looked up and paid attention to the sighing tree. He wanted to find out what it was and interrupted his reading; at that moment death could take him.

This story, looked at from the point of view of modern science is just as unintelligible and just as unacceptable as the Sambation story. Medical man will refute such a cause of death as primitive utterance, just as other scientists will characterize the Sambation story as a primitive legend. Yet this anecdote about David tells us a lot, if only one understands the terminology, if only one realizes what reading in the Bible means, if one understands what looking at a tree with one's senses implies, and if one understands what is meant with life and death.

Hence we must not look for the river Sambation here. If we understand the structure of the world, as set forth by the Bible, we will realize that we will find 'ten tribes' just as much in this world as the men in the moon, or Mars, or Venus. And in saying that they do not exist at all, one acts like those who assume that the celestial bodies examined with the help of radio-waves or rockets represent *heaven;* that all those stories about angels, heaven, etc. are purely based on primitive imagination; that there is only science and its observations.

Either approach does injustice to the Bible. The river Sambation is the very boundary of this world of the seventh day, and the 'ten tribes' as well as all the bodies which got lost in course of time are on the other side of that border. One should not measure these things with the criteria of this world. The Bible gives the standards to measure things by correctly; and the results of the experiences with *those* standards ever show how marvellous these standards are. They always bear the proof of their correctness in themselves, and therewith lead us from one surprise to another.

PART FOUR

The Return

27

The Threshold to the Eighth

The first of the five books with which the Bible begins ends with the story of Joseph. These five books, Pentateuch, together form one unit. They contain the root-story for what follows. And these five books are also arranged according to the structure we have become familiar with, the 1–4. In the first book, in fact, all is essentially present which is to unfold itself in the next four. The next four are an extension in another plane of that which the first contains.

Thus the departure of Jacob, after his death in Egypt, a departure which he had so particularly stressed, is the substance of all that happens as told in the next four books in the Exodus from Egypt and the preparation and arrangement of the entrance into Canaan. And the actual entrance into Canaan, set forth in the next four books, Exodus, Leviticus, Numbers and Deuteronomy, is not experienced alive either. Moses, the leader on that journey, remains in the desert, on the way from Egypt to Canaan; on the borders of Canaan, he dies. He beholds what is coming, it is true, from one end to the other, but he himself does not reach it. This *coming into Canaan* is something taking place outside, beyond those five books. The five books are the expression of the essential in this world of our phenomenal form, the world which in our terminology we have come to know as the world of the seventh day. That is why, according to tradition, Moses passes away in the late afternoon of the seventh day, immediately before the entrance into the eighth day, which in the biblical systematism of time, just as every day, begins at the setting of the previous day, hence at 'night fall'.

In this world of the seventh day one does not – as we term it – pass 'alive' into the next day. In this world of our phenomenal form the transition into the next day still takes place through 'death'. Moses as the leader through the seventh day dies just before the coming of the eighth day. King David, too, is said to have died about that hour. For he, indeed, is the seventh; a seventh generation and a seventh son. However much he might pray for it, he could not see the solid house of God in this world, either. God promised him that his son should build it. Just as Moses – according to tradition it happened in an intensely dramatic way – implored *yet* to be granted to keep alive and enter alive into that other world. It is the heartfelt desire and the secret hope of every man that he may be granted to tread this path to the coming world alive, not through death.

But it is the foundation of his existence in this world, it is that through which he expresses himself here, his growing, developing body, this basis of his existence, which is at the same time the cause of his death in this world. Man exists here physically just because he has eaten of the 'tree that makes fruit', the tree of the knowledge of good and evil, and through this very existence he can realize the principal purpose of creation, viz. reunion with the origin, with the divine; because of his faith in God, the faith that things are right. Eating of the tree of the knowledge is part of creation; it is that part which causes the extreme development directed away from the source, as well as the greatest bliss at reunion. It is this paradox which man thinking along lines of causality cannot fathom, viz. that man *had* to eat of the tree of knowledge, if life was to come forth on earth at all, and that on the other hand death came for man on account of this act. Our thought in the world of duality is always 'one thing or the other', good or bad, life or death; here it never can be good *and* bad, united simultaneously in harmony. This is not an earthly harmony; it is of a different order. Nevertheless man should realize that this harmony is an existing fact; that it even forms the foundation of existence.

But that argumentation about it using earthly criteria, thought born from observation and perception, is impossible. Owing to the character of duality of this world we shall always come up against the opposite. For this world it is a question of 'predestination', or 'free will', and according to logical, earthly thought it is quite right. However, in essence, predestination and free will are two aspects of the same phenomenon, just as the jots together form the 'one', the 'aleph'. It is just because they are there together that the harmony of unity is formed. But this is the harmony of another world, the world of unity; whereas we still live here, *on our way* to unity.

Thus death here on earth is diametrically opposed to life, and all the more so in proportion to the distance we are removed from the point of union. Death, as it were, counterbalances the world which is whole, and it also shows what may be called material causality. In this world, owing to our perception and the experience based on it, there is the law of cause and effect. When I put something on the fire, it will get hot; if I throw something into water it will get wet. If I drop something fragile, it will break into fragments. Here with us there is no question of anything breaking into fragments, yet remaining whole.

Thinking along the lines of causality creates the principle of wages; if a person acts properly, he is rewarded; if he acts badly, he is punished. This thinking along lines of causality man extends towards God as well. He thinks that if he has been decent, has acted correctly, he must be rewarded, and that similarly a person acting badly should be punished. This calculating of interests make of life and virtue something attractive. Anybody seeing a dutiful person remaining in good health, well-to-do, living on and on forever, having friends only; would leave off all his other pursuits and apply himself to being good all the time. No science, nor planning could match it either.

Therefore death forms part of creation. For with death a completely new element is added, viz. that causality *does not hold*. One acts well, yet is persecuted, is poor, is ill and suffering. Whoever acts well dies all the same, sometimes even at an earlier age than a bad man who is in glorious health. The wicked man prospers, he lives a peaceful life. At least, there is as much chance for his doing so as for the decent man. Briefly, fate shows no logical connection with moral behaviour. A man may pray fervently for freedom, yet he is hanged. He that bribes the gaoler or the judge, gets free. The number of examples one can put forward is legion.

The new element brought forward with death, with the elimination of this perceptible causality, therefore is the introduction of the principle of faith, belief, readiness to sacrifice oneself without tangible profit. For it is these principles from the plane of the soul which are the divine principles. Those of causality are, in a sense, mechanical principles; c.f. the examples of putting things on the fire, or throwing things into water. These mechanical principles are merely one aspect of the question; since they are incomplete on account of it, they are not true. The so-called mechanical principles form part of the general principles, such as love, faith; belief; they form the expression of it in matter. And whoever stops at that expression and does not return to the essence together with the image, has no conception of the purpose of the world.

God has not made the world from calculation, to derive advantages from it. God has created it to bestow man – whom He does not owe anything, nor could He either – the greatest bliss; the bliss God Himself knows in the harmony of the great completeness.

This is a gift, a boon, granted for nothing. To realize this immense happiness as well, man has to proceed from the same sentiments. He, too, will have to act, for nothing, from love, from self-surrender, from belief and faith. Only then will man be on a level with the divine and will reunion be appreciated by him as such.

Coming to God is not a question of earthly logic, of cunning or subtlety, it is not a thing to be measured by earthly standards.

If man thinks so and acts accordingly, he takes of the tree of the knowledge, which is for God only, because to God only, good and bad are 'one'.

To man there is in that case either good or bad, and he creates duality for himself, which expresses itself as suffering, as desire for getting benumbed, as losing face altogether.

Thus death in this world of the seventh day counterbalances material causality and lifts man into a sphere of different causality, where it is not a matter of life or death, but where life and death are *together* in a harmony, inimitable to earthly perceptive thought. The good action will assuredly be rewarded, but death may form an intermediate stage between the action and the reward, for the good action is only good, if faith and the will-to-good, eventually eliminating all thought of reward, sustain it. *Together* they form a unity which translates the action into another world. The reward is not a 'business deal', it is of an altogether different order. It forms part of the love, the goodness with which God made creation, to bestow on man the bliss of reuniting with the source.

The appraising in the material sense, of action and reward or punishment, the watching narrowly whether one can actually collect the reward even here, is what I called the mentality of the 'business deal'. It is the mentality of 'if *that* can happen and is permitted, then there is no God', or 'then God is not interested, or cruel, etc.' The name Canaanite in Hebrew indeed means 'merchant'. It is the characteristic of the world which must be expelled by the 'Ibri', the man coming from the 'other side', from another world.

Thus there is death at the end of this world of the seventh day to bestow on man, living in the sphere of earthly causality, the foundation for standards of an entirely different order. Owing to the fact that there is death, man has received these standards and factors inherent in himself even in this life, and whether he likes it or not, they determine all his doings, both in the positive and negative sense.

For that reason the first book of the Bible, Genesis, ends with the death of Jacob and Joseph, just as the whole of Pentateuch ends with the death of the leader in the other four books, the death of Moses.

In the subsequent books of the Bible also everything is ever expressed in the structure of the seventh day and everything shows at the end what this world shows at the end, viz. ruin and death, and besides, like Moses at the end of Pentateuch, the prophets 'see' the coming world, which is not yet realized.

Here again there is at the end the barrier of darkness expressing the duality of life and death, of this world and of the world to come.

Here again on account of it there arises in man that supermundane, non-material seal of criteria, implying love, self-surrender, faith and belief.

When unity has been attained in the eighth day, when man has similarly passed into the new world, after crossing the river Jordan with Joshua, then indeed arises a new condition. Attaining unity implies that there is no longer a contrast between life and death as in the seventh day, as in this world. This is the sense of life 'eternal' in the coming world, a sense unintelligible, incomprehensible to our sensory criteria. It is different from our conception 'infinite', indicating the bounds of the senses which cannot get beyond. Between the seventh and the eighth day there still is the threshold of death. He that has passed beyond, enters the eighth day. This transition is there also for the whole world. When this boundary has been crossed, it is the eighth day to all the world and then life and death assume a different character to all mankind; they then form a harmonious whole.

We saw that the Bible in its initial five books has the temporal structure of the 10–5. This also implies that the '5' of the world, the second 5 of the

10–5–6–5 can ever merely offer and see one side, life or death, good or bad, predestination or free will. Not until the '5' of the world has united with the 10–5, which always and everywhere advances towards us, will there be for man, too, that harmony between all phenomena presenting themselves as opposites. And this reunion of the '5' of the world with the '5' above, is what is attained in the Bible, in the root-story, i.e. in the Pentateuch, with the revelation on Mount Sinai on the 50th day after the exodus from Egypt, in the 'eighth'. Whenever and however the 'eight' or 'eighth' makes its appearance here, it already bears the stamp of revelation, of recognition and living-experience of that harmony which eliminates all opposites. It even gives an anticipation of what the world of the eighth day shall be.

When Jacob dies in Egypt, he desires to be brought to Canaan, 'in the cave that is in the field of Ephron, the Hittite; in the cave that is in the field of Machpelah' (Gen. 49:29–30) where Abraham had buried Sarah (Gen. 23).

The name Machpelah means 'double'. It is the place where the patriarchs and matriarchs in the story of the Bible come after their death in this world. What is double, is united there in that one place, the divorce is terminated. Double implies this being together of this world and that other, coming world. It similarly is the male and female gathered in harmony. Briefly, it is like the 'one', the 'aleph', the gathering of the opposites.

It is this place that Abraham buys from Ephron, the Hittite. The name Ephron is spelt 70–80–200–6–50. The root of the word is 70–80–200 and it has exactly the same structure as the word 'dust', when God said that man was dust and should return to dust. We came across the word, when we discussed the conception 3½ (or 350) which indeed renders the time-structure of matter.

In the name Ephron, however, the conception dust finishes with the ending 'nun', 50, indicating that in this Ephron in that place, dust is already connected with the coming world, when unity shall have been accomplished in the eighth day.

The 'double' of the name Machpelah, in which the opposites are united, just as the patriarchs and matriarchs are gathered together there, implies the condition of the eighth day, and in the name Ephron this is stated about that dust.

Moreover Ephron is the Hittite, which name actually means the 'eight' – apart from the fact that in its earthly phenomenal form it indicates a nation, the Hittites, which indeed also has its meaning. The name is spelt cheth-taf-jot, 8–400–10, meaning 'he that is of Cheth'; now we know Cheth as the 'eight' in the numerical significance of the word, hence in the original significance. So Ephron the Hittite is 'Ephron who is of the eight'. Another indication – in fact the third – that there is something which has to do with the eighth day.

And to end up with, there are in Machpelah the 'double', eight persons, viz. (according to ancient lore) Adam and Eve, and besides, according to the biblical story, Abraham and Sarah, Isaac and Rebekah and Jacob and Leah. It ever is the woman who comes there first, who therefore is the first to die in this world. Remember the description of body and soul in connection with the land of Joseph and the land of Judah. There, too, we saw that in principle the realm of Joseph is first to disappear and that the realm of Judah continues alive a little longer.

So, even in this root-story there is the statement that the body, the woman, disappears here sooner than that which is the expression of the soul, of the man.

Jacob comes as the eighth to Machpelah, and with this 'eighth', just as with the eighth day, its destination is completed. With it, in fact, ends the first book of the Bible.

In this way does the 'eight' come into prominence here in all places, indicating that this storing away has to do with the 'eight'. That this storing away is characteristic of the eighth day, that dying here means a transition to the field of Ephron, the 3½ with the 50, i.e. matter passing into the eighth, to Ephron, the Hittite, which again means the 'eight', and into the place where indeed the 'eight' are present.

We also see Ephron demanding 400 shekels of silver from Abraham, which ancient lore takes to be unworthy of Ephron because it is an exorbitant amount of money. Indeed, this 400 implies that matter, the 3½, demands the whole duration of this world, the uttermost, the endless, as the price for this eighth day.

He demands 400 shekels, spelt 300–100–30, with a sum-total of 430. And this is the number we already know as the expression for servitude in Egypt, servitude to the forces of development of the body. We also saw that the word 'nefesh', the bodily soul, has this number 430, hence that servitude essentially is servitude to this power of the body. So the amount Ephron demands as price is the 400 and the 430, two numbers rendering servitude in Egypt as duration in time. To acquire the place Machpelah, this long distance through the world must be covered, a course which seems endless. The 'silver' too, of the 400 shekels of silver, is connected with this place. For indeed silver is the metal which takes the second place in the systematism of the metals. Gold is the first and silver the second. So it has the place of the moon, the woman, body, covering, on the left side. Hence what is given for that place of the eighth day is everything of this life, the 400 and the 430, that which is the extreme duration and that which is the bodily soul, expressed in silver, given in the form of the physical, of that which appears on the left.

We see, for instance in Exod. 30:11–16, that the shekel is used as 'atonement for life'. The text mentions the ransom again for the 'nefesh'. Thus in that place again, the shekel of silver, here as 'half shekel' for 'nefesh'. The shekel which is 430 for the 'nefesh', which itself is 430.

So at the end of the book Genesis, Jacob is brought to this Machpelah as the last, as the eighth. It is a most uncommon journey, emphatically set forth in the

Bible. Ancient lore gives many more details about it. The whole shows a kind of Exodus of Jacob from Egypt, an exodus with pomp and circumstance and with great emphasis. And Joseph who then returns again with his family demands emphatically to be taken from Egypt. For, says Joseph, the purpose of life is that *all* shall finally leave Egypt. The purpose of life is not Egypt, this world of duality; but leaving it verily is. And Joseph who had formed the foundation of existence in that world of Egypt, desires that he himself shall also he removed from Egypt. The purpose of existence is the Exodus from Egypt.

28
The Pangs of Development

The exodus from Egypt is the axis round which everything revolves, also for the four books subsequent to Genesis. For these four books are an elaboration of what has been established in the first book, in Genesis. It is indeed that which is expressed as 'the merit of the fathers', by whom in the next four books the exodus is accomplished and the preparations are made for the occupation of Canaan, the coming world. 'Because God hath loved the fathers', the exodus and the journey to Canaan is accomplished, in the course of the four books. And that which in Genesis was enacted within the circle of a few people now comes to expression in immense multiplicity in the four subsequent books. That is why the four books can, in a certain sense, be looked upon as a world which is essentially already determined by the happenings in the book Genesis. What enacts itself in Genesis in the root, expands in immense multiplicity in the four books following Genesis.

The Bible tells us that the children of Israel, who had come down to Egypt as highly esteemed men, were getting suppressed there; that they were subjected to inexpressibly hard toil. The story in itself is most dramatic and the suffering of the children of Israel in Egypt and their emancipation from their yoke is a happening which appeals to a great many people.

Nevertheless, just because it concerns the Bible, we should not stop at the historical picture, however fascinating it may be owing to the real power which expresses itself in this image, but try and discover here too what are those essential forces, what the structure of the story is like, that we may realize from it that the exodus from Egypt is something taking place every day, that it is a communication from God, as to how life is made, what it is made for and what happens with it.

We have already seen that the name for Egypt, Mizraim, implies 'suffering in duality' and we have also pointed out the relationship between suffering and form. So that it expresses at the same time that there is a form in duality which because of it effects suffering.

The duality of Egypt, however, is not a duality in harmony, in tranquillity, but to the contrary, the duality of opposites, of clashing extremes. That is why there is suffering in Egypt; it is the suffering through contrast, through the inability of reconciling the opposites.

This contrast also embraces that of the present with the past and the future. There is no harmony between past and future, the two extremes which we are ever submitted to in the present. And this absence of rest, of harmony, demonstrates itself in a continual change of condition. That is what we call development. That is why the forces of development are inherent in the condition of disharmony of duality. Thus we saw that the serpent, bent on destroying the harmony of the Garden of Eden, became the cause of development in time; in the generations. The forces of development are rooted in that which disturbed harmony which the Bible sums up as the 'serpent'.

It is also what we know as wave-motion, with which everything appears that has to do with form in time.

Thus Egypt as duality without harmony has unleashed these forces of development. Now it is in this world that the children of Israel live.

The children of Israel already descended into Egypt in a previous phase, in Genesis. Joseph had just bridged the duality of Egypt, whose opposites could not be reconciled – remember the dream of Pharaoh – he had made the connection for the times of famine with the times of abundance and fullness. But this harmony, established by Joseph in that world of duality, had been disturbed in this period of the 'four' as contrasted with the period of the 'one', which proportion is similarly expressed between the four books following Genesis and Genesis itself. The new king of Egypt did not know anything about Joseph at all; he had no idea of the possibilities of bridging duality and reconciling it. As far as Egypt was concerned, there was no link between the time of Exodus and that of Genesis. In our terminology it means: the connection between the 'one' and the 'four' has been severed; the 'four' is now isolated.

On the other hand, the children of Israel prove still to be as they were. Tradition points out how their names, with which Genesis ends, are immediately mentioned again in the beginning of Exodus, and that with it the connection has been made between the 'one' and the 'four', in contradistinction with Pharaoh, who proves not to know Joseph any more.

Egypt, which had severed the connection with the 'one', is the power of material development, which is eager to develop away from the origin; it is the body in the grip of that intoxication which intimates that through developing ever more it will gather such impetus it will be able to rule as a god on earth.

The children of Israel who still have the connection with the 'one', who indeed have the connection with the origin, have therefore landed in a world which does not understand them at all. They are like the soul, with its divine origin, incarcerated in a body which absolutely refutes that origin, and, to the contrary, develops ever farther away from that origin.

Now Egypt incorporates the children of Israel into the life determined by the forces of development. It is the fear of Egypt that Israel might one day leave the land, that it should relinquish growth, that it should join the powers bent on disturbing this world of Egypt, bent on preventing and destroying development. Egypt is also scared at the enormous power this soul has acquired, a power, as biblical Egypt expresses it, which is greater than Egypt itself, greater and more numerous. This mighty power, with its bond with the origin, is felt by Egypt as an ever-impending danger. That is why Pharaoh decides to curtail this power through incorporating it in building up the world of development. So now the children of Israel are compelled to pay attention to the world of Egypt in the way the Egyptians who have severed themselves from the 'one', regard that world. They are incorporated in the service to the earth, the building of cities, stocking supplies towards an earthly future, making that earthly future secure. The soul thus diverted from its real duty, would thus lose strength, be enslaved, it would no longer find any opportunity to turn away from the world which had severed the bond with the 'one'.

But the more they were oppressed, the more the children of Israel gained in strength. As the soul is faced with the forces of development, it becomes aware of its destination all the more.

For that is the suffering in Egypt; it is the suffering of the soul which is compelled to serve the body in its obsession for development. It is not the suffering of the body, forced to toil, under the kicks and lashes of the overseers. It is the suffering of the man who cannot occupy himself with his humane task, but is diverted from it to perform tasks ensuing from that sham-world which a man creates for himself, as soon as he has severed himself from the origin.

A man knows he has to make an effort, get excited, overtired, ill, neurotic just for show, and this awareness constitutes suffering.

It is the suffering of man in a world imprisoned in an illusion of material development.

Tradition makes it clear, one should not consider servitude in Egypt as a kind of inferior slavish toil, while the Egyptians had fine positions.

From tradition we learn that oppressed Israel was not at all oppressed in the way the picture suggests. For the children of Israel are reported to have crowded the 'circuses and theatres' of Egypt, which does not quite tally with the picture one forms for oneself of slaves belaboured with whips.

Imprisonment is implicitly imprisonment in a world which does not know and does not want to know about the origin; a world which only sees a future in material prosperity ever richer and made more secure; a world which builds up a culture of cities, competitions, art which serves that society; a world stimulating the will and the disposition to plunge ever more and ever farther into this spiral of development.

And this imprisonment was not felt as such by all the children of Israel. Ancient lore has it that the greater part of Israel had turned with zest to this culture of Egypt, that it had joined in the activities for all they were worth. Therefore, emancipation did not come for all, most of them remained in Egypt and perished there; they lost themselves in multiplicity.

In Exod. 13:18 a certain passage reads in translation: 'the children of Israel went up harnessed out of the land of Egypt.' In the Hebrew text the word, translated as 'harnessed' is 'chamushin', which translated literally would be 'in fives', or 'one fifth'. Some translations, earlier ones, render it by: 'in rows of five'.

At any rate this fits in more logically with the story than the translation 'as one fifth did the Israelites march out of the land of Egypt.' Yet, this is actually what the literal translation should be.

Ancient lore has it that merely one fifth, i. e. one to every five of the children of Israel out of Egypt was saved; that four out of every five remained behind, because they had not suffered under the culture of the world of duality, of the world of development, because that was where they belonged and therefore got lost, just as the multiplicity of that world got lost.

I rather think the reader will have observed that there again the structure of the 1–4 shows up. And that here, too, the 'one' means life, the way which leads people alive from that world of Egypt, and the 'four' means death, perishing in multiplicity. Those that had gone the way of the tree of life in Egypt, the way of the 'one' had suffered under the development of culture, which had been entirely directed towards the earth; which saw emancipation as a final phase of development.

It was not their world and therefore they were saved from it. Those, however, who had gone the way of the tree of knowledge, of the 'tree that makes fruit', who therefore had regarded development as the central factor of the life of the world; had felt at home in the world of Egypt; they had taken delight in that culture. And that was why they had gone the way which ultimately is the way of those who have eaten of the tree of knowledge, the way of death and destruction, in ignorance, believing until the very end in the forces of development, even when these already show they are in-effectual.

Therefore the word 'one-fifth' i. e. the 'one' over against the 'four', is indeed identical with the word 'harnessed', 'fitted out for battle'. For he that has the quality of the 'one', who has the way of the tree of life in which the 'four' is bound to 'one', he is 'harnessed' in the sense of the Bible, in the sense which brings with it the exodus from the world of duality, from Egypt.

Thus we see that the suffering of the children of Israel in Egypt was not a kind of racial persecution to which all Jacob's descendants were subjected. To the contrary, the majority, according to tradition, felt very comfortable there. To them an exodus from that world was as much an abhorrence as it was to the Egyptians themselves. The separation therefore is different from what one might infer from the image. It was not a division along racial or national lines, but ensuing from people's disposition towards life.

Ancient lore also says that the tribe of Levi was exempt from work for Egypt. For the very simple reason that the tribe of Levi was occupied with God's word, making it their object of life to study the purpose of life, the purpose of creation, and desiring to pass it on to others. It is rather difficult to conciliate the scheme of things called up by the picture, with the Egyptians' exempting this very group of people from service to the world. One would have thought they were the ones most likely to be suppressed. The tribe of Levi, to the contrary, fall outside the scope of the census of the children of Israel; they had a private census, a census of their own.

This statement of ancient lore shows that whoever occupies himself positively with the matter with which the tribe of Levi busied themselves is free from service to this world. These people size up the things of this world, so that, whatever they may or may not do, they will never feel subject to the forces of this world. They are so utterly detached from, so utterly beyond the world of Egypt, that it does not affect them. It is something they observe, judge with the standards of creation; then they know it for what it is and whither it leads. Such people cannot be subjugated in the sense the Bible really means it.

Who has *actually* suffered in Egypt? Ancient lore states that Egypt had begun to pay 'wages' to the children of Israel for their work. If something, taking up the place of the soul in the story, receives wages, it means that these wages *gratify* the soul. For thus indeed is the way. The world offers all its attractions to man, it gives the impression of storing mighty secrets; it provokes man by showing *something* and leaving the rest to be surmised; it shows concspicuous laws, relationships, etc.

Briefly it is a challenge to the hunt. The hunter cannot resist the pursuit, after the animal has shyly, fearfully, enticed him, and subsequently hidden itself. It is also like the woman who, overflowing with the forces of development — called sex nowadays — provokes the man to pursue her in order to win her. Such a man is as proud as the hunter of his trophy, but he very soon looks out for the next. For it is motion, the hunt, the pursuit which provokes him, not possession of the *animal*.

In the same way does the world promise wages; it holds out the prospect of certain things, thus appealing to man. So man begins his service to the world, he begins to follow it in its movements, in its constant changing of place and aspect. It seems fascinating enough, this investigation of the world. It shows its manifold varieties. One can serve it for wages in the field of science, chemistry, biology, sociology, economics, technology, etc. And the wages certainly mean satisfaction; one presumes one is on one's way to the high wages, the glorious and formidable animal of legend, the discovery of the grand secret of life, of the universe.

But — thus ancient lore continues its tale — once the children of Israel, through the wages they received at first, had got used more or less to working for Egypt, their wages continued decreasing little by little. They had, however, got wrapped up so much in their work, they hardly noticed the decrease. In this way the wages decreased more and more, till finally they were stopped altogether. But by then the children of Israel could not stop working any more; they had got captivated by their work. Egypt had reached its goal; it had incorporated the soul, divine man, in the work on matter, in the service of the world of duality.

This story of the decreasing wages, which were in the end stopped altogether in the service of Egypt, is a most important aspect which helps comprehend what service to Egypt actually means. For the service of the world which at first holds out great promise – keeping before man in his first spell of enthusiastic optimism that he may discover the secret of life, the purpose of life, and provoking him to the pursuit in showing him partial successes – this service of the world entails man's getting obsessed with the hunt. This hunter, who as it says in the Bible, desires to be a 'mighty hunter before the Lord, a mighty man in the earth'. Man loses sight of the fact that the goal held out before him keeps dwindling down all the time; he has not discovered the secret of life, it is true, but indeed very interesting relationships and afterwards he is content with relationships in more limited fields, getting excited about *such* niggling results that any outside person will wonder how it is that sensible people can bother about these trifles which have nothing to do with the purpose of life. Their goal is shifting all the time; it is also divided into so many portions.

But man is in the grip of this obsession. It is very much like smoking and drinking; just as one may derive some joy from one's first cigarette, similarly from one's first strong drink, but once one has started that way, it is not the pleasure which urges one on, but one simply cannot stop. By that time Egypt need not pay any more wages, for then one has got so much addicted to one's work, one simply cannot leave off. One has no longer got the taste, but is gripped in the intoxication. So much so, one would not even *desire* to stop. Thus everything, approaching the world along the lines of the running, moving 'four', the 'four' that has not been bound, becomes an obsession. Obsession, intoxication, is inherent to the substance of this 'four' as expression of multiplicity, and one cannot stop it any more. This holds good for every aspect of this power of development, which expresses itself as the non-bound 'four', whether it concerns opium, morphia, nicotine, alcohol, sex, business, research, or economics, whenever one has taken this course, enticed by the wages at the beginning, one considers it impossible to stop. One had rather accept the obvious ruin and destruction than discontinue any further action in this sphere of intoxication.

As a matter of fact there would not be anything wrong with the world, if one did stop. It would be incomparably better for the world anyway. But people think it cannot be; people have sham-constructions of the world and development in their minds, and they take these sham-constructions for reality. When a formidable war comes down on these structures like a bolt from the blue and smashes them up, showing that the world has different standards, people close their eyes for a moment and then go on unconcernedly building up these structures anew, at best adding yet another over the guilty ones and the indemnities in connection with the war.

Thus did Egypt get the children of Israel in its grip. They worked for the world of Egypt, because they simply could not do otherwise any more; because they thought the world should end in chaos, if they were to stop.

The 'four' of the children of Israel who like Egypt had severed themselves from the 'one', thought that life in this way was good, that this was life. And they enjoyed their social status in this work, never realizing that there was something else. Just think of the story of Cain, and see how all these stories ever show this relationship. Whoever has cut himself off from the 'one', i.e. has killed Abel, will plunge into that culture on purpose to banish death, to him death is unsocial and should be forgotten. Intoxication is the very means to forget; intoxication in the culture of this world of Egypt.

But the '*one*' of the children of Israel, first enticed by the promised wages in their idealism and their eagerness to understand the purpose of life, are quick to see that those wages are delusive, and they sigh in this world of Egypt. They suffer on account of time lost, energy wasted and unnecessary excitement. They have to run in harness since they have chosen that course, but they suffer under that world, their souls sigh and lament. They look out for help, for a saviour, who is to set them free from the world of duality with its character of never-ending development. They do not believe emancipation will come as the final phase of development.

Egypt fears that saviour. Again it is ancient lore which sets forth that Egypt actually knew there would be a saviour. After all, ever since creation this notion has been inherent in duality; an inkling about the return to the source of origin. The only thing is that duality refuses to admit the fact. Just as the man given to duality refuses to know about death. Therefore Egypt desires to thwart the coming of the saviour. First with the help of the so-called midwives Sifra and Pua. It seems rather strange that two midwives should suffice for those hundreds of thousands of people. Very often the image in itself urges us to concentrate on the essential, since its expression in phenomenal form cannot adequately satisfy our earthly logic. According to ancient lore, these two women were Jochebed, Moses' mother, and Miriam, Moses' sister. It is the 'two', who are also present at the birth of Moses.

Now it is these two that get Pharaoh's command to kill all the boys immediately at their birth. They do not obey, motivating it with the statement that the children of Hebrew women are born differently from those of Egyptians; that the child of the Hebrew woman lives even before the midwives arrive. Actually it means that the Egyptian children are born as the 'two' – here expressed in the image of the two midwives who allow those that are at the gate, to be born into this world – hence when the 'two' are on the spot. They are born into a world past the 'two', going towards multiplicity. The 'two' can carefully watch whether they shall come or not. But the children of the Hebrew women, i.e. of the women bearing the name of 'Ibri', coming from another world, come from the world of the 'one', the world previous to the 'two'. There where the 'two' stands at the command of Pharaoh, there the 'Ibri' is already alive, since he comes from another world. The power of the 'Ibri', the Hebrew, is his very bond with the 'one'. Hence the Ibri cannot be attacked in the world of duality; the weapons of that world do not worry him, since he is of a different quality.

The midwives were rewarded by God, because they had not affected the 'one' of the sons who were born, because they had not cut off the sons from their connection with the origin, but allowed them to grow up in the world *with* that bond with the 'one' which they bore as a special characteristic, as it was expressed by their name 'Ibri'. The reward consisted in these women receiving 'houses'. Translation here gives the word 'families', which as a translation indeed is not illogical (Exod. 1:21). The reward was that they got a 'two' — the 'two' as a letter, as we know, means 'house' — a 'two' which, in agreement with their acting towards the newly born sons, was also united with the 'one'. For immediately after, it says in Exod. 2:1 that 'there went a man of the house of Levi and took to wife a daughter of Levi', i.e. Jochebed, one of the two 'midwives', and that Moses was born to them. Keeping alive at its entrance into this world that which actually descends from the other world, from the other side, and emphasizing the bond which connects it with the origin, yields a 'two', a 'house', in which similarly the bond with the 'one' is also present, in which therefore the saviour is born. Of the things which come here from the other world, whose image we perceive here, we must not take this image as their only existing reality, we must not sever it from its origin and thus kill it. We should rather allow the image to live by *not* cutting it off from its substance; to the contrary we should clearly show that bond. Then a 'two' will come to us, i.e. an image in this world, a phenomenon in this world, which bears the bond with the origin so as to unite everything of this world with that origin, bringing everything of this world back to the origin. Thus did Moses, the saviour in the world of Egypt, come into the 'house', the 'two' of Jochebed.

The 'house' which the other midwife, Miriam, received, according to ancient lore, was the house with Caleb. We saw that Caleb, of Judah, and Joshua, were the only ones to come alive from the desert into Canaan although they belonged to the generation which was to die in the desert.

When Pharaoh realizes that the bond with the 'one' exists in the 'Ibri' — in that which also expresses itself as soul — this bond which implies the danger of an exodus from Egypt, because this bond permits of the coming of the saviour, there comes a new phase in the attempt to prevent the saviour from making his appearance here. It entails throwing all the sons that are born, into the river and allowing the daughters to live. The daughters, as body, as 'outward appearance' were greatly beloved in Egypt. According to ancient lore Egypt placed the daughters in the very centre for the sake of adultery. As the world with the character of duality, with the 'Phar', the power of development for its 'god', Egypt keeps a place apart for the woman, for the body. Indeed, the body serves to make this development possible at all; it becomes the pivot of this development. With it the body is cut off from its destination of uniting with the 'origin', with the soul. The soul is killed, is kept in servitude, and the body is emancipated with a purpose of its own, a destination of its own. This is what is virtually implied by adultery with the woman.

The sons, however, must be thrown into the river. We have already seen that water is connected with the left side, and that it expresses multiplicity without individuality, without personality. Throwing a thing into the water, into the expression, into the image of our phenomenal form, means that one desires to drown that thing, to have it merged in a vast whole, make it imperceptible. It also implies death to the one that is thrown into the water. Thus there is also a death in the substance, if one makes something lose its personality, its individuality; merges it into a colourless mass which covers it. For that is the actual meaning of throwing all the 'sons' into the river. It is the world's moulding that vast uniform mass, desiring to submerge in it everything that has individuality, the 'root'. It is the constraint to uniformity, the ban on conspicuousness, the compulsion to adapt oneself to society in its development. It means fixing criteria for the colourless man, the submersion of anyone deviating from this standard. It is Pharaoh's endeavour to make it unlikely for the saviour to come. If everything which yet desires to maintain the bond with the origin; if everything which is 'son', virile, aware of the significance of the essential to this world; if all this is constrained by the form of society resulting from the laws of development to become uniform with the masses, to assume the character of multiplicity, it is choked in its chances of life; then it is killed as 'son', as man, as potential redeemer.

Thus Pharaoh tried not only to incorporate the soul into labour for the ideals of Egypt, for material development, but at the same time he created the form to thwart any termination of this condition, the form of drowning the 'sons' in the masses. On account of this world of Egypt did that part of the children of Israel suffer, which pertained to the 'one' of the (1–4). It realized the purposelessness of the so-called work for the world, which aimed at something entirely different from that which might give purpose to life in this world. It suffered from the foolishness and the lack of understanding of the world; it also saw that redemption was frustrated by the forms of society which would send out of bounds anybody trying to put forward anything different; and would hold him up to ridicule and make him unacceptable. And their power and insight increased as the world tried to commit the soul more firmly to itself. Thus did the children of Israel increase in power and number.

Now this suffering was seen by God, and the sighs and lamentations of this subjugated man were heard. For, if man complains of that, then there is contact with God. If a man complains about a world which incorporates the soul for material development; which refuses to give the soul a chance of following its own way; which only pays attention to increase of the 'national produce', to research into more and more details about earthly matter or extra-terrestrial matter; which takes the children and from an early age incorporates them into this service of matter which stifles every chance of a new vision; *then* that man is heard. For then he complains about the impending dissolution of all remaining bonds with the origin. Then he shows that he has still got those bonds and is sighing and groaning about the world turning away more and more from the source of origin; about this wilful disruption of even the last bonds with the origin. And whoever has still got this bond and would feel happy at the strengthening of that bond and at seeing this bond restored everywhere, most assuredly has contact with God and his sighs are heard. Indeed, it is the one attitude possible, bearing testimony before God of one's experience and sentiments with such a world. Neither fighting nor shouting is of any avail. At best a statement to other people about the things one observes and feels.

Sighing before God and formulating one's suffering on account of making no progress in the world; having to plod for exams in the field of science; complaining about feeling poorly because one has to work so hard and runs the risk of heart-complaint or haemorrhage of the brain or nervous breakdowns, and praying for health in order to plunge again into advertising campaigns, expansion of production, increase of efficiency, party-politics, conferences, etc. I have my doubts whether such sighing and groaning really establishes the contact with God which the victim imagines. For his complaints are concerned with his lack of speed in his pursuit of the evasive, ever hiding 'four'. He prays for help to become a better hunter. If his prayer be such that it is heard – and under any circumstances, wherever man may be, a prayer can restore the connection with God, for it means that man has turned his face towards the origin, if even for that fraction of a minute – it would only be heard to set him free from the pursuit, to make him retrace his steps. At first he may look upon it as a wrong effect of his prayer, since everything he has been praying for is taken from him. But he may yet come to see that God made him empty in regard to the pursuit to return to the right course. Sighing to break the bond with God still further, even if it is done in good faith, since one knows no better, certainly does not yield the effect prayed for. A psychologist in that case is the proper person to turn to, rather than God.

Those that sigh because of the lashes, and hope that they in their turn may soon be allowed to wield the whip to lash the others; those that sigh because of material oppression or oppression of national pride, do not sigh because of what Egypt makes the children of Israel suffer in the Bible. They sigh like one Egyptian because of the oppression by another Egyptian. They sigh like Cain on his way as 'a fugitive and a vagabond'.

But whoever suffers from the abuse of man, from this humiliation of the divine soul being incorporated in the labour for this world, this suffering of the soul because of the senselessness of it all, this suffering brings emancipation. The soul that can 'quite well adapt itself' to this world; that 'does not think the world a bad place'; that 'sees great possibilities opening up'; that 'thinks people quite reasonable' and above all dislikes exaggeration, that soul pertains to the four fifths that did not leave Egypt; pertains to the 'four'. Whoever feels comfortable, at ease, in this world, a substantial citizen 'on holiday far away', who does not feel like crying out with misery for what he should see every day but does not, pertains to those that were destroyed in Egypt together with the others who enjoyed themselves. Only he that really suffers for the true reason of suffering, who daily sighs under it, only he is heard. That is the meaning of the story of the suffering in Egypt. These people's sighing for *that* reason brings salvation.

29
The Laws Governing the Return

Ancient lore gives a good deal of information on the birth of Moses. Pharaoh's measures to have all the newborn sons thrown into the water, fell in the period before Moses' birth. Owing to the oppressiveness of the times, says ancient lore, Amram and Jochebed, the parents-to-be of Moses, had decided not to have any more children. If children were to meet with that fate, it would be better to save them as well as the parents themselves from grief and renounce on conjugal life.

Thereupon Miriam, their six-year-old daughter, reproached her parents with this attitude – we see how tradition almost compels us to abandon the outward image and try to grasp the meaning of the story; for Miriam at that time had already been the midwife. Even if there should only be daughters, i.e even if the body alone were allowed to come into this world, it was not for them to judge from the standpoint of this world what purpose it served. As husband and wife their married intercourse should be physically fruitful as well, that was what they had become husband and wife for in this world. Man had similarly come into the world to eat and drink through the body.

The same situation according to ancient lore, arose with Adam and Eve, after Cain had killed his brother Abel. Then, too, the parents decided to have no more children since it merely resulted in one killing the other. There, too, it was Abel the reflection of the conception 'soul' who was killed by the physical, by Cain, just as Pharaoh desired to drown the sons and use the daughters.

Adam, according to the statements, subsequently had intercourse with Lilith, a femal entity of the night, of the demonic sphere. The name Lilith and the word for night 'laila' have the same root. Having intercourse with a woman without begetting children is described as having intercourse with a nocturnal demon. What they created in their intercourse was demons with which they filled the world. According to tradition demons are beings which make their appearance here in a body, but never come to a consummation of it. They are beings which feel attracted by the earth and are dangerous to man on his way to reunion. Now it is this kind of beings the man brings forth, if, arguing that having children produces disaster, he substitutes intercourse with the 'demon of the night' for that with his wife of flesh and blood.

The reader is begged to realize it is of course not merely a question of conjugal intercourse without the desire for the fruit, or even with the fear of eventual fruit. The term 'male and female' bears on the encounter of any pair of opposites. And if one brings the opposites to an encounter without the intention of reconciling them to unity, if any idea in that direction is evaded, if one derives pleasure from the reality of the contrast, then these 'demons' are produced in that plane, too. What is not directed towards reunion, creates demons, creates this multiplicity which permeates everything with the thought of further development, of continuing existing conditions. That is why these demons are called very attractive. For they exercise a strong temptation in the same way as the conception 'serpent' did.

So one should not make a mental picture of these demons as creatures with tails and horns. In their outward appearance they are just 'ordinary' people. They are, however, rooted in a non-human world and they do not reach completion like human beings. According to tradition every final phase is crowded with demons.

According to tradition Adam lived with Lilith for 130 years. When he returned from that evil way, he begot Seth, the son from whom indeed completion came, who was again in His image, after His likeness. The 300–400 of the name of Seth was completed in the 500. Seth came instead of Abel, as it says in the Bible and from this generation ultimately arose the 500 of the tree of life, the 500 which also began with the coming of Abraham and which ended in the Revelation of God on Mount Sinai.

The time which lapsed between the 'descent' of the children of Israel with Jacob into Egypt, i.e. in 2238, and Miriam's pointing at the wrong attitude in the renunciation, in 2368, similarly is 130 years. Thus we again see it confirmed what this 130 means in the structure of the Bible. In either case it means the conclusion of wrong intercourse of a man and a woman, and also of soul and body, and of all opposites; and that with the 130, through right encounter, there comes the fruit which brings salvation.

The word Sinai, too, spelt Samech-jot-nun-jot, 60–10–50–10, has a sum-total of 130. For indeed, there too reunion was accomplished: on Mount Sinai as terminus of the way of the 500 years since Abraham and as the 50th day after the exodus from Egypt, there was the reunion between God and the world: God descending on Mount Sinai – the name through its part 'Sin' has to do with the moon, hence with form, with body, with the world of the left side – therewith intimating the purpose of life.

And also, for instance, the ladder which Jacob saw (Gen. 28:10–22), set up on the earth and the top of it reaching to heaven; thus uniting heaven and earth, has this value of 130. The name for that ladder is 'sulam', spelt samech-lamed-mem, 60–30–40. In every phenomenal form of ladder there is this essential principle of 'ascending'. One should, however, always unite the image to the substance. To wind up with, let me remind the reader of the structure of the word 'one', which similarly gives the sum-total of 13.

So we see that the structure of chronology in the Bible and that of the words ever fit together, and that correct understanding of the meaning of the whole can only ensue if we know this structure. For it is only on the ground of the structure of the Bible that an explanation can have sense. Otherwise it becomes something arbitrary, sprung from human sentiments or human criteria.

Thus, when the 130 has been attained, there is this transformation and with it the saviour is born.

It may be useful to point again at the situation in the image, which shows anew that one should not translate the image as such into this world, but that one should understand it in its substance. Thus, for instance, Jochebed, the mother of Moses, appears to be the daughter of Levi (Exod.6:13–26). According to tradition, she was born on the way from Canaan to Egypt, in 2238, that is. If one goes the way towards this world of servitude, the world of duality, even on the way thither the mother of the saviour is born. On the way to duality salvation is in fact determined. Just remember the structure of the word 'create', which similarly implies things ending up in the 'one'. The exodus from Egypt is in 2448, i.e. 210 years after the 'descent'. Moses is then 80 years old; he was born, as stated above, in 2368. This means that Jochebed was then 130 years old. And Aaron and Mirian had been born respectively 3 and 6 years previously, when Jochebed was 127 and 124 years old. All this shows that one should be very careful in handling the image. It has an entirely different meaning and is an expression for an entirely different world.

Thus there came the most important decision on the part of Amram and Jochebed, in spite of everything, to follow the course of the 'be fruitful and multiply', decreed by God. As discussed above, this principle in Hebrew is 'pru urebu', with a sum-total of 500. So it represents the way, expressed physically, to attain the 500, the coming world. As the principle '500' it evades the criteria of earthly causality. In its true sense, however, in its world of the 500, it expresses very clearly that following this course brings salvation; that it leads beyond this world. That is why God had imparted this 'pru urebu' as first principle to all living things. For this way would be the physical fulfilment of the principle of salvation. In man, as contrasted with the rest of nature, the fulfilment of this principle is a matter for him to decide. Man can argue that ruin and destruction await the children, and then refuse to obey the principle. With it, however, making use of his own standards to come to a decision, he would stand in the way of the fulfilment of the 500, a principle of a world beyond ours, beyond the 400.

The decision of Amram and Jochebed to do as man is enjoined to do, in spite of the ruin to be expected for their son, leaving it to God to lead the world by His standards, is very much the same situation as that of Abraham, when in obedience to God's command he is to sacrifice, to kill the only son bestowed on him with many promises; and who yet goes *all the same,* realizing that God purposed better with his son than he as the father in this world, since he himself could not distinguish which was good or bad essentially. It is also the situation with the tree of life and the tree of knowledge. According to the tree of knowledge, man fixing for himself the criteria of good and bad by virtue of his sensory perception and experience, would have to argue that it was madness to want any children with the prospect of having one's son drowned in the waters. But Amram and Jochebed leave the tree of knowledge to God and perform the things in life according to the standards of the tree of life, according to the standards God gave them that they might see *how* good everything was. And that attitude of Amram and Jochebed means the '130', it implies that one acts *in spite of* that which the senses and the logic, based on it, present as conclusion. And it is exactly from acting *like this* that the saviour comes forth.

The word 'saviour', 'god', implies that the 'one' has been brought into the form in matter. 'Goel is spelt gimmel-aleph-lamed, 3–1–30. And the word for the soulless body, for that which lives without a soul, is 'golem', gimmel-lamed-mem, 3–30–40. The root 'gal', 3–30, represents this life in which the soul as deliverer is lacking. Thus the word for the exile, the captivity, is 'galuth', 3–30–400. It is the life of the form, yet without a soul which can give purpose to life. That is why the word 'saviour' has the 'one' in that same root of the 3–30, hence it is 3–1–30. Thus it indicates that introducing the 'one' into the form, like the soul into the body, brings the saviour. It is this introduction of the other standards, the standards of the 'one', into the form which causes the saviour to come.

The child which has come in this way, is *not* cast into the waters, like the others for it is laid in an 'ark of bulrushes' and it is set afloat in the waters of the river, by the brink of the river. Now this word translated as 'ark of bulrushes' is exactly the same word which in the story of the Great Flood is translated by 'ark', for it is the word we are familiar with, the 'teba'.

Again we see a life remaining in existence, there where all the others are drowned, viz. by placing it in the 'word'. It also means: by uniting everything with the word and therefore with the substance, man keeps *alive* in times of superficiality and ruin.

Not only does he keep alive, but his is even found by the daughter of Pharaoh and smuggled into the king's palace to grow up there. Suddenly an altogether different, strange causality comes into effect. Pharaoh who was so much afraid of the coming of a saviour who would put an end of the world of duality, his world; who took all kinds of measures to forestall the coming of the saviour, without realizing it, is obliged to let the redeemer grow up in his house. Merely because Moses entered the river in the 'teba', because he entered time in the 'word'. Because on account of it he was connected with the substance of things. The world suffers the saviour to grow up in its midst, because he came with the 'teba', with the word. Even though they have their suspicions that the saviour has thus come – tradition tells a great deal about these misgivings on the part of Pharaoh and his councillors – yet everything compels them to let him live and grow up. When the world desires to give death, the coming with the word compels them to give life.

The story of the 'teba' raises the question why the other children were not put in a *teba*, why the other children were thrown into the water without more ado. They, too, would have stood a better chance of keeping alive in a *teba*. The answer can be given the more easily now that we know what *teba* means. In times of superficiality, of getting lost in the mass, parents must be able to pass on the 'word' to their children to keep them alive. It is only parents like Amram and Jochebed who prove to be able through their mode of life, to make this *teba*, thus paving the way for the saviour against all causal expectations.

Through this *teba* the name of Moses too comes into existence, viz. 'taken from the water'. So the saviour of that root-story is he that was taken from the water. All the rest get drowned, are submerged by multiplicity. Since he came into that multiplicity with the word, with the teba, he became conspicuous, he was different, he was a real Ibri, the one coming from another world. Thus does Pharaoh's daughter characterize him. And because of the *teba* he is drawn from the water.

The name of the saviour indicates what he is. He is the one that is drawn from multiplicity, who does not get drowned in uniformity, who is 'different'. For him another law of creation obtains. For it is the 'daughter' of substance of this earth, who feels driven to save him and educate him. This was already prepared and predestined from before creation. Whatever the name Moses may mean in Egyptian, in the language of the Bible it means 'he that was drawn from the water'; and the language of the Bible is unique in its connecting image and substance. To the other languages the way back to the essence has become undiscoverable in consequence of the 'dividing', the 'splitting into two' by the Haflaga.

That the redeemer grows up in the palace of Pharaoh, also means that he learns to know the reality of this world; for Pharaoh represents the nucleus of the world of Egypt, of duality.

We shall not here expatiate on the arguments for Moses' flight. The sum and substance of it is that he was recognized as the future destroyer of Egypt. Ancient lore is very comprehensive, in its details about what happened to Moses in the period between his seventeenth year when he was recognized and had to make his escape, and his eightieth year when God revealed Himself to him in the same place where God later on revealed Himself to all.

But I should like to point at the bush (Exod. 3:2) which was burning, yet was not consumed, called in Hebrew 'sne', spelt 60–50–5. The root is the same as that of the word Sinai, the place where it happens, which also has the 60–50 for its root. And the happening itself, the burning without being consumed is that which we have learnt to know as the reconciliation of the opposites, hence something inherent in God's revelation of Himself. For logic based on perception implies that a bush burning with fire must be consumed. But when one has reached the place of reunion, the contrast proves to be a harmony; then it appears that what consumes things in this world of ours is not consumed at all.

According to ancient lore Moses merely came to this spot, because he had gone after a lamb which had strayed away from the flock, to bring it back. It is again as we saw, for instance, in the case of Jacob at the ford Jabbok, the interest in the apparently futile, the attention of man to small things, for things abandoned by others as not being worth while, which brings him to the place of reunion. So he does not measure in accordance with the masses, not according to the weight in this world, not with the standards of this world.

At that bush, the 'sne', Moses is directed by God to accomplish the exodus of all the children of Israel from Egypt as their leader. I cannot, within the scope of this book, elaborate on this story either. I only want to point at Moses' resistance to obey (Exod. 2:23–4:17). It is, as tradition points out, the resistance of man to coming into this world and again the fear of leaving this world. It is also like the fear of Jacob about going and getting his father Isaac's blessing, when Esau was to have it.

To make existence in this world possible for man, God covered him with a body, just as Rebekah covered Jacob with the skins of the kids of the goats prepared for a meal, and with the garments of Esau. Thus God finally says to Moses that his brother Aaron would come from Egypt to meet him: 'he shall be to thee instead of a mouth, and thou shalt be to him instead of God' (Exod. 4:16). Again it means that the relationship between Moses and Aaron is like that between soul and body. That Aaron shall be the outward appearance of Moses, while Moses as being, as nucleus, as God, shall lead that outward appearance. That is why in the systematism Moses is on the right, under Abraham, and Aaron is on the left on the side of Isaac, of the body. That is also why Aaron has to do with the 'korban', the offerings, bringing the body to God. Just as with Isaac, the first 'korban' of the body was brought, the first binding of the 'four' to 'one' took place already. That is also the reason why it was Aaron who was concerned with the making of the golden calf, when people did not believe any more that Moses would return from Mount Sinai. At man's appearance in this world it is the body which goes to meet him and receive him, the body which is there for the very purpose of being brought by man before God. Through this body man's existence has a purpose, man can obtain the blessing in this world. But at the same time this body brings with it the potentiality of deviating, if it unites itself with the forces of development.

Moses' fear of going, his imploring almost to be excused from going therefore is also an expression of the principle which has voiced itself ever since creation, the fear of going into the captivity of the earth, even though being aware that one shall return from the exile with the blessing, and even though knowing that through this exile one shall save all the rest as well. Thus in going down to Egypt Moses will make the exodus from Egypt possible, he will bring the great emancipation there. Going down to Egypt is like having to be born into this world in order to leave it again at one's death. One comes from elsewhere and goes back somewhere else. It is like the rod of Moses which turned into a serpent, afterwards to become a rod again, and like his hand which became 'leprous' afterwards became a hand again.

According to ancient lore, every child that will be born has the same fear of the world here, but it is sent down all the same to be received by the body which through the intercourse of the parents has been made ready to receive the child. And there is the same resistance, the same fear of departing from this world, when at a different level a similar situation arises.

At first one dislikes leaving the condition in which one experiences reunion, just as Moses at the 'one', to expose oneself to the danger of the world of duality. But at this departure, one finds oneself in the same situation which God created for Himself when He made this world and man, to go as Lord God into 'exile' with this world. In ancient lore it is called the 'exile of the Shechinah'. 'Shechinah' can be described as 'God immanent in this world'.

The act of God in creating together with this world the greatest happiness for man implied God's going into captivity as the 'shechinah', taking upon Himself the suffering of the exile. Just as God said to Jacob (Gen. 46:3–4) when he was going to descend into Egypt, that He would accompany him thither and back again. It is the name Lord God expressing itself in the (10–5–6–5) structure of the 26 generations down to the Revelation.

To give the world this creation, God took it upon Himself to go the way of the exile, that He might accompany the world to the extreme point and come back with it, bring it back with Him to the source of origin. The way to the farthest extreme, to this world of duality, ever is an exile. But this journey abroad is the condition, it is the offering, relinquishing one's own abode of peace, of harmony, so that the joy of reunion with creation may be experienced.

So that man as a divine being, made in the image of God, after His likeness, shall accomplish this same reunion of everything, therefore does God send man into the same exile, He took upon Himself; therefore is the name Lord God expressed in the generations of man; therefore there is the fear of man at taking that way. But it is only through this exile that the immense happiness of reunion can be tasted, for it is only through this exile one can do everything 'for nothing', one can fulfil the foundations of the conception 'reunion' in yielding faith, affection; in surrender. There, in that captivity, one has only got one's own criteria of perception, of that world of duality, which shows contrast and contradiction, which opposes death to life. One can only come to reunion with the same qualities God expressed when He made creation and went into exile with man, for man's sake.

So, from the same principle there is this long conversation between Moses and God at the 'sne', at the place of unity, because the journey into the captivity is a very, very difficult way. And Aaron is like the body, which comes to meet him to receive him. Together like a unity they will bring deliverance, and on their way to reunion, from Egypt to Mount Sinai and to Canaan they will play the part of the leaders.

When Moses is on his way to Egypt, a curious scene is enacted in the 'inn', giving the impression that God assailed Moses to kill him. (Exod. 4:20–27). Moses descends into Egypt with his wife and sons. He sets them upon an ass, and starts on the journey which is to lead to the emancipation of the children of Israel from the world of duality. God tells him about the principle of the conflict with Egypt. Egypt keeps Israel imprisoned, the body oppresses the soul, sets the soul to do the senseless work in the service of the transient things of this world. Israel, as the expression of what in principle is the soul, is to God even His first-born. To the world of duality, to Egypt, the first-born is the body tied to the forces of development. Emancipation means liberating the soul, the substance, the nucleus, from the oppression of the body which is subject to continual change through development. If the body insists on oppressing and abusing the nucleus in this way, then something will have to be done to that body. If Pharaoh, the Phar, the maker of multiplicity, the lord of the world of duality, refuses to refrain from oppressing the soul, then this Pharaoh will experience the loss of his power, of the oppressing body in its ceaseless activity of striving after multiplicity. Now this is, as we have already seen, the meaning of circumcision. There too, it is a forcing back of the body, of that which covers the substance, in order to emancipate the nucleus.

Now the same thing happens to Moses, on his way down to Egypt, on the border of Egypt, on his way to liberate the children of Israel. On the night-side of the world, where man abides, before he makes his appearance on the day-side – just think of the words 'and the evening and the morning were', where the night ever precedes the day, just as the body precedes the soul – on this night-side, in the 'inn' does Moses appear, himself similarly covered with this encompassing body; together with his wife and children and the ass. The deliverer comes together with the body, in order to emancipate it. What pertains to him at his coming into this world, this covering which chokes the nucleus, is still present. This covering brings death to him just as much as to Pharaoh, who stifles the nucleus within himself, Pharaoh, who emphasizes and accords priority to the developing body. Liberation means setting the nucleus free. That is what man shall conquer death with. But in anybody, oppressing this nucleus, according priority to perceptibility, the attack will always be directed at the covering. At perceiving the utter nakedness of what to him is the principal, the most important, the first-born, he will experience death. The experience of death will always take place, as long as that covering, has not been circumcised and turned back, pushed back; as long as it causes duality. That which Moses is to accomplish in Egypt is very much the same thing enacted in the world-of-night, in the inn, in the form of the coming of death and emancipation from it, because the covering is pushed back and the nucleus is set free. The exodus from Egypt already takes place in the inn, in the abode of the night; the attack in order to kill is like the impending suffocation of the soul, of Israel in servitude to the world of multiplicity; and the emancipation from death is like the exodus from Egypt. That which will be enacted in the day-world which Moses is now going to enter, appears in this form on the night-side. And it is Zipporah, the wife, the body, who recognizes the forces of development and rejects them. She is the mediator who achieves liberation for her husband; just as Rebekah did. Just as, in the reverse sense, Eve had been the mediator to send the serpent to her husband, thus giving the nucleus for the generating of the growing, developing and dying body.

Ancient lore has it a.o. that Moses was attacked in the inn by the serpent, and that Zipporah saved his life by circumcising their son Eliezer. Zipporah had recognized the cause of death. Again it was the body which had recognized why and when the serpent can make an attack, and it had removed the cause in weakening the covering of the nucleus.

She showed it to Moses, passed it on to him pointing out to him that it had brought death to the body which is subjected to the forces of development and feels affinity with those forces; and that she, the woman, the body, had recognized it and therewith had headed off death. She had reduced the forces of the body, she had removed them altogether from certain places and thus given the body its destination on the way to the origin.

As ancient lore puts it, the angel of God turned into a serpent, and this serpent made an attack. There where the forces of development still operate unrestrainedly, the Lord God functions as assailant; in removing this condition, He seems to be the destroyer of life. However He is merely destructive to that which threatens to stifle actual life; He is destructive to the principal force of Egypt, the first-born of Egypt, with whom He deals in the same way. To the germ of life, to the first-born of God, however, He is redeeming, emancipating. The serpent is merely dangerous to the body which surrenders itself to the forces of development, which desires to move ever farther away from the origin; which sees salvation as the final phase of self-directed planning and development.

In this connection one might for instance think of the story in Numbers 21:4–9, i.e. that of the 'serpent of brass'. Briefly, the substance of it is this, that people were getting discouraged because of the long distance of this way to Canaan, and desired to return to Egypt, the world of duality. In this situation the serpent appeared with its deadly venom to prevent it. When people realize they have acted wrongly and turn to God again, God gives away the secret of this serpent. For whoever is bitten by the serpent on earth and thereafter desires to turn to God, finds the cure coming from the serpent, too. That the serpent is only lethal, if one is bent on taking the wrong way; that what was deadly at first, can be life-giving, if only one follows the right way. This indeed is the deeper meaning of the fact that the value of the numbers of the word 'serpent' is identical with that of the word 'Messiah'; and that the Lord God who sends Moses down to Egypt to emancipate Israel, desires to kill him, when he appears on the border of Egypt with his uncircumcised son, Eliezer, with the nucleus covered by the forces of development.

The word for serpent and the happenings with the serpent of brass induce me to say a word or two on the systematism, as it is expressed in the phenomenon of metals. For metals are also subdivided into groups in connection with the systematism in creation. We have already seen that gold has the place of the first day and silver that of the second day. Thus brass has the place of the sixth day. It was not done at random, since a division had to be made anyway, but because among metals brass expresses the essence of the sixth day; and because metals in themselves express a very special aspect of the world.

Now the serpent appears on the sixth day. It is determinative for the happenings then. In fact it causes the transition to the seventh day in bringing death with it, and also the weakening of the forces of development. That Moses had to make a serpent of brass is logically determined by this systematism.

But there is more to it. The word for 'serpent' is, as we have seen before, 'nachash', nun-cheth-shin, 50–8–300. The word for brass is 'nechosheth', spelt nun-cheth-shin-taf, 50–8–300–400 in which the final letter has the character of a suffix. So the word brass and the word serpent are indentical as regards structure, both of them having the structure 50–8–300. This shows why it is that brass has the sixth place in systematism, the place where the serpent determines the development. And why it is that the two words have the same structure. And then it becomes clearer still why Moses made a 'brass' serpent, for, if we read the text as numbers, he made a 50–8–300–50–8–300–400.

So the serpent brings death at the end of the sixth day. It is the bite of the serpent, because man is impatient and thinks the way he is going is 'dull and insipid', because he desires the stimulus of the world of duality, hence wants to go to Egypt, wants the tree of knowledge.

But then, when death makes its appearance, man sees how and why his ways were wrong and he turns back. Then it is again the serpent he encounters, but this time it is life-giving, now it is forming the transition from this world where rules the bite of the serpent, to the coming world where through beholding the serpent one keeps alive instead. There the serpent forms the transition from death to life; there its value of '358' is the value of the Messiah.

That is why the Bible in that text also calls it the 'fiery serpent', the 'serpent of fire' which characterizes that ending. The word for 'fiery serpent' is 'saraph', spelt sin-resh-peh, 300–200–80. The value is 580. And we have already seen the structure of '58' as expressive of the end of this world of the seventh day. This fiery serpent which Moses had to make and which people had to look upon to remain alive, is the situation arising at the end of time, when one shall see, if one is aware that one had gone the wrong way, that it is also the serpent which leads man from death to life, from the seventh day to the eighth day.

Hence that it was not the serpent, the forces of development that caused death, but that it was the attitude of man towards these forces of development. That they also lead him to life, as the saviour, when he approaches them on the way via the tree of life, which is also the tree 'that makes fruit' besides having the quality of being the 'tree which is fruit'.

I take it that after this exposition of fact, the notion of serpent and circumcision will have become a little clearer.

It now remains for us to discuss the relationship in structure between the word 'night's abode' and the happening there, the circumcision. This relationship exists merely in connection with the structure of the words. Grammatically the word 'night's abode' derives from a root altogether different from that of the word 'circumcise'. This complete difference in grammatical root notwithstanding, the relationship in the structure of the words points to coherence; a coherence, however, which does not come to expression in this phenomenal form.

Now the word for night's abode, 'malon' is spelt 40–30–6–50. The happening there, characterizing this night's abode, the circumcising, is 40–30, mem-lamed. In the night-world, where one takes lodging for the night, this circumcising, the removal of the oppressing covering, is the characteristic element. It is the entrance of emancipation, of liberation into the day-side of our world.

After the circumcision Zipporah calls her husband 'blood-bridegroom'. Here too there is a structural relationship through the word. On account of the fact that the power of development of the covering has been removed, man is taken up in the coming world, which expresses itself in the systematism as the eighth day. For that reason, indeed, circumcision takes place physically on the eighth day after the birth into this world. And the word 'bridegroom', as we have seen, is also connected with the eighth day, for it is the word 'chathan', 8–400–50, with the 'cheth', 8–40, the letter 'eight', for its root-construction. Thus Zipporah's recognizing the serpent, the subsequent transition through the serpent into the eighth day, and the circumcision on the eighth day, on all sides are connected with each other. And with it we recognize the purpose of Moses' coming to Egypt.

Moses – I point to the fact again – at that moment is eighty years old. He has then reached the twice forty years in proportion to the coming once forty of his life. He is here at the transition from the 'two' of Egypt, the opposing extremes, to the 'one' of the way to Canaan, the harmony of the opposites.

30
How the World is Left

Pharaoh does not let the children of Israel go. To the contrary when he finds there is a serious chance of their emancipation; when the struggle commences; when the impending turning-point in the development has been reached; he intensifies the oppression. The children of Israel are now compelled to gather straw for which they have to spread out all over Egypt. This straw serves the purpose of giving coherence to the 'bricks', the building-material for the works in Egypt. Straw is the dry covering of what at one time was the fruit of the tree of the knowledge. This naked covering is to bring coherence to that which is the ideal of the world of duality: building with the help of earthly material, loam and water. Until then this straw had been provided by Pharaoh; effecting coherence was no problem as yet; the substance of Pharaoh supplied it. Towards the end, however, even *this* is lost; the earthly ideal loses its purpose. And from this substance, from this Pharaoh, there comes this diffusion over the face of the earth, in order to find that which might effect coherence. There comes the great unrest, the urge to move, to transport oneself, to migrate from one country to another, from one house to another, to seek everywhere, to see lots of things, merely for the sake of coherence, which for the world of Egypt after all is an empty covering, something devoid of life. Nor does all this searching yield any but the same results people had previously, when it had not been necessary for them to go and find that straw for the coherence of the life of Egypt.

Whereas formerly people had enjoyed a certain amount of rest, because this 'coherence', 'this binding together' formed no problem, now that rest is gone, too; now there is this hurrying to and fro to find the coherence somewhere. The earth goes on building; it only gives people this restlessness, this compulsion to transport themselves, looking for straw; looking for something which will make man suffer still more, since he has come to consider the dryness, the hollowness of straw as binding material for the life of Egypt. It is the stir and commotion on the face of the earth which the end of time brings with it.

Bringing offerings to God in the desert is, as Moses expresses it to Pharaoh, the purpose of the exodus. Bringing the offerings in Egypt itself, as Pharaoh suggests once or twice (Exod. 8:25–27), is rejected by Moses as utterly impossible, since the Egyptians themselves would not be able to bear it. Just as little as the Egyptians can appreciate herding cattle and flocks, 'for every shepherd is an abomination unto the Egyptians' (Gen. 46:34).

For indeed it is the purpose of the soul to bring the body to God; it is, as we saw, the purpose of the 'korban'. One cannot bring this body to God if the world of duality reigns supreme. That is why the offering had to be brought into the temple, the place of the measurings of the 500, where in fact duality, development, has become 'one'. And in the temple itself the offering is only accomplished, if there, too, in the expression in the substance, man has got beyond the 'two'. For in the temple the korban is only accomplished beyond the first two courts, after one has got into the third court. Therefore it is that Moses says to Pharaoh that the offerings can only be brought at 'three days journey from Egypt into the wilderness' (Exod. 8:27). Not until one has achieved this alienation from the world of the opposites, will this bringing nearer of the body be at all possible. Therefore the offering can only take place in the world of the measures of the 'five hundred', and even then only in the third phase and not in the world of the measures of the 'four hundred'.

In Egypt itself, however, the offering is altogether out of the question. There it would mean severing the body from life, killing the body. In Egypt there is the contrast life-death; the phenomenon Egypt is even built up on that contrast. Therefore in a world of duality, the conception 'offering' in that sense is impossible. One may talk about it, one may eventually understand, but one cannot bring it. Bringing the body nearer is, in reality, something taking place outside this world of duality, in another phase of life, hence in another world. To do so, one should first have left this world of duality.

Thus in the expression of this life here, bringing the body nearer is possible only if one has altogether alienated oneself from the condition 'Egypt', the condition of the opposites in this world; if, in other words, one passes out of that world, not in a state of trance, but alive and aware, very clear and distinct, and if one sees the other world, with the other standards, similarly clear, alive, distinct.

But relinquishing this world, both as regards passing away, after this life here and forsaking it through turning towards the other life even while in one's phenomenal form here, rouses the great revolt, the great fear of Egypt. To Egypt the animal is 'god'. The body with its power of development, as Pharaoh, as cow or bull, as moon, this is the divinity, this the purpose of life; on it is concentrated one's thought, one's forming ideals, 'one's planning'. All knowledge of Egypt is 'evolutionary' knowledge, calculating with continuity, hiding from discontinuity. Everything is measured with the standard of development, of 'progress'. Everything is to be perceptible, or at any rate to be figured out from the perceptible.

Therefore a shepherd who desires to guide the animal is an abomination in himself. For it is the 'animal' in its many phenomenal forms which one adapts oneself to, and that animal is not led, that animal is 'god', itself leads. One subjects oneself to the reality of development, to material standards, to perception and experiment. Whoever desires to lead the animal, is suspect. That is why the children of Israel do not live in Egypt proper, but in Goshen. The name Goshen means 'nearby'. One lives in this world, if one is a child of Israel, but one does not live in it completely; one can only live 'nearby', because one has received the knowledge handed on from the fathers that one has to lead the animal, ultimately to bring it as the 'korban' before God. It is the conviction, the doctrine of the fathers, that one has to lead the animal.

Pharaoh's suggestion of bringing the offering inside Egypt, represents an impossibility. It is the suggestion often heard also, one may on the one hand quite well serve the world and on the other hand serve God. Bringing the body nearer to God as a 'korban' is altogether out of the question, if one is to serve the world at the same time. This world will crush every initiative to bring a 'korban' of the body to God.

Service to God means bringing the 'korban', bringing the body and the world to God. It is not a kind of philosophy, a mental occupation, building up satisfactory theories about God having withdrawn Himself, finding God back in flowers and animals, in rocks and in colours. Indeed, such mental occupation does not disturb Egypt; it may even contribute to people's resignation to the harness of the labour for the world of duality.

However, it is impossible for Egypt to allow the children of Israel to leave Egypt for the sake of the 'korban'; for that would imply the end of this world.

It is incomprehensible to Pharaoh that Moses should have to act so uncompromisingly (Exod. 10:8–10).

When Pharaoh asks him what is implied in the 'korban', hoping, just as he himself had suggested, it might only then concern the men, and that anyway what makes up physical life, the 'nefesh', the bodily soul, viz. the women, the little children, the animals, were to remain behind, even then he has to be disappointed.

Moses tells him that literally everything is to go. Because bringing nearer to God does not merely mean the soul, but everything pertaining to this world, everything the soul has acquired as support, unto the veriest details. Literally nothing shall be left behind.

Pharaoh fails to understand this reasoning and this attitude. For it just means that life here, as calculated by the standards of this world, is to end in horrible death; and that this world in itself is senseless. Therefore he says (Exod.10:10): 'Look to it; for evil is before you'.

The word translated as 'evil' in Hebrew is 'raa', meaning 'bad, evil'. Tradition has it that Pharaoh with his earthly knowledge, the knowledge of natural law, came to the conclusion that, if the children of Israel were actually to leave Egypt in that way, this would be to them identical with death, in the desert, in the world they were journeying through.

'Raa' is a constellation, which according to tradition, indicates within the situation obtaining at the moment, that leaving Egypt must end in the children of Israel's dying in the desert. That which is meant with the expression 'constellation' in connection with Egypt, is what in our times is formulated as a cosmic necessity.

To us the conception 'constellation' in that sense has got lost as science and has been substituted by what we now call a natural constellation.

So Pharaoh points out this consequence to Moses. Measured with earthly standards, considered from the standpoint of natural law, leaving this world means death.

From this point of view of this earth it cannot be looked at otherwise. To earthly standards it is also implied in the principle of circumcision. These standards recognize no other life except that contained in the contrast life-death.

That the exodus from Egypt should, however, mean an ascent into real life, free from the oppression of evolution, of change, is a thing which cannot be understood from the standpoint of earthly standards.

Man in Egypt merely beholds death, if he should leave Egypt and therefore he resists it.

Everything turns on the decisive point in the structure, it is the end of the 'two' and the beginning of the 'one', both in regard to Egypt, with the numerical value of '380', whence the journey starts to Canaan with the sum-total of 190 — hence the journey from the 2 × 190 to the 1 × 190 — and in regard to the life of the leader, Moses, who has left the 2 × 40 behind and is starting on the 1 × 40 of his life of 120 years. To the world of duality, that which is impending must be identical with death, with disappearance into the void, into a condition where *this* life cannot exist.

With its standards of that world of duality it merely knows the life to which it gave development and it cannot imagine any other sort of life.

If it should exist, it is just as uncanny as death and therefore is to be rejected.

31
The Principle of the Half

Everything points to the fact that a new world is beginning; that this world is passing. God says to Moses and Aaron: 'This month shall be unto you the beginning of months' (Exod. 12:2). This form of the world which has now set in, will be the beginning for the coming world. That month is the month Nissan. It is the seventh month after that of creation.

What is going to take place now is the story of the 'seventh' again, just as the Bible is the story of the seventh day, the day after the six days of creation. This seventh month, however, will be the beginning of the census; people will reckon, starting from this world. For in this world does the decisive moment come of the transition to real life. The moon of this world, this development, this growing form, will demonstrate the decision. On account of that happening this world will be the first. Therefore in the practice of Judaism people count the years from the month of creation, the month Tishri; and the months from the seventh month, from the month of Nissan. In this seventh month, which is now the first, in the evening of the fifteenth, exactly in the middle of the month, this very special thing will happen, the transition from this world to the other. At midnight at that, hence in the middle of the night. So here again there is an uncommon relationship in the structure. God begins dividing the twelve months into two parts. The second part is the new beginning. Then this seventh month in turn is divided into two parts. Where the second part begins, there is the exodus from Egypt and there is the new beginning. But the night, in which it happens, is itself divided into two parts. In the first part there is the preparation of the new, and at the beginning of the second half of the night the new life commences. This principle of the halving, we have also beheld in the 'ten' dividing itself into the twice 'five', where the half also became the decisive point in the structure of the 10–5–6–5. We also saw it in the halving of time of the year 1656–1657–1658, in which the half indeed indicated the decisive point of the entrance into Canaan, the end of the way leading to the coming world. Also the letter 'one', the 'aleph', as we saw, consists of two halves, the two 'jots'.

This halving, as it is expressed in the fundamental structure of the 10–5–6–5 in the coming of the 10–5, implied that at the consummation of this 10–5 one half was fulfilled, the half of removal from the source of origin, whereas with the coming half, the 6–5, was accomplished the return to the origin.

Calling to mind the diagram which I tried to render schematically the course of the world through multiplicity back to its origin, we shall try by means of a similar design to find an explanation for the meaning of that 'half'.

Moving away from the origin takes place in the awareness of there being two extremes, beginning and ending, between which one always finds oneself. Perceiving, considering, observing things in this situation, one lives in the world of duality.

But at the point of the farthest extreme, as the 'Haflaga', the division of the 15th generation, represented it at the 10–5, there is the power of the name Lord, of the God who accompanied man into the exile to bring the world back again, God who in the exile makes the curve, back to the origin. That is the point where we have got 'half-way', where the second half of the circle is beginning. In the cycle of the year it is the beginning of the seventh month, which God pointed out to Moses and Aaron, to understand the significance of growth, of form. In the cycle of the month it is the night of the 15th day, when the 14½ has come to an end. And in the cycle of the night it is the moment of midnight.

In our drawing it is:

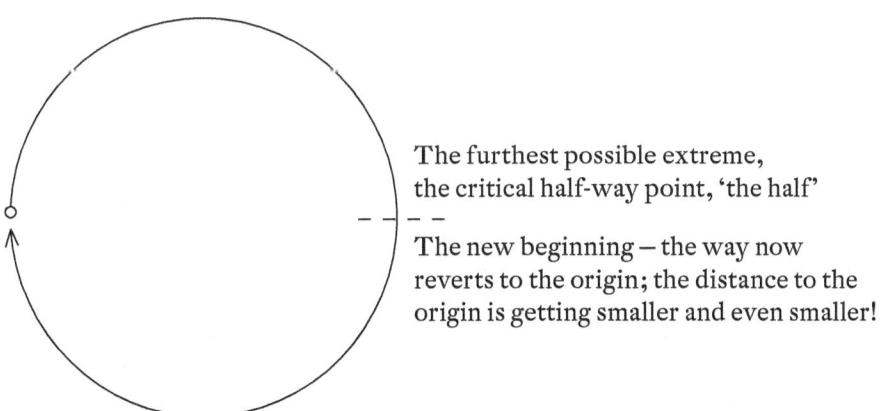

The furthest possible extreme, the critical half-way point, 'the half'

The new beginning – the way now reverts to the origin; the distance to the origin is getting smaller and even smaller!

For that reason the world was halved together with the whole period of time of the Pentateuch. For Pentateuch gives the 10–5 in time, gives the world as it appears to us, at the utter extreme of development.

In fact that is the situation in which man always finds himself. He always finds himself between the two extremes, half-way, at the point of extreme development. Every new life means 'extreme development' at that moment and may form a preliminary to the way back. And every moment which one experiences is such a point of extreme development, and therefore the way back may begin at any moment. That is why the 10–5 is every present, it ever presents itself to us as the one extreme, that it may be bound by us to the 6–5, to the harmony of unity. And therefore the 'five books', as expressive of the whole way, have that signature of the 10–5 in the structure of time. They offer us creation, the world, life, at any moment; and at any moment we can start on our way back to the origin.

This continual abiding at the point 'half-way', at that point of 'midnight', between the two extremes, according to the law of creation mentioned in the Bible, implies that at the point of the 10–5 the 6–5 will ever *have* to follow. At this point the circle curves back to the point of origin. It is at that critical moment that the law of creation, which is also signed with this 10–5–6–5, comes into operation.

So we continually live at this point of the 'half', knowing for certain that through the operation of the law of creation, we shall return to the source of origin. For this is the meaning of the 'exodus from Egypt', every day of our life. Because God has created the world so as to embrace this principle of the return half-way, because He has also created this exodus from the world of the two, we daily experience this regress, this reversal of the way. And that is the meaning of the statements in the Bible. It means that in the happenings in the Bible it has been essentially established what will happen in time; that because of it, it has become a certainty for the further phenomena.

It means that therefore it has become a law of creation. We have also been formed by it. In our lives, we, too, are an expression of the Bible, just as the whole world, the whole of creation, is an expression of the Bible.

Tradition here states that the children of Israel had already been gripped so much by the power, the force of attraction of Egypt, that they were on the point of being lost for ever. As tradition expresses it, they had already 'passed through forty-nine gates of impurity'. If they had passed within the fiftieth gate of impurity, there would never been any possibility of a way back. They were on the point of passing through that gate.

By now we know enough of this terminology to understand that with this 49 is meant that whatever possibilities of removal from the origin there may be in the expression of the seventh day, had already been exhausted. If this world had developed one step further, it would have been lost forever.

This condition also shows that man could not of his own accord have accomplished the emancipation from Egypt, for the simple reason that his way is that of further evolution. He cannot accomplish it any more than he can set back time. It is only because it is a law of creation anticipating God's interference in this evolution, that there is liberation from Egypt. According to man's ideas on evolution, the moon would have to grow and develop after the 15th of the month. The law of creation, however, implies that the sphere is the farthest possible expansion and that after the 15th of the month a new situation arises, viz. that of the waning moon, which reverts to the origin, when it likewise emerged from the void.

The same situation presented itself at the end of the sixth day in Paradise. Through the contact with the serpent and through absorbing the will to determine for himself on the standards of the world, to operate with them through the body and his observation, and by means of this develop the world ever further, man had reached the condition in which he would find himself forever on this way of further development without end, ever further removed from the origin, and with it he would have deprived creation of its purpose. For creation was there on purpose to unite man again with the origin, therewith to bestow on him the supreme bliss, that of reunion.

Thus there was in the sixth day the reversal, decreed by God, thwarting the conceptions of man, who saw it coming to him as death. Thus it is the same principle that is active in Egypt. When the children of Israel get submerged in the multiplicity of Egypt, when they have completely given themselves up to the culture of Egypt, when according to our standards of the world they have reached the extreme degree of removal from the origin, then it is that God intervenes, then there is God's law of creation which operates and which effects a curve in the line shooting away into the infinite, ultimately causing it to revert to the origin.

The period of this month of decision is subdivided again so as to show the meaning of the structure of time. For on the tenth day of the month the lamb is taken and kept in readiness to be killed at the end of the fourteenth day and eaten on the fifteenth before midnight (Exod. 12:3–11).

Again we see that something special is coming on the tenth day, which continues to exist for five days and serves to be 'eaten' at the end of those five days – and at that very moment the fifteenth day of the month sets in. So the 15 days are divided into the 10–5. This 10–5 in its turn precedes the coming of the new, of the reversal, back to the origin, hence it preceded the coming 6–5. This 10–5, which is at the same time expressive of the splitting-up and of the (2–1) principle, is again seen as the condition for what is to come. What comes in the '5' of this 10–5 is the perceptible lamb, known as the means to accomplish the exodus, the transition to the coming world. So it is like the time which with the 828–829 years (of 1658–2487) is half the time of the first two 'ele toldoth', the time up to 1658. So the period from 1658–2487 is the period in which the lamb is kept ready. It is the '5' of the 'whole time' of Pentateuch, which is the 10–5.

This lamb comes into every house. It emphatically must not be divided about more houses. This 'whole' lamb according to the systematism of the animals, pertains to the animal at the first place, where the ram is, or to that at the tenth place, where the goat is. Because it remains *whole* itself, because it remains 'one', this lamb which becomes the 'korban' binds the house unto unity. For the house is the letter 'beth', the 'two'. This 'two' is bound unto the 'one' by the lamb which will be the 'korban' at the end of the period of five days. In all things one has to calculate in accordance with that which will make the 'two' unto 'one'. *Operating* with the body, which in substance is expressed in the form of this lamb, makes the 'two' unto 'one', gives sense to the house, to life in this world.

When the moment has come for the exodus, the lamb binds the children of

Israel to the house. Within the *house* does the 'two' become 'one', i.e. in the 'two' is found the 'one'. It is not *they* who force the exodus, it is God who then makes His appearance in Egypt and removes everything which was made by Egypt unto a 'god', and everything which had been looked upon by the Egyptians as 'first', as 'principal'. Development is reversed. The line which had moved away from the origin curves back, reverts. None of the words people had ever built on, had counted on, proves enduring.

It is an emancipation in which man is allotted a very special duty. He is to remain within the house, together with the family and with everything counted thereto by the lamb which has to remain 'one'. It is emphatically pointed out that it is not man who works emancipation in for instance fighting against Egypt, in leaving Egypt with violence. Man has to accomplish his duty at home, among the family. He that is in the house and has the blood of the lamb on the doorpost, on that which is the 'four' – the letter daleth, meaning door – he has *not* gone the way of development, he proves to have retraced his steps.

The 'two', the house – the letter beth – he must not left. One is not to go out through the door, the letter 'four' towards further development. For everything which proves to be 'outside', which desired to go on developing, *that* is removed by God. That which at the transition has the sign of the 'one', the blood of the lamb which is whole, which is 'one', is that which remains indoors, inside the 'two'. It is bound there by the lamb which makes the house unto 'one'.

And the lamb must be finished, 'eaten', before the 'half' is there, before midnight. At midnight time is past. On the outside of the house, on the door, the 'four', that is, the eating of the lamb, is expressed by the blood, visible on the doorpost. There that is seen as blood in the 'four', which inside the house appears to be a meal, a joyous gathering. It is only this 'two', bound up into the 'one' which remains at the transition, at the end of time. All the rest is removed.

According to ancient lore at that moment the children of Israel circumcised themselves, i.e. they performed that which made the exodus possible; removing the forces of development which had taken possession of the body.

And the blood which was visible, was similarly this blood of the circumcision. For circumcision is identical with killing the lamb; it means removing the forces of development. The lamb is the body which is brought to God. That body must be 'whole', must be seen as a unity. Only in this way does it fulfil its purpose.

There is also the instruction given by God (Exod.12:15–21) never to have any leaven in the house, when the time in the world coincides with the time of the exodus. The house which at the exodus is bound by the lamb unto 'one' must have removed all leaven and anything in the catergory of the principle leaven, in its phenomenal form in this world where in our place the exodus is ever repeated, in every cycle. For indeed, leaven is that which like yeast, rises, makes multiplicity, expands, makes the dough 'grow'. It is the power of development, the power which has got hold of the body. It has the disposition to split up, ever to make multiplicity, hence doing exactly that which is the strength of the world of duality, of Egypt.

And the exodus is therefore identical with removing that power, wherever it may be found. One has in a way to make oneself and one's surroundings entirely free from these bacteria which merely purpose all the time to make multiplicity in the world, which can only regard the world in multiplicity and measure it in multiplicity. On the basis of the knowledge of what the world is and what the phenomenal forms express of the essential, it is elucidated in tradition what it is in these phenomenal forms that has to do with those forces of development. The expression in leaven is the expression in the domain of bread, the fruit of wheat, where leaven proves to be the power which has given to the fruit of wheat this inflation, this fluffiness. Wheat, as an expression also of the 'tree of knowledge' through leaven has become like the body through contact with the serpent: exploding into multiplicity. Therefore leaving Egypt not only means destroying everything in any plane which has to do with this tendency to expand in and with this world, but also to eat of the bread made *without* this leaven. There, midway, where the world reverts to the source of origin, man receives the tree of life. For the tree of life implies the tree which *is* fruit and *makes* fruit. Then one sees indeed this growth, this reaching the goal. But without that emphasis, without the characteristics of this world, after growth as such. This growth by then has consummated its task and is now taken away, taken back. It is as with circumcision: the prepuce is not altogether removed, but only partly, and the remainder is folded back, so that the nucleus becomes visible. Circumcision, essentially, does not mean *taking away, removing* the body, but merely a body made less arrogant, a body divested of the forces which see their destination merely in multiplicity, in material power. Eating this bread without leaven therefore is eating in the world which is facing the return to the origin. In this way do time and the happenings of the exodus express themselves in every further cycle of life. For that was the substance; that was what the exodus was consummated with.

So the meal (Exod. 12:11) taken that night, is an expression for life on the borderline of the transition. As has been mentioned before, all our life bears the signature of this transition, is this principle of the 'half' of the 10–5 facing the 6–5, the purpose of life, of reunion, of integration. Therefore this meal on the borderline is the expression of all life in concentrated form. The border where the meal is taken, is also the fifteenth of the month, is also the ending of the 10–5, as that month is emphatically subdivided into the 10 and the 5. On that borderline the way to reunion is starting. The meal at that moment is therefore the expression of the whole of life. This life is the transition. If one belongs to those who have cleared away the leaven, if one has the lamb for the 'korban' within the house, if one remains inside, does not allow oneself to be tempted to go out from the 'two', since it is for God to act outside, then one's life implies that one is ready at any moment to take the way back. 'The loins girded, one's shoes on one's feet, and one's staff in one's hand; in haste.' Everything directed towards the exodus. What is enacted at the meal on the border, is an expression of what life virtually is. In Egypt, in this world, one was a stranger; from the outset, from the moment one got there, the purpose of it was to depart from there again. That God might remember, as spoken in the 'one', in Genesis, to the Patriarchs, and that God should bestow the coming world on that aspect of the Patriarchs, on the 'one', which would express itself in the 'four' of the subsequent books after Genesis. This waiting for the fulfilment of the word of God, expresses itself in substance, in concentrated form in the meal, at which one passes the time of this world. In the image of this meal, the Bible expresses how life essentially is, how it waits, how it has made itself ready to set out to the coming world.

Pharaoh is opposed to this exodus. The world of multiplicity, of the 'leaven', does not understand the purpose of it, it merely sees meaningless death. Whatever theories it might have built up to explain death, they remained and simply had to remain vague, unsatisfactory hypotheses. For the standards of that world of duality cannot possibly be used to measure life in another, a coming world.

One might wonder why God made Pharaoh's heart so stubborn that from the outset he was condemned to go down. All the so-called 'plagues' were seen in advance to be useless against Pharaoh.

The answer is found in what the Bible previously states about Pharaoh. As a matter of fact he had severed the bond with the origin. He did not remember 'Joseph', who had established unity in the life of the world of opposites. With this severing of the bond, with this cutting-off the 'four' from the 'one', Pharaoh had done what Cain had done also when he killed Abel. The Bible states that if man severs the connection with the 'one', his life will assume a very definite character. Pharaoh will then see the soul as something pertaining to this world, something which is to serve this world. Like Cain, Pharaoh built the cities, he was obsessed with working for the world of development, of multiplicity. Because he had no connection any more with the 'one', he judged the children of Israel absolutely wrongly. His judgement was only determined by the criteria this world gave him, and this world has no criteria for the soul, for the 'one'. Therefore Pharaoh knew of nothing else except incorporating the soul in the interest of the affairs of this world of multiplicity.

This severing oneself from the 'one' is stated by the Bible in a great many other cases as well. Thus for instance 'being cut off from among one's people', a thing often mentioned in the Bible as a consequence of certain actions, is such a severing.

The word translated as 'cutting off', 'koreth', literally means cut off. The bond with the essence of the people, as the Bible sees that people, means a bond with the origin of things, the bond with God. For at that stage this people is the people giving expression to the Bible in its life, concretizing the Bible. And the bond with it is severed by certain actions, upon whose significance I cannot of course enter here. The 'punishment' therefore is that people have severed the bond, that they have cut themselves into halves, that they have left the 'four' to itself in severing the bond with the 'one' which gave the purpose of life to the 'four'. Whoever has done that, thereupon goes the way of Cain, of Pharaoh, the way of the world with its culture, its sciences, its technology. And such a man will entirely misunderstand the goal, and he will judge the soul with the criteria of the 'four', just as Cain and Pharaoh did.

Now God said to Cain that he would not be killed. This means that Cain's lack of understanding of life after the act of severing, had given him that terrible fear of death. His further life would be a turning away from death, a denial of death. Until even his actual death, as is stated, represents a kind of mishap, a careless action. Even the manner of death is senseless. The way of Cain was to be that of a 'fugitive and a vagabond'. For Cain there was no other return except through meeting death at the end of his journey as a 'fugitive and a vagabond'. Only beyond death he might be liberated.

Now this is the state of Pharaoh. Owing to his refusal to recognize Joseph — tradition has it that he actually turned his face away and refused — he came to enslaving Israel which, with Joseph, had been a boon to Egypt. And because of all this now Pharaoh too started on his way to the end as one 'severed off'; he too went as 'a fugitive and a vagabond' through his earthly culture and therefore Pharaoh could not behave otherwise. His delivery therefore came with death.

For that reason Pharaoh has the terrible fear of the migration of the children of Israel. To him it means what death implies to man. When the blows hit him, he sometimes repents, because he fears ruin and destruction, having to go without this world, and then he promises all sorts of things, even bringing the 'korban'. But as soon as the world is again what he considers normal, he forgets his promises, his intentions, he even has no time to remember them. He cannot; not because he is so stupid, or so bad, but because the bond with the 'one' is severed. His good intentions somehow have their origin in the fear of death, the fear of a judgement in an uncanny world and as soon as that fear has gone, the intentions are gone as well. Whoever has got the bond with the one, performs things not because he is afraid of death or of judgement in another world, he does it from love, from faith, from profound conviction. He would do it even if he knew he would land in 'hell', because even there he would love God. Pharaoh's action is that of the man who has severed the bond with the 'one'. It is likewise the way of the body which, owing to eating of the tree of the knowledge, i.e. of the 'four', has cut off for himself the way to the tree of life. The angels with the fiery sword which keeps revolving, simply block the way.

Therefore Pharaoh undergoes the 'plagues' as a terrible sensation. The Bible states that the children of Israel who lived in Goshen, who kept away from the world of duality, who were shepherds and leaders of the 'animals', were not subjected to the plagues. Only he that lives in the world of duality, feels them as plagues. For virtually these ten plagues cause the new world to be born, just as the ten words of creation caused everything in the world to arise, and just as the ten words of God on Mount Sinai reveal the structure of man and of the world and therewith create the new man. Pharaoh, however, experiences this birth as a destruction. For to him the world of duality is everything; outside that world nothing can exist. With these plagues the Bible tells us how the ten acts of creation are seen from the standpoint of the world of duality. As an opposite, as the other extreme. What is 'good' in creation, to the world of duality means 'death'.

Even in the first part of this book, at the discussion of the systematism I showed in an example that these plagues, too, possess a distinct systematism; that they are not some accidental fancy, in what way this wicked Pharaoh might be tormented. They have a fixed structure, because they form part of creation, they express how the birth of a new world takes place as experienced in the world with the body which is driven by the forces of development; the body filled with the 'leaven'. The plagues show they too are rooted in the time-structure of the Bible. For the total value of the letters, building up the names of these ten plagues, also indicates the time they take place in, the time of the exodus. The numerical values of the ten plagues are respectively 44, 444, 110, 272, 206, 358, 206, 208, 328, 272. Added together this makes 2448, the year of the plagues and of the exodus. In the word 'shgin', the sixth plague, spelt 300–8–10–50, the 10 which merely serves as vowel is omitted. Thus the Bible sometimes spells the word Kinim, the third plague, with the 10, sometimes without the 10, which similarly represents a vowel there.

From this, too, it can be seen that they form an indispensable part of this world; that they also render the world in duration, as time is experienced by people in the world of opposites, who have severed the bond with the 'one', with the origin. This example too shows what wonderful relationships, considered practically impossible, there are in the Bible; how systematism, word-structure, time-structure, everything is interrelated, fits in with everything else, even out-marvelling creation of the universe and life.

So Pharaoh refuses to let go. It is like the body of the mother, resisting the birth of the child; it cannot help wanting to hold it. And the birth-pangs compel it more and more to give up combating. Until in the end the mother cannot but thrust it out, if she is not to succumb herself. Thus Egypt has to thrust out the children of Israel, that they may be born into the new world.

When those departed are to start their way to freedom, they reach the sea, which on the one hand prevents their crossing it, while on the other hand they prove not to be altogether free from Egypt which pursues them, desiring to drag them back. And just as the water bursts through from the matrix at the birth of the child, thus the boundaries of the sea also burst through. When the child ultimately enters into the new world, it is still bound to the mother by the navel-cord. It is the pursuit of the Egyptians across the sea, the pursuit of that which is escaping. Not until the navel-cord has been cut through will the newcomer really be born an independent. In accordance with ancient usage the afterbirth was held up before the eyes of the newly-born, if it showed little vitality. All this on the analogy of the story of the Bible that the children of Israel did not feel free until they saw the Egyptians lying dead on the shores of the sea. For indeed the people saw the departure from Eypt expressed in the happenings, the various phases of childbirth. This childbirth followed the pattern of what is told in the Bible about the essence of the coming of the new.

Just as birth is a departure from an old world where one had come to maturity where one was due to depart from the old world, thus it is with what we call 'dying'.

At a person's death, the same pattern unfolds. To us, however, on account of bodily perception, with a reversed effect. At a person's death, too, there is the battle of the body's refusal to let go. Owing to its taking of the tree of knowledge, the body merely knows the standards of this world, and therefore takes up the same attitude as Pharaoh. At death, too, there is the crossing of a sea which suddenly dries up to let one through; a sea which at first had served as bounds to close off. There, too, the body comes in pursuit, it refuses to let go, to the horror of that which is trying to escape. Until at long last one sees the body, cut off, and one starts on the new life.

About this further life the Bible also tells us in the story of the journey across the desert, to Canaan. It has the same pattern as that which expresses itself here in this world, only it is then in a different plane, it has different standards.

In this world of the form, of the body, God pointed at the moon to Moses and Aaron because in this world we base our calculations on the moon. Just as the moon emerges from the 'void', if one only knows life through the duration of the body, the form, thus this life ends with the waning of the moon. This waning is like a reflection of the crescence. To a life reckoned by the mere duration of this moon, the commencement is called birth and the ending death. They form the opposites, the duality characteristic of everything converning this life of constant change. He that knows the moon as something which ever renews itself, however, will not worry about its waning at the end of a lunar month. He will state it as one of the aspects of life on the night-side. For that reason did God point to the moon, and tell Moses and Aaron that this renewal which was then just beginning, was the commencement of many renewals. Hence that one should look upon life as a series of lives, the present life having left a great many behind and a great number in store yet. As far as that was concerned, one had got exactly half-way. And that was what made life here so very important. In this life here it happens; here and now one takes the way back to the origin. As we have seen from so many examples, this life appears at the end of the 10–5 and the beginning of the 6–5. What we observe here as time, is merely the time as it expresses itself in this one life, in this so-called seventh day. It naturally seems endless, because it knows nothing except this life, this phenomenal form. And with the standards of observation one cannot find any other time. Therefore the Bible mentions the times of other worlds and through the word it gives the opportunity to measure these times. It is only through the word that times can be measured; observation would make us draw wrong conclusions.

The children of Israel leave Egypt promptly at midnight, when one half is past, the 10–5 of that month; when the second half starts. And they take a great deal with them from Egypt, jewels of silver and jewels of gold and raiment which they had received from the Egyptians (Exod. 12:35–36). It is not a kind of last minute robbery when the Egyptians were not in the mood to take better care. It is not that any more than that there was servitude with the whip. If one has suffered a lot, because the world compelled one to go the way of multiplicity, of material development, if one has sighed because man was incorporated into all that labour which merely served to keep up the pretence of eternity, one has in that life set free a great deal of this world, and one takes along a great deal on one's journey to the coming world, to the 'one'. With it is built the tabernacle in the desert and everthing that is therein. It is taken up into the great harmony. That is what every man takes along with him from this world to the next, when he follows that way as a way leading to emancipation. It is the 'one', the one-fifth, of the children of Israel starting on the exodus, having fulfilled the purpose of existence in this world, in taking with them everything of that world, in emptying that world. The word, translated by 'spoiled' (Exod. 12:36) does not mean 'robbing' in Hebrew, but 'emptying'. The ultimate purpose of creation is that everything of this world is taken along by man on his way to reunion. Without man's agency it cannot get there.

32
Crossing the Border

When in every house, in every 'beth', i. e. in every 'two', Egypt has one dead (Exod. 12:30); when in contrast with that world of duality in every house in every 'two' of the children of Israel there is the 'whole' lamb and the meal, and everything is in readiness for the departure from that world, the exodus takes place. At that moment the body still imagines it can live without the soul, that only the soul indeed is the cause of all misery. But when the children of Israel have gone forth from Egypt, there is the experience that without them there is no life left, that it was the soul which had made the body into a live being. Then there is the last effort. The sea has not yet been crossed. It forms the boundary between this world and the other. This sea in Hebrew is called 'jam suf', translated as 'Red Sea'. The word 'suf', however, which means reed or rush, in its structure of samech-waw-peh, 60–6–80, also means 'end'. The sea at the border is also the sea of the end. The word for sea, 'jam', jot-mem, is 10–40. We have already seen the connection between the mist, the 'ed' as 1–4 and the sea as 10–40; it is identical, but then in the plane of the decads.

This border, the sea of the end, the time of the end, seems impassable. Indeed, to those standards and even to the greatest marvels of technology and magic, this border is impassable. The standards of this world are dashed to pieces against it. They form a different boundary from the infinite which is, in fact, not a boundary, but merely a representation arising in man, when he wants to measure the conceptions space-time.

There at the border the body is seen approaching again, in terror of death, in a last endeavour yet to catch life.

The body approaches with the 'six'. For it is the exodus from the sixth day. Egypt merely knows the 'six' as highest power and therefore takes the six-hundred chariots to catch those escaping (14:7). And it takes the horses. The word for horses is 'sus', spelt 60–6–60. It is the characteristic phenomenon of Egypt, through the very six in the structure of the word. Horses are always connected with Egypt (cf. Deut. 17:16).

Tradition has it that at the terrific multiplying of the children of Israel in Egypt every woman always had sextuplets. Again a conspicuously impossible physical happening. But again this statement will be understood if it is considered in connection with the structure of the story. In the sixth day birth, multiplying, finds its highest expression in the six. Getting innumerable is there expressed in terms of the six.

But at the moment of the exodus the number of children of Israel setting forth is given as 'about 600,000' (Exod. 12:37). For it is exactly the border that will be crossed between the six and the seven. Then there is no longer the solid measure of the six. And the first census of those that have set forth yields the number 603,550 (Numbers 2:32). The border has been crossed, they have outgrown the sixth day, they have burst forth into a new world. The seventh day has begun. And in the 3,550 with which it begins, this seventh day again contains the 3½ with which the seventh day is always associated. Just think of the 3½ with which Noah's seventh day was marked.

So people live in terror, the extremes face each other at the farthest possible remove. In front of them there is the border, the end. There is the impassable barrier; they cannot get away from it; they can only be drowned in it. And there is the body in full assault, desiring to drag the soul along, back to the world of duality. The problems cannot be solved; people are in a panic. In the circumstances people see no chance of continuing on their way. They only see death, one way or another. And then, according to tradition, Nachshon, of Judah, of the generation from which David will come forth and the Messiah of the future, wades into the sea of the end. Since this way had been pointed out by God, he goes, although logically only death through drowning awaits him. He goes without an inkling of any reward for this deed. The only knowledge he may possess is that of causal reasoning, that on this way death is awaiting him. It is the kind of going Abraham undertook when he went with Isaac to Mount Moriah. Nachshon, too, is reduced to the last extremity; he is facing death.

Nachshon is a typical name. It is spelt 50–8–300–6–50, the 6–50 forming a suffix, indicating the '50' of the end, of the eighth day. The word 50–8–300, i. e. the word for serpent, forms the root. Here at the end there is again the identification with the conception 50–8–300. It is the leader from one world to the next. Viewed from one side, it is that which brings death, from the other side it is that which bears across to the new life.

This Nachshon shows in his action that he does not operate with the criteria of the experience predicting death, but that he goes that way, because God had shown it him as the right way. He is not afraid of being the only one to go. For none dare follow him on this way contrary to experience; but through Nachshon's action everything falling under the category of natural law proves to have been inoperative. A way *actually* proves to exist beyond this end. At the same time because of it God is seen to interfere. It is seen. It is also seen that the so-called pillar of cloud and the pillar of fire, the opposites of the left and right sides, of water and fire, with God are *one* (Exod. 14). People become aware of it in wonder and astonishment. With it, with this elimination of the contrasts, God leads them, shows them the way. And when Nachshon is able to prove it, they all follow him.

Egypt, too, comes to this border. Drawn by the soul, the forces of development also come within that time of the end, time which suddenly ceases to flow, time which splits up, which suddenly forms a solid wall, on the right and on the left. People can look through time, according to tradition. They see how everything goes, whither it goes and why. What was considered infinite, proves to cease close by.

The forces of development, too, at this moment of stress and strain, of the extremes touching each other, try to transgress the confines of time, suddenly opening up. But Egypt cannot get beyond those confines. The contrast cannot penetrate into the plane where the 'one' obtains. Suddenly the chariots' wheels cease to revolve; the circular characterizing this world has become ineffective. And Egypt is faced simultaneously with the pillar of the cloud and the pillar of fire. The contrast which ceased to exist, takes them aback and confuses them. The body with the forces of development only recognizes the flowing, the continual, the ever-moving circular, i.e. that which can only exist by virtue of everlasting contrast.

But the circular has ceased to function. Motion proves to be something different, originating from a different source. The world of the body therefore crashes down; it finds its ending there in that sea of the end. All conditions of its existence have dropped away; it has simply ceased to function. It has reached the terminus of its journey, after having severed the bond with the 'one'. By another route, as 'a fugitive and a vagabond' it would have to make its return.

According to tradition this Pharaoh who succumbed there, became the king of Nineveh in another world, and as it is stated in the book Jonah, he reacted with a return to God, together with his people, at Jonah's announcement that Nineveh was to be destroyed after forty days, i.e. that death was waiting at the 'end' of earthly duration expressed as 'forty'. This Pharaoh had come to know God in that root-story, at the sea of the end, and he knew that God used different standards from those of the world of opposites. He knew that the standards of mercy, goodness, love, for which there were no measures in this world of duality, applied in the substance, and that the return was a discontinuous phenomenon. With his ruin and destruction in the sea at the end of the root-story, he had experienced that return to God changes everything for the better at once. He had recognized it in the destruction of the body, ruled by the forces of development. This destruction was similarly a deed of mercy, for it had brought him back to the origin after the way he had had to go as 'a fugitive and a vagabond'. It is not just for nothing that ancient lore points to this identity of the King of Nineveh and Pharaoh.

The passage through the Red Sea has been set forth circumstantially and in great detail by ancient lore; it shows that one should decidedly not try to find an image to explain how the sea came to dry up. For the Bible tells a most important and essential story, representing an incomparably greater miracle than some natural phenomenon of a small sized (emphatically small-sized!) sea running dry. All this enacted itself in a world of a different quality from ours. It was not only the sea that ran dry, but God appeared, literally, according to the Bible, in a pillar of cloud and a pillar of fire. One should not turn that into a symbol either. The appearance of God is a greater miracle yet. Moreover the sea did not dry up; it was even more contrary to the natural phenomenon: the water rose like a wall, on the right and on the left. In that world of those qualities it certainly must have been like that. The only thing is that it is foolish to look for that sea somewhere here and to try to explain how it could be that it ran dry. People will not trace back that sea, and the explanation they imagine they have found has nothing to do with what the Bible states as literally happening. According to tradition the passage through the sea was even more surprising. Every tribe, for instance, followed its own way; the sea stood still like crystal, etc.

Whoever tries to discover and explain it with the criteria of observation, behaves like Pharaoh who was bent on driving across with his chariots. He got drowned in that sea.

In the terminology of tradition this happening is called the 'splitting of the Jam Suf', of the sea of the end. For the sea suddenly stood still; time suddenly ceased to operate. Yet the children of Israel passed through it alive. Such is the miracle of the passage from one world to the next.

This passage took place on the seventh day after the exodus from Egypt. For six days people had been still bound to Egypt.

On the seventh day there is the severing from the bonds with Egypt, the crossing of the domain whither Egypt cannot follow. It is the way from duality back to unity. This is characteristic always and everywhere of the seventh day, of this world. On the eighth day the people were entirely free of Egypt; they saw how it had been cut off; they were aware of being in another world, in a world from which Egypt was perceived as dead.

Just as one has the covering of the nucleus for seven days, and on the eighth day circumcision takes place. The eighth day ever indicating emancipation in every respect. So here, too, we see this pattern expressing itself in the happenings of the exodus from Egypt.

Thus there are seven days of the exodus. And these seven days, according to the Bible, are also the time of the Passover. During these seven days there is no leaven, for it is indeed, a detaching from the Egypt of multiplicity. In those seven days there is the bread which is *free* from this force of making multiplicity. In these seven days people set themselves free from the yoke of Egypt. Thus the whole of creation is an emancipation from the forces of development. Up to and including this seventh day, there is still the contact. In this seventh day there is again the decision; then Egypt, i.e. the body, with the forces of development, gets drowned in the sea of the end. On the eighth there is the salvation. It is the day of the Song of Moses at the sea (Exod. 15).

Immediately from the outset of the exodus, as the story goes, side by side with the perceptible transition from the sixth day into the seventh, there was present the transition from the seventh into the eighth day, into ultimate salvation.

For there is the story of the children of Israel journeying from Rameses to Succoth (Exod. 12:37). These are the only indications of place-names given at the beginning of the exodus. What for? In order to retrace things with the spade or on the map in our highly-civilized times, then to confirm that the Bible stated the place names correctly? By now, we know better, I expect.

Rameses, whence the children of Israel started, is spelt 200–70–40–60–60, with a sum-total of 430. It is the 430 of the oppression, expressed in time as the 430 years and also expressed in the word as the conception 'nefesh', the bodily soul. This city of Rameses, according to the story (Exod. 1:11) had been built in Egypt even at the time of servitude. They themselves had built their servitude, they themselves had built the city, expressive of servitude, the city where the supplies of Egypt, the sureties for the future could be garnered; where the world of duality — indeed they had built two cities — could he fortified.

Now people journeyed from Rameses to Succoth, according to the Bible. Succoth is spelt 60–20–400. The sum-total of the components being 480. So from Rameses to Succoth the journey is from 430 to 480, i.e. a journey of 50. Now that is the purpose of giving names of cities. The exodus meant following this way of the 50, a way, incomprehensible, untraceable to the world. It is the way beyond the 40, it is the way to another world, to another life. It is the way beyond this seventh day, entering into the eighth day. That is the substance too of the exodus from Egypt. With the setting forth from the sixth day, a journey which can only take place through God's interference, there is already present in the bud the entrance into the eighth day. For the seventh day *leads* to unity; that is what this seventh day was made for by God, with a very specific character, therefore this seventh day is called 'blessed and hallowed'.

The place where they went, Succoth, is indeed characterized by its name. At our discussion of the tabernacle we came across this word as the Hebrew name for tabernacles. People used to leave the place where they suffered unworthy labour and went to the place where they could see heaven through the roof, where the fictitious surety formed by the roof is eliminated. Where one could see through the contrast. That *too* is the way from one world to another. This transition is measured with '50'.

33
The Condition: Creating Order

From Rameses to Succoth it is a distance of '50'. Thus, from the exodus from Egypt there is a period of seven weeks until the revelation of the purpose of it all, God descending on Mount Sinai, can take place on the fiftieth day.

This union of heaven and earth comes on that fiftieth day, i.e. in the eighth week. Here again the eighth is a termination, the crowning of the happenings in the seven previous phases; again the eighth is an expression of the condition of the coming world. It pertains to the pattern of creation, hence it expresses itself also in this world of the seventh day, at which it assumes the forms of this world of the seventh day. Only in the coming world is there the form proper of the eighth day, and everything expresses itself in *that* form.

Just as people on the eighth day after the exodus from Egypt see how they have been emancipated, in an incredible way indeed, from a condition they have thought it impossible ever to escape, thus in the eighth week after the exodus, there is this revelation on Mount Sinai. Another experience of something considered impossible.

Before the happening of the revelation on Mount Sinai – the place which, as the name denotes, is an expression of the world of form, of the left side, of the lunar side – we see Jethro coming to Moses. The reader gets the impression about this visit that Jethro is giving Moses a kind of efficiency advice. All his good qualities notwithstanding, Moses does not seem to know a great deal about the doctrine of organization. Everybody wants to ask him questions, from all sides people thrust themselves on him to hear his judgement or to ask him questions. Every day is an exhausting chaos and Moses does not arrive at results (Exod. 18). Now Jethro shows Moses a simple way of planned schedules and hierarchic gradation to escape from the chaotic pressure of everbody wanting to consult him.

What Jethro does, has of course a more profound significance in substance. Here we see again, just as in the case of the slaves, how the essential is expressed in humane terms.

The word *Midian* – for Jethro is the priest of Midian – is closely related to the word Mida, which means measure and faculty. Midian, in fact, is 40–4–10–50, and Mida is 40–4–5. They have the same root.

According to ancient lore, Jethro had seven names, i.e. he presented himself in seven forms, like the seven days of the world. With the happening on Mount Sinai on the fiftieth day, the seven days have come to an end. So Jethro comes as phenomenal form of the 'seven' and indicates the measure of the happening, the structure of the world. It is a revelation of the structure, the measure, which precedes the revelation accomplished on Mount Sinai by the reunion of heaven and earth in the eighth day. This revelation on Mount Sinai presents itself in the seventh day as the great secret. To get the secret divulged, there must first be put order, measure, structure in the chaos which bears down upon man with a great number of stories and events in the time of the seventh day. On the basis of this order the secret of the coming world can be divulged.

Jethro gets Moses to put order in the masses and make groups of one thousand, a hundred, fifty and ten. And knowledge, the explaining of the why and wherefore of things, will come through this ordering of multiplicity. Now there will come an end of the chaos of multiplicity: now one will be able to penetrate to the nucleus.

The explanation of the reality of things is expressed in the image as judgement. For judgement is the elimination of the opposites, the restoring of harmony. If one suffers from the contrast life-death, then in the image there is a judgement: people want to know who is right and what is everybody's place. And the judge in his wisdom sees the relationships and restores harmony.

The condition of chaos in judgement implies that there is no system in the approach of the essence, in this case, Moses. People want to eliminate the opposites through incidental approaches, without knowing the place of everything and every word. On all sides the problems, the 'lawsuits' come rushing in; they demand restoration of harmony, but the enormous mass of questions, without any system, without knowledge of the structure of the approach, cause chaos. Countless numbers of interpretations, running crisscross in utter confusion, in contradiction with themselves, creating the impression of arbitrariness, such is the condition, as long as the structure of the approach is not yet known.

So that is what Jethro brings. He explains how the systematism is, the structure. If one introduces it, there is order in the mass at once, things are conveniently arranged; it is no longer that terrible exhaustion of not knowing where to begin and where to end. And it is on this basis of order, of creating structure, that the eighth day can make its entry. The seventh day can end with this creating of structure, after one has pronounced judgement all day long, in many lawsuits, most of which could not be solved, because there was still chaos in the system of approaching the nucleus, Moses. Moses' father-in-law, coming from the side of the physical form, comes and tells about the measures of creation, the measures of the world.

Now, what are they like exactly? We see again how profound the relationships are. For Jethro institutes *four* groups over against Moses; those of a thousand, a hundred, fifty and ten. Moses stands as the *one* opposite them and unites them with God. The way leads through these four, starting with the simple statement of the first, outermost group, penetrating more and more into the following groups, and if these 'four' should be unable to give the answer to the why and wherefore, then the contrast is laid before Moses, the 'one', and through his connection as 'one' with God, he is *ever* able to give the answer, to restore harmony.

So we see that the condition for the divulgence of the secret, the basis on which the secret of the other world can rest, is the introduction of the (1–4) structure. Not until this has been created, will there be a chance of penetrating to the heart, the essence of things, of reaching the heart, and 'pronouncing judgement'. And then the seventh day can be ended, and Jethro can go again; then the eighth day will come with the revelation of the secret, with the revealing of the miracle of the Thora to man. The story of the Bible is made public; one can look across it. For the very reason that Jethro had indicated the measure, the structure.

That is why that piece of the Bible in which occurs the story of the revelation, bears the title of Jethro. For in providing a measure, Jethro laid the basis for the entrance into a new world, a world which to an outside person bears the character of the great secret.

34
The Structure of Man

The way leading through the twenty-six generations is consummated on Mount Sinai and it is there that the purpose of the way is revealed. It is then that one *sees* what previously one could only have believed, trusted in. God comes down to the earth, on Mount Sinai — as we saw, the word Sinai is the expression of the moon, hence the left side, form, matter — and through the fact of His coming, His descent onto the form of the earth, into matter, He expresses by means of the word what He is, what man is and what the world is. Then the story in the Bible, and especially the story in the nucleus, Pentateuch, is presented, as the form in which the substance expresses itself in this world.

This is the situation in the eighth day. Then the revelation, expressing itself on Mount Sinai, in the form of the seventh day, is an uninterrupted, ever-present one.

Of this revelation, that which indicates man's place in the world, that which in a word, supports all the rest, that which is the mediator between the world and God is expressed in the so-called 'ten words' on the 'stone tables'. People often talk about the 'Ten Commandments' or of the 'law', but these names are misleading. In ancient lore no reference is ever made to the ten '*commandments*', but always to the 'ten words'. Commandments in ancient lore have not got the character of injunctions, they are rather indications of the right way which, because of its goodness, one should be eager to follow. If one tells a marl to put on his overcoat, because there is a biting wind, it is not so much a commandment as an admonition, in the interests of the party concerned. Or if one tells a man not to follow a certain route, because one knows it makes dangerous curves along precipices, is full of holes and other obstacles, which will almost certainly cause him to fall headlong down the precipice, that is not a commandment either, in common parlance. Remember what has been said above about the offering. It could only be brought if the sacrificer did so with conviction, full of joy and purpose. Otherwise it would be mere desecration, hypocrisy, stupidity and lack of interest in things of the highest value. Man should consider it his duty to know what the world is; he should be interested first and foremost in the purpose of his being here and in the meaning of the world. Then he will experience that these indications of the way he has to go are based on an amazing structure, revealing what man really is and what he is doing here in this life. He will realize that in following this way he brings the marvel of the Bible to life in his own existence; that his life will then show the same structure as creation, reverting to the source of things.

These 'ten words' are the expression of man's place in the world; they formulate what man is and how he is to reach his destination. That is why they have been written by God Himself on stone tables. None but God, from His world, can indicate what the structure of man is. These standards must emphatically come from another world. Written down by a man, they could inevitably only be related to this life, this world. They might then have a 'useful' character for this life, but they could not possibly extend their meaning beyond death and other lives.

We have also seen that the word for stone, *eben,* renders the idea of the immutable throughout. In this world anything permanent, 'eternal', cannot be expressed in images of matter except in the hardest, collective conception of 'stone', immutable under any circumstances. For the expression in this world, these words were engraved by God on tables of the hardest precious stone, to be written on by no other than God. That which was explicitly to do with *man* is given this invariable way of expression. Man's shape on the human level has been unalterably established by God. That which makes man into a divine being, his attitude towards God and the world, is something God has already established in its immutable form. Only thus, not otherwise, does man's way lead to his destination.

The tables have been given as 'two'. Though they form a unit, they emphatically consist of two parts. We have already come across this principle in the *aleph,* the 'one' consisting of the two *jots,* we know it as the fact, so often manifesting itself in the foregoing, of unity as a harmony of opposites. The 'five' above reflecting itself in the 'five' below and forming a unity with it. The two sides are united, are connected by the very life of man.

The harmony of the duality in these stone tables is also expressed in the statement that the letters had been engraved athwart the stone so as to appear engraved on the other side as well. Now a statement like that, in tradition, in our world would mean that the letters on the other side would be in mirror-writing. Nevertheless ancient lore holds that either side shows the same writing. That which in our world *must* express itself as duality proves in essence to manifest the miracle that, although perceptible on either side, yet it represents the same thing. The two sides show a unity, inexplicable to our world.

Now what is the sense of these ten words, the twice 'five'? They denote what man is in substance and therefore they have to be considered in that sense. They are not laws, moral, hygienic, or social, etc.; those are the images of the ten words. The image, of course, has sense for this life. But only if it is connected with the substance, it will have sense for further lives as well, far beyond this life and this world. About this a few hints are necessary, limited again by the character of this book which is merely intended as an introduction.

If the sixth word says 'thou shalt not kill', of course it also means literally that one must not kill another person. If, however, one were to think that this is all that this sixth word conveys, he again stops at the image, commits idolatry, and will not make any headway. His way to the tree of life, to the essence of things, is cut off.

The principle of 'thou shalt not kill' embraces all human life in all its expressions, in all planes. Tradition, elaborating these principles, includes for instance making a person ashamed. Thus there is a story about a great man who was conscious of having violated this principle in having kept a woman, who had come to ask him a question, waiting without looking up because he was just tying his shoelaces. To that woman, who was deeply impressed by entering into the presence of such a famous man, this moment's waiting, though very short, was confusing. Thus, rebuking another person in the presence of other people is ranged under the principle of 'shedding blood'. Even showing one's anger without any witnesses except the person concerned, may imply 'killing'. All this indicates that man simultaneously lives on several 'planes', and that it is not only the physical plane one is concerned with. And the 'thou shalt not kill' has to do anywhere, in any world, with non-injuring man in his dignity and in his totality as divine being. This 'sixth word' is opposite to the 'first word' on the other side of the two tables of 'five words' each, in which God establishes what He is. Man as phenomenon on earth after the likeness of God, must be treated in the same way, even to the very detail. Man is not a social being, a cog in the wheel, a minor part in the productive machinery. He is all that only in an unimportant, secondary way. Only in Egypt, in the world of duality, where man is statistically observed and measured, where he is a digit in an index file, he is all that in the first place. For in Egypt the covering of the physical, the material, is oppressive; there the covering has not yet been removed and turned back. Man, however, is essentially of divine origin, and one should not impair his unity and totality any more than God's.

The 'first word' states that God effected the exodus from Egypt. One might wonder, if God could not have given another and wider characterization of Himself on these eternal tables. Yet, if the reader has been able to follow the argument so far, he will realize that this characterization is indeed the most embracing, the only possible. For all creation is based on this return from Egypt. The conception 'create' implies making duality, i.e. reducing man to servitude of multiplicity, just as God Himself descended with this creation to have reunion, fruition, realized. And the marvel of creation indeed lies in the fact that through this descent of God, this accompanying as Lord God in duration, in history, the further development of the forces of matter is stopped at the extreme point, the farthest possible point, contrary to all logic of science, and that at this farthest point the return is effected. At the farthest point suddenly God's interference is manifest, an interference embedded in the word 'create' which pertained to the Plan even before creation, to the idea which led to creation. This reversal of the development 1 → 2 to that of 2 → 1 is the miracle which in the world of man is expressed as the exodus from Egypt. The reversal of the way can only be effected by the 'one' of God in the origin. That is what God expresses Himself by in the world. Any return from duality to the 'one' can only take place because God expresses Himself thus in the world. The purpose of life and of the world is the reunion, i. e. the exodus from duality. And it is God who has established this way, at creation. So it is *the* characterization, the formulation of the essence of God in this world: emancipation from servitude in the 'two' and guidance on the way to the 'one'.

Man, created by God in His image, yearns just as much for this reunion. Man seeks it in every plane. He may have been led astray by the forces of development, but this delusion rouses annoyance in him, since it is contrary to the purpose of his existence. He then plunges into all the varieties of excitement, intoxication, he grows desperate, falls ill, gets unbalanced. Therefore it is essential for anybody to regard his fellowman as a creature, similarly made after God's likeness and similarly craving for the harmony of oneness to be accomplished. Every man has within himself this yearning to bring creation to tranquillity and every man has within himself this sentiment that he himself is creation. So one should behold in every man the reflection of God. Whoever underestimates a man; sets *less* value upon him; kills this consciousness in him, and as ancient lore expresses it, it is as if one were destroying all creation.

Whoever deters anybody from this exodus from Egypt, from duality, through this fact rejects the principle of God's expression in this world. And at the same time he kills that man in this life, he deprives him of the purpose of life. Even though the victim may live to be a hundred on this earth, in affluence and good health.

Tradition points to the fact that, just as the ten words of creation began with the 'two', the *beth* of the word 'in the beginning', thus the ten words at the end of the 26 generations begin with the 'one', the *aleph* of the word 'I', in Hebrew 'anochi', spelt 1–50–20–10. For here ends the world of duality. God Himself has brought salvation from duality for the twentysixth generation, and in the eighth cycle after their salvation He has brought that generation to a place where heaven is visible, where the purpose of existence is clear and distinct, where the essence of man and of the world is revealed. Now this revelation begins with the 'one', just as creation started with the 'two'. Here the way has essentially attained its destination. The way led through the four birth-stories, man got emancipated from the forces of development, from the poison of the bite of the serpent. At the end of the way man sees the 'one' again, the 'one' with which the ten words begin on the tables eternal.

The 'second word' deals with the prohibition of making images. We have repeatedly discussed this principle. Again we are not concerned with the outer appearance of 'images' here. If it were nothing but that; that people should rightly or wrongly hold images to be gods, then in that case the whole principle of the 'second word' would stand or fall with a historic phase; then the 'ten words' would be deprived of their bases. For if mankind should 'develop' to the insight that images could not possibly be gods; that the image 'gods' even renders a primitive conception; and if they should reject the images, they had first worshipped, as primitive stuff and nonsense, then the 'second word' would simultaneously be dated through evolution. For 'cultured' mankind the 'second word' might in that case be struck out.

These images, however, will always continue to exist as long as this world goes on showing this form, in which the substance expresses itself. And as long as man bases his reasoning on observation; as long as his objects in view and his ideals are based on standards of observation; as long as he does not realize that the outward appearance should be connected with the substance into unity; there will be idolatry. The 'second word', however, conveys that man virtually cannot worship images. Eternal man in his structure knows no idolatry. To him the images are connected with their origin. Man robs the substance of something, if he severs it from its image, and then uses the form for the purpose of this life only, for enjoying the forces of development.

The form pertains to the substance, and it means breaking up unity if man cuts through the connection with the substance that he may use the form for this earth. Form belongs to the substance as much as woman to man. Together they are a unity, and whoever breaks this unity is like an adulterer.

For that reason as the second word in the other five, i.e. as the 'seventh word', there is the 'thou shalt not commit adultery'. For disturbing this unity of 'man-woman' in the atmosphere of man is much the same as upsetting harmony through judging things from their form, from what observation states about it.

The woman forms a unity with the man; one should not judge of her by herself. Just as man has meaning as a being in this world, if he forms a unity with a woman. The harmony man-woman is analogous to the harmony between substance-appearance, and one should leave both intact. Therefore non-adultery implies deference to this harmony in every respect. One must not commit adultery in thought either, and regarding woman in any way as mere outward appearance is a desecration of the purpose of woman's existence. It cuts her off from her connection with the substance; it is idolatry.

This 'seventh word' embraces everything which impairs the unity of harmonized contrast, which is bent on severing appearance from substance. It is parallel to the 'second word', which similarly demands not to look on the form, the image, as if it were the substance, God.

Taking the name of the Lord God in vain, thus also shows a connection with stealing; taking the name of the Lord God in vain implies breaking the unity of the name. If one assumes that something pertains to A, when in reality it belongs to B, one has broken up a unity, created a disharmony, a lie.

God's name expresses that very harmony of unity. Relating disharmony to the name of God makes this interference a serious affair.

The same thing happens in stealing. One creates a lie, one disrupts a unity, a harmony. Tradition extends this conception of stealing, just like the other conceptions, over all details of human life. Thus, for instance, giving a wrong representation of facts, creating a wrong impression, is similarly something falling under this heading. It breaks unity, which is expressed by truth.

Taking the name of the Lord God in vain also embraces relating this name to situations which have nothing to do with any intention of accomplishing reunion. The name of God indeed expresses unity; and connecting it with the superficial, the mundane, which does not change the condition of duality at all; which lets multiplicity be as before; all this is a reversal of the purpose of creation. It is like servitude imposed on the soul.

Thus one should not deter people from their destination. Neither should one steal time for worldly things. One should not use time without connecting it with the source. Whatever a man does, with others and with oneself; this connection with the origin must be the primary object. One should not use in vain the time of one's own life; one cannot deter oneself from one's destination.

Remembering the Sabbath day of course is not a question of a little breathing-space after which one takes matters in hand with all the more energy. In these modern times one should he very circumspect in drawing everything within the range of the economically and socially useful. Society has a pupose entirely different from merely creating a welfare state. It most decidedly is not the purpose of creation and the history of mankind. The structure of man points in an altogether different direction.

The seventh day is to take a very special place, because every seventh day intersects the line of the seventh day in the nucleus, in creation. This seventh day in the nucleus implies that everything concerning development is finished. This mission of man as the 'one' opposite the multiplicity of development lies in bringing together the opposites. As soon as he does so, he fulfils the purpose of his existence and has the joy for which the world was created. This bringing together of the opposites, ipso facto, is meant for every plane. Also doing good for instance, falls under this heading, it eliminates a contrast which expresses itself as suffering. Any action, indeed, can imply the elimination of a contrast, or the continuation or even creation of a contrast. The same holds good for the thoughts, intentions and the attitude of man. Through this elimination of dualism, man puts a stop to development in the sense we have discussed. Development can only exist, if there is duality.

In the terminology of the exodus from Egypt, which indeed was a journey from the sixth day into the seventh, a hurrying to get into the seventh day, we saw how arrestingly this development expressed itself in casting out the leaven, the fermenting, the making of multiplicity, and eating *unleavened* bread, free from this cause of multiplicity.

Thus in the whole of his life in this world of the seventh day, mans bears the stamp of the seventh. All his life he stands as the 'one' facing the many, and he must be fully awake to the conviction that God consummated everything in the previous phase; that it was all 'very good', and that man can now connect all creation with the origin. On this his attention should be fixed; his interest should go out to these things, whatever the field of his activities, wherever he may be faced with matter and multiplicity. On all sides he is to activate this principle through his attitude and actions. With it he is the true witness to creation, to God's purpose in regard to creation and the world. With it he bears witness that everything is complete; that it is good and purposeful as soon as man sets himself to uniting it with the origin. But if he lets things be, or if he is desirous of developing things further in his own way, then it remains severed from the origin; it remains duality.

If man should be *bent* on developing things further in this seventh day, if he should devote his interest and energy to this, he bears false witness to the purpose of the world. Then he testifies that God had not yet developed the world well enough; that it is up to man to see that it develops further materially, through his views of good and bad; and in so doing he bears false witness. Now this is the 'ninth word', facing the 'fourth', that about the Sabbath in the first 'five'. With his life and with his actions man bears witness to God and all His creation. He testifies either that there can be peace in material development on the seventh day, and that to his mind God has made creation well, or he testifies to the contrary. In the latter case he shows with his testimony that he does not possess the structure of man, as it is present in the eternal. And every testimony which disturbs a harmony, a truth, breaks that existing peace and leads to the continuation of development. A lie brings multiplicity over against the 'one' of truth.

The 'fifth word' concerns honouring one's father and mother. It has its place with the first 'five', i.e. there where man's attitude towards God is established, and not, as one might have expected, on the side where man's attitude towards God is expressed in man's attitude towards the world.

The 'honour thy father and thy mother', as a matter of fact, is a principle which has to do with the attitude of man towards God. It turns man's attention towards the origin. It convinces man that the past was not inferior to the present; that one merely comes to that conclusion by using the wrong standards; by taking material development as a standard, and not the divine which expresses itself in man's sentiments and attitude.

The principle of this 'fifth word' therefore is the opposite to the principle of evolution. It gives deference to things ancient, because in that direction also extends reverence of God. So it does not mean that one should honour his father and his mother to keep peace at home, or because father and mother have more experience of life, or because there must be a head of the family. Of course it extends far beyond this. For the grandparents are honoured by the parents, and so it continues to the first man. The man who as the 'one' faces multiplicity which has been brought to him through development.

So, according to this principle one cannot maintain for instance that biblical Israel behaved badly in the wilderness with its almost continual rebellion against God; or that Adam because of his rather primitive sin ruined all humanity. All the past had to be like that, otherwise it would not have been expressed in the Bible in that wonderful way. And that Adam and biblical Israel in the wilderness were nearer to God anyway, appears indeed from the statements in the Bible, that God spoke to them, that things happened whose implications are beyond our conception. They were all much nearer to God; their phase of the way of development was in its initial stage yet. Our attitude of turning away from the origin, has brought with it a development so far removed from the origin, that we have completely alienated ourselves from it. We idolize expansion, the very opposite of the return from mulitplicity to the 'one', of coming to ourselves too.

The 'tenth word' about 'not coveting' therefore expresses the same principle as regards the relationship of man to the world. It also implies turning away from expansion in the material sense, from ambition as to social status, from records in production. It causes man to turn to other things; to the contrary, restricting this urge for development. It gives him the chance of directing energy and attention to the real purpose of life.

Modern man is inclined to say: 'but, it's impossible; for then the whole economic structure would come crashing down. For indeed it is based on the continual increase of production per head of the population; for only in this way will there really be a further rise of the standard of the living.'

This, however, is the argumentation which tradition states so circumstantially, of the generation of the 'Great Flood', of the times of the 'Haflaga' and of 'Egypt'. All of them ever ended in catastrophe; their world went down. And then there is no standard of living any longer to measure things by. The Bible always registers such a destruction as a law of creation. As soon as this expansion comes, it always swells to the farthest extreme and then there is the inexorable catastrophe, the return through the removal of all the forces which effected that expansion.

In view of these laws of creation, one should realize that going back *at present* would be a great deal better than going on. Quite apart from the fact that at a return now the criteria would change; that man would place himself and the world in a different plane, where most of the burning questions of these times would suddenly assume a different aspect. Most problems would simply stop existing. The only thing is that man would first have to believe all that, he would have to undertake it because of faith in God and God's expression of the plan of creation in the Bible. If he should desire to calculate in advance the consequences of a way back, in order to investigate if the results were worth while, he would do exactly the same thing as the man taking from the tree of knowledge at the commencement of his way in this world. The way back is the way of the tree of life, i. e. the tree with the number 'one' and that way does not know about the mechanical reaction of output of work and wages, it does not know this duality. The way back is measured with expressions such as confidence, goodness, help for nothing; the will to give joy.

I entered for a moment into a rather strange speculation. I rather think the world *cannot* turn back. The numerous prophets in the form of planners, sociologists, politicians, etc. spell peace and prosperity, if only 'so and so', and 'this and that' would co-operate. But 'so and so' and 'this and that' have been put into the world by God, because this way of prosperity for ever, of disarmament, space-exploitation, peaceful use of nuclear energy, represents the same utopia as that which the generation of the Haflaga conjured up as a mental picture; the same utopia which the serpent held up at each of these situations as an ideal, far-removed but attainable through human effort. Paradise is *not* accomplished along the road of material development; to the contrary one moves away from it; one runs along that road to meet catastrophe.

The 'true' prophet never could do anything except point at this destruction. For he knew through the Bible and through his life as part of the Bible that development *must* ever lead to catastrophe; he knew the stories of Paradise, of the Flood, the Haflaga and Egypt.

All the same, one prophet who did not foretell everlasting prosperity, but ruin and destruction, ruin of a flourishing culture, inescapable destruction, found a hearing. This prophet was Jonah and his prophecy saved the world. The king of Nineveh was the Pharaoh who himself had experienced in this world of Egypt what the other standards meant, the standards of the return, of the 'one'.

According to tradition people striving after a high standard of life, the conquerors of heaven of the world of the Haflaga had to lower their standards considerably. Their descendants are said to be the primitive savages, and even the apes are called remnants of that period of growth and development.

Belief in expansion, in the fruits of science and technology nowadays is such that people cannot imagine another world as the ideal world except one with highly developed technology, where everything can be arranged by pressing the button. Clever electrical engineers, scientific research-people, organizers and politicians, leading everything in the right orbits of expansion, are leading the way. Even if inhabitants of other planets are made to descend on earth to help this world, they are beings of highly advanced technical ability, and the great masters of all kinds of movements speak about energy, electricity, etc. as powers of other worlds.

And people live in hope that man's soul may get accustomed to all this electrical perfection; that society may adapt itself to this progress; that the nations' organizations may realize that this progress should be cherished and upheld. And they do not even realize how horribly uncanny a world must be with such a summit of research-institutes and engineers and organizers, and that all these things are signs of a development, so far removed from the origin that indeed it has reached the 'point of no return'. But exactly at this point, where and whenever it is reached, God interferes and accomplishes the return for those that believe in evolution, not in a sense they will rejoice in, on account of their very belief.

One also sees that in a world of evolution, youth ever is the symbol. Whoever is young still possesses the power of development. On the other hand the Bible always mentions the 'elders' as the symbols of the world. The elders know the purpose of life; they are nearer the origin. It is the grey-haired man that is honoured. In the world of development, however, the grey-haired man makes an effort to look youthful, just to show that in him the forces of development are still active.

The 'ten words' of the two tables form a harmony of 'five' and 'five'. The first 'five' are opposite the second 'five', yet they form a unity. The attitude of man towards God and the attitude of man towards his fellow men are to form a harmony, a unity, just as these two tables form a unity. The two 'fives' are opposite each other so that they may be united together, just as it is the case with the two 'fives' of the name Lord God. In the two stone tables it is expressed that this union already exists in substance, and in their words and letters it is expressed what the essential looks like in this world.

Just like everything appearing here in this world of the seventh day, the 'ten words' have the form of the alternative. Man stands facing duality. He can either follow this one way of the images, of evolution, or he can follow the way which brings the 'two' back to the 'one'. In that case he unites the images with the substance, he brings development to the origin.

This principle is expressed in the fact that the number of words in these 'ten' is 172, the value of the word 'ekeb' which means 'if'. Man, standing on the boundary line, at the very extreme of development, is 'free' to choose as regards his attitude towards God. God has established everything except the attitude of man towards Himself. For the purpose that man in his return may have himself guided by the divine properties of love, faith, goodness, doing things for nothing; and not by the urge to have things mechanically weighed against each other.

Man can consummate reunion in this life, *if* he lives in accordance with this structure of the divine. On the other hand, he can choose *not* to go that way; he can follow the way of the process of material development. In that case reunion will *not* be in this life. Then it will come after that long, long way full of the terror of death, the way of Cain, as a 'fugitive and a vagabond'.

These 'ten words' demand an attitude towards God and the world; they do not require any interference with the world. This interference in the world is the province of God, even if man often imagines it was he himself that took the initiative. Man's way in this world is his attitude towards this alternative.

Now the number of the letters of these 'ten words' is 620. These 620 letters taken together form the structure of that which has been established for all eternity as the way of man towards reunion. This number 620 is also the number expressing the value of the components of the word 'kether', 20–400–200, the word which means 'crown' and which expresses the unity of God. In the manner of representation in the kabbalah it is the primeval, the initial beginning, the condition of oneness, from which God brought forth creation.

Thus in the whole of the 'ten words' there is the structure of the oneness as it exists in God. Just like the outward appearance of the two tables engraved in such a particular way on *two* sides, these 'ten words' mean the condition of the harmony of the opposites. This harmony is the structure of man, as it has been engraved by God in eternally enduring form. The kinetic element in this structure, that which 'makes fruit', is the word which makes an image and which bears the signature of the 172, of the alternative, of the 'if'.

For this, our world, the harmony of unity expresses itself in the sign of the alternative. The word itself implies this alternative. For it expresses an image as well as the substance. One can look upon it as a mere image, or as an image which is the form of expression of the substance. According to his disposition, man will let it either remain an image, or he will look upon image and substance as 'one'.

The letters, taken alone, do not express an image. Only of course in their names, which, however, through this fact make words at once. The letters in themselves are mere substance, and the 620 letters of the two stone tables therefore build up the conception implied in 'kether', the uppermost Sephirah. It is the part that 'is fruit'.

So when God in the fiftieth day proclaims this structure of man as His eternal form, expressing itself in behalf of this world of material phenomena in the two stone tables, coming from God and engraved by God, then on that day there is the condition of the coming world; then there prevails the condition of the eighth day.

Moses in this condition is with God and unites the world with God. According to ancient lore, God on Mount Sinai, i.e. on the 'form' reveals to him how the substance expresses itself in this life, how one is to regard and judge of the things and events of this life from the standpoint of the substance, and how by means of it, life can be lived. This revelation of God is expressed in the established structure of the words given by God, which together form the five books of the beginning, the 1–4 of the nucleus of the Bible. And this revelation at the same time expresses itself in the statements concerning the purpose of life, concerning the significance of the daily way of life, concerning the why and wherefore of things. They give the expression of the substance established in Pentateuch, in the phenomenal form of the different worlds, among which the one we live in now. This complex of statement, without which it is impossible to regard, let along understand the Bible in this world, and which in a way forms the body of the Bible, is the complex of ancient lore. Just as the body makes its appearance in every generation again, though in practically the same form yet ever with its own features, thus these statements of ancient lore ought to be passed on to every new generation by the previous one. They form the part of revelation which appears here as life. They can only live, if the life-breath is breathed through the word of the teacher into the pupil, through the word of the parents into the children. Therefore this part of the revelation bears the name of ancient lore. The first time God created this bodily part of revelation in imparting it to Moses. And just as children come to life through the will-to-create of the parents, thus this bodily part has kept alive because Moses imparted it to his pupil Joshua; he in his turn to his pupil, continuing the line until about two thousand years ago. Just because the body in every generation must be generated anew, albeit according to the same principles, with the same general forms and features, therefore these statements were never established in writing. The mouth imparted them; the breath, the life.

In times of great upheaval, when the knowledge of the substance of things got lost, over two thousand years ago, the knowledge of this oral revelation threatened to get lost as well. There arose points of doubt; there arose various deviating conceptions. That is why at about that time people began all the same to establish this complex in writing, a process which covered many centuries. Nevertheless people continue to call this complex the 'oral Thorah'. For even now on account of the very special, profoundly considered form of expression, it can only be imparted from teacher to pupil; it will only be understood if brought to life in constant practice. So the special character remained intact and every generation is to receive the ancient lore breathed into their ears by the previous one.

The name 'oral Thorah' in fact also means that it is more directly connected with our world. Our world, as we have stated, is the world on the left side of the systematism. It is on the side of hearing, of things oral. On the other hand the Bible, 'the written Thorah', is on the right side of the systematism. What is written is seen, what is spoken is heard. And seeing, together with the light, is on the right side. And it is exactly because the Bible is on the right side of systematism that it cannot, without more ado, be applied in our world of the left side. Just remember the examples given as regards jurisdiction.

Together, the written and the oral Thorah form one indivisible complex; it is again the well-known harmony between substance and appearance, body and soul.

He that enters the eighth day, like Moses in the biblical story on Mount Sinai, receives this revelation. On Mount Sinai, in the world of form, that is, encountering God; God who reveals everything; in which the contrast day-night, and waking-sleeping is eliminated, in which duality no longer exists as contrast. Moses on Mount Sinai does not eat, does not drink; because in him everything has been consummated on the Mount (Exod. 34:28).

In the 26th generation completion is attained. This encounter in the form, the body, on Mount Sinai, between God and Moses is the end in view of the way which started at creation. Now that it has been achieved in the nucleus and has found expression in the world, the cycle of the 10–5–6–5 is completed. This revelation is the tree of life, the 'one', which with the measure of the 500 opens up the way from earth to heaven. Through this happening everything bears the stamp of this completion. The biblical story following thereon, shows how it is expressed in time.

35
The Circle and the Fragments

But then why does the story go on? On Mount Sinai the goal is reached; the way of the 26 generations is completed.

The story goes on, because life goes on. The story shows what life is like *after* the revelation of its purpose, after the revelation of the tree of life. It shows in the first place that whoever is emancipated from Egypt, will follow this way to the revelation in accordance with the law of creation. It also shows that whoever is emancipated from Egypt, and therefore has been a witness to the flash of light of the eighth day at Mount Sinai, *cannot* go back to Egypt any more. The way back to duality, even if one should sometimes long for it, is closed off. Whoever pertains to the 'one' which has been emancipated from Egypt in contradistinction to the 'four', journeys on towards the world of Canaan, towards the eighth day. He can enter there 'alive' and, if not, he will get there in another form, as it is expressed in the statement that the children arrived there, when the fathers died in the wilderness in consequence of their 'sin'.

But do not let us anticipate. Emancipation from Egypt, and coming as far as Mount Sinai, in the first place has its consequence in regard to the measure of time. What expressed itself in Egypt as 400 years, therewith indicating an endlessly long time, the longest time possible, has now become shorter in reality. The journey through the desert is also signed by the 'four' of time, now no longer as 400, but as 40. One may say that duration essentially decreases, even though 40 years expresses an infinitely long duration. So it means that when one is on one's way from duality to the 'one', the inner experience of time is shorter. Just as man also feels it in this life in miserable periods or in joyful ones. In evil times the day lasts very long and one sighs 'if only it were night again' or 'if only it were morning again' (Deut. 28:67). But joyful days pass quickly, in joy one experiences the phenomenon time less acutely. Therefore time, measured in connection with Mount Sinai, is shorter and the 'four' expresses itself as 40 days.

Tradition puts it very clearly and flexibly, that the constellations, and especially those of the Zodiac, after the eating of the tree of knowledge revolve more slowly. So the measurement of time gets longer.

It is as if life leaps to another plane, to a circle closer to the centre or further removed from it. That is why the experience in the various circles differs.

What is impossible in Egypt, does happen in the wilderness; and at Mount Sinai things happen which were out of the question in the desert. Schematically one might represent it as follows, keeping in mind, however, that it is merely a method of presentation, no more (see figures on page 447).

The distance AB on p.447 is the reality of 'duality' expressing itself in the cycle of the 400 years. The distance B'C' is the reality in the condition on the way from the 'two' to the 'one', expressing itself in the cycle of the 40 years. This reality cannot be experienced on the outer circle as well, it will not be understood when it is expressed in BC. One will have to translate it from BC into B'C', where it prevails as reality. In BC, for instance, an 'angel' is unreal, a tabernacle is unreal. Thus the happening at Mount Sinai, in the 40 days there, expressed in the graphic in the distance C"D", cannot be comprehended in the circle of the 40 years, in the distance C'D'. One will have to translate again from that condition into the condition of C"D", where the event *actually* took place. And most assuredly the man in the outer circle, on CD, will not be able to comprehend it in his images. We have already seen how this retranslation into the substance can take place through the word, which forms the bridge between image and substance.

The exodus from Egypt also implies a leap from one plane to another. In our graphic this leaping takes place on BB'. And the condition of the 40 days at Mount Sinai similarly means a leaping to another plane. After the events with the spies there is another leap, this time downwards and outwards. The 40 days now become 40 years.

Now the Bible is expressed in what we call the forms of the seventh day. This is the world after the exodus from 'duality', from Egypt. In our drawing it is the circle of the 40 years. For in the seventh day, indeed, there occurs the flash of light of the eighth day, of Mount Sinai. If one lives and thinks in the forms of the man who is not yet emancipated, i. e. if one reasons from the standpoint of duality, of Egypt, because in one's life one is turned in that direction, then the events on the circle of 40 years are not real; neither should one look upon them as real on that outer circle of the 400 years. There one only sees the images and nothing else. One will always have to realize that one has to translate images with the help of the word into the inner circle. With it one puts oneself in the situation of the exodus from Egypt, for with it one connects image and substance; hence one is on one's way from the 'two' to the 'one'. For this is one of the meanings of reading the Bible truly and taking it in. One emancipates from the servitude to 'duality'.

As soon as one gets emancipated from servitude to 'duality' in Egypt, the spiral of time which until then had been expanding, begins to contract, the way 1 → 2 merges gradually into the way from the 2 → 1.

And therefore one of the first encounters on this way from 2 → 1 is that of Mount Sinai. Whoever goes this way very soon experiences the revelation of the tree of life, which was hidden as long as one was on the way from 1 → 2. And whatever may happen further on this way from 2 → 1, everything bears the mark of the revealed purpose for all that. This revelation cannot he undone, it also marks the attitude of the man on the way which is opening now. A way leading to the eighth day, a way inexorably blocking a return to Egypt. Everybody emancipated from Egypt and because of it having the experience of Mount Sinai, now participates of the eighth day, of the coming world. The way thither is the content of the story, unfolding itself *after* the revelation on Mount Sinai.

The first thing that happens is Moses abiding on the mountain for 40 days, separated from his people. Previous to these 40 days, Moses had also spent one day on Mount Sinai; but on that day there still was the connection between him and the others, and he had passed on to them the words of God. In contradistinction, however, with that single day spent in joy and glory, from the moment he ascended Mount Sinai again, to stay away for 40 days, there was no connection any more between below and above (Exod. 19:20–25 and Exod. 24).

These 40 days again express for our world that the period of separation was of infinitely long duration. The duration, however, is much shorter, since one is now at Mount Sinai, close to the centre. Nevertheless, in essence this 40 implies being compelled to wait an unendurably long time. And this waiting in time, implying an every further removal from the origin, like all such removals, finally gets to the breaking-point, upon which severing oneself from every connection is possible. It is the point, well known to us by now, the point of the 'half', the point of the crisis, of the decision.

Thus the story of the Bible tells us how at the end of the 40 days people got tired of waiting, how doubts began to arise of Moses ever getting back. And then there is the well-known story of the golden calf (Exod. 32).

The people begged for leadership, they wanted to have a leader to take them to the promised land, the time had come for fulfilment of the promise, the 40 was quickly coming to an end. Thus the calf was produced with the gold eagerly offered for the purpose. The consequence was that God's stone tables were broken; there was sorrow and ruin. A most dismal story following so shortly after the miracles at the exodus from Egypt and at Mount Sinai. How was it that people came to adore a *calf* as their leader after all those miracles? Is not this 'primitive' element of the adoration of a golden calf a flat contradiction of the grandeur preceding it? Were these nomads of the desert after all so uncivilized as present-day evolutionists like to present them? Was it a 'dance round the golden calf', as those that love symbolism like to express the adoration of money? After the preceding we shall all of us easily understand that neither manner of explanation has anything to do with the true significance of the story.

After the grand experience of the descent of God on Mount Sinai, at which according to tradition, literally everybody surveyed space and time from one extreme to the other; at which the purpose of everything was revealed to everybody; at which heaven and earth were 'one'; a division was accomplished.

He that had accomplished the connection between below and above, became invisible. He was supposed to be above, and above was completely divorced from below. Again we see here how, after the condition of unity, the 'two' is effected. Hence a duality again, which had for its purpose the return of him that had made the connection, Moses, this time with the two tables containing the eternal structure of man, with the knowledge concerning body and soul through the revelation. For the purpose of ultimately accomplishing this unity again, a unity with a harmony much more profoundly understood and inwardly realized, a unity now expressed in the stone tables; for this purpose had 'duality' been made; had the division been effected again with the pattern of creation.

During that time of division, the great gift is prepared 'above'; and 'below' there is the abiding in time, in faith of the coming of reunion. So again it is the making of duality for the sake of the bliss of reunion. For that reason the duration of duality also is the duration of the world. That is why in this bit of cloth of that specific colour of Joseph's coat of many colours, the 40 days present the picture of the whole world, how it is waiting for ultimate reunion, after having tasted this oneness, in a different quality, before the commencement of this period of 40 days.

According to tradition, before his departure, Moses had said that his absence would last forty days, i. e. that the separation, duality, would continue throughout the time of this world, till the end of this time. For on that fortieth day he would return, then to lead this world to the great harmony, to the world of the coming day.

Now in this period of separation the time comes of the approaching end. The development of multiplicity, ever inherent in existence in duality, is approaching its farthest extreme, the point of the 'half'. It is, in fact, the point which, expressed in time, ever is the present moment; *this* very moment, *this* very life, *this* time and *this* world. It is the point where we are faced with the 10–5, and where the 6–5 is to start. And therefore it is also the moment where the serpent comes to point at the splendour and the glory of development, of youth as the symbol of development, therewith propounding the alternative.

It is in that sense, that, according to ancient lore, towards the end of the time of separation between Moses and the people, when the 'forty' was running to an end, Satan came along and began to draw people's attention to the promised salvation failing to materialize; the promised return of the original saviour who had gone up to God and stayed there, to all intents and purposes. Satan *figured* out that the fortieth day, i. e. the last day of this world, was running to an end and that Moses had not yet appeared. Who and what was to make people enter the promised land? What was to give the lead in this Messianic time, in this time of the end?

In the time of the end the forces of development are strongest; the seduction going forth from them is greatest then. Owing to development the distance to the origin has become exceedingly great, people are simply sheathed in the phases of development and they even fail to see the significance of that origin. The origin is regarded as a very distant phase; away back in the past; there where development had started. So very far back, one could only guess at that vague beginning. How had man grown to be human at all? How had he been able to take the leap from dull, mechanical matter to the present high level of intellect with its numerous standards of good and bad and the organization built up thereon? What had brought him thither, who was the God that had emancipated him from matter; the God who was to lead him further to a world full of the good?

The man Moses, drawn from the water, was a fairy-tale, quite likely or may be people had misunderstood things! What did it really mean that he was in heaven, and what was heaven anyway! Heaven had bestowed on earth laws of its own and a development of its own and one had to take these realities into account. Everything was full of promise of having attained the 'last phase of development', a phase which had given the world an entirely new aspect. A new era, a new world enticed, if only people would persevere.

When the times are ripe for this thought, the serpent comes. It is the serpent which always appears towards the end of worn conditions on the border of the new. In various countries there is a saying even heard nowadays that if a serpent if found inside the house it means one will shortly remove to another place.

The fortieth day drew to a close, and Moses did not come. Satan seemed to be right, after all. People would like to see the gods; they insisted on knowing for sure; the secret ought to be unveiled now. People turned to Aaron, the aspect of the original unity Moses-Aaron, who had stayed behind.

For indeed, in the systematism Moses takes the place on the right in the second triad, and Aaron the place on the left. The left place, the side of the body, is the only side present in the world of the 40 days. The other side in that period is the 'imperceptible', it is 'in heaven'. Now Aaron, as expression of the leader in this world, is required to 'make' these gods. People wanted these gods at the hands of him that was on earth, the visible, tangible, perceptible. And Aaron claimed the offering of that which gave the body its attractiveness, which imparted to 'women, sons and daughters' the outward semblance of glory. According to tradition Aaron hoped that people would not be prepared to sacrifice so much and would be willing to wait, even though time was running out.

Aaron, the one that brings the body nearer to God, who makes unity between this world and the other, hopes that in the dynamic time of the end, this body which wants to sever itself from the origin, will not care to make this sacrifice. It is made difficult for this life to follow the way of development. There are conflicts; family life is disrupted; there is discontent through the numerous sacrifices one has to bring to training, education, studies, society; there is disquiet; war and revolution. The body gets ill, nervous, full of complaints and minor ailments in consequence of dynamism and the subsequent tensions. The reverse of seductive development becomes perceptible in the form of sacrifices required. It is the final effort made by Aaron to prevent people from going the way pointed by Satan. But people bring all these sacrifices; they are prepared to offer all this, that they may find the energies which will bring them to the promised land, to the ideal future. What people had ever relied on, the coming of the saviour from heaven where he was supposed to abide with God, had proved to be a hollow phrase. People would have to take the initiative into their own hands.

Again Aaron tried to postpone. Ancient lore points to the fact that Aaron says: 'tomorrow is a feast unto the Lord' (Exod. 32:5). Aaron still cherished hopes of Moses' return, even though the time predicted was past, even though the fortieth day had gone and Moses had not come back.

Next morning, i. e. at the beginning of the forty-first day, people rose early and brought the offering to the god they had made for themselves, the god, come forth from the offerings people had ungrudgingly sacrificed for the sake of finding him. This god had indeed come forth from the offerings and people had proclaimed him as such. He proved to be alive.

There is an immense dynamic power to serve that god at this time. Satan made people rise up early to devote themselves entirely to this newly-proclaimed god. All Aaron's postponement had proved unavailing. Such was the pace of time, there was no restraining it. People had turned to this new god and they counted on the promised land, the ideal future, through the mediation of this god.

But then, how is it with the calf? Why exactly was it a calf that was made into a god? Again it is the image which deludes us as long as we merely live and think in a world of images. Here again we shall have to learn to know the substance of the image, that we may understand. Therefore we shall have to study the structure of the word calf.

The word for calf is 'egel', spelt 70–3–30. Now the word for circle is similarly built up of the identical letters, it is also 70–3–30. So the calf is connected with the circular, and the circular finds its expression in the form of 'calf'.

We can also approach this identity through the systematism we have got rather familiar with. For the calf is the animal of the second place, hence on the left side of systematism. Indeed in the Zodiacal constellations, it is the place of the 'bull'. And the left side is at the same time the side of the covering, of the garment, of the circle surrounding this centre. Indeed the left world, as principle, ever presents itself as a cycle, as wave-motion, as a coming and going, as a turning wheel. In translation of course *calf* and *circle* have nothing in common any more than they have in their outward appearance. In substance, however, they are identical, and the word shows us this identity.

To enter more profoundly into this identity of calf and circle, I will for the moment drop the subject of the golden calf, presently to take it up again. We shall then understand even better what these conceptions mean.

There is a story in tradition, for instance, pointing out that Jacob did not know for sure that Joseph was still alive, until he 'saw the wagons which Joseph had sent' (Gen. 45:27). For, says the story the last principle Jacob had discussed with Joseph before his disappearance to Egypt was that which occurs in the Bible in Deut. 21:1–9. This passage mentions finding a man slain in the field and nobody knowing who has slain him. In that case the elders of the nearest city must take a heifer, which means a calf, and break its neck. In Hebrew the word for 'heifer' naturally is the same as that for calf, with the only difference that in the case of the heifer, the word has the feminine ending, since in this case it is a *female* animal. The word for the golden calf, which is a young *bull*, is 70–3–30, and that for the heifer is 70–3–30–5.

Now in the story in ancient lore about Joseph being found again, the *wagon*, spelt 70–3–30–5, is connected with the heifer, spelt 70–3–30–5, without the connection becoming apparent anywhere, except in the first place from the structure of the word. The wagon, the Hebrew word for which is derived from wheel, from the circular, from the circle, superficially has no connection whatsoever with a calf. That Jacob therefore, when seeing the wagons, should immediately link them up to his last discussion with Joseph on the heifer in connection with the 'man slain and the unknown perpetrator', points in the direction of a deeper connection. Otherwise one might rightly ask why Joseph had not rather sent a calf instead of posing this riddle with the wagon.

Besides, the reader may wonder how it was that Jacob could have discussed anything with Joseph which was to be dealt with in the Bible hundreds of years afterwards. I do hope, however, that the reader has come to realize by now that the Bible is not a history book, but that it is the expression of the substance, of the principles of creation and of life, given by God in the forms of space-time. And since creation these principles had naturally been known to those people who had preserved the tie with the origin, with the substance, or had restored it. These principles merely take form through the word in the happening the Bible describes, and therefore that happening itself is important too. The principles, however, are the principles known to the first man, who spoke with God.

Thus tradition, for instance, although well aware that it took place much earlier, has it that Lot, when the angels came to him in Sodom to destroy it and to lead him away, offered them unleavened bread (Gen. 19:3) because it was Passover, the day, that is, of the exodus from Egypt. Yet this is not accidental either. For the destruction of Sodom, too, means God interfering at the extreme point of development. Going further would be impossible, it would be contradictory to the principle of creation, which indeed, implies a return to the source of origin. The swelling of the ferment, the leaven, had attained its maximum. It would now be removed. Lot, however, ate the unleavened bread, he also received guests from another world, beyond Sodom.

There, again, the reversal; the forces of development being removed at the very moment when for creation, for the substance, the condition sets in of saving the world from the grip of development. Lot, who ate the unleavened bread, is saved from destruction. Sodom goes down at Passover, which runs parallel with the fall of Egypt at Easter. And the birth of the new world, of Isaac, is announced. This new world, too, comes forth at Easter. The essential conception of 'salvation at the point of extremity' always finds expression, and always this wonderful wellnigh incredible, utterly unexpected salvation, takes place at Easter.

Thus there also is a principle of 'the man slain and the unknown perpetrator', which principle is ever expressed under specific circumstances. And his principle is quite well known of course to everyone who knows the foundations of the world, who knows the purpose of creation. Therefore one should regard the substance of the Bible, that whither the word of the Bible leads us, as something ever present and always operative. The image the Bible uses, is the image created by God to express this substance in terms of time and therewith to create unity between image and substance.

The principle of 'the man slain and the unknown perpetrator' is a very important principle in the world. Briefly and broadly stated it comes to this that 'man dies and nobody knows how it is'. There must be a cause – this does not mean a cause such as a certain disease or an accident, but a cause for dying at all – but people do not understand the cause, they do not know where to look for it; they can at best trace back one link in the causal sequence, the nearest 'town'; but what will be the outcome, or whether it is the right direction for investigation, nobody knows.

This ignorance concerning the cause of events, the cause of the contrast life-death, the why and wherefore of the sudden departure from this world, has to do with the fact of our living in the world of the left side, in the world of form, of the body. This world in its way of expression on the left side of systematism, on the side where the forces of development can unfold to the utmost extreme, is the world of the compassing by the body. The substance within is hardly to be recognized. Thus Isaac did not recognize Jacob under the garment of Esau, even though the voice, the word, rather puzzled him. In this way does the body compass the soul, thus 'does the woman compass the man', the circle compasses the centre. Hence the characteristic of this world is the circle, the 70–3–30. And the substance crystallizes into the physical, which we call 'calf', which therefore is also 70–3–30, and in the systematism of the animals it therefore is in the second place, on the left.

The cause of the ignorance whence death derives, is indeed that calf, that circle; is the fact that we live on the left side, the side where the real, the substance, is hidden; remains compassed. The leaders, the 'elders', in fact, are guilty of this ignorance. The 'elders' should have explained it clearly and distinctly; they ought to have made the connection between right and left, soul and body, substance and appearance. Then they might have told people what death is and what it is for. The 'elders', the leaders of the generation, that is, ought to have given the 'tree of life' to their world. Then the cause of death would *certainly* have become clear. Then there would not have been the dishonour of death in public, in the field, in the world without people knowing how it was and whence it had come. The 'elders' cherished a circular world, a world of circular reasonings, revolving in circles, without ever catching the centre. The elders had the calf, the world which could be gripped by development. They omitted connecting the opposites into unity.

Therefore they have now to bring that heifer and the heifer's neck has to be struck off. Which means that the circle must be broken through; that which gives the circle life, existence, must be broken.

The neck connects the head with the trunk, the 'one' with the 'four'. This connection must not blur the difference. The 'one' is to remain 'one' and for that very reason gives meaning to the 'four'. Therefore the neck is the supple movable part, through which the 'one' and the 'four' are connected as well as distinguished. Only thus will there be the harmony of the opposites. If, however, the neck is 'stiff', it means that there is no difference between head and trunk, between the 'one' and the 'four', that there exists a continuum, where there should have been a harmony of opposites. The word for the expression 'stiff' has the letters 100–300 as its root, with a sum-total of 400. It is this 400 which characterizes the whole. There is now formed a continued circle, in which the distinction between head and trunk is eradicated, where one no longer knows what is cause and what is effect. It is in this sense that the term 'stiff-necked' people is used, of people who are similarly unwilling to make unity in the sense of harmony of opposites, but try to find the way in a kind of continuum, in an evolution, gradually moving towards an apparent goal, which however is no goal, because they keep revolving in the circle.

The word 'neck' in Hebrew is 'oref', spelt 70–200–80. The sum-total is 350. It is the 3½ which is somewhat familiar to us; the 3½ which indicates how the substance unites with expansion in time. Now this 3½ forms the connection between head and trunk, between the 'one' and the 'four'. It denotes how the 'four' is seen from the point of view of the 'one'. And this connection is a matter of principle; it ever has to denote the distinction, it forms the decisive hinge. It must not become the cause of a continuity between the 'one' and the 'four'. The 'one' does not pass into the 'four' as an evolution of one thing into the other; the place of the transition is both connection and distinction; it is a most sensitive, decisive place. Where the connection consists of a stiff neck, a stiff 3½, a 3½ characterized by the 400, there the neck, the 3½, must be struck off.

Thus the elders, i.e. the wise men, the leaders, have to strike off this stiff neck. They have to show *what* is the cause of ignorance; that they were living in the world of the cycle, of the circle, of evolution, of the gradual, and it was that which caused ignorance.

If this has been done, they can plead 'not guilty'. When one has left the old way, the guilt is wiped out. It was not they who had shed that blood. But the fact they had found the slain man in the field was due all the same to the existence of this live heifer, of that operative circle. It has got to be broken publicly.

It goes without saying that in this our world the neck of the heifer should not be stuck off any more than anybody's tooth or eye may be knocked out, because he had done it to somebody else; it is no more permissible than bringing an animal offering nowadays. These are absolute situations which can only become a reality in another world. We already discussed this principle in the chapters on jurisdiction and the offerings. As regards this heifer, the all-important thing is in the first place to realize what is involved. The physical act is to the purpose only, if here too one has a living experience of substance and appearance.

This principle it was which formed the last discussion between Jacob and Joseph, before the latter was sold into Egypt. In that case too, there was a happening arising from an obscure cause with an unknown purpose. Jacob did not know the perpetrators of the sale. Joseph was carried off from his father, who thought he was dead, into a world with which no contacts were possible. According to ancient lore, from the moment of the sale of Joseph, Jacob was no longer called Israel, because the clear consciousness of unity, which had made him like a prophet, left him. For the name Israel indeed implies the harmony of the opposites, the union of the two sides. The left side, however, now dissociated itself from the name Israel and lived an independent existence. Therefore Jacob did not see through the purpose of the happening and suffered so much from the loss of Joseph.

But when Jacob saw the wagons, i.e. the circle, which Joseph had sent, he suddenly understood, and, after having been called Israel for the last time in Gen. 37:13, now when his spirits revived, he was called Israel again (Gen. 45:28). Jacob realized that the point at issue was the heifer whose neck should be struck off. In doing so he all at once saw the relationships, the causes, and harmony was restored in him. The whole story of the sale of Joseph is this story of the 'slain man and nobody knowing the perpetrator'. It starts with Jacob and Joseph facing the principle and it ends with the wagons, the circle which Joseph showed to 'strike off the heifer's neck', to conclude the story with which Joseph departed from Jacob. When the circle is broken through, then the separation, the duality between Jacob and Joseph and between Jacob and Israel is eliminated.

Now let us return to the story of the golden calf. When at the end of the fortieth day the offerings are brought abundantly and eagerly in order to learn to know and to serve the power of the earth, which is to lead mankind to the condition of the promised land, of the ideal world, now that people no longer cherish any belief of a potential saviour coming from another world, there *naturally* comes forth that calf, the circular. Aaron did not mould a calf; it came forth of its own accord. When people go that way, the consequence is an image of the cyclic world. Things present themselves to us as circular, as closed off. Suddenly it all seems to tally. Also when one operates with it. According to ancient lore, even Aaron saw how that calf lived and ate. In fact, it produced wonderful results.

Towards the end everything proceeds more quickly; things seem to come of their own accord. Ancient lore has it that Satan, i. e. the power of development, he that prevents the return, speeds up everything in the final phase. Everything seems to come to people automatically, everything looks well-ordered and right. People discover all sorts of secrets about matter; even young children appear to be able to discover these things. They all at once lie ready to hand. People had hoped and counted on a quiet, balanced, civilized development. But things go quicker and quicker; the circular overpowers everybody, there are explosions of energetic activity and of discoveries.

Once people see how all the circular fits together, because after all everything is round in this world of phenomena, in this material world, they get blind to all that might eventually he beyond it. People simply refuse to see it, for it might have a disturbing effect on all this delightful illusion they are enjoying now. Whoever lives in illusion, dislikes all interference, he dislikes suggestions of the unreality of the world which he conjures up before himself. People get dangerously aggressive when they are compelled to give up their illusions. Hur, the son of Miriam and Caleb, according to ancient lore, wanted to point at the foolishness of taking the circular, the cycle for one's guidance, to accept it as one's god. He was killed by the world. People brook no interference.

Thus the circular, this cyclic, is proclaimed which encloses because it excludes all others; thus earthly, experimental causality is exalted as a god. With it is proved (Exod. 32:4), that emancipation from Egypt was a matter of that circular, of evolution, that everything hinged on the mechanical laws of the cyclic. Thus man had also developed ever further, had freed himself more and more from the shackles which bound him to the earth. Physically and psychically he rose above the earth. Admittedly, it was a process of many thousands of years, probably many hundred thousands of years. And how grand, how absolutely different would everything be again when mankind had advanced another hundred thousand years. That they themselves would not be there any more, that they had not even got an idea where they would be themselves within a few decades, all this was outside the ken of the circle. The circle enclosed this material, perceptible world. It was only this that the game, the intoxication confined itself to. And for this material world, thus did the theory of the circular inform people, would this god, boasting of how he had emancipated man from the bonds of servitude to the earth, also be the guide on the way to the ideal future full of peace and opulence. On this earth, of course.

To that god everything was offered now. He yielded results, whereas the so-called redeemer, abiding in heaven, had in fact, never come. The 40 days were gone, the fortyfirst day had begun. They had been chasing a phantom, a symbol, thinking it might be a reality to this world; they had failed, just as this saviour had failed to return and prove his existence.

Finally people ate and drank with that god of the circular, and there was rejoicing. The purpose of existence is fulfilled – think of the discussion of the real meaning of the conception eating – in the presence of that god, according to his standards. And there were rejoicings. According to ancient lore this also implied committing adultery and manslaughter. Development in the continuum, in the circular, brings other criteria with it. These sacrifices are duly to be brought for the sake of progress, and it is these very sacrifices that rouse the kind of joy that struck Moses with horror. For the word, translated here as rejoicing, is not the ordinary word for it. In this text it is the word 'tsachek', which implies ridicule, mockery, irony, cynicism; because one does not believe in it; it is the laughter of the intoxicated. From this word the name Isaac is derived in which similarly, though in a different sense, is expressed the contrast between reality and the predicted ideal. People simply cannot believe it any more and give utterance to it in derision.

Thus there is in the end this kind of joy which is not real joy; it is the rejoicing of abandonment, of so-called relaxation, of shouting, yelling, the boisterous, foolish enjoyment, noise for the sake of noise.

The world at the zenith of its enthusiasm for development, suddenly becomes aware of the saviour yet descending from on high. The saviour from above stands face to face with the god which the world had made for itself, face to face with the fascinating enclosing circular, which excludes everything else. And everything breaks into fragments at this confrontation, the tables which were to bring man eternal, and the calf which had conjured up the round world.

In all this we recognize again the story of the tree of knowledge. Man, following the indications of the serpent, forms the world of development and with it he breaks man eternal into fragments; scatters him in the endless multiplicity of the generations, in space-time. The forces which had caused this development are weakened, pushed back. And man is taken to another world in which to follow the way to reunion.

After the 'calf', too, there comes a new world, a different world. The tabernacle of the congregation which had been in the centre of the camp is pitched outside, afar off from the camp (Exod. 33:7–11). The centre, the essence is not perceptible any more. One has now first to step outside one's own world to be able to see the substance. And the ornament, in Hebrew a word with the root 70–4, is laid aside. These ornaments, according to ancient lore, were the crowns people had received during the revelation on Mount Sinai. The word contains the 70 and the 4; either of them as we saw being the expression of multiplicity with which the word Eden has also been composed. After this happening man lays aside the faculty of seeing through multiplicity. It was this very 70–4 which had been his crown. So in every respect can be retraced the pattern of the transition from the world of the Garden of Eden to a lower world, another world.

The day when Moses returned and encountered the 'calf' was the seventeenth day of the fourth month. Again we see the 17 appearing as the end of a phase of development. In another plane, this seventeenth day of the fourth month spelt the end of biblical Jerusalem. There, too, a development was arrested, since the removal from the source had reached the farthest extreme, since there too people had resorted to seeking a redeemer in the earthly sphere, besides God in whom they continued to believe in a general way. There too followed the period of an 'endless' exile, of a 'forty' in the essential. Just think of the word 'good' with which in the story of creation one day passes into the other, and which has this same number 17 as its total value.

As a matter of fact, man ever stands at this point of furthest removal. At every moment that point comes to expression in every man's life. And at every moment he is faced with this alternative, this crossing of ways. He sees that the redeemer from heaven is not there. At that point furthest removed from the source of origin, as every moment represents it to each individual, he yearns to see him in an earthly form, measure him with earthly criteria, as an earthly home. The redeemer should be in accordance with the standards of that point. And when the redeemer from heaven does not even react, so that it even begins to seem foolish to go on counting on him in earthly things, then one gives all one's time and energy, all one's thoughts and feelings to an ideal in this world; then one offers all this to the forces of development. With it one has voted for the way which leads to that godhead looming up before our eyes and our minds which implies the circular, the cyclic. And the 'calf' has emerged. Now that is the way which leads to destruction. For the saviour from heaven *does* come after all, and the whole way is reversed.

Whoever does not vote for the way of the redeemer as an earthly power of development – as, according to ancient lore, the tribe of Levi did, which even in Egypt had kept themselves free from the servitude to duality – attains real salvation even in this life. It is the well-known pattern again: whoever takes the way of the tree of life, has the tree that 'is fruit and makes fruit'. To him the way to unity is not a way filled with fear and despair, he does not follow it as a 'fugitive and a vagabond'. To him life does not break into the fragments of the generations, ever bringing death and exile anew.

This farthest point of removal from the origin expresses itself in every individual life at every moment which is experienced as the present, the 'now'. It also expresses itself, however, in every time for groups of people belonging together and for mankind as a totality. For this collective reaction, too, there is the alternative; there is always the crossways. These farthest points of development of every individual life, however, and of the life of mankind as a whole, acquire a very special character as this 'now' coincides with the time when the world approaches its farthest point of development, the point expressed a.o. in the principle of the 58. Then the forces active in those conditions are naturally especially intensified. Then, indeed, in every respect it is the period in which one offers energy and time towards a salvation measured with the standards of the earth. Then there emerges the circular with all the more intensive power. The alternative shows up more distinctly, there is no vagueness any more. Where the world will approach the extreme point of development, certainly *cannot* be calculated with the methods of the 'circular', as they are applied for measuring the physical, the material. The standards which the Bible gives of such turning-points of worlds, however, afford some insight. What has been brought forward about these standards in the foregoing, together with what has already been indicated about the moment of expulsion from Paradise, the generation of Cain, that of the Flood, that of the splitting-up, the Haflaga, about the exodus from Egypt, the calf in the wilderness, yields various facets, pointing the way to the standards by which to measure the end of time in this world.

Our astronomic conceptions of years and of centuries lies in a different plane; we see them merely from the mechanical point of view. The real standards of time, however, are vibrant with life, man helps to form them. With those standards does the story of the Bible calculate.

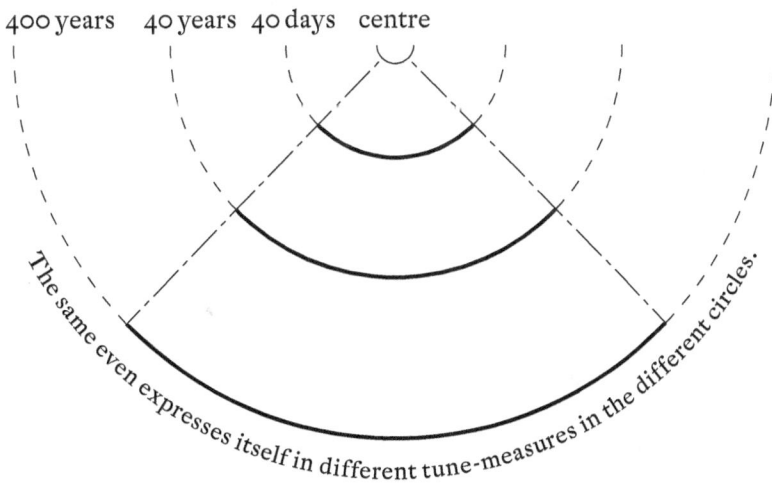

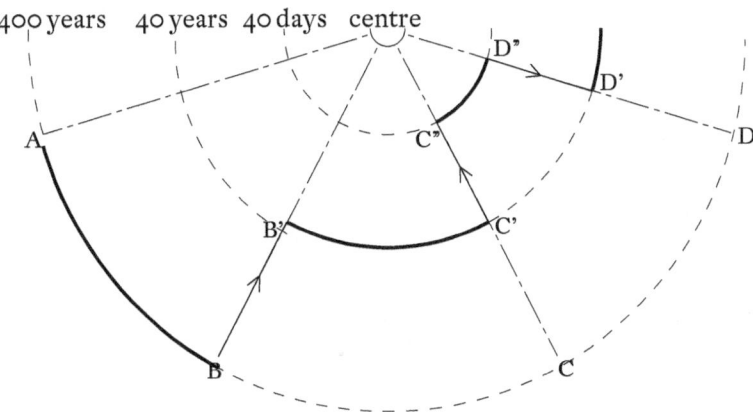

36
The Method of Counting

So far we have kept back the answer to the question how it was that Moses did *not* return on the fortieth day, as he himself had promised. All that tragic story with the calf could not have presented itself, if only Moses had come back in time. For people indeed had a perfect right to cherish doubts about his return, of his existence even, when the time had visibly passed and that which had been promised had not been fulfilled.

According to ancient lore, Satan played in that calculation of the time of the end and through it caused confusion. Then there follows some arithmetic, rather simple at first sight, which however states the very principle of chronology.

According to these statements, Moses ascended Mount Sinai on the seventh of the third month (Exod. 24:9–18). It was a very special day for Moses as well as for the others. A day of pomp and circumstances, a day of realizing what until then had been considered impossible (Exod. 24:10–11). When Moses is with God, a new phase sets in for the others. For then begins the period of the divorce, the period of the 40 days. Those 40 days express the time when Moses is alone with God and the people are alone down below.

Now Satan lets the 40 days start from the beginning of that day, the seventh day of the third month, whereas in fact they begin to count from the moment of separation, the moment when duality arises between Moses and the others. That moment occurs much later on that day. According to Satan's reckoning the 40 days are past at the end of the sixteenth day of the fourth month, the seventeenth being the fortyfirst day, whereas, when reckoned from the moment of separation the 40 days run to an end only in the course of the seventeenth of the fourth month.

When one reads all this, one is rather inclined to say, as with so many of those statements of tradition, it is rather far-fetched to bring all this misery of the calf and the broken tables over the people in consequence of such a trifling misunderstanding. One might rightly say Moses ought to have stated a little more exactly when he was going to return, and that moreover apart from all this, the method of reckoning of the children of Israel was not sinful. By now we know enough about the profound significance of the statements of ancient lore not to wave aside this bit of arithmetic as mere hair-splitting. For what is the meaning of this method of reckoning?

The story of tradition aims at making it clear that the time when Moses was still in the company of the others, when they witnessed and experienced the unbelievable together, falls outside the counting of the '40'. At that moment there still was the harmony Moses-Aaron; at that moment everything had an aspect different from that which began with the '40'. In that period they saw God and lived. With the '40' an absolutely new condition begins. People are cut off from above, they cannot do anything except 'wait', the characteristic expression of the symptom time, of that which presents itself as '40'. The condition of 'one' obtains when Moses together with Aaron, Nadab, Abihu and the seventy elders, see God and have the living experience of unity; and there is a condition of 'forty' when Moses is alone, imperceptible, divorced from the others; the latter having nothing to do except 'waiting' for the passing of that condition. Here again it is the 'one' facing multiplicity or, translated into the terminology we are now familiar with, the 'one' facing the 'four'.

So the error did not lie in the confusion as regards the calculation of the '40' days, but in the fact that people made a continuity of two entirely different conditions; that people considered the 'one' and the 'four' as coming from the same plane; that they did not understand, from the standpoint of the 'four', that the 'one' represented something entirely different, another world; that they considered the greatest miracles of that 'one' as something pertaining to the 'four', as part of it; as a condition, at any rate, not different from the 'four'. So people were 'stiff-necked', they did not show any understanding of the harmony between the 'one' and the 'four'. They had no notion of the fact that in the one plane there obtain standards entirely different from those of the other; they made everything flowing, liquid, applying what we see and think as colouring and measure. Now that is not an error in arithmetic, it is called sit. It is the consequence of a certain disposition, an attitude of man towards God and the world.

Therefore ancient lore speaks of the appearance of Satan. He it was that suggested this reckoning of ordinary arithmetic. The forces of development merely know this continual flowing; and whoever binds himself to those forces, gets the vision of everything evolving gradually and the standards acquired from evolution as being the only ones. Then one gets caught up within the circle; then one serves the 'calf'. Then one has the disposition to measure what is holy, what belongs to a different level, with the standards of the world of multiplicity. It actually is the 'stiff neck', the stiff 3½ which had to be struck off in the calf.

A similar happening, similarly based on an apparent misunderstanding in the calculation of time, is mentioned in a story in tradition, known as the exodus of the sons of Ephraim from Egypt.

The story is that the sons of Ephraim, a very vigorous family, knew about the 400 years of exile in Egypt. They also knew that God had foretold this exile of 400 years to Abraham in the biblical year 2018 (Gen. 15:13). Hence servitude was to end in 2418. It started at the pronouncing of the fact of the oppression; from the moment Abraham knew about it, the exile became a reality.

Therefore in 2418, thirty years before the actual exodus from Egypt, they bestirred themselves to leave Egypt and occupy Canaan. Since they were exceedingly strong — remember: Emphraim, the physical side of the unity Judah-Joseph — they won their liberty with their weapons, and entered Canaan. They did not follow the long way from the east to the west, but straightway made their entry from Egypt into the west. There they were defeated and killed by the inhabitants of the country. The dry bones which Ezekiel saw — as mentioned before — were the bones of the apparently over-rash sons of Ephraim.

They too had made *the* miscalculation and to them too that error was catastrophic. Abraham, indeed, even in 2018, knew about the 400 years' exile and the emancipation following it. He knew even then about the reunion after the separation. But there was not yet that which could go along that way, which could have the living experience of the reunion. Life in this world, in the world of the left side, had not yet come and everything pointed to the fact that it could not *ever* come.

The wonder of the creation of this world, similarly crystallizing in the miracle of Isaac's coming, had not yet been consummated, and all knowledge and every law pointed to the fact that it was utterly out of the question.

For thirty years Abraham had lived in the faith, in the conviction that it would come all the same, however improbable, even impossible, it might look to him. Only after thirty years did the unbelievable come true, did Isaac arrive. When *that* incredible thing made its appearance, a further continuation of the miracle, of exile and emancipation, of duality and reunion, was not really so difficult to believe in any more. Concretizing in fact made its entrance with Isaac's arrival, with the coming of this world of the left side, which had been considered impossible. Therefore the 30 years of faith, of belief from conviction, as a measure of time, are considered wholly apart from the ensuing 400 years. They pertain to a different level; they form the 'one' over against the multiplicity to come. Here, too, one should realize that the 400 contain a world in themselves, a world of development, of duration, of waiting for salvation. And that there is no continuity possible between a condition previous to the 400 and this all-embracing 400. The world which Abraham believed in the impossible, lived up to it, stands as a 'one' facing the world of seeing and perceiving, which made its entrance with Isaac. One should not, must not, mix up these two situations; one cannot make them into a continuity.

So the mistake of the sons of Ephraim, like that of the makers of the 'calf' is that they measured eveything with the same standards; that to them there did not exist any difference between things sacred and multiplicity. It is mixing up the saviour with the promise of development. Thus the sons of Ephraim approached the calculations about the end with the criteria of this world, with the causality of the circular. That is why they felt they absolutely had every right when, with the signs of the ending of a world actually about them, they took their swords to do what was theirs to do, to reap the promise of salvation with the standards of development. Their activity, again in accordance with the law of creation, was rewarded with an enormous success in the first instance. The exodus was a success, but the entry into the coming world meant the entry into death.

It is the precipitousness of physical man who draws conclusions from developments and cannot refrain from attaching himself to them. Not realizing that he is the victim of an enormous confusion, that he is caught up in a circle made by himself.

Therefore, when Moses descended into Egypt and people wanted to know whether he really was the redeemer, they turned to Sarah, the daughter of the eighth son, Asher. Since she pertained to the eight, she would be able to recognize the characteristics of the true saviour. Many redeemers had already announced themselves as such, and ever again after having heard their arguments and claims, she had rejected them as untrue saviours. She had, likewise, refuted the theories of the sons of Ephraim. When, however, she heard that the words of Moses (Exod. 4:31) were identical with those with which Joseph had predicted the saviour (Gen. 50:25) she said, 'This time it is the true saviour.' These words – in Hebrew in both texts literally the same – imply that God will remember; that God will do it. For real emancipation is something utterly outside the scope of evolution. It is an interference coming from another world. It is a principle established with creation that liberation is to come from another world, from the origin, and that it is *not* a consequence, *not* an extrapolation of the line of evolution, of further progress. There is merely a return from the point of development attained, through this interference. However sensible, wise, clever or good a man may be, salvation comes to all as a surprise.

We shall get a clearer insight in the special position of the 30 years in regard to the 400, if the structure of that period is more closely observed. We see, as it has indeed been discussed before, that 190 years of those 400 years are still spent in Canaan, albeit as 'stranger' because the Canaanite yet occupied the land of the origin, because the world as a whole had not yet returned to the condition of harmony in the 'one'. These 190 years in Canaan therefore have the same value as the word Canaan, which indeed is 20–50–70–50, with a sum-total of 190. After this come the 210 years in Egypt, the years with the value of the word 'descend', the word 'redu' which, as we have also seen is spelt 200–4–6, with a sum-total of 210. These 210 form the actual sojourn in the world of duality, in Egypt. Now the 30 of Abraham determine, lead, these 210 in Egypt. Owing to the qualities and the attitude of Abraham these 30 are like a 'one' over against the experience, the suffering of the exile in duality.

These properties, the qualities of Abraham, create a standard, also of 'time'. For the Hebrew word for measure and standard, i.e. *midah*, 40–4–5, is the same word as that for quality, property. When, for instance, in Exod. 34:6-7 God sums up His qualities, known in ancient lore as the 'thirteen qualities' it reads 'thirteen measures' just as well. For in substance it is the same. That which expresses itself here as measure, as proportion, is created in the substance, through properties, through qualities. And expressing things here in a certain measure is analogous with the happenings in the essential in qualities. The word is an example of it. It makes its appearance here as a measure, as a certain structure, but it is an expression of something alive, of a purpose, of a quality. When a thing expresses itself here as 'four', or as 'one fifth', or as 'a third', etc., then it means a translation of course into the world of forms of something alive in the substance which has no mechanical significance there, but an inner meaning. This meaning may be called human or divine. From this point of view, the moon can speak, fields can hop and skip, rivers can 'clap their hands'.

Thus Abraham's quality to live according to a conviction in opposition to all perceptible or imaginable probability, that God's prediction shall come true in spite of all that, gives a certain standard, also to time. And that standard also comes to expression in the proportion of those 30 years of faith over against the 210 years of submersion in duality. These 30 are to the 210 as 1:7. The 210, according to the standard created by Abraham form an expression of the 'seven', of the seven days of the world. They are determined, directed by the 30, i.e. by the 'one' of Abraham.

This principle of the 'one' as opposed to the 'seven' therefore is a most important principle. Only by means of it can the secret of this world be understood. This world of the 'seven', expressing itself in this seventh day of the world, is directed from the 'one', with the standards of the 'one'. This 'one' ever stands outside the 'seven' yet forms a unity with it. It is like the 'one' standing opposite the 'four' in the harmony of the 1-4. I have already pointed at the relationship of the 'four' and the 'seven'.

So it is of paramount importance ever to distinguish the 'one' over against the 'four' or over against the 'seven'. Not to have done so, to have confused these conceptions, means that one has been caught up in the circle, in the forces of development, in service to the god of the circular, the 'calf'. Thus did the sons of Ephraim fail. They did not know the difference between the 'one' and the other; to them the world was merely continuity, merely development. And this is not merely an error; it is a sin.

When the high-priest enters the holy of holies on that one and only day in the cycle of the year, on the tenth day of the seventh month, when he brings the blood of the *korban* to the place of the ark, where obtains the harmony of the opposites and where therefore is the place of God in this world, he sprinkles this blood, coming from that which expresses itself as body, before God. The body has then penetrated to the extreme point in the origin; man has brought it thither with him. It then finds itself at the place of the 'one'; it has attained reunion. With the high-priest things come to reunion.

Now the sprinkling of the blood, according to tradition, happens as follows. There is counting; for along with the measure in the material, there is a reality in the substance. The counting which forms that reality is as follows, 'one', 'one and one', 'one and two', 'one and three', 'one and four', 'one and five', 'one and six', 'one and seven'.

There in the holy of holies, where the secret of the world is known, *this* kind of counting prevails. Not one, two, three, etc, but everything placed opposite the all-directing 'one', the all-determining 'one'. Every condition, however it may express itself, merely exists because it is brought in a position which contains the original 'one' as a criterion by itself. Thus the 210 in Egypt are as 'seven' to the 30 of Abraham as 'one'. There too, the counting is 'one', 'one and one', 'one and two', etc., up to and including the 'one and seven'. This is the secret underlying all.

Thus to life and to the world the 'one' of the Bible is the all-directing 'one'. In it God has laid down the standards with which the 'seven' of the world are determined. In having the 'one' ever present, in any situation, whether one counts 'one and four', 'one and five'; that situation is united with the 'one'. And that is what reunion of the opposites implies in the essential. Then one has found the harmony in the opposites. And this is indeed the purpose of life.

37
The Secret of the Reversal of the Laws of Nature

For the man who at the end of time forms the circular, the eternal tables cannot continue to exist as a unity. They break up into many fragments. This means that at the end of time the comprehension concerning the unity of the miracle of creation, of the word, cannot be preserved, it breaks up into many fragments. People only see the fragments, they only know verses or passages of the Bible, which they use or abuse at their own discretion. It is a law of creation that this unity breaks as soon as one has made the circle, which in its turn broke a unity, and which similarly excluded everything that lay outside the scope of material perception. This action of forming the god that has the circle for his sign, causes the unity of insight in the Bible, the substance, to be lost. In exactly the same manner in which unity broke in the Haflaga, and confusion, multiplicity, came instead. The wonder, made by God, can no longer be seen, and understood as unity. And it remains broken until something new, a new world arises.

Man in his enthusiasm at the results of development at the end of the '40', had discovered the circular as sign of evolution. The circular which, as indicated above, also has the character of confining itself to the field encompassed by the circle. The 'egel', the 'calf', reduces man to a frame of mind which makes him think and act as if the field encompassed by the circle, *were everything*. People feel perturbed, irritated, when they are reminded of the existence of worlds outside this circle. Similarly people have conceptions of an ideal world, excluding many other things. Now, supposing at the end of such a journey through development there should come a generation able to live in peace and liberty, without ailments worth mentioning, and in great prosperity. Then what about all those generations that have lived up to that moment, what about the parents, the grandparents etc? What about the many that suffered and died in the midst of their grief? Forgotten? Excluded from the circle of satisfaction? Then is that really an ideal world, an ideal creation, where all that is past and gone by stays away for ever? As long as oneself has a snug and cosy and enjoyable life? And what is the ending for the inhabitants of this world of prosperity? They may live to be 150, perhaps even 300. But for them there will be the departure too, a departure for all eternity. Then, what? Is the result worth all that trouble, all that sorrow and grief, all those sacrifices for the condition of prosperity? A result which excludes the point at issue: having the knowledge and the living experience of a world eternal? For *whatever* the circle may create, it must, needs exclude *that*. People may console themselves with a heaven and scatter about all sorts of sweet stories concerning it; they can camouflage cemeteries and through cremation try to arouse more interest in hygiene, but man will always go on enquiring about the purpose of life, the why and wherefore of happenings; he will always want to see the bridge between the opposites of life and death, and he will suffer terribly, unfathomably, as long as the contrast continues to exist. He will continue to feel himself to be in servitude to Egypt. There is no consolation in a heaven with which there exists no connection whatsoever during this life; a heaven which exists as an entirely unreal, disconnected phenomenon outside the whole of this life, merely makes the contrast greater and deeper. For the people of this circular world, the tables break up into fragments, the unity which might have been won, has got lost. They merely see the fragments.

When the end was approaching perceptibly, Aaron said, as mentioned above, 'tomorrow is a feast to the Lord'. Tradition specially points at Aaron's optimism. It was an optimism which contributed to the coming of the 'calf'. Aaron counted on everything to take a turn for the better yet and meanwhile he did as people desired at his hands. He hoped that development would take a turn for the better through Moses' return. Development, however, cannot lead to the good; in the end it will *yet* call forth the circular, the new and marvellous god. It is the optimism of people who like to hope there may be achieved balance between technical development and the human soul, that some great man may appear who in his wisdom will be able to put things right and divert everything into the right channels.

According to tradition Aaron cast the gold offered into the fire, hoping that nothing important might come of it. For people could not imagine that in consequence of it such a powerful god might emerge. They thought the dangerous aspects might prove not so bad after all; it was not likely that that calf was to come forth.

But in the times of the end everything is different. Up above, things are coming to a close; Moses is on the point of returning. Therefore, in the image below there is that amazing, incomprehensible rate of speed. Everything is apparently coming of its own accord; people invent all sorts of things simultaneously. And Aaron is amazed at the results. His optimism veers round to bewilderment, and he is powerless to do anything. Development and its godhead have taken things in hand.

We cannot go on counting on people, if we mix the idea of 'doing one's bit' with the hope of 'a great man to divert development into the right channels'. This 'doing one's bit' leaves us powerless; a mighty god comes into prominence, and the 'great man', nor the 'wise generation' ever make their appearance as such. When the saviour appears, he is the great enemy of the god of development and he smashes it to pieces. And he asks man how it was he could do such a thing. To that man unity breaks into fragments. He will not to be able to recognize the unity of the miracle. There is no possibility of adapting oneself to the speed of development; the only possible thing is resistance or austerity. Thus the Bible in this text states what happens to development.

After this blow there are 'forty days' again. A new world begins, a world with an entirely different aspect. The fact that 'at one time', in another phase, one participated in the emancipation from Egypt, and that one had the living experience of the miracle of the revelation of the word, gives this new man a new manner of reacting. It is the situation analogous to the moment of the expulsion from Paradise. There man shunts off his guilt on circumstances, the quality of creation, his natural weakness facing the forces before him. The man, however, who has experienced emancipation from duality, who has been a witness to the happenings of Mount Sinai, knows his grandeur, is aware of the wonder of his existence. And he is conscious of the fact that now he *does* possess the qualities to act differently, and that it would therefore imply failure on his part, if the forces of development were to overpower him. Just as the forces of development *had* to operate in order to accomplish his body for him, so he now has to curb them as they threaten to invade his mind. Man in Paradise was faced with a 'must', when capitulating to the serpent, because the body was yet to come; man after the emancipation from Egypt and the Revelation, has *not* got that 'must'. His situation is comparable to the position of the head as regards that of the body in the story before the emancipation from Egypt. Now the situation obtains, when the soul can dominate, since it is liberated from the leadership of the body.

Therefore this new man can now react differently. He sees the cause of his failure and he knows the way of the return. There is repentance and remorse, and in that condition there is the possibility of contact with God. Man *of his own accord* lays aside his ornament, which contains the 70 and the 4, and with which he can see through space-time and survey the whole range from beginning to end. This implies a journey to a new world. A more modest life, a quieter life begins and there is nothing left of the sensation of the 'calf'. Just as there is not a vestige left of all that time of ecstasy about development.

So there is once more the same condition as at the expulsion from Paradise when both man and the forces of development were weakened by God. There too, man entered into a new world, more modest, more quiet, but this time vibrant with potentialities for the return.

After this period of 40 days of reversal, of undergoing the lowering of level and also experiencing the decrease of the forces of development living in him, there comes yet another phase of 40 days.

So we see that over against the 1×40 days before the fall with the calf, now twice 40 days are to follow. So there is a very distinct development 1–2. It is once more the same condition which existed at creation, when from the 'one' emerged the 'two', and it is the same condition obtaining when man had to give up the 'one' of Paradise in order to enter into the duality of the world, a duality which he was to bind to 'one', just as in the case of all creation, which was to make man again into 'one'. And it is similarly the condition in the pattern of the 10–5–6–5, where the 10 splits up into the two fives with the purpose of reuniting them again.

Thus the twice forty days are facing each other like a 'two', that they may eventuate into a new condition of unity. The breaking of the tables means the break of the 'one', into many fragments, to eventuate in the coming forth of the new tables, as a new unity again (Exod. 33 and 34).

These twice 40 days – ancient lore indicates them precisely – are signed with the consciousness of responsibility on the part of men, because of their yearning to have God in their midst. They are in powerful contrast with the condition in the once 40 days, when the exuberant splendour – just remember the splendour and grandeur of man in the Garden of Eden – caused the disposition to attach himself to the forces of development to increase so much. Now, however, there is silence, there is modesty, there is a turning to God, a yearning to be guided by God to the promised land, to the condition of the 'one'. The colour come forth from the emancipation from Egypt and from the Revelation is now very clearly perceptible in the pattern.

This man, too, could fall; and he did; with the exception of the tribe of Levi; as already discussed. But this man now knows the way back; he knows the causes, the forces; he knows what everything is for; so he knows also how to restore himself.

The forces of duality in creation here too come to expression, but now they allow *man* to come forward stronger and more distinctly; man is subject to duality, it is true, but at the same time he knows the purpose both of duality and reunion. The image of the divine man shows up distinctly in the pattern.

Therefore the divine qualities come to expression (Exod. 33:12–34:7) in the middle of the twice forty days. In this condition of the return of the will to seek God with all one's might, as it is interpreted by Moses for his people, God reveals His way. This way is determined by the so-called 13 Middoth, i.e. the 13 qualities of God. I have already pointed out the connections between quality and measure. The 13 qualities of God – think of the number 13 as value of the word 'one' – are given in standards of goodness (Exod. 33:19), because they are the translation of the conceptions of God, which would otherwise be unintelligible to us. These unintelligible conceptions for instance, are infinitude, eternity, creator, filler of all worlds; they imply that if man knows these qualities of God's goodness and as image of God tries to imitate them, he at once approaches the qualities of infinitude, eternity, etc., and that at the same time man therefore exalts himself above this world. These conceptions: infinitude, eternity, etc., are not, as man in this world might think, principles of science, technology, or magic, but they are, expressed on the divine level in the words and proportions of the '13 middoth' (Exod. 34:6–7).

It is with these '13 measures', the world is measured and changed. Chronology is not something mechanical or astronomic. Chronology is a live principle, directed by such conceptions as are expressed in these 13 middoth. They determine God's way in the world.

We saw it already when discussing the 10–5–6–5. However, we see it coming into prominence again in these 13 measures. For these 13 measures are connected with the 58, we are by now quite familiar with, duration as it expresses the physical. God gives them to Moses on the 'tsur', the rock, which is also the word for 'form'. The sum-total of the components of these 13 measures in fact is 5857. We remember the numbers 5845 and 5848 and the principle of the 5800 in connection with the 3½ and the 'time' of the 1656–1657–1658.

That which expresses itself in conceptions, translated as mercy, grace, benevolence, truth, in reality is standards of time. One gets to know them, if after the fall with the 'circle', one realizes one's responsibility as man and one's potentialities as well, and if then one manages to take the way back and yearns for God's guidance on this way. Then God *shows* this way and that is the beginning of the second 40. The second 40 which will lead to unity.

This way is shown in retrospect. When measuring the happenings of the past with standards, one sees that everything has the structure of these '13 measures'. Then one also knows that the future is not a mechanical-astronomical datum, that therefore one *cannot* see the future from the human point of view in this world. For the measures of the future are not mechanically fixed and computable, but like the measures of the past, they are dependent on these '13 measures', i.e. on conceptions like mercy, grace, truth, charity, etc. They are measures which are accomplished by man's life and God's answer to it. They are living, changeable measures, dependent on the qualities and the attitude of man.

In this atmosphere new tables are achieved, a new man is formed, similar to the previous one which had fallen and broken into fragments. It is again in accordance with the pattern of the 'one' of the end which comes after the way of the 1 → 2. The 'one' of the end is like the *aleph*, like the 'one' of the beginning. They are each other's reflection, just as the cherubs are opposite each other.

Yet this 'one' of the end is different from the 'one' of the beginning as regards the accomplishing. The second set of tables consisted of matter from down here, prepared by Moses and brought to God who engraved the 'ten words' in them, just as in the first tables. The first tables, however, had been altogether made by God, and as they had been made, they were given to Moses.

So, in spite of the identical final result, there is a difference in principle in the way. The 'one' of the end is accomplished by reunion of the matter of down below with the soul which God engraves in it. Now it is man who prepares the material to be taken on high; now man has his share in it.

The first man is created like the first tables. God takes the body from the dust and engraves the soul in it. Through the confrontation with the tree of the knowledge, the forces of development, this man is broken into multiplicity and thus he is brought into the world. Inherent in these fragments is the yearning for reunion; humanity in its broken status yearns for the harmony of the origin. And on this way God shows the purpose of everything, He shows the '13 measures'. Thus the new man is accomplished below, the man who now forms the right foundation to get the eternal values engraved in himself by God. This man it is that becomes the man of the end, in every respect identical with the man in the origin, in the same harmony with God.

It is the purpose of history, of life, that this man should be formed down here. His formation is the integration down here. It is the man who has conquered duality, who has been emancipated from it. This man then receives the soul with life eternal from God. It is now an eternal body with an eternal soul, it is the new stone tables. In everything there is again duality in harmony.

It is not very difficult to recognize again the pattern of the name Lord God, who puts His stamp on everything in this world. For had not indeed the name Lord God divided itself from the condition of the first 'ten' into the two 'fives', according to the way 1–42, afterwards to have the two fives meet again and join together to form a new 'ten'? And was not that the tracing of the way from 2 → 1? The second set of tables is this joining of the two fives, of the five below with the five above. The man of down here who forms the 5–6–5, who with the 620 letters of the 'ten words' also gets the crown engraved in himself, which makes him into God's image.

Ancient lore computes with precision the dates of the period of the first 40 days after the fall with the 'calf', and then that of the adjoining twice 40 days. This second period of 40 days ends on the tenth day of the seventh month. Now this day in the Bible stands wholly apart from this story of the second period of 40 days after the event with the 'calf', a very special day; (Lev. 23:27–32). It is the day which in the seventh month completes the cycle of the 'ten'. Biblical years, starting at creation, are numbered from the first day of the seventh month; it is the day of the creation of man. On the tenth day this cycle is closed, and so this day forms a transition to the condition of another world. On that day in the fiftieth year, the return was proclaimed of everything which was removed from the origin. Therefore man spends that day as one not living in this world; neither eating nor drinking, all day long in every respect concentrated on another life, relinquishing this life altogether, being to this life as one dead. It is the day called 'the Day of Atonement', because on this tenth day, when man experiences the complete return before God, this return compensates, atones for all man's failings throughout the cycle of the year.

Therefore it is the day when in the Jewish practice of life the story of Jonah is read. For there too the miracle is seen that undertaking a complete reversal eliminates a destruction already determined on.

Now that day in the biblical story is identical with the last day of the second period of 40 days, when Moses has received from God the new tables, the new man, when the previous failure has been eliminated by the complete return to God. It is also shown here that a destruction, as definite as a law of nature, is eliminated; that death presumed as a fact, is suddenly diverted. It shows again that the world is not ruled by immutable laws of nature, but that the qualities and attitude of man can effect a change in the operation of these laws.

So it is not sheer coincidence, but on the contrary a characteristic confirmation of the the structure that the end of the twice 40 days coincides with the day on which God reverts the course of nature, if man on his way turns back to God. One might also put it like this, that the tenth day of the seventh month has this character, because on that day the 'two' of the twice forty days came to an end and the new 'one' began. All this coincidence, is one whole. It shows the deep significance of the structure of the Bible. The day when the first set of tables broke after the once 40 days, is the seventeenth of the fourth month, a day characterized by this 17, which, as discussed before, has a very specific character of destruction of a world. So the seventeenth coincides with everything that is stamped with the 17; just as this tenth day upon which the twice 40 days end, coincides with that very specific character of the tenth day of the seventh month. The story of the tables fits in completely with the structure of the whole of the biblical story and shows again the unity of the biblical story.

Tradition also points out another facet in the various ways of accomplishing the first and second sets of tables. When the first tables were to be collected by Moses, there was great pomp at his ascent of Mount Sinai. He covered the first stretch accompanied by a great host; besides, all the people witnessed the event. There were great rejoicings and many miracles became manifest.

The world emanating from this manner of approach, was that of the once 40 days. This world eventuated in an enormous development. Satan penetrated into this world, and stimulated by the manifestness of the miracles at Moses' ascent, people now started computations about the end; they felt the need of expressing the imperceptible, the non-material, in terms of matter and the result booked was the 'circular', the 'calf'. This 'circular' was to express in earthly terms what people were lacking, because of the inexpressibility, in consequence of the absence of Moses who seemed to abide in another world. And the 'circular' brought with it the earthly marvels and destruction.

If one ascends with pomp, surrounded by many, the multitude will avail themselves of it on the lower level in accordance with their standards. They will use it to acquire riches, scientific success, cures of the body only, and then it takes the forms of here below, the circular forms of the 'calf'. And people assume that this circular will even enable them to attain the ideal world.

The great feast Aaron promises, eventuates in a grand terrestrial feast with the earthly criteria of the 'circular'. For indeed people presume it must be an earthly feast. For that purpose did they make the god of the 'circular'. People also availed themselves of the powers of the secret they had tasted at the manifest ascent of Moses.

When on the other hand Moses ascended Mount Sinai for the second time, i.e. in the cycle of the twice 40 days, at the beginning of the second 40 days, after the repentance and decrease in forces during the first 40 days thereof, he went all by himself, in silence. He sees the miracles alone by himself, learns to know the way of God, the way of the '13 qualities'. And people below experience these 40 days in the conscious restrictions of the forces of development, culminating in the fortieth day, when they turn away altogether from things earthly, as if dead to the earth, to be able to direct themselves to God completely. That very fortieth day, which with the first set of tables was the day of the grand earthly feast, is now become a day of festively turning oneself away from the earth. On this fortieth day which is the tenth day of the seventh month, men below as well as Moses up above are divested of everything earthly. There is now identity in attitude, because the ascent has taken place in silence, as a mystery. This time there is the faith in the miracle and not the endeavour to accomplish the miracle with the help of a material god.

This is what tradition points at. Only when the ascent takes place as a mystery, closed to the many, will it bring the new man. If one desires to approach the heart of things and bring it back, unbroken, to the world, one has to go in silence; alone. And return, alone. Then the abiding above is not interrupted by a fall down below. And then one can translate it for the world into the proportions of the world.

The transition to the new world needs this threshold of the tenth day of the seventh month. That last day indeed, which at the same time is the fortieth of the twice 40 days and which lends itself so perfectly to make of it a feast of earthly rejoicings; that day which runs parallel with the final phase of time, when Satan penetrates and urges people on to make computations themselves in the form of a continuum; that very day must needs be one of earthly retirement, devoid of any dealings with the world. It must be signed by the practice of the yearly recurrent tenth day of the seventh month, which because of it produces the miracle of the reversion of the laws of nature. *Thus* one experiences the miracle of the stone tables down here; thus they get down here, unbroken.

And then a new world begins. Immediately at the end of this tenth day the building is started of the dwelling for God on this earth, the tabernacle. Then the 'measures' are made known, the proportions, in which God's immanence in this world is expressed. For now the connection between heaven and earth is become transparent, now 'duality' is become a harmony.

In the Jewish practice of life of every year at the end of this tenth day, people start building the 'tabernacle', the dwelling-place of man during the journey from Egypt to Canaan, from the 'two' to the 'one'. And this dwelling-place similarly has the proportions established in accordance with tradition, expressing the essential of man's dwelling-place here on earth. It is the dwelling with the 'transparent' roof, the roof through which one must be able to see heaven.

This dwelling is ready on the fifteenth of the seventh month. So people work at it for 5 days. These 5 days are to the 10 previous days, starting from the day of the creation of man, again as 5:10, hence 1:2. For the time of building this house with the well-known measurements, is the phase of the 'one' facing the previous phase as the 'two' opposite. And the transition of the 'two' to the 'one' is formed by that very special tenth day of the seventh month, when man turns away in every respect from things earthly.

Just to point at a single parallel here, we saw that on the tenth of the first month, the month of the exodus from Egypt, the lamb had to be put in readiness which on the fifteenth of that month was to bring the 'one' into the house, into the 'two'. And that there too this period of 5 days was to the period of the previous 10 days, as 'one' to the 'two' thus formed. Everywhere one will discover anew the structure of the Bible, since the Bible is a greater miracle yet then the creation of the universe. This way from the 'two' to the 'one' is the purpose of creation. Creation without the Bible is empty, void. The Bible imbues it with life, and content.

38
The Fourth Dimension

The tabernacle is the place where God's immanence on earth comes to expression. In those proportions and with that structure, the place is created where God appears. I have already said a few words about the principle of this structure, when discussing the temple which differed from the tabernacle mainly in that the temple represents a solid house, whereas the tabernacle is charactized by the fact that it can be removed.

The tabernacle is the place of God's immanence on earth during the seventh day of the world, during the journey from Egypt to Canaan, from the 'two' to the 'one'. This seventh day is the journey across the desert, hence a continual migrating. Going from the 'two' to the 'one' implies a continual motion, an everlasting change of place, of proportion. That is why there are such circumstantial directions as to how the tabernacle is to be constructed, how it is to be pulled down again, how it is to be carried from one place to another, and by whom it is to be carried. For one cannot move from the 'two' to the 'one' by stopping in one place. Everything is based on onward motion in a certain direction. He that is on his way to the 'one' cannot afford to remain standing still in the seventh day, in this day-of-the-world.

Life teaches man a great deal. He always imagines that now he knows, and in a sense he is content. But life drags him on again; his mind proves to discover new aspects; life purifies him through this constant change. And in this way man approaches the 'one', the 'coming world' ever more, until in the end it is only the boundary-river – expressing itself in the name Jordan and again forming the barrier of waters of impassable time – which forms the barrier to the coming world.

He that is emancipated from Egypt, leads a life of migration. He simply has to go on, it pertains to the law of those that have left the 'two'. This migration, however, has quite a definite character. For the principle motive for travelling onwards is the fact that the 'cloud' on the tabernacle lifts. As soon as the pillar of cloud abides on the tabernacle again, it is a sign that a new stage on the way from the 'two' to the 'one' has been reached. This cloud in our terms and forms is the expression of the presence of God. The cloud is merely perceptible on the tabernacle. It reflects in this image the assuming of the subtlest form of matter, just getting perceptible, it is the boundary between perceptibility and imperceptibility. Just think of the ed, the mist, as incipient perceptibility, forming the foundation for this world's arising in progressive perceptibility. It is not just an ordinary cloud, but a cloud upon earth, covering the tabernacle and especially rooted in the tabernacle, in its nucleus, on the mercy-seat between the two cherubs. The cloud conveys to us that God has approached to the very boundary of perceptibility, yet simultaneously with this incipient perceptibility, has covered himself with imperceptibility. This is the manner of expression in the image and one has naturally to revert from the image to the substance. It amounts to this: God can only be perceived, if on one's way from the 'two' to the 'one' one has been able to build this potentiality of God's immanence on earth, so that as Betsalel – meaning 'in the shadow of God' – one has the wisdom and the insight to express these proportions in matter (Exod. 31). If a man has created this possibility, then in the very heart of it, he can become aware of God at the boundary, at the transition from the material into the non-material. But this awareness covers it up simultaneously, hides the innermost heart, makes it imperceptible again.

He that is on his way from the 'two' to the 'one' might become aware of this perceptibility, if he had been able to create the abode for it. And then the 'cloud' will tell him, whether he can abide at that spot during his life, or whether he has to leave there, because God desires to lead him somewhere else. He will then have to begin to eliminate the proportions of God's abode, make the very heart of his life invisible, cover it up, pack it up to move away elsewhere, wherever the cloud may guide him. The other place may in a certain phenomenal form also mean another life. Then he will have to build up this abode of the nucleus in a similar way. The abode with its proportions ever remains the same, however much the places and the other proportions may vary.

Ancient lore tells us a great deal about this 'cloud', naturally. From it one can immediately conclude that we are not concerned here with the clouds of our perception, such as rain-clouds or clouds of smoke. Thus ancient lore mentions the presence of seven clouds, one of which was the cloud which showed the way, and the other six of which were grouped in a very special way around the four parts into which the 'people' were divided. The cloud in front levelled the hills and filled up the dales, and only the place where the tabernacle was set up in the centre always showed itself to be an elevation. The seven clouds encompassed everything, they also screened off the people from view, they caused them to radiate within in the same way as God Himself, since because of the cloud there was the inner light.

The word for cloud 'anan' has the structure of 70–50–50. It is a connection therefore of the concrete 70 with the 50 of the other world, thus in the word itself expressing the condition of transition between two worlds, the boundary. The connections of the 70 and the 4 we have already learned to know as the all-embracing in this space-time world. The 70 with the 40 reflects a similar principle. The word for 'people', for instance, has this 70–40 structure, also the word 'with', implying the inclusion of something in a great whole. The word 70–400 is the expression for time, hence likewise something of this world. Thus the combination 70–50 expresses the leap beyond this world of the 4. The 70 of this world remains, the 40, however, has become the 50 of the other, the coming world.

Man, on his way from the 'two' to the 'one' therefore travels through the desert. One may wonder why he is to travel through a desert at all, and why in the image of this earth there must be a desert between Egypt and Canaan. The phenomenon of the desert as a way expresses the idea that the way itself is not for loitering on. The essential man does not attach himself to a wilderness, he regards it as something to pass through, because the goal of the journey is elsewhere.

According to tradition the definition of 'desert' is not 'a region of sands and rocks, of heat and uninhabitableness.' That is the impression the conception desert awakens in man. According to ancient lore, however, the desert is 'a place where people pasture their cattle, and which is studded with cities and villages.' What ancient lore means to convey is that the desert (i.e. wilderness) is this world, this seventh day, that notwithstanding its being studded with cities and villages, notwithstanding the fact that it yields profit to the cattle, i.e. the body, yet it must be sensed as the place which one passes through, which is *not* the goal of man; what man was *not* made for.

So in this desert there is an incessant progress towards the 'one'. And he that is able to see the 'cloud' in the place at the centre, will realize that it is God, decreeing when and whither to travel onwards. In Egypt there was the solid, unchangeable place; in the desert, however, one travels, just because one can see the 'cloud' there and because one realizes what is the purpose of this cloud's leading the way. One knows that there is guidance proceeding exactly towards the goal. In the life in the desert all attention is directed towards building the abode of God's immanence towards bringing the 'korban' thither, towards the contact with the leader who is called Moses in the world.

Going through this world of the seventh day is not a going in accordance with one's own standards, but a going with the gaze directed at the 'cloud' in that special place. It is having oneself led by criteria which one can find in the Bible, in the revelation of this way through the world. Thus we see, for instance, how Noah goes this way from the sixth day through the seventh: *not* in a ship in which he takes the wheel, pointing out the direction; but in an 'ark' which, regarded from the human point of view, cannot be controlled and which is steered by God. It is a natural analogy to this journey through the desert, led by the ever visible 'cloud'.

The journey across the desert takes place according to a fixed systematism. Wherever they pitch their tents, the tabernacle forms the centre. About it are grouped the 'four' armies (Num. 2 and 3). Within the circle of these four armies are grouped the Levites, as if in an inner circle, similarly in four parts. The 1–4 structure is apparent. From that centre, from the 'one' comes all wisdom and insight, comes all knowledge and thither is directed all surrender. The tribe of Levi mediates the contact with this 'one', guides the approach of it and explains its purpose. The 'four' encompasses, surrounds the 'one'. From the 'one' comes the signal to start on the journey and then people travel to another spot. And when the signal is given to pitch the tents, they settle there. People *see* the centre and none imagine that this coming and going is the result of their own human decisions. They see that there is an entirely different causality. In everything God is seen as the power determining the migrations through life, whether in this life or in the life in other worlds, after death.

And when people have to migrate, the nucleus in the centre migrates too, proceeded by two groups and followed by two of the four groups. The 1–4 structure is ever maintained. The minute directions as to how this centre has to be set up and pulled down again to be built up anew in another place, show in what way this world and this life arise and in what way they disappear from here in order to occupy a place somewhere else.

That is why ancient lore considers the story about the structure and the construction of the tabernacle a detailed parallel of the way in which God made the world. It is an expression of creation in the weights and measure of that miraculous nucleus, the marvellous 'one' facing the surrounding 'four'. On this ground does ancient lore translate the actions to build up the tabernacle into the actions accomplished by God to form the world.

On the human level those actions express themselves in the actions which people had to perform to get the tabernacle ready and build it up. If therefore in human life of the seventh day our consciousness should be that God had already completed the creation of the world, that creation was good just as it was, and that no actions were required any more after those six days to complete the world as yet in the seventh, then ancient lore also sees this complex of God's acts to make the world repeated in the complex of actions to get the tabernacle completed. And just as it applies for the whole of the seventh-day-of-the-world that man in that world should have a certain attitude, thus for ancient lore it applies for every seventh day in course of time that man should abstain from acts of creation, as they are also expressed in the actions required to complete the tabernacle. The rules of abstaining from actions on the Sabbath in the Jewish practice of life are therefore based on these actions to complete the tabernacle, for the very reason that the tabernacle in that place is identical with the whole of creation.

This seventh day is 'motion', a migration towards a goal beyond that day. That is why the tabernacle is constructed in such a way that putting it up and pulling it down without much ado form an important part of it. It is, like all life in the world of the desert, a tent, a cabin. It is purposely not a house yet. It cannot be that until the eighth day. Thus David who in the cycle after the 26 generations, is the seventh, cannot yet build a house; the tent has to be preserved by him, and it is only his son, the eighth, who can build the house. Then migrating has come to an end.

It is only this seventh-day-of-the-world which knows the phenomenon of motion, of constant change of place and situation, therefore also the constant change of form. In this seventh-day-of-the-world, therefore, something is fulfilling itself through this motion; it is growing towards its destination. In the eighth day it has reached its destination, and there is no longer this character of growing towards something. In our world it expresses itself in the phenomenon time which carries on everything. Time is the dimension in development, it is ever completing itself. It is what is called nowadays the fourth dimension. In the eighth day it will be completed and therefore the coming world cannot be imagined in our space-time thought. In our world three dimensions are completed; the fourth represents life in this world. Therefore time is always measured as a way for completing the 30 or the 400. It is exactly the fourth that completes itself therewith. It is this fourth dimension which carries us from the sixth day into the eighth.

Ancient lore has it that during the journey across the desert the covering of man also grew. Through growing, it made it possible for him to live in this world. The story expresses it in the statement that the garments and footwear grew with man; that they ever kept in good condition to make going possible to man.

Thus this story of the desert is characterized by the completion of a new dimension, a dimension which the world of the desert did not yet know. Tradition expresses it in its well-known way in stating that in the desert there were only 'three' winds; the fourth, the 'north wind' was not there yet. It did not come until people had passed through the desert and had entered Canaan. Now in the 'north', according to ancient lore, there is the element 'ruach', i. e. wind, also meaning spirit. That which is completing itself in the desert, is exactly that which here in the image we know as what is moving: wind. It is, however, at the same time that which as 'ruach' has its place in between the other two expressions for soul, between 'nefesh' the bodily soul, and 'neshamah', the divine soul. The spirit, which is completing itself, the 'ruach' at its completion unites the nefesh with the neshamah, i. e. body and soul. And that was, indeed, the purpose of the seventh day and the reality of the coming day, the eighth. The eighth day is the marriage of the male and the female, a marriage prepared during the seven days. That is the living, the human element, in the mathematical fourth dimension.

39
Economic Problems

The journey through the desert is also characterized by the special nature of anxiety concerning the sustenance of life.

On the one hand we notice an almost ceaseless fear and complaint of those that were emancipated from Egypt, about their sustenance; on the other hand there is a very special way of supplying things in the form of 'Man' (manna) and water, acquired in a striking way.

Those that had left Egypt ever showed their worry about these problems and their rebelliousness for the main part can be ascribed to these economic problems if we may use this modern term. It simply seems an incredible thing that on the way from the 'two' to the 'one' sustenance should be an affair God has taken upon Himself to see to.

Besides, people cannot brook it that they can no longer build up this material existence for themselves, and that they have to do without the incentive of ambition, of the struggle for life, of the victory over the rival, of the expansion of production and of sales, of continual increase of power, of the record. This incentive had given zest to the life in Egypt, had created a sham-world there, which could obscure the true purpose of existence. In the hard existence in the world of duality of the opposites, from which there was no escape, they easily came to conjuring up a world which barred the true problems. They conjured up a world of their own with ambitions and goals of their own, just as children like to play at schools, joyously keeping out the harsh reality of the genuine school. In this self-created world in which they could determine on criteria for themselves, they could similarly create for themselves the feeling of satisfaction, of 'we have got there', 'we have reached our goal'. They had gained a certain standard of life, and people should not spoil the game in asking what is so pithily summed up in the words 'and so what?' For how much had not been barred in stating their satisfaction. People may hygienically camouflage cemeteries, lunatic asylums and hospitals, and similarly prisons, houses of correction and concentration camps. These things continue to exist all the same, and to banish them from view, after the purpose of their game was achieved, they created what is nowadays called relaxation. In all its forms of detective-stories, thrillers, illustrated magazines and hobbies, down to cruises across the high seas.

Yet they had done all this themselves in Egypt, in their decisions on themselves and others they felt like gods, and for these gods palaces were built accordingly.

On the way from the 'two' to the 'one' this kind of fun is utterly impossible. The reality of the purpose of existence is distinctly perceptible; under God's guidance one is on one's way to the fulfilment of happiness beyond dreams.

The incentive to distinguish oneself from another in power, in the struggle for the possession of the power of development, ceases to be. Even the ambition to come into prominence as a dictator, as a tin god on wheels, cannot be realized; by this time, other criteria prevail.

Now, how is it, that man who had sighed so much in Egypt under the oppression of duality, who had so much hoped for the emancipation considered impossible, in fact, nevertheless after the miraculous salvation should suddenly yearn for Egypt? Is not there a contradiction somehow?

According to ancient lore, this ever-present inclination to return to Egypt was not caused by those that sighed under the oppression in Egypt, not by the 'one' which was redeemed in contradistinction to the 'four', but by what is called in the Bible the 'ereb rab', translated as a 'mixed multitude' or 'all conditions of men' (Exod. 12:38).

For when at the end of time, shortly before the emancipation, the miracles of Israel became perceptible, when the world of duality crashed down on all sides, when that world was affected in its core, then there arose a large-scale enthusiasm to unite with Israel. It was obvious then that Israel was right, that they possessed the world of the future and that the world of duality was going under. Everybody could perceive it for himself and many there were to join departing Israel.

It was they who, on their way to the 'one', felt the lack of the stimulus of life in duality, and who ever yearned for Egypt. It was they too who made the 'calf' and were continually subject to attraction by gravity, by matter in the world of duality.

What is expounded here of course is not a chauvinistic distinction between 'real' Israel and the satellite Egyptians. Besides in our post-biblical world the distinctions between Israel and other nations are no longer of the nature expressed in the Bible. What is told here, rather, stresses, that salvation could merely exist for those who believed in that salvation, trusted to it, when everything still pointed at its sheer impossibility in this world of matter; those that nevertheless precisely for that reason had trusted in it. Therefore they followed the way to the 'one' with joy.

Those, however, who see in salvation a 'paying proposition', who make up their minds to join Israel on its way, because they see that way yields success, not only in this world, but also concrete prospects of success in a coming world, prospects of 'rewards', it is they that form the persistent tempter, the everlasting stumbling-block. Their motives were not those of the image of God, the 'doing for nothing', the 'faith against all probability'; their motives were those of the trader, the Canaanite; they had weighed the pros and cons and had seen the scales turn.

According to ancient lore, overjoyed at the great number of Egyptians who had decided to join the departing children of Israel at the time of the end, Moses had not paused to consider that their coming along was based on the manifest successes of Israel, that their motives were entirely different from those of the real wanderers. When therefore this 'ereb rab' had caused the fall with the calf and God reproached Moses (Exod. 32:7) … '*thy* people which thou broughtest out of the land of Egypt, have corrupted themselves', ancient lore states that God impressed on Moses how short-lived is the reliability of those that join others for the sake of the promised reward. If the reward does not appear at their fixed standards of time, i.e. within *their* time-reckoning, their assessment of the 40 days, then they become the serpent, the tempters, they turn against the purpose of creation.

Therefore it is wrong to persuade people to choose the way to God, or to support them in pointing out to them the advantages it brings even for this life, referring to their own successes, both spiritual and material, or in convincing them of some reward in another world, stressing it with statements about their own views concerning it. Such people will come along from their own interests and on their way to the 'one' they will become stumbling-blocks for the others as well. They will never cease yearning for Egypt and will create a god of their own in the end. In a choice like this no self-interest whatsoever must be involved. The real way to God can only be trodden from 'gratuitous love', without the least thought of an eventual reward. One should be perfectly willing to tread the path without any wages at all, with sacrifices only, because one does it from love of God, from love in comparison with which all other motives pale into insignificance.

The 'mixed multitude', the 'ereb rab', is like the body's power of development compassing the soul and setting the tune in the outer world, the world of the left side. The word for 'murmur' or 'grumble' in Hebrew has the root 30–50, which is at the same time the word for 'spend the night'. Therefore murmuring in the wilderness always is 'a revolt at night', a revolt of the left side, a discontent, since one does not see the right relationships, does not know them because of this compassing by the forces of development, by darkness, night. A night effected by the coming along of the 'ereb rab'.

Therefore it is wrong to state that biblical Israel was rather thankless, unmanageable, stupid, primitive, etc., because they ever failed anew on their way to Canaan. One had better recognize that the biblical story tells what the way from the 'two' to the 'one' is exactly like. The reactions of biblical Israel were determined even before creation, so to speak, they pertained to the plan of creation. The story tells us that on the way to the 'one' the power of attraction of the earth is always operative; the force which in material sense expresses itself also as gravity. It is the force which in the essence in the Bible is called the disposition ever to want to return to Egypt. There is always this pull by the earth, by the forces of development of matter, by the female; Satan pulls and the serpent pulls and they mingle as forces of development also in that which has been emancipated. There is the everlasting rebelliousness against the way to the 'one', as it is indicated by God and there ever is the preference for a leader able to lead people back to Egypt. But ever again they are forced to continue on their way to the 'one'; it is a way established in the plan of creation. For the seventh day is blessed and hallowed by God, it leads of its own accord to the 'one' that is. People cannot put the clock back in the seventh day; time operates under the law of creation towards its fulfilment. The exodus from Egypt happened on the 'half'; from the 'half' the way turns back of its own accord. People cannot help themselves.

Yet we see that in spite of the 'ereb rab' coming along, this journey across the desert is a good thing. For every failure owing to the operation of this gravity is followed by insight into the error, by repentance, by a more intense turning to God and by a return to God. This reaction lends sense to failure, delivers it from the covering and binds it to the good. The purpose is exactly that evil is set free by the return; it has fulfilled its purpose as power on the way of development; it gets its ultimate significance in that it becomes the cause of insight, of the realization of the significance of the alternative at the extreme point of development. This insight leads to that which in a man's sentiments is expressed as remorse at not recognizing the purpose of life, and to man's uniting with the origin. Sin becomes significant in that it can become the cause of a dialogue with God and of retracing one's steps. It may be put this way, sin is waiting, just as everything in the world is yearning for the contact with man so that it may be united with God.

According to ancient lore, biblical Israel failed ten times in the desert, having a fall caused by the 'mixed multitude'. But every time there followed a dialogue with God, the insight, the return, thus lending purpose to the accompaniment of the 'ereb rab'. This coming along shows how God made the world. For it was also God who gave the forces of development that they might operate in the world at creation. Man will not be able to prevent this coming along any more than his own physical development. Nevertheless, for this very reason he will have to detach himself from these forces. For indeed, man is at this point of the 'half', at the farthest extreme, and will ever be supported by the consciousness of having to return now, of having to steer clear of these forces of development *now*. The exodus from Egypt demands the throwing away of the leaven and the eating of the unleavened bread.

The ten plagues did not yield this result for Pharaoh. Pharaoh tried to react tactically on these blows, but he was cut off from all possibility of return. Like Cain he had to cover the way back as a 'fugitive and a vagabond', because he had enslaved and killed the soul.

Israel, however, which had sighed under this servitude, which had therefore had the experience of the exodus and the revelation of Mount Sinai, reacts in the right way. Sin lies on man's way every day; that is why Israel fails in the desert fully 'ten' times. But every time they united the fall with the origin, thus setting themselves free.

There also is the grumbling about their sustenance. People do not understand how sustenance can be received for all those masses, unless they occupy themselves with the production thereof. On the way to the 'one' these pursuits consist of building and constructing the tabernacle, the bringing of the 'korban', the contact with Moses concerning the purpose of existence. How can the process of production be continued, how can these vast masses be supported? Is not that an irresponsible policy, a reckless pursuit of a dream with the existence of all humanity on earth as stakes? People had got used to anticipating in the economic field, to planning, organizing, and even then there were difficulties galore. And now they are required to give up this attitude altogether; they are to pay attention principally to the thoughts and actions on this way to the promised land, where evidently standards prevail so entirely different as to frighten them out of their wits.

God's answer to this grumbling, so easy to understand and so logical when viewed from the standpoint of this world, is His pointing at the specific way of nutrition, of sustenance in this seventh day. It is 'Man', or, as it is often called in translation: manna (Exod. 16).

The word 'Man' is spelt 40–50. Yet another characteristic expression of the boundary. It is the 40 of time in this world, bound to the 50 of the coming world. It also means that this is the food consumed on the way from the 40 to the 50, on the way through the wilderness that is, the way from the seventh day to the eighth.

The characteristic of manna is that it is given in a miraculous way by God to the man who journeys from the 'two' to the 'one'. It means that the man who goes this way sees that sustenance is God's affair, that no activities on the part of man can alter the share destined to him. That it is mere delusion to think one can decide on that share for oneself. It similarly shows that man on his way to Canaan *cannot* act any other way. If he should want to gather more than he needs for the day, the harvest begins to rot and smell bad. It has a pernicious influence on him. That he should imagine that his achievements determine the size of his share, is the outcome of a mistaken causality. The causes lie in a different plane from what man thinks.

Besides, the story of the manna implies that man should work every day for his share. It does not come to him, if he remains passive; he has to gather it in himself for himself and his family. This means that man is required to have contact with matter. A contact, however, of the character of manna. One should see in matter the transition from the 40 to the 50, as it is expressed in the word manna. This implies that the contact should hallow matter, unite it with the origin. The contact must not be utilitarian, directed towards the earth; as is shown by the example of the wise shoemaker who united heaven and earth in his work, the contact should be directed at the emancipation of matter and to its integration with the source of origin.

The gathering-in must not turn away man's attention from the main purpose on this way through the desert. Manna could only be gathered during part of the day. The sun caused it to melt afterwards. This means that essentially man fulfils his duty towards matter, and towards his material sustenance, if he devotes part of the day to it, but that the climax of the day, when the sun is powerful, should be devoted to other affairs. This need not be a question of hours of employment. Essentially it rather implies that the point of gravity of man's attention and the main part of his energy should be directed towards other things besides gathering-in for sustenance. Sustenance is dependent on causes different from the sacrifices made by man towards it. This is what the Bible hammers into us with this story about manna.

According to tradition, manna acquired the taste people gave to it themselves; it was man himself therefore who decided on this taste. And this in its turn means that the standard of life, as viewed from the standpoint of the way to Canaan, gives the satisfaction man himself bestows on it. To one man the same manna is as sweet as honey, to the other it has a dull and dry taste. To one man it is ready for immediate consumption, to another – the man who lives in the wrong way, according to ancient lore – it must first undergo all kinds of preparation, of grinding and dressing before it can give satisfaction.

All these statements merely imply that it is wrongly directed causality which makes man stress the economic side; that it shows non-understanding of the true causalities. On his way through the desert, however, man is supposed to be able to perceive this causality every day, just as he perceives the tabernacle and the cloud. It is exactly in Egypt that there is this oppressive anxiety about sustenance, this exhausting toil for it. Only he that is not yet emancipated from Egypt cannot free himself from this mental picture that all one's attention should be directed at economics. Egypt builds Pithom and Rameses as treasure-cities (Exod. 1:11); manna, however, can not be stored.

On the seventh day no manna is to be found. On the sixth day the share comes for the seventh day as well. So it runs parallel to creation. On the sixth day everything was completed; in the seventh day there was no need any longer to seek things; it had already been seen to in the sixth day. So it again stresses the fact that in this seventh day of the world the proportions for sustenance have also been established. What is expressed in this phenomenon of manna in the wilderness, in the seventh day that is, is the previous establishment of proportions. The only thing which is not established, is man's attitude towards it, the taste he bestows on it and the preparations which to his mind manna has yet to undergo.

This vision on the matter of sustenance is decisive for man's being on the way from the 'two' to the 'one'. Its significance is also expressed in the fact that Aaron is to fill a pot with an omer of this manna to be kept for his generations (Exod. 16:32–34). Manna is not only a historic event, it is the conception of life in regard to the sustenance on one's way to the promised land, to the coming world. And that way is this world. Existence in this world is based on this principle of manna. If one lives in accordance with this principle, one is on one's way to the promised land. If one does not live according to this principle, one most decidedly does *not* go that way. Manna is the sign: he that lives on manna, is signed with it.

That is why Aaron was told to preserve this manna and lay it up before the Testimony to be kept. Eternal man, i. e. man who is able to live in this world in accordance with the principles of the 'ten words' can only do so, if he lives on manna. Every other man will fail on that way. The Testimony and the manna pertain to each other. The one cannot be without the other.

In the desert there is also the problem of water. Just as in the mental picture of the desert, water plays an important part, thus it is in the substance. On the way from the 'two' to the 'one' there is the great desire for water.

We have already discussed that water is the vital element for the world of the left side. Without the mist, the ed arising, life in this world could not even come about. The anxiety concerning the water therefore is the anxiety about life, about the time allotted.

In tradition water in the desert is connected with Miriam. It is woman who is in relationship with water. Tradition has many wonderful stories about the 'source of Miriam'. From those communications one can see that the purpose of the story is not the supplying with water of a nomadic tribe in the desert, but that here is stated the purpose of the whole world.

In Egypt life had been visualized in its earthly causality. All the rest people had been able to bar. Egypt looked upon itself as eternal and also expressed it in all forms of life. The 'korban' was out of the question in Egypt, since the body such as it was, meant the purpose of life. People desired to make this body everlasting as well.

In the desert there is a complete reversal of conditions. The physical is united with another life, through the 'korban'. And this life passes by, without much ado; no causalities are based hereon. It is an entirely different world.

Therefore from the very outset of the journey through the desert there was the anxiety about water, about the vital element, about the time allotted, the income, the health. They were yearning for the mental picture which Egypt had conjured up (Exod. 17:1–7).

Then the water had come. God showed how it welled up out of the 'rock'. We saw already that the word for rock and for form are related to each other. God showed that time was related to form. According to ancient lore the rock ever travelled on with the people, the water constantly emerging from it flowed into the outer court of the tabernacle.

The conception 'form', like the conception 'woman' is a principle of the left side of systematism. The court of the tabernacle at the same time is the female side; it is the outside. That is why the outer court of the temple was called the court of the women. Thus this miraculous source of time was connected with the woman, with Miriam.

When Miriam died, however, the water ceased to flow from the source and there arose a great fear that it would never come again (Num. 20:1–13). They had come to know a certain causality and now that at the end of time the bearer of the cause was no longer there, they reasoned correctly that the effects too would fail.

Now it pleased God to show that causalities have no binding effect, that at decisive moments laws obtained, 'measures' prevailed, completely different from those which man expects. Man wants to know through the tree of the knowledge, and God has prepared for man the tree of life. Through the tree of life man can see that the true causes are entirely different from what he has ever supposed. In getting to know the true causes, man learns to connect the happenings with God, and God is hallowed.

Moses, however, irritated by the ceaseless conflict, gives in to the insistence of the people requiring a logical, causal explanation. He himself knows better, of course, but he thinks people will be more satisfied with a causal explanation; they might not even understand anything else. Therefore he acts, as if water, time, appears in a causal way. He shows the explanation, he demonstrates the happening. With it he has closed off the possibility of the miracle. Everything seems circular now; he knocks 'visibly', people can observe things for themselves.

Thus he creates the fall which always takes place at the end of a world. It is creating the impression of a logical continual development, with causes and effects, all in the atmosphere of the earthly.

Such a fall will ever bring with it, not only the end of a world, but also the arising of a new world. So what is happening here is identical to all phases of the end. Even Moses does not unite the world with the 'one' in pointing to the divine, miraculous origin of the water, of time, of life, but in giving an explanation of it, which adapted itself to the desire of the times. Thus making duality; keeping the divine divorced from things earthly. Indeed, he beat 'twice' with his staff on the rock.

From the human point of view, we cannot speak of a failure of Moses. He failed as Adam failed. What he did agreed with the structure of creation. We can rather state that with this making of duality at the end he also gave the world and our life the appearance of the seventh day-of-the-world. Just as in making the 'two' at creation God called the whole world into appearance.

God making the 'two' implied that God Himself sent His 'shechinah', His quality with which He made this creation, to accompany the world. It went, as tradition expresses it, into exile with the world for the duration of time. Just as

God had said He was descending with Jacob into Egypt, to stay with him and Israel all the time, till at the exodus God would accompany them again to Canaan, to reunion. We saw this fact expressed in the (10–5–6–5) structure in the 26 generations.

Living this life implies self-sacrifice therefore, as it is also expressed in the conception 'exile of the shechinah'. Physically also, in the projection in the body of man, the forming of descendants means a commencement of man's dying on earth. The body is built in that way and life has this connection with it.

The happening with the water which means death to Moses, his continuing in the seventh day, is analogous with this principle. It means that the world got this root-story, this 10–5 from Moses to live on it, to unite it in every life to the 6–5.

Of course we cannot say that Moses consciously sacrificed himself for it. It is, however, a fact that his whole life tended towards this event happening in the end. An event, analogous to the principle of creation, hence manifest in his life.

Thus the leader on the way from the 'two' to the 'one' himself is ever present on this way, as long as the seventh day lasts. 'Causal' water gave rise to this life in this world. Moses led the world into this seventh day and he will journey on again with the world out of this seventh day when it is consummated. Ancient lore points to the fact that the word 'shiloh', meaning the ultimate bringer of the coming world, (Gen. 49:10), has the same numerical value as the word Moses. They are respectively spelt 300–10–30–5 and 40–300–5; either word has the sum total of 345. Until that time has arrived, everything will be expressed in the form of the seventh day, the root-story of which is formed by the 'five books of Moses'. Together with duality for himself, Moses brought that tree of life which bestows the joy and happiness of reunion to the world. With his duality he continues to be the leader on the way from the 'two' to the 'one'.

And this is the secret of the man Moses.

40
Looking Into the Future

The story of the twelve spies (Num. 13 and 14) means a turning-point in the journey through the wilderness. The journey of the spies ended in a call on the people to return to Egypt, definitely to give up the way to the 'one', since the spies themselves had decided it was utterly out of the question that man should ever occupy this world of the 'one' and remain alive. The challenge rather to return to Egypt ended in a change of level of the story. The journey through the wilderness which was at this moment coming to a close, suddenly became 'forty years'; very, very long, that is. The chronology of the 40 days passed into one of 40 years. So there is a lowering of level, a leap to a circle further outward. And at the same time there was the announcement that the whole generation which had journeyed away from Egypt and which at the moment of the exodus was twenty years old or older yet, should perish in the wilderness.

Now what does this story mean? How is it that it was these very spies who should turn the scales and decide that all were to die in the wilderness; and that the journey was to last 40 years now? And how is it that the people take the radical decision to appoint a new leader and to return to Egypt?

They are on the way to the 'one' and on this way continually experience miracles. Every moment this way has surprises in every sphere. The whole day and all life are full of the most fascinating aspects. It means a never-ending joy to be able to go this way.

There are, however, pious and learned men, the greatest and wisest men of the generation, and they want to know this instant how things are in that world of the 'one'; they want this instant to penetrate into that other world to get to know it. And they would like eventually to make reports about it to the others. And those others also wonder what things are like there, what are the proportions prevailing there, what it will be like when ultimately they themselves have got there.

If people on this way across the wilderness are so inclined, God leaves things open and Moses even gives directions as to how they are to approach the world of the 'one'. From the south in the direction east-west, and then in the west, northwards.

The twelve spies, representing every part of total man, come, indeed, into that other world. They experience, as tradition tells us circumstantially, great and mightily strange things, they are overwhelmed by impressions. For forty days they stay there, again a very long time.

At their return, ten of them have brought all kinds of fruit from that other world. That which is fruit there, object realized, to the world of the wilderness is unimaginably great, incalculable, hardly to be borne. And they also have many things to report.

Those reports, translated into the criteria of duality, similarly translated into the standards of the way through the wilderness, are shattering. They imply that no mental picture of life in the coming world can convey any idea at all of the realities there. Those realities implied that it was out of the question for man to live there; that life there merely consisted of fright and horror; that the opposing powers were so immense, so fearful, as to crush the man who should happen to penetrate into the land. It was indeed a grand world, awe-inspiring, but decidedly not a world for man. And then there was the desire to rush into the intoxication of Egypt, to stay there; to ban all the rest again. All the rest was too awful.

The 'sin' of the spies was not so much that they had wanted to penetrate into the world of the 'one', although their desire implied a very dangerous undertaking. For that reason Moses had altered the name of Joshua, one of the spies. The name had originally been Hosea, 5–6–300–70 and Moses made it into 10–5–6–300–70. The whole 10 of the name Lord God was united to the 5–6–300–70 which was as yet unconnected with it. The latter part of the name, the 300–70, is built into the human names, according to the principle of the name Lord, instead of the second 5. It represents the expression of this 5 in the phenomenon of this world. We cannot, however, expatiate on the subject. Let it suffice here to state that the name of Joshua was made whole, bound into a unity, at the beginning of this journey.

The sin of the spies was that they wanted to measure the 'one' with the standards of the 'two', or with the standards of the way towards the 'one'. It is man's inability to detach himself from the standards of his world. Indeed, if measured with the proportions of this world, everything in the 'one' is incongruous, paralysing, creating the impression of being fatal. The coming world can only be accepted with the qualities of faith, of belief in the intentions of the creator. Standards arising from sensory images are diametrically opposed to those arising from faith, love, affection, loyalty. Sensory images can be said to exist on purpose to create that contrast; that one will not be able to build up things on logical, sensory conclusions, to base everything exclusively on human and divine 'measures', the non-mechanical 'measures'.

According to tradition, it was those very ten spies who had brought with them 'proofs' from the other world. They wanted to impress people with the grand possibilities obtaining in the 'one'; they wanted to demonstrate the miracle. And then one will discover that everything operates the other way round. It creates fright and people only want to turn away from the other world. It was precisely after the demonstrations with the 'fruits' that the decision was made to revert the whole way, to go back to the world of the opposites.

So the story also wants to convey that, if one really decides to fathom the secret of the 'one', the profoundest secret of the purpose of existence, one should first of all realize that one must leave unused all standards of this life which are based on sensory perceptions. Besides, one should never come with proofs of that other world to our world. The craving for demonstrations will cause both the bringer of the proof and the hearer to fall.

The two spies who did not bring any proofs with them, Caleb and Joshua, were preserved to pass 'alive' from this seventh day into the eighth. Ancient lore tells about Caleb that he visited the place in the 'one' where the Patriarchs and Matriarchs were, and did not do anything there. It means that he sought the original 'one' in the coming 'one' and recognized it, and that this too gave him the assurance of the goodness of the coming world. People would come home again to the previous generations, to everything which had been here and had left here.

The fall of the ten spies, however, dragged all the people along on the way to the coming world. Demonstrating the experiences of the 'one' and wanting to impress people with the proofs, brings with it the lowering of level to all and also death. The 'one' would only be attained after 40 years, only after a long, an endlessly long time. Hence the saying that one must not penetrate into the secret until one is forty; that until then the same fall may take place as with the spies who wanted to know the 'one' even before the 40 years had passed.

Non-understanding of the potentialities of the coming world repeatedly expresses itself in various fields, because people ever try, in good faith, to grasp the future with the criteria of this world. People ask where everybody will be able to live, how they will be nourished, how long they will live, if children will go on being born. They ask if technology and its results will continue to exist, if they will go on being perfected, what people will be occupied with. People want to know where all the dead ones – eventually resurrected – will be, what will be their age and what they will look like, whom one will frequent, etc. None of these questions can possibly be answered with the standards of this life, and the standards of that other world frighten us in this life, for the very reason that they do away with this life, in fact make it impossible. And all the spies of the future, who give information in any way, whether reasoning logically or through real or imagined visions, cause for themselves and the others the same results as described for the ten spies in the biblical story.

Only the attitude of Joshua and Caleb is fitting for such future espionage. One should point at the qualities of faith in God and point at the numerous miracles God has already revealed in creation which is concentrated in the Bible especially for man. If God already shows these numerous miracles in the Bible, indicates therein the structure of the way, tells about man's journey through the various worlds, about the succession of times and periods, and also indicates in the manner of expression of this world how the future can be seen, He will assuredly make the coming world possible for man to live in and allow him to occupy it.

The attitude towards a coming world, a world which in our terminology we express as the world of the eighth day, also projects itself in our world of today, in the seventh day. In this world too there are spies for the coming world and these spies too bring a mental picture with them, which must cause despair. Thus there are such telling us that development will continue for thousands upon thousands of years, that one generation will follow after the other, that individual life is as nothing in comparison with all that immensity and vastness of thousands upon thousands of years. But then, what is the purpose of individual life? It gets lost like a grain of sand in the desert. Others predict plans for the future, in which the individual cannot play a part. Others again tell about the enormous technical developments, the conquests of the universe, contacts with other heavenly bodies. And the individual feels still more lost in those immense oceans in space-time. What is his value as compared to this, what is his significance? Refined instruments take his place more and more and he is left merely to seek forgetfulness.

These spies of the future bring great despair. Rather than meet such a future full of fear on account of his littleness, man would go back to Egypt; exclude all thoughts other than the material occupations and pleasures of life in duality.

As soon as a period of time ceases to offer man mental pictures of the future, to stimulate him to self-consciousness, to convince him of the great significance of every individual life; as soon as, to the contrary, the mental picture of the future reduces him to despair, it will rouse the desire for the return to Egypt. Then people will appoint leaders to accomplish the return to Egypt. Leaders will be those figures who manage to stage the play of pretending that economics or sports, or the cinema, or politics are exceptionally important, as if the salvation of mankind depended on decisions taken in that direction. Such leaders will set the greatest value on the conception relaxation, recreation; they will create the illusion that everything they do is of definite significance to the world. Just as all illusion destroys the vision of right proportions, right relationships. Everything will then revolve round the moment's satisfaction and pleasure, and the rest will all be barred growlingly. It is the atmosphere in which the unredeemed 'four' of Israel in Egypt felt so comfortable. And the spies themselves in similar despair plunge into the illusion of the return to Egypt. They belong to the front ranks who feel appalled at the picture of the future they saw themselves.

The voices of Joshua and Caleb who point out that God will never allow man to go to destruction in this infinite mass in space-time, in a 'land that eateth up the inhabitants thereof' (Num. 13:32); in a world of giants to whom the men of this world are like grasshoppers; that God had not brought man into the world for that, had not made him go through all his experience merely to lead him to this time of the present which created such a horrible vision of the future; these voices of Joshua and Caleb are not listened to. Would God have given man the miracle of the Bible, and then allow him to be eaten up in this inhuman future?

One recognizes the technocracy and culture-pessimism of the end of a period in all these expressions: man on the threshold of the seventh day in Paradise, Cain as 'a fugitive and a vagabond', the generation of the Flood, etc.

Here again it is the 'ereb rab', the 'mixed multitude', the power of development which sets the tune. And just as in the story of Paradise, it brings death with it. For the way to Egypt is cut off. Man does not get the opportunity to continue the game of his god. It is not his destination. The phenomenon expressing itself as death for this world, puts an end to it.

Around the 'calf' people had called for the leader, visible in this world, able to lead mankind to the promised land. With the spies, however, people desire the guide who leads them back to Egypt. The dehumanized picture of the future is the most serious fall, it is the sign that nothing can bring salvation, except death.

Ancient lore points out that the biblical day of the fall with the 'calf', the seventeenth of the fourth month, is the same day when in another cycle of time biblical Jerusalem fell. The day of the rebellion of the spies, however, is the ninth of the fifth month, and this day in the later cycle of time is the moment when the temple, the established house of God, disappeared. With the fall of the spies, God ceases to speak with Moses, and through him with the people. Not until the end of the 40 years, at the end of an infinitely long cycle does God speak with Moses again to announce the end of the world of the seventh day and to prepare the entrance into the new. The silence of God during the 40 years in the wilderness from that ninth day of the fifth month, in the second year after the exodus from Egypt, runs parallel to the silence because of God leaving the solid house in this world on the same day, in another cycle of time.

Just as the happening with the calf, in accordance with the structure in the biblical story, is the cause of the arising of a duality, expressing itself in the twice 40 days after the once 40 days *previous* to it, thus the fall of the spies similarly means a duality. Every fall implies a duality and a lowering of level. It is the principle of creation this duality, so that the 'one' may come forth from it.

Now where is this duality found in the structure of the story of the spies? Duality in this case has the widest possible bearing. It leads to death. Thus it is opposite the first duality, that of creation itself and man eating of the tree of the knowledge.

Yet it is an entirely different duality, since it comes after the exodus and after the happenings of Mount Sinai.

Reunion of the duality now arisen is at the same time the realization of the eighth day, is at the same time therefore the end of this world. It is the last making-of-the-two in the root story. That is why, according to ancient lore, it signs the last destruction of the temple, the last withdrawal of God from this world.

The new temple and the new appearance of God will at the same time imply the concretizing of the eighth day, which has never appeared yet. This coming reunion is beyond the root-story of the Bible; it is predicted in Pentateuch, but not yet realized.

The journey through the wilderness is characterized by going from one place to the next, for indeed it is a journey from one condition to the other, on the way from the 'two' to the 'one'.

All in all they pass through 42 places (Num. 33). Besides a great number of other aspects, which we cannot enter upon here, the number 42 characterizes the way of the seventh day. For the completed sixth day is expressed by 6², the completed seventh day by 7². The completed sixth day on its way to the completed seventh day finds its form in these proportions as $(6½)^2$, which makes 42.

The spies go on their way after the people moved from Hazeroth and pitched in the wilderness of Paran; (Num. 12:16 and 13:3).

According to the enumeration of the 42 places in Num. 33, the place Hazeroth proves to be the fourteenth. So the people have passed 14 places, when the spies are sent forth; a number also specially mentioned by tradition. So it means that 14 places had been passed through, when the spies were sent forth, and that *from* that moment a number of 28 places lay ahead. The place coming after Hazeroth in the enumeration of Num. 33 is Rithma; and with Rithma began the series of 28 places. Which shows, therefore, that at the moment the spies were sent forth, the exact proportion of 1:2 obtained.

So the happening of the spies means that there arose a duality in the number of places of the whole journey. Just as after the making of the calf there came the twice 40 days, so here there are the twice 14 places over against the once 14 before that fall.

Once more we see that an established structure in the Bible is evident in all parts. The places of the journey through the wilderness also bear this signature. The spies made the fracture of the 'one' into the 'two', they are in the point of fracture.

The significance of their fall comes to expression in the fact that the 'two' they created will only have come to an end, when the 42 places have been completed. It means that this duality will continue to the end of the root-story. The reunion of *this* duality will take place after the root-story; will not take place in Pentateuch, as is the case with the other reunions of created dualities. It is a reunion which has not yet been fulfilled in the root-story. For man in this world also it will therefore take place beyond this life, beyond this world.

Opposite the way from Egypt to Canaan, expressing itself as a way from the 'two' to the 'one', there is in that same journey through the wilderness a way from the 'one' to the 'two'. It is the situation we have come across in the fact that in the 26 generations up to and including Moses, the name 10–5–6–5 is consummated, the reunion of the two fives has taken place, whereas in the chronological structure of these 26 generations it is only the principle of the 10–5 which comes to expression, so that a duality has been created and the two 'fives' are still opposed to each other to be united into the unity in the 10–5–6–5. The completed 'one' in either case faces a 'two' which is placed opposite man in time, for the purpose of completion. The 'tree which is fruit and makes fruit', the tree of life that is, again comes to expression here. The part which 'is fruit', is the way from the 'two' to the 'one' which is completed, and in the 10–5–6–5 of the 26 generations which are completed, which are fruit already. The part which 'makes fruit' is opposite us in the duality created by the spies, which comes to reunion in this world through life and death, just as is the case with the 10–5 of the chronological structure of the 26 generations, which in the reality of this life shall become 'one' with the 6–5.

It is also the harmony of the opposites, which comes to expression in the Pentateuch, just as it does of course in the further story of the Bible. The 2 → 1 forms a harmonic whole with the 1 → 2. For indeed *that* is why is the tree of life, since it embraces life and death as a unity.

41
At the End of the Journey, the Giants

When time is running out, when the journey through the wilderness expressing itself in the 40 has reached its last year, there is the confrontation with the giants Sihon and Og (Num. 21:21–55). At the border of the world, where the time of this world runs out, where the water, the river Jordan, forms the boundary between two worlds, that is where the giants live. The time to be spent at the end of the seventh day, is the time when the development of the forces of matter has reached its pinnacle. These forces have by that time assumed immense proportions; they seem invincible. It is this period people have to pass through at the end.

Miriam and Aaron are not here any longer. On the left side, the physical side of the man approaching the end of time, a great deal has changed.

The battles against the seemingly invincible giants of matter are won and the border of time is reached. This border is formed by the fields of Moab (Num. 22:13) which are at the same time the last of the 42 places of the journey from the 'two' to the 'one'. The seventh day is running to an end.

The word Moab is spelt 40–6–1–2, having 49 as sum-total. For it is the last thing to appear on the way of the seventh day, hence its value of the completed seven. We have already discussed that Ruth came from Moab to Bethlehem, thus laying the foundation for the coming of the saviour, who leads from the seventh day to the eighth. So Ruth comes from Moab, which has the value of 49, to Bethlehem, which as we saw, has the sum-total of 490. It is the end of the seventh day which expresses itself thus in the substance of the word.

Sihon and Og indeed are the apparently invincible giants. Their forces are circumstantially described in ancient lore. The struggle with them runs parallel to the battle which at the end of the seventh day is also expressed in the wars of Gog and Magog. The stories about the power of Sihon and Og show that ancient lore ascribes potencies to them, far surpassing those encountered before. The Hebrew terms 'Sihon, King of the Amorites' and 'Og, King of Bashan' in fact express these enormous potencies in the essential. The numbers of the components of these names are respectively 60–10–8–50, 40–30–20, 5–1–40–200–10 and 70–6–3, 40–30–20, 5–2–300–50.

Together they form the number 1,000, which we have already come across as a special expression of the 'one'. Nevertheless these giants, taking their stand at the end of time, are slain by man advancing towards the coming world.

People at that moment are in the fields of Moab, the final place of the journey, the place with the significance of the completed seventh day. Moab saw what had happened to the giants Sihon and Og, and greatly feared that now indeed the end of time had come, that the world of development would be destroyed in the form it had had so far. Therefore Balak, king of Moab, turned to Balaam (Num. 22–25). The forces of Balaam at the end of time are considered incontestable. Balaam has the contact with the substance, with heaven, God speaks with him. To the world at the time of the end he is the power to determine what is to happen to the world.

According to ancient lore Balaam was one of the counsellors of Pharaoh at the time when Moses was to be born. At that time he foresaw what Moses was going to do with the world and he advised Pharaoh to kill Moses at once. Even the decision to cast all the male children into the river, originated with Balaam. Therewith he intended to have the redeemer, augured by him, killed immediately after his birth. Hence the position of Balaam is that of the defender of the world of the forces of development, he is the enemy of the eliminator of this development, of the leader to a coming world.

Balaam is connected with Midian. I should like to point here at a specific facet of Midian in the structure of the whole. Midian is the son of Keturah, the wife of Abraham (Gen. 25:1–2). According to ancient lore Keturah is identical with Hagar (Gen. 16), the mother of Ishmael. In a later phase Hagar retraced her steps and thus she became the real wife of Abraham. About Ishmael too a wending of the way is mentioned in his later years. So Midian and Ishmael are brothers and in a sense Midian can also be looked upon as an expression for a later phase of Ishmael, just as Keturah is that for Hagar. So it is not sheer accident that Midianites and Ishmaelites together should play a part at the sale of Joseph, in which readers without inside knowledge get the impression that these two names are sometimes confused with each other.

Now Midian always makes his appearance when a world comes to an end and a new world is announced. It bears upon the fact that this transformation is also expressed in Hagar-Keturah. We have seen that Ishmael appears before Abraham as a messenger, that the appearance of the incredible is potentially present. Then we see Midian playing a part in the sale of Joseph when again the way is opened to a new world and an old world ceases to be. Before his return to Egypt to put an end to the old world and start the new, Moses visits Jethro, the priest of Midian (Exod. 2:15–22 and Exod. 4:18–19). We have already discussed the fact of Jethro coming from Midian to visit Moses, when the 'seven' runs to an end, and the eighth day expressing itself in the revelation on Mount Sinai, is to come. Thus we similarly see Balaam appearing when a cycle is running to an end, when the seventh day approaches the end, the boundary.

And here again we see how order is accomplished, measure is given, from the part of Midian. Balaam, the antagonist of Moses, in whom he recognizes the eliminator of this world – i. e. the world represented by Balaam, – contrary to his personal desires and intentions, is compelled to indicate the order of the transition to the coming world. For it is Balaam who in the *'four'* statements announces the structure of this transition, which establishes the coming of the saviour in the root-story (Num. 24:17) and marks out the end of the world in development (Num. 24:18–24). Just as Jethro of Midian formed the four groups at Mount Sinai, thus on his part preparing the transition to the eighth day, so now Balaam of Midian gives the four statements which establish the position of this identical transition, this time in the expression of the final phase of the journey from the 'two' to the 'one'. This pronouncing and therewith establishing of the structure of the 'four' at the transition to the coming world, in the story of the Bible again is an action originating from Midian.

That Balaam has to speak words different from his original thoughts again shows that the transition does come, even though everything is bent on proving logically and causally that it is not coming, that it even cannot come. In the same way Balaam had taken all logical measures to prevent Moses descending into Egypt, after he had foreseen the coming developments. But even then there arose the almost comic situation that Balaam was first compelled to behold Moses growing up in Pharaoh's house of all places, in the house of his future victim, and that afterwards everything happened contrary to Balaam's counsels and interference. The coming is just as unavoidable as one second passing to make place for the next in our mechanistic times. However much one might like to hold on to time, the way from the 'two' to the 'one' is a motion, not to be arrested.

Balaam himself is killed in the end, when after the events with Baal-Peor – which I cannot enter upon in this connection – the children of Israel defeat the Midianites (Num. 25:1–18 and Num. 31). With the help of the Baal-Peor, Balaam had ventured a last effort to avert the tide; he imagined he had found the weak spot in that which was to come. It was Phinehas the son of Eleazar, who was able to prevent the catastrophe resulting from this final assault. According to tradition, it bestowed life eternal on Phinehas; and Phinehas is identical with the prophet Elijah and thus the messenger of the coming of the Messiah. Arresting the assault of Baal-Peor is identical with announcing the coming of salvation.

But – again without entering into details in this connection – I should like to point at the circumstantial specification of the spoils secured on Midian. Nowhere in the Bible is it done with such minuteness as in this case. It is not only that the total amounts are stated of these spoils, divided and subdivided, but the whole is repeated once more when half of it has to be counted; again when a five-hundredth part has to be computed and finally when a fiftieth part is figured out. One is inclined to say that anybody would have been able to do that for himself. But here we are concerned with Midian, that which had indicated the measure, and now this measure is taken and divided. The manner of dividing, the making of the two, and then the binding of each of the halves to the origin, via the proportions of one to fifty and one to five-hundred, shows clearly that here we are told what happens in the end to the giver of the measure. The battle against Midian is the final one in the root-story.

When everything has been won and the people are at the boundary between the seventh and eighth days, there is the request on the part of the tribes of Reuben and Gad with regard to their numerous flocks and herds, to occupy the land which had belonged to Sihon and Og (Num. 32). This land of Sihon and Og lies on the side of the seventh day, on the side of the journey from the 'two' to the 'one'. So the desire of Reuben and Gad is to be allowed to live in the land where there still is the development, where one is still progressing towards the goal.

We have already discussed the relationship in the substance between the body of man and the beasts, which as the three kinds of beasts of sacrifice also occur in the Zodiac. The numerous flocks and herds of Reuben and especially of Gad therefore mean that the mass of the body is specially concentrated there. And it is on behalf of this body that the land is desired where development is still possible, and especially that place where the power of development acquired such intensity as Sihon and Og could cause to arise. It is the plane expressing itself in terms of time as the pinnacle of development at the end of the seventh day of the world. Reuben and Gad want to continue to occupy this land, this cycle of time, and renounce on participating in the coming world, in the eighth day. Reuben and Gad are the first and seventh sons of Jacob. They encompass exactly the period of the seven days which they desire to occupy; they refuse to step outside their circle, they are content to possess these seven days, since the seven days are completely in the hands of the children of Israel.

This request rouses a violent reaction in Moses. With Reuben and Gad it is the fear of relinquishing the world of the seventh day; it is the fear of the coming, unknown and terrible world, which comes to expression here. That is why Moses points at the catastrophe caused by the spies with their vision of the future, their measuring with the wrong standards, their leaving out of the reckoning the miracle which the eighth day ever shows in every crystallization. He points at death which then promptly appears as the alternative, the contrast.

Moses' referring to that which was the beginning of the '40', the long, long way through the world, finally to attain the moment of the present, which had been the cause of the phenomenon death; the fact that death did verily come as soon as one made the divorce, made duality; all this caused understanding to dawn on Reuben and Gad. It may be put in this way. In the Bible Moses showed them what were the consequences of an attitude of mind which desired the duality of the seventh day – eighth day to continue.

At the end of the way reunion appears to be a reality after all. For Reuben and Gad tell Moses that they shall pioneer for the others and help to occupy the land of the 'one' for them. The name of Gad implies the conception 'fighting power', and the fact that he is the seventh also shows that it is this seventh day of the world which forms the fighting power for conquering the coming world. It is the very destination of this seventh day that it sets out to force a decision. That is why this seventh world is continually at the front. Anybody setting out from this world, belongs to the conquerors of the promised land.

It is the men that set out; the women and children and the flocks and herds remain waiting here for them until such time as they shall return, after having co-operated as pioneers to occupy the land of the 'one' as a whole on behalf of the others. It is the soul which sets forth from the manifestness of this physical world, leaving behind everything of the body and of the forces of development here to wait for its return. For it is a fact that Reuben and Gad shall come back, i.e. that the soul of the life of this seventh day similarly comes back here, again to have the experience of this world as it has developed unto its final stage.

There is the condition that the land must first be conquered, before there can be life in that domain at the end of the seventh day, the land for Reuben and Gad. For one must first have the tree of life before one can understand the purpose of development. First one has to know and possess the 'fruit', the goal, before one can get busy about what is called making the fruit. For first of all the seventh day must have conquered the 'one' and occupied it, before it can turn itself to 'development'. For in this land of the seventh day, and especially the most highly developed part, that of the giants Sihon and Og, there is the part that 'makes fruit' and that part cannot come to life until the part 'tree which *is* fruit' has come to fulfilment. It is only when the fruit is there, when it exists, that the part 'which makes fruit' spells joy and happiness; only then it is become what God purposes with the world.

Therefore Moses has this fear – when he hears the desire of Reuben and Gad to remain on the side of the seventh day – this fear that people will again eat of the tree of the knowledge, the tree 'that makes fruit', with the consequence again of the miserable and long way of death, of the 'fugitive and the vagabond', of ignorance and suffering through ignorance.

At the end, however, there is no longer this eating of the tree of the knowledge; they have then got beyond development, just as at the end of every life, development has been left behind. Now Gad, the seventh, sets forth to the new world to occupy it; Gad is leading the way. After this he may return, back across the river Jordan, the boundary between the two worlds, to the part which expresses 'being on the way'. On condition, however, that there will ever be the contact with the land itself. Only in a 'tree which is fruit and makes fruit' can there be present the growing towards a goal. This goal then is already present and is at the same time experienced. It is the being together of the opposites which are aware that they belong together and which unceasingly experience the joy of finding each other anew. When Reuben and Gad were thus promised that in the future they were to experience the part that 'makes fruit' and that this part was to remain connected with the part which 'is fruit', Moses gave them the tribe of Manasseh to accompany them as the connection (Num. 32:33). For together with this decision Moses determined that half the tribe of Manasseh was to abide with Reuben and Gad, and the other half in the land of the 'one', in the part which 'is fruit'. So Manasseh is like a bridge connecting the two worlds, the world of the seventh day with that of the eighth day; the world of development with the world of the 'one'.

The Hebrew word for Manasseh is spelt 40–50–300–5. And the word for soul, 'Neshamah', is spelt 50–300–40–5. So there are exactly the same proportions as building-bricks in the two words. Just as the soul makes the connection between the two worlds, just as the soul effects the harmony and has been bestowed by God on man for that purpose, thus Moses gives Manasseh as the connecting-link to the side of the bodily life, the side with the numerous 'herds'. The soul lives in both worlds.

Now, why did Manasseh get this place? With Ephraim, Manasseh is the son of Joseph. And to the world of duality, to Egypt in the story of Genesis, the primeval story, Joseph is he that brings unity. Joseph, too, makes the connection between the two extremes, between the opposites. And this same principle is transmitted to Ephraim and Manasseh. Ephraim is the thirteenth of the tribes, hence the one fulfilling the word 'one', therewith bringing the 12, the still incomplete part of the tribe, to unity, to completeness. And Joshua, the leader for the eighth day, for the day expressing unity, is of Ephraim.

The same principle in another plane also comes to expression in Manasseh as son of Joseph. Just as Ephraim makes-the-one, unites, so does Manasseh. Ephraim as the younger one is expression for the new body, just as it was evident in Joseph, because of which Jacob cherished such a love for Joseph. With Manasseh comes into prominence what in Judah was facing Joseph, namely the side of the soul.

Jacob says (Gen. 48:20) that in the future Israel shall give his blessing in saying: 'God make thee as Ephraim and as Manasseh'. Blessing means bringing duality to unity; therefore, because of it, making that which is blessed eternal and harmonious. Thus God blesses the seventh day, making the seventh day therewith into a unity (Gen. 2:3). Therefore blessing with the words: 'God make thee as Ephraim and as Manasseh', also implies that in the person thus blessed this unity is accomplished; the unity in the plane of Ephraim and unity in the plane of Manasseh. In this way the person blessed receives the complete harmony. Therefore it still is the custom of Jewry for the father to bless the son with these words, especially at the entrance into the seventh day. For indeed one enters the seventh day as a duality to acquire unity in that day.

When the land has been conquered, Reuben, Gad and half the tribe of Manasseh return across the river Jordan to live in the part which all through this period had been virtually without any life. And then, as it says in Joshua 22, they set up a sign on the border, which continues to give life to this bond;

which, as the tribe of Manasseh does, connects the part which 'is fruit' with the part which 'makes fruit' as a unity, thus concretizing the tree of life in the times of the world. All the time, however, similarly coming to expression in the story of Joshua, there is the fear that people will vote for the side of development and lose the connection with the 'one'. For taking of the power of development is the great temptation of this world. There is always the fear that man will eat of the tree of the knowledge anew. But the story shows that at the end of the journey the connection is consciously maintained, that man by then sees the meaning of it, thus showing he has realized the purpose of creation.

42
A Realistic and Serious Conclusion

In bringing the children of Israel to the border of the coming world, the mission of the leader on that way from the 'two' to the 'one' is accomplished. Moses himself, however, remains in the seventh day, in this world, as long as this seventh day continues as a fact to the world. He remains here as long as the 10–5 of his 'five books' have not yet been completely united with the 6–5 of time, as long as there still are people here, going their way through this world. This 10–5 is the root which imbues all existence in time with life, until complete unity of the 10–5–6–5 has been accomplished in time as well.

It is also the continuing of man's life on this side of the border, so that reunion with God may ensue from the faith, and the loyalty and the yearning man gives Him. Just as there was not anything changing in Moses' attitude towards God, when he knew he was not going to the other world alive.

But the man who has followed this way as far as the boundary of the coming world, just like Moses who fosters this man's existence, has the knowledge and the awareness of that which is to come, the full survey thereof. As regards this, he is able to experience all that is to come within his own consciousness. God shows him everything, to the veriest details (Deut. 34:1–4). Tradition reveals what this vision of Moses implies, that he surveyed all times 'unto the hindmost sea'. This 'hindmost sea', the hindmost jot-mem, the 10–40, is at the same time the hindmost or 'final day', the 10–6–40.

Moses who had in his life passed through the '49 gates of insight', who had absorbed all the insight the seven days have to offer, went and climbed Mount Nebo in the fields of Moab, hence again the fields of the 49. From this top he had this survey of all things.

In ancient lore it says that he covered the way of the fields of Moab, the 49, to the top of Mount Nebo in one step, although there were many steps. Mount Nebo is spelt in Hebrew 50–2–6, having a sum-total of 58. By now we have acquired some knowledge about this number 58. It is the proportion which expresses the end of the way of this material phenomenon. At that point Moses too dies eventually. And at that point God shows him all that is to come, shows him again in fact the world from beginning to end, and then there is man's power of vision once more, as it was before his taking of the tree of the knowledge.

There is a story in ancient lore in which we are told in great detail what happens to man even before his birth, from the moment of his conception to his death and thereafter. The story contains a.o. that the soul at the moment it is marked out to enter into the body for which the seeds are then laid, implores not to be sent down into this world of duality. It is informed, however, it has to go, since it will thus learn the purpose of creation. And before the birth of the body, the soul is shown everything about creation, that it may understand and realize the sublimity of it all. The soul then sees all cycles of time and all worlds, from one end to the other. During that time the body grows in the womb, develops till the moment comes of entering into a new world, till the moment which is called birth. When the soul has been shown everything and it has understood everything, all this knowledge is again wiped out from its consciousness. This divesting of knowledge and insight expresses itself physically in the dual character of the upper lip. Forgetfulness came so that man might go the way to unity 'for nothing', without *knowledge* about the reward such a way gives in the form of joy and happiness. That man might go this way trusting in God who would tell him during his life that the way was really good. A faith based on love and veneration.

The angel who shows the soul everything, at the moment this forgetfulness is to be imprinted, tells her that he will meet her again as soon as she has reached the end of her way through this life when she has reached unity on that way. And indeed, when man is on the point of departure from this world of the seventh day, there is a recapitulation of the happenings which took place before birth. Again man implores not to have to leave the world he lives in. But then, suddenly, he meets the angel of the beginning, who lifts his pre-natal forgetfulness from him and he sees and understands everything again. Once more he sees everything from beginning to end and he realizes the sublimity and experiences the bliss thereof.

This story of ancient lore runs parallel to the happening in the biblical story and the legends concerning it. Before man enters this world of the seventh day, he sees everything in space-time in one mighty sweep. It is the situation at the end of the sixth day, on Friday afternoon. Man is most unwilling to leave that world from which he is literally driven out. In the world into which he is then born, in the seventh day, all the knowledge and the insight of the previous world is lost. He can only attain unity through the divine attributes of trust, faith, loyalty, gratuitous love. And at the end of the way through this world, when man has attained the point of extreme development, the 49 and the 58, he is able to survey again everything from one end to the other. And then he has crossed the threshold and has got beyond the fear of that which is to come; to the contrary, he marvels at the sublimity that exists.

Moses' dying in fact is an expression of death in this world of the seventh day. It is also an expression of the end of the seventh day as a whole.

It takes place in the fields, in the plain, of Moab. We now know that all this expresses the 49, the completeness of the seventh day in the proportions of the substance. But in those plains rises Mount Nebo, which expresses the conception 58 in the substance. Moses ascends Mount Nebo, so that God may show him everything, the survey of the great whole with all the details. According to ancient lore there are many steps before the top of Mount Nebo is reached. To attain this understanding of the survey from the 58, one has to ascend from the plain of the 49. Moses achieved the ascent in one step. For the 58 is not only the end of the material phenomenon, it is for that reason at the same time the whole root-story of the Bible, the story of the 'five books of Moses', which, as discussed before, contain the 5,845 parts, the verses which, each in itself, forms a unity. From these 5,845 of the root-story one has the survey which Moses had on Mount Nebo with which the root-story ends. When God tells Moses to ascend Mount Nebo, the mount 58, exactly 5,800 verses are completed (Deut. 32:49). He that goes thus to the coming world, when at the end of the seventh day in the plains of Moab, the 49, he can ascend Mount Nebo, this 58 of the creation of God in the word, the most miraculous creation, he goes as the true man of the seventh day, like Moses.

The age of Moses is indeed 120 years, the measure God gives to man in this world. In the whole of the Pentateuch, Moses is the only one that actually has this measure. It means that this is the measure of man in the seventh day. That is why even nowadays in the practice of Jewish life, people wish each other 'a hundred and twenty years'. It does not mean that our bodily form should have exactly this measure as counted in our years; people may die older or younger. It means that people wish each other to fulfil this life of the seventh day as the true man. It is not just accidentally that Moses, and Moses alone, completes these 120 years.

When God gives man this measure in time (Gen. 5:3), the end of the 120 years allotted there coincides with the Flood, in 1656–1657 of biblical chronology. And we have already seen that together with the measure of the 3½, discussed before – the measure which is also the expression of the fact that 'the fourth wind', the fourth dimension, is fulfilling itself in this world, is on its way to fulfilment in this world – the 1656–1657 bring the 5,800. There where the 120 years of man come to an end, as also the 120 years of Moses, in 1656–1657, there the measure of the multiplier 3½ yields exactly that 58 of Mount Nebo and of the number of verses of the 'five books of Moses' and at the same time the real 120 years of Moses' life. These 120 years here at the end and there at the beginning, where the first 'time' comes to expression, shows clearly how profound the significance is of the measure of 58.

No one knows of Moses' sepulcher unto this day. For none can know from the point of view of this world whither man goes. God Himself accords him the place. That place is somewhere in a valley in Moab, in the 49. According to ancient lore, Mount Nebo lies in the land of Reuben, but the sepulcher of Moses lies in the land of Gad, the seventh. In the land of the pioneer who wins the 'one', thereupon to return and once more have the experience of the 'seven'.

The man who has died here is irretrievable to this world. It serves no purpose to look for him in this seventh day-of-the-world. Whatever passes by here, at any moment of time, cannot be found here any more. It is only in the 'one', in the 'eighth day', that everything of the 'four corners of the earth' is gathered in again and it becomes apparent that nothing has got lost. Then everything pertaining to man has also been gathered in, not only the condition of his last moment but that of all the moments of his life. In this regard, too, there obtains a unity, unimaginable to our organs and senses which are focused on passing along the way; and not to be expressed in the mental pictures reflecting this same world.

Moses' death takes place at the end of this seventh day of the world, also expressed in his presence in the fields of Moab which have the completed seventh day in their numerical proportions. His grave is in the land of the seventh son, of Gad, who in his own name, 3–4, has the seven, and about whom the Bible states that he has seven sons. And according to tradition Moses' death also occurred towards the end of the seventh day of the week. Besides, that day is on the seventh day of the twelfth month.

In everything it comes to expression that at the end of the 'seven' there is death. A death which means a transition to the world where unity, established in principle in the seventh day, has been realized. The new world of the eighth day *has* that unity.

In our chronology the year is divided into twelve months, because our time does not know of unity yet. In our time everything passes, everything flows, everything is broken into fragments in endless multiplicity. A thirteenth month would express that unity, just as the word 'one' has the value of 'thirteen' and just as 'thirteen' everywhere expresses this unity. A thirteenth month lies beyond our times, just like a twentyfifth hour and an eighth day. Chronology is based on this knowledge of the limits of 7 and 12.

In Jewish chronology we start from lunar months for the classification of the years. Nevertheless the year is ultimately corrected in accordance with the solar year. It is done by inserting a thirteenth month every so many years. This calendar is most emphatically not based on the so-called practical usefulness for society. The purpose of the calendar is that life is also an expression of the rhythm which the substance has in other dimensions. Now the substance means that time is as yet determined by the conception 'moon' which implies that everything is flowing, changing, on its way. But it also implies that there is ever present this being focused on the permanent, the invariable, the constant. Therefore there is the correction of the whole through the conception 'sun'. And this correction is made through the indication that this being focused on the permanent, the invariable, i. e. on the 'one', implies that the 'twelve' of the calculation of months and of the Zodiac passes into the 'thirteen'. If there is 'one', there necessarily is 'thirteen'.

That Moses should die on the seventh day of the twelfth month means that it happens at the extreme limit of what is possible in this time of flow; that the eight and the thirteen imply unity. Therefore, when in the Bible there is this going towards the eighth day such as crossing the sea in the exodus from Egypt, which crossing, as discussed before, was a journey towards the eighth day of the exodus; or at the crossing of the river Jordan, after the way through the wilderness; then time stops, the water stands still and forms a wall, a dam. The flowing has an end for the man who enters into the eighth day. Crossing the river Jordan at the end of the journey through the wilderness similarly shows this special aspect of the flow of time ceasing (Joshua 3 and 4).

Thus the consecration of the tabernacle takes seven days and it is not taken into actual use until the eighth day (Lev. 8:33–9:7). Thus too in the first story of creation, the creation of man is the eighth act of creation. The seventh is that of the beast. It is physical man still in development. And that beast is brought as 'korban' before God on the eighth day. That is why an animal must stay with its dam up to and including the seventh day after its birth, and it can only be brought as 'korban' before God on the eighth day (Lev. 22:27).

All this shows that the eighth day is the purpose of the whole; that the seventh represents the way thither and that at the end of the seventh day the way is completed and one can enter into the new world. Therefore the real story of the Bible winds up with the conclusion of the seventh day, with the end of this world, that is.

One may wonder why the Bible has not an 'agreeable' ending; why it does not end up with the reality of an ideal society. Again the answer is: the Bible is the expression of the essential in this world of the seventh day. Therefore the Bible tells us very seriously that the seventh day passes by and that another day will come. The Bible even indicates the nature of this seventh day, i.e. that it is passing, flowing, moving.

This also implies that an ideal society in this seventh day will *have* to exclude all kinds of realities, viz. the *reality* of death, however long life may last; and the reality of the disappearance and impossibility of recovery of past generations and of past moments of personal experience. Under the circumstances there can never arise a satisfactory world, a world which actually makes people happy. The world will ever bear the stamp of this flowing, this passing, also on account of the consciousness that there can or must exist another world with which one has no contact from this world. The purpose of existence will always depend on whether or not that other is real. It is what we ever understood to be the world of duality, which will always be the background as long as one has not found the 'one'.

The Bible is serious, it points out the realities. It does not content itself with conjuring up a utopian world before man, where it cannot exist. To the contrary, the Bible tells us that this world will end, a reality which presents itself in every life, as expressive of the character of this world. But the Bible also tells us why and how this world ends and what comes after. The coming world is not a matter of speculation in the Bible, but it is part of the structure. The eighth day in the Bible is a reality quite as distinct as the sixth day or the seventh. If it were not so, death at the end of the seventh day would necessarily be a fact leading to despair. Through the reality, however, of the structure which lends to the eighth day a place quite as distinct as that of the seventh, death acquires an absolutely different character. As long as this seventh day continues to exist, death proves to be the transition to the eighth day. So the coming world is not merely a question of hope but at the same time of certainty.

This certainty it is which makes the Bible identical with the tree of life, the tree with the measure of the five-hundred, the tree that is 'one' facing multiplicity. He that knows the Bible as such a unity, extending to life before this world, embracing life in all aspects of this world, and similarly embracing the life of the coming world, he knows the tree of life. And for him that knows the tree of life and takes it to himself, there is no death. He will then know that going from this world to the coming world is the transition from the seventh day to the eighth, like going from today to tomorrow. For that very reason has the Bible been bestowed on man in this seventh day, in order that death shall be eliminated for him through the Bible.

On the point of the 49 he can ascend this 58, and he will be aware that he has the tree of life.

Epilogue

The story of the Pentateuch ends with the death of Moses, just as the story of the whole Bible ends with the destruction of the temple, and the life we perceive also ends always in death. These are undeniable facts, this is reality, and nobody can escape from this reality. Indeed, the Bible in its story speaks of this reality, it tells what everybody in all times has seen and what everybody has undergone.

Yet, at the same time the Bible tells something different. This other, however, is not the story of what people see happening. It is that which comes into prominence if one grasps the real structure of the story, of time, of the words. This other is only thrown into relief, when we learn to know the Bible in its deepest essence. Then we shall see how this deepest essence gives life and the purpose of life to the story of the outer happenings, just as the soul does to the body.

For we have seen that a development from the 'one' to the 'two' ever goes together with a development in the opposite sense, from the 'two' to the 'one', and that these two contradictory developments form an indivisible unity indeed. The former is the development towards multiplicity, towards death; the latter is that towards unity, towards all-embracing life. The first mentioned is the outwardly perceptible, the physical, it is the progress of the story, of the images; the other is the progress one can only become aware of if one has become acquainted with the substance; if, as we have shown by means of a few examples from the Bible, one has approached the inner, imperceptible structure. This imperceptible structure is not to be found in the image; this structure is not present in a 'translation' either, because a translation transfers one image to another. It is merely the word in the language with which the Bible was created, which offers the bridge to the substance.

He that merely reads the outer story, meets that which actually happens with the external. It gets lost, just as everything appearing in space-time must flow away, disappear from sight. And it is only he that at the same time knows the hidden inner story — the story which is like a soul that vitalizes the body — *recognizes* that the outward disappearance forms part of life eternal, that is the part which 'makes fruit', of the tree which 'is fruit and makes fruit', of the tree which for that reason is called the tree of life. It is this certainty which the Bible gives, which it communicates penetratingly and insurpassably clearly and distinctly in showing that it embraces in its story the unity of the two opposite ways.

Therefore the Bible *proves* through its structure, through the miracle of the word, that it is merely the outer story which leads to death, just as one experiences it through one's senses which perceive the exterior; but that it is this same story which in its inner structure informs us that it is exactly the opposite which happens in the substance. That it is only the man, who continues to cling to the outer story with all its eventual interpretations, who has the fear of death, who feels the despair which merely through rousing the intoxicating illusion can pass into a tragic gaiety, negating the substance and ever taking to flight. He that has fathomed the Bible in his soul, in its power which actuates and determines the story, he knows the meaning of the opposites; he knows that real life is indeed built up of the synthesis of 'going to the two' and 'going to the one'. He also knows that life bears the secret signature of the name Lord which name also contains within itself this unity of the opposites.

Practically everywhere in the world and almost at all times mankind has intuitively felt it would be senseless, purposeless, if death actually meant the end of everything. People have always been more or less aware that there must be something else opposite this perceptible death, which somehow formed a contrast and a synthesis therewith. Where even this awareness is lost, there remains nothing except despair and the craving for the profoundest numbness of spirit.

Throughout the centuries mankind has in many ways given expression to this feeling that death was not the end, and of this hope of an inner purpose, of justice, love, forgiveness. They have sometimes been sublime testimonies of that hope, of that belief. Very often they are sad self-deception, it forms part of the stimulants which serve to make a life without purpose, without understanding of the substance, at least materially worth living. Theories have been built up about a life hereafter, people forcibly conjured up visions, deceived themselves and deceived other people. To large numbers of people it was the way which we learned to know as that of a 'fugitive and a vagabond'. Sometimes there was hope, sometimes fear, now one was preponderant, now the other. There never was any definite cognizance, however.

Now this is the difference in principle with what the Bible reveals through its marvellous structure, on account of which in ancient lore it bears the name of 'tree of life'. With this structure the Bible shows that life essentially consists of the unity of this life in development, lunar life, and the life in unity, solar life. Day and night together form a unit, just as man and woman, just as everything which appears here as opposites, as it is also expressed by the letter aleph, the 'one'.

Supposing the Bible were a book written in antiquity by clever and inspired people, and supposing the book should inform us that people could feel comforted; that there really was a hereafter; that everything remaining unanswered here as injustice and grief was bound to come right; then we would feel prompted to ask the question 'How do they *know*? Were they present at it; did they witness it?' The answer would always have to be evasively negative. For indeed what man, what historical Moses or whoever else, could really know? At best they could believe it honestly and intensely.

But since the Bible proves to be a creation with a structure which it is impossible for any or for mankind to imitate, let alone create originally, with a structure which goes deeper and farther than the creation of the universe, of nature, already defined as unsurpassable miracles, for the very reason that the structure of the Bible embraces both the mechanistic and the marvellously human, therefore all this information of the Bible has an entirely different character and a much wider purport, exactly because of its unity of the opposites of the exterior, the physical, and the inner, live miracle.

Since this Bible, this miracle, this unbelievable creation, contains the information, pervading all its parts, and coming to expression in all its aspects, that the opposites essentially represent the fullest harmony, that there is only a contrast, if one severs the exterior from the substance, if one makes duality, it consequently means something entirely different from any utterance of hope or expectation from any man whatsoever, who indeed is himself subject to this perceptible death, who therefore is a party interested and can therefore only have a subjective opinion. Since the Bible in this fascinating language of the structure, of the proportions, of this world created as a miracle, establishes irrefutably, for this world and for everything that existed previous to it and all that is beyond it, how this life makes its appearance here, what is its meaning, what happens to it, how it brings about the unity of the opposites on the way from Egypt to Canaan, from the seventh day to the eighth day, all this is no longer a subject for speculations, for hope, but it is at least as firmly established as the fact that there is a universe, a world. I used the qualification 'at least', because the universe is only manifest as a material phenomenon, whereas the Bible in its structure proves to be more embracing to go far beyond the world of material perceptibility, how infinite it may appear to be in its measures.

In its story the Bible does not say a word about a hereafter. The story, the expression in the outward happening, quite rightly merely speaks of the end, called 'death'. A story expressed in mental pictures can never speak about a hereafter. Wherever such a thing might occur, it can only be deceit, fiction. The Bible tells us about the eternal in its structure, in its soul. There one does see what the seventh day means and what the eighth day; there one does see how all the opposites become a unity forever bound in a harmony, unimaginable to this world of duality. All this properly means that just because this creation, bearing the name of Bible, contains this structure of life, it represents a certainty. It is just as certain as the fact that the sun and the moon represent a certainty to this world. It can be ascertained from the Bible in a manner even more fascinating than any astronomic or scientific statement of our perception.

Whoever can thus approach the Bible and penetrate into the depth of its being, whoever, in a word, can enter into a marriage with it, has this certainty. To him it is 'knowledge', 'cognizance'. He has in this world and in this life the tree of life, the tree with the measures of the 'five-hundred'; he has even in this life got beyond the 'four-hundred' which indeed forms the boundary. He needs no longer hope in the way of the ignorant man, of the man who is a 'fugitive and a vagabond'. His hope merely consists of waiting for the day when for the whole world that way of the 'four-hundred' shall have come to an end, when the whole world receives the 'five-hundred' for their measure. Then it will not be necessary for him either to disappear into imperceptibility, because this world cannot yet behold the 'one'. Then there will be an end to the sorrow of the world which in ignorance, in hope and despair, has to follow the way. The belief of this man is a faith built up on certainties. He knows for sure that it will come in this way; he knows through the miracle of the Bible which he received as a present in this world. And his great joy in this life, the bliss of his existence here, is his daily communion with this miracle, which shows him new depths every moment. The sublimity of this belief in this world is that it is experienced with such self-evidence, when everything from observation points to the opposite. Such a man believes in life eternal, in justice, righteousness, in bliss and harmony, when observation every day screams into his face that there is death, miserable and unintelligible; that there is unrighteousness, sorrow, strife. It is the sublimity of this life and of this world, that with the Bible one has the certainty to live with this belief, which defies all realities. That is why the word belief has the structure 1–40–50, a structure which shows that it surpasses the word truth, which as 1–40–400, does not get beyond the 'four'. In this world this belief, just because it is opposed to the reality of daily life, is so fundamental, because it forms the oneness of the opposites even here. It unites the cognizance of the substance with the outward form of reality.

It is the purpose of this book that the reader should become aware that this belief is possible and accessible, since it is based on an inner experience of the miracle and therewith acquires the actuality of certainty about the purpose of life. A great many things have been discussed in this book, but there is very much more which necessarily had to be left out. Please consider this book as a day trip through a new land. To become better acquainted with this land one should live there for many years. On this day trip I could only point out the most striking things we met on our way. A great deal more, much more impressive, overwhelming, was too far removed from our route and to my regret I had to make up my mind not to refer to them lest the reader should feel disappointed at hearing things mentioned without being shown them. What one does not know one does not realize one is missing. Besides during such a short trip the impression can sometimes hardly be avoided that a good many landmarks are too hurriedly passed, owing to which the surroundings there leave no clear impression. It may serve to encourage the reader to spend a little more time on these points during a more leisurely visit.

I therefore trust that this short visit of orientation may induce some people to abide a little longer by and by, or even induce a desire to settle down in this land. Then one will experience many more miracles still, everyone on the very way he treads in this life. These miracles may bring the great reversal individually and collectively. Let the reader realize that they lie ready to hand for people of the right disposition. One only needs eyes to see them.

Appendix

Notes and Records

Page 73, first paragraph. As soon as man faces the woman formed out of him, there is the encounter with the serpent. In ancient lore it is even formulated thus, 'when woman was created, Satan was created along with her' (Midrash Bereshith Rabba 17:9). For as soon as there is development in the material sense, as soon as there is the circle, there is at the same time the power of temptation. The seducer desires to be taken.

Page 77, fourth paragraph. The word 'secret' in Hebrew is 'sod', 60–6–4. And the word for 'foundation', 'basis', is 'jesod', 10–60–6–4. What all the rest is built on, what must stand firmly, immovably, in the substance of the language is closely related to the conception 'secret'. The sephirah of the sixth day bears the name of 'jesod', foundation. Just as this world of the seventh day is clearly and distinctly based on the sixth day, thus the insight into the substance must also be clear. And then, as every basis, also in the phenomenal form of this life, shows, it must be protected and covered.

Page 84. Although physical observations must on no account be used to illustrate the Bible with – let alone to prove the correctness thereof – I should like to point out here that the whole time of one revolution of the Zodiac is 26,000 years. Of course this may be coincidence. All the same it is a striking coincidence, since those 26,000 years indeed represent the complete revolution. In fact this time of revolution is only rounded off to 26,000 years; in reality it is a little less. In an ancient legend, not discussed in this book, we are told about a sinful world of wrong actions, the world of the generation of Enos, that is (Gen. 4:24). Their sin consisted in their 'invoking the name of the Lord'. The translation creates the impression they were really doing the right thing. The meaning of the text, however, implies 'making use' of the name of the Lord on behalf of the earth. According to tradition the face of the earth changed its aspect on account of it. This generation of Enos occurs 235 years after the coming of Adam, as we can see from Gen. 5. The manifest revolution of these 26,000 years, as based on this tradition, therefore starts from the moment they began to invoke the name of the Lord – 'to read', it says literally – 235 years later, that is. Owing to this the manifest time of revolution is only 25,765 years. The generation of Enos brought with it an alteration in the expression of time.

It may be rather useful also to mention here that the letter 'aleph', the 'one', has 111 as sum-total of its components – aleph-lamed-peh, 1–30–80, i.e. the 'one' in centuples, in decads and in units, representing the 1 in three planes.

The 1–30–80 is also the word, in its structure, of the number 1,000, eleph which number is the highest expression to be attained through the letters of the word. For the highest number is 400, and just as the 4 implies the 10, thus the 400 has the

1,000 as its supreme potentiality, i.e. as 400+300+200+100=1,000.

Page 85, last paragraph. The word 'mercy' in Hebrew is 'rachem', 200-8-40. The root is closely related to the word 'rechem' 200-8-40, meaning 'womb'. So mercy is related to the sentiment of the mother for the child growing in her. It is the protective, the feminine, which is the basis for this quality.

We saw that the name Lord also contains the number 72. Now this number also represents the value of the components of the word 'chesed'. This word means goodness, love; it is sometimes translated as grace. It is the expression of an active affection, a desire to give of oneself to do good to the other. The first Sephirah, in the place of the first day of creation, with which creation begins, bears the name of 'chesed'. This word 'chesed' is spelt 8-60-4 and has a sum-total of components of 72. So there is a close relationship, a close identity between this name Lord and the conception 'chesed'.

Pages 104-105. The 'three' and the 'four' as contrast between the male and the female are the sign for the seventh day, for $3+4=7$. But at the completion of the seventh day, it is $3^2+4^2=5^2$. That is the purpose of the seventh day. Always when the opposites have found each other, there is the fruit. Always when the 'two' become 'one', there is the new, the unbelievable. The new is always the 5, the 50, and the 500.

Pages 108-109. The 'seven' as measure in the phenomenal form of this world expresses itself a.o. in music as the seven notes of the scale. The tone cannot be manifest beyond this seven.

Page 112, second paragraph. Compare this word 'yetsirah' with its root etsel, close by, with the word for shadow (tsel), side (tsela) and image (tselem), which words are discussed on pages 91 (bottom) – 92.

tsel	90–30
etsel	1–90–30
tsela	90–30–70
tselem	90–30–40

Page 122, second paragraph. The door as 'four' in Jewish life therefore knows the 'one' in the form of the so-called Mezoozah, which binds the 'four' and connects them with the source of origin.

Pages 179-108. Connecting the 10-5 with the 6-5 similarly always occurs in the oral formulation of the preparation of certain important actions in Jewish life. For indeed those actions are supposed to form the connection of the 10-5 with the 6-5. The expression in Hebrew is 'lejacheed Shem Jod-Hee be-Waw-Hee', which in translation is 'to unite (in fact it says to make 'one') the Name 10-5 with the 6-5'. For that is the purpose of every action.

Page 184, sixth paragraph. Another word for garment is 'beged', 2-3-4, and that word also means 'false', 'falsify'. For covering up implies an obscuring, i.e. exteriorizing is a falsifying of the nucleus.

Page 186, third paragraph. In cases where, just as here with the 227, I make a connection between the total values of the components of the conceptions, the relationship is present of course in other ways as well, albeit very often not outwardly perceptible. There is more hidden in the numbers than can be brought into prominence in this book.

Page 186, fifth paragraph. This connection between the 'third' in the place of the 'child' in systematism, and the 'second', in systematism the place of the 'mother', which connection brings evil to the world, may very well prove to be the background of the story of Oedipus. It is the connection where the word 'good' is missing.

Page 190, second paragraph. That the fig tree represents this principle of the tree of the knowledge is probably also expressed in the numerous 'seeds' in the phenomenal form of this fruit, thus showing the urge to multiplicity, to the great fruitfulness. That is why in man's act of eating of the tree of the knowledge is also seen the sexual act. And through it one can also understand the purpose of the happening with the tree of the knowledge. For on the one hand there is the 'be fruitful and multiply', which God gives to man as the ninth word of creation and on the other hand there is the instruction not to eat of that tree. With God's utterance to be fruitful it is established that man is meant to eat of the tree of the knowledge. With it mankind comes into existence, man creates the next generation and with it accepts death. It expresses itself everywhere when it is a question of creating. With death as the consequence of the 'be fruitful and multiply', man is able to serve God 'gratuitously'. The conception 'creating' as the word expresses it, proceeds via the 'two', therefore also via the crossing of the threshold of death, so that after the 490 of this world man may enter the 500 of the coming world.

Just because the sexual act is an expression of eating of the tree of knowledge, it is essential that man does not accomplish this act for the sake of enjoyment, but only for the sake of the coming generation, taking upon himself the suffering of uncertain death in order to confer life. For this reason that this world may come to the realization of the real, the written Thorah the 'oral Thorah' contains a mighty complex of instructions concerning sexual relationships, endowing the paradox of the 'must' versus the 'shalt not' with the form through which it can indeed become a blessing in this life.

There is also a statement in tradition — not as contradiction but as an approach from another point of view — that the tree of knowledge is the tree on which grows the ultimate product of wheat. And that after eating of the tree of knowledge we must necessarily undergo the similar lengthy process of the wheat before the ultimate product, bread, is accomplished. Now wheat and fig, as first and fourth in systematism, are similarly connected.

On page 291 the subject of wheat and fig as tree of knowledge is entered into in greater detail.

Page 197, first paragraph. Since the tree of knowledge is taken on 'Friday afternoon', the Friday afternoon — also in its expression in our world — is a 'dangerous' moment for worldly initiatives. Therefore Jewish life has arranged things so as to enable people on Friday afternoon to concentrate on the coming of the Sabbath and on the preparations thereof, for the purpose of turning away from any contact with the world 'in development'. One therefore starts the Sabbath earlier than the day begins, astronomically.

Characteristic in this connection, also as regards the view of the early Chassidim in these things, is a story from Chassidic circles that the Riziner, one of the famous leaders of the Chassidim at the beginning of last century, was found one Friday afternoon in his room covered in clouds of smoke from his pipe. The Riziner told a story of a man who had lost his way in the forest on Friday afternoon and finally came upon a house, which he entered. Within he found a robber holding a gun. The traveller quickly seized the gun, thinking, 'if I get him with this shot, it is right; if not, the room will at any rate be filled with smoke because of the shot, and I can escape.' At that very moment the Riziner put down his pipe and said 'Sabbath'.

It is quite clear that the story points at the danger of the Friday afternoon, at man coming into the world and on entering this 'house' of the world being faced with a robber; a threat which he will have to remove, if he is not to perish himself. At any rate recognizing the danger and man's ensuing action, will procure for him the smoke-curtain to escape unnoticed from the Friday afternoon of the world of the seventh day into the world of the Sabbath.

Page 223, first paragraph. In the splitting up into the multiplicity of the phenomena of this world, the animals too have adopted various forms. The unsurveyable variety in the expression of creation can be looked upon as the crystallization or condensation in matter of God's thoughts and words which called into existence this creation. Every thought thus found its materialization in one of the innumerable forms of creation. The great variety of things created contains the endless variety and the all-embracing potentialities of God's thoughts concerning this world. That which is thought 'above' becomes form 'below'.

Pages 229–230. The attitude of man towards the things of the world is a.o. outlined in the following story from tradition (T.B. Sabbath 33b). In the presence of Rabbi Simon bar Jochai the Roman world was praised one day for its high culture and its sublime organization. Examples mentioned were its marketing-system, the monetary transactions, and hygiene. Simon bar Jochai, however, attacked Roman culture because to his mind the fundamental motives were vulgar egoism and propensity for sensual pleasure.

This negative, critical attitude brings him into conflict with the Roman authorities. To save his skin he has to make his escape with his son. They hide in a cave, where they remain for twelve years and in that period they make a profound study of the Thorah. In that cave they miraculously find sustenance, because a bread-tree grows there and there also is a well of clear water. At the end of those twelve years the prophet Elijah comes up to the entrance of the cave, calling out that the emperor has died and the danger for Simon bar Jochai is over. On leaving the cave they see people ploughing and sowing. This rouses their wrath, and they say: 'These people neglect the things of the life eternal and they busy themselves about things temporal.' And wherever Simon bar Jochai and his son direct their gaze, everything is burnt down. Then a voice is heard from heaven, saying, 'have you got out of the cave merely to destroy my world? Go back into your cave.' They return and take up their abode in the cave for another year. At the end of that time a voice from heaven makes them leave the cave anew. Back in the world they say a.o. 'A miracle has befallen us, therefore we want to do good.' Thereupon Simon bar Jochai goes and establishes markets, organizes the monetary system and takes measure in the field of hygiene. That is the end of the story!

However, everything has been said. Man is only able and allowed to approach matter, after he has learned to understand the purpose of life. When he occupies himself with development without knowing the purpose thereof, he is a Roman and can only have motives in the field of ambition, social status, voluptuousness. It is man's duty to renounce that world, just as Simon bar Jochai did, and to accept the consequences, being cast out by society. This expulsion from society indeed brings him to see the wonder of the world. When at the end of time – for the 'twelve' is identical with the end of time – he thinks he can judge the world, he is unfavourably disposed towards every material occupation. How can a man occupy himself with such foolish things, when the miracle of the Thorah exists, a miracle pointing the way to life eternal. This attitude, however, is destructive, it disregards the purpose of creation, which to the contrary insists on man's occupying himself with the world. The purpose of the world one cannot learn to know in the 'twelve', in 'time'. For up to and including that moment Simon bar Jochai has merely been in the 'twelve'.

Therefore now he enters the thirteenth year, the year granted to him anew in the cave after the 'twelve'. The 'thirteen' is outside time, and it is only then one learns to know the purpose of existence. Not until then does one see that it is incumbent on man to occupy himself with the world, most intensively, to the very details. For it is exactly through this occupation with the world on the part of the man who knows the purpose of things, that this world can be united with the origin again. The tree of life is the tree that is fruit and makes fruit. The part that 'makes fruit' is just as indispensable to that tree as the part that 'is fruit'. The right attitude towards that part which makes fruit, which is development, however, cannot be adopted until one has entered the world beyond time. Just as Reuben and Gad could not occupy the land of the giants until they had entered the land of the coming world. Only then one is able to live in this world and unite it to the other world (vide pages 488 and 489).

So the story of Simon bar Jochai, like so many other stories from ancient lore, tells us that there must definitely be contact with matter, with development but that it depends on what kind of man has that contact, and that one can only have contact with good, if one is pervaded by good through abiding in another world. Then one has oneself become like the 'tree that is fruit', which through its contact with the world, with development, comes to realization of the tree of life, through uniting the 'tree that makes fruit' with itself. This unity of the 'one' with the 'four' is the secret of this life.

Page 290, fourth paragraph. Wheat as the first of the seven fruits therefore means the beginning of multiplicity, just as the first day of creation was the beginning with the 'two'. Wheat therefore is not the 'one'. This 'one' stands outside the seven of the multiplicity of this world. With the wheat, in fact, multiplicity starts and therefore it has the place of the tree of knowledge, just as the fig has got that place in the second triad in the systematism of the seven fruits.

Page 309, penultimate paragraph. This world as the world of the left side, the female world, therefore has the character of desiring to receive, desiring to wait for things. It is ready, like the woman, to receive the man. It is looking out for the man, like the woman in the Song of Solomon.

Page 310, last paragraph. Concerning the significance of disproving statements of the witnesses as a matter of principle in order to rule out the execution of 'capital punishment', let me quote the pronouncement of Rabbi Tarphon and Rabbi Akiba (Mishnajoth Makkoth 1:10) 'If we had held a seat in the Sanhedrin, no man would ever have been executed.' These two held that they would have been able to show under any circumstances that one must never base definite conclusions on observations in this world.

Page 320, sixth paragraph. To Esau, who cannot understand this sorrow, this unassimilated grief becomes the foundation of his view of life. That is why he cannot bring the 'korban'. For it must be brought full of joy. And if unassimilated grief becomes the basis of thought, a sham-world is created to escape into. Setbacks drive man to this sham-world. Esau was shocked at death and did not know the purpose of it.

Page 321, second paragraph. Tradition tells about Esau that he pondered on the question, whether one had to pay tithes on salt and straw. Esau is willing to bring as offerings that which is practically useless to his own life. That which is valuable to this life in the world of development to his mind must not be involved. It is the tragedy of the man who does not realize that it is this very body, this very life here, which should be hallowed, united with God; and that in letting this life ostensibly 'free', yet claiming for himself that other thing, the blessing, he cannot get anywhere except in an illusory world, poisoned by intoxication.

Page 348, second paragraph. In the outer court of the women, there was the so-called lesser Sanhedrin where the legal cases appeared. The great Sanhedrin, principally treating on affairs of state and religious matters, had a place within the wall of the second court.

Page 349. Acting with the body in our world, involving the body and its actions in one's search for God, therefore is equivalent to bringing the animal back from the atmosphere of development to the source of origin. The point at issue is the animal, the body, which has got to be emancipated through man's breaking away from development. Through it man achieves the union of the two extremes, of soul and body, here in this world.

Page 350, second and third paragraphs. The feast of the tabernacles, in the expression of this world is the time of the end. Then the world of the seventh day ceases to exist. Therefore during this feast there is the so-called 'pouring out of the water' (Mishnajoth Sukkah IV and V). With great rejoicings water is brought into the temple and poured on the altar. It therefore means that in that place where image and substance are 'one', water, i.e. time, is poured out, where the body ever departed in consequence of time, where it passed from this world to the other. Now time comes to an end, and it is experienced with immense joy at that place. During all this happening, the Levites stand on the fifteen steps, leading from the court of Israel to the court of the women. They descend these fifteen steps with music and singing. These fifteen steps are associated with the 15 Psalms, 120–134. They are also known to us as the 10–5 of the name Lord God, which has to be connected with the 6–5. The Levites therefore do not descend these 15 steps straightaway, but they first go down 5 steps and then 10 steps, before going to the entrance-gate, where they make the statement that the fathers had still been conscious of time – at that moment they are facing the east, in the direction of the origin of time – but that people now only see God. Viewed from the world these 15 steps of the transition are the 10–5.

Page 369, second paragraph. The world of Canaan, as it is promised, is a world entirely different from this our world. The Bible characterizes it in saying that people will live in houses they have not built themselves, that they will gather grapes from vineyards they have not planted themselves. With it the Bible expresses the world of the eighth day, the world of the tree of life, of the tree that 'is fruit and makes fruit'. Everything is ready there, is fruit already, just like the land of Cockaigne of the fairy-tale where people could enter only after removing innumerable obstacles.

Page 387, fourth and fifth paragraphs. Adam's intercourse with Lilith is the result of non-assimilation of the grief coming over him on account of Cain and Abel. It is therefore maintained that deep, uncomprehended sorrow, in any field brings people to sexual dissipation or sexual aberrations. This is also included in 'intercourse with Lilith'.

Pages 416–417, last and first paragraphs. On the eighth day there is the salvation, then one sees that one is emancipated from the forces of development, from the covering. Therefore the eighth day is the day of circumcision. And therefore it is the custom at a circumcision in the Synagogue, that the man who has performed the circumcision, should in unison with the others recite line by line the so-called Hymn of Moses, where occurs the passage through the 'sea' and the destruction of the Egyptians (Exod. 15).

Page 424, third paragraph. The serpent's poison remains active throughout the seventh day. It is the power of development which makes everything grow and change, which therefore kills also. Owing to this change every previous moment dies. Not until the seventh day is past, will the 'poison' have ceased working and be eliminated.

Pages 473, third paragraph, 474 and 475, first three paragraphs. The attitude of life in the desert, on the way from the 'two' to the 'one', is entirely different from that of the world of duality. And from the Egyptian point of view the rebellion against this change is quite intelligible. Ancient lore gives some characteristic details about it. One of them in Talmud Babli, Sanhedrin 109b–110a, for instance tells about a case on which Korach based his criticism on the way of Moses. A poor widow who could just manage to make both ends meet on the produce of a small patch of land, every time she tried to extend her property was urged by Moses now to forgo this, now that, and not to try to make any productive improvements. So the widow sold her field and bought two sheep that she might be clothed with the wool and live on the sale of the lambs. But the first lamb and the wool were claimed by Aaron who took it away again from this world. When therefore she made up her mind she had better kill the animals, Aaron came again and claimed a large share. In despair at these constant demands on the part of Moses and Aaron she put a ban on the meat of the animals. But then Aaron took everything since all that is banned is altogether for God. On the ground of such things Korach was brought to rebellion.

Now it was this sort of life in which not a single action is 'free', in which everything was referred to God, to another world, which was unbearable to Korach and his followers. It is the universal revolt against relating everything in this life to God, against lack of freedom to develop according to one's own standards, just as in Egypt, in the world of duality, everything could develop. For indeed, the 'poor widow', i.e. man in this world, never gets a chance of expanding on this way to the 'one'. If man wants that, he will undergo Moses and Aaron as a constant plague, as an exasperating nuisance. Only he that really desires to go the way to Canaan, will experience joy in this attitude of life which represents an inner experience of the Bible in this world. As for the others: one should not think scornfully of Korach's revolt. It is the everlasting rebellion of the many against the path of the solitary.

Page 486, third paragraph. The service to Baal-Peor implies unrestrained sexual life, sexual depravity in word, custom and behaviour, with the physical woman as the centre of the service, such as it always expresses itself at the end of time. It is the way of Moab and Midian who appear both of them at the end of the journey across the wilderness. At that point, of time, it spells great danger and it is the point at which the world undertakes its last assault. When everything on the way has been conquered, even the giants, and although the sublime future has been proclaimed, the world comes with the seductive woman, with the temptation of matter and development, and causes a castastrophe. It shows the greatness of Phinehas who according to ancient lore for that very reason continues to live as Elijah, that he may be able to arrest this fall. Because of it he indeed becomes Elijah and the harbinger of ultimate salvation.

Statement of the Sources of Sagas Employed

In this register most passages in which 'sagas' are mentioned have been verified by stating one or more sources from this vast field. It is impossible to enumerate all the sources of every saga. For, as often as not, the same subjects are elucidated in their various aspects in diverse places. I have, however, endeavoured to supply the interested reader with a statement of the sources, as complete and illustrative as possible for the purpose of this book. One will thus be able to form an idea how an insight into the purpose of existence can be built up like a mosaic for which were borrowed building-bricks from the inexhaustible treasures scattered about everywhere in the vast complex of these sagas. The reader is begged to regard the mosaic shown in this book as the mere floor of a humble anteroom from which he is eventually to gain entrance to the palace.

Abbreviations will be used of some works or collections frequently mentioned in the statement of the sources. They are:

T. B. Talmud Babli (The treatise referred to will be mentioned in toto after the T. B.)
M. R. Midrash Rabbah (Behind the M. R. is mentioned which part is meant)
M. T. Midrash Tanchumah
P. E. Pirke de-Rabbi Eliezer
S. J. Sepher ha-Jashar

Of the smaller collections no detailed indications are given. Their arrangement is sometimes dependent on specific editions and the passages moreover are fairly easy to find in the majority of cases, since they run parallel with the text of the story of the Bible.

Page 23 Nimrod throws Abraham into the lime-kiln: T. B. Pesachim 118 a; Midrash Shirha-Shirim I; M. T. Toldoth; S. J.; P. E.; on Abraham and Nimrod in general, vide M. R. Bereshith 38; Seder Elijahu Zuttah; Midrash ha-Gadol and most especially S. J.

Page 66 'let us make men': T. B. Sanhedrin 38 b; M. R. Bereshith 17:5; Midrash ha-Neelam.

Page 75 Only in very special circumstances and in a very special place can the name Lord God be pronounced: T. B. Jomah 66 a.

Page 77 The way which started from the tree of the knowledge, ends at Mount Sinai: T. B. Jebamoth 103 b; T. B. Aboda Zarah 22 b.

Page 79 God looked in the Thorah and by means of it created the world: M. R. Bereshith 1:2.

Page 90 The two countenances of primeval man: M. R. Bereshith 8:1.

Page 91 Adultery with the beasts: T. B. Jebamoth 63 a.

Page 100 Compass of the tree of life: M. R. Bereshith 15:7.

Page 104 The Eben Shetijah: Tosseftah Jomah III:6.

Page 118 be-Abraham: M. R. Bereshith 12:8.

Page 128 Paradise: Targum Jonathan on Gen. 3:24 and Targum Jerushalmi on same; T. B. Berachoth 17 a.

Page 129 No circumcision in the wilderness: T. B. Jebamoth 71 b–72 a.

Page 134 The 'spirits' at the end of the sixth day: M. R. Bereshith 7:7; P. E.; Mishnajoth Aboth v:9.

Page 135 Adam thinks the world is destroyed; but the Sabbath comes: T. B. Aboda Zara 8 a; P. E.; Aboth de-Rabbi Nathan; Pessikta de-Rabbi Kahana; Pessikta Rabbathi.

Page 135 Moses and David die on the afternoon of the Sabbath: Seder Olam; Jalkuth Shimeoni; T. B. Sabbath 33 a–b.

Page 135 After the Sabbath comes the Messiah: T. B. Sanhedrin 97 a; T. B. Megillah 17 b.

Page 137 Serah: S. J.

Page 139 Serah in Egypt: Midrash Agada on Exod. 13:17; P. E.; Aboth de-Rabbi Nathan.

Page 139 Serah lives to be very old: S. J.

Page 142 Pupils of Akibah: T. B. Jebamoth 62 b.

Page 144 Dudaim: Midrash ha-Galuj.

Page 151 Stars removed: T. B. Rosh ha-Shana l lb–12 a.

Page 155 The land Canaan 400 Parsa: M. T. Shelach.

Page 155 Man covers a distance of 10 parsa a day: T. B. Pesachim 94 a.

Page 156 Solomon: Targum Sheni I:2.

Page 165 The 86 years: P. E.

Page 167 Abraham 70 years: S. J.

Page 185 Samael and the Camel: P. E.

Page 188 The eyes of man: Midrash Shir ha-Shirim; M. T. Wajikra; M. R. Bamidbar 13:7; T. B. Sanhedrin 38 a–b; T. B. Chigiga 12 a.

Page 190 The figtree: T. B. Sanhedrin 70 b; T. B. Berachoth 40 a; M. R. Bereshith 15:8; M. T.

Page 193 Ajeka: M. R. Bereshith 19:18.

Page 197 The Speed of Time: M. R. Bereshith 10:4.

Page 197 The earlier worlds: Aboth de-Rabbi Nathan; Midrash haNeelam; Emek ha-Melech.

Page 198 Thorah is the Tree of Life: Mishnajoth Aboth VI:7; M. R. Bereshith 12:5; Targum Jonathan and Targum Jerushalmi on Gen. 3:24.

Page 200 The 26th generation: T. B. Jabamoth 103 b; T. B. Aboda Zara 22 h.

Page 201 Tob mend: M. R. Bereshith 9:5.

Page 214 The earth is also 'cursed':vide Rashie on Gen. 1:11.

Page 224 The flame on Abel's offering: S. J.

Page 232 Cain's death: M. T. Bereshith; S. J.

Page 236 Reuben and the 13: T. B. Sabbath 55 b; M. R. Bereshith 98:7.

Page 238 Egypt and the daughters: M. R. Shemoth 1:22.

Page 243 Adam recites psalm 92: P. E.

Page 249 The teba: M. R. Bereshith 31:13; vide also Rashie on Gen. 6:16.

Page 253 The beasts block the entrance: S. J.

Page 257 The distress in the teba: M. R. Bereshith 32:20; cf. also Rashie on Gen. 7:23.

Page 260 The dove and the oliveleaf: T. B. Sanhedrin 108 b; P. E.

Page 270 Ham sees Noah: T. B. Sanhedrin 70 a.

Page 273 Canaan sees Noah: M. R. Bereshith 36:8.

Page 278 Details about the pinnacle: M. R. Bereshith 38; M. T. Noah; P.E; S. J.; Tossefta Sanhedrin XIII:7; Midrash ha-Gadol; Jalkuth Reubeni; Berith Menucha.

Page 278 The language of the Bible: M. R. Bereshith 18:6; Midrash ha-Gadol.

Page 279 Details about the tower: S. J.

Page 279 The six thousand years: T. B. Sanhedrin 97 a–b.

Page 282 The catastrophe of the Haflaga: S.J.

Page 285 Shem and Heber: M.R. Bereshith 37:10, 63:15 and 66:16 and 20; S.J.

Page 285 Pishon-Nile: according to Gaon Saadja, Rashie, Ibn Ezra, Nachmanides.

Page 286 Solomon rules the world: Targum Sheni I:2.

Page 287 Legend about Abraham: S.J.

Page 288 Abraham's Departure: Midrash ha-Neelam.

Page 288 Haran imitating Abraham: S.J.

Page 288 Lot as the Serpent: Midrash ha-Neelam.

Page 293 God leading Abraham outside: M.R. Bereshith 44:12–15.

Page 294 Stories about Sodom: S.J.; M.R. Bereshith 49:9ff; T.B. Sanhedrin 109 a–b; P.E.

Page 294 Mine is Mine; Mishnajoth Aboth v:13.

Page 296 Isaac looks like Abraham: T.B. Baba Metsia 87a; M.R. Shemoth 1:1.

Page 297 The two servants: S.J.

Page 297 Keturah is Hagar: M.R. Bereshith 61:4.

Page 300 The beast of the Akedah has been ready ever since creation: S.J.; Talmud Jerushalmi Taanith 65; Mishnajoth Aboth v:9.

Page 301 Details about the Akedah: S.J.; M.T.; P.E.; Aboth de-Rabbi Nathan; T.B. Sanhedrin 89b; M.R. Bereshith 55 end and 56; Midrash ha-Gadol.

Page 301 Satan and the Akedah: S.J.

Page 302 Isaac 37 years: P.E.; Jalkuth ('Toldoth); M.R. Shemoth 1:1.

Page 302 Isaac dies at the Akedah: P.E.; Midrash ha-Gadol.

Page 304 A kid of the goats before the Lord: T.B. Chulin 60b; M.R. Bereshith 6:4.

Page 304 Sun and Moon: T.B. Chulin 60b.

Page 308 The division into three parts of man: cf. Abraham ibn Ezra on Gen. 3:23.

Page 308 Rebekah as Eve: Nof Ets Chaim; Midrash ha-Gadol.

Page 310 Esau's wives make Isaac blind: M.T. Toldoth.

Page 310 Justice: T.B. Sanhedrin 17a; T.B. Makkoth 7a.

Page 311 Moses at the well: folktale in tradition with reference to T.B. Berachoth 7a and T.B. Makkoth 1013.

Page 313 Birth of Isaac: T.B. Rosh ha-Shana 11a.

Page 315 The beast hiding itself: M.T. Toldoth; P.E.; Midrash ha-Gadol.

Page 316 The appearance of Elijah: T.B. Sabbath 33b and 109b; T.B. Jebamoth 63a; T.B. Berachoth 4b; T.B. Aboda Zara 17h; Midrash Esther Rabba; Tana de-be Elijahu; Pessikta Rabbathi; on ground a living legend, also in the course of centuries since.

Page 320 The lentils, the mess of pottage; S.J.; P.E.; M.R. Bereshith 63:16–20; Midrash ha-Gadol; T.B. Baba Bathra 16b.

Page 321 Jacob learns the Thorah: M.R. Bereshith 63:15; M.R. Shemoth 1:1.

Page 324 Dust whirling up to heaven: T.B. Chulin 91a.

Page 324 The 'sae of Esau: T.B. Chulin 92a; M.R. Bereshith 77:2.

Page 325 Biting and Kissing: M.R. Bereshith 78:12.

Page 325 Esau returning by himself: M.R. Bereshith 78:19.

Page 325 The small jar: T.B. Chulin 91a.

Page 328 The various patches: cf. Redak on Gen. 37:3.

Page 329 The snail-shell: Zohar on beginning of Genesis.

Page 331 Joseph sees the image of Jacob: T.B. Sota 36b.

Page 344 The ten sons of Benjamin: M.R. Bereshith 94:7.

Page 347 Jacob and Joseph: S.J.; Aboth de-Rabbi Nathan.

Page 347 Tabernacle and Creation: M. T. Pekudeh; M. R. Bamidbar 13:8.
Page 349 Leviathan: T. B. Baba Bathra 74–75 a; Midrash Konen (in Beth ha-Midrash); Emek ha-Melech.
Page 350 Tabernacles in the wilderness: Lev. 23:43.
Page 350 Gog and Magog: T. B. Pesachim 118 a.
Page 353 The strip of Judah through Benjamin: T. B. Zebachim 53 b–54 a.
Page 362 The two Messiahs: T. B. Sukkah 52 a–b.
Page 363 Sambation: T. B. Sanhedrin 65 b; Talmud Jerushalmi Sanhedrin 10; M. R. Bereshith 73:5; Pessikta Rabbathi; Echa Rabbathi.
Page 365 David and the tree: T. B. Sabbath 33 a–b; cf. also Mishnajoth Aboth III:9.
Page 369 Death of Moses: T. B. Sota 13 b; Sifreh Debarim; M. R. Debarim 2, 7, 11; P. E.; Mechilthah Beshallach; M. T. We-Etchanan; Midrash ha-Gadol.
Page 373 Adam and Eve in Machpela: M. R. Bereshith 58:4.
Page 377 Connecting the names: cf. Rashie on Exod. 1:1.
Page 378 The welfare of the 'oppressed' in Egypt: M. R. Shemoth 14:3.
Page 379 Levi exempt from work: S. J.
Page 380 At first wages were paid: S. J.
Page 382 Egypt knows the Saviour shall come: S. J.
Page 382 Shifrah and Puah: M. R. Shemoth 1:17.
Page 383 Miriam and Caleb: T. B. Sota 11 b.
Page 383 Adultery with the daughters: M. R. Shemoth 1:22.
Page 387 The birth of Moses: T. B. Sota 12 a–b; S. J.
Page 387 Lilith and Adam: T. B. Chagigah 17 a.
Page 387 The Shedim: T. B. Chulin 105 b; T. B. Chagigah 16 a; Talmud Jerushalmi Berachoth 5, 6; Aboth de-Rabbi Nathan.
Page 389 Jochebed born at the boundary: T. B. Sota 12 a; M. R. Bereshith 94:8.
Page 390 Pharaoh has misgivings: S. J.
Page 391 Moses after his flight: S. J.
Page 392 The fear of being born: Mishnajoth Aboth IV:29; Seder Jetsirah ha-Wlad (in Beth ha-Midrash).
Page 395 Moses in the inn: T. B. Nedarim 31 b–32 a; cf. also Rashie on Exod. 4:24.
Page 400 Raa: Midrash Jalkuth.
Page 406 The blood of the circumcision: Mechiltha Bo.
Page 409 Pharaoh refuses to know Joseph: M. T. Shemoth.
Page 411 Afterbirth: cf. Preuss: Biblisch Talmudische Medizin.
Page 413 The sextuples: M. T. Pekudeh.
Page 414 Seeing at the end: P. E.; Midrash Wajosha (in Beth ha-Midrash); Jalkuth Shimeoni (Deut); Mechiltha Beshallach; T. B. Sota 30 b.
Page 415 Pharaoh in Nineveh: S. J.; Midrash Wajosha (in Beth ha-Midrash).
Page 418 The seven names of Jethro; M. R. Shemoth 1:39.
Page 422 The letters on two sides: T. B. Sabbath 104 a.
Page 424 Man is the world: Mishnajoth Sanhedrin IV:5.
Page 424 The poison of the serpent ceases to operate at Mount Sinai: T. B. Jebamoth 103 b; T. B. Abodah Zarah 22 b.
Page 429 The descendants of the Haflaga: S. J.
Page 434 The constellations revolve more slowly: M. R. Bereshith 10:4.
Page 436 The revelation transforms the world: T. B. Sabbath 88 b; M. T. Jethro; M. R. Wajikra 3; Midrash Tehillim on Ps. 8; P. E.; Mechilthah Jethro.
Page 437 Satan at Mount Sinai: T. B. Sabbath 89 a; M. R. Shemoth 41:10.

Page 438 Aaron claims offerings: P.E.; M.T. Ki Tissah; T.B. Sabbath 89 a.

Page 440 The Wagons of Joseph: M.R. Bereshith 94:3.

Page 440 In Sodom, Passover: M.R. Bereshith 50:22.

Page 443 The Calf came as a matter of course: M.T. Ki Tissah.

Page 444 I-lur: M.R. Shemoth 41:10; M.T. Wajakhel.

Page 444 The rejoicings round the calf: M.R. Shemoth 41:11; cf. also Rashie on Exod. 32:6 and on Exod. 32:18.

Page 445 Taking off the ornaments: T.B. Sabbath 88 a.

Page 446 Levi keeps apart: P.E.

Page 448 Satan throws the calculation into confusion: T.B. Sabbath 89 a; M.R. Shemoth 41:10.

Page 449 The exodus of Ephraim: Mechiltha Beshallach; P.E.; Pessikta de-Rabbi Kahana; S.J.

Page 451 Serah points at Moses: Midresh Agadah on Exod. 13:17; P.E.; M.R. Shemoth 3:11.

Page 452 The highpriest counts: T.B. Jomah 66 a.

Page 455 The optimism of Aaron: M.R. Shemoth 41:10.

Page 459 The calculation of the dates: cf. Rashie on Exod. 32:1.

Page 460 The Difference in the tables' coming about: M.T. Ki Tissah.

Page 463 The cloud over the Tabernacle; M.R. Debarim 7:10; Sifreh; cf. also Rashie on Num. 9:17–18.

Page 465 Definition of the Wilderness: M.T. on Deut. 29:4; M.R. Shemoth 44:1; cf. also commentary Jacob Emden on Perek Shirah I.

Page 467 Garments in the wilderness: M.R. Debarim 7:11.

Page 467 The North-wind: T.B. Jebamoth 71 b–72 a.

Page 469 The ereb rab: M.T. Shemoth.

Page 470 The accompanying for the sake of the advantage: M.T. Shemoth.

Page 471 Failing ten times in the wilderness: T.B. Erechin 15 a; Mishnajoth Aboth v:7.

Page 472 Manna: T.B. Joma 75 a–b; Sifreh (Numbers); Mechiltha.

Page 474 The well of Miriam: T.B. Tossefta on Sota III:11; M.T.

Page 475 Exile of the Shechinah: T.B. Megillah 29 a; cf. Kabbalah Literature.

Page 476 Shiloh is Moses: Bereshith Rabbathi.

Page 477 The spies: T.B. Sota 34 b–35 a; T.B. Baba Bathra 15 a; 118 b; Talmud Jerushalmi Taanith IV; Jelamdenu; T.B. Menachoth 53 b; M.T. Shelach; Seder Elijahu Rabba; Targum on Gen. 6:4; Othioth de-Rabbi Akiba.

Page 484 Sihon and Og: S.J.; Midrash Tehillim; M.T. Mishpattim; M.T. Chukkath; M.R. Debarim 1:21–22; T.B. Berachoth 54 b; T.B. Nidda 61 a.

Page 485 Bileam: M.T. Mattoth; M.T. Balak; Sifreh (Num.); M.R. Bamidhar 22:5; Jelamdenu; S.J.

Page 491 Moses surveys the whole at the end: Mechiltha Beshallach; Sifreh (Num. and Deut.)

Page 491 The 49 gates of insight with Moses: T.B. Rosh ha-Shanah 21 b; T.B. Nedarin 38 a.

Page 491 The steps up Mount Nebo: T.B. Sota 13 b.

Page 492 Prenatal man: Seder Jetsirath ha-Wlad (in Beth ha-Midrash).

Page 493 Mount Nebo in Reuben and sepulchre in Gad: T.B. Sota 13 b.

Page 495 The end of the seventh day: Seder Olam; Jalkuth Shimeoni.

Bibliography
of the main sources of Tradition

Ancient lore can be subdivided into halacha, agada, midrash and targum. The halacha means 'going', 'the way' and it contains the directions for the daily practice of life, that it may be in every one of its expressions an inner experience, a realization, and concretization in this world of the structure which the Thorah reveals of the substance of the world and of man.

With agada (from Aramaic 'agadete', which in Hebrew is 'hagada', meaning story, explanation, information, instruction) is generally meant the body of information about the meaning of the Bible, very often clothed in the form of stories.

In the oral doctrine they form the commentary on the Bible, handed down by word of mouth 'from Mount Sinai', thus forming the bridge from the Bible to the practice of life, and thus giving content to the halacha. As it is expressed in the Sifri commentary in Deuteronomy (Ekeb): 'if you desire to recognize Him who spoke, learn to know the agada.'

Midrash (from the word 'derash', meaning search, examine, investigate, explain, elucidate) like agada forms a complex of information on the Bible, handed down by word of mouth and for the greater part collected severally at a later date and taken down in writing. Targum (the word means 'translation') is an explanatory translation from Hebrew into Aramaic of the text of the Pentateuch and other parts of the Bible. Through a paraphrastic translation Targum often gives indications as to the direction in which the explanation must be sought.

The concise bibliography given herewith contains the principal works and collections of the oldest sagas which have appeared in print. Several of these works have been repeatedly published, also recently. There are also a great number of new collections and anthologies.

It seems superfluous to state that all publications merely contain the exterior text and the exterior commentaries of the sagas, and that, without knowledge of the master key, about which this book has tried to give some information, they can hardly be more than strange, sometimes interesting but often quite unintelligible stories and communications.

Of a number of these works there are translations, also in the form of anthologies. One of the most conveniently arranged, is the collection of M.J. bin Gorion: Die Sagen der Juden. The objection mentioned previously of the meaning being obscure, ipso facto applies in a still higher degree to the translations. Nevertheless, if one has understood the purport of my prudently conceived introductory book, one will be able to penetrate a little more deeply

through the outer skin of the stories into the works mentioned. At any rate one will have learnt to be very careful with one's personal interpretations.

Aboth de-Rabbi Nathan (a Midrash on Pirke Aboth')

Agada Agadoth (a collection of Midrashim)
Agadath Bereshith (Midrash-explanation of Genesis)
Baraitha de-Shmoeel ha Katan (Midrash in the field of astronomy) Bereshith Rabbathi (Midrash on Genesis)
Beth ha-Midrash (collection of Midrashim)
Derech Erets Zuttah (treatise on mode of living)
Ein Jacob (collection of the agadaic parts of the Talmud)
Ektan de-Mar Jacob (Midrashim)
Jalkuth Eliezer (collection from Midrash and Talmud)
Jalkuth Shimeoni (collection from Midrash and Talmud, arranged in accordance with the Bible)
Jalkuth Sippurim (collection of stories from the Talmud and the Midrash)
Likkutim me-Midrash ele ha-Debarim Zuttah (Midrash on Deuteronomy)
Lekketh Midrashim (collection of Midrashim)
Mechilthah (halachaic Midrash on Exodus)
Midrash Agada (Agada-commentary on Pentateuch)
Midrash Chaseroth we-Jetheroth (Midrash-collection)
Midrash ha-Gadol (Midrash-collection on Genesis)
Midrash Koheleth Rabba (Midrash on Ecclesiastes)
Midrash Lekach Tob (Agada-commentary on Genesis and Exodus) Midrash Mishle (Midrash on Proverbs)
Midrash Othioth de-Rabbi Akibah (Midrash on the alphabet)
Midrash Rabbah (Extensive Midrash-commentary on Pentateuch, subdivided after the five books: Bereshith Rabbah (commentary on Genesis), Shmoth Rabbah (explanation on Exodus), Wajikrah Rabbah (explanation of Leviticus), Bamidhar Rabbah (explanation of Numbers) and Debarum Rabbah (commentary on Deuteronomy)
Midrash Sechel Tob (Midrash on Genesis and Exodus)
Midrash Shir ha-Shirim (Midrash on the Song of Solomon)
Midrash Shmoeel (Midrash on Samuel)
Midrash Tadshe (Midrash on Pentateuch)
Midrash Tanaim (Midrash on Deuteronomy)
Midrash Tanchumah (also called 'Jelamdenu'. Midrash on Pentateuch)
Midrash Tehillim (also called 'Shocher Tob'. Midrash on Psalms)
Midrash Zuttah (explanations of the Song of Solomon, Ruth, Lamentations and Ecclesiastes)
Mishnajoth (the earliest written part of the oral Thorah, containing 6 vols.)
Otsar Agadoth (anthology from Midrash and Talmud)
Otsar Midrashim Kitwe Jad (collection of Midrashim)
Perek Shirah (characteristic savings on heaven and earth, the heavenly bodies, men, animals and plants)
Pesiktah de-Rab Kahanah (Midrash on the feasts and the Sabbath) Pesikta Rabbathi (Midrash on the feasts)
Pirke de-Rabbi Eliezer (stories in Midrash-form on Pentateuch)
Seder Elijahu Rabba (also called 'Tana de-be-Elijahu'. Book with Agada-character, according to tradition inspired by the prophet Elijah)
Seder Olam Rabba (ancient chronicle)
Sepher ha-Jashar (legends, analogous to the story of the Bible)
Sepher ha-Likkutim (collection of Midrashim)
Sifrah (halachaic Midrash on Leviticus)
Sifre de-agadete (Midrash on Esther)
Sifri (halachaic Midrash on Numbers and Deuteronomy)
Talmud Babli (the Babylonic Talmud, the oral Thorah ultimately written down,

in which are incorporated the 'Mishnajoth', 36 extensive treatises, collected in six divisions)
Talmud Jerushalmi (the Jerusalem Talmud; similarly containing the oral Thorah, but much less comprehensive than the Babylonian Talmud)
Targum Jerushalmi
 (Targum of Pentateuch)
Targum Jonathan
 (Targum of Pentateuch)
Targum Onkelos
 (Targum of Pentateuch)
Targum Sheni
 (Targum of the Book Esther)

In the commentaries on the Bible of Solomon Jitschaki (Rashi) and David Kimchi (Redak), accomplished respectively in the eleventh and thirteenth centuries, the sagas mentioned above still play an important part as starting-point for the explanations. In our times, however, they in their turn require ample elucidation to grasp the relationships indicated, and this elucidation is difficult to give without the reader's knowledge of the structure of the substance. Yet one can, exteriorly, draw a good deal of information from these commentaries, if one has understood the contents of this book. These explanations will then point the right way to the sagas.

The halachaic part of the sagas, forming the basis for the daily conduct of life, practised throughout the centuries, were systematically grouped together in the work 'Mishne Thorah' of Moses ben Maimon (Rambam of Maimonides) in the twelfth century, when insight and vision were rapidly deteriorating. In this domain later on were as yet accomplished the 'Arbaa Turim' of Jacob Asheri (beginning of the fourteenth century) and the 'Shulchan Aruch' of Joseph Karo (sixteenth century) which books on Jewish life are similarly of great repute. Without knowledge of this halacha, the Bible cannot be understood. But even to grasp the meaning of this halacha, insight into the structure of the substance is likewise a conditio sine qua non.

Index
(for oe read u)

Aaron 349, 388, 392, 393, 402, 403, 411, 437–439, 443, 449, 454–456, 461, 473, 484
Abel 73, 104, 221–222, 223–227, 228, 231, 237, 241–242, 276–277, 303, 323, 328–329, 356–357, 382, 387, 407–408
Abimelech 23, 303
Abraham 22, 23, 25, 74, 81, 100–101, 117–119, 128–129, 145–146, 148, 163, 165, 167, 168, 170–172, 251, 286, 291, 292–295, 303, 308, 320, 323, 349, 364, 373–374, 414, 449–450, 451–452, 484–485
Accompany 349–350
Adam 43, 80, 81–82, 134–135, 199–200, 228–229, 236–237, 243–244, 252–253, 308, 313, 364, 373, 387, 388, 427–428, 475
Ages 81–82
Ai 288–289, 292–293
Ajeka 193
Ajin 41, 196, 208–209, 231, 274
Akeda, *see also* Bind 302, 308, 313–314, 351–352
Akiba 142
Aleph 39–43, 83–85, 87–91, 102–103, 114–115, 132–133, 138, 174–175, 196, 208, 209–210, 300, 303–304, 316–317, 347–348, 370, 373, 402, 421–422, 458
Alphabet 40–41, 66–67, 99
Altar 298–299, 347–348, 352–353, 355
Alternative 66–67, 78–79, 87–88, 94, 122–125, 129–130, 132–133, 145–146, 191, 194–195, 272–273, 429–431, 446, 447, 471, 487–488
Amalek 358–359

Amen 199–200
Ammon 275–277
Amram 81–82, 163–164, 387, 388–390
Anantomy 145–146, 267
Anochi 424
Angels 151–152, 158, 193–194, 245, 342–343, 395, 440
Approaching downfall 279–280
Aprons 189–190, 195
Ararat 251–252, 253, 255
Ark of Covenant 132–133, 175, 178–179, 236, 298–299, 347–349, 355–356, 452, 463–464
Ark of Noah, *see* Teba
Art 230, 231
Ashamed 98, 188–189, 195–196, 307
Asher 131–133, 135–136, 138–142, 450–451
Asnath 337–338
Ass 144–147, 297–299, 393–394
Assur 360
Atonement, Day of 316, 459–460
Attack 191
Attractive power 197–199, 219, 227–228, 233–235, 246–247, 280–281, 387, 468–469, 470–471
Automatic protection 196–197, 200

Baal-Peor 486–487
Baal-Shem 76
Babel 59–61, 177–178, 246–247, 281
Baker 331–333
Balak 484–485
Beast 20, 23–24, 32–33, 44–45, 62–66, 73–74, 91–95, 106, 146–147, 155–156, 167, 191–192, 196, 222–223, 232–233,

253–254, 266–267, 269–270, 297–300, 309, 316–319, 321, 328–329, 347–355, 364, 398–401, 409–410, 486–487, 495
Beginning 65–66, 82
Beginning- In the 56, 63–70, 72, 83 (foot)–84, 98–104, 116–117, 178–179, 209, 424
Behibaram 116–117, 118
Belief, *see* Faith
Benjamin 184–185, 327, 341, 343–345, 352–355, 358–359, 361–362
Bereshith, *see* Beginning- In the
Beth 39–41, 56, 78–79, 116–117, 119–120, 179–180, 208, 332, 405–406, 413, 424
Bethel 288–290, 292–293
Bethlehem 290–291, 327, 330–331, 484
Bethuel 148
Betsalel 463–464
Bileam 484–487
Bilha 22, 327–328
Bind, *see also* Akeda 299–300, 302, 306–307, 312, 329–330, 351–352, 392
Birds 167
Birth 122, 128–129, 245, 382–383, 411, 413–414, 491–492
Birth pangs 254, 323–324
Bitter 260–261
Blessing 25, 73–74, 131, 270, 277, 313, 315, 316–323, 489
Blind 25–26, 309–310, 313
Blood 43–44, 298–299, 329–330, 352–353, 406, 452–453
Boaz 291
Bondage 73–74, 85–86, 95, 99–100, 122, 125–126, 139–141, 149–150, 168–171, 271 (foot)–238, 241, 272–273, 290, 308 (foot)–309, 374, 388–389, 408–409, 411 (foot)–412, 417, 423–424, 446, 454 (foot)–455, 471
Bones, *see* Dry bones
Boundary 362–363, 464–465, 472, 484, 485–486, 489 (foot)–491
Brains 164–165

Brass – serpent of brass 395, 396
Bread 105, 204, 291, 330–334, 355, 406–407, 416–417, 426–427
Bride 135 (foot)–136
Brother 343–344
Bull 306–307, 335, 351, 399
Burning Bush, *see* Sne
Burst 196 (foot)–197, 456–457, 458–459, 481 (foot)–482
Butler 331–336

Cain 73, 104–105, 221–222, 223–237, 241 (foot)–242, 243–244, 252–253, 268–270, 276–277, 303, 308, 318–320, 326, 328–329, 356–357, 381–382, 385, 387, 407–409, 430 431, 446 (foot)–447, 471, 481
Caleb 357–358, 383–384, 443–444, 478–481
Calf 250–251, 392, 436, 439–461, 468 (foot)–469, 481–482
Camel 40–41, 184–186
Canaan (land) 58, 59–60, 123–124, 125–126, 126, 127–128, 141–142, 143, 154 (foot)–155, 164–165, 167–168, 173–174, 175, 176, 177–178, 227, 260–261, 264–265, 287–288, 320–321, 341, 343–344, 349–354, 356–357, 358–359, 400–402, 411, 449–450, 451–452, 461–462, 463, 464–465, 467, 470–471, 472, 472–473, 475–476, 482–483
Canaan (entrance, occupation) 173–174, 248, 369, 376, 411
Canaan (person) 271–273, 276–277
Canaanite 165–166, 177, 288–289, 469–470 Canaanitish (servant) 273, 275 (foot)–276 Candlestick 347 (foot)–348, 355
Catastrophe 94, 281, 428–429, 449–450, 486–487
Cattle, *see* Beast
Cham 269–277, 286 (foot)–287, 308, 317 (foot)–318, 326
Channuka 133–134
Charan 287 (foot)–288
Characteristic, *see* Midda

520 APPENDIX

Chariots 414 (foot)–415, 439–440, 442 (foot)–443
Cherubim 132 (foot)–133, 174–175, 347 (foot)–348, 356 (foot)–357, 458
Cherubs, *see* Cherubim
Cheth 41, 241, 373
Child 24–25, 26–27, 30–31, 46, 56–57, 98, 100, 104–105, 111 (foot)–112, 121, 264 (foot)–265, 390, 392 (foot)–393
Choice, *see* Alternative
Circle 82, 194, 228–229, 298 (foot)–299, 304 (foot)–305, 352–354, 402 (foot)–403, 439440, 441 (foot)–444, 450–451, 452, 454
Circumcision 117–118, 128–129, 129–130, 293–294, 295–296, 323, 394, 406–407, 416–417
Clean 129–130, 264–265, 279 (foot)–280
Cloud, *see also* Column of smoke 463–465, 472 (foot)–473
Coat of many colours, we Ketoneth Passim
Column of fire 414–415, 415–416
Column of smoke 414–415, 415–416, 463
Come 64–65
Coming World, *see* Land, Promised
Commandments 33, 61–62, 79, 89–90, 104–105, 168 (foot)–169, 305–306, 409–410, 424
Complete 95 (foot)–96
Conflict 286 (foot)–287
Consciousness of guilt 227, 455 (foot)–456, 470–471
Constellation – stars (Zodiac) 19–21, 23 (foot)–24, 42, 62, 106 (foot)–107, 151–152, 267 (foot)–268, 305–306, 316 (foot)–317, 335, 351, 400–401, 434, 439, 486–487, 494
Continuation 134–135, 150–154, 193–194, 247–248, 328–329, 399, 442 (foot)–443, 444, 448 (foot)–449, 450–451, 452, 461–462, 475
Counting 27 (foot)–29, 141–142, 452–453
Covenant, between the parts 22, 117–118, 312, 313 (foot)–314
Covering, cover, circle 45, 62, 68–69, 70–72, 74–75, 78–79, 117–118, 128–129, 146–147, 183 (foot)–184, 185, 196–197, 241 (foot)–242, 243, 269 (foot)–270, 293–296, 308 (foot)–310, 312–317, 327 (foot)–328, 359–360, 374, 392, 395, 398, 416–417, 435, 439–442, 448 (foot)–449, 454, 463 (foot)–466, 467, 470–472
Cow 167, 306–307, 335–336, 399, 439
Cross 99, 308 (foot)–309
Cubit 254
Culture 229–230, 231–232, 276–277, 378–379, 409–410, 441 (foot)–442
Culture – pessimism 480–481
Cunning 189–190, 193–194
Curve 68–69, 196 (foot)–198, 242–243, 245 (foot)–246, 262, 404–405

Daleth 40–43, 78–79, 122, 208–209, 231, 406
Damascus 292
Date 189–190
Daughter 62, 119 (foot)–120, 237 (foot)–239, 241 (foot)–243, 383–387, 391, 438–439
David 73 (foot)–74, 120–121, 131 (foot)–132, 135 (foot)–136, 143, 144, 147, 177 (foot)–178, 221, 291, 319–320, 358–359, 364–365, 365–369, 413 (foot)–414, 466–467
David, son of 361 (foot)–362
Day 19, 107–108, 261, 304 (foot)–305, 356, 491
Deed 107 (foot)–108, 111–113, 119, 122–124, 146–147, 191, 405, 442 (foot)–443
Deliverance, *see also* Exodus 85–86, 140–141, 168 (foot)–169, 241, 404–405
Demons (spirits) 134, 387, 388
Demonstrate 475, 478–479
Dependence 272, 275–276, 304 (foot)–305, 317 (foot)–318
Descend, *see also* Redu 63, 91, 164 (foot)–165, 387 (foot)–388
Devil, *see also* Satan and Samael 232, 306–307
Discontinuity 151–153, 328–329, 363–364, 399, 415–416

Door 40–41, 78–79, 121–123, 406
Dove 168, 255–256, 259–261
Draw nearer, see Korban
Dream 124–125, 259–260, 335–336
Dress 146–148, 183 (foot)–185, 195–196, 270, 316–317, 325–326, 328–329, 331, 392, 439440, 467
Drown 414
Dry bones 361, 449–450
Dudaim 139 (foot)–141, 143–144, 144–148, 341 (foot)–342
Dwell 170–171

Ear 121–123, 274
Ear (of corn) 335
East 40–41, 347 (foot)–348, 356 (foot)–357, 449 (foot)–450, 478
Easter 140–144, 218, 332 (foot)–334, 349–350, 356, 416, 440–441
Eat 32–34, 45, 48, 59, 71, 87–88, 94–97, 110, 130, 140–141, 191–192, 266–267, 387, 406, 444–445, 471
Ecclesiastes 350
Ed, see Mist
Eden – Garden of Eden, Paradise 32–34, 42, 45, 48, 62, 73, 77, 87, 96, 97–100, 106, 110 (foot)–111, 134, 183, 192, 197–200, 203, 205, 206–209, 210 (foot)–211, 214–218, 222, 231, 242–243, 262, 270, 276–277, 279, 280–281, 285, 289–290, 300–302, 303 (foot)–304, 308, 324, 328–329, 330–331, 356 (foot)–357, 404–405, 429, 445, 447, 455 (foot)–457, 481
Edom, see Esau
Efraim (Ephraim) 237, 335, 357–358, 359–360, 361 (foot)–362, 449 (foot)–450, 489
Efraim (Ephraim) sons of 449 (foot)–450, 450–451, 452
Efron (Ephron) 373, 374
Egoistic 294–295
Egypt 51, 59 (foot)–61, 73 (foot)–74, 123 (foot)–126, 134, 136–137, 139, 144, 152, 156–157, 163 (foot)–165, 168–169, 173 (foot)–176, 215 (foot)–216, 227–228, 237, 241, 246 (foot)–247, 250 (foot)–251, 260261, 275 (foot)–277, 279, 292, 320, 323, 329–330, 332, 335–336, 339–340, 341 (foot)–342, 343–347, 349–354, 357 (foot)–359, 361 (foot)–363, 369, 376 (foot)–386, 391 (foot)–394, 398–408, 410–417, 423, 428429, 434–435, 439, 441, 442 (foot)–443, 446, 449 (foot)–451, 461–462, 463, 464 (foot)–465, 468–470, 472 (foot)–478, 480483, 489
Egypt – bondage in, see Bondage
Elder, see also First-born 221, 341 (foot)–343, 357 (foot)–358
Eleph 114 (foot), 209 (foot)–210
Ele toldoth, see Toldoth
Elia 73 (foot)–74, 135 (foot)–136, 296, 316, 486–487
Eliezer 292, 297
Emoenah (Emunah) see Faith
End (end of time, end of the world) 28 (foot)–29, 65–66, 68–69, 98, 127 (foot)–128, 135 (foot)–136, 213, 237 (foot)–238, 250 (foot)–251, 267–268, 279–280, 287 (foot)–288, 291, 307, 318–319, 321, 350, 355, 362–363, 371–372, 387 (foot)–388, 396 (foot)–397, 413–416, 424, 436 (foot)–438, 443–444, 446 (foot)–447, 454, 458–461, 469 (foot)–470, 475–476, 480–481, 484–490, 492 (foot)–494
Enoch 80, 139 (foot)–140
Ereb-rab 469 (foot)–471, 481
Esau 22–23, 25–26, 96 (foot)–97, 184–185, 234–235, 237, 266, 303, 306–307, 308–310, 312–326, 331, 332 (foot)–333, 358–359, 392, 441
Eternal 121–125, 308 (foot)–309
Ets ose pri, see Tree of Knowledge
Ets pri ose pri, see Tree of Life
Euphrate 285–286
Eve 221 (foot)–222, 308, 373, 387, 394–395
Evening 107
Everlasting, see Eternal
Evolution 36–37, 60–61, 65–66, 106, 154,

204, 226, 228–229, 239–240, 270, 328
    (foot)–329, 427–428, 430, 442–444
Exile 127, 138, 250 (foot)–251, 287
    (foot)–288, 360, 389–390, 392
    (foot)–394, 446, 450–452, 475–476
Exodus from Egypt 95, 120–121, 124–125,
    139, 149 (foot)–150, 163–164, 218, 227
    (foot)–228, 236, 248, 257 (foot)–258,
    264 (foot)–265, 279–280, 333, 369,
    375–376, 394–395, 400 (foot)–402,
    403 (foot)–408, 410, 413, 416–418,
    423–424, 435, 440, 444–445, 447,
    455–456, 462, 471, 475, 481
    (foot)–482, 494
Expulsion 106, 110 (foot)–111, 134
Extremes 19, 106, 110 (foot)–111, 113,
    147–148, 171, 177 (foot)–178
Eye, an – for an – 240–241, 297, 309
    (foot)–310, 311–312
Eyes 97 (foot)–98, 188–189, 196, 274, 312
Ezechiel 100 (foot)–101, 361–364, 449
    (foot)–450

Fairy-tales 145
Faith 162, 198–203, 288–289, 292
    (foot)–293, 300–301, 304, 314,
    358–359, 370 (foot)–372, 428, 430,
    449 (foot)–450, 452, 469 (foot)–470,
    478 (foot)–480, 491–493
Fall 44 (foot)–45, 50–51
Family 139, 405–406
Fast 74–75, 197, 434–436
Father 46, 56–57, 61–62, 64 (foot)–65,
    78–79 83, 96 (foot)–97, 119 (foot)–121,
    157, 270 (foot)–271, 299–300, 331,
    427–428
Faust 232
Fear 159 (foot)–160, 162
Feast, *see also* Easter, Pentecost and
    Tabernacles (feast of) 356
Fecundate 104–105
Feet 197 (foot)–198
Feeling(s) 38–39, 44 (foot)–45, 58
Figtree 57–58, 189–190, 290
Filled 103–104, 339 (foot)–340
Fire 22–23, 25–26, 33–34, 331, 414
    (foot)–415

First-born – birthright 23, 221–223, 236,
    303, 320, 323–328, 341–342, 347
    (foot)–348
Fish 127, 349, 351
Flood 251 (foot)–252, 257, 259–261, 262,
    279, 281–282, 285, 328 (foot)–329,
    428–429, 447
Forecourt 347 (foot)–348, 349, 356
    (foot)–357, 474–475
Free will 370, 372–373
Friday afternoon 196 (foot)–197, 491
    (foot)–492
Friday evening 143–144
Fruit 30, 73, 207–208, 330–331, 478–479
Fruitful, be- and multiply 19 (foot)–20,
    30, 71, 100 (foot)–101, 107 (foot)–108,
    118, 196, 210 (foot)–211, 213, 217–219,
    227 (foot)–228, 232, 335–336, 354,
    387–389
Fugitive and a vagabond 227–231, 268,
    318 (foot)–319, 385, 408 (foot)–409,
    414 (foot)–415, 430 (foot)–431, 446,
    471, 481, 488
Future 99, 479–480

Gad 131, 486–489, 493–494
Galoeth (Galuth) see Exile
Game 188 (foot)–189, 190, 286
    (foot)–287, 328 (foot)–329, 353–354,
    444–445, 468–469, 480–481
Gan, *see* Garden
Garden 190–191, 206–207, 208
Gass 205 (foot)–206
Gate 196
Gathering 493–494
Gedi, *see* Goat
Generations (book of) see also Toldoth
    194 195, 305 (foot)–306
Gephen, *see* Vine
Ger 170 (foot)–171
Giants 241 (foot)–242, 480 (foot)–481,
    484–485
Gilgal 128 (foot)–129
Gimmel 40–41, 184 (foot)–185, 210
    (foot)–211
Globular shape 109–110, 127 (foot)–128,
    139, 153, 193–194, 262, 286, 440, 443

(foot)–447, 450–451, 454–455, 460
(foot)–461, 475
Goat 23, 167, 304, 306 (foot)–307, 316,
  317 (foot)–318, 329–330, 392, 405
Goat's hoofs 306–307
Gog and Magog 136, 350–351, 361
  (foot)–362, 484
Gold 24–25, 26, 374
Golem 389–390
Good 251–252
Goshen 169–170, 400, 409 (foot)–410
Grain 290, 350
Gratuitous 198–199, 201, 280–281,
  371–372, 428, 430, 469 (foot)–470, 491
  (foot)–493
Gravitation, see Attractive power
Grease 131, 224–225
Greek 40–41
Grief 140–141

Haflaga, see also Tower of Babel 281, 285,
  287–288, 319–320, 356 (foot)–357,
  402 (foot)–403, 428–429, 446
  (foot)–447, 454
Hagar 292, 297, 484 (foot)–485
Flair 196
Half (halve) 90–91, 92 (foot)–93, 114, 177
  (foot)–178, 256, 262, 281, 285, 332
  (foot)–333, 402–404, 406–407, 411
  (foot)–412, 436–437, 470–471
Half of the time 263 (foot)–265
Hand 45, 238
Haran 148, 288–289
Harvest (wheat -) 139 (foot)–141, 142
Hasmonees 133–134
Hazeroth 482
Head 165–166, 196, 308, 441 (foot)–442
Heart 164–165
Heber 81, 285–287
Hee 41, 76, 116–119
Herbs 355–356
Hereafter 59
Hide 190, 192 (foot)–193, 195, 233–234
High places 297 (foot)–298
High Priest 356–357, 452
Hizkia 150–151
Holy 35 (foot)–36, 54, 60–61, 472

Holy of Holies, the–347 (foot)–348, 352
  (foot)–353, 355, 356 (foot)–357, 453
Honey 189–190, 472 (foot)–473
Hook 77 (foot)–78, 81, 84–85, 147–148,
  287 (foot)–288
Horeb, see Sinai
Horn, see also Shofar 222 (foot)–223, 232
  (foot)–233, 265–266, 306–307
Horse 405–406
Hospitality (guests) 294–296
House 39 (foot)–40, 64 (foot)–65,
  78–79, 95, 97–98, 183 (foot)–184, 197,
  319–320, 321, 332–333, 347
  (foot)–348, 349, 351, 352 (foot)–353,
  354–355, 382 (foot)–383, 405–406,
  413, 462, 466–467
House of God see Temple
Hunger 103–104, 340
Hunter (hunting) 233–234, 286
  (foot)–288, 309, 315, 317, 380–381, 385
Hur 443–444

Ibex 306–307
Ibri 285–287, 331, 336, 339–344,
  353–354, 382–383
Idol 286 (foot)–287, 325–326
Idolatry 205 (foot)–206, 222 (foot)–223,
  230, 286 (foot)–287, 309 (foot)–310,
  360
Illusion 286 (foot)–287
Independent persons 275–276
Individuality 246, 247–248, 249,
  383–384
Infinite, see Eternal
Inn 393–394
Intoxication 55 (foot)–56, 125–126,
  179–180, 234–235, 238 (foot)–239,
  269–270, 272, 308 (foot)–309, 315,
  319–320, 381, 424, 444–445, 480–481
Isaac 22–23, 25, 34, 73 (foot)–74, 81
  (foot)–82, 148, 163, 165–166, 168
  (foot)–169, 172, 286 (foot)–287,
  293–294, 295–301, 303, 306–319, 323,
  330, 348–349, 351 (foot)–352, 373,
  392, 413 (foot)–414, 441, 449(foot)–451
Ishmael 292, 293 (foot)–294, 297, 399
  (foot)–400, 485 (foot)–486

Israel (children of) 23, 57–58, 124, 126, 163 (foot)–164, 168 (foot)–169, 175–176, 177 (foot)–178, 215 (foot)–216, 227 (foot)–228, 246 (foot)–247, 260–261, 273, 276 (foot)–277, 285, 359–362, 364, 376 (foot)–382, 385, 398, 400 (foot)–401, 403 (foot)–404, 405, 408 (foot)–416, 427–428, 468 (foot)–471, 475, 486–487, 491
Israel (Jacob) 22, 26, 324, 346 (foot)–347, 442 (foot)–443

Jabbok 323 (foot)–324, 332 (foot)–333, 392
Jacob 22–23, 25–26, 73 (foot)–74, 79, 81 (foot)–82, 96 (foot)–97, 131, 133, 136 (foot)–137, 139 (foot)–140, 148, 165–166, 169–170, 172, 184–185, 221, 236–237, 266, 286 (foot)–287, 290, 303, 308 (foot)–309, 313–329, 332 (foot)–333, 341 (foot)–342, 346–348, 357 (foot)–358, 369, 371–374, 379–380, 388 (foot)–389, 392–393, 439443, 475, 489
Jacob (sons of) 131, 142–143, 163 (foot) 164, 236, 339 (foot)–341, 352–353
Jafeth 269–270, 271-3
Jam Suf (Jam Soef) 326, 328 (foot)–329
Jar 324 (foot)–326
Jerusalem 230, 352 (foot)–353, 445, 481
Jethro 418–420, 485 (foot)–486
Jochebed 381 (foot)–384, 387–390
Jod 41, 76, 87 (foot)–89, 132 (foot)–133, 175, 300–301
Joktan 80 (foot)–82
Jonah 414 (foot)–415, 429, 459 (foot)–460
Jonathan 358–359
Jordan 247 (foot)–248, 372–373, 463, 484, 488, 489 (foot)–490, 494
Joseph 23, 100 (foot)–101, 136 (foot)–137, 138–139, 164 (foot)–165, 166, 221, 237, 250, 251, 327, 329–332, 335–348, 352 (foot)–354, 357 (foot)–363, 369, 371–372, 373, 375, 376 (foot)–377, 407 (foot)–409, 436 (foot)–437, 439–440, 442 (foot)–444, 449 (foot)–451, 484 (foot)–486, 489

Joseph (son of -) 361 (foot)–362
Joshua 126, 127 (foot)–129, 131 (foot)–132, 135 (foot)–136, 150–151, 173 (foot)–174, 247–248, 357–358, 361 (foot)–362, 372–373, 431–432, 477 (foot)–480, 489–490
Joy 137
Jubilee year 122, 273
Juda (Judah) 100 (foot)–101, 341–345, 352 (foot)–355, 357–363, 373, 383–384, 413 (foot)–414, 449 (foot)–450, 489
Juda (Judah) Kingdom of 177 (foot)–178

Kabbala 39 (foot)–40, 48 (foot)–50, 68–69, 76–77, 286
Kaf 41
Kahen (Cohen), *see* Priest
Kehath 81 (foot)–82, 163 (foot)–164
Ketoneth Passim 327 (foot)–328, 329–330, 341 (foot)–342, 346, 363, 436 (foot)–439
Keturah 297, 484 (foot)–486
Klippoth, *see* Covering
Kof 41
Koreth, *see* Sever the connection
Kriath Shma 209–210
King's son 65
Kush 287

Laban 23, 25, 73 (foot)–74, 148, 323, 327, 328 (foot)–329, 342 (foot)–343
Labour 198–199
Ladder 388
Lamb 404–406, 413, 462
Lamech 80, 231 (foot)–233, 234
Lamed 41
Land, Promised 57–58, 77, 123 (foot)–127, 135 (foot)–136, 141–142, 200, 247–248, 286, 292, 350, 357 (foot)–358, 376, 431–432, 436–437, 439, 463, 469 (foot)–470, 472, 473 (foot)–474, 476, 479–480, 481, 487, 491, 492 (foot)–493
Last moment 242–243
Laugh 293 (foot)–294, 295–296, 444–445
Law, *see* Commandments
Law of Creation 106, 115 (foot)–116,

INDEX 525

121–122, 134, 154, 199–200, 216–217, 228 (foot)–229, 274 (foot)–275, 281, 391, 403 (foot)–405, 428, 434, 450–451, 454, 470–471

Law of Nature 35, 49–50, 53–54, 66–67, 84 (foot)–85, 95, 126, 188, 292–293, 297 (foot)–298, 301, 400 (foot)–401, 414 (foot)–415, 449 (foot)–450, 459 (foot)–460, 461–462

Lea 22–24, 26, 131, 139 (foot)–140, 148, 327–328, 328, 341–342, 373

Leaven 406–408, 410, 416–417, 426 (foot)–427, 440, 471

Lechem, *see* Bread

Left, left side, left side world 20–21, 24 (loot)-25, 26, 33–34, 45–47, 73–74, 87, 102, 110, 113, 119 (foot)–120, 124–125, 183 (foot)–190, 196, 205 (foot)–206, 221, 247–248, 261, 303–304, 308–315, 318 (foot)–319, 323–324, 332, 333 (foot)–337, 347 (foot)–348, 349, 351–352, 360, 374, 383–384, 418, 421, 432, 437 (foot)–438, 441–443, 449 (foot)–450, 470–471, 473 (foot)–474, 484

Lentils 23

Leviathan 349–350, 351–352

Levy 81–82, 349–350, 351 (foot)–352, 379–380, 388 (foot)–389, 446, 457, 465–466

Light 19–25, 30, 33–34, 42, 61–62, 68–69, 73, 133–134, 196, 221, 304 (foot)–305

Lilith 387–388

Lime kiln 23, 286 (foot)–287

Loam 146

Look, *see also* See 269 (foot)–270

Lost, be–95

Lot 288–289, 293 (foot)–296, 440

Love, *see also* Mercifulness 85–86, 95, 198–200, 429 (foot)–430

Love-apples (Mandrakes), *see* Dudaim

Lunar year 261

Luz 290

Mabbul (Mabul), *see* Flood

Maccabees 132 (foot)–133

Machpela 373

Magic 205

Magog, *see* Gog and Magog

Malon, *see* Inn

Manasseh 237, 357 (foot)–358, 488–490

Manna 130, 468, 472–474

Mask 315 (foot)–317

Materializing 19 (foot)–20, 22, 27, 43, 205 (foot)–206, 450–451, 481 (foot)–482

Matriarchs 27, 28 (foot)–29, 147–148, 323, 346–347, 373, 478 (foot)–479

Matter, development of 58–59, 60 (foot)–61, 66–67, 87, 92, 99 (foot)–100, 106, 118, 119 (foot)–120, 121, 127 (foot)–128, 129–134, 138, 145 (foot)–146, 192, 197 (foot)–198, 205 (foot)–206, 219 (foot)–220, 222–223, 230, 233–234, 237 (foot)–244, 257, 271–272, 277, 279, 280 (foot)–281, 286 (foot)–288, 293 (foot)–296, 307, 315, 317 (foot)–319, 321, 323, 325–326, 329–330, 337–338, 345, 347, 378–379, 384–385, 421, 427–428, 430 (foot)–431, 437 (foot)–438, 444–445, 447, 457–458, 460 (foot)–461, 463 (foot)–464, 468–473, 484, 491

Meal 191, 332–334, 407–408

Meat 92, 145 (foot)–147, 183 (foot)–184

Mechanic 32, 35 (foot)–36, 48, 54, 267–268, 370 (foot)–371, 428–429, 430, 437 (foot)–438, 444, 452, 457–458, 478 (foot)–479

Mem 41, 43, 73 (foot)–74, 210 (foot)–211, 247–248, 259–260

Mercifulness, Love, Grace 85–86, 95, 154, 415–416, 458

Merchant 371–372, 469 (foot)–470

Merkabah 364 (foot)

Messiah 94, 106, 108–109, 131 (foot), 136, 137, 144, 152–153, 195, 260–261, 278–280, 289–290, 291, 295–296, 303 (foot)–304, 316, 361 (foot)–363, 396, 437 (foot)–438, 486–487

Metals 24–25, 396

Methusalah 80, 140, 150, 252–253

Midda 418–419, 451–452

Middle 20, 24–25, 26, 34, 45–48, 51–52, 87–88, 355
Mid 418–419, 484 (foot)–487
Midnight 402–406, 411 (foot)–412
Midwives 124–125, 381 (foot)–382
Mila, *see* Circumcision
Milk 305 (foot)–306
Milka 148
Miriam 382 (foot)–387, 443–444, 473–475, 484
Mirror 83, 84 (foot)–85, 87 (foot)–89, 102, 132 (foot)–133, 175, 198–199, 347 (foot)–348, 411, 421 (foot)–422, 491 (foot)–492
Missing stone 257
Mist 32–33, 42–46, 47–48, 40–51, 56, 59, 62, 73 (foot)–74, 87, 107, 110, 115, 120–121, 166, 205 (foot)–206, 207, 218, 221, 247 (foot)–248, 352, 413, 463 (foot)–464, 473–474
Mitsraim, *see* Egypt
Moab 275–277, 295–296, 484–485, 491, 492 (foot)–493
Moed, *see* Feasts
Moon 20–21, 24–25, 26, 42, 107, 108–109, 261, 268, 303 (foot)–307, 312, 314, 327, 335, 358–359
Maria 297–302, 348–349, 354, 414
Moses 73 (foot)–74, 81–82, 124, 126–127, 131, 135 (foot)–136, 141–142, 164, 169–170, 172, 173 (foot)–174, 221, 236, 245, 246 (foot)–247, 248, 250–251, 264 (foot)–265, 310–311, 349, 354, 356, 369, 372, 382 (foot)–383, 387, 388 (foot)–389, 390–403, 411, 416, 418–420, 431–432, 436–438, 445, 448–449, 450–451, 445, 457–461, 465–466, 469 (foot)–470, 472, 474–477, 481, 482–494
Mother 46, 56–57, 61–62, 87, 96 (foot)–97, 111 (foot)–112, 119 (foot)–120, 161 (foot)–170, 222, 304, 305 (foot)–306, 427–428
Motion 463, 466–467, 482, 486–487
Mountain 258–259
Mouth 267
Month 107, 402, 494

Mystic, *see* Kabbala
Mythology 145, 151–152

Nachash, *see* Serpent
Nachshon 413 (foot)–415
Nahor 81 (foot)–82, 148
Naked 97 (foot)–98, 188 (foot)–190, 193, 195, 269–270
Name 285
Nature 35, 53, 67, 96 (foot)–97, 158
Navel 104–105
Navel-cord 410
Nebo 491, 492 (foot)–493
Neck 442–443, 449–450
Nephesh 44 (foot)–45, 50–51, 168–169, 298 (foot)–299, 352 (foot)–353, 354–355, 361, 374, 400, 416–417, 467
Neshamah, *see also* Soul 44 (foot)–45, 93–94, 111 (foot)–112, 192, 361, 467, 489
New Moon 305–306, 307, 358–359, 363–364 New Year 260–261, 265–266
Night 19, 261, 304 (foot)–306, 314, 355–356, 394–395, 402, 411, 470–471
Night wife, *see* Lilith
Nile 285–286
Nimrod 23, 234–235, 275 (foot)–276, 287–289, 364–365
Nineveh 414 (foot)–416, 429
Nissan 260–261, 402
Noah 79–81, 173, 237 (foot)–238, 242–249, 251–260, 262–264, 269–274, 276–279, 285, 307, 323, 388 (foot)–389, 465–466
North 129, 347 (foot)–348, 352 (foot)–353, 355, 467, 478
Nun 41, 126–127, 206–207, 208, 210 (foot)–211, 231, 241 (foot), 373

Og 484, 488
Oil 131–132, 133, 144, 260–261, 355
Olive 189–190, 260–261, 355
Optimism 454 (foot)–456
Oral Thora 136 (foot)–137, 431–433
Ornament 445, 456–457
Ox 351

Paradise, *see* Eden
Param 481 (foot)–482
Parents 31, 427–428
Passive 23, 26, 34, 74, 139, 146 (foot)–147, 198–199, 222, 259–260
Patriarchs 22–27, 28 (foot)–29, 73 (foot)–74, 176, 177 (foot)–178, 277, 303, 319–320, 373, 408, 478 (foot)–479
Peh 41, 267
Peleg 81–82, 172, 281–282, 285
Pentecost 140 (foot)–142, 144, 218, 349–350
Perez 221, 357 (foot)–358
Periodical system 108–109
Periods 150 (foot)–151, 305 (foot)–306
Pesach, *see* Easter
Phar 335–337, 341 (foot)–344, 351, 393 (foot)–394
Pharaoh 124–125, 166–167, 169–170, 238, 335–339, 377–378, 383–384, 387, 390, 393 (foot)–394, 398–399, 400 (foot)–401, 407 (foot)–411, 414 (foot)–416, 429, 471, 485
Pinchas (Pinehas) 486–487
Pinnacle (of development) 134, 278, 287, 484, 487–488
Pishon 285
Pithom 473
Poison 184, 185, 194, 309, 424–425
Pomp 460
Potiphar 330, 335
Potiphar's wife 330–331, 337–338, 357–358
Practice-school 286 (foot)–287
Predestination 370, 372–373
Pria, *see also* Circumcision 128 (foot)–129
Priest (- blessing) 316 (foot)–318
Primitive 28 (foot)–29, 39 (foot)–40, 43, 45–46, 55(foot)–56, 58–59, 67–68, 75–76, 83, 96 (foot)–97, 149, 172 (foot)–173, 180, 188, 204–206, 239–240, 250, 270, 319–320, 364–365, 424–425, 436–437, 470–471
Produce 471–472
Prophet 99–101, 158, 360, 372–373, 429
Psalm(s) 135

Pyramid 250, 257
Pythagoras 28, 31, 115

Raa 400
Raämses 168 (foot), 416–418, 473
Rachel 22–24, 26, 74, 139 (foot)–140, 148, 236–237, 327–328, 341 (foot)–342, 343–344
Rain 205 (foot)–206
Ram 167, 306–307, 335
Raven 255–256, 259–260
Rebekah 23–24, 26, 74, 148, 308, 312, 313–316, 324, 373, 392, 394–395
Redeem 206 (foot)–207
Redeemer 94, 108–109, 124–125, 169–170, 260–261, 279, 382, 388 (foot)–390, 391, 414, 443–444, 445–446, 450–451, 455 (foot)–456, 484–486
Redeemers, two 361 (foot)–362
Redemption 85–86, 95, 111, 135 (foot)–136, 137, 139–140, 152–153, 194–195, 280–281, 376, 378–379, 389 (foot)–390, 393 (foot)–394, 405–406, 416, 451, 468 (foot)–470, 486–487
Redu 63, 166, 451–452
Relaxation 349–350, 445, 468 (foot)–469, 480
Resh 41
Rest (remainder) 142–143
Resurrection 100 (foot)–101, 361, 363–364
Return 66–67, 94, 99, 103, 228 (foot)–229, 238 (foot)–239, 262, 280–281, 304, 323, 361, 423–424, 427–430, 443–444, 451, 455 (foot)–456, 457–460, 470–471
Reunion 92 (foot)–93, 98–99, 105–106, 108–109, 110 (foot)–112, 130, 135 (foot)–136, 192 (foot), 201, 206 (foot)–207, 214 (foot), 224–225, 262, 315, 345–346, 393 (foot)–394, 404–405, 407
Revelation, *see* Sinai
Revenge 311–312
Reversal, *see* Curve
Rhythm 481 (foot)–482

Rib 32–33, 37–38
Richess 460 (foot)–461
Right 20–21, 24–25, 26, 33.34, 42, 45–48, 102, 184–185, 308, 332, 335, 349–350, 360, 432, 437 (foot)–438, 441 (foot)–442
Righteousness 85–86, 95
River 32–34, 42–43, 47–48, 49–50, 75–76, 124–125, 285, 301, 323 (foot)–324, 335, 383–384
Rock 457, 474–475
Roof 351, 461–462
Round (round world) 110, 127 (foot)–128, 139, 153, 193–195, 262, 286, 440, 443–444, 446–447, 450–451, 454–455, 460 (foot)–461, 475
Ruach 361, 467
Ruhen (Reuben) 140, 144–145, 147, 236–237, 486–489, 493
Ruin 295–296, 459 (foot)–460
Ruth 140 (foot)–141, 291, 295–296, 484

Sabbath 102–105, 134–135, 362–363, 426, 466
Sabbath-year 130
Sacred (things) 347 (foot)–348, 352 (foot)–353, 450–451
Sacrificial animals 222 (foot)–223, 265–266, 306–307, 316
Sacrifice 23, 25, 151–152, 158, 167–168, 170–171, 222–225, 297–299, 302, 304, 305–306, 320, 347–355, 356 (foot)–357, 364, 392, 398–400, 405–406, 407 (foot)–408, 409–410, 421, 442 (foot)–443, 452, 465466, 472, 474–475, 495
Sacrifice of Isaac, *see* Akeda
Samael, *see also* Satan, and Devil 183 (foot)–187, 189–190
Sambation 362–365
Samech 41, 183 (foot)–184
Sar 324
Sarah 24, 25, 148, 302, 323 (foot), 374
Saraph 396
Satan, *see also* Samael and Devil 301, 324 (foot)–325, 329–330, 437 (foot)–439,

443 (foot)–444, 448–449, 460 (foot)–461, 470–471
Saul 358–359, 361–362
Science 55 (foot), 205–206, 228 (foot)–230 270 (foot)–271, 321, 408 (foot)–409, 429, 460 (foot)–461
Sea of the end, *see also* Jam Suf 416–417
Secret 28 (foot)–29, 53, 82, 108–109, 122, 135 (foot)–136, 178–179, 191, 259–260, 281, 316, 418 (foot)–420, 452–453, 460-(foot)–461, 478 (foot)–479
See 162, 196, 421, 465–466, 491
Seir, *see also* Esau 266–267, 306–307, 316, 321, 324 (foot)–325
Seir, *see* Goat
Sephiroth 49–50, 69, 111 (foot)–112, 170–171, 174–175, 311–312
Serah 136 (foot)–140, 450–451
Series 317 (foot)–318
Serpent 34, 44 (foot)–45, 50–51, 69, 71–74, 77, 92 (foot)–93, 94, 106, 108, 109, 121, 123, 134, 184 (foot)–187, 190–194, 197 (foot)–198, 200, 243, 268, 278, 280 (foot), 288–289, 301, 303 (foot)–305, 307–309, 315, 318 (foot)–319, 323–325, 329–330, 347, 352 (foot)–353, 377, 387 (foot)–388, 394–395, 404–405, 407, 414, 424–425, 437, 445, 455 (foot)–456, 469 (foot)–471
Servant, *see* Bondage
Set of teeth 267
Sever the connection 407 (foot)–409, 410, 471
Sextuplets 413
Sham world 188 (foot)–191, 309 (foot)–310, 318–319, 321, 377 (foot)–378, 381, 412, 442, 468
Shechinah 392 (foot)–393, 475
Sheep 306–307
Shem 79–80, 80(foot)–81, 149 (foot)–150,
172 (foot)–173, 178 (foot)–179, 269–270, 271–273, 277–278, 281–288, 308, 323–324
Shemen, *see* Oil
Shepherd 399 (foot)

Sheth 80, 104–105, 236–237, 241 (foot)–242, 276–277, 387 (foot)–388
Shetijah 104–105, 297 (foot)–299, 354–355
Shibboleth 184 (foot)–185
Shilo 476
Shin 41, 104–105, 183 (foot)–185, 196
Ship 245 (foot)–246, 247–248, 249 (foot)–250, 465–466
Shoes 147
Shofar 265–266
Shut-out 454 (foot)–455, 468, 477 (foot)–478, 480–481, 495
Side 91 (foot)–92
Sifra (Shifra) 381 (foot)–382
Sigh 385
Sihon 484–488
Silence 460(foot)–461
Silver 24–25, 26, 374
Sin (letter Sin/Shin) 41, 183 (foot)–184, 196
Sin 448 (foot)–449, 452, 471–472, 477 (foot)–478
Sin – offering 303 (foot)–304, 305 (foot)–306, 307
Sinai – Revelation 73 (foot)–74, 75–76, 77–78, 81–82, 83, 85–86, 96 (foot)–97, 100 (foot)–101, 129, 142–143, 144, 160–161, 169 (foot)–170, 171–172, 184–185, 191, 200, 201 (foot)–202, 215 (foot)–217, 236, 241, 257 (foot)–258, 264 (foot)–265, 269, 279 (foot)–280, 354–355, 373, 388–389, 391–392, 409–410, 418–419, 421, 431 (foot)–437, 455 (foot)–456, 459–461, 471–472, 481 (foot)–482, 485 (foot)–486
Skeleton 145 (foot)–146
Skin 195–196
Smell 356
Sne- Burning bush 391–394
Society 108–109, 121, 179–180, 230, 239–240, 384, 425 (foot)–426, 429
Sodom 23, 293 (foot)–296, 440
Sukkoth (Sukoth) 168 (foot)–169, 416–418
Solar system 108–109

Solar year 261, 494
Solomon 120–121, 132, 136, 155 (foot)–156, 171, 286, 319–320, 327, 359–360, 364–365
Son 62, 64 (foot)–65, 119 (foot)–121, 169 170, 238–239, 383–384, 389–390, 438–439, 466
Song of Solomon 88–89, 105, 113, 143–144, 346
Soul, *see also* Nefesh, Neshamah 44 (foot)–45.92–93, 96 (foot)–97, 100–101, 105–108, 111 (foot)–112, 115–117, 120, 130, 138, 143, 146 (foot)–147, 183 (foot)–184, 187, 189–190, 192, 195, 221–228, 238–243, 260 261, 272–273, 281–282, 293, 295–296, 303–304, 314, 316, 321, 323–327, 329–330, 341–344, 355–358, 360–363, 373–374, 378, 380, 383–387, 389–390, 392–393, 399, 407 (foot)–408, 413, 414–415, 426, 431, 437, 441–442, 445–456, 458, 459, 470–471, 487 489, 491 (foot)–492
Sound 38–39, 75–76
South 347 (foot)–348, 352 (foot)–353, 355, 477
Space, space-time 115–116, 297 (foot)–298
Sphynx 92 (foot)–93, 94
Spies 357 (foot)–358, 435, 452–483, 487–488
Spirits, *see* Demons
Standard of life 468, 472 (foot)–473–474
State dress, *see* Ketoneth Passim
Stiff-necked 441 (foot)–442, 448 (foot)–449
Stone 119 (foot)–120, 121–122, 421 (foot)–422
Stranger, *see* Ger
Straw 398
Stored 473
Stupefaction, *see* Intoxication
Substance 264 (foot)–265, 323 (foot)–324, 373–374
Success 469 (foot)–470
Suffer 92 (foot)–93, 99–100, 105–106, 107 (foot)–108, 122, 123–126, 127,

141–142, 164–165, 168 (foot)–169, 176, 194–195, 214, 251–252, 355 (foot)–356, 348–349, 357 (foot)–358, 376–378, 379, 384, 385, 418 (foot)–419, 426 (foot)–427, 454 (foot)–455, 488
Sun 19 (foot)–21, 23 (foot)–25, 26, 42, 107, 150–151, 261, 268, 303 (foot)–304, 305–306, 307, 363, 364, 494
Surprise 95 (foot)–96, 136–137, 200, 353–354, 357 (foot)–359, 362–363, 451–452, 477
Sustenance 468, 471–474
Sweet incense 347 (foot)–348, 355–356
Symbolic 55

Tabernacles (Feast of -) 349–352, 417, 461–462
Tabernacle 132 (foot)–133, 347 (foot)–348, 411 (foot)–412, 461–462, 463–467, 472–473, 474–475, 495
Table 332 (foot)–333
Table with shewbreads 347 (foot)–348, 355
Taf 41, 99 (foot)–100, 104–105, 114, 138
Tamar 357 (foot)–358
Tear to pieces 192
Teba 155 (foot)–156, 245–250, 252–261, 262 (foot)–263, 264 (foot)–265, 272–273, 277, 351 (foot)–352, 390–391, 465–466
Technology 205 (foot)–206, 228–233, 270 (foot)–271, 279 (foot)–280, 321, 380, 408 (foot)–409, 413, 429, 454 (foot)–455, 479–480
Tekia 265–266
Temple 104–105, 120–121, 131, 132, 133, 149 (foot)–150, 151–152, 154 (foot)–155, 177 (foot)–178, 297 (foot)–298, 319–320, 344–345, 347–349, 352–358, 364, 399, 463, 481–482
Temptation 106, 185, 194–195, 227 (foot)–228, 292 (foot)–293, 306–307, 437 (foot)–438, 469 (foot)–470
Tent 319–321, 445, 466–467
Terah 81–82, 148, 287 (foot)–288
Teth 41

Thorns and thistles 195
Threshold 95, 461–462, 492–493
Thumb 45–46
Time – calculation 148–149, 151–152, 261, 267, 388 (foot)–389, 448, 457, 494
Time of the end, *see* End
Time (half) 177 (foot)–178
Time (whole) 177 (foot)–178
Time-period 77 (foot)–78
Time, space-time 38–40, 59 (foot)–61, 64, 71, 73, 74 (foot)–76, 78 (foot)–87, 97 (foot)–98, 100 (foot)–101, 107–108, 110, 122–125, 135, 141–142, 149–157, 171, 180, 183, 188 (foot)–189, 196–197, 215 (foot)–216, 231, 236–237, 243, 247–249, 257, 263–264, 266, 268, 275 (foot)–276, 286, 292 (foot)–294, 297, 313, 319–320, 323 (foot)–324, 335 (foot)–336, 344–345, 347 (foot)–348, 351, 356–357, 390, 402 (foot)–403, 413–414, 434, 436 (foot)–437, 440, 445–449, 451–452, 456–457, 463, 464 (foot)–465, 466–467, 470–471, 472, 473–475, 477 (foot)–478, 480–487, 491–492, 494–495
Time – structure 162 (foot)–163, 166, 173 (foot)–174, 177, 244, 262 (foot)–263, 267, 313, 373, 410, 494
Tishri 260–261, 402
Toldoth 77 (foot)–81, 129, 172 (foot)–173, 174–175, 178 (foot)–179, 237 (foot)–238, 242–243, 244, 262 (foot)–263, 276–277, 278, 280 (foot)–281, 285, 287 (foot)–288, 301, 308, 312–313, 323 (foot)–324, 328 (foot)–329, 405–406
Tongue 246 (foot)–247
Totalitarian 35 (foot)–36
Tower of Babel, *see also* Haflaga 279 (foot)–281
Town-builder 229–232, 252–253, 278, 319–320, 408 (foot)–409, 416, 441
Tree 210–212, 213, 219
– of Knowledge 33, 45–48, 49–51, 56–57, 59, 62, 73, 75–76, 77, 78–79, 87–88, 96–97, 108–109, 110, 115–116, 119 (foot)–124, 129130, 134, 140–141,

INDEX 531

150–151, 166, 184–190, 192 (foot)–198, 200–202, 204, 206 (foot)–207, 212, 214–218, 222, 227–228, 233–234, 242 (foot)–243, 249, 251–252, 264 (foot)–265, 268–273, 274 (foot)–279, 281, 290–291, 292 (foot)–294, 302, 307, 313–314, 330–333, 363–364, 370, 379–380, 389–390, 398, 407, 411, 441, 445, 459, 474–475, 482, 489, 491 (foot)
— of Life 33, 45–48, 49–51, 53, 56–57, 59, 87 (foot)–88, 99 (foot)–101, 105, 115–117, 119 (foot)–120, 166, 184–185, 193–194, 197–198, 199–200, 201 (foot)–202, 206–207, 212, 214 (foot)–218, 249, 251–252, 288–289, 290, 293, 302, 313–314, 326–328, 337–338, 344–345, 363, 378–379, 389–390, 407, 422 (foot)–423, 428–436, 442, 445–446, 474–475, 476, 482 (foot)–483, 488–490, 495 (foot)–496
— that is fruit and makes fruit 212, 214, 216–217, 280–281, 288–289, 293 (foot)–294, 295–296, 326, 337 (foot)–338, 344–345, 354–355, 363, 407, 446, 482 (foot)–483, 488
— that makes fruit 212, 216 (foot)–218, 219(foot), 223 (foot)–224, 227–228, 233 (foot)–234, 239, 249–251, 270, 275–276, 285, 290–291, 301, 304–306, 310, 337, 354, 370, 379–380, 488 (foot)–489
Trunk 308, 442
Tsade 41
Tubal-Cain 230–231, 232 (foot)–233, 234–235
Turning, *see* Curve
Twins 22, 24, 26, 303

Uncle 147–148
Unclean 129–130, 264 (foot)–265
Universe 35, 39, 49 (foot)–50, 53, 66–67, 96 (foot)–97, 100, 114, 150–153, 203–204, 339, 480–481
Utmost, point of development 28–30, 57–58 62, 66–67, 77 (foot)–78, 92 (foot)–93, 94, 114–115, 138, 192, 199–200, 215–216, 223–224, 249, 257, 270, 304, 306–307, 309, 316, 318–319, 339, 374, 393, 403 (foot)–404, 423–424, 428, 440–441, 445–446, 471, 492–493
Uzza 236

Veil 347 (foot)–348
Very good 201, 251 (foot)–252
Vine 44 (foot)–45, 57–58, 189–190, 332
Vineyard 269

Wages 370 (foot)–371, 380–383, 428, 469 (foot)–470, 491 (foot)–492
War 291
Water (-world, -side) 19, 20–26, 33–34, 36 (foot)–39, 42–43, 73–76, 96 (foot)–97, 110, 113, 124–125, 169–170, 205 (foot)–206, 221, 238, 246–249, 254–257, 261, 281, 301, 303, 309, 312, 324, 332, 335, 351–352, 383–387, 390–391, 398, 414(foot)–416, 437 (foot)–438, 468, 473–475, 484, 494
Wave, wave motion 247–248, 377, 439
Waw 41, 76, 77 (foot)–78, 81, 84, 287 (foot)–288
Wedding 143–144, 241–242
Week 107
Well 23, 25, 74, 303, 310–311, 473 (foot)–474
West 347 (foot)–348, 356 (foot)–357, 449 (foot)–450, 478
Wheat 139 (foot)–141, 189 (foot)–190, 290–291, 330–332, 355, 465 (foot)–466
Wilderness 73 (foot)–74, 115, 123–127, 129, 132, 135 (foot)–136, 141–142, 152–153, 154, 176, 227, 248, 264 (foot)–265, 277, 320, 349–350, 364, 369, 383–384, 400 (foot)–401, 412, 427–428, 434–435, 436, 447, 463–468, 470–471, 471–475, 477–478, 481–483, 495
Window 255, 260
Wine 45, 333–334
Witness 207–208, 310–312, 426–428

Word, *see also* Teba 246–249, 251(foot)–253, 257 (foot)–261, 390
Work, *see* Labour

Year 107, 150–151, 154, 266–267, 494
Younger (the -) 221, 223–224, 303, 341 (foot)–342, 489

Zafnath Paaneach 337 (foot)
Zajin 41, 248 (foot)–249
Zilpa 22, 327 (foot)
Zippora 74, 394–395, 397
Zodiac, *see* Constellation

Numbers

⅕ 336 (foot)–337, 339, 378–380, 386, 411 (foot)–412
⅔ 259–260
1½ 177 (foot)–178, 263 (foot)–264
1-2 64 (foot)–65, 177, 423–424, 435–436, 456 (foot), 458–459, 482 (foot)–483
1:2 165, 461–462, 482
1-2-184 (foot)–86, 93–94, 176–177, 197 (foot)–198, 228 (foot)–229, 346
1-4 42, 43 (foot)–44, 45–51, 53, 54, 56, 59, 61–62, 71, 73–74, 78–79, 87, 107–108, 109–110, 115, 117–121, 130, 163–164, 166, 169–171, 205 (foot), 207–208, 218, 221, 249, 254–255, 267, 286, 298 (foot)–299, 302, 308, 312, 317 (foot)–318, 229–330, 333, 337, 339–341, 343–345, 352, 354, 369, 377, 378 (foot)–380, 382, 384, 392, 407 (foot)–410, 413, 420, 431–432, 434, 442–443, 449, 452, 466–467, 469
1-7 452–453
1st day 19–25, 26, 74–75
1st 3 days 19 (foot)–20, 21–22, 29–30, 42–43, 111 (foot)–112
1st word 422–424
2-164 (foot)–65, 174–178, 259–260, 312, 405, 423–424, 435–436, 459, 482–483
2:1 125–126, 141–142, 173 (foot)–175, 227–228, 231
2-200-1 67–68, 98, 116–117
2nd day 19–26, 65–66, 246 (foot)–248
2nd 3 days 20–21, 29–30, 42–43, 56–57, 111 (foot)–112
2nd word 424–425

3, 3rd 22–33, 39 (foot)–41, 51–53, 62, 71 (foot)–72, 80 (foot)–82, 98–99, 104–105, 111 (foot)–112, 113, 119 (foot)–120, 129–131, 184–185, 206–207, 218, 236, 263 (foot)–264, 303, 305–306, 308–309, 312, 316 (foot)–317, 448
3½ 263–267, 279 (foot)–280, 307, 373–374, 414, 442–443, 449 (foot)–450, 458, 493–494
3rd day 19–22, 56–57, 65–66, 211–212, 214 (foot)–215, 279 (foot)–280, 297
3 days 22–23, 27 (foot)–28, 29–30, 102, 104–105, 249
3 dimensions 467
3 half-times 264 (foot)–265, 279 (foot)–280
3 days of Creation 24, 26, 27, 62, 80, 305–306
4, 4th, 4 times 22, 24, 26–33, 39–48, 50–51, 59, 61–64, 66–67, 71 (foot)–73, 75–82, 89, 95, 98–99, 104–105, 107 (foot)–108, 111 (foot)–112, 113–117, 119–120, 125–131, 147, 155, 163, 169–170, 189–190, 193–194, 208–209, 214, 218, 231, 236, 249, 254–255, 257 (foot)–259, 263 (foot)–265, 267, 271 (foot)–272, 274, 285–286, 292–293, 305 (foot)–306, 309, 313, 315, 320, 324, 328 (foot)–329, 336 (foot)–337, 339, 347 (foot)–348, 349–350, 356 (foot)–357, 361 (foot)–362, 381, 385, 406, 417, 419 (foot)–420, 445, 448, 459 (foot)–460, 465–466, 481, 485 (foot)–486

4 acts of Creation 22, 24, 26–28, 29–30, 43, 78–79, 104, 305–306
4 corners 286, 298 (foot)–299, 493–494
4 cubits 155, 258–259
4 exiles 258–259, 286
4 formtakings 286
4th day 19–21, 65
4th dimension 466–467, 493–494
4 elements 28–29, 285, 303
4 half-times 264 (foot)–265
4 Kingdoms 258–259
4 registers of birth 424
4 rivers 286
4th word 426 (foot)–427
4 worlds 111 (foot)–112, 113, 129–130, 285, 303
5, 5th 27, 30–33, 81–82, 92 (foot)–93, 99, 105, 108, 111–119, 130, 172, 177, 178 (foot)–179, 180, 244, 262, 272–273, 317, 343 (foot)–345, 349–350, 372–373, 402, 405, 407, 422–423, 430, 459, 478, 481, 482 (foot)–483
5–6–5 111–112, 115–116, 218, 262, 264 (foot)–265, 287 (foot)–288, 459
5th day 19–21, 62
5th word 427–428
6, 6th 28 (foot)–30, 32–33, 77 (foot)–78, 81, 83–85, 147–148, 232 (foot)–233, 242 (foot)–243, 246, 263 (foot)–264, 287 (foot)–288, 387, 413–414
6–5 113, 135, 177–180, 217–218, 258–259, 264 (foot)–265, 281, 301, 333 (foot)–334, 337–338, 402 (foot)–404, 405–406, 407, 411 (foot)–412, 437, 475–476, 482 (foot)–483, 491
6th day 19–22, 62–63, 105–106, 110 (foot)–111, 112–113, 124–125, 130, 134–137, 143144, 197, 242 (foot)–243, 251 (foot)–252, 259–260, 262, 275 (foot)–276, 279–280, 301, 304 (foot)–305, 355, 395, 404–405, 413–414, 417, 426 (foot)–427, 465 (foot)–466, 472 (foot)–473, 482, 492, 495 (foot)–496
6 days 22, 30, 102, 107 (foot)–108, 110, 112 (foot)–113, 191, 402, 416, 466

6th word 423
7, 7th 32–33, 103,   105, 109, 119–121, 132, 140–141, 195–196, 236, 242–244, 246, 248, 251–252, 257–258, 263–264, 265–266, 273–274, 276–277, 302, 317, 319–320, 327, 351, 355–356,   414, 448, 452–453, 459, 460 (foot)–461, 461–462, 464–467, 485 (foot)–486, 487–488, 493–494
7th day 30, 102–113, 119–131, 134–144, 147–148, 168, 173 (foot)–175, 177 (foot)–178, 192 (foot), 196, 206–207, 234–236, 241, 242–243, 246, 248, 251–252, 257–259, 262, 264 (foot)–265, 266–267, 271–272, 275–281, 291, 295–296, 308, 328, 349–352, 355–356, 363–364, 369, 397, 402, 412, 414, 416–420, 426–427, 430, 435, 452, 463, 464 (foot)–471, 472–476, 478 (foot)–494
7 days 129–130, 133–134, 165–166, 195, 242, 250, 253–254, 264 (foot)–265, 349–350, 418 (foot), 487–488, 491, 495
7 fruits 140 (foot)–141, 189–190, 260–261
7th generation 230, 232 (foot)–233, 237, 291
7 half-times 264 (foot)–265
7 nations 165–166, 175–176
7 weeks see also 49, 218, 418
7th word 425
8, 8th 30, 32 (foot)–33, 120–121, 131–132, 133–134, 135 (foot)–136, 139–141, 236, 241 (foot)–242, 252–253, 257 (foot)–258, 267, 327, 372–373, 418, 424, 450–451, 466, 494–495
8th day 119–121, 123, 126–131, 133–134, 135 (foot)–138, 144, 147–148, 176, 177 (foot), 192 (foot), 195, 199, 206–208, 218, 241–242, 258 (foot)–261, 264 (foot)–265, 272, 274, 277, 279 (foot), 291, 295–296, 312–313, 337 (foot)–338, 350–353, 355, 362, 363, 369, 372–374, 397, 416–417, 419 (foot)–421, 431–435, 466–467, 472, 479–480, 481 (foot), 484, 485 (foot)–487, 489, 493–496
8th generation 320

9, 9th 30, 32–33, 51, 130, 251–252, 254, 481
9th word 426–427
10, 10th 30, 33, 79–80, 84 (foot)–86, 88–93, 98–99, 108, 144, 169–170, 179, 207–208, 262, 264 (foot)–266, 272–273, 295–296, 305 (foot)–306, 316–317, 328, 340, 356, 402, 404–405, 407, 430, 452, 459–460, 461–462, 471, 478
10–5 92 (foot), 113, 135, 172–180, 216, 217–218, 258–259, 264 (foot)–265, 282, 333 (foot), 337 (foot)–338, 345, 373, 402 (foot)–407, 411 (foot), 437, 475, 483, 491
10–5–6–5 75–76, 80, 81 (foot)–85, 112–114, 166, 171, 175, 176–180, 217–218, 244, 246 (foot), 258–259, 262, 272, 282, 287 (foot)–288, 308, 313, 324, 358, 373, 393, 402–404, 433, 456 (foot)–458, 475 (foot)–476, 483, 491
10 generations 237, 253–254
10 plagues 51–52, 124–125, 168 (foot)–169, 407 (foot)–408, 409–410, 471
10 tribes 361, 363, 365
10 words of Creation 33, 61–62, 79–80, 89–90, 104, 168 (foot)–169, 305 (foot)–306, 409 (foot)–410, 424
10th word 428
10 words 421–424, 430–431
11 255, 258–259
12 23, 32, 236–237, 293 (foot)–294, 351, 477, 489, 494–495
13 236–237, 293 (foot)–294, 350–351, 388 (foot)–389, 457–458, 489, 494–495
13 Middoth 451–452, 457–458, 459, 460 (foot)–461
14 481 (foot)–482
15 316 (foot)–318, 320, 402 (foot)–406, 461–462
15 cubits 155–156, 254–256, 258–259
17 250–252, 254–255, 257 (foot)–258, 261, 307, 329–330, 335, 391, 445–446, 448, 459 (foot)–460, 481
19 255
22 99 (foot)–100, 138
26 76, 197, 258 (foot)–259, 316 (foot)–317
26 generations 82–84, 86–87, 98, 129–130, 165–166, 171–172, 177–180, 197, 200, 208, 215 (foot)–217, 217–219, 269, 319–320, 392–393, 421–424, 432–434, 466–467, 475–476, 482 (foot)–483
28 481 (foot)–482
30 168 (foot)–169, 246, 255, 257, 450–452
33rd day 141–142
37 25–26, 301
40, 40th 25, 39 (foot)–40, 43–44, 73 (foot)–74, 78–79, 107 (foot)–108, 115, 125–127, 154–155, 175–176, 199–200, 207–208, 210 (foot)–211, 224–225, 247–248, 250, 251–252, 256, 259–260, 265–266, 306–307, 308 (foot)–309, 329–330, 403 (foot)–405, 414 (foot)–415, 417, 434, 435 (foot)–439, 443–445, 446–449, 454–457, 458–462, 464 (foot)–465, 467, 469 (foot)–470, 472, 477–479, 481, 484, 487
42 places 481 (foot)–482, 484
49 49th 119, 120–121, 122, 140–143, 168 (foot)–169, 207–208, 257, 274, 286 (foot)–287, 291, 403 (foot)–405, 418, 484, 491, 492 (foot)–494, 495 (foot)–496
50, 50th 62, 108, 120–121, 122–123, 127, 140–141, 142–143, 144, 168 (foot)–169, 192 (foot)–193, 199–200, 206–207, 214, 216–217, 218, 231, 241–242, 246, 257–258, 259–261, 265–267, 273–274, 316 (foot)–317, 329–330, 372–373, 374, 403 (foot)–404, 417–419, 430 (foot)–431, 459, 464 (foot)–465, 472
58 263–268, 274, 279 (foot)–280, 307, 316 (foot)–317, 321, 446, 457–458, 491, 492 (foot)–493, 495 (foot)–496
70 195–196, 207–209, 214, 218, 231, 245, 274, 333 (foot)–334, 350–351, 464 (foot)–465
70–4 209, 216–217, 356, 445
70 Children of Jacob 163 (foot)–164, 196
70 elders 448 (foot)–449
70 languages 196

NUMBERS   535

70 nations 196, 209, 350 (foot)–351
70 sciences 196
72 76–77
80 126, 141–142, 163 (foot)–164, 169–170, 267
86 168 (foot)–169
100 162 (foot)–163, 207–208, 336 (foot)–337, 111, 316 (foot)–317
120 58, 141–142, 245–246, 249, 252–253, 492 (foot)–494
130 236, 245, 274, 387 (foot)–388, 389–390
148 333 (foot)–334
172 430–431
179 289–290, 302
190 125–126, 451–452
200 63 (foot)–65, 66–67, 84 (foot)–85, 104–105
210 166–167, 451–453
227 185–186
233 46–47, 193–194
248 145 (foot)–146
260 269
272 104–105, 340
286 100 (foot)–101
300 71 (foot)–72, 99 (foot)–100, 103–105, 183 (foot)–184, 196, 245 (foot)–246
300–10–400 98–99
300–400 104–105, 387 (foot)–388
340 285
345 476
350 193–194, 232 (foot)–233, 263, 373, 442
355 261
358 94, 185–186, 289–290, 301, 396
359 301, 324 (foot)–325
365 145 (foot)–147, 261
372 340
389 125–126
400 43 (foot)–44, 62, 66–67, 71 (foot)–72, 78–79, 95, 98–105, 107 (foot)–108, 114–115, 122, 125–126, 127, 138, 155, 163, 164 (foot)–165, 166–167, 168 (foot)–169, 170 171, 199, 207–208, 213, 215, 236, 245, 247–248, 265–266, 274, 286, 290, 293, 302, 309, 324 (foot)–325, 329–330, 333, 337, 357, 364, 374, 434–435, 442–443, 449 (foot)–452, 467
400 parsa 155
430 150, 163 (foot)–165, 167–171, 417
434 79
444 292
451 292
480 150, 417
490 291, 484
500 98–99, 99 (foot)–100, 105, 107 (foot)–108, 114, 119 120, 138, 150, 155, 163, 171, 210, 215, 236, 266–267, 286, 291, 302, 304, 337, 344–345, 357, 388, 389–390, 432–433, 495 (foot)–496
541 324 (foot)–325
580 265–267, 306–307, 316, 321, 396
600 172 (foot)–173, 249, 251–252, 279, 413
613 145 (foot)–146
620 430 (foot)–431, 459
828 337–338
828–829 405–406
829 173 (foot)–174, 177
932 47
974 former worlds 197
1,000 114 (foot)–115, 197, 207–208, 209, 484 (foot)
1656 173, 250, 263
1656–1657 493
1656–1657–1658 263, 337 (foot), 402, 458
1657 263, 264 (foot)–265, 267
1658 173–174, 177–179, 263, 405
1,671 266
1996 285
2238 388
2418 449 (foot)
2448 167
2488 265
5,800 263, 266–267, 268, 458, 492 (foot)–494 5, 845 266, 458, 492 (foot)–493
5,848 266, 458
5,857 458
6,000 279
10,000 114 (foot)–115
600,000 114 (foot)–115, 123, 279, 280, 413 (foot)–414

www.ingramcontent.com/pod-product-compliance
Lightning Source LLC
Chambersburg PA
CBHW081156230426
43666CB00016B/2834